T0323622

Introduction to the Mathematical and Statistical Foundations of Econometrics

This book is intended for use in a rigorous introductory Ph.D.-level course in econometrics or in a field course in econometric theory. It covers the measure–theoretical foundation of probability theory, the multivariate normal distribution with its application to classical linear regression analysis, various laws of large numbers, and central limit theorems and related results for independent random variables as well as for stationary time series, with applications to asymptotic inference of M-estimators and maximum likelihood theory. Some chapters have their own appendixes containing more advanced topics and/or difficult proofs. Moreover, there are three appendixes with material that is supposed to be known. Appendix I contains a comprehensive review of linear algebra, including all the proofs. Appendix II reviews a variety of mathematical topics and concepts that are used throughout the main text, and Appendix III reviews complex analysis. Therefore, this book is uniquely self-contained.

Herman J. Bierens is Professor of Economics at the Pennsylvania State University and part-time Professor of Econometrics at Tilburg University, The Netherlands. He is Associate Editor of the *Journal of Econometrics* and *Econometric Reviews*, and has been an Associate Editor of *Econometrica*. Professor Bierens has written two monographs, *Robust Methods and Asymptotic Theory in Nonlinear Econometrics* and *Topics in Advanced Econometrics* (Cambridge University Press 1994), as well as numerous journal articles. His current research interests are model (mis)specification analysis in econometrics and its application in empirical research, time series econometrics, and the econometric analysis of dynamic stochastic general equilibrium models.

Themes in Modern Econometrics

Managing editor

PETER C. B. PHILLIPS, *Yale University*

Series editors

RICHARD J. SMITH, *University of Warwick*
ERIC GHYSELS, *University of North Carolina, Chapel Hill*

Themes in Modern Econometrics is designed to service the large and growing need for explicit teaching tools in econometrics. It will provide an organized sequence of textbooks in econometrics aimed squarely at the student population and will be the first series in the discipline to have this as its express aim. Written at a level accessible to students with an introductory course in econometrics behind them, each book will address topics or themes that students and researchers encounter daily. Although each book will be designed to stand alone as an authoritative survey in its own right, the distinct emphasis throughout will be on pedagogic excellence.

Titles in the series

Statistics and Econometric Models: Volumes 1 and 2
CHRISTIAN GOURIEROUX and ALAIN MONFORT
Translated by QUANG VUONG

Time Series and Dynamic Models
CHRISTIAN GOURIEROUX and ALAIN MONFORT
Translated and edited by GIAMPIERO GALLO

Unit Roots, Cointegration, and Structural Change
G. S. MADDALA and IN-MOO KIM

Generalized Method of Moments Estimation
Edited by LÁSZLÓ MÁTYÁS

Nonparametric Econometrics
ADRIAN PAGAN and AMAN ULLAH

Econometrics of Qualitative Dependent Variables
CHRISTIAN GOURIEROUX
Translated by PAUL B. KLASSEN

The Econometric Analysis of Seasonal Time Series
ERIC GHYSELS and DENISE R. OSBORN

Semiparametric Regression for the Applied Econometrician
ADONIS YATCHEW

INTRODUCTION TO THE MATHEMATICAL AND STATISTICAL FOUNDATIONS OF ECONOMETRICS

HERMAN J. BIERENS
Pennsylvania State University

CAMBRIDGE
UNIVERSITY PRESS

CAMBRIDGE UNIVERSITY PRESS
Cambridge, New York, Melbourne, Madrid, Cape Town, Singapore,
São Paulo, Delhi, Dubai, Tokyo, Mexico City

Cambridge University Press
The Edinburgh Building, Cambridge CB2 8RU, UK

Published in the United States of America by Cambridge University Press, New York

www.cambridge.org
Information on this title: www.cambridge.org/9780521542241

First published 2005

A catalogue record for this publication is available from the British Library

Library of Congress Cataloguing in Publication Data
Bierens, Herman J., 1943-
Introduction to the mathematical and statistical foundations of econometrics /
Herman J. Bierens.
p. cm. – (Themes in modern econometrics)
Includes bibliographical references and index.
ISBN 0-521-83431-7 - ISBN 0-521-54224-3 (pb.)
1. Econometrics. I. Title. II. Series.
HB139.B527 2004
330'.01'5195 - dc22   2004040792

ISBN 978-0-521-83431-5 Hardback
ISBN 978-0-521-54224-1 Paperback

Contents

Preface

This book is intended for use in a rigorous introductory Ph.D.-level course in econometrics or in a field course in econometric theory. It is based on lecture notes that I developed during the period 1997–2003 for the first-semester econometrics course "Introduction to Econometrics" in the core of the Ph.D. program in economics at the Pennsylvania State University. Initially, these lecture notes were written as a companion to Gallant's (1997) textbook but have been developed gradually into an alternative textbook. Therefore, the topics that are covered in this book encompass those in Gallant's book, but in much more depth. Moreover, to make the book also suitable for a field course in econometric theory, I have included various advanced topics as well. I used to teach this advanced material in the econometrics field at the Free University of Amsterdam and Southern Methodist University on the basis of the draft of my previous textbook (Bierens 1994).

Some chapters have their own appendixes containing the more advanced topics, difficult proofs, or both. Moreover, there are three appendixes with material that is supposed to be known but often is not – or not sufficiently. Appendix I contains a comprehensive review of linear algebra, including all the proofs. This appendix is intended for self-study only but may serve well in a half-semester or one-quarter course in linear algebra. Appendix II reviews a variety of mathematical topics and concepts that are used throughout the main text, and Appendix III reviews the basics of complex analysis, which is a subject needed to understand and derive the properties of characteristic functions.

At the beginning of the first class, I always tell my students, "Never ask me how. Only ask me why." In other words, don't be satisfied with recipes. Of course, this applies to other economics fields as well – in particular if the mission of the Ph.D. program is to place its graduates at research universities. First, modern economics is highly mathematical. Therefore, in order to be able to make original contributions to economic theory, Ph.D. students need to develop a "mathematical mind." Second, students who are going to work in an applied econometrics field like empirical Industrial Organization (IO) or labor need to be able to read the theoretical econometrics literature in order to keep up-to-date with the latest econometric techniques. Needless to say, students interested in contributing to econometric theory need to become professional mathematicians and statisticians first. Therefore, in this book I focus on teaching "why" by providing proofs, or at least motivations if proofs are too complicated, of the mathematical and statistical results necessary for understanding modern econometric theory.

Probability theory is a branch of measure theory. Therefore, probability theory is introduced in Chapter 1 in a measure-theoretical way. The same applies to unconditional and conditional expectations in Chapters 2 and 3, which are introduced as integrals with respect to probability measures. These chapters are also beneficial as preparation for the study of economic theory – in particular modern macroeconomic theory. See, for example, Stokey, Lucas, and Prescott (1989).

It usually takes me three weeks (on a schedule of two lectures of one hour and fifteen minutes per week) to get through Chapter 1 with all the appendixes omitted. Chapters 2 and 3 together, without the appendixes, usually take me about three weeks as well.

Chapter 4 deals with transformations of random variables and vectors and also lists the most important univariate continuous distributions together with their expectations, variances, moment-generating functions (if they exist), and characteristic functions. I usually explain only the change-of-variables formula for (joint) densities, leaving the rest of Chapter 4 for self-tuition.

The multivariate normal distribution is treated in detail in Chapter 5 far beyond the level found in other econometrics textbooks. Statistical inference (i.e., estimation and hypotheses testing) is also introduced in Chapter 5 in the framework of the classical linear regression model. At this point it is assumed that the students have a thorough understanding of linear algebra. This assumption, however, is often more fiction than fact. To test this hypothesis, and to force the students to refresh their linear algebra, I usually assign all the exercises in Appendix I as homework before starting with Chapter 5. It takes me about three weeks to get through this chapter.

Asymptotic theory for independent random variables and vectors – in particular the weak and strong laws of large numbers and the central limit theorem – is discussed in Chapter 6 together with various related convergence results. Moreover, the results in this chapter are applied to M-estimators, including nonlinear regression estimators, as an introduction to asymptotic inference. However, I have never been able to get beyond Chapter 6 in one semester, even after skipping all the appendixes and Sections 6.4 and 6.9, which deal with asymptotic inference.

Chapter 7 extends the weak law of large numbers and the central limit theorem to stationary time series processes, starting from the Wold (1938) decomposition. In particular, the martingale difference central limit theorem of McLeish (1974) is reviewed together with preliminary results.

Maximum likelihood theory is treated in Chapter 8. This chapter is different from the standard treatment of maximum likelihood theory in that special attention is paid to the problem of how to set up the likelihood function if the distribution of the data is neither absolutely continuous nor discrete. In this chapter only a few references to the results in Chapter 7 are made – in particular in Section 8.4.4. Therefore, Chapter 7 is not a prerequisite for Chapter 8, provided that the asymptotic inference parts of Chapter 6 (Sections 6.4 and 6.9) have been covered.

Finally, the helpful comments of five referees on the draft of this book, and the comments of my colleague Joris Pinkse on Chapter 8, are gratefully acknowledged. My students have pointed out many typos in earlier drafts, and their queries have led to substantial improvements of the exposition. Of course, only I am responsible for any remaining errors.

Introduction to the Mathematical and Statistical Foundations of Econometrics

1 Probability and Measure

1.1. The Texas Lotto

1.1.1. Introduction

Texans used to play the lotto by selecting six different numbers between 1 and 50, which cost $1 for each combination.[1] Twice a week, on Wednesday and Saturday at 10 P.M., six ping-pong balls were released without replacement from a rotating plastic ball containing 50 ping-pong balls numbered 1 through 50. The winner of the jackpot (which has occasionally accumulated to 60 or more million dollars!) was the one who had all six drawn numbers correct, where the order in which the numbers were drawn did not matter. If these conditions were still being observed, what would the odds of winning by playing one set of six numbers only?

To answer this question, suppose first that the order of the numbers does matter. Then the number of *ordered* sets of 6 out of 50 numbers is 50 possibilities for the first drawn number times 49 possibilities for the second drawn number, times 48 possibilities for the third drawn number, times 47 possibilities for the fourth drawn number, times 46 possibilities for the fifth drawn number, times 45 possibilities for the sixth drawn number:

$$\prod_{j=0}^{5}(50 - j) = \prod_{k=45}^{50} k = \frac{\prod_{k=1}^{50} k}{\prod_{k=1}^{50-6} k} = \frac{50!}{(50 - 6)!}.$$

---

[1] In the spring of 2000, the Texas Lottery changed the rules. The number of balls was increased to fifty-four to create a larger jackpot. The official reason for this change was to make playing the lotto more attractive because a higher jackpot makes the lotto game more exciting. Of course, the actual intent was to boost the lotto revenues!

The notation $n!$, read "n factorial," stands for the product of the natural numbers 1 through n:

$$n! = 1 \times 2 \times \cdots \times (n-1) \times n \quad \text{if } n > 0, \qquad 0! = 1.$$

The reason for defining $0! = 1$ will be explained in the next section.

Because a set of six given numbers can be permutated in 6! ways, we need to correct the preceding number for the 6! replications of each unordered set of six given numbers. Therefore, the number of sets of six *unordered* numbers out of 50 is

$$\binom{50}{6} \stackrel{\text{def.}}{=} \frac{50!}{6!(50-6)!} = 15,890,700.$$

Thus, the probability of winning such a lotto by playing only one combination of six numbers is $1/15,890,700.$[2]

1.1.2. Binomial Numbers

In general, the number of ways we can draw a set of k *unordered* objects out of a set of n objects *without* replacement is

$$\binom{n}{k} \stackrel{\text{def.}}{=} \frac{n!}{k!(n-k)!}. \tag{1.1}$$

These (binomial) numbers,[3] read as "n choose k," also appear as coefficients in the binomial expansion

$$(a+b)^n = \sum_{k=0}^{n} \binom{n}{k} a^k b^{n-k}. \tag{1.2}$$

The reason for defining $0! = 1$ is now that the first and last coefficients in this binomial expansion are always equal to 1:

$$\binom{n}{0} = \binom{n}{n} = \frac{n!}{0!n!} = \frac{1}{0!} = 1.$$

For not too large an n, the binomial numbers (1.1) can be computed recursively by hand using the *Triangle of Pascal*:

---

[2]   Under the new rules (see Note 1), this probability is $1/25,827,165.$

[3]   These binomial numbers can be computed using the "Tools → Discrete distribution tools" menu of *EasyReg International*, the free econometrics software package developed by the author. *EasyReg International* can be downloaded from Web page http://econ.la.psu.edu/~hbierens/EASYREG.HTM

$$
\begin{array}{ccccccccccc}
 & & & & & 1 & & & & & \\
 & & & & 1 & & 1 & & & & \\
 & & & 1 & & 2 & & 1 & & & \\
 & & 1 & & 3 & & 3 & & 1 & & \\
 & 1 & & 4 & & 6 & & 4 & & 1 & \\
 1 & & 5 & & 10 & & 10 & & 5 & & 1 \\
1 & \cdots & & \cdots & & \cdots & & \cdots & & \cdots & & 1
\end{array}
\qquad (1.3)
$$

Except for the 1's on the legs and top of the triangle in (1.3), the entries are the sum of the adjacent numbers on the previous line, which results from the following easy equality:

$$
\binom{n-1}{k-1} + \binom{n-1}{k} = \binom{n}{k} \quad \text{for} \quad n \geq 2, \ k = 1, \ldots, n-1. \quad (1.4)
$$

Thus, the top 1 corresponds to $n = 0$, the second row corresponds to $n = 1$, the third row corresponds to $n = 2$, and so on, and for each row $n + 1$, the entries are the binomial numbers (1.1) for $k = 0, \ldots, n$. For example, for $n = 4$ the coefficients of $a^k b^{n-k}$ in the binomial expansion (1.2) can be found on row 5 in (1.3): $(a + b)^4 = 1 \times a^4 + 4 \times a^3 b + 6 \times a^2 b^2 + 4 \times ab^3 + 1 \times b^4$.

1.1.3. Sample Space

The Texas lotto is an example of a statistical experiment. The set of possible outcomes of this statistical experiment is called the *sample space* and is usually denoted by Ω. In the Texas lotto case, Ω contains $N = 15{,}890{,}700$ elements: $\Omega = \{\omega_1, \ldots, \omega_N\}$, where each element ω_j is a set itself consisting of six different numbers ranging from 1 to 50 such that for any pair ω_i, ω_j with $i \neq j$, $\omega_i \neq \omega_j$. Because in this case the elements ω_j of Ω are sets themselves, the condition $\omega_i \neq \omega_j$ for $i \neq j$ is equivalent to the condition that $\omega_i \cap \omega_j \notin \Omega$.

1.1.4. Algebras and Sigma-Algebras of Events

A set $\{\omega_{j_1}, \ldots, \omega_{j_k}\}$ of different number combinations you can bet on is called an *event*. The collection of all these events, denoted by $\mathscr{F}$, is a "family" of subsets of the sample space Ω. In the Texas lotto case the collection $\mathscr{F}$ consists of all subsets of Ω, including Ω itself and the empty set $\emptyset$.[4] In principle, you could bet on all number combinations if you were rich enough (it would cost you \$15,890,700). Therefore, the sample space Ω itself is included in $\mathscr{F}$. You could also decide not to play at all. This event can be identified as the empty set $\emptyset$. For the sake of completeness, it is included in $\mathscr{F}$ as well.

---

[4] Note that the latter phrase is superfluous because $\Omega \subset \Omega$ signifies that every element of Ω is included in Ω, which is clearly true, and $\emptyset \subset \Omega$ is true because $\emptyset \subset \emptyset \cup \Omega = \Omega$.

Because, in the Texas lotto case, the collection $\mathscr{F}$ contains all subsets of Ω, it automatically satisfies the conditions

$$\text{If } A \in \mathscr{F} \quad \text{then} \quad \tilde{A} = \Omega \backslash A \in \mathscr{F}, \tag{1.5}$$

where $\tilde{A} = \Omega \backslash A$ is the *complement* of the set A (relative to the set Ω), that is, the set of all elements of Ω that are not contained in A, and

$$\text{If } A, B \in \mathscr{F} \quad \text{then} \quad A \cup B \in \mathscr{F}. \tag{1.6}$$

By induction, the latter condition extends to any finite union of sets in $\mathscr{F}$: If $A_j \in \mathscr{F}$ for $j = 1, 2, \ldots, n$, then $\cup_{j=1}^{n} A_j \in \mathscr{F}$.

Definition 1.1: *A collection $\mathscr{F}$ of subsets of a nonempty set Ω satisfying the conditions (1.5) and (1.6) is called an algebra.*[5]

In the Texas lotto example, the sample space Ω is finite, and therefore the collection $\mathscr{F}$ of subsets of Ω is finite as well. Consequently, in this case the condition (1.6) extends to

$$\text{If } A_j \in \mathscr{F} \quad \text{for} \quad j = 1, 2, 3, \ldots \quad \text{then} \quad \overset{\infty}{\underset{j=1}{\cup}} A_j \in \mathscr{F}. \tag{1.7}$$

However, because in this case the collection $\mathscr{F}$ of subsets of Ω is finite, there are only a finite number of distinct sets $A_j \in \mathscr{F}$. Therefore, in the Texas lotto case the countable infinite union $\cup_{j=1}^{\infty} A_j$ in (1.7) involves only a finite number of distinct sets A_j; the other sets are replications of these distinct sets. Thus, condition (1.7) does not require that all the sets $A_j \in \mathscr{F}$ are different.

Definition 1.2: *A collection $\mathscr{F}$ of subsets of a nonempty set Ω satisfying the conditions (1.5) and (1.7) is called a σ-algebra.*[6]

1.1.5. Probability Measure

Let us return to the Texas lotto example. The odds, or probability, of winning are $1/N$ for each valid combination ω_j of six numbers; hence, if you play n different valid number combinations $\{\omega_{j_1}, \ldots, \omega_{j_n}\}$, the probability of winning is $n/N : P(\{\omega_{j_1}, \ldots, \omega_{j_n}\}) = n/N$. Thus, in the Texas lotto case the probability $P(A)$, $A \in \mathscr{F}$, is given by the number n of elements in the set A divided by the total number N of elements in Ω. In particular we have $P(\Omega) = 1$, and if you do not play at all the probability of winning is zero: $P(\emptyset) = 0$.

[5] Also called a *field*.
[6] Also called a *σ-field* or a *Borel field*.

The function $P(A), A \in \mathscr{F}$, is called a probability measure. It assigns a number $P(A) \in [0, 1]$ to each set $A \in \mathscr{F}$. Not every function that assigns numbers in $[0, 1]$ to the sets in $\mathscr{F}$ is a probability measure except as set forth in the following definition:

Definition 1.3: *A mapping* $P: \mathscr{F} \to [0, 1]$ *from a* σ-*algebra* $\mathscr{F}$ *of subsets of a set* Ω *into the unit interval is a probability measure on* $\{\Omega, \mathscr{F}\}$ *if it satisfies the following three conditions:*

For all $A \in \mathscr{F}$, $P(A) \geq 0$, $\qquad\qquad\qquad\qquad\qquad\qquad\qquad$ (1.8)

$P(\Omega) = 1$, $\qquad\qquad\qquad\qquad\qquad\qquad\qquad\qquad\qquad$ (1.9)

For disjoint sets $A_j \in \mathscr{F}$, $P\left(\bigcup_{j=1}^{\infty} A_j\right) = \sum_{j=1}^{\infty} P(A_j).$ $\qquad\qquad$ (1.10)

Recall that sets are *disjoint* if they have no elements in common: their intersections are the empty set.

The conditions (1.8) and (1.9) are clearly satisfied for the case of the Texas lotto. On the other hand, in the case under review the collection $\mathscr{F}$ of events contains only a finite number of sets, and thus any countably infinite sequence of sets in $\mathscr{F}$ must contain sets that are the same. At first sight this seems to conflict with the implicit assumption that countably infinite sequences of *disjoint* sets always exist for which (1.10) holds. It is true indeed that any countably infinite sequence of disjoint sets in a finite collection $\mathscr{F}$ of sets can only contain a finite number of nonempty sets. This is no problem, though, because all the other sets are then equal to the empty set $\emptyset$. The empty set is disjoint with itself, $\emptyset \cap \emptyset = \emptyset$, and with any other set, $A \cap \emptyset = \emptyset$. Therefore, if $\mathscr{F}$ is finite, then any countable infinite sequence of disjoint sets consists of a finite number of nonempty sets and an infinite number of replications of the empty set. Consequently, if $\mathscr{F}$ is finite, then it is sufficient to verify condition (1.10) for any pair of disjoint sets A_1, A_2 in $\mathscr{F}$, $P(A_1 \cup A_2) = P(A_1) + P(A_2)$. Because, in the Texas lotto case $P(A_1 \cup A_2) = (n_1 + n_2)/N$, $P(A_1) = n_1/N$, and $P(A_2) = n_2/N$, where n_1 is the number of elements of A_1 and n_2 is the number of elements of A_2, the latter condition is satisfied and so is condition (1.10).

The statistical experiment is now completely described by the triple $\{\Omega, \mathscr{F}, P\}$, called the *probability space*, consisting of the sample space Ω (i.e., the set of all possible outcomes of the statistical experiment involved), a σ-algebra $\mathscr{F}$ of events (i.e., a collection of subsets of the sample space Ω such that the conditions (1.5) and (1.7) are satisfied), and a probability measure $P: \mathscr{F} \to [0, 1]$ satisfying the conditions (1.8)–(1.10).

In the Texas lotto case the collection $\mathscr{F}$ of events is an algebra, but because $\mathscr{F}$ is finite it is automatically a σ-algebra.

1.2. Quality Control

1.2.1. Sampling without Replacement

As a second example, consider the following case. Suppose you are in charge of quality control in a light bulb factory. Each day N light bulbs are produced. But before they are shipped out to the retailers, the bulbs need to meet a minimum quality standard such as not allowing more than R out of N bulbs to be defective. The only way to verify this exactly is to try all the N bulbs out, but that will be too costly. Therefore, the way quality control is conducted in practice is to randomly draw n bulbs *without* replacement and to check how many bulbs in this sample are defective.

As in the Texas lotto case, the number M of different samples s_j of size n you can draw out of a set of N elements without replacement is

$$ M = \binom{N}{n}. $$

Each sample s_j is characterized by a number k_j of defective bulbs in the sample involved. Let K be the actual number of defective bulbs. Then $k_j \in \{0, 1, \ldots, \min(n, K)\}$.

Let $\Omega = \{0, 1, \ldots, n\}$ and let the σ-algebra $\mathscr{F}$ be the collection of all subsets of Ω. The number of samples s_j with $k_j = k \le \min(n, K)$ defective bulbs is

$$ \binom{K}{k}\binom{N-K}{n-k} $$

because there are "K choose k" ways to draw k unordered numbers out of K numbers without replacement and "$N - K$ choose $n - k$" ways to draw $n - k$ unordered numbers out of $N - K$ numbers without replacement. Of course, in the case that $n > K$ the number of samples s_j with $k_j = k > \min(n, K)$ defective bulbs is zero. Therefore, let

$$ P(\{k\}) = \frac{\binom{K}{k}\binom{N-K}{n-k}}{\binom{N}{n}} \quad \text{if } 0 \le k \le \min(n, K), $$

$$ P(\{k\}) = 0 \text{ elsewhere}, \tag{1.11} $$

and for each set $A = \{k_1, \ldots, k_m\} \in \mathscr{F}$, let $P(A) = \sum_{j=1}^{m} P(\{k_j\})$. (*Exercise*: Verify that this function P satisfies all the requirements of a probability measure.) The triple $\{\Omega, \mathscr{F}, P\}$ is now the probability space corresponding to this statistical experiment.

The probabilities (1.11) are known as the *hypergeometric* (N, K, n) probabilities.

1.2.2. Quality Control in Practice[7]

The problem in applying this result in quality control is that K is unknown. Therefore, in practice the following decision rule as to whether $K \leq R$ or not is followed. Given a particular number $r \leq n$, to be determined at the end of this subsection, assume that the set of N bulbs meets the minimum quality requirement $K \leq R$ if the number k of defective bulbs in the sample is less than or equal to r. Then the set $A(r) = \{0, 1, \ldots, r\}$ corresponds to the assumption that the set of N bulbs meets the minimum quality requirement $K \leq R$, hereafter indicated by "accept," with probability

$$P(A(r)) = \sum_{k=0}^{r} P(\{k\}) = p_r(n, K), \tag{1.12}$$

say, whereas its complement $\tilde{A}(r) = \{r + 1, \ldots, n\}$ corresponds to the assumption that this set of N bulbs does not meet this quality requirement, hereafter indicated by "reject," with corresponding probability

$$P(\tilde{A}(r)) = 1 - p_r(n, K).$$

Given r, this decision rule yields two types of errors: a Type I error with probability $1 - p_r(n, K)$ if you reject, whereas in reality $K \leq R$, and a Type II error with probability $p_r(K, n)$ if you accept, whereas in reality $K > R$. The probability of a Type I error has upper bound

$$p_1(r, n) = 1 - \min_{K \leq R} p_r(n, K), \tag{1.13}$$

and the probability of a Type II error upper bound

$$p_2(r, n) = \max_{K > R} p_r(n, K). \tag{1.14}$$

To be able to choose r, one has to restrict either $p_1(r, n)$ or $p_2(r, n)$, or both. Usually it is the former option that is restricted because a Type I error may cause the whole stock of N bulbs to be trashed. Thus, allow the probability of a Type I error to be a maximal α such as $\alpha = 0.05$. Then r should be chosen such that $p_1(r, n) \leq \alpha$. Because $p_1(r, n)$ is decreasing in r, due to the fact that (1.12) is increasing in r, we could in principle choose r arbitrarily large. But because $p_2(r, n)$ is increasing in r, we should not choose r unnecessarily large. Therefore, choose $r = r(n|\alpha)$, where $r(n|\alpha)$ is the minimum value of r for which $p_1(r, n) \leq \alpha$. Moreover, if we allow the Type II error to be maximal β, we have to choose the sample size n such that $p_2(r(n|\alpha), n) \leq \beta$.

As we will see in Chapters 5 and 6, this decision rule is an example of a statistical test, where $H_0 : K \leq R$ is called the null hypothesis to be tested at

---

[7] This section may be skipped.

the $\alpha \times 100\%$ significance level against the alternative hypothesis $H_1 : K > R$. The number $r(n|\alpha)$ is called the critical value of the test, and the number k of defective bulbs in the sample is called the test statistic.

1.2.3. Sampling with Replacement

As a third example, consider the quality control example in the previous section except that now the light bulbs are sampled *with* replacement: After a bulb is tested, it is put back in the stock of N bulbs even if the bulb involved proves to be defective. The rationale for this behavior may be that the customers will at most accept a fraction R/N of defective bulbs and thus will not complain as long as the actual fraction K/N of defective bulbs does not exceed R/N. In other words, why not sell defective light bulbs if doing so is acceptable to the customers?

The sample space Ω and the σ-algebra $\mathscr{F}$ are the same as in the case of sampling without replacement, but the probability measure P is different. Consider again a sample s_j of size n containing k defective light bulbs. Because the light bulbs are put back in the stock after being tested, there are K^k ways of drawing an *ordered* set of k defective bulbs and $(N - K)^{n-k}$ ways of drawing an *ordered* set of $n - k$ working bulbs. Thus, the number of ways we can draw, with replacement, an ordered set of n light bulbs containing k defective bulbs is $K^k(N - K)^{n-k}$. Moreover, as in the Texas lotto case, it follows that the number of *unordered* sets of k defective bulbs and $n - k$ working bulbs is "n choose k." Thus, the total number of ways we can choose a sample with replacement containing k defective bulbs and $n - k$ working bulbs in any order is

$$\binom{n}{k} K^k(N - K)^{n-k}.$$

Moreover, the number of ways we can choose a sample of size n with replacement is N^n. Therefore,

$$P(\{k\}) = \binom{n}{k} \frac{K^k(N - K)^{n-k}}{N^n}$$
$$= \binom{n}{k} p^k(1 - p)^{n-k}, \quad k = 0, 1, 2, \ldots, n, \tag{1.15}$$

where $p = K/N$, and again for each set $A = \{k_1, \ldots, k_m\} \in \mathscr{F}, P(A) = \sum_{j=1}^{m} P(\{k_j\})$. Of course, if we replace $P(\{k\})$ in (1.11) by (1.15), the argument in Section 1.2.2 still applies.

The probabilities (1.15) are known as the *binomial* (n, p) probabilities.

1.2.4. Limits of the Hypergeometric and Binomial Probabilities

Note that if N and K are large relative to n, the hypergeometric probability (1.11) and the binomial probability (1.15) will be almost the same. This follows from the fact that, for fixed k and n,

$$P(\{k\}) = \frac{\binom{K}{k}\binom{N-K}{n-k}}{\binom{N}{n}} = \frac{\frac{K!(N-K)!}{K!(K-k)!(n-k)!(N-K-n+k)!}}{\frac{N!}{n!(N-n)!}}$$

$$= \frac{n!}{k!(n-k)!} \times \frac{\frac{K!(N-K)!}{(K-k)!(N-K-n+k)!}}{\frac{N!}{(N-n)!}}$$

$$= \binom{n}{k} \times \frac{\frac{K!}{(K-k)!} \times \frac{(N-K)!}{(N-K-n+k)!}}{\frac{N!}{(N-n)!}}$$

$$= \binom{n}{k} \times \frac{\left(\prod_{j=1}^{k}(K-k+j)\right) \times \left(\prod_{j=1}^{n-k}(N-K-n+k+j)\right)}{\prod_{j=1}^{n}(N-n+j)}$$

$$= \binom{n}{k} \times \frac{\left[\prod_{j=1}^{k}\left(\frac{K}{N}-\frac{k}{N}+\frac{j}{N}\right)\right] \times \left[\prod_{j=1}^{n-k}\left(1-\frac{K}{N}-\frac{n}{N}+\frac{k}{N}+\frac{j}{N}\right)\right]}{\prod_{j=1}^{n}\left(1-\frac{n}{N}+\frac{j}{N}\right)}$$

$$\to \binom{n}{k} p^k (1-p)^{n-k} \quad \text{if } N \to \infty \quad \text{and} \quad K/N \to p.$$

Thus, the binomial probabilities also arise as limits of the hypergeometric probabilities.

Moreover, if in the case of the binomial probability (1.15) p is very small and n is very large, the probability (1.15) can be approximated quite well by the Poisson(λ) probability:

$$P(\{k\}) = \exp(-\lambda)\frac{\lambda^k}{k!}, \quad k = 0, 1, 2, \ldots, \tag{1.16}$$

where $\lambda = np$. This follows from (1.15) by choosing $p = \lambda/n$ for $n > \lambda$, with $\lambda > 0$ fixed, and letting $n \to \infty$ while keeping k fixed:

$$P(\{k\}) = \binom{n}{k}p^k(1-p)^{n-k}$$

$$= \frac{n!}{k!(n-k)!}(\lambda/n)^k(1-\lambda/n)^{n-k} = \frac{\lambda^k}{k!} \times \frac{n!}{n^k(n-k)!}$$

$$\times \frac{(1-\lambda/n)^n}{(1-\lambda/n)^k} \to \exp(-\lambda)\frac{\lambda^k}{k!} \quad \text{for} \quad n \to \infty,$$

because for $n \to \infty$,

$$\frac{n!}{n^k(n-k)!} = \frac{\prod_{j=1}^{k}(n-k+j)}{n^k} = \prod_{j=1}^{k}\left(1-\frac{k}{n}+\frac{j}{n}\right) \to \prod_{j=1}^{k} 1 = 1$$

$$(1-\lambda/n)^k \to 1$$

and

$$(1 - \lambda/n)^n \rightarrow \exp(-\lambda). \tag{1.17}$$

Due to the fact that (1.16) is the limit of (1.15) for $p = \lambda/n \downarrow 0$ as $n \rightarrow \infty$, the Poisson probabilities (1.16) are often used to model the occurrence of *rare* events.

Note that the sample space corresponding to the Poisson probabilities is $\Omega = \{0, 1, 2, \ldots\}$ and that the σ-algebra $\mathscr{F}$ of events involved can be chosen to be the collection of *all* subsets of Ω because any nonempty subset A of Ω is either countable infinite or finite. If such a subset A is countable infinite, it takes the form $A = \{k_1, k_2, k_3, \ldots\}$, where the k_j's are distinct nonnegative integers; hence, $P(A) = \sum_{j=1}^{\infty} P(\{k_j\})$ is well-defined. The same applies of course if A is finite: if $A = \{k_1, \ldots, k_m\}$, then $P(A) = \sum_{j=1}^{m} P(\{k_j\})$. This probability measure clearly satisfies the conditions (1.8)–(1.10).

1.3. Why Do We Need Sigma-Algebras of Events?

In principle we could define a probability measure on an algebra $\mathscr{F}$ of subsets of the sample space rather than on a σ-algebra. We only need to change condition (1.10) as follows: For disjoint sets $A_j \in \mathscr{F}$ such that $\cup_{j=1}^{\infty} A_j \in \mathscr{F}$, $P(\cup_{j=1}^{\infty} A_j) = \sum_{j=1}^{\infty} P(A_j)$. By letting all but a finite number of these sets be equal to the empty set, this condition then reads as follows: For disjoint sets $A_j \in \mathscr{F}$, $j = 1, 2, \ldots, n < \infty$, $P(\cup_{j=1}^{n} A_j) = \sum_{j=1}^{n} P(A_j)$. However, if we confined a probability measure to an algebra, all kinds of useful results would no longer apply. One of these results is the so-called strong law of large numbers (see Chapter 6).

As an example, consider the following game. Toss a fair coin infinitely many times and assume that after each tossing you will get one dollar if the outcome is heads and nothing if the outcome is tails. The sample space Ω in this case can be expressed in terms of the winnings, that is, each element ω of Ω takes the form of a string of infinitely many zeros and ones, for example, $\omega = (1, 1, 0, 1, 0, 1\ldots)$. Now consider the event: "After n tosses the winning is k dollars." This event corresponds to the set $A_{k,n}$ of elements ω of Ω for which the sum of the first n elements in the string involved is equal to k. For example, the set $A_{1,2}$ consists of all ω of the type $(1, 0, \ldots)$ and $(0, 1, \ldots)$. As in the example in Section 1.2.3, it can be shown that

$$P(A_{k,n}) = \binom{n}{k}(1/2)^n \quad \text{for} \quad k = 0, 1, 2, \ldots, n,$$

$$P(A_{k,n}) = 0 \quad \text{for} \quad k > n \text{ or } k < 0.$$

Next, for $q = 1, 2, \ldots$, consider the events after n tosses the average winning k/n is contained in the interval $[0.5 - 1/q, 0.5 + 1/q]$. These events correspond to the sets $B_{q,n} = \cup_{k=[n/2-n/q)]+1}^{[n/2+n/q]} A_{k,n}$, where $[x]$ denotes the smallest integer $\geq x$. Then the set $\cap_{m=n}^{\infty} B_{q,m}$ corresponds to the following event:

From the nth tossing onwards the average winning will stay in the interval $[0.5 - 1/q, 0.5 + 1/q]$; the set $\cup_{n=1}^{\infty} \cap_{m=n}^{\infty} B_{q,m}$ corresponds to the event there exists an n (possibly depending on ω) such that from the nth tossing onwards the average winning will stay in the interval $[0.5 - 1/q, 0.5 + 1/q]$. Finally, the set $\cap_{q=1}^{\infty} \cup_{n=1}^{\infty} \cap_{m=n}^{\infty} B_{q,m}$ corresponds to the event the average winning converges to $1/2$ as n converges to infinity. Now the strong law of large numbers states that the latter event has probability 1: $P[\cap_{q=1}^{\infty} \cup_{n=1}^{\infty} \cap_{m=n}^{\infty} B_{q,m}] = 1$. However, this probability is only defined if $\cap_{q=1}^{\infty} \cup_{n=1}^{\infty} \cap_{m=n}^{\infty} B_{q,m} \in \mathscr{F}$. To guarantee this, we need to require that $\mathscr{F}$ be a σ-algebra.

1.4. Properties of Algebras and Sigma-Algebras

1.4.1. General Properties

In this section I will review the most important results regarding algebras, σ-algebras, and probability measures.

Our first result is trivial:

Theorem 1.1: *If an algebra contains only a finite number of sets, then it is a σ-algebra. Consequently, an algebra of subsets of a finite set Ω is a σ-algebra.*

However, an algebra of subsets of an *infinite* set Ω is not necessarily a σ-algebra. A counterexample is the collection $\mathscr{F}_*$ of all subsets of $\Omega = (0, 1]$ of the type $(a, b]$, where $a < b$ are *rational* numbers in $[0, 1]$ together with their *finite* unions and the empty set $\emptyset$. Verify that $\mathscr{F}_*$ is an algebra. Next, let $p_n = [10^n \pi]/10^n$ and $a_n = 1/p_n$, where $[x]$ means truncation to the nearest integer $\leq x$. Note that $p_n \uparrow \pi$; hence, $a_n \downarrow \pi^{-1}$ as $n \to \infty$. Then, for $n = 1, 2, 3, \ldots, (a_n, 1] \in \mathscr{F}_*$, but $\cup_{n=1}^{\infty}(a_n, 1] = (\pi^{-1}, 1] \notin \mathscr{F}_*$ because π^{-1} is irrational. Thus, $\mathscr{F}_*$ is *not* a σ-algebra.

Theorem 1.2: *If $\mathscr{F}$ is an algebra, then $A, B \in \mathscr{F}$ implies $A \cap B \in \mathscr{F}$; hence, by induction, $A_j \in \mathscr{F}$ for $j = 1, \ldots, n < \infty$ implies $\cap_{j=1}^{n} A_j \in \mathscr{F}$. A collection $\mathscr{F}$ of subsets of a nonempty set Ω is an algebra if it satisfies condition (1.5) and the condition that, for any pair $A, B \in \mathscr{F}, A \cap B \in \mathscr{F}$.*

Proof: Exercise.
Similarly, we have

Theorem 1.3: *If $\mathscr{F}$ is a σ-algebra, then for any countable sequence of sets $A_j \in \mathscr{F}, \cap_{j=1}^{\infty} A_j \in \mathscr{F}$. A collection $\mathscr{F}$ of subsets of a nonempty set Ω is a σ-algebra if it satisfies condition (1.5) and the condition that, for any countable sequence of sets $A_j \in \mathscr{F}, \cap_{j=1}^{\infty} A_j \in \mathscr{F}$.*

These results will be convenient in cases in which it is easier to prove that (countable) intersections are included in $\mathscr{F}$ than to prove that (countable) unions are included:

If $\mathscr{F}$ is already an algebra, then condition (1.7) alone would make it a σ-algebra. However, the condition in the following theorem is easier to verify than (1.7):

Theorem 1.4: *If $\mathscr{F}$ is an algebra and A_j, $j = 1, 2, 3, \ldots$ is a countable sequence of sets in $\mathscr{F}$, then there exists a countable sequence of disjoint sets B_j in $\mathscr{F}$ such that $\cup_{j=1}^{\infty} A_j = \cup_{j=1}^{\infty} B_j$. Consequently, an algebra $\mathscr{F}$ is also a σ-algebra if for any sequence of disjoint sets B_j in $\mathscr{F}$, $\cup_{j=1}^{\infty} B_j \in \mathscr{F}$.*

Proof: Let $A_j \in \mathscr{F}$. Denote $B_1 = A_1$, $B_{n+1} = A_{n+1}\backslash(\cup_{j=1}^{n} A_j) = A_{n+1} \cap (\cap_{j=1}^{n} \tilde{A}_j)$. It follows from the properties of an algebra (see Theorem 1.2) that all the B_j's are sets in $\mathscr{F}$. Moreover, it is easy to verify that the B_j's are disjoint and that $\cup_{j=1}^{\infty} A_j = \cup_{j=1}^{\infty} B_j$. Thus, if $\cup_{j=1}^{\infty} B_j \in \mathscr{F}$, then $\cup_{j=1}^{\infty} A_j \in \mathscr{F}$. Q.E.D.

Theorem 1.5: *Let $\mathscr{F}_{\theta}$, $\theta \in \Theta$, be a collection of σ-algebras of subsets of a given set Ω, where Θ is a possibly uncountable index set. Then $\mathscr{F} = \cap_{\theta \in \Theta} \mathscr{F}_{\theta}$ is a σ-algebra.*

Proof: Exercise.

For example, let $\mathscr{F}_{\theta} = \{(0, 1], \emptyset, (0, \theta], (\theta, 1]\}$, $\theta \in \Theta = (0, 1]$. Then $\cap_{\theta \in \Theta} \mathscr{F}_{\theta} = \{(0, 1], \emptyset\}$ is a σ-algebra (the trivial σ-algebra).

Theorem 1.5 is important because it guarantees that, for any collection $\mathfrak{C}$ of subsets of Ω, there exists a smallest σ-algebra containing $\mathfrak{C}$. By adding complements and countable unions it is possible to extend $\mathfrak{C}$ to a σ-algebra. This can always be done because $\mathfrak{C}$ is contained in the σ-algebra of all subsets of Ω, but there is often no unique way of doing this except in the case in which $\mathfrak{C}$ is finite. Thus, let $\mathscr{F}_{\theta}$, $\theta \in \Theta$ be the collection of all σ-algebras containing $\mathfrak{C}$. Then $\mathscr{F} = \cap_{\theta \in \Theta} \mathscr{F}_{\theta}$ is the smallest σ-algebra containing $\mathfrak{C}$.

Definition 1.4: *The smallest σ-algebra containing a given collection $\mathfrak{C}$ of sets is called the σ-algebra generated by $\mathfrak{C}$ and is usually denoted by $\sigma(\mathfrak{C})$.*

Note that $\mathscr{F} = \cup_{\theta \in \Theta} \mathscr{F}_{\theta}$ is not always a σ-algebra. For example, let $\Omega = [0, 1]$ and let, for $n \geq 1$, $\mathscr{F}_n = \{[0, 1], \emptyset, [0, 1 - n^{-1}], (1 - n^{-1}, 1]\}$. Then $A_n = [0, 1 - n^{-1}] \in \mathscr{F}_n \subset \cup_{n=1}^{\infty} \mathscr{F}_n$, but the interval $[0, 1) = \cup_{n=1}^{\infty} A_n$ is not contained in any of the σ-algebras $\mathscr{F}_n$; hence, $\cup_{n=1}^{\infty} A_n \notin \cup_{n=1}^{\infty} \mathscr{F}_n$.

However, it is always possible to extend $\cup_{\theta \in \Theta} \mathscr{F}_{\theta}$ to a σ-algebra, often in various ways, by augmenting it with the missing sets. The smallest σ-algebra containing $\cup_{\theta \in \Theta} \mathscr{F}_\theta$ is usually denoted by

$$\vee_{\theta \in \Theta} \mathscr{F}_\theta \overset{\text{def.}}{=} \sigma\left(\cup_{\theta \in \Theta} \mathscr{F}_\theta\right).$$

The notion of smallest σ-algebra of subsets of Ω is always relative to a given collection $\mathfrak{C}$ of subsets of Ω. Without reference to such a given collection $\mathfrak{C}$, the smallest σ-algebra of subsets of Ω is $\{\Omega, \emptyset\}$, which is called the *trivial* σ-algebra.

Moreover, as in Definition 1.4, we can define the smallest algebra of subsets of Ω containing a given collection $\mathfrak{C}$ of subsets of Ω, which we will denote by $\alpha(\mathfrak{C})$.

For example, let $\Omega = (0, 1]$, and let $\mathfrak{C}$ be the collection of all intervals of the type $(a, b]$ with $0 \leq a < b \leq 1$. Then $\alpha(\mathfrak{C})$ consists of the sets in $\mathfrak{C}$ together with the empty set $\emptyset$ and all finite unions of disjoint sets in $\mathfrak{C}$. To see this, check first that this collection $\alpha(\mathfrak{C})$ is an algebra as follows:

(a) The complement of $(a, b]$ in $\mathfrak{C}$ is $(0, a] \cup (b, 1]$. If $a = 0$, then $(0, a] = (0, 0] = \emptyset$, and if $b = 1$, then $(b, 1] = (1, 1] = \emptyset$; hence, $(0, a] \cup (b, 1]$ is a set in $\mathfrak{C}$ or a finite union of disjoint sets in $\mathfrak{C}$.

(b) Let $(a, b]$ in $\mathfrak{C}$ and $(c, d]$ in $\mathfrak{C}$, where without loss of generality we may assume that $a \leq c$. If $b < c$, then $(a, b] \cup (c, d]$ is a union of disjoint sets in $\mathfrak{C}$. If $c \leq b \leq d$, then $(a, b] \cup (c, d] = (a, d]$ is a set in $\mathfrak{C}$ itself, and if $b > d$, then $(a, b] \cup (c, d] = (a, b]$ is a set in $\mathfrak{C}$ itself. Thus, finite unions of sets in $\mathfrak{C}$ are either sets in $\mathfrak{C}$ itself or finite unions of disjoint sets in $\mathfrak{C}$.

(c) Let $A = \cup_{j=1}^n (a_j, b_j]$, where $0 \leq a_1 < b_1 < a_2 < b_2 < \cdots < a_n < b_n \leq 1$. Then $\tilde{A} = \cup_{j=0}^n (b_j, a_{j+1}]$, where $b_0 = 0$ and $a_{n+1} = 1$, which is a finite union of disjoint sets in $\mathfrak{C}$ itself. Moreover, as in part (b) it is easy to verify that finite unions of sets of the type A can be written as finite unions of disjoint sets in $\mathfrak{C}$.

Thus, the sets in $\mathfrak{C}$ together with the empty set $\emptyset$ and all finite unions of disjoint sets in $\mathfrak{C}$ form an algebra of subsets of $\Omega = (0, 1]$.

To verify that this is the smallest algebra containing $\mathfrak{C}$, remove one of the sets in this algebra that does not belong to $\mathfrak{C}$ itself. Given that all sets in the algebra are of the type A in part (c), let us remove this particular set A. But then $\cup_{j=1}^n (a_j, b_j]$ is no longer included in the collection; hence, we have to remove each of the intervals $(a_j, b_j]$ as well, which, however, is not allowed because they belong to $\mathfrak{C}$.

Note that the algebra $\alpha(\mathfrak{C})$ is not a σ-algebra because countable infinite unions are not always included in $\alpha(\mathfrak{C})$. For example, $\cup_{n=1}^\infty (0, 1 - n^{-1}] = (0, 1)$ is a countable union of sets in $\alpha(\mathfrak{C})$, which itself is not included in $\alpha(\mathfrak{C})$. However, we can extend $\alpha(\mathfrak{C})$ to $\sigma(\alpha(\mathfrak{C}))$, the smallest σ-algebra containing $\alpha(\mathfrak{C})$, which coincides with $\sigma(\mathfrak{C})$.

1.4.2. Borel Sets

An important special case of Definition 1.4 is where $\Omega = \mathbb{R}$ and $\mathbb{C}$ is the collection of all open intervals:

$$\mathbb{C} = \{(a, b) : \forall a < b, a, b \in \mathbb{R}\}. \tag{1.18}$$

Definition 1.5: *The σ-algebra generated by the collection (1.18) of all open intervals in $\mathbb{R}$ is called the Euclidean Borel field, denoted by $\mathscr{B}$, and its members are called the Borel sets.*

Note, however, that $\mathscr{B}$ can be defined in different ways because the σ-algebras generated by the collections of open intervals, closed intervals $\{[a, b] : \forall a \leq b, a, b \in \mathbb{R}\}$ and half-open intervals $\{(-\infty, a] : \forall a \in \mathbb{R}\}$, respectively, are all the same! We show this for one case only:

Theorem 1.6: $\mathscr{B} = \sigma(\{(-\infty, a] : \forall a \in \mathbb{R}\})$.

Proof: Let

$$\mathbb{C}_* = \{(-\infty, a] : \forall a \in \mathbb{R}\}. \tag{1.19}$$

(a) If the collection $\mathbb{C}$ defined by (1.18) is contained in $\sigma(\mathbb{C}_*)$, then $\sigma(\mathbb{C}_*)$ is a σ-algebra containing $\mathbb{C}$. But $\mathscr{B} = \sigma(\mathbb{C})$ is the smallest σ-algebra containing $\mathbb{C}$; hence, $\mathscr{B} = \sigma(\mathbb{C}) \subset \sigma(\mathbb{C}_*)$.

To prove this, construct an arbitrary set (a, b) in $\mathbb{C}$ out of countable unions or complements of sets in $\mathbb{C}_*$, or both, as follows: Let $A = (-\infty, a]$ and $B = (-\infty, b]$, where $a < b$ are arbitrary real numbers. Then $A, B \in \mathbb{C}_*$; hence, $A, \tilde{B} \in \sigma(\mathbb{C}_*)$, and thus

$$\sim (a, b] = (-\infty, a] \cup (b, \infty) = A \cup \tilde{B} \in \sigma(\mathbb{C}_*).$$

This implies that $\sigma(\mathbb{C}_*)$ contains all sets of the type $(a, b]$; hence, $(a, b) = \cup_{n=1}^{\infty}(a, b - (b - a)/n] \in \sigma(\mathbb{C}_*)$. Thus, $\mathbb{C} \subset \sigma(\mathbb{C}_*)$.

(b) If the collection $\mathbb{C}_*$ defined by (1.19) is contained in $\mathscr{B} = \sigma(\mathbb{C})$, then $\sigma(\mathbb{C})$ is a σ-algebra containing $\mathbb{C}_*$. But $\sigma(\mathbb{C}_*)$ is the smallest σ-algebra containing $\mathbb{C}_*$; hence, $\sigma(\mathbb{C}_*) \subset \sigma(\mathbb{C}) = \mathscr{B}$.

To prove the latter, observe that, for $m = 1, 2, \ldots, A_m = \cup_{n=1}^{\infty}(a - n, a + m^{-1})$ is a countable union of sets in $\mathbb{C}$; hence, $\tilde{A}_m \in \sigma(\mathbb{C})$, and consequently $(-\infty, a] = \cap_{m=1}^{\infty} A_m = \sim(\cup_{m=1}^{\infty} \tilde{A}_m) \in \sigma(\mathbb{C})$. Thus, $\mathbb{C}_* \subset \sigma(\mathbb{C}) = \mathscr{B}$.

We have shown now that $\mathscr{B} = \sigma(\mathbb{C}) \subset \sigma(\mathbb{C}_*)$ and $\sigma(\mathbb{C}_*) \subset \sigma(\mathbb{C}) = \mathscr{B}$. Thus, $\mathscr{B}$ and $\sigma(\mathbb{C}_*)$ are the same.   Q.E.D.[8]

The notion of Borel set extends to higher dimensions as well:

---

[8]   See also Appendix 1.A.

Definition 1.6: $\mathcal{B}^k = \sigma(\{\times_{j=1}^k (a_j, b_j) : \forall a_j < b_j, a_j, b_j \in \mathbb{R}\})$ *is the k-dimensional Euclidean Borel field. Its members are also called Borel sets (in $\mathbb{R}^k$).*

Also, this is only one of the ways to define higher-dimensional Borel sets. In particular, as in Theorem 1.6 we have

Theorem 1.7: $\mathcal{B}^k = \sigma(\{\times_{j=1}^k (-\infty, a_j] : \forall a_j \in \mathbb{R}\}).$

1.5. Properties of Probability Measures

The three axioms (1.8), (1.9), and (1.10) imply a variety of probability measure properties. Here we list only the most important ones.

Theorem 1.8: *Let $\{\Omega, \mathcal{F}, P\}$ be a probability space. The following hold for sets in $\mathcal{F}$:*

(a) $P(\emptyset) = 0,$
(b) $P(\tilde{A}) = 1 - P(A),$
(c) $A \subset B$ *implies* $P(A) \le P(B),$
(d) $P(A \cup B) + P(A \cap B) = P(A) + P(B),$
(e) *If* $A_n \subset A_{n+1}$ *for* $n = 1, 2, \ldots,$ *then* $P(A_n) \uparrow P(\cup_{n=1}^\infty A_n),$
(f) *If* $A_n \supset A_{n+1}$ *for* $n = 1, 2, \ldots,$ *then* $P(A_n) \downarrow P(\cap_{n=1}^\infty A_n),$
(g) $P(\cup_{n=1}^\infty A_n) \le \sum_{n=1}^\infty P(A_n).$

Proof: (a)–(c): Easy exercises. (d) $A \cup B = (A \cap \tilde{B}) \cup (A \cap B) \cup (B \cap \tilde{A})$ is a union of disjoint sets; hence, by axiom (1.10), $P(A \cup B) = P(A \cap \tilde{B}) + P(A \cap B) + P(B \cap \tilde{A})$. Moreover, $A = (A \cap \tilde{B}) \cup (A \cap B)$ is a union of disjoint sets; thus, $P(A) = P(A \cap \tilde{B}) + P(A \cap B)$, and similarly, $P(B) = P(B \cap \tilde{A}) + P(A \cap B)$. Combining these results, we find that part (d) follows. (e) Let $B_1 = A_1, B_n = A_n \backslash A_{n-1}$ for $n \ge 2$. Then $A_n = \cup_{j=1}^n A_j = \cup_{j=1}^n B_j$ and $\cup_{j=1}^\infty A_j = \cup_{j=1}^\infty B_j$. Because the B_j's are disjoint, it follows from axiom (1.10) that

$$P\left(\bigcup_{j=1}^\infty A_j\right) = \sum_{j=1}^\infty P(B_j)$$

$$= \sum_{j=1}^n P(B_j) + \sum_{j=n+1}^\infty P(B_j) = P(A_n) + \sum_{j=n+1}^\infty P(B_j).$$

Part (e) follows now from the fact that $\sum_{j=n+1}^\infty P(B_j) \downarrow 0$. (f) This part follows from part (e) if one uses complements. (g) Exercise.

1.6. The Uniform Probability Measure

1.6.1. Introduction

Fill a bowl with ten balls numbered from 0 to 9. Draw a ball randomly from this bowl and write down the corresponding number as the first decimal digit of a number between 0 and 1. For example, if the first-drawn number is 4, then write down 0.4. Put the ball back in the bowl, and repeat this experiment. If, for example, the second ball corresponds to the number 9, then this number becomes the second decimal digit: 0.49. Repeating this experiment infinitely many times yields a random number between 0 and 1. Clearly, the sample space involved is the unit interval: $\Omega = [0, 1]$.

For a given number $x \in [0, 1]$ the probability that this random number is less than or equal to x is x. To see this, suppose that you only draw two balls and that $x = 0.58$. If the first ball has a number less than 5, it does not matter what the second number is. There are five ways to draw a first number less than or equal to 4 and 10 ways to draw the second number. Thus, there are 50 ways to draw a number with a first digit less than or equal to 4. There is only one way to draw a first number equal to 5 and 9 ways to draw a second number less than or equal to 8. Thus, the total number of ways we can generate a number less than or equal to 0.58 is 59, and the total number of ways we can draw two numbers with replacement is 100. Therefore, if we only draw two balls with replacement and use the numbers involved as the first and second decimal digit, the probability that we will obtain a number less than or equal to 0.58 is 0.59. Similarly, if we draw 10 balls with replacement, the probability that we will obtain a number less than or equal to 0.5831420385, for instance, is 0.5831420386. In the limit the difference between x and the corresponding probability disappears. Thus, for $x \in [0, 1]$ we have $P([0, x]) = x$. By the same argument it follows that for $x \in [0, 1]$, $P(\{x\}) = P([x, x]) = 0$, that is, the probability that the random number involved will be exactly equal to a given number x is zero. Therefore, for a given $x \in [0, 1]$, $P((0, x]) = P([0, x)) = P((0, x)) = x$. More generally, for any interval in $[0, 1]$ the corresponding probability is the length of the interval involved regardless of whether the endpoints are included. Thus, for $0 \leq a < b \leq 1$, we have $P([a, b]) = P((a, b]) = P([a, b)) = P((a, b)) = b - a$. Any finite union of intervals can be written as a finite union of disjoint intervals by cutting out the overlap. Therefore, this probability measure extends to finite unions of intervals simply by adding up the lengths of the disjoint intervals involved. Moreover, observe that the collection of all finite unions of subintervals in $[0, 1]$, including $[0, 1]$ itself and the empty set, is closed under the formation of complements and finite unions. Thus, we have derived the probability measure P corresponding to the statistical experiment under review for an *algebra* $\mathscr{F}_0$ of subsets of $[0, 1]$, namely,

$$\mathscr{F}_0 = \{(a, b), [a, b], (a, b], [a, b), \forall a, b \in [0, 1], a \leq b,$$

$$\text{and their finite unions}\}, \tag{1.20}$$

where $[a, a]$ is the singleton $\{a\}$ and each of the sets (a, a), $(a, a]$ and $[a, a)$ should be interpreted as the empty set $\emptyset$. This probability measure is a special case of the Lebesgue measure, which assigns each interval its length.

If you are only interested in making probability statements about the sets in the algebra (1.20), then you are done. However, although the algebra (1.20) contains a large number of sets, we cannot yet make probability statements involving arbitrary Borel sets in $[0, 1]$ because not all the Borel sets in $[0, 1]$ are included in (1.20). In particular, for a countable sequence of sets $A_j \in \mathscr{F}_0$, the probability $P(\cup_{j=1}^{\infty} A_j)$ is not always defined because there is no guarantee that $\cup_{j=1}^{\infty} A_j \in \mathscr{F}_0$. Therefore, to make probability statements about arbitrary Borel set in $[0, 1]$, you need to extend the probability measure P on $\mathscr{F}_0$ to a probability measure defined on the Borel sets in $[0, 1]$. The standard approach to do this is to use the *outer measure*.

1.6.2. Outer Measure

Any subset A of $[0, 1]$ can always be completely covered by a finite or countably infinite union of sets in the algebra $\mathscr{F}_0$: $A \subset \cup_{j=1}^{\infty} A_j$, where $A_j \in \mathscr{F}_0$; hence, the "probability" of A is bounded from above by $\sum_{j=1}^{\infty} P(A_j)$. Taking the infimum of $\sum_{j=1}^{\infty} P(A_j)$ over all countable sequences of sets $A_j \in \mathscr{F}_0$ such that $A \subset \cup_{j=1}^{\infty} A_j$ then yields the *outer measure*:

Definition 1.7: *Let $\mathscr{F}_0$ be an algebra of subsets of Ω. The outer measure of an arbitrary subset A of Ω is*

$$P^*(A) = \inf_{A \subset \cup_{j=1}^{\infty} A_j, A_j \in \mathscr{F}_0} \sum_{j=1}^{\infty} P(A_j). \tag{1.21}$$

Note that it is *not* required in (1.21) that $\cup_{j=1}^{\infty} A_j \in \mathscr{F}_0$.

Because a union of sets A_j in an algebra $\mathscr{F}_0$ can always be written as a union of disjoint sets in the algebra $\mathscr{F}_0$ (see Theorem 1.4), we may without loss of generality assume that the infimum in (1.21) is taken over all *disjoint* sets A_j in $\mathscr{F}_0$ such that $A \subset \cup_{j=1}^{\infty} A_j$. This implies that

$$\text{If } A \in \mathscr{F}_0 \quad \text{then} \quad P^*(A) = P(A). \tag{1.22}$$

The question now arises, For which other subsets of Ω is the outer measure a probability measure? Note that the conditions (1.8) and (1.9) are satisfied for the outer measure P^* (*Exercise*: Why?), but, in general, condition (1.10) does not hold for arbitrary sets. See, for example, Royden (1968, 63–64). Nevertheless, it is possible to extend the outer measure to a probability measure on a σ-algebra $\mathscr{F}$ containing $\mathscr{F}_0$:

Theorem 1.9: *Let P be a probability measure on $\{\Omega, \mathscr{F}_0\}$, where $\mathscr{F}_0$ is an algebra, and let $\mathscr{F} = \sigma(\mathscr{F}_0)$ be the smallest σ-algebra containing the algebra $\mathscr{F}_0$. Then the outer measure P^* is a unique probability measure on $\{\Omega, \mathscr{F}\}$, which coincides with P on $\mathscr{F}_0$.*

The proof that the outer measure P^* is a probability measure on $\mathscr{F} = \sigma(\mathscr{F}_0)$ that coincides with P on $\mathscr{F}_0$ is lengthy and is therefore given in Appendix I.B. The proof of the uniqueness of P^* is even longer and is therefore omitted.

Consequently, for the statistical experiment under review there exists a σ-algebra $\mathscr{F}$ of subsets of $\Omega = [0, 1]$ containing the algebra $\mathscr{F}_0$ defined in (1.20) for which the outer measure P^*: $\mathscr{F} \to [0, 1]$ is a unique probability measure. This probability measure assigns its length as probability in this case to each interval in $[0, 1]$. It is called the *uniform* probability measure.

It is not hard to verify that the σ-algebra $\mathscr{F}$ involved contains all the Borel subsets of $[0, 1]$: $\{[0, 1] \cap B$, for all Borel sets $B\} \subset \mathscr{F}$. (*Exercise*: Why?) This collection of Borel subsets of $[0, 1]$ is usually denoted by $[0, 1] \cap \mathscr{B}$ and is a σ-algebra itself (*Exercise*: Why?). Therefore, we could also describe the probability space of this statistical experiment by the probability space $\{[0, 1], [0, 1] \cap \mathscr{B}, P^*\}$, where P^* is the same as before. Moreover, defining the probability measure μ on $\mathscr{B}$ as $\mu(B) = P^*([0, 1] \cap B)$, we can also describe this statistical experiment by the probability space $\{\mathbb{R}, \mathscr{B}, \mu\}$, where, in particular

$$\mu((-\infty, x]) = 0 \quad \text{if } x \leq 0,$$
$$\mu((-\infty, x]) = x \quad \text{if } 0 < x \leq 1,$$
$$\mu((-\infty, x]) = 1 \quad \text{if } x > 1,$$

and, more generally, for intervals with endpoints $a < b$,

$$\mu((a, b)) = \mu([a, b]) = \mu([a, b)) = \mu((a, b])$$
$$= \mu((-\infty, b]) - \mu((-\infty, a]),$$

whereas for all other Borel sets B,

$$\mu(B) = \inf_{B \subset \cup_{j=1}^{\infty}(a_j, b_j)} \sum_{j=1}^{\infty} \mu((a_j, b_j)). \tag{1.23}$$

1.7. Lebesgue Measure and Lebesgue Integral

1.7.1. Lebesgue Measure

Along similar lines as in the construction of the uniform probability measure we can define the Lebesgue measure as follows. Consider a function λ that assigns its length to each open interval (a, b), $\lambda((a, b)) = b - a$, and define for all other Borel sets B in $\mathbb{R}$,

$$\lambda(B) = \inf_{B \subset \cup_{j=1}^{\infty}(a_j, b_j)} \sum_{j=1}^{\infty} \lambda((a_j, b_j)) = \inf_{B \subset \cup_{j=1}^{\infty}(a_j, b_j)} \sum_{j=1}^{\infty}(b_j - a_j).$$

This function λ is called the Lebesgue measure on $\mathbb{R}$, which measures the total "length" of a Borel set, where the measurement is taken from the outside.

Similarly, now let $\lambda(\times_{i=1}^{k}(a_i, b_i)) = \prod_{i=1}^{k}(b_i - a_i)$ and define

$$\lambda(B) = \inf_{B \subset \cup_{j=1}^{\infty}\{\times_{i=1}^{k}(a_{i,j}, b_{i,j})\}} \sum_{j=1}^{\infty} \lambda\left(\times_{i=1}^{k}(a_{i,j}, b_{i,j})\right)$$

$$= \inf_{B \subset \cup_{j=1}^{\infty}\{\times_{i=1}^{k}(a_{i,j}, b_{i,j})\}} \sum_{j=1}^{\infty} \left\{ \prod_{i=1}^{k}(b_{i,j} - a_{i,j}) \right\},$$

for all other Borel sets B in $\mathbb{R}^k$. This is the Lebesgue measure on $\mathbb{R}^k$, which measures the area (in the case $k = 2$) or the volume (in the case $k \geq 3$) of a Borel set in $\mathbb{R}^k$, where again the measurement is taken from the outside.

Note that, in general, Lebesgue measures are not probability measures because the Lebesgue measure can be infinite. In particular, $\lambda(\mathbb{R}^k) = \infty$. However, if confined to a set with Lebesgue measure 1, this measure becomes the uniform probability measure. More generally, for any Borel set $A \in \mathbb{R}^k$ with positive and finite Lebesgue measure, $\mu(B) = \lambda(A \cap B)/\lambda(A)$ is the uniform probability measure on $\mathcal{B}^k \cap A$.

1.7.2. Lebesgue Integral

The Lebesgue measure gives rise to a generalization of the Riemann integral. Recall that the Riemann integral of a nonnegative function $f(x)$ over a finite interval $(a, b]$ is defined as

$$\int_a^b f(x)dx = \sup \sum_{m=1}^{n} \left(\inf_{x \in I_m} f(x) \right) \lambda(I_m),$$

where the I_m's are intervals forming a finite partition of $(a, b]$ – that is, they are disjoint and their union is $(a, b]$: $(a, b] = \cup_{m=1}^n I_m$ – and $\lambda(I_m)$ is the length of I_m; hence, $\lambda(I_m)$ is the Lebesgue measure of I_m, and the supremum is taken over all finite partitions of $(a, b]$. Mimicking the definition of Riemann integral, the Lebesgue integral of a nonnegative function $f(x)$ over a Borel set A can be defined as

$$\int_A f(x)dx = \sup \sum_{m=1}^n \left(\inf_{x \in B_m} f(x) \right) \lambda(B_m),$$

where now the B_m's are Borel sets forming a finite partition of A and the supremum is taken over all such partitions.

If the function $f(x)$ is not nonnegative, we can always write it as the difference of two nonnegative functions: $f(x) = f_+(x) - f_-(x)$, where

$$f_+(x) = \max[0, f(x)], \qquad f_-(x) = \max[0, -f(x)].$$

Then the Lebesgue integral over a Borel set A is defined as

$$\int_A f(x)dx = \int_A f_+(x)dx - \int_A f_-(x)dx$$

provided that at least one of the right-hand integrals is finite.

However, we still need to impose a further condition on the function f in order for it to be Lebesgue integrable. A sufficient condition is that, for each Borel set B in $\mathbb{R}$, the set $\{x : f(x) \in B\}$ is a Borel set itself. As we will see in the next chapter, this is the condition for Borel measurability of f.

Finally, note that if A is an interval and $f(x)$ is Riemann integrable over A, then the Riemann and the Lebesgue integrals coincide.

1.8. Random Variables and Their Distributions

1.8.1. Random Variables and Vectors

In broad terms, a random variable is a numerical translation of the outcomes of a statistical experiment. For example, flip a fair coin once. Then the sample space is $\Omega = \{H, T\}$, where H stands for heads and T stands for tails. The σ-algebra involved is $\mathscr{F} = \{\Omega, \emptyset, \{H\}, \{T\}\}$, and the corresponding probability measure is defined by $P(\{H\}) = P(\{T\}) = 1/2$. Now define the function $X(\omega) = 1$ if $\omega = H$, $X(\omega) = 0$ if $\omega = T$. Then X is a random variable that takes the value 1 with probability $1/2$ and the value 0 with probability $1/2$:

$$P(X = 1) \stackrel{\text{(shorthand notation)}}{=} P(\{\omega \in \Omega : X(\omega) = 1\}) = P(\{H\}) = 1/2,$$

$$P(X = 0) \stackrel{\text{(shorthand notation)}}{=} P(\{\omega \in \Omega : X(\omega) = 0\}) = P(\{T\}) = 1/2.$$

Moreover, for an arbitrary Borel set B we have

$$P(X \in B) =$$

$$P(\{\omega \in \Omega : X(\omega) \in B\}) \begin{cases} = P(\{H\}) & = 1/2 & \text{if } 1 \in B & \text{and} & 0 \notin B, \\ = P(\{T\}) & = 1/2 & \text{if } 1 \notin B & \text{and} & 0 \in B, \\ = P(\{H, T\}) & = 1 & \text{if } 1 \in B & \text{and} & 0 \in B, \\ = P(\emptyset) & = 0 & \text{if } 1 \notin B & \text{and} & 0 \notin B, \end{cases}$$

where, again, $P(X \in B)$ is a shorthand notation[9] for $P(\{\omega \in \Omega : X(\omega) \in B\})$.

In this particular case, the set $\{\omega \in \Omega : X(\omega) \in B\}$ is automatically equal to one of the elements of $\mathscr{F}$, and therefore the probability $P(X \in B) = P(\{\omega \in \Omega : X(\omega) \in B\})$ is well-defined. In general, however, we need to confine the mappings $X : \Omega \to \mathbb{R}$ to those for which we can make probability statements about events of the type $\{\omega \in \Omega : X(\omega) \in B\}$, where B is an arbitrary Borel set, which is only possible if these sets are members of $\mathscr{F}$:

Definition 1.8: *Let $\{\Omega, \mathscr{F}, P\}$ be a probability space. A mapping $X : \Omega \to \mathbb{R}$ is called a random variable defined on $\{\Omega, \mathscr{F}, P\}$ if X is measurable $\mathscr{F}$, which means that for every Borel set B, $\{\omega \in \Omega : X(\omega) \in B\} \in \mathscr{F}$. Similarly, a mapping $X : \Omega \to \mathbb{R}^k$ is called a k-dimensional random vector defined on $\{\Omega, \mathscr{F}, P\}$ if X is measurable $\mathscr{F}$ in the sense that for every Borel set B in $\mathscr{B}^k$, $\{\omega \in \Omega : X(\omega) \in B\} \in \mathscr{F}$.*

In verifying that a real function $X : \Omega \to \mathbb{R}$ is measurable $\mathscr{F}$, it is not necessary to verify that for *all* Borel sets B, $\{\omega \in \Omega : X(\omega) \in B\} \in \mathscr{F}$, but only that this property holds for Borel sets of the type $(-\infty, x]$:

Theorem 1.10: *A mapping $X : \Omega \to \mathbb{R}$ is measurable $\mathscr{F}$ (hence X is a random variable) if and only if for all $x \in \mathbb{R}$ the sets $\{\omega \in \Omega : X(\omega) \leq x\}$ are members of $\mathscr{F}$. Similarly, a mapping $X : \Omega \to \mathbb{R}^k$ is measurable $\mathscr{F}$ (hence X is a random vector of dimension k) if and only if for all $x = (x_1, \ldots, x_k)^\mathsf{T} \in \mathbb{R}^k$ the sets $\cap_{j=1}^k \{\omega \in \Omega : X_j(\omega) \leq x_j\} = \{\omega \in \Omega : X(\omega) \in \times_{j=1}^k (-\infty, x_j]\}$ are members of $\mathscr{F}$, where the X_j's are the components of X.*

Proof: Consider the case $k = 1$. Suppose that $\{\omega \in \Omega : X(\omega) \in (-\infty, x]\} \in \mathscr{F}, \forall x \in \mathbb{R}$. Let $\mathscr{D}$ be the collection of all Borel sets B for which $\{\omega \in \Omega : X(\omega) \in B\} \in \mathscr{F}$. Then $\mathscr{D} \subset \mathscr{B}$ and $\mathscr{D}$ contains the collection of half-open intervals $(-\infty, x]$, $x \in \mathbb{R}$. If $\mathscr{D}$ is a σ-algebra itself, it is a σ-algebra containing

---

[9] In the sequel we will denote the probability of an event involving random variables or vectors X as P ("expression involving X") without referring to the corresponding set in $\mathscr{F}$. For example, for random variables X and Y defined on a common probability space $\{\Omega, \mathscr{F}, P\}$, the shorthand notation $P(X > Y)$ should be interpreted as $P(\{\omega \in \Omega : X(\omega) > Y(\omega)\})$.

the half-open intervals. But $\mathscr{B}$ is the smallest σ-algebra containing the half-open intervals (see Theorem 1.6), and thus $\mathscr{B} \subset \mathscr{D}$; hence, $\mathscr{D} = \mathscr{B}$. Therefore, it suffices to prove that $\mathscr{D}$ is a σ-algebra:

(a) Let $B \in \mathscr{D}$. Then $\{\omega \in \Omega : X(\omega) \in B\} \in \mathscr{F}$; hence,

$$\sim \{\omega \in \Omega : X(\omega) \in B\} = \{\omega \in \Omega : X(\omega) \in \tilde{B}\} \in \mathscr{F},$$

and thus $\tilde{B} \in \mathscr{D}$.

(b) Next, let $B_j \in \mathscr{D}$ for $j = 1, 2, \ldots$. Then $\{\omega \in \Omega : X(\omega) \in B_j\} \in \mathscr{F}$; hence,

$$\cup_{j=1}^{\infty}\{\omega \in \Omega : X(\omega) \in B_j\} = \{\omega \in \Omega : X(\omega) \in \cup_{j=1}^{\infty} B_j\} \in \mathscr{F},$$

and thus $\cup_{j=1}^{\infty} B_j \in \mathscr{D}$.

The proof of the case $k > 1$ is similar.   Q.E.D.[10]
The sets $\{\omega \in \Omega : X(\omega) \in B\}$ are usually denoted by $X^{-1}(B)$:

$$X^{-1}(B) \overset{\text{def.}}{=} \{\omega \in \Omega : X(\omega) \in B\}.$$

The collection $\mathscr{F}_X = \{X^{-1}(B), \forall B \in \mathscr{B}\}$ is a σ-algebra itself (*Exercise*: Why?) and is called the σ-algebra *generated* by the random variable X. More generally,

Definition 1.9: *Let X be a random variable $(k = 1)$ or a random vector $(k > 1)$. The σ-algebra $\mathscr{F}_X = \{X^{-1}(B), \forall B \in \mathscr{B}^k\}$ is called the σ-algebra generated by X.*

In the coin-tossing case, the mapping X is one-to-one, and therefore in that case $\mathscr{F}_X$ is the same as $\mathscr{F}$, but in general $\mathscr{F}_X$ will be smaller than $\mathscr{F}$. For example, roll a dice and let $X = 1$ if the outcome is even and $X = 0$ if the outcome is odd. Then

$$\mathscr{F}_X = \{\{1, 2, 3, 4, 5, 6\}, \{2, 4, 6\}, \{1, 3, 5\}, \emptyset\},$$

whereas $\mathscr{F}$ in this case consists of *all* subsets of $\Omega = \{1, 2, 3, 4, 5, 6\}$.

Given a k-dimensional random vector X, or a random variable X (the case $k = 1$), define for arbitrary Borel sets $B \in \mathscr{B}^k$:

$$\mu_X(B) = P\big(X^{-1}(B)\big) = P(\{\omega \in \Omega : X(\omega) \in B\}). \tag{1.24}$$

Then $\mu_X(\cdot)$ is a probability measure on $\{\mathbb{R}^k, \mathscr{B}^k\}$

(a) for all $B \in \mathscr{B}^k$, $\mu_X(B) \geq 0$;
(b) $\mu_X(\mathbb{R}^k) = 1$;
(c) for all disjoint $B_j \in \mathscr{B}^k$, $\mu_X(\cup_{j=1}^{\infty} B_j) = \sum_{j=1}^{\infty} \mu_X(B_j)$.

---

[10] See also Appendix 1.A.

Thus, the random variable X maps the probability space $\{\Omega, \mathscr{F}, P\}$ into a new probability space, $\{\mathbb{R}, \mathscr{B}, \mu_X\}$, which in its turn is mapped back by X^{-1} into the (possibly smaller) probability space $\{\Omega, \mathscr{F}_X, P\}$. The behavior of random vectors is similar.

Definition 1.10: *The probability measure $\mu_X(\cdot)$ defined by (1.24) is called the probability measure induced by X.*

1.8.2. Distribution Functions

For Borel sets of the type $(-\infty, x]$, or $\times_{j=1}^k (-\infty, x_j]$ in the multivariate case, the value of the induced probability measure μ_X is called the distribution function:

Definition 1.11: *Let X be a random variable $(k = 1)$ or a random vector $(k > 1)$ with induced probability measure μ_X. The function $F(x) = \mu_X(\times_{j=1}^k (-\infty, x_j])$, $x = (x_1, \ldots, x_k)^\mathsf{T} \in \mathbb{R}^k$ is called the distribution function of X.*

It follows from these definitions and Theorem 1.8 that

Theorem 1.11: *A distribution function of a random variable is always right continuous, that is, $\forall x \in \mathbb{R}, \lim_{\delta \downarrow 0} F(x + \delta) = F(x)$, and monotonic nondecreasing, that is, $F(x_1) \leq F(x_2)$ if $x_1 < x_2$, with $\lim_{x \downarrow -\infty} F(x) = 0$, $\lim_{x \uparrow \infty} F(x) = 1$.*

Proof: Exercise.

However, a distribution function is not always left continuous. As a counterexample, consider the distribution function of the binomial (n, p) distribution in Section 1.2.2. Recall that the corresponding probability space consists of sample space $\Omega = \{0, 1, 2, \ldots, n\}$, the σ-algebra $\mathscr{F}$ of all subsets of Ω, and probability measure $P(\{k\})$ defined by (1.15). The random variable X involved is defined as $X(k) = k$ with distribution function

$$F(x) = 0 \qquad \text{for} \quad x < 0,$$
$$F(x) = \sum_{k \leq x} P(\{k\}) \quad \text{for} \quad x \in [0, n],$$
$$F(x) = 1 \qquad \text{for} \quad x > n.$$

Now, for example, let $x = 1$. Then, for $0 < \delta < 1$, $F(1 - \delta) = F(0)$, and $F(1 + \delta) = F(1)$; hence, $\lim_{\delta \downarrow 0} F(1 + \delta) = F(1)$, but $\lim_{\delta \downarrow 0} F(1 - \delta) = F(0) < F(1)$.

The left limit of a distribution function F in x is usually denoted by $F(x-)$:

$$F(x-) \overset{\text{def.}}{=} \lim_{\delta \downarrow 0} F(x - \delta).$$

Thus, if x is a continuity point, then $F(x-) = F(x)$; if x is a discontinuity point, then $F(x-) < F(x)$.

The binomial distribution involved is an example of a *discrete* distribution. The uniform distribution on [0, 1] derived in Section 1.5 is an example of a *continuous* distribution with distribution function

$$
\begin{aligned}
F(x) &= 0 \quad \text{for} \quad x < 0, \\
F(x) &= x \quad \text{for} \quad x \in [0, 1], \\
F(x) &= 1 \quad \text{for} \quad x > 1.
\end{aligned}
\tag{1.25}
$$

In the case of the binomial distribution (1.15), the number of discontinuity points of F is finite, and in the case of the Poisson distribution (1.16) the number of discontinuity points of F is countable infinite. In general, we have that

Theorem 1.12: *The set of discontinuity points of a distribution function of a random variable is countable.*

Proof: Let D be the set of all discontinuity points of the distribution function $F(x)$. Every point x in D is associated with a nonempty open interval $(F(x-), F(x)) = (a, b)$, for instance, which is contained in [0, 1]. For each of these open intervals (a, b) there exists a rational number q such $a < q < b$; hence, the number of open intervals (a, b) involved is countable because the rational numbers are countable. Therefore, D is countable.   Q.E.D.

The results of Theorems 1.11 and 1.12 only hold for distribution functions of random *variables*, though. It is possible to generalize these results to distribution functions of random vectors, but this generalization is far from trivial and is therefore omitted.

As follows from Definition 1.11, a distribution function of a random variable or vector X is completely determined by the corresponding induced probability measure $\mu_X(\cdot)$. But what about the other way around? That is, given a distribution function $F(x)$, is the corresponding induced probability measure $\mu_X(\cdot)$ unique? The answer is yes, but I will prove the result only for the univariate case:

Theorem 1.13: *Given the distribution function F of a random vector $X \in \mathbb{R}^k$, there exists a unique probability measure μ on $\{\mathbb{R}^k, \mathscr{B}^k\}$ such that for $x = (x_1, \ldots, x_k)^{\mathrm{T}} \in \mathbb{R}^k$, $F(x) = \mu(\times_{i=1}^{k}(-\infty, x_i])$.*

Proof: Let $k = 1$ and let $\mathfrak{I}_0$ be the collection of all intervals of the type

$$
\begin{aligned}
&(a, b), [a, b], (a, b], [a, b), (-\infty, a), (\infty, a], (b, \infty), \\
&[b, \infty), \ a \le b \in \mathbb{R}
\end{aligned}
\tag{1.26}
$$

together with their finite unions, where $[a, a]$ is the singleton $\{a\}$, and (a, a), $(a, a]$, and $[a, a)$ should be interpreted as the empty set $\emptyset$. Then each set in $\mathfrak{F}_0$ can be written as a finite union of *disjoint* sets of the type (1.26) (compare (1.20)); hence, $\mathfrak{F}_0$ is an algebra. Define for $-\infty < a < b < \infty$,

$$\mu((a, a)) = \mu((a, a]) = \mu([a, a)) = \mu(\emptyset) = 0$$
$$\mu(\{a\}) = F(a) - \lim_{\delta \downarrow 0} F(a - \delta), \quad \mu((a, b]) = F(b) - F(a)$$
$$\mu([a, b)) = \mu((a, b]) - \mu(\{b\}) + \mu(\{a\}),$$
$$\mu([a, b]) = \mu((a, b]) + \mu(\{a\})$$
$$\mu((a, b)) = \mu((a, b]) - \mu(\{b\}), \quad \mu((-\infty, a]) = F(a)$$
$$\mu([-\infty, a)) = F(a) - \mu(\{a\}), \quad \mu((b, \infty)) = 1 - F(b)$$
$$\mu([b, \infty)) = \mu((b, \infty)) + \mu(\{b\})$$

and let $\mu(\cup_{j=1}^{n} A_j) = \sum_{j=1}^{n} \mu(A_j)$ for *disjoint* sets $A_1, \ldots, A_n$ of the type (1.26). Then, the distribution function F defines a probability measure μ on $\mathfrak{F}_0$, and this probability measure coincides on $\mathfrak{F}_0$ with the induced-probability measure μ_X. It follows now from Theorem 1.9 that there exists a σ-algebra $\mathfrak{F}$ containing $\mathfrak{F}_0$ for which the same applies. This σ-algebra $\mathfrak{F}$ may be chosen equal to the σ-algebra $\mathscr{B}$ of Borel sets.   Q.E.D.

The importance of this result is that there is a one-to-one relationship between the distribution function F of a random variable or vector X and the induced probability measure μ_X. Therefore, the distribution function contains all the information about μ_X.

Definition 1.12: *A distribution function F on $\mathbb{R}^k$ and its associated probability measure μ on $\{\mathbb{R}^k, \mathscr{B}^k\}$ are called absolutely continuous with respect to Lebesgue measure if for every Borel set B in $\mathbb{R}^k$ with zero Lebesgue measure, $\mu(B) = 0$.*

We will need this concept in the next section.

1.9. Density Functions

An important concept is that of a density function. Density functions are usually associated to differentiable distribution functions:

Definition 1.13: *The distribution of a random variable X is called absolutely continuous if there exists a nonnegative integrable function f, called the density function of X, such that the distribution function F of X can be written as the (Lebesgue) integral $F(x) = \int_{-\infty}^{x} f(u) du$. Similarly, the distribution of a random* vector $X \in \mathbb{R}^k$ *is called absolutely continuous if there exists a nonnegative integrable function f on* $\mathbb{R}^k$, *called the joint density, such that the distribution function F of X can be written as the integral*

$$F(x) = \int_{-\infty}^{x_1} \cdots \int_{-\infty}^{x_k} f(u_1, \ldots, u_k) du_1 \ldots du_k,$$

where $x = (x_1, \ldots, x_k)^{\mathrm{T}}$.

   Thus, in the case $F(x) = \int_{-\infty}^{x} f(u) du$, the density function $f(x)$ is the derivative of $F(x)$: $f(x) = F'(x)$, and in the multivariate case $F(x_1, \ldots, x_k) = \int_{-\infty}^{x_1} \ldots \int_{-\infty}^{x_k} f(u_1, \ldots, u_k) du_1 \ldots du_k$ the joint density is $f(x_1, \cdots, x_k) = (\partial/\partial x_1) \ldots (\partial/\partial x_k) F(x_1, \ldots, x_k)$.

   The reason for calling the distribution functions in Definition 1.13 *absolutely continuous* is that in this case the distributions involved are absolutely continuous with respect to Lebesgue measure. See Definition 1.12. To see this, consider the case $F(x) = \int_{-\infty}^{x} f(u) du$, and verify (*Exercise*) that the corresponding probability measure μ is

$$\mu(B) = \int_B f(x) dx, \tag{1.27}$$

where the integral is now the Lebesgue integral over a Borel set B. Because the Lebesgue integral over a Borel set with zero Lebesgue measure is zero (*Exercise*), it follows that $\mu(B) = 0$ if the Lebesgue measure of B is zero.

   For example, the uniform distribution (1.25) is absolutely continuous because we can write (1.25) as $F(x) = \int_{-\infty}^{x} f(u) du$ with density $f(u) = 1$ for $0 < u < 1$ and zero elsewhere. Note that in this case $F(x)$ is not differentiable in 0 and 1 but that does not matter as long as the set of points for which the distribution function is not differentiable has zero Lebesgue measure. Moreover, a density of a random variable always integrates to 1 because $1 = \lim_{x \to \infty} F(x) = \int_{-\infty}^{\infty} f(u) du$. Similarly, for random vectors $X \in \mathbb{R}^k : \int_{-\infty}^{\infty} \int_{-\infty}^{\infty} \cdots \int_{-\infty}^{\infty} f(u_1, \ldots, u_k) du_1 \ldots du_k = 1$.

   Note that continuity and differentiability of a distribution function are *not* sufficient conditions for absolute continuity. It is possible to construct a continuous distribution function $F(x)$ that is differentiable on a subset $D \subset \mathbb{R}$, with $\mathbb{R} \backslash D$ a set with Lebesgue measure zero, such that $F'(x) \equiv 0$ on D, and thus in this case $\int_{-\infty}^{x} F'(x) dx \equiv 0$. Such distributions functions are called singular. See Chung (1974, 12–13) for an example of how to construct a singular distribution function on $\mathbb{R}$ and Chapter 5 in this volume for singular multivariate normal distributions.

1.10. Conditional Probability, Bayes' Rule, and Independence

1.10.1. Conditional Probability

Consider a statistical experiment with probability space $\{\Omega, \mathscr{F}, P\}$, and suppose it is known that the outcome of this experiment is contained in a set B with $P(B) > 0$. What is the probability of an event A given that the outcome of the experiment is contained in B? For example, roll a dice. Then $\Omega = \{1, 2, 3, 4, 5, 6\}$, $\mathscr{F}$ is the σ-algebra of all subsets of Ω, and $P(\{\omega\}) = 1/6$ for $\omega = 1, 2, 3, 4, 5, 6$. Let B be the event The outcome is even ($B = \{2, 4, 6\}$), and let $A = \{1, 2, 3\}$. If we know that the outcome is even, then we know that the outcomes $\{1, 3\}$ in A will not occur; if the outcome is contained in A, it is contained in $A \cap B = \{2\}$. Knowing that the outcome is 2, 4, or 6, the probability that the outcome is contained in A is therefore $1/3 = P(A \cap B)/P(B)$. This is the conditional probability of A, given B, denoted by $P(A|B)$. If it is revealed that the outcome of a statistical experiment is contained in a particular set B, then the sample space Ω is reduced to B because we then know that the outcomes in the complement of B will not occur, the σ-algebra $\mathscr{F}$ is reduced to $\mathscr{F} \cap B = \{A \cap B, A \in \mathscr{F}\}$, the collection of all intersections of the sets in $\mathscr{F}$ with B (*Exercise*: Is this a σ-algebra?), and the probability measure involved becomes $P(A|B) = P(A \cap B)/P(B)$; hence, the probability space becomes $\{B, \mathscr{F} \cap B, P(\cdot|B)\}$. See Exercise 19 for this chapter.

1.10.2. Bayes' Rule

Let A and B be sets in $\mathscr{F}$. Because the sets A and $\tilde{A}$ form a partition of the sample space Ω, we have $B = (B \cap A) \cup (B \cap \tilde{A})$; hence,

$$P(B) = P(B \cap A) + P(B \cap \tilde{A}) = P(B|A)P(A) + P(B|\tilde{A})P(\tilde{A}).$$

Moreover,

$$P(A|B) = \frac{P(A \cap B)}{P(B)} = \frac{P(B|A)P(A)}{P(B)}.$$

Combining these two results now yields Bayes' rule:

$$P(A|B) = \frac{P(B|A)P(A)}{P(B|A)P(A) + P(B|\tilde{A})P(\tilde{A})}.$$

Thus, Bayes' rule enables us to compute the conditional probability $P(A|B)$ if $P(A)$ and the conditional probabilities $P(B|A)$ and $P(B|\tilde{A})$ are given.

More generally, if A_j, $j = 1, 2, \ldots, n$ ($\leq \infty$) is a partition of the sample space Ω (i.e., the A_j's are disjoint sets in $\mathscr{F}$ such that $\Omega = \cup_{j=1}^n A_j$), then

$$P(A_i|B) = \frac{P(B|A_i)P(A_i)}{\sum_{j=1}^n P(B|A_j)P(A_j)}.$$

Bayes' rule plays an important role in a special branch of statistics (and econometrics) called Bayesian statistics (econometrics).

1.10.3. Independence

If $P(A|B) = P(A)$, knowing that the outcome is in B does not give us any information about A. In that case the events A and B are described as being *independent*. For example, if I tell you that the outcome of the dice experiment is contained in the set $\{1, 2, 3, 4, 5, 6\} = \Omega$, then you know nothing about the outcome: $P(A|\Omega) = P(A \cap \Omega)/P(\Omega) = P(A)$; hence, Ω is independent of any other event A.

Note that $P(A|B) = P(A)$ is equivalent to $P(A \cap B) = P(A)P(B)$. Thus,

Definition 1.14: *Sets A and B in $\mathscr{F}$ are (pairwise) independent if $P(A \cap B) = P(A)P(B)$.*

If events A and B are independent, and events B and C are independent, are events A and C independent? The answer is not necessarily. As a counterexample, observe that if A and B are independent, then so are $\tilde{A}$ and B, A and $\tilde{B}$, and $\tilde{A}$ and $\tilde{B}$ because

$$P(\tilde{A} \cap B) = P(B) - P(A \cap B) = P(B) - P(A)P(B)$$
$$= (1 - P(A))P(B) = P(\tilde{A})P(B),$$

and similarly,

$$P(A \cap \tilde{B}) = P(A)P(\tilde{B}) \quad \text{and} \quad P(\tilde{A} \cap \tilde{B}) = P(\tilde{A})P(\tilde{B}).$$

Now if $C = \tilde{A}$ and $0 < P(A) < 1$, then B and $C = \tilde{A}$ are independent if A and B are independent, but

$$P(A \cap C) = P(A \cap \tilde{A}) = P(\emptyset) = 0,$$

whereas

$$P(A)P(C) = P(A)P(\tilde{A}) = P(A)(1 - P(A)) \neq 0.$$

Thus, for more than two events we need a stronger condition for independence than pairwise independence, namely,

Definition 1.15: *A sequence A_j of sets in $\mathscr{F}$ is independent if for **every** subsequence $A_{j_i}, i = 1, 2, \ldots, n$, $P(\cap_{i=1}^n A_{j_i}) = \prod_{i=1}^n P(A_{j_i})$.*

By requiring that the latter hold for all subsequences rather than $P(\cap_{i=1}^\infty A_i) = \prod_{i=1}^\infty P(A_i)$, we avoid the problem that a sequence of events would be called independent if one of the events were the empty set.

The independence of a pair or sequence of random variables or vectors can now be defined as follows.

Definition 1.16: *Let X_j be a sequence of random variables or vectors defined on a common probability space $\{\Omega, \mathscr{F}, P\}$. X_1 and X_2 are pairwise independent if for all Borel sets B_1, B_2 the sets $A_1 = \{\omega \in \Omega : X_1(\omega) \in B_1\}$ and $A_2 = \{\omega \in \Omega : X_2(\omega) \in B_2\}$ are independent. The sequence X_j is independent if for all Borel sets B_j the sets $A_j = \{\omega \in \Omega : X_j(\omega) \in B_j\}$ are independent.*

As we have seen before, the collection $\mathscr{F}_j = \{\{\omega \in \Omega : X_j(\omega) \in B\}, B \in \mathscr{B}\}\} = \{X_j^{-1}(B), B \in \mathscr{B}\}$ is a sub-σ-algebra of $\mathscr{F}$. Therefore, Definition 1.16 also reads as follows: *The sequence of random variables X_j is independent if for arbitrary $A_j \in \mathscr{F}_j$ the sequence of sets A_j is independent according to Definition 1.15.*

Independence usually follows from the setup of a statistical experiment. For example, draw randomly *with* replacement n balls from a bowl containing R red balls and $N - R$ white balls, and let $X_j = 1$ if the jth draw is a red ball and $X_j = 0$ if the jth draw is a white ball. Then $X_1, \ldots, X_n$ are independent (and $X_1 + \cdots + X_n$ has the binomial (n, p) distribution with $p = R/N$). However, if we drew these balls without replacement, then $X_1, \ldots, X_n$ would not be independent.

For a sequence of random variables X_j it suffices to verify only the condition in Definition 1.16 for Borel sets B_j of the type $(-\infty, x_j], x_j \in \mathbb{R}$:

Theorem 1.14: *Let $X_1, \ldots, X_n$ be random variables, and denote, for $x \in \mathbb{R}$ and $j = 1, \ldots, n$, $A_j(x) = \{\omega \in \Omega : X_j(\omega) \leq x\}$. Then $X_1, \ldots, X_n$ are independent if and only if for arbitrary $(x_1, \ldots, x_n)^\mathsf{T} \in \mathbb{R}^n$ the sets $A_1(x_1)$, $\ldots, A_n(x_n)$ are independent.*

The complete proof of Theorem 1.14 is difficult and is therefore omitted, but the result can be motivated as follow. Let $\mathscr{F}_j^0 = \{\Omega, \emptyset, X_j^{-1}((-\infty, x]),$ $X_j^{-1}((y, \infty)), \forall x, y \in \mathbb{R}$ together with all finite unions and intersections of the latter two types of sets$\}$. Then $\mathscr{F}_j^0$ is an algebra such that for arbitrary $A_j \in \mathscr{F}_j^0$

the sequence of sets A_j is independent. This is not too hard to prove. Now $\mathscr{F}_j = \{X_j^{-1}(B), B \in \mathscr{B}\}\}$ is the smallest σ-algebra containing $\mathscr{F}_j^0$ and is also the smallest monotone class containing $\mathscr{F}_j^0$. One can show (but this is the hard part), using the properties of monotone class (see Exercise 11 below), that, for arbitrary $A_j \in \mathscr{F}_j$, the sequence of sets A_j is independent as well.

It follows now from Theorem 1.14 that

Theorem 1.15: *The random variables $X_1, \ldots, X_n$ are independent if and only if the joint distribution function $F(x)$ of $X = (X_1, \ldots, X_n)^{\mathrm{T}}$ can be written as the product of the distribution functions $F_j(x_j)$ of the X_j's, that is, $F(x) = \prod_{j=1}^n F_j(x_j)$, where $x = (x_1, \ldots, x_n)^{\mathrm{T}}$.*

The latter distribution functions $F_j(x_j)$ are called the *marginal* distribution functions. Moreover, it follows straightforwardly from Theorem 1.15 that, if the joint distribution of $X = (X_1, \ldots, X_n)^{\mathrm{T}}$ is absolutely continuous with joint density function $f(x)$, then $X_1, \ldots, X_n$ are independent if and only if $f(x)$ can be written as the product of the density functions $f_j(x_j)$ of the X_j's:

$$f(x) = \prod_{j=1}^n f_j(x_j), \quad \text{where} \quad x = (x_1, \ldots, x_n)^{\mathrm{T}}.$$

The latter density functions are called the *marginal* density functions.

1.11. Exercises

1. Prove (1.4).

2. Prove (1.17) by proving that $\ln[(1 - \mu/n)^n] = n \ln(1 - \mu/n) \to -\mu$ for $n \to \infty$.

3. Let $\mathscr{F}_*$ be the collection of all subsets of $\Omega = (0, 1]$ of the type $(a, b]$, where $a < b$ are *rational* numbers in $[0, 1]$, together with their *finite disjoint* unions and the empty set $\emptyset$. Verify that $\mathscr{F}_*$ is an algebra.

4. Prove Theorem 1.2.

5. Prove Theorem 1.5.

6. Let $\Omega = (0, 1]$, and let $\mathfrak{C}$ be the collection of all intervals of the type $(a, b]$ with $0 \le a < b \le 1$. Give as many distinct examples as you can of sets that are contained in $\sigma(\mathfrak{C})$ (the smallest σ-algebra containing this collection $\mathfrak{C}$) but not in $\alpha(\mathfrak{C})$ (the smallest algebra containing the collection $\mathfrak{C}$).

7. Show that $\sigma(\{[a, b] : \forall a \le b, \quad a, b \in \mathbb{R}\}) = \mathscr{B}$.

8. Prove part (g) of Theorem 1.8.

9. Prove that $\mathscr{F}_0$ defined by (1.20) is an algebra.

10. Prove (1.22).

11. A collection $\mathscr{F}$ of subsets of a set Ω is called a *monotone class* if the following two conditions hold:

$$A_n \in \mathscr{F}, A_n \subset A_{n+1}, n = 1, 2, 3, \ldots \text{ imply } \cup_{n=1}^{\infty} A_n \in \mathscr{F},$$
$$A_n \in \mathscr{F}, A_n \supset A_{n+1}, n = 1, 2, 3, \ldots \text{ imply } \cap_{n=1}^{\infty} A_n \in \mathscr{F}.$$

Show that an algebra is a σ-algebra if and only if it is a monotone class.

12. A collection $\mathscr{F}_\lambda$ of subsets of a set Ω is called a λ-system if $A \in \mathscr{F}_\lambda$ implies $\tilde{A} \in \mathscr{F}_\lambda$, and for *disjoint* sets $A_j \in \mathscr{F}_\lambda, \cup_{j=1}^{\infty} A_j \in \mathscr{F}_\lambda$. A collection $\mathscr{F}_\pi$ of subsets of a set Ω is called a π-system if $A, B \in \mathscr{F}_\pi$ implies that $A \cap B \in \mathscr{F}_\pi$. Prove that if a λ-system is also a π-system, then it is a σ-algebra.

13. Let $\mathscr{F}$ be the smallest σ-algebra of subsets of $\mathbb{R}$ containing the (countable) collection of half-open intervals $(-\infty, q]$ with *rational* endpoints q. Prove that $\mathscr{F}$ contains all the Borel subsets of $\mathbb{R} : \mathscr{B} = \mathscr{F}$.

14. Consider the following subset of $\mathbb{R}^2 : L = \{(x, y) \in \mathbb{R}^2 : y = x, 0 \le x \le 1\}$. Explain why L is a Borel set.

15. Consider the following subset of $\mathbb{R}^2 : C = \{(x, y) \in \mathbb{R}^2 : x^2 + y^2 \le 1\}$. Explain why C is a Borel set.

16. Prove Theorem 1.11. *Hint*: Use Definition 1.12 and Theorem 1.8. Determine first which parts of Theorem 1.8 apply.

17. Let $F(x) = \int_{-\infty}^{x} f(u)du$ be an absolutely continuous distribution function. Prove that the corresponding probability measure μ is given by the Lebesgue integral (1.27).

18. Prove that the Lebesgue integral over a Borel set with zero Lebesgue measure is zero.

19. Let $\{\Omega, \mathscr{F}, P\}$ be a probability space, and let $B \in \mathscr{F}$ with $P(B) > 0$. Verify that $\{B, \mathscr{F} \cap B, P(\cdot|B)\}$ is a probability space.

20. Are disjoint sets in $\mathscr{F}$ independent?

21. (Application of Bayes' rule): Suppose that a certain disease, for instance HIV+, afflicts 1 out of 10,000 people. Moreover, suppose that there exists a medical test for this disease that is 90% reliable: If you don't have the disease, the test will confirm that with probability 0.9; the probability is the same if you do have the disease. If a randomly selected person is subjected to this test, and the test indicates that this person has the disease, what is the probability that this person actually has this disease? In other words, if you were this person, would you be scared or not?

22. Let A and B in $\mathscr{F}$ be pairwise independent. Prove that $\tilde{A}$ and B are independent (and therefore A and $\tilde{B}$ are independent and $\tilde{A}$ and $\tilde{B}$ are independent).

23. Draw randomly *without* replacement n balls from a bowl containing R red balls and $N - R$ white balls, and let $X_j = 1$ if the jth draw is a red ball and $X_j = 0$ if the jth draw is a white ball. Show that $X_1, \ldots, X_n$ are *not* independent.

APPENDIXES

1.A. Common Structure of the Proofs of Theorems 1.6 and 1.10

The proofs of Theorems 1.6 and 1.10 employ a similar argument, namely the following:

Theorem 1.A.1: *Let $\mathfrak{C}$ be a collection of subsets of a set Ω, and let $\sigma(\mathfrak{C})$ be the smallest σ-algebra containing $\mathfrak{C}$. Moreover, let ρ be a Boolean function on $\sigma(\mathfrak{C})$, that is, ρ is a set function that takes either the value "True" or "False." Furthermore, let $\rho(A) =$ True for all sets A in $\mathfrak{C}$. If the collection $\mathfrak{D}$ of sets A in $\sigma(\mathfrak{C})$ for which $\rho(A) =$ True is a σ-algebra itself, then $\rho(A) =$ True for all sets A in $\sigma(\mathfrak{C})$.*

Proof: Because $\mathfrak{D}$ is a collection of sets in $\sigma(\mathfrak{C})$ we have $\mathfrak{D} \subset \sigma(\mathfrak{C})$. Moreover, by assumption, $\mathfrak{C} \subset \mathfrak{D}$, and $\mathfrak{D}$ is a σ-algebra. But $\sigma(\mathfrak{C})$ is the smallest σ-algebra containing $\mathfrak{C}$; hence, $\sigma(\mathfrak{C}) \subset \mathfrak{D}$. Thus, $\mathfrak{D} = \sigma(\mathfrak{C})$ and, consequently, $\rho(A) =$ True for all sets A in $\sigma(\mathfrak{C})$.   Q.E.D.

This type of proof will also be used later on.

Of course, the hard part is to prove that $\mathfrak{D}$ is a σ-algebra. In particular, the collection $\mathfrak{D}$ is not automatically a σ-algebra. Take, for example, the case in which $\Omega = [0, 1]$, $\mathfrak{C}$ is the collection of all intervals $[a, b]$ with $0 \le a < b \le 1$, and $\rho(A) =$ True if the smallest interval $[a, b]$ containing A has positive length: $b - a > 0$ and $\rho(A) =$ False otherwise. In this case $\sigma(\mathfrak{C})$ consists of all the Borel subsets of $[0, 1]$ but $\mathfrak{D}$ does not contain singletons, whereas $\sigma(\mathfrak{C})$ does, and thus $\mathfrak{D}$ is smaller than $\sigma(\mathfrak{C})$ and is therefore not a σ-algebra.

1.B. Extension of an Outer Measure to a Probability Measure

To use the outer measure as a probability measure for more general sets that those in $\mathscr{F}_0$, we have to extend the algebra $\mathscr{F}_0$ to a σ-algebra $\mathscr{F}$ of events for which the outer measure is a probability measure. In this appendix it will be shown how $\mathscr{F}$ can be constructed via the following lemmas.

Lemma 1.B.1: *For any sequence B_n of disjoint sets in Ω, $P^*(\cup_{n=1}^{\infty} B_n) \le \sum_{n=1}^{\infty} P^*(B_n)$.*

Proof: Given an arbitrary $\varepsilon > 0$ it follows from (1.21) that there exists a countable sequence of sets $A_{n,j}$ in $\mathscr{F}_0$ such that $B_n \subset \cup_{j=1}^{\infty} A_{n,j}$ and $P^*(B_n) >$

$\sum_{j=1}^{\infty} P(A_{n,j}) - \varepsilon 2^{-n}$; hence,

$$\sum_{n=1}^{\infty} P^*(B_n) > \sum_{n=1}^{\infty} \sum_{j=1}^{\infty} P(A_{n,j}) - \varepsilon \sum_{n=1}^{\infty} 2^{-n} = \sum_{n=1}^{\infty} \sum_{j=1}^{\infty} P(A_{n,j}) - \varepsilon.$$

(1.28)

Moreover, $\cup_{n=1}^{\infty} B_n \subset \cup_{n=1}^{\infty} \cup_{j=1}^{\infty} A_{n,j}$, where the latter is a countable union of sets in $\mathscr{F}_0$; hence, it follows from (1.21) that

$$P^* \left(\overset{\infty}{\underset{n=1}{\cup}} B_n \right) \leq \sum_{n=1}^{\infty} \sum_{j=1}^{\infty} P(A_{n,j}).$$

(1.29)

If we combine (1.28) and (1.29), it follows that for arbitrary $\varepsilon > 0$,

$$\sum_{n=1}^{\infty} P^*(B_n) > P^* \left(\overset{\infty}{\underset{n=1}{\cup}} B_n \right) - \varepsilon.$$

(1.30)

Letting $\varepsilon \downarrow 0$, the lemma follows now from (1.30).   Q.E.D.

Thus, for the outer measure to be a probability measure, we have to impose conditions on the collection $\mathscr{F}$ of subsets of Ω such that for any sequence B_j of disjoint sets in $\mathscr{F}$, $P^*(\cup_{j=1}^{\infty} B_j) \geq \sum_{j=1}^{\infty} P^*(B_j)$. The latter is satisfied if we choose $\mathscr{F}$ as follows:

Lemma 1.B.2: *Let $\mathscr{F}$ be a collection of subsets B of Ω such that for **any** subset A of Ω:*

$$P^*(A) = P^*(A \cap B) + P^*(A \cap \tilde{B}).$$

(1.31)

*Then for all countable sequences of **disjoint** sets $A_j \in \mathscr{F}$, $P^*(\cup_{j=1}^{\infty} A_j) = \sum_{j=1}^{\infty} P^*(A_j)$.*

Proof: Let $A = \cup_{j=1}^{\infty} A_j$, $B = A_1$. Then $A \cap B = A \cap A_1 = A_1$ and $A \cap \tilde{B} = \cup_{j=2}^{\infty} A_j$ are disjoint; hence,

$$\begin{aligned} P^* \left(\cup_{j=1}^{\infty} A_j \right) = P^*(A) &= P^*(A \cap B) + P^*(A \cap \tilde{B}) \\ &= P^*(A_1) + P^* \left(\cup_{j=2}^{\infty} A_j \right). \end{aligned}$$

(1.32)

If we repeat (1.32) for $P^*(\cup_{j=k}^{\infty} A_j)$ with $B = A_k$, $k = 2, \ldots, n$, it follows by induction that

$$\begin{aligned} P^* \left(\cup_{j=1}^{\infty} A_j \right) &= \sum_{j=1}^{n} P^*(A_j) + P^* \left(\cup_{j=n+1}^{\infty} A_j \right) \\ &\geq \sum_{j=1}^{n} P^*(A_j) \quad \text{for all} \quad n \geq 1; \end{aligned}$$

hence, $P^*(\cup_{j=1}^{\infty} A_j) \geq \sum_{j=1}^{\infty} P^*(A_j)$.   Q.E.D.

Note that condition (1.31) automatically holds if $B \in \mathscr{F}_0$: Choose an arbitrary set A and an arbitrary small number $\varepsilon > 0$. Then there exists a covering $A \subset \cup_{j=1}^{\infty} A_j$, where $A_j \in \mathscr{F}_0$, such that $\sum_{j=1}^{\infty} P(A_j) \le P^*(A) + \varepsilon$. Moreover, because $A \cap B \subset \cup_{j=1}^{\infty} A_j \cap B$, where $A_j \cap B \in \mathscr{F}_0$, and $A \cap \tilde{B} \subset \cup_{j=1}^{\infty} A_j \cap \tilde{B}$, where $A_j \cap \tilde{B} \in \mathscr{F}_0$, we have $P^*(A \cap B) \le \sum_{j=1}^{\infty} P(A_j \cap B)$ and $P^*(A \cap \tilde{B}) \le \sum_{j=1}^{\infty} P(A_j \cap \tilde{B})$; hence, $P^*(A \cap B) + P^*(A \cap \tilde{B}) \le P^*(A) + \varepsilon$. Because ε is arbitrary, it follows now that $P^*(A) \ge P^*(A \cap B) + P^*(A \cap \tilde{B})$.

I will show now that

Lemma 1.B.3: *The collection $\mathscr{F}$ in Lemma 1.B.2 is a σ-algebra of subsets of Ω containing the algebra $\mathscr{F}_0$.*

Proof: First, it follows trivially from (1.31) that $B \in \mathscr{F}$ implies $\tilde{B} \in \mathscr{F}$. Now, let $B_j \in \mathscr{F}$. It remains to show that $\cup_{j=1}^{\infty} B_j \in \mathscr{F}$, which I will do in two steps. First, I will show that $\mathscr{F}$ is an algebra, and then I will use Theorem 1.4 to show that $\mathscr{F}$ is also a σ-algebra.

(a) *Proof that $\mathscr{F}$ is an algebra*: We have to show that $B_1, B_2 \in \mathscr{F}$ implies that $B_1 \cup B_2 \in \mathscr{F}$. We have

$$P^*(A \cap \tilde{B}_1) = P^*(A \cap \tilde{B}_1 \cap B_2) + P^*(A \cap \tilde{B}_1 \cap \tilde{B}_2),$$

and because

$$A \cap (B_1 \cup B_2) = (A \cap B_1) \cup (A \cap B_2 \cap \tilde{B}_1),$$

we have

$$P^*(A \cap (B_1 \cup B_2)) \le P^*(A \cap B_1) + P^*(A \cap B_2 \cap \tilde{B}_1).$$

Thus,

$$\begin{aligned} P^*(A \cap (B_1 \cup B_2)) + P^*(A \cap \tilde{B}_1 \cap \tilde{B}_2) &\le P^*(A \cap B_1) \\ + P^*(A \cap B_2 \cap \tilde{B}_1) + P^*(A \cap \tilde{B}_2 \cap \tilde{B}_1) \\ = P^*(A \cap B_1) + P^*(A \cap \tilde{B}_1) &= P^*(A). \end{aligned} \tag{1.33}$$

Because $\sim(B_1 \cup B_2) = \tilde{B}_1 \cap \tilde{B}_2$ and $P^*(A) \le P^*(A \cap (B_1 \cup B_2)) + P^*(A \cap (\sim(B_1 \cup B_2)))$, it follows now from (1.33) that $P^*(A) = P^*(A \cap (B_1 \cup B_2)) + P^*(A \cap (\sim(B_1 \cup B_2)))$. Thus, $B_1, B_2 \in \mathscr{F}$ implies that $B_1 \cup B_2 \in \mathscr{F}$; hence, $\mathscr{F}$ is an algebra (containing the algebra $\mathscr{F}_0$).

(b) *Proof that $\mathscr{F}$ is a σ-algebra*: Because we have established that $\mathscr{F}$ is an algebra, it follows from Theorem 1.4 that, in proving that $\mathscr{F}$ is also a σ-algebra, it suffices to verify that $\cup_{j=1}^{\infty} B_j \in \mathscr{F}$ for disjoint sets $B_j \in \mathscr{F}$. For such sets we have $A \cap (\cup_{j=1}^n B_j) \cap B_n = A \cap B_n$ and $A \cap (\cup_{j=1}^n B_j) \cap \tilde{B}_n = A \cap (\cup_{j=1}^{n-1} B_j)$; hence,

$$P^* \left(A \cap \left(\overset{n}{\underset{j=1}{\cup}} B_j \right) \right)$$

$$= P^* \left(A \cap \left(\overset{n}{\underset{j=1}{\cup}} B_j \right) \cap B_n \right) + P^* \left(A \cap \left(\overset{n}{\underset{j=1}{\cup}} B_j \right) \cap \tilde{B}_n \right)$$

$$= P^*(A \cap B_n) + P^* \left(A \cap \left(\overset{n-1}{\underset{j=1}{\cup}} B_j \right) \right).$$

Consequently,

$$P^* \left(A \cap \left(\overset{n}{\underset{j=1}{\cup}} B_j \right) \right) = \sum_{j=1}^n P^*(A \cap B_j). \tag{1.34}$$

Next, let $B = \cup_{j=1}^{\infty} B_j$. Then $\tilde{B} = \cap_{j=1}^{\infty} \tilde{B}_j \subset \cap_{j=1}^n \tilde{B}_j = \sim(\cup_{j=1}^n B_j)$; hence,

$$P^*(A \cap \tilde{B}) \leq P^* \left(A \cap \left(\sim \left[\overset{n}{\underset{j=1}{\cup}} B_j \right] \right) \right). \tag{1.35}$$

It follows now from (1.34) and (1.35) that for all $n \geq 1$,

$$P^*(A) = P^* \left(A \cap \left(\overset{n}{\underset{j=1}{\cup}} B_j \right) \right) + P^* \left(A \cap \left(\sim \left[\overset{n}{\underset{j=1}{\cup}} B_j \right] \right) \right)$$

$$\geq \sum_{j=1}^n P^*(A \cap B_j) + P^*(A \cap \tilde{B});$$

hence,

$$P^*(A) \geq \sum_{j=1}^{\infty} P^*(A \cap B_j) + P^*(A \cap \tilde{B}) \geq P^*(A \cap B) + P^*(A \cap \tilde{B}), \tag{1.36}$$

where the last inequality is due to

$$P^*(A \cap B) = P^* \left(\overset{\infty}{\underset{j=1}{\cup}} (A \cap B_j) \right) \leq \sum_{j=1}^{\infty} P^*(A \cap B_j).$$

Because we always have $P^*(A) \leq P^*(A \cap B) + P^*(A \cap \tilde{B})$ (compare Lemma 1.B.1), it follows from (1.36) that, for countable unions $B = \cup_{j=1}^{\infty} B_j$ of disjoint sets $B_j \in \mathscr{F}$,

$$P^*(A) = P^*(A \cap B) + P^*(A \cap \tilde{B});$$

hence, $B \in \mathscr{F}$. Consequently, $\mathscr{F}$ is a σ-algebra and the outer measure P^* is a probability measure on $\{\Omega, \mathscr{F}\}$.   Q.E.D.

Lemma 1.B.4: *The σ-algebra $\mathscr{F}$ in Lemma 1.B.3 can be chosen such that P^* is unique: any probability measure P_* on $\{\Omega, \mathscr{F}\}$ that coincides with P on $\mathscr{F}_0$ is equal to the outer measure P^*.*

The proof of Lemma 1.B.4 is too difficult and too long (see Billingsley 1986, Theorems 3.2–3.3) and is therefore omitted.

If we combine Lemmas 1.B.2–1.B.4, Theorem 1.9 follows.

2 Borel Measurability, Integration, and Mathematical Expectations

2.1. Introduction

Consider the following situation: You are sitting in a bar next to a guy who proposes to play the following game. He will roll dice and pay you a dollar per dot. However, you have to pay him an amount y up front each time he rolls the dice. Which amount y should you pay him in order for both of you to have equal success if this game is played indefinitely?

Let X be the amount you win in a single play. Then in the long run you will receive $X = 1$ dollars in 1 out of 6 times, $X = 2$ dollars in 1 out of 6 times, up to $X = 6$ dollars in 1 out of 6 times. Thus, on average you will receive $(1 + 2 + \cdots + 6)/6 = 3.5$ dollars per game; hence, the answer is $y = 3.5$.

Clearly, X is a random variable: $X(\omega) = \sum_{j=1}^{6} j \cdot I(\omega \in \{j\})$, where here, and in the sequel, $I(\cdot)$ denotes the indicator function:

$$I(\text{true}) = 1, \qquad I(\text{false}) = 0.$$

This random variable is defined on the probability space $\{\Omega, \mathscr{F}, P\}$, where $\Omega = \{1, 2, 3, 4, 5, 6\}$, $\mathscr{F}$ is the σ-algebra of all subsets of Ω, and $P(\{\omega\}) = 1/6$ for each $\omega \in \Omega$. Moreover, $y = \sum_{j=1}^{6} j/6 = \sum_{j=1}^{6} j P(\{j\})$. This amount y is called the mathematical expectation of X and is denoted by $E(X)$.

More generally, if X is the outcome of a game with payoff function $g(X)$, where X is discrete: $p_j = P[X = x_j] > 0$ with $\sum_{j=1}^{n} p_j = 1$ (n is possibly infinite), and if this game is repeated indefinitely, then the average payoff will be

$$y = E[g(X)] = \sum_{j=1}^{n} g(x_j)p_j. \tag{2.1}$$

Some computer programming languages, such as Fortran, Visual Basic, C++, and so on, have a built-in function that generates uniformly distributed random numbers between zero and one. Now suppose that the guy next to you at the bar pulls out his laptop computer and proposes to generate random numbers

37

and pay you X dollar per game if the random number involved is X provided you pay him an amount y up front each time. The question is again, Which amount y should you pay him for both of you to play even if this game is played indefinitely?

Because the random variable X involved is uniformly distributed on $[0, 1]$, it has distribution function $F(x) = 0$ for $x \leq 0$, $F(x) = x$ for $0 < x < 1$, $F(x) = 1$ for $x \geq 1$ with density function $f(x) = F'(x) = I(0 < x < 1)$. More formally, $X = X(\omega) = \omega$ is a nonnegative random variable defined on the probability space $\{\Omega, \mathscr{F}, P\}$, where $\Omega = [0, 1]$, $\mathscr{F} = [0, 1] \cap \mathscr{B}$, that is, the σ-algebra of all Borel sets in $[0, 1]$, and P is the Lebesgue measure on $[0, 1]$.

To determine y in this case, let

$$
X_*(\omega) = \sum_{j=1}^{m} \left[\inf_{\omega \in (b_{j-1}, b_j]} X(\omega) \right] I(\omega \in (b_{j-1}, b_j])
$$

$$
= \sum_{j=1}^{m} b_{j-1} I(\omega \in (b_{j-1}, b_j]),
$$

where $b_0 = 0$ and $b_m = 1$. Clearly, $0 \leq X_* \leq X$ with probability 1, and, as is true for the dice game, the amount y involved will be greater than or equal to $\sum_{j=1}^{m} b_{j-1} P((b_{j-1}, b_j]) = \sum_{j=1}^{m} b_{j-1}(b_j - b_{j-1})$. Taking the supremum over all possible partitions $\cup_{j=1}^{m}(b_{j-1}, b_j]$ of $(0, 1]$ then yields the integral

$$
y = E(X) = \int_0^1 x dx = 1/2. \tag{2.2}
$$

More generally, if X is the outcome of a game with payoff function $g(X)$, where X has an absolutely continuous distribution with density $f(x)$, then

$$
y = E[g(X)] = \int_{-\infty}^{\infty} g(x) f(x) dx. \tag{2.3}
$$

Now two questions arise. First, under what conditions is $g(X)$ a well-defined random variable? Second, how do we determine $E(X)$ if the distribution of X is neither discrete nor absolutely continuous?

2.2. Borel Measurability

Let g be a real function and let X be a random variable defined on the probability space $\{\Omega, \mathscr{F}, P\}$. For $g(X)$ to be a random variable, we must have that

For all Borel sets B, $\{\omega \in \Omega : g(X(\omega)) \in B\} \in \mathscr{F}$. \hfill (2.4)

It is possible to construct a real function g and a random variable X for which this is not the case. But if

$$\text{For all Borel sets } B, A_B = \{x \in \mathbb{R} : g(x) \in B\} \text{ is a Borel set itself,}$$
$$(2.5)$$

then (2.4) is clearly satisfied because then, for any Borel set B and A_B defined in (2.5),

$$\{\omega \in \Omega : g(X(\omega)) \in B\} = \{\omega \in \Omega : X(\omega) \in A_B\} \in \mathscr{F}.$$

Moreover, if (2.5) is not satisfied in the sense that there exists a Borel set B for which A_B is not a Borel set itself, then it is possible to construct a random variable X such that the set

$$\{\omega \in \Omega : g(X(\omega)) \in B\} = \{\omega \in \Omega : X(\omega) \in A_B\} \notin \mathscr{F};$$

hence, for such a random variable X, $g(X)$ is not a random variable itself.[1] Thus, $g(X)$ is guaranteed to be a random variable if and only if (2.5) is satisfied. Such real functions $g(x)$ are described as being Borel measurable:

Definition 2.1: *A real function g is Borel measurable if and only if for all Borel sets B in $\mathbb{R}$ the sets $A_B = \{x \in \mathbb{R} : g(x) \in B\}$ are Borel sets in $\mathbb{R}$. Similarly, a real function g on $\mathbb{R}^k$ is Borel measurable if and only if for all Borel sets B in $\mathbb{R}$ the sets $A_B = \{x \in \mathbb{R}^k : g(x) \in B\}$ are Borel sets in $\mathbb{R}^k$.*

However, we do not need to verify condition (2.5) for all Borel sets. It suffices to verify it for Borel sets of the type $(-\infty, y]$, $y \in \mathbb{R}$ only:

Theorem 2.1: *A real function g on $\mathbb{R}^k$ is Borel measurable if and only if for all $y \in \mathbb{R}$ the sets $A_y = \{x \in \mathbb{R}^k : g(x) \le y\}$ are Borel sets in $\mathbb{R}^k$.*

Proof: Let $\mathscr{D}$ be the collection of all Borel sets B in $\mathbb{R}$ for which the sets $\{x \in \mathbb{R}^k : g(x) \in B\}$ are Borel sets in $\mathbb{R}^k$, including the Borel sets of the type $(-\infty, y]$, $y \in \mathbb{R}$. Then $\mathscr{D}$ contains the collection of all intervals of the type $(-\infty, y]$, $y \in \mathbb{R}$. The smallest σ-algebra containing the collection $\{(-\infty, y]$, $y \in \mathbb{R}\}$ is just the Euclidean Borel field $\mathscr{B} = \sigma(\{(-\infty, y], y \in \mathbb{R}\})$; hence, if $\mathscr{D}$ is a σ-algebra, then $\mathscr{B} \subset \mathscr{D}$. But $\mathscr{D}$ is a collection of Borel sets; hence, $\mathscr{D} \subset \mathscr{B}$. Thus, if $\mathscr{D}$ is a σ-algebra, then $\mathscr{B} = \mathscr{D}$. The proof that $\mathscr{D}$ is a σ-algebra is left as an exercise.   Q.E.D.

The simplest Borel measurable function is the *simple* function:

---

[1] The actual construction of such a counterexample is difficult, though, but not impossible.

Definition 2.2: *A real function g on $\mathbb{R}^k$ is called a simple function if it takes the form $g(x) = \sum_{j=1}^{m} a_j I(x \in B_j)$, with $m < \infty$, $a_j \in \mathbb{R}$, where the B_j's are disjoint Borel sets in $\mathbb{R}^k$.*

Without loss of generality we may assume that the disjoint Borel sets B_j's form a *partition* of $\mathbb{R}^k$: $\cup_{j=1}^{m} B_j = \mathbb{R}^k$ because, if not, then let $g(x) = \sum_{j=1}^{m+1} a_j I(x \in B_j)$, with $B_{m+1} = \mathbb{R}^k \backslash (\cup_{j=1}^{m} B_j)$ and $a_{m+1} = 0$. Moreover, without loss of generality we may assume that the a_j's are all different. For example, if $g(x) = \sum_{j=1}^{m+1} a_j I(x \in B_j)$ and $a_m = a_{m+1}$, then $g(x) = \sum_{j=1}^{m} a_j I(x \in B_j^*)$, where $B_j^* = B_j$ for $j = 1, \ldots, m - 1$ and $B_m^* = B_m \cup B_{m+1}$.

Theorem 2.1 can be used to prove that

Theorem 2.2: *Simple functions are Borel measurable.*

Proof: Let $g(x) = \sum_{j=1}^{m} a_j I(x \in B_j)$ be a simple function on $\mathbb{R}^k$. For arbitrary $y \in \mathbb{R}$,

$$\{x \in \mathbb{R}^k : g(x) \le y\} = \left\{x \in \mathbb{R}^k : \sum_{j=1}^{m} a_j I(x \in B_j) \le y\right\} = \underset{a_j \le y}{\cup} B_j,$$

which is a finite union of Borel sets and therefore a Borel set itself. Because y was arbitrary, it follows from Theorem 2.1 that g is Borel measurable. Q.E.D.

Theorem 2.3: *If $f(x)$ and $g(x)$ are simple functions, then so are $f(x) + g(x)$, $f(x) - g(x)$, and $f(x) \cdot g(x)$. If, in addition, $g(x) \ne 0$ for all x, then $f(x)/g(x)$ is a simple function.*

Proof: Exercise
Theorem 2.1 can also be used to prove

Theorem 2.4: *Let $g_j(x)$, $j = 1, 2, 3, \ldots$ be a sequence of Borel-measurable functions. Then*

(a) *$f_{1,n}(x) = min\{g_1(x), \ldots, g_n(x)\}$ and $f_{2,n}(x) = max\{g_1(x), \ldots, g_n(x)\}$ are Borel measurable;*

(b) *$f_1(x) = inf_{n \ge 1} g_n(x)$ and $f_2(x) = sup_{n \ge 1} g_n(x)$ are Borel measurable; and*

(c) *$h_1(x) = liminf_{n \to \infty} g_n(x)$ and $h_2(x) = limsup_{n \to \infty} g_n(x)$ are Borel measurable;*

(d) *if $g(x) = lim_{n \to \infty} g_n(x)$ exists, then g is Borel measurable.*

Proof: First, note that the min, max, inf, sup, liminf, limsup, and lim operations are taken *pointwise* in x. I will only prove the min, inf, and liminf cases for Borel-measurable real functions on $\mathbb{R}$. Again, let $y \in \mathbb{R}$ be arbitrary. Then,

(a) $\{x \in \mathbb{R} : f_{1,n}(x) \le y\} = \cup_{j=1}^{n} \{x \in \mathbb{R} : g_j(x) \le y\} \in \mathcal{B}$.

(b) $\{x \in \mathbb{R} : f_1(x) \le y\} = \cup_{j=1}^{\infty} \{x \in \mathbb{R} : g_j(x) \le y\} \in \mathcal{B}$.

(c) $\{x \in \mathbb{R} : h_1(x) \le y\} = \cap_{n=1}^{\infty} \cup_{j=n}^{\infty} \{x \in \mathbb{R} : g_j(x) \le y\} \in \mathcal{B}$.

The max, sup, limsup, and lim cases are left as exercises.   Q.E.D.

Because continuous functions can be written as pointwise limits of step functions and step functions with a finite number of steps are simple functions, it follows from Theorems 2.1 and 2.4(d) that

Theorem 2.5: *Continuous real functions are Borel measurable.*

Proof: Let g be a continuous function on $\mathbb{R}$. Define for natural numbers n, $g_n(x) = g(x)$ if $-n < x \le n$ but $g_n(x) = 0$ elsewhere. Next, define for $j = 0, \ldots, m - 1$ and $m = 1, 2, \ldots$

$$B(j, m, n) = (-n + 2n \cdot j/m, -n + 2(j + 1)n/m].$$

Then the $B(j, m, n)$'s are disjoint intervals such that $\cup_{j=0}^{m-1} B(j, m, n) = (-n, n]$; hence, the function

$$g_{n,m}(x) = \sum_{j=0}^{m-1} \left(\inf_{x \in B(j,m,n)} g(x_*) \right) I(x \in B(j, m, n))$$

is a step function with a finite number of steps and thus a simple function. Because, trivially, $g(x) = \lim_{n \to \infty} g_n(x)$ pointwise in x, $g(x)$ is Borel measurable if the functions $g_n(x)$ are Borel measurable (see Theorem 2.4(d)). Similarly, the functions $g_n(x)$ are Borel measurable if, for arbitrary fixed n, $g_n(x) = \lim_{m \to \infty} g_{n,m}(x)$ pointwise in x because the $g_{n,m}(x)$'s are simple functions and thus Borel measurable. To prove $g_n(x) = \lim_{m \to \infty} g_{n,m}(x)$, choose an arbitrary fixed x and choose $n > |x|$. Then there exists a sequence of indices $j_{n,m}$ such that $x \in B(j_{n,m}, m, n)$ for all m; hence,

$$0 \le g_n(x) - g_{n,m}(x) \le g(x) - \inf_{x_* \in B(j_{n,m},m,n)} g(x_*)$$

$$\le \sup_{|x-x_*| \le 2n/m} |g(x) - g(x_*)| \to 0$$

as $m \to \infty$. The latter result follows from the continuity of $g(x)$.   Q.E.D.

Next, I will show in two steps that real functions are Borel measurable if and only if they are limits of simple functions:

Theorem 2.6: *A nonnegative real function $g(x)$ is Borel measurable if and only if there exists a nondecreasing sequence $g_n(x)$ of nonnegative simple functions such that pointwise in x, $0 \le g_n(x) \le g(x)$, and $\lim_{n \to \infty} g_n(x) = g(x)$.*

Proof: The "if" case follows straightforwardly from Theorems 2.2 and 2.4. For proving the "only if" case let, for $1 \leq m \leq n2^n$, $g_n(x) = (m-1)/2^n$ if $(m-1)/2^n \leq g(x) < m/2^n$ and $g_n(x) = n$ otherwise. Then $g_n(x)$ is a sequence of simple functions satisfying $0 \leq g_n(x) \leq g(x)$ and $\lim_{n \to \infty} g_n(x) = g(x)$ pointwise in x.   Q.E.D.

Every real function $g(x)$ can be written as a difference of two nonnegative functions:

$$g(x) = g_+(x) - g_-(x), \quad \text{where} \quad g_+(x) = \max\{g(x), 0\},$$
$$g_-(x) = \max\{-g(x), 0\}. \tag{2.6}$$

Moreover, if g is Borel measurable, then so are g_+ and g_- in (2.6). Therefore, it follows straightforwardly from (2.6) and Theorems 2.3 and 2.6 that

Theorem 2.7: *A real function $g(x)$ is Borel measurable if and only if it is the limit of a sequence of simple functions.*

Proof: Exercise.
Using Theorem 2.7, we can now generalize Theorem 2.3 to

Theorem 2.8: *If $f(x)$ and $g(x)$ are Borel-measurable functions, then so are $f(x) + g(x)$, $f(x) - g(x)$, and $f(x) \cdot g(x)$. Moreover, if $g(x) \neq 0$ for all x, then $f(x)/g(x)$ is a Borel-measurable function.*

Proof: Exercise.

2.3. Integrals of Borel-Measurable Functions with Respect to a Probability Measure

If g is a step function on $(0, 1]$ – for instance, $g(x) = \sum_{j=1}^{m} a_j I(x \in (b_j, b_{j+1}])$ – where $b_0 = 0$ and $b_{m+1} = 1$, then the Riemann integral of g over $(0, 1]$ is defined as

$$\int_0^1 g(x)dx = \sum_{j=1}^{m} a_j(b_{j+1} - b_j) = \sum_{j=1}^{m} a_j \mu((b_j, b_{j+1}]),$$

where μ is the uniform probability measure on $(0, 1]$. Mimicking these results for simple functions and more general probability measures μ, we can define the integral of a simple function with respect to a probability measure μ as follows:

Definition 2.3: *Let μ be a probability measure on $\{\mathbb{R}^k, \mathcal{B}^k\}$, and let $g(x) = \sum_{j=1}^{m} a_j I(x \in B_j)$ be a simple function on $\mathbb{R}^k$. Then the integral of g with* *respect to μ is defined as*

$$\int g(x)d\mu(x) \stackrel{\text{def.}}{=} \sum_{j=1}^{m} a_j\, \mu(B_j).^2$$

For nonnegative continuous real functions g on $(0, 1]$, the Riemann integral of g over $(0, 1]$ is defined as $\int_0^1 g(x)dx = \sup_{0 \leq g_* \leq g} \int_0^1 g_*(x)dx$, where the supremum is taken over all step functions g_* satisfying $0 \leq g_*(x) \leq g(x)$ for all x in $(0, 1]$. Again, we may mimic this result for nonnegative, Borel-measurable functions g and general probability measures μ:

Definition 2.4: *Let μ be a probability measure on $\{\mathbb{R}^k, \mathfrak{B}^k\}$ and let $g(x)$ be a nonnegative Borel-measurable function on $\mathbb{R}^k$. Then the integral of g with respect to μ is defined as*

$$\int g(x)d\mu(x) \stackrel{\text{def.}}{=} \sup_{0 \leq g_* \leq g} \int g_*(x)d\mu(x),$$

where the supremum is taken over all simple functions g_* satisfying $0 \leq g_*(x) \leq g(x)$ for all x in a Borel set B with $\mu(B) = 1$.

Using the decomposition (2.6), we can now define the integral of an arbitrary Borel-measurable function with respect to a probability measure:

Definition 2.5: *Let μ be a probability measure on $\{\mathbb{R}^k \, \mathfrak{B}^k\}$ and let $g(x)$ be a Borel-measurable function on $\mathbb{R}^k$. Then the integral of g with respect to μ is defined as*

$$\int g(x)d\mu(x) = \int g_+(x)d\mu(x) - \int g_-(x)d\mu(x), \qquad (2.7)$$

where $g_+(x) = max\{g(x), 0\}, g_-(x) = max\{-g(x), 0\}$ provided that at least one of the integrals at the right-hand side of (2.7) is finite.[3]

Definition 2.6: *The integral of a Borel-measurable function g with respect to a probability measure μ over a Borel set A is defined as $\int_A g(x)d\mu(x) \stackrel{\text{def.}}{=} \int I(x \in A)g(x)d\mu(x)$.*

All the well-known properties of Riemann integrals carry over to these new integrals. In particular,

---

[2] The notation $\int g(x)d\mu(x)$ is somewhat odd because $\mu(x)$ has no meaning. It would be better to denote the integral involved by $\int g(x)\mu(dx)$ (which some authors do), where dx represents a Borel set. The current notation, however, is the most common and is therefore adopted here too.

[3] Because $\infty - \infty$ is not defined.

Theorem 2.9: *Let $f(x)$ and $g(x)$ be Borel-measurable functions on $\mathbb{R}^k$, let μ be a probability measure on $\{\mathbb{R}^k, \mathcal{B}^k\}$, and let A be a Borel set in $\mathbb{R}^k$. Then*

(a) $\int_A (\alpha g(x) + \beta f(x)) d\mu(x) = \alpha \int_A g(x) d\mu(x) + \beta \int_A f(x) d\mu(x)$.

(b) *For disjoint Borel sets A_j in $\mathbb{R}^k$,* $\int_{\cup_{j=1}^\infty A_j} g(x) d\mu(x) = \sum_{j=1}^\infty \int_{A_j} g(x) d\mu(x)$.

(c) *If $g(x) \geq 0$ for all x in A, then $\int_A g(x) d\mu(x) \geq 0$.*

(d) *If $g(x) \geq f(x)$ for all x in A, then $\int_A g(x) d\mu(x) \geq \int_A f(x) d\mu(x)$.*

(e) $\left| \int_A g(x) d\mu(x) \right| \leq \int_A |g(x)| d\mu(x)$.

(f) *If $\mu(A) = 0$, then $\int_A g(x) d\mu(x) = 0$.*

(g) *If $\int |g(x)| d\mu(x) < \infty$ and $\lim_{n\to\infty} \mu(A_n) = 0$ for a sequence of Borel sets A_n, then $\lim_{n\to\infty} \int_{A_n} g(x) d\mu(x) = 0$.*

Proofs of (a)–(f): Exercise.

Proof of (g): Without loss of generality we may assume that $g(x) \geq 0$. Let

$$C_k = \{x \in \mathbb{R} : k \leq g(x) < k+1\} \quad \text{and}$$
$$B_m = \{x \in \mathbb{R} : g(x) \geq m\} = \cup_{k=m}^\infty C_k.$$

Then $\int_\mathbb{R} g(x) d\mu(x) = \sum_{k=0}^\infty \int_{C_k} g(x) d\mu(x) < \infty$; hence,

$$\int_{B_m} g(x) d\mu(x) = \sum_{k=m}^\infty \int_{C_k} g(x) d\mu(x) \to 0 \quad \text{for} \quad m \to \infty. \qquad (2.8)$$

Therefore,

$$\int_{A_n} g(x) d\mu(x) = \int_{A_n \cap B_m} g(x) d\mu(x) + \int_{A_n \cap (\mathbb{R} \setminus B_m)} g(x) d\mu(x)$$
$$\leq \int_{B_m} g(x) d\mu(x) + m\mu(A_n);$$

hence, for fixed m, $\limsup_{n\to\infty} \int_{A_n} g(x) d\mu(x) \leq \int_{B_m} g(x) d\mu(x)$. Letting $m \to \infty$, we find that part (g) of Theorem 2.9 follows from (2.8).   Q.E.D.

Moreover, there are two important theorems involving limits of a sequence of Borel-measurable functions and their integrals, namely, the monotone convergence theorem and the dominated convergence theorem:

Theorem 2.10: *(Monotone convergence) Let g_n be a nondecreasing sequence of nonnegative Borel-measurable functions on $\mathbb{R}^k$ (i.e., for any fixed $x \in \mathbb{R}^k$, $0 \leq g_n(x) \leq g_{n+1}(x)$ for $n = 1, 2, 3, \ldots$), and let μ be a probability measure* *on* $\{\mathbb{R}^k, \mathscr{B}^k\}$. *Then*

$$\lim_{n \to \infty} \int g_n(x)d\mu(x) = \int \lim_{n \to \infty} g_n(x)d\mu(x).$$

Proof: First, observe from Theorem 2.9(d) and the monotonicity of g_n that $\int g_n(x)d\mu(x)$ is monotonic nondecreasing and that therefore $\lim_{n \to \infty} \int g_n(x)d\mu(x)$ exists (but may be infinite) and $g(x) = \lim_{n \to \infty} g_n(x)$ exists (but may be infinite) and is Borel-measurable. Moreover, given that for $x \in \mathbb{R}^k$, $g_n(x) \leq g(x)$, it follows easily from Theorem 2.9(d) that $\int g_n(x)d\mu(x) \leq \int g(x)d\mu(x)$; hence, $\lim_{n \to \infty} \int g_n(x)d\mu(x) \leq \int g(x)d\mu(x)$. Thus, it remains to be shown that

$$\lim_{n \to \infty} \int g_n(x)d\mu(x) \geq \int g(x)d\mu(x). \tag{2.9}$$

It follows from the definition on the integral $\int g(x)d\mu(x)$ that (2.9) is true if, for any simple function $f(x)$ with $0 \leq f(x) \leq g(x)$,

$$\lim_{n \to \infty} \int g_n(x)d\mu(x) \geq \int f(x)d\mu(x). \tag{2.10}$$

Given such a simple function $f(x)$, let $A_n = \{x \in \mathbb{R}^k : g_n(x) \geq (1 - \varepsilon) f(x)\}$ for arbitrary $\varepsilon > 0$, and let $\sup_x f(x) = M$. Note that, because $f(x)$ is simple, $M < \infty$. Moreover, note that

$$\lim_{n \to \infty} \mu(\mathbb{R}^k \backslash A_n) = \lim_{n \to \infty} \mu(\{x \in \mathbb{R}^k : g_n(x) \leq (1 - \varepsilon)f(x)\}) = 0.$$
$$\tag{2.11}$$

Furthermore, observe that

$$\int g_n(x)d\mu(x) \geq \int_{A_n} g_n(x)d\mu(x) \geq (1 - \varepsilon) \int_{A_n} f(x)d\mu(x)$$

$$= (1 - \varepsilon) \int f(x)d\mu(x) - (1 - \varepsilon) \int_{\mathbb{R}^k \backslash A_n} f(x)d\mu(x)$$

$$\geq (1 - \varepsilon) \int f(x)d\mu(x) - (1 - \varepsilon)M\mu(\mathbb{R}^k \backslash A_n).$$
$$\tag{2.12}$$

It follows now from (2.11) and (2.12) that, for arbitrary $\varepsilon > 0$, $\lim_{n \to \infty} \int g_n(x)d\mu(x) \geq (1 - \varepsilon) \int f(x)d\mu(x)$, which implies (2.10). If we combine (2.9) and (2.10), the theorem follows.   Q.E.D.

Theorem 2.11: *(Dominated convergence) Let g_n be sequence of Borel-measurable functions on $\mathbb{R}^k$ such that pointwise in x, $g(x) = \lim_{n \to \infty} g_n(x)$,* *and let $\bar{g}(x) = \sup_{n\geq 1}|g_n(x)|$. If $\int \bar{g}(x)d\mu(x) < \infty$, where μ is a probability measure on $\{\mathbb{R}^k, \mathfrak{B}^k\}$, then*

$$\lim_{n\to\infty} \int g_n(x)d\mu(x) = \int g(x)d\mu(x).$$

Proof: Let $f_n(x) = \bar{g}(x) - \sup_{m\geq n}g_m(x)$. Then $f_n(x)$ is nondecreasing and nonnegative and $\lim_{n\to\infty}f_n(x) = \bar{g}(x) - g(x)$. Thus, it follows from the condition $\int \bar{g}(x)d\mu(x) < \infty$ and Theorems 2.9(a,d)–2.10 that

$$\int g(x)d\mu(x) = \lim_{n\to\infty} \int \sup_{m\geq n} g_m(x)d\mu(x)$$

$$\geq \lim_{n\to\infty}\sup_{m\geq n} \int g_m(x)d\mu(x) = \limsup_{n\to\infty} \int g_n(x)d\mu(x).$$

$$(2.13)$$

Next, let $h_n(x) = \bar{g}(x) + \inf_{m\geq n}g_m(x)$. Then $h_n(x)$ is nondecreasing and nonnegative and $\lim_{n\to\infty}h_n(x) = \bar{g}(x) + g(x)$. Thus, it follows again from the condition $\int \bar{g}(x)d\mu(x) < \infty$ and Theorems 2.9(a,d)–2.10 that

$$\int g(x)d\mu(x) = \lim_{n\to\infty} \int \inf_{m\geq n} g_m(x)d\mu(x) \leq \lim_{n\to\infty}\inf_{m\geq n} \int g_m(x)d\mu(x)$$

$$= \liminf_{n\to\infty} \int g_n(x)d\mu(x).$$

$$(2.14)$$

The theorem now follows from (2.13) and (2.14).   Q.E.D.

In the statistical and econometric literature you will encounter integrals of the form $\int_A g(x)dF(x)$, where F is a distribution function. Because each distribution function $F(x)$ on $\mathbb{R}^k$ is uniquely associated with a probability measure μ on $\mathfrak{B}^k$, one should interpret these integrals as

$$\int_A g(x)dF(x) \stackrel{\text{def.}}{=} \int_A g(x)d\mu(x),$$

$$(2.15)$$

where μ is the probability measure on $\mathfrak{B}^k$ associated with F, g is a Borel-measurable function on $\mathbb{R}^k$, and A is a Borel set in $\mathfrak{B}^k$.

2.4. General Measurability and Integrals of Random Variables with Respect to Probability Measures

All the definitions and results in the previous sections carry over to mappings $X : \Omega \to \mathbb{R}$, where Ω is a nonempty set, with $\mathfrak{F}$ a σ-algebra of subsets of Ω. Recall that X is a random variable defined on a probability space $\{\Omega, \mathfrak{F}, P\}$ if, for all Borel sets B in $\mathbb{R}$, $\{\omega \in \Omega : X(\Omega) \in B\} \in \mathfrak{F}$. Moreover, recall that it suffices to verify this condition for Borel sets of the type $B_y = (-\infty, y]$,

$y \in \mathbb{R}$. These generalizations are listed in this section with all random variables involved defined on a *common* probability space $\{\Omega, \mathscr{F}, P\}$.

Definition 2.7: *A random variable X is called simple if it takes the form $X(\omega) = \sum_{j=1}^{m} b_j I(\omega \in A_j)$, with $m < \infty$, $b_j \in \mathbb{R}$, where the A_j's are disjoint sets in $\mathscr{F}$.*

Compare Definition 2.2. (Verify as was done for Theorem 2.2 that a simple random variable is indeed a random variable.) Again, we may assume without loss of generality that the b_j's are all different. For example, if X has a hypergeometric or binomial distribution, then X is a simple random variable.

Theorem 2.12: *If X and Y are simple random variables, then so are $X + Y$, $X - Y$, and $X \cdot Y$. If, in addition, Y is nonzero with probability 1, then X/Y is a simple random variable.*

Proof: Similar to Theorem 2.3.

Theorem 2.13: *Let X_j be a sequence of random variables. Then $max_{1 \le j \le n} X_j$, $min_{1 \le j \le n} X_j$, $sup_{n \ge 1} X_n$, $inf_{n \ge 1} X_n$, $limsup_{n \to \infty} X_n$, and $liminf_{n \to \infty} X_n$ are random variables. If $lim_{n \to \infty} X_n(\omega) = X(\omega)$ for all ω in a set A in $\mathscr{F}$ with $P(A) = 1$, then X is a random variable.*

Proof: Similar to Theorem 2.4.

Theorem 2.14: *A mapping $X: \Omega \to \mathbb{R}$ is a random variable if and only if there exists a sequence X_n of simple random variables such that $lim_{n \to \infty} X_n(\omega) = X(\omega)$ for all ω in a set A in $\mathscr{F}$ with $P(A) = 1$.*

Proof: Similar to Theorem 2.7.

As in Definitions 2.3–2.6, we may define integrals of a random variable X with respect to the probability measure P in four steps as follows.

Definition 2.8: *Let X be a simple random variable: $X(\omega) = \sum_{j=1}^{m} b_j I(\omega \in A_j)$, for instance. Then the integral of X with respect to P is defined as $\int X(\omega) dP(\omega) \stackrel{def.}{=} \sum_{j=1}^{m} b_j P(A_j)$.*[4]

Definition 2.9: *Let X be a nonnegative random variable (with probability 1). Then the integral of X with respect of P is defined as $\int X(\omega) dP(\omega) = sup_{0 \le X_* \le X} \int X(\omega)_* dP(\omega)$, where the supremum is taken over all simple random variables X_* satisfying $P[0 \le X_* \le X] = 1$.*

[4] Again, the notation $\int X(\omega) dP(\omega)$ is odd because $P(\omega)$ has no meaning. Some authors use the notation $\int X(\omega) P(d\omega)$, where $d\omega$ represents a set in $\mathscr{F}$. The former notation is the most common and is therefore adopted.

Definition 2.10: *Let X be a random variable. Then the integral of X with respect to P is defined as $\int X(\omega)dP(\omega) \overset{def.}{=} \int X_+(\omega)dP(\omega) - \int X_-(\omega)\, dP(\omega)$, where $X_+ = max\{X, 0\}$ and $X_- = max\{-X, 0\}$, provided that at least one of the latter two integrals is finite.*

Definition 2.11: *The integral of a random variable X with respect to a probability measure P over a set A in $\mathscr{F}$ is defined as $\int_A X(\omega)dP(\omega) = \int I(\omega \in A)X(\omega)dP(\omega)$.*

Theorem 2.15: *Let X and Y be random variables, and let A be a set in $\mathscr{F}$. Then*

(a) $\int_A (\alpha X(\omega) + \beta Y(\omega))dP(\omega) = \alpha \int_A X(\omega)dP(\omega) + \beta \int_A Y(\omega)dP(\omega)$.

(b) *For disjoint sets A_j in $\mathscr{F}$,* $\int_{\cup_{j=1}^{\infty} A_j} X(\omega)dP(\omega) = \sum_{j=1}^{\infty} \int_{A_j} X(\omega)dP(\omega)$.

(c) *If $X(\omega) \geq 0$ for all ω in A, then $\int_A X(\omega)dP(\omega) \geq 0$.*

(d) *If $X(\omega) \geq Y(\omega)$ for all ω in A, then $\int_A X(\omega)dP(\omega) \geq \int_A Y(\omega)dP(\omega)$.*

(e) $\left| \int_A X(\omega)dP(\omega) \right| \leq \int_A |X(\omega)|dP(\omega)$.

(f) *If $P(A) = 0$, then $\int_A X(\omega)dP(\omega) = 0$.*

(g) *If $\int |X(\omega)|dP(\omega) < \infty$ and for a sequence of sets A_n in $\mathscr{F}$, $lim_{n \to \infty} P(A_n) = 0$, then $lim_{n \to \infty} \int_{A_n} X(\omega)dP(\omega) = 0$.*

Proof: Similar to Theorem 2.9.

Also the monotone and dominated-convergence theorems carry over:

Theorem 2.16: *Let X_n be a monotonic, nondecreasing sequence of nonnegative random variables defined on the probability space $\{\Omega, \mathscr{F}, P\}$, that is, there exists a set $A \in \mathscr{F}$ with $P(A) = 1$ such that for all $\omega \in A$, $0 \leq X_n(\omega) \leq X_{n+1}(\omega)$, $n = 1, 2, 3, \ldots$. Then*

$$\lim_{n \to \infty} \int X_n(\omega)dP(\omega) = \int \lim_{n \to \infty} X_n(\omega)dP(\omega).$$

Proof: Similar to Theorem 2.10.

Theorem 2.17: *Let X_n be a sequence of random variables defined on the probability space $\{\Omega, \mathscr{F}, P\}$ such that for all ω in a set $A \in \mathscr{F}$ with $P(A) = 1$, $Y(\omega) = lim_{n \to \infty} X_n(\omega)$. Let $\bar{X} = sup_{n \geq 1} |X_n|$. If $\int \bar{X}(\omega)dP(\omega) < \infty$, then $lim_{n \to \infty} \int X_n(\omega)dP(\omega) = \int Y(\omega)dP(\omega)$.*

Proof: Similar to Theorem 2.11.

Finally, note that the integral of a random variable with respect to the corresponding probability measure P is related to the definition of the integral of a Borel-measurable function with respect to a probability measure μ:

Theorem 2.18: *Let μ_X be the probability measure induced by the random variable X. Then $\int X(\omega)d P(\omega) = \int x d\mu_X(x)$. Moreover, if g is a Borel-measurable* *real function on $\mathbb{R}^k$ and X is a k-dimensional random vector with induced probability measure μ_X, then $\int g(X(\omega))dP(\omega) = \int g(x)d\mu_X(x)$. Furthermore, denoting in the latter case $Y = g(X)$, with μ_Y the probability measure induced by Y, we have $\int Y(\omega)dP(\omega) = \int g(X(\omega))dP(\omega) = \int g(x)d\mu_X(x) = \int y d\mu_Y(y)$.*

Proof: Let X be a simple random variable: $X(\omega) = \sum_{j=1}^{m} b_j I(\omega \in A_j)$, for instance, and recall that without loss of generality we may assume that the b_j's are all different. Each of the disjoint sets A_j are associated with disjoint Borel sets B_j such that $A_j = \{\omega \in \Omega : X(\omega) \in B_j\}$ (e.g., let $B_j = \{b_j\}$). Then $\int X(\omega)dP(\omega) = \sum_{j=1}^{m} b_j P(A_j) = \sum_{j=1}^{m} b_j \mu X(B_j) = \int g_*(x)d\mu_X(x)$, where $g_*(x) = \sum_{j=1}^{m} b_j I(x \in B_j)$ is a simple function such that

$$g_*(X(\omega)) = \sum_{j=1}^{m} b_j I(X(\omega) \in B_j) = \sum_{j=1}^{m} b_j I(\omega \in A_j) = X(\omega).$$

Therefore, in this case the Borel set $C = \{x : g_*(x) \neq x\}$ has μ_X measure zero: $\mu_X(C) = 0$, and consequently,

$$\int X(\omega)dP(\omega) = \int_{\mathbb{R}\backslash C} g_*(x)d\mu_X(x) + \int_C g_*(x)d\mu_X(x)$$

$$= \int_{\mathbb{R}\backslash C} x d\mu_X(x) = \int x d\mu_X(x). \tag{2.16}$$

The rest of the proof is left as an exercise.   Q.E.D.

2.5. Mathematical Expectation

With these new integrals introduced, we can now answer the second question stated at the end of the introduction: How do we define the mathematical expectation if the distribution of X is neither discrete nor absolutely continuous?

Definition 2.12: *The mathematical expectation of a random variable X is defined as $E(X) = \int X(\omega)dP(\omega)$ or equivalently as $E(X) = \int x dF(x)$ (cf.(2.15)), where F is the distribution function of X, provided that the integrals involved are defined. Similarly, if $g(x)$ is a Borel-measurable function on $\mathbb{R}^k$ and X is a random vector in $\mathbb{R}^k$, then, equivalently, $E[g(X)] = \int g(X(\omega))dP(\omega) = \int g(x)dF(x)$, provided that the integrals involved are defined.*

Note that the latter part of Definition 2.12 covers both examples (2.1) and (2.3).

As motivated in the introduction, the mathematical expectation $E[g(X)]$ may be interpreted as the limit of the average payoff of a repeated game with payoff function g. This is related to the strong law of large numbers, which we will discuss in Chapter 7: Let X_1, X_2, X_3, ... be a sequence of independent random variables or vectors each distributed the same as X, and let g be a Borel-measurable function such that $E[|g(X)|] < \infty$. Then

$$P\left(\lim_{n\to\infty} (1/n)\sum_{j=1}^{n} g(X_j) = E[g(X)]\right) = 1.$$

There are a few important special cases of the function g – in particular the variance of X, which measures the variation of X around its expectation $E(X)$ – and the covariance of a pair of random variables X and Y, which measures how X and Y fluctuate together around their expectations:

Definition 2.13: *The m's moment ($m = 1, 2, 3, ...$) of a random variable X is defined as $E(X^m)$, and the m's central moment of X is defined by $E(|X - \mu_x|^m)$, where $\mu_x = E(X)$. The second central moment is called the variance of X, $var(X) = E[(X - \mu_x)^2] = \sigma_x^2$, for instance. The **covariance** of a pair (X, Y) of random variables is defined as $cov(X, Y) = E[(X - \mu_x)(Y - \mu_y)]$, where μ_x is the same as before, and $\mu_y = E(Y)$. The correlation (coefficient) of a pair (X, Y) of random variables is defined as*

$$corr(X, Y) = \frac{cov(X, Y)}{\sqrt{var(X)}\sqrt{var(Y)}} = \rho(X, Y).$$

The correlation coefficient measures the extent to which Y can be approximated by a linear function of X, and vice versa. In particular,

$$\text{If exactly } Y = \alpha + \beta X, \quad \text{then} \quad corr(X, Y) = 1 \quad \text{if } \beta > 0,$$
$$corr(X, Y) = -1 \quad \text{if } \beta < 0. \tag{2.17}$$

Moreover,

Definition 2.14: *Random variables X and Y are said to be uncorrelated if $cov(X, Y) = 0$. A sequence of random variables X_j is uncorrelated if, for all $i \neq j$, X_i and X_j are uncorrelated.*

Furthermore, it is easy to verify that

Theorem 2.19: *If $X_1, ..., X_n$ are uncorrelated, then* $var(\sum_{j=1}^{n} X_j) = \sum_{j=1}^{n} var(X_j)$.

Proof: Exercise.

2.6. Some Useful Inequalities Involving Mathematical Expectations

There are a few inequalities that will prove to be useful later on – in particular the inequalities of Chebishev, Holder, Liapounov, and Jensen.

2.6.1. Chebishev's Inequality

Let X be a nonnegative random variable with distribution Function $F(x)$, and let $\varphi(x)$ be a monotonic, increasing, nonnegative Borel-measurable function on $[0, \infty)$. Then, for arbitrary $\varepsilon > 0$,

$$E[\varphi(X)] = \int \varphi(x)dF(x) = \int_{\{\varphi(x)>\varphi(\varepsilon)\}} \varphi(x)dF(x)$$

$$+ \int_{\{\varphi(x)\leq\varphi(\varepsilon)\}} \varphi(x)dF(x) \geq \int_{\{\varphi(x)>\varphi(\varepsilon)\}} \varphi(x)dF(x) \geq \varphi(\varepsilon)$$

$$\times \int_{\{\varphi(x)>\varphi(\varepsilon)\}} dF(x) = \varphi(\varepsilon) \int_{\{x>\varepsilon\}} dF(x) = \varphi(\varepsilon)(1 - F(\varepsilon));$$

$$\tag{2.18}$$

hence,

$$P(X > \varepsilon) = 1 - F(\varepsilon) \leq E[\varphi(X)]/\varphi(\varepsilon). \tag{2.19}$$

In particular, it follows from (2.19) that, for a random variable Y with expected value $\mu_y = E(Y)$ and variance σ_y^2,

$$P\left(\left\{\omega \in \Omega : |Y(\omega) - \mu_y| > \sqrt{\sigma_y^2/\varepsilon}\right\}\right) \leq \varepsilon. \tag{2.20}$$

2.6.2. Holder's Inequality

Holder's inequality is based on the fact that $\ln(x)$ is a concave function on $(0, \infty)$: for $0 < a < b$, and $0 \leq \lambda \leq 1$, $\ln(\lambda a + (1 - \lambda)b) \geq \lambda\ln(a) + (1 - \lambda)\ln(b)$; hence,

$$\lambda a + (1 - \lambda)b \geq a^\lambda b^{1-\lambda}. \tag{2.21}$$

Now let X and Y be random variables, and put $a = |X|^p/E(|X|^p)$, $b = |Y|^q/E(|Y|^q)$, where $p > 1$ and $p^{-1} + q^{-1} = 1$. Then it follows from (2.21), with $\lambda = 1/p$ and $1 - \lambda = 1/q$, that

$$p^{-1}\frac{|X|^p}{E(|X|^p)} + q^{-1}\frac{|Y|^q}{E(|Y|^q)} \geq \left(\frac{|X|^p}{E(|X|^p)}\right)^{1/p}\left(\frac{|Y|^q}{E(|Y|^q)}\right)^{1/q}$$

$$= \frac{|X \cdot Y|}{(E(|X|^p))^{1/p}(E(|Y|^q))^{1/q}}.$$

Taking expectations yields Holder's inequality:

$$E(|X \cdot Y|) \leq (E(|X|^p))^{1/p}(E(|Y|^q))^{1/q},$$

$$\text{where} \quad p > 1 \quad \text{and} \quad \frac{1}{p} + \frac{1}{q} = 1. \tag{2.22}$$

For the case $p = q = 2$, inequality (2.22) reads $E(|X \cdot Y|) \leq \sqrt{E(X^2)}\sqrt{E(Y^2)}$, which is known as the Cauchy–Schwartz inequality.

2.6.3. Liapounov's Inequality

Liapounov's inequality follows from Holder's inequality (2.22) by replacing Y with 1:

$$E(|X|) \leq (E(|X|^p))^{1/p}, \quad \text{where} \quad p \geq 1.$$

2.6.4. Minkowski's Inequality

If for some $p \geq 1$, $E[|X|^p] < \infty$ and $E[|Y|^p] < \infty$, then

$$E(|X + Y|) \leq (E(|X|^p))^{1/p} + (E(|Y|^p))^{1/p}. \tag{2.23}$$

This inequality is due to Minkowski. For $p = 1$ the result is trivial. There-fore, let $p > 1$. First note that $E[|X + Y|^p] \leq E[(2 \cdot \max(|X|, |Y|))^p] = 2^p E[\max(|X|^p, |Y|^p)] \leq 2^p E[|X|^p + |Y|^p] < \infty$; hence, we may apply Liapounov's inequality:

$$E(|X + Y|) \leq (E(|X + Y|^p))^{1/p}. \tag{2.24}$$

Next, observe that

$$
\begin{aligned}
E(|X + Y|^p) = E(|X + Y|^{p-1}|X + Y|) &\leq E(|X + Y|^{p-1}|X|) \\
&+ E(|X + Y|^{p-1}|Y|).
\end{aligned}
\tag{2.25}
$$

Let $q = p/(p - 1)$. Because $1/q + 1/p = 1$ it follows from Holder's inequality that

$$
\begin{aligned}
E(|X + Y|^{p-1}|X|) &\leq \left(E(|X + Y|^{(p-1)q})\right)^{1/q}(E(|X|^p))^{1/p} \\
&\leq (E(|X + Y|^p))^{1-1/p}(E(|X|^p))^{1/p},
\end{aligned}
\tag{2.26}
$$

and similarly,

$$E(|X + Y|^{p-1}|Y|) \leq (E(|X + Y|^p))^{1-1/p}(E(|Y|^p))^{1/p}. \tag{2.27}$$

If we combine (2.24)–(2.26), Minkowski's inequality (2.23) follows.

2.6.5. Jensen's Inequality

A real function $\varphi(x)$ on $\mathbb{R}$ is called convex if, for all $a, b \in \mathbb{R}$ and $0 \leq \lambda \leq 1$,

$$\varphi(\lambda a + (1 - \lambda)b) \leq \lambda \varphi(a) + (1 - \lambda)\varphi(b).$$

It follows by induction that, then also,

$$\varphi\left(\sum_{j=1}^{n} \lambda_j \, a_j\right) \leq \sum_{j=1}^{n} \lambda_j \, \varphi(a_j),$$

$$\text{where} \quad \lambda_j > 0 \quad \text{for} \quad j = 1, \ldots, n, \quad \text{and} \quad \sum_{j=1}^{n} \lambda_j = 1.$$

(2.28)

Consequently, it follows from (2.28) that, for a simple random variable X,

$$\varphi(E(X)) \leq E(\varphi(X)) \text{ for all convex real functions } \varphi \text{ on } \mathbb{R}. \quad (2.29)$$

This is Jensen's inequality. Because (2.29) holds for simple random variables, it holds for all random variables. Similarly, we have

$$\varphi(E(X)) \geq E(\varphi(X)) \text{ for all concave real functions } \varphi \text{ on } \mathbb{R}.$$

2.7. Expectations of Products of Independent Random Variables

Let X and Y be independent random variables, and let f and g be Borel-measurable functions on $\mathbb{R}$. I will show now that

$$E[f(X)g(Y)] = (E[f(X)])(E[g(Y)]). \quad (2.30)$$

In general, (2.30) does not hold, although there are cases in which it holds for dependent X and Y. As an example of a case in which (2.30) does not hold, let $X = U_0 \cdot U_1$ and $X = U_0 \cdot U_2$, where U_0, U_1, and U_2 are independent and uniformly [0, 1] distributed, and let $f(x) = x, g(x) = x$. The joint density of U_0, U_1 and U_2 is

$$h(u_0, u_1, u_2) = 1 \quad \text{if } (u_0, u_1, u_2)^{\mathsf{T}} \in [0, 1] \times [0, 1] \times [0, 1],$$
$$h(u_0, u_1, u_2) = 0 \text{ elsewhere;}$$

hence,

$$\begin{aligned}
E[f(X)g(Y)] = E[X \cdot Y] &= E\left[U_0^2 \, U_1 \, U_2\right] \\
&= \int_0^1 \int_0^1 \int_0^1 u_0^2 u_1 u_2 du_0 \, du_1 \, du_2 \\
&= \int_0^1 u_0^2 \, du_0 \int_0^1 u_1 du_1 \int_0^1 u_2 du_2 \\
&= (1/3) \times (1/2) \times (1/2) = 1/12,
\end{aligned}$$

whereas

$$E[f(X)] = E[X] = \int_0^1 \int_0^1 \int_0^1 u_0 u_1 \, du_0 \, du_1 \, du_2$$

$$= \int_0^1 u_0 \, du_0 \int_0^1 u_1 \, du_1 \int_0^1 du_2 = 1/4,$$

and similarly, $E[g(Y)] = E[Y] = 1/4$.

As an example of dependent random variables X and Y for which (2.30) holds, now let $X = U_0(U_1 - 0.5)$ and $Y = U_0(U_2 - 0.5)$, where U_0, U_1, and U_2 are the same as before, and again $f(x) = x$, $g(x) = x$. Then it is easy to show that $E[X \cdot Y] = E[X] = E[Y] = 0$.

To prove (2.30) for independent random variables X and Y, let f and g be simple functions, $f(x) = \sum_{i=1}^m \alpha_i I(x \in A_i)$, $g(x) = \sum_{j=1}^n \beta_j I(x \in B_j)$, where the A_i's are disjoint Borel sets and the B_j's are disjoint Borel sets. Then

$$E[f(X)g(Y)] = E\left[\sum_{i=1}^m \sum_{j=1}^n \alpha_i \beta_j \, I(X \in A_i \quad \text{and} \quad Y \in B_j)\right]$$

$$= \int \left(\sum_{i=1}^m \sum_{j=1}^n \alpha_i \beta_j \, I(X(\omega) \in A_i \quad \text{and} \quad Y(\omega) \in B_j)\right) dP(\omega)$$

$$= \sum_{i=1}^m \sum_{j=1}^n \alpha_i \beta_j \, P(\{\omega \in \Omega : X(\omega) \in A_i\} \cap \{\omega \in \Omega : Y(\omega) \in B_j\})$$

$$= \sum_{i=1}^m \sum_{j=1}^n \alpha_i \beta_j \, P(\{\omega \in \Omega : X(\omega) \in A_i\})$$

$$\times P(\{\omega \in \Omega : Y(\omega) \in B_j\})$$

$$= \left(\sum_{i=1}^m \alpha_i \, P(\{\omega \in \Omega : X(\omega) \in A_i\})\right)$$

$$\times \left(\sum_{j=1}^n \beta_j \, P(\{\omega \in \Omega : Y(\omega) \in B_j\})\right)$$

$$= (E[f(X)]) (E[g(Y)])$$

because, by the independence of X and Y, $P(X \in A_i \text{ and } Y \in B_j) = P(X \in A_i)P(Y \in B_j)$. From this result the next theorem follows more generally:

Theorem 2.20: *Let X and Y be random vectors in $\mathbb{R}^p$ and $\mathbb{R}^q$, respectively. Then X and Y are independent if and only if $E[f(X)g(Y)] = (E[f(X)])(E[g(Y)])$ for all Borel-measurable functions f and g on $\mathbb{R}^p$ and $\mathbb{R}^q$, respectively, for which the expectations involved are defined.*

This theorem implies that independent random variables are uncorrelated. The reverse, however, is in general not true. A counterexample is the case I have considered before, namely, $X = U_0(U_1 - 0.5)$ and $Y = U_0(U_2 - 0.5)$, where U_0, U_1, and U_2 are independent and uniformly $[0, 1]$ distributed. In this case, $E[X \cdot Y] = E[X] = E[Y] = 0$; hence, $\text{cov}(X, Y) = 0$, but X and Y are dependent owing to the common factor U_0. The latter can be shown formally in different ways, but the easiest way is to verify that, for example, $E[X^2 \cdot Y^2] \neq (E[X^2])(E[Y^2])$, and thus the dependence of X and Y follows from Theorem 2.20.

2.8. Moment-Generating Functions and Characteristic Functions

2.8.1. Moment-Generating Functions

The moment-generating function of a bounded random variable X (i.e., $P[|X| \leq M] = 1$ for some positive real number $M < \infty$) is defined as the function

$$m(t) = E[\exp(t \cdot X)], t \in \mathbb{R}, \tag{2.31}$$

where the argument t is nonrandom. More generally:

Definition 2.15: *The moment generating function of a random vector X in $\mathbb{R}^k$ is defined by $m(t) = E[\exp(t^\mathsf{T} X)]$ for $t \in \mathsf{T} \subset \mathbb{R}^k$, where T is the set of nonrandom vectors t for which the moment-generating function exists and is finite.*

For bounded random variables the moment-generating function exists and is finite for all values of t. In particular, in the univariate bounded case we can write

$$m(t) = E[\exp(t \cdot X)] = E\left[\sum_{k=0}^{\infty} \frac{t^k X^k}{k!}\right] = \sum_{k=0}^{\infty} \frac{t^k E[X^k]}{k!}.$$

It is easy to verify that the jth derivative of $m(t)$ is

$$m^{(j)}(t) = \frac{d^j m(t)}{(dt)^j} = \sum_{k=j}^{\infty} \frac{t^{k-j} E[X^k]}{(k-j)!}$$

$$= E[X^j] + \sum_{k=j+1}^{\infty} \frac{t^{k-j} E[X^k]}{(k-j)!}; \tag{2.32}$$

hence, the jth moment of X is

$$m^{(j)}(0) = E[X^j].$$
(2.33)

This is the reason for calling $m(t)$ the "moment-generating function."

Although the moment-generating function is a handy tool for computing moments of a distribution, its actual importance arises because the shape of the moment-generating function in an open neighborhood of zero uniquely characterizes the distribution of a random variable. In order to show this, we need the following result.

Theorem 2.21: *The distributions of two random vectors X and Y in $\mathbb{R}^k$ are the same if and only if for all bounded continuous functions φ on $\mathbb{R}^k$, $E[\varphi(X)] = E[\varphi(Y)]$.*

Proof: I will only prove this theorem for the case in which X and Y are random variables: $k = 1$. Note that the "only if" case follows from the definition of expectation.

Let $F(x)$ be the distribution function of X and let $G(y)$ be the distribution function of Y. Let $a < b$ be arbitrary continuity points of $F(x)$ and $G(y)$ and define

$$\varphi(x) = \begin{cases} = 0 & \text{if } x \geq b, \\ = 1 & \text{if } x < a, \\ = \dfrac{b - x}{b - a} & \text{if } a \leq x < b. \end{cases}$$
(2.34)

Clearly, (2.34) is a bounded, continuous function and therefore, by assumption, we have $E[\varphi(X)] = E[\varphi(Y)]$. Now observe from (2.34) that

$$E[\varphi(X)] = \int \varphi(x)dF(x) = F(a) + \int_a^b \frac{b - x}{b - a}dF(x) \geq F(a)$$

and

$$E[\varphi(X)] = \int \varphi(x)dF(x) = F(a) + \int_a^b \frac{b - x}{b - a}dF(x) \leq F(b).$$

Similarly,

$$E[\varphi(Y)] = \int \varphi(y)dG(y) = G(a) + \int_a^b \frac{b - x}{b - a}dG(x) \geq G(a)$$

and

$$E[\varphi(X)] = \int \varphi(y)dG(y) = G(a) + \int_a^b \frac{b-x}{b-a}dG(x) \leq G(b).$$

If we combine these inequalities with $E[\varphi(X)] = E[\varphi(Y)]$, it follows that for arbitrary continuity points $a < b$ of $F(x)$ and $G(y)$,

$$G(a) \leq F(b), F(a) \leq G(b). \tag{2.35}$$

If we let $b \downarrow a$, it follows from (2.35) that $F(a) = G(a)$.   Q.E.D.

Now assume that the random variables X and Y are discrete, and take with probability 1 the values $x_1, \ldots, x_n$. Without loss of generality we may assume that $x_j = j$, that is,

$$P[X \in \{1, 2, \ldots, n\}] = P[Y \in \{1, 2, \ldots, n\}] = 1.$$

Suppose that all the moments of X and Y match: For $k = 1, 2, 3, \ldots, E[X^k] = E[Y^k]$. I will show that then, for an arbitrary bounded continuous function φ on $\mathbb{R}$, $E[\varphi(X)] = E[\varphi(Y)]$.

Denoting $p_j = P[X = j], q_j = P[Y = j]$, we can write $E[\varphi(X)] = \sum_{j=1}^n \varphi(j)P_j$, $E[\varphi(Y)] = \sum_{j=1}^n \varphi(j)q_j$. It is always possible to construct a polynomial $\rho(t) = \sum_{k=0}^{n-1} \rho_k t^k$ such that $\varphi(j) = \rho(j)$ for $j = 1, \ldots n$ by solving

$$\begin{pmatrix} 1 & 1 & 1 & \cdots & 1 \\ 1 & 2 & 2^2 & \cdots & 2^{n-1} \\ \vdots & \vdots & \vdots & \ddots & \vdots \\ 1 & n & n^2 & \cdots & n^{n-1} \end{pmatrix} \begin{pmatrix} \rho_0 \\ \rho_1 \\ \vdots \\ \rho_{n-1} \end{pmatrix} = \begin{pmatrix} \varphi(1) \\ \varphi(2) \\ \vdots \\ \varphi(n) \end{pmatrix}.$$

Then $E[\varphi(X)] = \sum_{j=1}^n \sum_{k=0}^{n-1} \rho_k j^k p_j = \sum_{k=0}^{n-1} \rho_k \sum_{j=1}^n j^k p_j = \sum_{k=0}^{n-1} \rho_k E[X^k]$ and, similarly, $E[\varphi(Y)] = \sum_{k=0}^{n-1} \rho_k E[Y^k]$. Hence, it follows from Theorem 2.21 that if all the corresponding moments of X and Y are the same, then the distributions of X and Y are the same. Thus, if the moment-generating functions of X and Y coincide on an open neighborhood of zero, and if all the moments of X and Y are finite, it follows from (2.33) that all the corresponding moments of X and Y are the same:

Theorem 2.22: *If the random variables X and Y are discrete and take with probability 1 only a finite number of values, then the distributions of X and Y are the same if and only if the moment-generating functions of X and Y coincide on an arbitrary, small, open neighborhood of zero.*

However, this result also applies without the conditions that X and Y are discrete and take only a finite number of values, and for random vectors as well, but the proof is complicated and is therefore omitted:

Theorem 2.23: *If the moment-generating functions $m_X(t)$ and $m_Y(t)$ of the random vectors X and Y in $\mathbb{R}^k$ are defined and finite in an open neighborhood $N_0(\delta) = \{x \in \mathbb{R}^k : \|x\| < \delta\}$ of the origin of $\mathbb{R}^k$, then the distributions of X and Y are the same if and only if $m_X(t) = m_Y(t)$ for all $t \in N_0(\delta)$*

2.8.2. Characteristic Functions

The disadvantage of the moment-generating function is that it may not be finite in an arbitrarily small, open neighborhood of zero. For example, if X has a standard Cauchy distribution, that is, X has density

$$f(x) = \frac{1}{\pi(1 + x^2)}, \tag{2.36}$$

then

$$m(t) = \int_{-\infty}^{\infty} \exp(t \cdot x)f(x)dx \begin{cases} = \infty & \text{if } t \neq 0, \\ = 1 & \text{if } t = 0. \end{cases} \tag{2.37}$$

There are many other distributions with the same property as (2.37) (see Chapter 4); hence, the moment-generating functions in these cases are of no use for comparing distributions.

The solution to this problem is to replace t in (2.31) with $i \cdot t$, where $i = \sqrt{-1}$. The resulting function $\varphi(t) = m(i \cdot t)$ is called the *characteristic function* of the random variable X : $\varphi(t) = E[\exp(i \cdot t \cdot X)]$, $t \in \mathbb{R}$. More generally,

Definition 2.16: *The characteristic function of a random vector X in $\mathbb{R}^k$ is defined by $\varphi(t) = E[\exp(i \cdot t^\mathsf{T} X)]$, $t \in \mathbb{R}^k$, where the argument t is nonrandom.*

The characteristic function is bounded because $\exp(i \cdot x) = \cos(x) + i \cdot \sin(x)$. See Appendix III. Thus, the characteristic function in Definition 2.16 can be written as

$$\varphi(t) = E[\cos(t^\mathsf{T} X)] + i \cdot E[\sin(t^\mathsf{T} X)], t \in \mathbb{R}^k.$$

Note that by the dominated convergence theorem (Theorem 2.11), $\lim_{t \to 0} \varphi(t) = 1 = \varphi(0)$; hence, a characteristic function is always continuous in $t = 0$.

Replacing moment-generating functions with characteristic functions, we find that Theorem 2.23 now becomes

Theorem 2.24: *Random variables or vectors have the same distribution if and only if their characteristic functions are identical.*

The proof of this theorem is complicated and is therefore given in Appendix 2.A at the end of this chapter. The same applies to the following useful result, which is known as the *inversion formula for characteristic functions*:

Theorem 2.25: *Let X be a random vector in $\mathbb{R}^k$ with characteristic function $\varphi(t)$. If $\varphi(t)$ is absolutely integrable (i.e., $\int_{\mathbb{R}^k} |\varphi(t)|dt < \infty$), then the distribution of X is absolutely continuous with joint density $f(x) = (2\pi)^{-k} \int_{\mathbb{R}^k} \exp(-i \cdot t^\top x)\varphi(t)dt$.*

2.9. Exercises

1. Prove that the collection $\mathcal{D}$ in the proof of Theorem 2.1 is a σ-algebra.

2. Prove Theorem 2.3.

3. Prove Theorem 2.4 for the max, sup, limsup, and lim cases.

4. Why is it true that if g is Borel measurable then so are g_+ and g_- in (2.6)?

5. Prove Theorem 2.7.

6. Prove Theorem 2.8.

7. Let $g(x) = x$ if x is rational and $g(x) = -x$ if x is irrational. Prove that $g(x)$ is Borel measurable.

8. Prove parts (a)–(f) of Theorem 2.9 for simple functions
$$g(x) = \sum_{i=1}^{n} a_i I(x \in B_i), \quad f(x) = \sum_{j=1}^{m} b_j I(x \in C_j).$$

9. Why can you conclude from Exercise 8 that parts (a)–(f) of Theorem 2.9 hold for arbitrary, nonnegative, Borel-measurable functions?

10. Why can you conclude from Exercise 9 that Theorem 2.9 holds for arbitrary Borel-measurable functions provided that the integrals involved are defined?

11. From which result on probability measures does (2.11) follow?

12. Determine for each inequality in (2.12) which part of Theorem 2.9 has been used.

13. Why do we need the condition in Theorem 2.11 that $\int \bar{g}(x)d\mu(x) < \infty$?

14. Note that we cannot generalize Theorem 2.5 to random variables because something missing prevents us from defining a *continuous* mapping $X : \Omega \to \mathbb{R}$. What is missing?

15. Verify (2.16) and complete the proof of Theorem 2.18.

16. Prove equality (2.2).

17. Show that $\mathrm{var}(X) = E(X^2) - (E(E))^2$, $\mathrm{cov}(X, Y) = E(X \cdot Y) - (E(X)) \cdot (E(Y))$, and $-1 \le \mathrm{corr}(X, Y) \le 1$. Hint: Derive the latter result from $\mathrm{var}(Y - \lambda X) \ge 0$ for all λ.

18. Prove (2.17).

19. Which parts of Theorem 2.15 have been used in (2.18)?

20. How does (2.20) follow from (2.19)?

21. Why does it follow from (2.28) that (2.29) holds for simple random variables?

22. Prove Theorem 2.19.

23. Complete the proof of Theorem 2.20 for the case $p = q = 1$.

24. Let $X = U_0(U_1 - 0.5)$ and $Y = U_0(U_2 - 0.5)$, where U_0, U_1, and U_2 are independent and uniformly $[0, 1]$ distributed. Show that $E[X^2 \cdot Y^2] \neq (E[X^2])(E[Y^2])$.

25. Prove that if (2.29) holds for simple random variables, it holds for all random variables. Hint: Use the fact that convex and concave functions are continuous (see Appendix II).

26. Derive the moment-generating function of the binomial (n, p) distribution.

27. Use the results in Exercise 26 to derive the expectation and variance of the binomial (n, p) distribution.

28. Show that the moment-generating function of the binomial (n, p) distribution converges pointwise in t to the moment-generating function of the Poisson (λ) distribution if $n \to \infty$ and $p \downarrow 0$ such that $n \cdot p \to \lambda$.

29. Derive the characteristic function of the uniform $[0, 1]$ distribution. Is the inversion formula for characteristic functions applicable in this case?

30. If the random variable X has characteristic function $\exp(i \cdot t)$, what is the distribution of X?

31. Show that the characteristic function of a random variable X is real-valued if and only if the distribution of X is symmetric (i.e., X and $-X$ have the same distribution).

32. Use the inversion formula for characteristic functions to show that $\varphi(t) = \exp(-|t|)$ is the characteristic function of the standard Cauchy distribution [see (2.36) for the density involved]. Hints: Show first, using Exercise 31 and the inversion formula, that

$$f(x) = \pi^{-1} \int_0^\infty \cos(t \cdot x) \exp(-t) dt,$$

and then use integration by parts.

APPENDIX

2.A. Uniqueness of Characteristic Functions

To understand characteristic functions, you need to understand the basics of complex analysis, which is provided in Appendix III. Therefore, it is recommended that Appendix III be read first.

In the univariate case, Theorem 2.24 is a straightforward corollary of the following link between a probability measure and its characteristic function.

Theorem 2.A.1: *Let μ be a probability measure on the Borel sets in $\mathbb{R}$ with characteristic function φ, and let $a < b$ be continuity points of $\mu : \mu(\{a\}) = \mu(\{b\}) = 0$. Then*

$$\mu((a,b]) = \lim_{T \to \infty} \frac{1}{2\pi} \int_{-T}^{T} \frac{\exp(-i \cdot t \cdot a) - \exp(-i \cdot t \cdot b)}{i \cdot t} \varphi(t) dt.$$

(2.38)

Proof: Using the definition of characteristic function, we can write

$$\int_{-T}^{T} \frac{\exp(-i \cdot t \cdot a) - \exp(-i \cdot t \cdot b)}{i \cdot t} \varphi(t) dt$$

$$= \int_{-T}^{T} \int_{-\infty}^{\infty} \frac{\exp(i \cdot t(x - a)) - \exp(i \cdot t \cdot (x - b))}{i \cdot t} d\mu(x) dt$$

$$= \int_{-T}^{T} \lim_{M \to \infty} \int_{-M}^{M} \frac{\exp(i \cdot t(x - a)) - \exp(i \cdot t \cdot (x - b))}{i \cdot t} d\mu(x) dt.$$

(2.39)

Next, observe that

$$\left| \int_{-M}^{M} \frac{\exp(i \cdot t(x - a)) - \exp(i \cdot t \cdot (x - b))}{i \cdot t} d\mu(x) \right|$$

$$\leq \left| \frac{\exp(-i \cdot t \cdot a) - \exp(-i \cdot t \cdot b)}{i \cdot t} \right| \mu([-M, M])$$

$$\leq \frac{|\exp(-i \cdot t \cdot a) - \exp(-i \cdot t \cdot b)|}{|t|} = \sqrt{\frac{2(1 - \cos(t \cdot (b - a)))}{t^2}}$$

$$\leq b - a.$$

Therefore, it follows from the bounded convergence theorem that

$$
\int_{-T}^{T} \frac{\exp(-i \cdot t \cdot a) - \exp(-i \cdot t \cdot b)}{i \cdot t} \varphi(t) dt
$$

$$
= \lim_{M \to \infty} \int_{-T}^{T} \int_{-M}^{M} \frac{\exp(i \cdot t(x - a)) - \exp(i \cdot t \cdot (x - b))}{i \cdot t} d\mu(x) dt
$$

$$
\times \lim_{M \to \infty} \int_{-M}^{M} \int_{-T}^{T} \frac{\exp(i \cdot t(x - a)) - \exp(i \cdot t \cdot (x - b))}{i \cdot t} dt d\mu(x)
$$

$$
= \int_{-\infty}^{\infty} \left[\int_{-T}^{T} \frac{\exp(i \cdot t(x - a)) - \exp(i \cdot t \cdot (x - b))}{i \cdot t} dt \right] d\mu(x).
$$

$$(2.40)$$

The integral between square brackets can be written as

$$
\int_{-T}^{T} \frac{\exp(i \cdot t(x - a)) - \exp(i \cdot t \cdot (x - b))}{i \cdot t} dt
$$

$$
= \int_{-T}^{T} \frac{\exp(i \cdot t(x - a)) - 1}{i \cdot t} dt - \int_{-T}^{T} \frac{\exp(i \cdot t \cdot (x - b)) - 1}{i \cdot t} dt
$$

$$
= \int_{-T}^{T} \frac{\sin(t(x - a))}{t} dt - \int_{-T}^{T} \frac{\sin(t(x - b))}{t} dt
$$

$$
= 2 \int_{0}^{T} \frac{\sin(t(x - a))}{t(x - a)} dt(x - a) - 2 \int_{0}^{T} \frac{\sin(t(x - b))}{t(x - b)} dt(x - b)
$$

$$
= 2 \int_{0}^{T(x-a)} \frac{\sin(t)}{t} dt - 2 \int_{0}^{T(x-b)} \frac{\sin(t)}{t} dt
$$

$$
= 2 \operatorname{sgn}(x - a) \int_{0}^{T|x-a|} \frac{\sin(t)}{t} dt - 2 \operatorname{sgn}(x - b) \int_{0}^{T|x-b|} \frac{\sin(t)}{t} dt,
$$

$$(2.41)$$

where $\text{sgn}(x) = 1$ if $x > 0$, $\text{sgn}(0) = 0$, and $\text{sgn}(x) = -1$ if $x < 0$. The last two integrals in (2.41) are of the form

$$
\int_0^x \frac{\sin(t)}{t} dt = \int_0^x \sin(t) \int_0^\infty \exp(-t \cdot u) du \, dt
$$

$$
= \int_0^\infty \int_0^x \sin(t) \exp(-t \cdot u) dt \, du
$$

$$
= \int_0^\infty \frac{du}{1 + u^2} - \int_0^\infty [\cos(x) + u \cdot \sin(x)] \frac{\exp(-x \cdot u)}{1 + u^2} du,
$$

$$(2.42)$$

where the last equality follows from integration by parts:

$$
\int_0^x \sin(t) \exp(-t \cdot u) dt
$$

$$
= -\int_0^x \frac{d\cos(t)}{dt} \exp(-t \cdot u) dt
$$

$$
= \cos(t) \exp(-t \cdot u)|_0^x - u. \int_0^x \cos(t) \exp(-t \cdot u) dt
$$

$$
= 1 - \cos(x) \exp(-x \cdot u) - u. \int_0^x \frac{d\sin(t)}{dt} \exp(-t \cdot u) dt
$$

$$
= 1 - \cos(x) \exp(-x \cdot u) - u \cdot \sin(x) \exp(-x \cdot u)
$$

$$
- u^2 \int_0^x \sin(t) \exp(-t \cdot u) dt.
$$

Clearly, the second integral at the right-hand side of (2.42) is bounded in $x > 0$ and converges to zero as $x \to \infty$. The first integral at the right-hand side of (2.42) is

$$
\int_0^\infty \frac{du}{1 + u^2} = \int_0^\infty d\arctan(u) = \arctan(\infty) = \pi/2.
$$

Thus, the integral (2.42) is bounded (hence so is (2.41)), and

$$
\lim_{T \to \infty} \int_{-T}^{T} \frac{\exp(i \cdot t(x - a)) - \exp(i \cdot t \cdot (x - b))}{i \cdot t} dt
$$
$$
= \pi [\operatorname{sgn}(x - a) - \operatorname{sgn}(x - b)]. \tag{2.43}
$$

It follows now from (2.39), (2.40), (2.43), and the dominated convergence theorem that

$$
\lim_{T \to \infty} \frac{1}{2\pi} \int_{-T}^{T} \frac{\exp(-i \cdot t \cdot a) - \exp(-i \cdot t \cdot b)}{i \cdot t} \varphi(t) dt
$$
$$
= \frac{1}{2} \int [\operatorname{sgn}(x - a) - \operatorname{sgn}(x - b)] d\mu(x)
$$
$$
= \mu((a, b)) + \frac{1}{2}\mu(\{a\}) + \frac{1}{2}\mu(\{b\}). \tag{2.44}
$$

The last equality in (2.44) follow from the fact that

$$
\operatorname{sgn}(x - a) - \operatorname{sgn}(x - b) = \begin{cases} 0 & \text{if } x < a \text{ or } x > b, \\ 1 & \text{if } x = a \text{ or } x = b, \\ 2 & \text{if } a < x < b. \end{cases}
$$

The result (2.38) now follows from (2.44) and the condition $\mu(\{a\}) = \mu(\{b\}) = 0$. Q.E.D.

Note that (2.38) also reads as

$$
F(b) - F(a) = \lim_{T \to \infty} \frac{1}{2\pi} \int_{-T}^{T} \frac{\exp(-i \cdot t \cdot a) - \exp(-i \cdot t \cdot b)}{i \cdot t} \varphi(t) dt,
$$
$$
\tag{2.45}
$$

where F is the distribution function corresponding to the probability measure μ.

Next, suppose that φ is absolutely integrable: $\int_{-\infty}^{\infty} |\varphi(t)| dt < \infty$. Then (2.45) can be written as

$$
F(b) - F(a) = \frac{1}{2\pi} \int_{-\infty}^{\infty} \frac{\exp(-i \cdot t \cdot a) - \exp(-i \cdot t \cdot b)}{i \cdot t} \varphi(t) dt,
$$

and it follows from the dominated convergence theorem that

$$F'(a) = \lim_{b \downarrow a} \frac{F(b) - F(a)}{b - a}$$

$$= \frac{1}{2\pi} \int_{-\infty}^{\infty} \lim_{b \downarrow a} \frac{1 - \exp(-i \cdot t \cdot (b - a))}{i \cdot t \cdot (b - a)} \exp(-i \cdot t \cdot a) \varphi(t) dt$$

$$= \frac{1}{2\pi} \int_{-\infty}^{\infty} \exp(-i \cdot t \cdot a) \varphi(t) dt.$$

This proves Theorem 2.25 for the univariate case.

In the multivariate case Theorem 2.A.1 becomes

Theorem 2.A.2: *Let μ be a probability measure on the Borel sets in $\mathbb{R}^k$ with characteristic function φ. Let $B = \times_{j=1}^{k}(a_j, b_j]$, where $a_j < b_j$ for $j = 1, 2, \ldots, k$, and let ∂B be the border of B, that is, $\partial B = \{\times_{j=1}^{k}[a_j, b_j]\} \setminus \{\times_{j=1}^{k}(a_j, b_j)\}$. If $\mu(\partial B) = 0$; then*

$$\mu(B) = \lim_{T_1 \to \infty} \cdots \lim_{T_k \to \infty} \int_{\times_{j=1}^{k}(-T_j, T_j)} \prod_{j=1}^{k} \left[\frac{\exp(-i \cdot t_j \cdot a_j) - \exp(-i \cdot t_j \cdot b_j)}{i \cdot 2\pi t_j} \right]$$

$$\times \varphi(t) dt, \qquad (2.46)$$

where $t = (t_1, \ldots, t_k)^{\mathrm{T}}$.

This result proves Theorem 2.24 for the general case.

Moreover, if $\int_{\mathbb{R}^k} |\varphi(t)| dt < \infty$, (2.46) becomes

$$\mu(B) = \int_{\mathbb{R}^k} \prod_{j=1}^{k} \left[\frac{\exp(-i \cdot t_j \cdot a_j) - \exp(-i \cdot t_j \cdot b_j)}{i \cdot 2\pi t_j} \right] \varphi(t) dt,$$

and by the dominated convergence theorem we may take partial derivatives inside the integral:

$$\frac{\partial^k \mu(B)}{\partial a_1 \ldots \partial a_k} = \frac{1}{(2\pi)^k} \int_{\mathbb{R}^k} \exp(-i \cdot t^{\mathrm{T}} a) \varphi(t) dt, \qquad (2.47)$$

where $a = (a_1, \ldots, a_k)^{\mathrm{T}}$. The latter is just the density corresponding to μ in point a. Thus, (2.47) proves Theorem 2.25.

3   Conditional Expectations

3.1. Introduction

Roll a die, and let the outcome be Y. Define the random variable $X = 1$ if Y is even, and $X = 0$ if Y is odd. The expected value of Y is $E[Y] = (1 + 2 + 3 + 4 + 5 + 6)/6 = 3.5$. But what would the expected value of Y be if it is revealed that the outcome is even: $X = 1$? The latter information implies that Y is 2, 4, or 6 with equal probabilities $1/3$; hence, the expected value of Y, conditional on the event $X = 1$, is $E[Y|X = 1] = (2 + 4 + 6)/3 = 4$. Similarly, if it is revealed that $X = 0$, then Y is 1, 3, or, 5 with equal probabilities $1/3$; hence, the expected value of Y, conditional on the event $X = 0$, is $E[Y|X = 0] = (1 + 3 + 5)/3 = 3$. Both results can be captured in a single statement:

$$E[Y|X] = 3 + X. \tag{3.1}$$

In this example the conditional probability of $Y = y$, given, $X = x$ is[1]

$$P(Y = y|X = x) = \frac{P(Y = y \text{ and } X = x)}{P(X = x)}$$

$$= \frac{P(\{y\} \cap \{2, 4, 6\})}{P(\{2, 4, 6\})} = \frac{P(\{y\})}{P(\{2, 4, 6\})}$$

$$= \frac{1}{3} \quad \text{if } x = 1 \quad \text{and} \quad y \in \{2, 4, 6\}$$

$$= \frac{P(\{y\} \cap \{2, 4, 6\})}{P(\{2, 4, 6\})} = \frac{P(\emptyset)}{P(\{2, 4, 6\})}$$

$$= 0 \quad \text{if } x = 1 \quad \text{and} \quad y \notin \{2, 4, 6\}$$

---

[1] Here and in the sequel the notations $P(Y = y|X = x)$, $P(Y = y \text{ and } X = x)$, $P(X = x)$, and similar notations involving inequalities are merely shorthand notations for the probabilities $P(\{\omega \in \Omega : Y(\omega) = y\}|\{\omega \in \Omega : X(\omega) = x\})$, $P(\{\omega \in \Omega : Y(\omega) = y\} \cap \{\omega \in \Omega : X(\omega) = x\})$, and $P(\{\omega \in \Omega : X(\omega) = x\})$, respectively.

$$= \frac{P(\{y\} \cap \{1, 3, 5\})}{P(\{1, 3, 5\})} = \frac{P(\{y\})}{P(\{1, 3, 5\})}$$

$$= \frac{1}{3} \quad \text{if } x = 0 \quad \text{and} \quad y \in \{1, 3, 5\}$$

$$= \frac{P(\{y\} \cap \{1, 3, 5\})}{P(\{1, 3, 5\})} = \frac{P(\emptyset)}{P(\{1, 3, 5\})}$$

$$= 0 \quad \text{if } x = 0 \quad \text{and} \quad y \notin \{1, 3, 5\}; \tag{3.2}$$

hence,

$$\sum_{y=1}^{6} y P(Y = y | X = x) \begin{cases} = \dfrac{2 + 4 + 6}{3} = 4 & \text{if } x = 1 \\[2mm] = \dfrac{1 + 3 + 5}{3} = 3 & \text{if } x = 0 \end{cases} = 3 + x.$$

Thus, in the case in which both Y and X are discrete random variables, the conditional expectation $E[Y|X]$ can be defined as

$$E[Y|X] = \sum_{y} y p(y|X), \quad \text{where}$$

$$p(y|x) = P(Y = y | X = x) \quad \text{for} \quad P(X = x) > 0.$$

A second example is one in which X is uniformly $[0, 1]$ distributed, and given the outcome x of X, Y is randomly drawn from the uniform $[0, x]$ distribution. Then the distribution function $F(y)$ of Y is

$$\begin{aligned}
F(y) &= P(Y \le y) = P(Y \le y \text{ and } X \le y) + P(Y \le y \text{ and } X > y) \\
&= P(X \le y) + P(Y \le y \text{ and } X > y) \\
&= y + E[I(Y \le y) I(X > y)] \\
&= y + \int_0^1 \left(\int_0^x I(z \le y) x^{-1} \, dz \right) I(x > y) \, dx \\
&= y + \int_y^1 \left(\int_0^{\min(x,y)} x^{-1} \, dz \right) dx \\
&= y + \int_y^1 (y/x) \, dx = y(1 - \ln(y)) \quad \text{for} \quad 0 \le y \le 1.
\end{aligned}$$

Hence, the density of Y is

$$f(y) = F'(y) = -\ln(y) \quad \text{for} \quad y \in (0, 1], \ f(y) = 0 \quad \text{for} \quad y \notin (0, 1].$$

Thus, the expected value of Y is $E[Y] = \int_0^1 y(-\ln(y))dy = 1/4$. But what would the expected value be if it is revealed that $X = x$ for a given number $x \in (0, 1)$? The latter information implies that Y is now uniformly $[0, x]$ distributed; hence, the conditional expectation involved is

$$E[Y|X = x] = x^{-1} \int_0^x y\,dy = x/2.$$

More generally, the conditional expectation of Y given X is

$$E[Y|X] = X^{-1} \int_0^X y\,dy = X/2. \tag{3.3}$$

The latter example is a special case of a pair (Y, X) of absolutely continuously distributed random variables with joint density function $f(y, x)$ and marginal density $f_x(x)$. The conditional distribution function of Y, given the event $X \in [x, x + \delta], \delta > 0$, is

$$P(Y \le y | X \in [x, x + \delta]) = \frac{P(Y \le y \text{ and } X \in [x, x + \delta])}{P(X \in [x, x + \delta])}$$

$$= \frac{\int_{-\infty}^y \frac{1}{\delta} \int_x^{x+\delta} f(u, v)dv\,du}{\frac{1}{\delta} \int_x^{x+\delta} f_x(v)dv}.$$

Letting $\delta \downarrow 0$ then yields the conditional distribution function of Y given the event $X = x$:

$$F(y|x) = \lim_{\delta \downarrow 0} P(Y \le y | X \in [x, x + \delta])$$

$$= \int_{-\infty}^y f(u, x)du/f_x(x), \text{ provided } f_x(x) > 0.$$

Note that we cannot define this conditional distribution function directly as

$$F(y|x) = P(Y \le y \text{ and } X = x)/P(X = x)$$

because for continuous random variables X, $P(X = x) = 0$.

The conditional density of Y, given the event $X = x$, is now

$$f(y|x) = \partial F(y|x)/\partial y = f(y, x)/f_x(x),$$

and the conditional expectation of Y given the event $X = x$ can therefore be defined as

$$E[Y|X = x] = \int_{-\infty}^{\infty} y f(y|x)dy = g(x), \text{ for instance.}$$

Plugging in X for x then yields

$$E[Y|X] = \int_{-\infty}^{\infty} y f(y|X) dy = g(X). \tag{3.4}$$

These examples demonstrate two fundamental properties of conditional expectations. The first one is that $E[Y|X]$ is a function of X, which can be translated as follows: Let Y and X be two random variables defined on a common probability space $\{\Omega, \mathscr{F}, P\}$, and let $\mathscr{F}_X$ be the σ-algebra generated by X, $\mathscr{F}_X = \{X^{-1}(B), B \in \mathscr{B}\}$, where $X^{-1}(B)$ is a shorthand notation for the set $\{\omega \in \Omega : X(\omega) \in B\}$ and $\mathscr{B}$ is the Euclidean Borel field. Then,

$$Z = E[Y|X] \text{ is measurable } \mathscr{F}_X, \tag{3.5}$$

which means that, for all Borel sets B, $\{\omega \in \Omega : Z(\omega) \in B\} \in \mathscr{F}_X$. Secondly, we have

$$E[(Y - E[Y|X])I(X \in B)] = 0 \quad \text{for all Borel sets } B. \tag{3.6}$$

In particular, in the case (3.4) we have

$$E[(Y - E[Y|X])I(X \in B)]$$

$$= \int_{-\infty}^{\infty} \int_{-\infty}^{\infty} (y - g(x)) I(x \in B) f(y, x) dy dx$$

$$= \int_{-\infty}^{\infty} \left(\int_{-\infty}^{\infty} y f(y|x) dy \right) I(x \in B) f_x(x) dx$$

$$- \int_{-\infty}^{\infty} \left(\int_{-\infty}^{\infty} f(y|x) dy \right) g(x) I(x \in B) f_x(x) dx$$

$$= \int_{-\infty}^{\infty} g(x) I(x \in B) f_x(x) dx - \int_{-\infty}^{\infty} g(x) I(x \in B) f_x(x) dx = 0. \tag{3.7}$$

Because $\mathscr{F}_X = \{X^{-1}(B), B \in \mathscr{B}\}$, property (3.6) is equivalent to

$$\int_A (Y(\omega) - Z(\omega)) dP(\omega) = 0 \quad \text{for all } A \in \mathscr{F}_X. \tag{3.8}$$

Moreover, note that $\Omega \in \mathscr{F}_X$, and thus (3.8) implies

$$E(Y) = \int_\Omega Y(\omega) dP(\omega) = \int_\Omega Z(\omega) dP(\omega) = E(Z) \tag{3.9}$$

provided that the expectations involved are defined. A sufficient condition for the existence of $E(Y)$ is that

$$E(|Y|) < \infty. \tag{3.10}$$

We will see later that (3.10) is also a sufficient condition for the existence of $E(Z)$.

I will show now that condition (3.6) also holds for the examples (3.1) and (3.3). Of course, in the case of (3.3) I have already shown this in (3.7), but it is illustrative to verify it again for the special case involved.

In the case of (3.1) the random variable $Y \cdot I(X = 1)$ takes the value 0 with probability $\frac{1}{2}$ and the values 2, 4, or 6 with probability $1/6$; the random variable $Y \cdot I(X = 0)$ takes the value 0 with probability $\frac{1}{2}$ and the values 1, 3, or 5 with probability $1/6$. Thus,

$$
\begin{array}{llll}
E[Y \cdot I(X \in B)] = E[Y \cdot I(X = 1)] = 2 & \text{if } 1 \in B & \text{and} & 0 \notin B, \\
E[Y \cdot I(X \in B)] = E[Y \cdot I(X = 0)] = 1.5 & \text{if } 1 \notin B & \text{and} & 0 \in B, \\
E[Y \cdot I(X \in B)] = E[Y] = 3.5 & \text{if } 1 \in B & \text{and} & 0 \in B, \\
E[Y \cdot I(X \in B)] = 0 & \text{if } 1 \notin B & \text{and} & 0 \notin B,
\end{array}
$$

which by (3.1) and (3.6) is equal to

$$
\begin{aligned}
E[(E[Y|X])&I(X \in B)] \\
&= 3E[I(X \in B)] + E[X \cdot I(X \in B)] \\
&= 3P(X \in B) + P(X = 1 \text{ and } X \in B) \\
&= 3P(X = 1) + P(X = 1) &&= 2 && \text{if } 1 \in B && \text{and} && 0 \notin B, \\
&= 3P(X = 0) + P(X = 1 \text{ and } X = 0) &&= 1.5 && \text{if } 1 \notin B && \text{and} && 0 \in B, \\
&= 3P(X = 0 \text{ or } X = 1) + P(X = 1) &&= 3.5 && \text{if } 1 \in B && \text{and} && 0 \in B, \\
&= 0 &&&& \text{if } 1 \notin B && \text{and} && 0 \notin B.
\end{aligned}
$$

Moreover, in the case of (3.3) the distribution function of $Y \cdot I(X \in B)$ is

$$
\begin{aligned}
F_B(y) &= P(Y \cdot I(X \in B) \le y) = P(Y \le y \text{ and } X \in B) + P(X \notin B) \\
&= P(X \in B \cap [0, y]) + P(Y \le y \text{ and } X \in B \cap (y, 1)) + P(X \notin B) \\
&= \int_0^y I(x \in B)dx + y \int_y^1 x^{-1} I(x \in B)dx + 1 - \int_0^1 I(x \in B)dx \\
&= 1 - \int_y^1 I(x \in B)dx + y \int_y^1 x^{-1} I(x \in B)dx \quad \text{for} \quad 0 \le y \le 1;
\end{aligned}
$$

hence, the density involved is

$$f_B(y) = \int_y^1 x^{-1} I(x \in B)dx \quad \text{for} \quad y \in [0, 1], \ f_B(y) = 0 \quad \text{for} \quad y \notin [0, 1].$$

Thus,

$$E[Y \cdot I(X \in B)] = \int_0^1 y \left(\int_y^1 x^{-1} I(x \in B) dx \right) dy$$

$$= \frac{1}{2} \int_0^1 y \cdot I(y \in B) dy,$$

which is equal to

$$E(E[Y|X]I(X \in B)) = \frac{1}{2} E[X \cdot I(X \in B)] = \frac{1}{2} \int_0^1 x \cdot I(x \in B) dx.$$

The two conditions (3.5) and (3.8) uniquely define $Z = E[Y|X]$ in the sense that if there exist two versions of $E[Y|X]$ such as $Z_1 = E[Y|X]$ and $Z_2 = E[Y|X]$ satisfying the conditions (3.5) and (3.8), then $P(Z_1 = Z_2) = 1$. To see this, let

$$A = \{\omega \in \Omega : Z_1(\omega) < Z_2(\omega)\}. \tag{3.11}$$

Then $A \in \mathscr{F}_X$; hence, it follows from (3.8) that

$$\int_A (Z_2(\omega) - Z_1(\omega)) dP(\omega) = E[(Z_2 - Z_1)I(Z_2 - Z_1 > 0)] = 0.$$

The latter equality implies $P(Z_2 - Z_1 > 0) = 0$ as I will show in Lemma 3.1. If we replace the set A by $A = \{\omega \in \Omega : Z_1(\omega) > Z_2(\omega)\}$, it follows similarly that $P(Z_2 - Z_1 < 0) = 0$. Combining these two cases, we find that $P(Z_2 \neq Z_1) = 0$.

Lemma 3.1: $E[Z \cdot I(Z > 0)] = 0$ *implies* $P(Z > 0) = 0$.

Proof: Choose $\varepsilon > 0$ arbitrarily. Then

$$0 = E[Z \cdot I(Z > 0)] = E[Z \cdot I(0 < Z < \varepsilon)] + E[Z \cdot I(Z \geq \varepsilon)]$$
$$\geq E[Z \cdot I(Z \geq \varepsilon)] \geq \varepsilon E[I(Z \geq \varepsilon)] = \varepsilon P(Z \geq \varepsilon);$$

hence, $P(Z > \varepsilon) = 0$ for all $\varepsilon > 0$. Now take $\varepsilon = 1/n, n = 1, 2, \ldots$ and let

$$C_n = \{\omega \in \Omega : Z(\omega) > n^{-1}\}.$$

Then $C_n \subset C_{n+1}$; hence,

$$P(Z > 0) = P\left[\bigcup_{n=1}^{\infty} C_n \right] = \lim_{n \to \infty} P[C_n] = 0. \tag{3.12}$$

Q.E.D.

Conditions (3.5) and (3.8) only depend on the conditioning random variable X via the sub-σ-algebra $\mathscr{F}_X$ of $\mathscr{F}$. Therefore, we can define the conditional expectation of a random variable Y relative to an arbitrary sub-σ-algebra $\mathscr{F}_0$ of $\mathscr{F}$, denoted by $E[Y|\mathscr{F}_0]$, as follows:

Definition 3.1: *Let Y be a random variable defined on a probability space $\{\Omega, \mathscr{F}, P\}$ satisfying $E(|Y|) < \infty$, and let $\mathscr{F}_0 \subset \mathscr{F}$ be a sub-σ-algebra of $\mathscr{F}$. The conditional expectation of Y relative to the sub-σ-algebra $\mathscr{F}_0$, denoted by $E[Y|\mathscr{F}_0] = Z$, for instance, is a random variable Z that is measurable $\mathscr{F}_0$ and is such that for all sets $A \in \mathscr{F}_0$,*

$$\int_A Y(\omega)dP(\omega) = \int_A Z(\omega)dP(\omega).$$

3.2. Properties of Conditional Expectations

As conjectured following (3.10), the condition $E(|Y|) < \infty$ is also a sufficient condition for the existence of $E(E[Y|\mathscr{F}_0])$. The reason is twofold. First, I have already established in (3.9) that

Theorem 3.1: $E[E(Y|\mathscr{F}_0)] = E(Y)$.

Second, conditional expectations preserve inequality:

Theorem 3.2: *If $P(X \leq Y) = 1$, then $P(E(X|\mathscr{F}_0) \leq E(Y|\mathscr{F}_0)) = 1$.*

Proof: Let $A = \{\omega \in \Omega : E(X|\mathscr{F}_0)(\omega) > E(Y|\mathscr{F}_0)(\omega)\}$. Then $A \in \mathscr{F}_0$, and

$$\int_A X(\omega)dP(\omega) = \int_A E(X|\mathscr{F}_0)(\omega)dP(\omega) \leq \int_A Y(\omega)dP(\omega)$$

$$= \int_A E(Y|\mathscr{F}_0)(\omega)dP(\omega);$$

hence,

$$0 \leq \int_A (E(Y|\mathscr{F}_0)(\omega) - E(X|\mathscr{F}_0)(\omega))dP(\omega) \leq 0. \tag{3.13}$$

It follows now from (3.13) and Lemma 3.1 that $P(\{\omega \in \Omega : E(X|\mathscr{F}_0)(\omega) > E(Y|\mathscr{F}_0)(\omega)\}) = 0$.   Q.E.D.

Theorem 3.2 implies that $|E(Y|\mathscr{F}_0)| \leq E(|Y|\,|\mathscr{F}_0)$ with probability 1, and if we apply Theorem 3.1 it follows that $E[|E(Y|\mathscr{F}_0)|] \leq E(|Y|)$. Therefore, the condition $E(|Y|) < \infty$ is sufficient for the existence of $E(E[Y|\mathscr{F}_0])$.

Conditional expectations also preserve linearity:

Theorem 3.3: *If $E[|X|] < \infty$ and $E[|Y|] < \infty$, then $P[E(\alpha X + \beta Y|\mathscr{F}_0) = \alpha E(X|\mathscr{F}_0) + \beta E(Y|\mathscr{F}_0)] = 1$.*

Proof: Let $Z_0 = E(\alpha X + \beta Y|\mathscr{F}_0)$, $Z_1 = E(X|\mathscr{F}_0)$, $Z_2 = E(Y|\mathscr{F}_0)$. For every $A \in \mathscr{F}_0$ we have

$$
\int_A Z_0(\omega)dP(\omega) = \int_A (\alpha X(\omega) + \beta Y(\omega))dP(\omega)
$$

$$
= \alpha \int_A X(\omega)dP(\omega) + \beta \int_A Y(\omega)dP(\omega),
$$

$$
\int_A Z_1(\omega)dP(\omega) = \int_A X(\omega)dP(\omega),
$$

and

$$
\int_A Z_2(\omega)dP(\omega) = \int_A Y(\omega)dP(\omega);
$$

hence,

$$
\int_A (Z_0(\omega) - \alpha Z_1(\omega) - \beta Z_2(\omega))dP(\omega) = 0. \tag{3.14}
$$

If we take $A = \{\omega \in \Omega : Z_0(\omega) - \alpha Z_1(\omega) - \beta Z_2(\omega) > 0\}$ it follows from (3.14) and Lemma 3.1 that $P(A) = 0$, if we take $A = \{\omega \in \Omega : Z_0(\omega) - \alpha Z_1(\omega) - \beta Z_2(\omega) < 0\}$ it follows similarly that $P(A) = 0$; hence, $P(\{\omega \in \Omega : Z_0(\omega) - \alpha Z_1(\omega) - \beta Z_2(\omega) \neq 0\}) = 0$. Q.E.D.

If we condition a random variable Y on itself, then intuitively we may expect that $E(Y|Y) = Y$ because then Y acts as a constant. More formally, this result can be stated as

Theorem 3.4: *Let $E[|Y|] < \infty$. If Y is measurable $\mathscr{F}$, then $P(E(Y|\mathscr{F}) = Y) = 1$.*

Proof: Let $Z = E(Y|\mathscr{F})$. For every $A \in \mathscr{F}$ we have

$$
\int_A (Y(\omega) - Z(\omega))dP(\omega) = 0. \tag{3.15}
$$

Take $A = \{\omega \in \Omega : Y(\omega) - Z(\omega) > 0\}$. Then $A \in \mathscr{F}$; hence, it follows from (3.15) and Lemma 3.1 that $P(A) = 0$. Similarly, if one takes $A = \{\omega \in \Omega : Y(\omega) - Z(\omega) < 0\}$, it follows that $P(A) = 0$. Thus, $P(\{\omega \in \Omega : Y(\omega) - Z(\omega) \neq 0\}) = 0$. Q.E.D.

In Theorem 3.4 I have conditioned Y on the largest sub-σ-algebra of $\mathscr{F}$ – namely $\mathscr{F}$ itself. The smallest sub-σ-algebra of $\mathscr{F}$ is $\mathcal{T} = \{\Omega, \emptyset\}$, which is called the *trivial* σ-algebra.

Theorem 3.5: *Let $E[|Y|] < \infty$. Then $P[E(Y|\mathcal{T}) = E(Y)] = 1$.*

Proof: Exercise, along the same lines as the proofs of Theorems 3.2 and 3.4.

The following theorem, which plays a key role in regression analysis, follows from combining the results of Theorems 3.3 and 3.4:

Theorem 3.6: *Let $E[|Y|] < \infty$ and $U = Y - E[Y|\mathcal{F}_0]$. Then $P[E(U|\mathcal{F}_0) = 0] = 1$.*

Proof: Exercise.

Next, let (Y, X, Z) be jointly continuously distributed with joint density function $f(y, x, z)$ and marginal densities $f_{y,x}(y, x)$, $f_{x,z}(x, z)$ and $f_x(x)$. Then the conditional expectation of Y given $X = x$ and $Z = z$ is $E[Y|X, Z] = \int_{-\infty}^{\infty} yf(y|X, Z)dy = g_{x,z}(X, Z)$, for instance, where $f(y|x, z) = f(y, x, z)/f_{x,z}(x, z)$ is the conditional density of Y given $X = x$ and $Z = z$. The conditional expectation of Y given $X = x$ alone is $E[Y|X] = \int_{-\infty}^{\infty} yf(y|X)dy = g_x(X)$, for instance, where $f(y|x) = f_{y,x}(y, x)/f_x(x)$ is the conditional density of Y given $X = x$ alone. If we denote the conditional density of Z given $X = x$ by $f_z(z|x) = f_{z,x}(z, x)/f_x(x)$, it follows now that

$$E\left(E[Y|X, Z]|X\right) = \int_{-\infty}^{\infty} \left(\int_{-\infty}^{\infty} yf(y|X, z)dy \right) f_z(z|X)dz$$

$$= \int_{-\infty}^{\infty} \left(\int_{-\infty}^{\infty} y\frac{f(y, X, z)}{f_{x,z}(X, z)}dy \right) \frac{f_{x,z}(X, z)}{f_x(X)}dz$$

$$= \int_{-\infty}^{\infty} y \left(\int_{-\infty}^{\infty} f(y, X, z)dzdy \right) \frac{1}{f_x(X)}$$

$$= \int_{-\infty}^{\infty} y\frac{f_{y,x}(y, X)}{f_x(X)}dy$$

$$= \int_{-\infty}^{\infty} yf(y|X)dy = E[Y|X].$$

This is one of the versions of the law of iterated expectations. Denoting by $\mathscr{F}_{X,Z}$ the σ-algebra generated by (X, Z) and by $\mathscr{F}_X$ the σ-algebra generated by X, we find this result can be translated as

$$E(E[Y|\mathscr{F}_{X,Z}]|\mathscr{F}_X) = E[Y|\mathscr{F}_X].$$

Note that $\mathscr{F}_X \subset \mathscr{F}_{X,Z}$ because

$$\begin{aligned}
\mathscr{F}_X &= \{\{\omega \in \Omega : X(\omega) \in B_1\}, B_1 \in \mathscr{B}\} \\
&= \{\{\omega \in \Omega : X(\omega) \in B_1, Z(\omega) \in \mathbb{R}\}, B_1 \in \mathscr{B}\} \\
&\subset \{\{\omega \in \Omega : X(\omega) \in B_1, Z(\omega) \in B_2\}, B_1, B_2 \in \mathscr{B}\} = \mathscr{F}_{X,Z}.
\end{aligned}$$

Therefore, the law of iterated expectations can be stated more generally as

Theorem 3.7: *Let $E[|Y|] < \infty$, and let $\mathscr{F}_0 \subset \mathscr{F}_1$ be sub-σ-algebras of $\mathscr{F}$. Then*

$$P[E(E[Y|\mathscr{F}_1]|\mathscr{F}_0) = E(Y|\mathscr{F}_0)] = 1.$$

Proof: Let $Z_0 = E[Y|\mathscr{F}_0]$, $Z_1 = E[Y|\mathscr{F}_1]$ and $Z_2 = E[Z_1|\mathscr{F}_0]$. It has to be shown that $P(Z_0 = Z_2) = 1$. Let $A \in \mathscr{F}_0$. Then also $A \in \mathscr{F}_1$. It follows from Definition 3.1 that $Z_0 = E[Y|\mathscr{F}_0]$ implies $\int_A Y(\omega)dP(\omega) = \int_A Z_0(\omega)dP(\omega)$, $Z_1 = E[Y|\mathscr{F}_1]$ implies $\int_A Y(\omega)dP(\omega) = \int_A Z_1(\omega)dP(\omega)$, and $Z_2 = E[Z_1|\mathscr{F}_0]$ implies $\int_A Z_2(\omega)dP(\omega) = \int_A Z_1(\omega)dP(\omega)$. If we combine these equalities, it follows that for all $A \in \mathscr{F}_0$,

$$\int_A (Z_0(\omega) - Z_2(\omega))\, dP(\omega) = 0. \tag{3.16}$$

Now choose $A = \{\omega \in \Omega : Z_0(\omega) - Z_2(\omega) > 0\}$. Note that $A \in \mathscr{F}_0$. Then it follows from (3.16) and Lemma 3.1 that $P(A) = 0$. Similarly, if we choose $A = \{\omega \in \Omega : Z_0(\omega) - Z_2(\omega) < 0\}$, then, again, $P(A) = 0$. Therefore, $P(Z_0 = Z_2) = 1$. Q.E.D.

The following monotone convergence theorem for conditional expectations plays a key role in the proofs of Theorems 3.9 and 3.10 below.

Theorem 3.8: *(Monotone convergence). Let X_n be a sequence of non-negative random variables defined on a common probability space $\{\Omega, \mathscr{F}, P\}$ such that $P(X_n \leq X_{n+1}) = 1$ and $E[sup_{n \geq 1} X_n] < \infty$. Then $P(lim_{n \to \infty} E[X_n|\mathscr{F}_0] = E[lim_{n \to \infty} X_n|\mathscr{F}_0]) = 1$.*

Proof: Let $Z_n = E[X_n|\mathscr{F}_0]$ and $X = lim_{n \to \infty} X_n$. It follows from Theorem 3.2 that Z_n is monotonic nondecreasing; hence, $Z = lim_{n \to \infty} Z_n$ exists. Let $A \in \mathscr{F}_0$ be arbitrary and $Y_n(\omega) = Z_n(\omega) \cdot I(\omega \in A)$, $Y(\omega) = Z(\omega) \cdot I(\omega \in$

A) for $\omega \in \Omega$. Then also Y_n is nonnegative and monotonic nondecreasing and $Y = \lim_{n \to \infty} Y_n$; hence, it follows from the monotone convergence theorem that $\lim_{n \to \infty} \int Y_n(\omega)dP(\omega) = \int Y(\omega)dP(\omega)$, which is equivalent to

$$\lim_{n \to \infty} \int_A Z_n(\omega)dP(\omega) = \int_A Z(\omega)dP(\omega). \tag{3.17}$$

Similarly, if we let $U_n(\omega) = X_n(\omega) \cdot I(\omega \in A)$, $U(\omega) = X(\omega) \cdot I(\omega \in A)$, it follows from the monotone convergence theorem that $\lim_{n \to \infty} \int U_n(\omega)dP(\omega) = \int U(\omega)dP(\omega)$, which is equivalent to

$$\lim_{n \to \infty} \int_A X_n(\omega)dP(\omega) = \int_A X(\omega)dP(\omega). \tag{3.18}$$

Moreover, it follows from the definition of $Z_n = E[X_n|\mathscr{F}_0]$ that

$$\int_A Z_n(\omega)dP(\omega) = \int_A X_n(\omega)dP(\omega). \tag{3.19}$$

It follows now from (3.17)–(3.19) that

$$\int_A Z(\omega)dP(\omega) = \int_A X(\omega)dP(\omega). \tag{3.20}$$

Theorem 3.8 easily follows from (3.20).   Q.E.D.

The following theorem extends the result of Theorem 3.4:

Theorem 3.9: *Let X be measurable $\mathscr{F}_0$, and let both $E(|Y|)$ and $E(|XY|)$ be finite. Then $P[E(XY|\mathscr{F}_0) = X \cdot E(Y|\mathscr{F}_0)] = 1$.*

Proof: I will prove the theorem involved only for the case in which both X and Y are nonnegative with probability 1, leaving the general case as an easy exercise.

Let $Z = E(XY|\mathscr{F}_0)$, $Z_0 = E(Y|\mathscr{F}_0)$. If

$$\forall A \in \mathscr{F}_0: \int_A Z(\omega)dP(\omega) = \int_A X(\omega)Z_0(\omega)dP(\omega), \tag{3.21}$$

then the theorem under review holds.

(a) First, consider the case in which X is discrete: $X(\omega) = \sum_{j=1}^{n} \beta_j I(\omega \in A_j)$, for instance, where the A_j's are disjoint sets in $\mathscr{F}_0$ and the β_j's are nonnegative numbers. Let $A \in \mathscr{F}_0$ be arbitrary, and observe that $A \cap A_j \in \mathscr{F}_0$ for $j = 1, \ldots, n$. Then by Definition 3.1,

$$\int_A X(\omega)Z_0(\omega)dP(\omega) = \int_A \sum_{j=1}^{n} \beta_j \, I(\omega \in A_j)Z_0(\omega)dP(\omega)$$

$$= \sum_{j=1}^{n} \beta_j \int_{A \cap A_j} Z_0(\omega)dP(\omega)$$

$$= \sum_{j=1}^{n} \beta_j \int_{A \cap A_j} Y(\omega)dP(\omega)$$

$$= \sum_{j=1}^{n} \beta_j \int_A I(\omega \in A_j)Y(\omega)dP(\omega)$$

$$= \int_A \sum_{j=1}^{n} \beta_j I(\omega \in A_j)Y(\omega)dP(\omega)$$

$$= \int_A X(\omega)Y(\omega)dP(\omega) = \int_A Z(\omega)dP(\omega),$$

which proves the theorem for the case in which X is discrete.

(b) If X is not discrete, then there exists a sequence of discrete random variables X_n such that for each $\omega \in \Omega$ we have $0 \le X_n(\omega) \le X(\omega)$ and $X_n(\omega) \uparrow X(\omega)$ monotonic; hence, $X_n(\omega)Y(\omega) \uparrow X(\omega)Y(\omega)$ monotonic. Therefore, it follows from Theorem 3.8 and part (a) that $E[XY|\mathscr{F}_0] = \lim_{n \to \infty} E[X_n Y|\mathscr{F}_0] = \lim_{n \to \infty} X_n E[Y|\mathscr{F}_0] = XE[Y|\mathscr{F}_0]$ with probability 1. Thus, the theorem under review holds for the case that both X and Y are nonnegative with probability 1.

(c) The rest of the proof is left as an exercise.   Q.E.D.

We have seen for the case in which Y and X are jointly, absolutely continuously distributed that the conditional expectation $E[Y|X]$ is a function of X. This holds also more generally:

Theorem 3.10: *Let Y and X be random variables defined on the probability space $\{\Omega, \mathscr{F}, P\}$, and assume that $E(|Y|) < \infty$. Then there exists a Borel-measurable function g such that $P[E(Y|X) = g(X)] = 1$. This result carries over to the case in which X is a finite-dimensional random vector.*

Proof: The proof involves the following steps:

(a) Suppose that Y is nonnegative and bounded: $\exists K < \infty : P(\{\omega \in \Omega : 0 \le Y(\omega) \le K\}) = 1$, and let $Z = E(Y|\mathscr{F}_X)$, where $\mathscr{F}_X$ is the σ-algebra generated by X. Then

$$P(\{\omega \in \Omega : 0 \le Z(\omega) \le K\}) = 1. \tag{3.22}$$

(b) Under the conditions of part (a) there exists a sequence of discrete random variables Z_m, $Z_m(\omega) = \sum_{i=1}^{m} \alpha_{i,m} I(\omega \in A_{i,m})$, where $A_{i,m} \in \mathscr{F}_X$, $A_{i,m} \cap A_{j,m} = \emptyset$ if $i \neq j$, $\cup_{i=1}^{m} A_{i,m} = \Omega$, $0 \leq \alpha_{i,m} < \infty$ for $i = 1, \ldots, m$ such that $Z_m(\omega) \uparrow Z(\omega)$ monotonic. For each $A_{i,m}$ we can find a Borel set $B_{i,m}$ such that $A_{i,m} = X^{-1}(B_{i,m})$. Thus, if we take $g_m(x) = \sum_{i=1}^{m} \alpha_{i,m} I(x \in B_{i,m})$, then $Z_m = g_m(X)$ with probability 1.

Next, let $g(x) = \limsup_{m \to \infty} g_m(x)$. This function is Borel measurable, and $Z = \limsup_{m \to \infty} Z_m = \limsup_{m \to \infty} g_m(X) = g(X)$ with probability 1.

(c) Let $Y_n = Y \cdot I(Y < n)$. Then $Y_n(\omega) \uparrow Y(\omega)$ monotonic. By part (b) it follows that there exists a Borel-measurable function $g_n(x)$ such that $E(Y_n | \mathscr{F}_X) = g_n(X)$. Let $g(x) = \limsup_{n \to \infty} g_n(x)$, which is Borel measurable. It follows now from Theorem 3.8 that

$$E(Y|\mathscr{F}_X) = \lim_{n \to \infty} E(Y_n|\mathscr{F}_X) = \limsup_{n \to \infty} E(Y_n|\mathscr{F}_X)$$
$$= \limsup_{n \to \infty} g_n(X) = g(X).$$

(d) Let $Y^+ = \max(Y, 0)$, $Y^- = \max(-Y, 0)$. Then $Y = Y^+ - Y^-$, and therefore by part (c), $E(Y^+|\mathscr{F}_X) = g^+(X)$, for instance, and $E(Y^-|\mathscr{F}_X) = g^-(X)$. Then $E(Y|\mathscr{F}_X) = g^+(X) - g^-(X) = g(X)$. Q.E.D.

If random variables X and Y are independent, then knowing the realization of X will not reveal anything about Y, and vice versa. The following theorem formalizes this fact.

Theorem 3.11: *Let X and Y be independent random variables. If $E[|Y|] < \infty$, then $P(E[Y|X] = E[Y]) = 1$. More generally, let Y be defined on the probability space $\{\Omega, \mathscr{F}, P\}$, let $\mathscr{F}_Y$ be the σ-algebra generated by Y, and let $\mathscr{F}_0$ be a sub-σ-algebra of $\mathscr{F}$ such that $\mathscr{F}_Y$ and $\mathscr{F}_0$ are independent, that is, for all $A \in \mathscr{F}_Y$ and $B \in \mathscr{F}_0$, $P(A \cap B) = P(A)P(B)$. If $E[|Y|] < \infty$, then $P(E[Y|\mathscr{F}_0] = E[Y]) = 1$.*

Proof: Let $\mathscr{F}_X$ be the σ-algebra generated by X, and let $A \in \mathscr{F}_X$ be arbitrary. There exists a Borel set B such that $A = \{\omega \in \Omega : X(\omega) \in B\}$. Then

$$\int_A Y(\omega)dP(\omega) = \int_\Omega Y(\omega)I(\omega \in A)dP(\omega)$$
$$= \int_\Omega Y(\omega)I(X(\omega) \in B)dP(\omega)$$
$$= E[YI(X \in B)] = E[Y]E[I(X \in B)],$$

where the last equality follows from the independence of Y and X. Moreover,

$$E[Y]E[I(X \in B)] = E[Y] \int_\Omega I(X(\omega) \in B)dP(\omega)$$

$$= E[Y] \int_\Omega I(\omega \in A)dP(\omega) = \int_A E[Y]dP(\omega).$$

Thus,

$$\int_A Y(\omega)dP(\omega) = \int_A E[Y]dP(\omega).$$

By the definition of conditional expectation, this implies that $E[Y|X] = E[Y]$ with probability 1.   Q.E.D.

3.3. Conditional Probability Measures and Conditional Independence

The notion of a probability measure relative to a sub-σ-algebra can be defined as in Definition 3.1 using the conditional expectation of an indicator function:

Definition 3.2: *Let $\{\Omega, \mathscr{F}, P\}$ be a probability space, and let $\mathscr{F}_0 \subset \mathscr{F}$ be a σ-algebra. Then for any set A in $\mathscr{F}$, $P(A|\mathscr{F}_0) = E[I_A|\mathscr{F}_0]$, where $I_A(\omega) = I(\omega \in A)$.*

In the sequel I will use the shorthand notation $P(Y \in B|X)$ to indicate the conditional probability $P(\{\omega \in \Omega : Y(\omega) \in B\}|\mathscr{F}_X)$, where B is a Borel set and $\mathscr{F}_X$ is the σ-algebra generated by X, and $P(Y \in B|\mathscr{F}_0)$ to indicate $P(\{\omega \in \Omega : Y(\omega) \in B\}|\mathscr{F}_0)$ for any sub-σ-algebra $\mathscr{F}_0$ of $\mathscr{F}$. The event $Y \in B$ involved may be replaced by any equivalent expression.

Recalling the notion of independence of sets and random variables, vectors, or both (see Chapter 1), we can now define conditional independence:

Definition 3.3: *A sequence of sets $A_j \in \mathscr{F}$ is conditional independent relative to a sub-σ-algebra $\mathscr{F}_0$ of $\mathscr{F}$ if for any subsequence j_n, $P(\cap_n A_{j_n}|\mathscr{F}_0) = \prod_n P(A_{j_n}|\mathscr{F}_0)$. Moreover, a sequence Y_j of random variables or vectors defined on a common probability space $\{\Omega, \mathscr{F}, P\}$ is conditional independent relative to a sub-σ-algebra $\mathscr{F}_0$ of $\mathscr{F}$ if for any sequence B_j of conformable Borel sets the sets $A_j = \{\omega \in \Omega : Y_j(\omega) \in B_j\}$ are conditional independent relative to $\mathscr{F}_0$.*

3.4. Conditioning on Increasing Sigma-Algebras

Consider a random variable Y defined on the probability space $\{\Omega, \mathscr{F}, P\}$ satisfying $E[|Y|] < \infty$, and let $\mathscr{F}_n$ be a nondecreasing sequence of sub-σ-algebras of $\mathscr{F} : \mathscr{F}_n \subset \mathscr{F}_{n+1} \subset \mathscr{F}$. The question I will address is, What is the limit of $E[Y|\mathscr{F}_n]$ for $n \to \infty$? As will be shown in the next section, the answer to this question is fundamental for time series econometrics.

We have seen in Chapter 1 that the union of σ-algebras is not necessarily a σ-algebra itself. Thus, $\cup_{n=1}^{\infty} \mathscr{F}_n$ may not be a σ-algebra. Therefore, let

$$\mathscr{F}_{\infty} = \bigvee_{n=1}^{\infty} \mathscr{F}_n \overset{\text{def.}}{=} \sigma \left(\overset{\infty}{\underset{n=1}{\cup}} \mathscr{F}_n \right), \tag{3.23}$$

that is, $\mathscr{F}_{\infty}$ is the smallest σ-algebra containing $\cup_{n=1}^{\infty} \mathscr{F}_n$. Clearly, $\mathscr{F}_{\infty} \subset \mathscr{F}$ because the latter also contains $\cup_{n=1}^{\infty} \mathscr{F}_n$.

The answer to our question is now as follows:

Theorem 3.12: *If Y is measurable $\mathscr{F}$, $E[|Y|] < \infty$, and $\{\mathscr{F}_n\}$ is a nondecreasing sequence of sub-σ-algebras of $\mathscr{F}$, then $\lim_{n\to\infty} E[Y|\mathscr{F}_n] = E[Y|\mathscr{F}_{\infty}]$ with probability 1, where $\mathscr{F}_{\infty}$ is defined by (3.23).*

This result is usually proved by using martingale theory. See Billingsley (1986), Chung (1974), and Chapter 7 in this volume. However, in Appendix 3.A I will provide an alternative proof of Theorem 3.12 that does not require martingale theory.

3.5. Conditional Expectations as the Best Forecast Schemes

I will now show that the conditional expectation of a random variable Y given a random variable or vector X is the best forecasting scheme for Y in the sense that the mean-square forecast error is minimal. Let $\psi(X)$ be a forecast of Y, where ψ is a Borel-measurable function. The mean-square forecast error (MSFE) is defined by $MSFE = E[(Y - \psi(X))^2]$. The question is, For which function ψ is the MSFE minimal? The answer is

Theorem 3.13: *If $E[Y^2] < \infty$, then $E[(Y - \psi(X))^2]$ is minimal for $\psi(X) = E[Y|X]$.*

Proof: According to Theorem 3.10 there exists a Borel-measurable function g such that $E[Y|X] = g(X)$ with probability 1. Let $U = Y - E[Y|X] = Y - g(X)$. It follows from Theorems 3.3, 3.4, and 3.9 that

$$E[(Y - \psi(X))^2 | X] = E[(U + g(X) - \psi(X))^2 | X]$$
$$= E[U^2 | X] + 2E[(g(X) - \psi(X))U | X]$$
$$+ E[(g(X) - \psi(X))^2 | X]$$
$$= E[U^2 | X] + 2(g(X) - \psi(X))E[U | X]$$
$$+ (g(X) - \psi(X))^2, \tag{3.24}$$

where the last equality follows from Theorems 3.4 and 3.9. Because, by Theorem 3.6, $E(U|X) = 0$ with probability 1, equation (3.24) becomes

$$E[(Y - \psi(X))^2 | X] = E[U^2 | X] + (g(X) - \psi(X))^2. \tag{3.25}$$

Applying Theorem 3.1 to (3.25), it follows now that

$$E[(Y - \psi(X))^2] = E[U^2] + E[(g(X) - \psi(X))^2],$$

which is minimal if $E[(g(X) - \psi(X))^2] = 0$. According to Lemma 3.1 this condition is equivalent to the condition that $P[g(X) = \psi(X)] = 1$. Q.E.D.

Theorem 3.13 is the basis for regression analysis. In parametric regression analysis, a dependent variable Y is "explained" by a vector X of explanatory (also called "independent") variables according to a regression model of the type $Y = g(X, \theta_0) + U$, where $g(x, \theta)$ is a known function of x and a vector θ of parameters, and U is the error term assumed to satisfy the condition $E[U|X] = 0$ (with probability 1). The problem is then to estimate the unknown parameter vector θ_0. For example, a Mincer-type wage equation explains the log of the wage, Y, of a worker from the years of education, X_1, and the years of experience on the job, X_2, by a regression model of the type $Y = \alpha + \beta X_1 + \gamma X_2 - \delta X_2^2 + U$, and thus in this case $\theta = (\alpha, \beta, \gamma, \delta)^T$, $X = (X_1, X_2)^T$, and $g(X, \theta) = \alpha + \beta X_1 + \gamma X_2 - \delta X_2^2$. The condition that $E[U|X] = 0$ with probability 1 now implies that $E[Y|X] = g(X, \theta_0)$ with probability 1 for some parameter vector θ_0. It follows therefore from Theorem 3.12 that θ_0 minimizes the mean-square error function $E[(Y - g(X, \theta))^2]$:

$$\theta_0 = \text{argmin}_\theta E[(Y - g(X, \theta))^2], \tag{3.26}$$

where "argmin" stands for the argument for which the function involved is minimal.

Next, consider a strictly stationary time series process Y_t.

Definition 3.4: *A time series process Y_t is said to be strictly station-ary if, for arbitrary integers $m_1 < m_2 < \cdots < m_k$, the joint distribution of $Y_{t-m_1}, \ldots, Y_{t-m_k}$ does not depend on the time index t.*

Consider the problem of forecasting Y_t of the basis of the past Y_{t-j}, $j \geq 1$, of Y_t. Usually we do not observe the whole past of Y_t but only Y_{t-j} for $j = 1, \ldots, t - 1$, for instance. It follows from Theorem 3.13 that the optimal MSFE forecast of Y_t given the information on Y_{t-j} for $j = 1, \ldots, m$ is the conditional expectation of Y_t given Y_{t-j} for $j = 1, \ldots, m$. Thus, if $E[Y_t^2] < \infty$, then

$$E[Y_t|Y_{t-1}, \ldots, Y_{t-m}] = \mathrm{argmin}_\psi E[(Y_t - \psi(Y_{t-1}, \ldots, Y_{t-m}))^2].$$

Similarly, as before, the minimum is taken over all Borel-measurable functions ψ on $\mathbb{R}^m$. Moreover, because of the strict stationarity assumption, there exists a Borel-measurable function g_m on $\mathbb{R}^m$ that does not depend on the time index t such that with probability 1,

$$E[Y_t|Y_{t-1}, \ldots, Y_{t-m}] = g_m(Y_{t-1}, \ldots, Y_{t-m})$$

for all t. Theorem 3.12 now tells us that

$$\lim_{m \to \infty} E[Y_t|Y_{t-1}, \ldots, Y_{t-m}] = \lim_{m \to \infty} g_m(Y_{t-1}, \ldots, Y_{t-m})$$
$$= E[Y_t|Y_{t-1}, Y_{t-2}, Y_{t-3}, \ldots], \qquad (3.27)$$

where the latter is the conditional expectation of Y_t given its whole past $Y_{t-j}, j \geq 1$. More formally, let $\mathscr{F}_{t-m}^{t-1} = \sigma(Y_{t-1}, \ldots, Y_{t-m})$ and $\mathscr{F}_{-\infty}^{t-1} = \bigvee_{m=1}^{\infty} \mathscr{F}_{t-m}^{t-1}$. Then (3.27) reads

$$\lim_{m \to \infty} E[Y_t|\mathscr{F}_{t-m}^{t-1}] = E[Y_t|\mathscr{F}_{-\infty}^{t-1}].$$

The latter conditional expectation is also denoted by $E_{t-1}[Y_t]$:

$$E_{t-1}[Y_t] \overset{\text{def.}}{=} E[Y_t|Y_{t-1}, Y_{t-2}, Y_{t-3}, \ldots] \overset{\text{def.}}{=} E[Y_t|\mathscr{F}_{-\infty}^{t-1}]. \qquad (3.28)$$

In practice we do not observe the whole past of time series processes. However, it follows from Theorem 3.12 that if t is large, then approximately, $E[Y_t|Y_{t-1}, \ldots, Y_1] \approx E_{t-1}[Y_t]$.

In time series econometrics the focus is often on modeling (3.28) as a function of past values of Y_t and an unknown parameter vector θ, for instance. For example, an autoregressive model of order 1, denoted by AR(1), takes the form $E_{t-1}[Y_t] = \alpha + \beta Y_{t-1}, \theta = (\alpha, \beta)^{\mathrm{T}}$, where $|\beta| < 1$. Then $Y_t = \alpha + \beta Y_{t-1} + U_t$, where U_t is called the error term. If this model is true, then $U_t = Y_t - E_{t-1}[Y_t]$, which by Theorem 3.6 satisfies $P(E_{t-1}[U_t] = 0) = 1$.

The condition $|\beta| < 1$ is one of the two necessary conditions for strict stationarity of Y_t, the other one being that U_t be strictly stationary. To see this, observe that by backwards substitution we can write $Y_t = \alpha/(1 - \beta) + \sum_{j=0}^{\infty} \beta^j U_{t-j}$, provided that $|\beta| < 1$. The strict stationarity of Y_t follows now from the strict stationarity of U_t.

3.6. Exercises

1. Why is property (3.6) equivalent to (3.8)?

2. Why is the set A defined by (3.11) contained in $\mathscr{F}_x$?

3. Why does (3.12) hold?

4. Prove Theorem 3.5.

5. Prove Theorem 3.6.

6. Verify (3.20). Why does Theorem 3.8 follow from (3.20)?

7. Why does (3.21) imply that Theorem 3.9 holds ?

8. Complete the proof of Theorem 3.9 for the general case by writing, for instance,

$$X = \max(0, X) - \max(0, -X) = X_1 - X_2, \text{ and}$$
$$Y = \max(0, Y) - \max(0, -Y) = Y_1 - Y_2$$

and applying the result of part (b) of the proof to each pair X_i, Y_j.

9. Prove (3.22).

10. Let Y and X be random variables with $E[|Y|] < \infty$ and Φ be a Borel-measurable one-to-one mapping from $\mathbb{R}$ into $\mathbb{R}$. Prove that $E[Y|X] = E[Y|\Phi(X)]$ with probability 1.

11. Let Y and X be random variables with $E[Y^2] < \infty$, $P(X = 1) = P(X = 0) = 0.5$, $E[Y] = 0$, and $E[X \cdot Y] = 1$. Derive $E[Y|X]$. *Hint:* Use Theorems 3.10 and 3.13.

APPENDIX

3.A. Proof of Theorem 3.12

Let $Z_n = E[Y|\mathscr{F}_n]$ and $Z = E[Y|\mathscr{F}_\infty]$, and let $A \in \cup_{n=1}^\infty \mathscr{F}_n$ be arbitrary. Note that the latter implies $A \in \mathscr{F}_\infty$. Because of the monotonicity of $\{\mathscr{F}_n\}$ there exists an index k_A (depending on A) such that for all $n \geq k_A$,

$$\int_A Z_n(\omega)dP(\omega) = \int_A Y(\omega)dP(\omega). \qquad (3.29)$$

If Y is bounded: $P[|Y| < M] = 1$ for some positive real number M, then Z_n is uniformly bounded: $|Z_n| = |E[Y|\mathscr{F}_n]| \leq E[|Y||\mathscr{F}_n] \leq M$; hence, it follows from (3.29), the dominated convergence theorem, and the definition of Z that

$$\int_A \lim_{n \to \infty} Z_n(\omega)dP(\omega) = \int_A Z(\omega)dP(\omega) \qquad (3.30)$$

for all sets $A \in \cup_{n=1}^\infty \mathscr{F}_n$. Although $\cup_{n=1}^\infty \mathscr{F}_n$ is not necessarily a σ-algebra, it is easy to verify from the monotonicity of $\{\mathscr{F}_n\}$ that $\cup_{n=1}^\infty \mathscr{F}_n$ is an algebra. Now let $\mathscr{F}_*$ be the collection of all subsets of $\mathscr{F}_\infty$ satisfying the following two conditions:

(a) For each set $B \in \mathscr{F}_*$ equality (3.30) holds with $A = B$.
(b) For each pair of sets $B_1 \in \mathscr{F}_*$ and $B_2 \in \mathscr{F}_*$, equality (3.30) holds with $A = B_1 \cup B_2$.

Given that (3.30) holds for $A = \Omega$ because $\Omega \in \cup_{n=1}^{\infty} \mathscr{F}_n$, it is trivial that (3.30) also holds for the complement $\tilde{A}$ of A:

$$\int_{\tilde{A}} \lim_{n\to\infty} Z_n(\omega) dP(\omega) = \int_{\tilde{A}} Z(\omega) dP(\omega);$$

hence, if $B \in \mathscr{F}_*$, then $\tilde{B} \in \mathscr{F}_*$. Thus, $\mathscr{F}_*$ is an algebra. Note that this algebra exists because $\cup_{n=1}^{\infty} \mathscr{F}_n$ is an algebra satisfying the conditions (a) and (b). Thus, $\cup_{n=1}^{\infty} \mathscr{F}_n \subset \mathscr{F}_* \subset \mathscr{F}_{\infty}$.

I will show now that $\mathscr{F}_*$ is a σ-algebra, and thus that $\mathscr{F}_{\infty} = \mathscr{F}_*$ because the former is the smallest σ-algebra containing $\cup_{n=1}^{\infty} \mathscr{F}_n$. For any sequence of **disjoint** sets $A_j \in \mathscr{F}_*$, it follows from (3.30) that

$$\int_{\cup_{j=1}^{\infty} A_j} \lim_{n\to\infty} Z_n(\omega) dP(\omega) = \sum_{j=1}^{\infty} \int_{A_j} \lim_{n\to\infty} Z_n(\omega) dP(\omega)$$

$$= \sum_{j=1}^{\infty} \int_{A_j} Z(\omega) dP(\omega) = \int_{\cup_{j=1}^{\infty} A_j} Z(\omega) dP(\omega);$$

hence, $\cup_{j=1}^{\infty} A_j \in \mathscr{F}_*$. This implies that $\mathscr{F}_*$ is a σ-algebra containing $\cup_{n=1}^{\infty} \mathscr{F}_n$ because we have seen in Chapter 1 that an algebra closed under countable unions of disjoint sets is a σ-algebra. Hence, $\mathscr{F}_{\infty} = \mathscr{F}_*$, and consequently (3.30), hold for all sets $A \in \mathscr{F}_{\infty}$. This implies that $P[Z = \lim_{n\to\infty} Z_n] = 1$ if Y is bounded.

Next, let Y be nonnegative: $P[|Y \geq 0] = 1$ and denote for natural numbers $m \geq 1$, $B_m = \{\omega \in \Omega : m - 1 \leq Y(\omega) < m\}$, $Y_m = Y \cdot I(m - 1 \leq Y < m)$, $Z_n^{(m)} = E[Y_m|\mathscr{F}_n]$ and $Z^{(m)} = E[Y_m|\mathscr{F}_{\infty}]$. I have just shown that for fixed $m \geq 1$ and arbitrary $A \in \mathscr{F}_{\infty}$,

$$\int_A \lim_{n\to\infty} Z_n^{(m)}(\omega) dP(\omega) = \int_A Z^{(m)}(\omega) dP(\omega) = \int_A Y_m(\omega) dP(\omega)$$

$$= \int_{A \cap B_m} Y(\omega) dP(\omega), \tag{3.31}$$

where the last two equalities follow from the definitions of $Z^{(m)}$ and Z_m. Because $Y_m(\omega) I(\omega \in \tilde{B}_m) = 0$, it follows that $Z_n^{(m)}(\omega) I(\omega \in \tilde{B}_m) = 0$; hence,

$$\int_A \lim_{n\to\infty} Z_n^m(\omega) dP\omega = \int_{A \cup B_m} \lim_{n\to\infty} Z_n^{(m)}(\omega) dP\omega$$

$$+ \int_{A \cap \tilde{B}_m} \lim_{n\to\infty} Z_n^{(m)}(\omega) dP(\omega)$$

$$= \int_{A \cap B_m} \lim_{n\to\infty} Z_n^{(m)}(\omega) dP\omega,$$

and thus by (3.31),

$$\int\limits_{A\cap B_m} \lim_{n\to\infty} Z_n^{(m)}(\omega)dP(\omega) = \int\limits_{A\cap B_m} Y(\omega)dP(\omega).$$

Moreover, it follows from the definition of conditional expectations and Theorem 3.7 that

$$Z_n^{(m)} = E[Y \cdot I(m-1 \le Y < m)|\mathscr{F}_n] = E[Y|B_m \cap \mathscr{F}_n]$$
$$= E[E(Y|\mathscr{F}_n)|B_m \cap \mathscr{F}_n] = E[Z_n|B_m \cap \mathscr{F}_n];$$

hence, for every set $A \in \cup_{n=1}^\infty \mathscr{F}_n$,

$$\lim_{n\to\infty} \int\limits_{A\cap B_m} Z_n^{(m)}(\omega)dP(\omega) = \lim_{n\to\infty} \int\limits_{A\cap B_m} Z_n(\omega)dP(\omega)$$
$$= \int\limits_{A\cap B_m} \lim_{n\to\infty} Z_n(\omega)dP(\omega)$$
$$= \int\limits_{A\cap B_m} Y(\omega)dP(\omega), \tag{3.32}$$

which by the same argument as in the bounded case carries over to the sets $A \in \mathscr{F}_\infty$. It follows now from (3.31) and (3.32) that

$$\int\limits_{A\cap B_m} \lim_{n\to\infty} Z_n(\omega)dP(\omega) = \int\limits_{A\cap B_m} Y(\omega)dP(\omega)$$

for all sets $A \in \mathscr{F}_\infty$. Consequently,

$$\int\limits_{A} \lim_{n\to\infty} Z_n(\omega)dP(\omega) = \sum_{m=1}^\infty \int\limits_{A\cap B_m} \lim_{n\to\infty} Z_n(\omega)dP(\omega)$$
$$= \sum_{m=1}^\infty \int\limits_{A\cap B_m} Y(\omega)dP(\omega) = \int\limits_{A} Y(\omega)dP(\omega)$$

for all sets $A \in \mathscr{F}_\infty$. This proves the theorem for the case $P[|Y \ge 0] = 1$. The general case is now easy using the decomposition $Y = \max(0, Y) - \max(0, -Y)$.

4   Distributions and Transformations

This chapter reviews the most important univariate distributions and shows how to derive their expectations, variances, moment-generating functions (if they exist), and characteristic functions. Many distributions arise as transformations of random variables or vectors. Therefore, the problem of how the distribution of $Y = g(X)$ is related to the distribution of X for a Borel-measure function or mapping $g(x)$ is also addressed.

4.1. Discrete Distributions

In Chapter 1 I introduced three "natural" discrete distributions, namely, the hypergeometric, binomial, and Poisson distributions. The first two are natural in the sense that they arise from the way the random sample involved is drawn, and the last is natural because it is a limit of the binomial distribution. A fourth "natural" discrete distribution I will discuss is the negative binomial distribution.

4.1.1. The Hypergeometric Distribution

Recall that a random variable X has a hypergeometric distribution if

$$P(X = k) = \frac{\binom{K}{k}\binom{N-K}{n-k}}{\binom{N}{n}} \quad \text{for} \quad k = 0, 1, 2, \ldots, \min(n, K),$$

$$P(X = k) = 0 \text{ elsewhere}, \tag{4.1}$$

where $0 < n < N$ and $0 < K < N$ are natural numbers. This distribution arises, for example, if we randomly draw n balls *without* replacement from a bowl containing K red balls and $N - K$ white balls. The random variable X is then the number of red balls in the sample. In almost all applications of this distribution, $n < K$, and thus I will focus on that case only.

The moment-generating function involved cannot be simplified further than its definition $m_H(t) = \sum_{k=0}^{m} \exp(t \cdot k) P(X = k)$, and the same applies to the characteristic function. Therefore, we have to derive the expectation directly:

$$E[X] = \sum_{k=0}^{n} k \frac{\binom{K}{k}\binom{N-K}{n-k}}{\binom{N}{n}} = \sum_{k=1}^{n} \frac{\frac{K!(N-K)!}{(k-1)!(K-k)!(n-k)!(N-K-n+k)!}}{\frac{N!}{n!(N-n)!}}$$

$$= \frac{nK}{N} \sum_{k=0}^{n-1} \frac{\frac{(K-1)!((N-1)-(K-1))!}{k!((K-1)-k)!((n-1)-k)!((N-1)-(K-1)-(n-1)+k)!}}{\frac{(N-1)!}{(n-1)!((N-1)-(n-1))!}}$$

$$= \frac{nK}{N} \sum_{k=0}^{n-1} \frac{\binom{K-1}{k}\binom{(N-1)-(K-1)}{(n-1)-k}}{\binom{N-1}{n-1}} = \frac{nK}{N}.$$

Along similar lines it follows that

$$E[X(X-1)] = \frac{n(n-1)K(K-1)}{N(N-1)}; \tag{4.2}$$

hence,

$$\mathrm{var}\,(X) = E[X^2] - (E[X])^2 = \frac{nK}{N}\left(\frac{(n-1)(K-1)}{N-1} + 1 - \frac{nK}{N}\right).$$

4.1.2. The Binomial Distribution

A random variable X has a binomial distribution if

$$P(X = k) = \binom{n}{k} p^k (1-p)^{n-k} \quad \text{for} \quad k = 0, 1, 2, \ldots, n,$$

$$P(X = k) = 0 \text{ elsewhere}, \tag{4.3}$$

where $0 < p < 1$. This distribution arises, for example, if we randomly draw n balls *with* replacement from a bowl containing K red balls and $N - K$ white balls, where $K/N = p$. The random variable X is then the number of red balls in the sample.

We have seen in Chapter 1 that the binomial probabilities are limits of hypergeometric probabilities: If both N and K converge to infinity such that $K/N \to p$, then for fixed n and k, (4.1) converges to (4.3). This also suggests that the expectation and variance of the binomial distribution are the limits of the expectation and variance of the hypergeometric distribution, respectively:

$$E[X] = np, \tag{4.4}$$

$$\mathrm{var}\,(X) = np(1-p). \tag{4.5}$$

As we will see in Chapter 6, in general, convergence of distributions does not imply convergence of expectations and variances except if the random variables involved are uniformly bounded. Therefore, in this case the conjecture is true because the distributions involved are bounded: $P[0 \leq X < n] = 1$. However, it is not hard to verify (4.4) and (4.5) from the moment-generating function:

$$
\begin{aligned}
m_B(t) &= \sum_{k=0}^{n} \exp(t \cdot k) \binom{n}{k} p^k (1-p)^{n-k} \\
&= \sum_{k=0}^{n} \binom{n}{k} (pe^t)^k (1-p)^{n-k} \\
&= (p \cdot e^t + 1 - p)^n.
\end{aligned}
\tag{4.6}
$$

Similarly, the characteristic function is

$$
\varphi_B(t) = (p \cdot e^{i \cdot t} + 1 - p)^n.
$$

4.1.3. The Poisson Distribution

A random variable X is Poisson(λ)-distributed if for $k = 0, 1, 2, 3, \ldots$ and some $\lambda > 0$,

$$
P(X = k) = \exp(-\lambda)\frac{\lambda^k}{k!}.
\tag{4.7}
$$

Recall that the Poisson probabilities are limits of the binomial probabilities (4.3) for $n \to \infty$ and $p \downarrow 0$ such that $np \to \lambda$. It is left as an exercise to show that the expectation, variance, moment-generating function, and characteristic function of the Poisson(λ) distribution are

$$
\begin{aligned}
E[X] &= \lambda, & (4.8)\\
\operatorname{var}(X) &= \lambda, & (4.9)\\
m_P(t) &= \exp[\lambda(e^t - 1)], & (4.10)\\
\varphi_P(t) &= \exp[\lambda(e^{i \cdot t} - 1)], & (4.11)
\end{aligned}
$$

respectively.

4.1.4. The Negative Binomial Distribution

Consider a sequence of independent repetitions of a random experiment with constant probability p of success. Let the random variable X be the total number of failures in this sequence before the mth success, where $m \geq 1$. Thus, $X + m$ is equal to the number of trials necessary to produce exactly m successes. The probability $P(X = k)$, $k = 0, 1, 2, \ldots$ is the product of the probability of obtaining exactly $m - 1$ successes in the first $k + m - 1$ trials, which is equal to the binomial probability

$$\binom{k+m-1}{m-1} p^{m-1}(1-p)^{k+m-1-(m-1)}$$

and the probability p of a success on the $(k+m)$th trial. Thus,

$$P(X=k) = \binom{k+m-1}{m-1} p^m(1-p)^k, \quad k=0,1,2,3,\ldots.$$

This distribution is called the negative binomial (m, p) – abbreviated NB (m, p) – distribution.

It is easy to verify from the preceding argument that an NB(m, p)-distributed random variable can be generated as the sum of m independent NB$(1, p)$-distributed random variables (i.e., if $X_{1,1}, \ldots, X_{1,m}$ are independent NB$(1, p)$ distributed, then $X = \sum_{j=1}^{n} X_{1,j}$ is NB(m, p) distributed.) The moment-generating function of the NB$(1, p)$ distribution is

$$m_{\text{NB}(1,p)}(t) = \sum_{k=0}^{\infty} \exp(k \cdot t) \binom{k}{0} p(1-p)^k$$

$$= p \sum_{k=0}^{\infty} \left((1-p) e^t\right)^k$$

$$= \frac{p}{1-(1-p) e^t}$$

provided that $t < -\ln(1-p)$, hence, the moment-generating function of the NB(m, p) distribution is

$$m_{\text{NB}(m,p)}(t) = \left(\frac{p}{1-(1-p) e^t}\right)^m, \quad t < -\ln(1-p). \tag{4.12}$$

Replacing t by $i \cdot t$ in (4.12) yields the characteristic function

$$\varphi_{\text{NB}(m,p)}(t) = \left(\frac{p}{1-(1-p) e^{i \cdot t}}\right)^m = \left(\frac{p(1+(1-p) e^{i \cdot t})}{1+(1-p)^2}\right)^m.$$

It is now easy to verify, using the moment generating function that, for an NB(m, p)-distributed random variable X,

$$E[X] = m(1-p)/p,$$
$$\text{var}(X) = m(1-p)/p^2.$$

4.2. Transformations of Discrete Random Variables and Vectors

In the discrete case, the question Given a random variable or vector X and a Borel measure function or mapping $g(x)$, how is the distribution of $Y = g(X)$ related to the distribution of X? is easy to answer. If $P[X \in \{x_1, x_2, \ldots\}] = 1$ and

$g(x_1), g(x_2), \ldots$ are all different, the answer is trivial: $P(Y = g(x_j)) = P(X = x_j)$. If some of the values $g(x_1), g(x_2), \ldots$ are the same, let $\{y_1, y_2, \ldots\}$ be the set of distinct values of $g(x_1), g(x_2), \ldots$ Then

$$P(Y = y_j) = \sum_{i=1}^{\infty} I[y_j = g(x_i)]P(X = x_i). \tag{4.13}$$

It is easy to see that (4.13) carries over to the multivariate discrete case.

For example, if X is Poisson(λ)-distributed and $g(x) = \sin^2(\pi x) = (\sin(\pi x))^2$ – and thus for $m = 0, 1, 2, 3, \ldots, g(2m) = \sin^2(\pi m) = 0$ and $g(2m + 1) = \sin^2(\pi m + \pi/2) = 1$ – then $P(Y = 0) = e^{-\lambda} \sum_{j=0}^{\infty} \lambda^{2j}/(2j)!$ and $P(Y = 1) = e^{-\lambda} \sum_{j=0}^{\infty} \lambda^{2j+1}/(2j + 1)!$

As an application, let $X = (X_1, X_2)^{\mathrm{T}}$, where X_1 and X_2 are independent Poisson(λ) distributed, and let $Y = X_1 + X_2$. Then for $y = 0, 1, 2, \ldots$

$$P(Y = y) = \sum_{i=0}^{\infty} \sum_{j=0}^{\infty} I[y = i + j]P(X_1 = i, X_2 = j)$$

$$= \exp(-2\lambda)\frac{(2\lambda)^y}{y!}. \tag{4.14}$$

Hence, Y is Poisson(2λ) distributed. More generally, we have

Theorem 4.1: *If for $j = 1, \ldots, k$ the random variables X_j are independent Poisson(λ_j) distributed, then $\sum_{j=1}^{k} X_j$ is Poisson ($\sum_{j=1}^{k} \lambda_j$) distributed.*

4.3. Transformations of Absolutely Continuous Random Variables

If X is absolutely continuously distributed, with distribution function $F(x) = \int_{-\infty}^{x} f(u)du$, the derivation of the distribution function of $Y = g(X)$ is less trivial. Let us assume first that g is continuous and monotonic increasing: $g(x) < g(z)$ if $x < z$. Note that these conditions imply that g is differentiable.[1] Then g is a one-to-one mapping – that is, for each $y \in [g(-\infty), g(\infty)]$ there exists one and only one $x \in \mathbb{R} \cup \{-\infty\} \cup \{\infty\}$ such that $y = g(x)$. This unique x is denoted by $x = g^{-1}(y)$. Note that the inverse function $g^{-1}(y)$ is also monotonic increasing and differentiable. Now let $H(y)$ be the distribution function of Y. Then

$$H(y) = P(Y \leq y) = P(g(X) \leq y)$$
$$= P(X \leq g^{-1}(y)) = F(g^{-1}(y)). \tag{4.15}$$

---

[1] Except perhaps on a set with Lebesgue measure zero.

Taking the derivative of (4.15) yields the density $H(y)$ of Y:

$$h(y) = H'(y) = f(g^{-1}(y))\frac{dg^{-1}(y)}{dy}. \tag{4.16}$$

If g is continuous and monotonic decreasing: $g(x) < g(z)$ if $x > z$, then $g^{-1}(y)$ is also monotonic decreasing, and thus (4.15) becomes

$$\begin{aligned}H(y) &= P(Y \leq y) = P(g(X) \leq y)\\ &= P(X \geq g^{-1}(y)) = 1 - F(g^{-1}(y)),\end{aligned}$$

and (4.16) becomes

$$h(y) = H'(y) = f(g^{-1}(y))\left(-\frac{dg^{-1}(y)}{dy}\right). \tag{4.17}$$

Note that in this case the derivative of $g^{-1}(y)$ is negative because $g^{-1}(y)$ is monotonic decreasing. Therefore, we can combine (4.16) and (4.17) into one expression:

$$h(y) = f(g^{-1}(y))\left|\frac{dg^{-1}(y)}{dy}\right|. \tag{4.18}$$

Theorem 4.2: *If X is absolutely continuously distributed with density f, and $Y = g(X)$, where g is a continuous, monotonic real function on $\mathbb{R}$, then Y is absolutely continuously distributed with density $h(y)$ given by (4.18) if $\min[g(-\infty), g(\infty)] < y < \max[g(-\infty), g(\infty)]$, and $h(y) = 0$ elsewhere.*

4.4. Transformations of Absolutely Continuous Random Vectors

4.4.1. The Linear Case

Let $X = (X_1, X_2)^{\mathrm{T}}$ be a bivariate random vector with distribution function

$$F(x) = \int_{-\infty}^{x_1}\int_{-\infty}^{x_2} f(u_1, u_2)\, du_1 du_2 = \int_{(-\infty, x_1]\times(-\infty, x_2]} f(u)\, du,$$
$$\text{where} \quad x = (x_1, x_2)^{\mathrm{T}}, \ u = (u_1, u_2)^{\mathrm{T}}.$$

In this section I will derive the joint density of $Y = AX + b$, where A is a (nonrandom) nonsingular 2×2 matrix and b is a nonrandom 2×1 vector.

Recall from linear algebra (see Appendix I) that any square matrix A can be decomposed into

$$A = R^{-1}L \cdot D \cdot U, \tag{4.19}$$

where R is a permutation matrix (possibly equal to the unit matrix I), L is a lower-triangular matrix with diagonal elements all equal to 1, U is an upper-triangular matrix with diagonal elements all equal to 1, and D is a diagonal matrix. The transformation $Y = AX + b$ can therefore be conducted in five steps:

$$
\begin{aligned}
Z_1 &= UX \\
Z_2 &= DZ_1 \\
Z_3 &= LZ_2 \\
Z_4 &= R^{-1} Z_3 \\
Y &= Z_4 + b.
\end{aligned}
\tag{4.20}
$$

Therefore, I will consider the first four cases, $A = U, A = D, A = L$, and $A = R^{-1}$ for $b = 0$ and then the case $A = I, b \neq 0$.

Let $Y = AX$ with A an upper-triangular matrix:

$$
A = \begin{pmatrix} 1 & a \\ 0 & 1 \end{pmatrix}.
\tag{4.21}
$$

Then

$$
Y = \begin{pmatrix} Y_1 \\ Y_2 \end{pmatrix} = \begin{pmatrix} X_1 + aX_2 \\ X_2 \end{pmatrix};
$$

hence, the joint distribution function $H(y)$ of Y is

$$
\begin{aligned}
H(y) &= P(Y_1 \leq y_1, Y_2 \leq y_2) = P(X_1 + aX_2 \leq y_1, X_2 \leq y_2) \\
&= E\left[I(X_1 \leq y_1 - aX_2)I(X_2 \leq y_2)\right] \\
&= E\left(E\left[I(X_1 \leq y_1 - aX_2)| X_2\right] I(X_2 \leq y_2)\right) \\
&= \int_{-\infty}^{y_2} \left(\int_{-\infty}^{y_1 - ax_2} f_{1|2}(x_1 \mid x_2)\, dx_1 \right) f_2(x_2)\, dx_2 \\
&= \int_{-\infty}^{y_2} \left(\int_{-\infty}^{y_1 - ax_2} f(x_1, x_2)\, dx_1 \right) dx_2,
\end{aligned}
\tag{4.22}
$$

where $f_{1|2}(x_1|x_2)$ is the conditional density of X_1 given $X_2 = x_2$ and $f_2(x_2)$ is the marginal density of X_2. If we take partial derivatives, it follows from (4.22) that for $Y = AX$ with A given by (4.21),

$$
\begin{aligned}
h(y) &= \frac{\partial^2 H(y)}{\partial y_1 \partial y_2} = \frac{\partial}{\partial y_2} \int_{-\infty}^{y_2} f(y_1 - ax_2, x_2) dx_2 \\
&= f(y_1 - ay_2, y_2) = f(A^{-1}y).
\end{aligned}
$$

Along the same lines, it follows that, if A is a lower-triangular matrix, then the joint density of $Y = AX$ is

$$h(y) = \frac{\partial^2 H(y)}{\partial y_1 \partial y_2} = f(y_1, y_2 - ay_1) = f(A^{-1}y). \tag{4.23}$$

Next, let $Y = AX$ with A a nonsingular diagonal matrix

$$A = \begin{pmatrix} a_1 & 0 \\ 0 & a_2 \end{pmatrix},$$

where $a_1 \neq 0, a_2 \neq 0$. Then $Y_1 = a_1 X_1$ and $Y_2 = a_2 X_2$; hence, the joint distribution function $H(y)$ is

$$H(y) = P(Y_1 \leq y_1, Y_2 \leq y_2) = P(a_1 X_1 \leq y_1, a_2 X_2 \leq y_2) =$$
$$P(X_1 \leq y_1/a_1, X_2 \leq y_2/a_2)$$
$$= \int_{-\infty}^{y_1/a_1} \int_{-\infty}^{y_2/a_2} f(x_1, x_2) dx_1 dx_2 \quad \text{if } a_1 > 0, \ a_2 > 0,$$
$$P(X_1 \leq y_1/a_1, X_2 > y_2/a_2)$$
$$= \int_{-\infty}^{y_1/a_1} \int_{y_2/a_2}^{\infty} f(x_1, x_2) dx_1 dx_2 \quad \text{if } a_1 > 0, \ a_2 < 0,$$
$$P(X_1 > y_1/a_1, X_2 \leq y_2/a_2)$$
$$= \int_{y_1/a_1}^{\infty} \int_{-\infty}^{y_2/a_2} f(x_1, x_2) dx_1 dx_2 \quad \text{if } a_1 < 0, \ a_2 > 0,$$
$$P(X_1 > y_1/a_1, X_2 > y_2/a_2)$$
$$= \int_{y_1/a_1}^{\infty} \int_{y_2/a_2}^{\infty} f(x_1, x_2) dx_1 dx_2 \quad \text{if } a_1 < 0, \ a_2 < 0. \tag{4.24}$$

It is a standard calculus exercise to verify from (4.24) that in all four cases

$$h(y) = \frac{\partial^2 H(y)}{\partial y_1 \partial y_2} = \frac{f(y_1/a_1, y_2/a_2)}{|a_1 a_2|} = f(A^{-1}y)|\det(A^{-1})|. \tag{4.25}$$

Now consider the case $Y = AX$, for instance, where A is the inverse of a permutation matrix (which is a matrix that permutates the columns of the unit matrix):

$$A = \begin{pmatrix} 0 & 1 \\ 1 & 0 \end{pmatrix}^{-1} = \begin{pmatrix} 0 & 1 \\ 1 & 0 \end{pmatrix}.$$

Then the joint distribution function $H(y)$ of Y is

$$H(y) = P(Y_1 \leq y_1, Y_2 \leq y_2) = P(X_2 \leq y_1, X_1 \leq y_2)$$
$$= F(y_2, y_1) = F(Ay),$$

and the density involved is

$$h(y) = \frac{\partial^2 H(y)}{\partial y_1 \partial y_2} = f(y_2, y_1) = f(Ay).$$

Finally, consider the case $Y = X + b$ with $b = (b_1, b_2)^{\mathrm{T}}$. Then the joint distribution function $H(y)$ of Y is

$$H(y) = P(Y_1 \leq y_1, Y_2 \leq y_2) = P(X_1 \leq y_1 - b_1, X_2 \leq y_2 - b_2)$$
$$= F(y_1 - b_1, y_2 - b_2);$$

hence, the density if Y is

$$h(y) = \frac{\partial^2 H(y)}{\partial y_1 \partial y_2} = f(y_1 - b_1, y_2 - b_2) = f(y - b).$$

Combining these results, we find it is not hard to verify, using the decomposition (4.19) and the five steps in (4.20), that for the bivariate case ($k = 2$):

Theorem 4.3: *Let X be k-variate, absolutely continuously distributed with joint density $f(x)$, and let $Y = AX + b$, where A is a nonsingular square matrix. Then Y is k-variate, absolutely continuously distributed with joint density $h(y) = f(A^{-1}(y - b))|\det(A^{-1})|$.*

However, this result holds for the general case as well.

4.4.2. The Nonlinear Case

If we denote $G(x) = Ax + b$, $G^{-1}(y) = A^{-1}(y - b)$, then the result of Theorem 4.3 reads $h(y) = f(G^{-1}(y))|\det(\partial G^{-1}(y)/\partial y)|$. This suggests that Theorem 4.3 can be generalized as follows:

Theorem 4.4: *Let X be k-variate, absolutely continuously distributed with joint density $f(x), x = (x_1, \ldots, x_k)^{\mathrm{T}}$, and let $Y = G(X)$, where $G(x) = (g_1(x), \ldots, g_k(x))^{\mathrm{T}}$ is a one-to-one mapping with inverse mapping $x = G^{-1}(y) = (g_1^*(y), \ldots, g_k^*(y))^{\mathrm{T}}$ whose components are differentiable in the components of $y = (y_1, \ldots, y_k)^{\mathrm{T}}$. Let $J(y) = \partial x/\partial y = \partial G^{-1}(y)/\partial y$, that is, $J(y)$ is the matrix with i, j's element $\partial g_i^*(y)/\partial y_j$, which is called the **Jacobian**. Then Y is k-variate, absolutely continuously distributed with joint density $h(y) = f(G^{-1}(y))|\det(J(y))|$ for y in the set $G(\mathbb{R}^k) = \{y \in \mathbb{R}^k : y = G(x), f(x) > 0, x \in \mathbb{R}^k\}$ and $h(y) = 0$ elsewhere.*

This conjecture is indeed true. Its formal proof is given in Appendix 4.B.

An application of Theorem 4.4 is the following problem. Consider the function

$$f(x) = c \cdot \exp(-x^2/2) \quad \text{if } x \geq 0,$$
$$= 0 \quad \text{if } x < 0. \tag{4.26}$$

For which value of c is this function a density?

To solve this problem, consider the joint density $f(x_1, x_2) = c^2 \exp[-(x_1^2 + x_2^2)/2]$, $x_1 \geq 0$, $x_2 \geq 0$, which is the joint distribution of $X = (X_1, X_2)^\mathsf{T}$, where X_1 and X_2 are independent random drawings from the distribution with density (4.26). Next, consider the transformation $Y = (Y_1, Y_2)^\mathsf{T} = G(X)$ defined by

$$Y_1 = \sqrt{X_1^2 + X_2^2} \in (0, \infty)$$
$$Y_2 = \arctan(X_1/X_2) \in (0, \pi/2).$$

The inverse $X = G^{-1}(Y)$ of this transformation is

$$X_1 = Y_1 \sin(Y_2),$$
$$X_2 = Y_1 \cos(Y_2)$$

with Jacobian

$$J(Y) = \begin{pmatrix} \partial X_1/\partial Y_1 & \partial X_1/\partial Y_2 \\ \partial X_2/\partial Y_1 & \partial X_2/\partial Y_2 \end{pmatrix} = \begin{pmatrix} \sin(Y_2) & Y_1\cos(Y_2) \\ \cos(Y_2) & -Y_1\sin(Y_2) \end{pmatrix}.$$

Note that $\det[J(Y)] = -Y_1$. Consequently, the density $h(y) = h(y_1, y_2) = f(G^{-1}(y))|\det(J(y))|$ is

$$h(y_1, y_2) = c^2 y_1 \exp\left(-y_1^2/2\right) \quad \text{for} \quad y_1 > 0 \quad \text{and} \quad 0 < y_2 < \pi/2,$$
$$= 0 \text{ elsewhere;}$$

hence,

$$1 = \int_0^\infty \int_0^{\pi/2} c^2 y_1 \exp\left(-y_1^2/2\right) dy_2 dy_1$$

$$= c^2(\pi/2) \int_0^\infty y_1 \exp\left(-y_1^2/2\right) dy_1$$

$$= c^2 \pi/2.$$

Thus, the answer is $c = \sqrt{2/\pi}$:

$$\int_0^\infty \frac{\exp(-x^2/2)}{\sqrt{\pi/2}} dx = 1.$$

Note that this result implies that

$$\int_{-\infty}^{\infty} \frac{\exp(-x^2/2)}{\sqrt{2\pi}} dx = 1. \tag{4.27}$$

4.5. The Normal Distribution

Several univariate continuous distributions that play a key role in statistical and econometric inference will be reviewed in this section, starting with the normal distribution. The standard normal distribution emerges as a limiting distribution of an aggregate of random variables. In particular, if $X_1, \ldots, X_n$ are independent random variables with expectation μ and finite and positive variance σ^2, then for large n the random variable $Y_n = (1/\sqrt{n}) \sum_{j=1}^{n} (X_j - \mu)/\sigma$ is approximately standard normally distributed. This result, known as the central limit theorem, will be derived in Chapter 6 and carries over to various types of dependent random variables (see Chapter 7).

4.5.1. The Standard Normal Distribution

The standard normal distribution is an absolutely continuous distribution with density function

$$f(x) = \frac{\exp(-x^2/2)}{\sqrt{2\pi}}, \quad x \in \mathbb{R}. \tag{4.28}$$

Compare this equation with (4.27). Its moment-generating function is

$$m_{N(0,1)}(t) = \int_{-\infty}^{\infty} \exp(t \cdot x) f(x) dx = \int_{-\infty}^{\infty} \exp(t \cdot x) \frac{\exp(-x^2/2)}{\sqrt{2\pi}} dx$$

$$= \exp(t^2/2) \int_{-\infty}^{\infty} \frac{\exp[-(x^2 - 2t \cdot x + t^2)/2]}{\sqrt{2\pi}} dx$$

$$= \exp(t^2/2) \int_{-\infty}^{\infty} \frac{\exp[-(x - t)^2/2]}{\sqrt{2\pi}} dx$$

$$= \exp(t^2/2) \int_{-\infty}^{\infty} \frac{\exp[-u^2/2]}{\sqrt{2\pi}} du = \exp(t^2/2), \tag{4.29}$$

which exists for all $t \in \mathbb{R}$, and its characteristic function is

$$\varphi_{N(0,1)}(t) = m(i \cdot t) = \exp(-t^2/2).$$

Consequently, if X is standard normally distributed, then

$$E[X] = m'(t)\big|_{t=0} = 0, \ E[X^2] = \text{var}(X) = m''(t)\big|_{t=0} = 1.$$

Given this result, the standard normal distribution is denoted by $N(0, 1)$, where the first number is the expectation and the second number is the variance, and the statement "X is standard normally distributed" is usually abbreviated as "$X \sim N(0, 1)$."

4.5.2. The General Normal Distribution

Now let $Y = \mu + \sigma X$, where $X \sim N(0, 1)$. It is left as an easy exercise to verify that the density of Y takes the form

$$f(x) = \frac{\exp\left(-\frac{1}{2}(x - \mu)^2/\sigma^2\right)}{\sigma\sqrt{2\pi}}, \quad x \in \mathbb{R}$$

with corresponding moment-generating function

$$m_{N(\mu,\sigma^2)}(t) = E[\exp(t \cdot Y)] = \exp(\mu t)\exp(\sigma^2 t^2/2), \quad t \in \mathbb{R}$$

and characteristic function

$$\varphi_{N(\mu,\sigma^2)}(t) = E[\exp(i \cdot t \cdot Y)] = \exp(i \cdot \mu t)\exp(-\sigma^2 t^2/2).$$

Consequently, $E[Y] = \mu$, $\text{var}(Y) = \sigma^2$. This distribution is the general normal distribution, which is denoted by $N(\mu, \sigma^2)$. Thus, $Y \sim N(\mu, \sigma^2)$.

4.6. Distributions Related to the Standard Normal Distribution

The standard normal distribution generates, via various transformations, a few other distributions such as the chi-square, t, Cauchy, and F distributions. These distributions are fundamental in testing statistical hypotheses, as we will see in Chapters 5, 6, and 8.

4.6.1. The Chi-Square Distribution

Let $X_1, \ldots X_n$ be independent $N(0, 1)$-distributed random variables, and let

$$Y_n = \sum_{j=1}^{n} X_j^2. \tag{4.30}$$

The distribution of Y_n is called the chi-square distribution with n degrees of freedom and is denoted by χ_n^2 or $\chi^2(n)$. Its distribution and density functions can be derived recursively, starting from the case $n = 1$:

$$G_1(y) = P[Y_1 \leq y] = P\left[X_1^2 \leq y\right] = P[-\sqrt{y} \leq X_1 \leq \sqrt{y}]$$

$$= \int_{-\sqrt{y}}^{\sqrt{y}} f(x)dx = 2 \int_0^{\sqrt{y}} f(x)dx \quad \text{for} \quad y > 0,$$

$$G_1(y) = 0 \quad \text{for} \quad y \leq 0,$$

where $f(x)$ is defined by (4.28); hence,

$$g_1(y) = G_1'(y) = f\left(\sqrt{y}\right)/\sqrt{y} = \frac{\exp(-y/2)}{\sqrt{y}\sqrt{2\pi}} \quad \text{for} \quad y > 0,$$

$$g_1(y) = 0 \quad \text{for} \quad y \leq 0.$$

Thus, $g_1(y)$ is the density of the χ_1^2 distribution. The corresponding moment-generating function is

$$m_{\chi_1^2}(t) = \frac{1}{\sqrt{1 - 2t}} \quad \text{for} \quad t < 1/2, \tag{4.31}$$

and the characteristic function is

$$\varphi_{\chi_1^2}(t) = \frac{1}{\sqrt{1 - 2 \cdot i \cdot t}} = \frac{\sqrt{1 + 2 \cdot i \cdot t}}{\sqrt{1 + 4 \cdot t^2}}. \tag{4.32}$$

It follows easily from (4.30) – (4.32) that the moment-generating and characteristic functions of the χ_n^2 distribution are

$$m_{\chi_n^2}(t) = \left(\frac{1}{1 - 2t}\right)^{n/2} \quad \text{for} \quad t < 1/2 \tag{4.33}$$

and

$$\varphi_{\chi_n^2}(t) = \left(\frac{1 + 2 \cdot i \cdot t}{1 + 4 \cdot t^2}\right)^{n/2},$$

respectively. Therefore, the density of the χ_n^2 distribution is

$$g_n(y) = \frac{y^{n/2-1} \exp(-y/2)}{\Gamma(n/2)2^{n/2}}, \tag{4.34}$$

where, for $\alpha > 0$,

$$\Gamma(\alpha) = \int_0^\infty x^{\alpha-1} \exp(-x)dx. \tag{4.35}$$

The result (4.34) can be proved by verifying that for $t < 1/2$, (4.33) is the moment-generating function of (4.34). The function (4.35) is called the Gamma function. Note that

$$\Gamma(1) = 1, \Gamma(1/2) = \sqrt{\pi}, \Gamma(\alpha + 1) = \alpha\Gamma(\alpha) \quad \text{for} \quad \alpha > 0. \quad (4.36)$$

Moreover, the expectation and variance of the χ_n^2 distribution are

$$E[Y_n] = n, \qquad \text{var}(Y_n) = 2n. \quad (4.37)$$

4.6.2. The Student's t Distribution

Let $X \sim N(0, 1)$ and $Y_n \sim \chi_n^2$, where X and Y_n are independent. Then the distribution of the random variable

$$T_n = \frac{X}{\sqrt{Y_n/n}}$$

is called the (Student's[2]) t distribution with n degrees of freedom and is denoted by t_n.

The conditional density $h_n(x|y)$ of T_n given $Y_n = y$ is the density of the $N(1, n/y)$ distribution; hence, the unconditional density of T_n is

$$h_n(x) = \int_0^\infty \frac{\exp(-(x^2/n)y/2)}{\sqrt{n/y}\sqrt{2\pi}} \times \frac{y^{n/2-1}\exp(-y/2)}{\Gamma(n/2)\,2^{n/2}}\,dy$$

$$= \frac{\Gamma((n+1)/2)}{\sqrt{n\pi}\,\Gamma(n/2)(1+x^2/n)^{(n+1)/2}}.$$

The expectation of T_n does not exist if $n = 1$, as we will see in the next subsection, and is zero for $n \geq 2$ by symmetry. Moreover, the variance of T_n is infinite for $n = 2$, whereas for $n \geq 3$,

$$\text{var}(T_n) = E\left[T_n^2\right] = \frac{n}{n-2}. \quad (4.38)$$

See Appendix 4.A.

The moment-generating function of the t_n distribution does not exist, but its characteristic function does, of course:

$$\varphi_{t_n}(t) = \frac{\Gamma((n+1)/2)}{\sqrt{n\pi}\,\Gamma(n/2)} \int_{-\infty}^\infty \frac{\exp(it \cdot x)}{(1+x^2/n)^{(n+1)/2}}\,dx$$

$$= \frac{2 \cdot \Gamma((n+1)/2)}{\sqrt{n\pi}\,\Gamma(n/2)} \int_0^\infty \frac{\cos(t \cdot x)}{(1+x^2/n)^{(n+1)/2}}\,dx.$$

---

[2] The t distribution was discovered by W. S. Gosset, who published the result under the pseudonym Student. The reason for this was that his employer, an Irish brewery, did not want its competitors to know that statistical methods were being used.

4.6.3. The Standard Cauchy Distribution

The t_1 distribution is also known as the standard Cauchy distribution. Its density is

$$h_1(x) = \frac{\Gamma(1)}{\sqrt{\pi}\,\Gamma(1/2)(1+x^2)} = \frac{1}{\pi(1+x^2)}, \tag{4.39}$$

where the second equality follows from (4.36), and its characteristic function is

$$\varphi_{t_1}(t) = \exp(-|t|).$$

The latter follows from the inversion formula for characteristic functions:

$$\frac{1}{2\pi}\int_{-\infty}^{\infty} \exp(-i \cdot t \cdot x)\exp(-|t|)dt = \frac{1}{\pi(1+x^2)}. \tag{4.40}$$

See Appendix 4.A. Moreover, it is easy to verify from (4.39) that the expectation of the Cauchy distribution does not exist and that the second moment is infinite.

4.6.4. The F Distribution

Let $X_m \sim \chi_m^2$ and $Y_n \sim \chi_n^2$, where X_m and Y_n are independent. Then the distribution of the random variable

$$F = \frac{X_m/m}{Y_n/n}$$

is said to be F with m and n degrees of freedom and is denoted by $F_{m,n}$. Its distribution function is

$$\begin{aligned}
H_{m,n}(x) &= P[F \leq x] \\
&= \int_0^\infty \left(\int_0^{m \cdot x \cdot y/n} \frac{z^{m/2-1}\exp(-z/2)}{\Gamma(m/2)2^{m/2}}dz \right) \\
&\quad \times \frac{y^{n/2-1}\exp(-y/2)}{\Gamma(n/2)2^{n/2}}dy, \quad x > 0,
\end{aligned}$$

and its density is

$$h_{m,n}(x) = \frac{m^{m/2}\,\Gamma(m/2+n/2)\,x^{m/2-1}}{n^{m/2}\,\Gamma(m/2)\Gamma(n/2)\,[1+m\cdot x/n]^{m/2+n/2}}, \quad x > 0 \tag{4.41}$$

See Appendix 4.A.

Moreover, it is shown in Appendix 4.A that

$$
\begin{aligned}
E[F] &= n/(n-2) & &\text{if } n \geq 3, \\
&= \infty & &\text{if } n = 1, 2,
\end{aligned}
$$

$$
\begin{aligned}
\text{var}(F) &= \frac{2n^2(m+n-4)}{m(n-2)^2(n-4)} & &\text{if } n \geq 5, \\
&= \infty & &\text{if } n = 3, 4, \\
&= \text{not defined} & &\text{if } n = 1, 2.
\end{aligned}
\tag{4.42}
$$

Furthermore, the moment-generating function of the $F_{m,n}$ distribution does not exist, and the computation of the characteristic function is too tedious an exercise and is therefore omitted.

4.7. The Uniform Distribution and Its Relation to the Standard Normal Distribution

As we have seen before in Chapter 1, the uniform [0, 1] distribution has density

$$
f(x) = 1 \quad \text{for} \quad 0 \leq x \leq 1, \qquad f(x) = 0 \text{ elsewhere.}
$$

More generally, the uniform $[a, b]$ distribution (denoted by $U[a, b]$) has density

$$
f(x) = \frac{1}{b-a} \quad \text{for} \quad a \leq x \leq b, \qquad f(x) = 0 \text{ elsewhere,}
$$

moment-generating function

$$
m_{U[a,b]}(t) = \frac{\exp(t \cdot b) - \exp(t \cdot a)}{(b-a)t},
$$

and characteristic function

$$
\begin{aligned}
\varphi_{U[a,b]}(t) &= \frac{\exp(i \cdot b \cdot t) - \exp(i \cdot a \cdot t)}{i \cdot (b-a)t} \\
&= \frac{(\sin(b \cdot t) + \sin(a \cdot t)) - i \cdot (\cos(b \cdot t) + \cos(a \cdot t))}{b-a}.
\end{aligned}
$$

Most computer languages such as Fortran, Pascal, and Visual Basic have a built-in function that generates independent random drawings from the uniform [0, 1] distribution.[3] These random drawings can be converted into independent random drawings from the standard normal distribution via the transformation

$$
\begin{aligned}
X_1 &= \cos(2\pi U_1) \cdot \sqrt{-2 \cdot \ln(U_2)}, \\
X_2 &= \sin(2\pi U_1) \cdot \sqrt{-2 \cdot \ln(U_2)},
\end{aligned}
\tag{4.43}
$$

---

[3] See, for example, Section 7.1 in Press et al. (1989).

where U_1 and U_2 are independent $U[0, 1]$ distributed. Then X_1 and X_2 are independent, standard normally distributed. This method is called the Box–Muller algorithm.

4.8. The Gamma Distribution

The χ_n^2 distribution is a special case of a Gamma distribution. The density of the Gamma distribution is

$$g(x) = \frac{x^{\alpha-1} \exp(-x/\beta)}{\Gamma(\alpha)\, \beta^\alpha}, \quad x > 0,\ \alpha > 0,\ \beta > 0.$$

This distribution is denoted by $\Gamma(\alpha, \beta)$. Thus, the χ_n^2 distribution is a Gamma distribution with $\alpha = n/2$ and $\beta = 2$.

The Gamma distribution has moment-generating function

$$m_{\Gamma(\alpha,\beta)}(t) = [1 - \beta t]^{-\alpha}, \quad t < 1/\beta \qquad (4.44)$$

and characteristic function $\varphi_{\Gamma(\alpha,\beta)}(t) = [1 - \beta \cdot i \cdot t]^{-\alpha}$. Therefore, the $\Gamma(\alpha, \beta)$ distribution has expectation $\alpha\beta$ and variance $\alpha\beta^2$.

The $\Gamma(\alpha, \beta)$ distribution with $\alpha = 1$ is called the *exponential distribution*.

4.9. Exercises

1. Derive (4.2).

2. Derive (4.4) and (4.5) directly from (4.3).

3. Derive (4.4) and (4.5) from the moment-generating function (4.6).

4. Derive (4.8), (4.9), and (4.10).

5. If X is discrete and $Y = g(x)$, do we need to require that g be Borel measurable?

6. Prove the last equality in (4.14).

7. Prove Theorem 4.1, using characteristic functions.

8. Prove that (4.25) holds for all four cases in (4.24).

9. Let X be a random variable with continuous distribution function $F(x)$. Derive the distribution of $Y = F(X)$.

10. The standard normal distribution has density $f(x) = \exp(-x^2/2)/\sqrt{2\pi}$, $x \in \mathbb{R}$. Let X_1 and X_2 be independent random drawings from the standard normal distribution involved, and let $Y_1 = X_1 + X_2$, $Y_2 = X_1 - X_2$. Derive the joint density $h(y_1, y_2)$ of Y_1 and Y_2, and show that Y_1 and Y_2 are independent. *Hint:* Use Theorem 4.3.

11. The exponential distribution has density $f(x) = \theta^{-1} \exp(-x/\theta)$ if $x \geq 0$ and $f(x) = 0$ if $x < 0$, where $\theta > 0$ is a constant. Let X_1 and X_2 be independent random drawings from the exponential distribution involved and let $Y_1 = X_1 + X_2$, $Y_2 = X_1 - X_2$. Derive the joint density $h(y_1, y_2)$ of Y_1 and Y_2. *Hints:* Determine first the support $\{(y_1, y_2)^\mathsf{T} \in \mathbb{R}^2 : h(y_1, y_2) > 0\}$ of $h(y_1, y_2)$ and then use Theorem 4.3.

12. Let $X \sim N(0, 1)$. Derive $E[X^{2k}]$ for $k = 2, 3, 4$, using the moment-generating function.

13. Let $X_1, X_2, \ldots, X_n$ be independent, standard normally distributed. Show that $(1/\sqrt{n}) \sum_{j=1}^{n} X_j$ is standard normally distributed.

14. Prove (4.31).

15. Show that for $t < 1/2$, (4.33) is the moment-generating function of (4.34).

16. Explain why the moment-generating function of the t_n distribution does not exist.

17. Prove (4.36).

18. Prove (4.37).

19. Let $X_1, X_2, \ldots, X_n$ be independent, standard Cauchy distributed. Show that $(1/n) \sum_{j=1}^{n} X_j$ is standard Cauchy distributed.

20. The class of standard stable distributions consists of distributions with characteristic functions of the type $\varphi(t) = \exp(-|t|^\alpha/\alpha)$, where $\alpha \in (0, 2]$. Note that the standard normal distribution is stable with $\alpha = 2$, and the standard Cauchy distribution is stable with $\alpha = 1$. Show that for a random sample $X_1, X_2, \ldots, X_n$ from a standard stable distribution with parameter α, the random variable $Y_n = n^{-1/\alpha} \sum_{j=1}^{n} X_j$ has the same standard stable distribution (this is the reason for calling these distributions stable).

21. Let X and Y be independent, standard normally distributed. Derive the distribution of X/Y.

22. Derive the characteristic function of the distribution with density $\exp(-|x|)/2$, $-\infty < x < \infty$.

23. Explain why the moment-generating function of the $F_{m,n}$ distribution does not exist.

24. Prove (4.44).

25. Show that if U_1 and U_2 are independent $U[0, 1]$ distributed, then X_1 and X_2 in (4.43) are independent, standard normally distributed.

26. If X and Y are independent $\Gamma(1, 1)$ distributed, what is the distribution of $X - Y$?

APPENDICES

4.A. Tedious Derivations

Derivation of (4.38):

$$E\left[T_n^2\right] = \frac{n\Gamma((n+1)/2)}{\sqrt{n\pi}\,\Gamma(n/2)} \int_{-\infty}^{\infty} \frac{x^2/n}{(1+x^2/n)^{(n+1)/2}} dx$$

$$= \frac{n\Gamma((n+1)/2)}{\sqrt{n\pi}\,\Gamma(n/2)} \int_{-\infty}^{\infty} \frac{1+x^2/n}{(1+x^2/n)^{(n+1)/2}} dx$$

$$- \frac{n\Gamma((n+1)/2)}{\sqrt{n\pi}\,\Gamma(n/2)} \int_{-\infty}^{\infty} \frac{1}{(1+x^2/n)^{(n+1)/2}} dx$$

$$= \frac{n\Gamma((n+1)/2)}{\sqrt{\pi}\,\Gamma(n/2)} \int_{-\infty}^{\infty} \frac{1}{(1+x^2)^{(n-1)/2}} dx - n$$

$$= \frac{n\Gamma((n-1)/2+1)}{\Gamma(n/2)} \frac{\Gamma(n/2-1)}{\Gamma((n-1)/2)} - n = \frac{n}{n-2}.$$

In this derivation I have used (4.36) and the fact that

$$1 = \int_{-\infty}^{\infty} h_{n-2}(x)dx$$

$$= \frac{\Gamma((n-1)/2)}{\sqrt{(n-2)\pi}\,\Gamma((n-2)/2)} \int_{-\infty}^{\infty} \frac{1}{(1+x^2/(n-2))^{(n-1)/2}} dx$$

$$= \frac{\Gamma((n-1)/2)}{\sqrt{\pi}\,\Gamma((n-2)/2)} \int_{-\infty}^{\infty} \frac{1}{(1+x^2)^{(n-1)/2}} dx.$$

Derivation of (4.40): For $m > 0$, we have

$$\frac{1}{2\pi} \int_{-m}^{m} \exp(-i \cdot t \cdot x)\exp(-|t|)dt$$

$$= \frac{1}{2\pi} \int_{0}^{m} \exp(-i \cdot t \cdot x)\exp(-t)dt + \frac{1}{2\pi} \int_{0}^{m} \exp(i \cdot t \cdot x)\exp(-t)dt$$

$$= \frac{1}{2\pi} \int_0^m \exp[-(1 + i \cdot x)t]dt + \frac{1}{2\pi} \int_0^m \exp[-(1 - i \cdot x)t]dt$$

$$= \frac{1}{2\pi} \frac{\exp[-(1 + i \cdot x)t]}{-(1 + i \cdot x)} \bigg|_0^m + \frac{1}{2\pi} \frac{\exp[-(1 - i \cdot x)t]}{-(1 - i \cdot x)} \bigg|_0^m$$

$$= \frac{1}{2\pi} \frac{1}{(1 + i \cdot x)} + \frac{1}{2\pi} \frac{1}{(1 - i \cdot x)} - \frac{1}{2\pi} \frac{\exp[-(1 + i \cdot x)m]}{(1 + i \cdot x)}$$

$$- \frac{1}{2\pi} \frac{\exp[-(1 - i \cdot x)m]}{(1 - i \cdot x)}$$

$$= \frac{1}{\pi(1 + x^2)} - \frac{\exp(-m)}{\pi(1 + x^2)}[\cos(m \cdot x) - x \cdot \sin(m \cdot x)].$$

Letting $m \to \infty$, we find that (4.40) follows.

Derivation of (4.41):

$$h_{m,n}(x) = H'_{m,n}(x)$$

$$= \int_0^\infty \frac{m \cdot y}{n} \times \frac{(m \cdot x \cdot y/n)^{m/2-1} \exp(-(m \cdot x \cdot y/(2n))}{\Gamma(m/2) \, 2^{m/2}}$$

$$\times \frac{y^{n/2-1} \exp(-y/2)}{\Gamma(n/2) \, 2^{n/2}} dy$$

$$= \frac{m^{m/2} x^{m/2-1}}{n^{m/2} \, \Gamma(m/2)\Gamma(n/2) \, 2^{m/2+n/2}}$$

$$\times \int_0^\infty y^{m/2+n/2-1} \exp\left(-[1 + m \cdot x/n] \, y/2\right) dy$$

$$= \frac{m^{m/2} x^{m/2-1}}{n^{m/2} \, \Gamma(m/2)\Gamma(n/2) \, [1 + m \cdot x/n]^{m/2+n/2}}$$

$$\times \int_0^\infty z^{m/2+n/2-1} \exp\left(-z\right) dz$$

$$= \frac{m^{m/2} \, \Gamma(m/2 + n/2) \, x^{m/2-1}}{n^{m/2} \, \Gamma(m/2)\Gamma(n/2) \, [1 + m \cdot x/n]^{m/2+n/2}}, \quad x > 0.$$

Derivation of (4.42): It follows from (4.41) that

$$\int_0^\infty \frac{x^{m/2-1}}{(1 + x)^{m/2+n/2}} dx = \frac{\Gamma(m/2)\Gamma(n/2)}{\Gamma(m/2 + n/2)};$$

hence, if $k < n/2$, then

$$\int_0^\infty x^k h_{m,n}(x)dx$$

$$= \frac{m^{m/2}}{n^{m/2}} \frac{\Gamma(m/2+n/2)}{\Gamma(m/2)\Gamma(n/2)} \int_0^\infty \frac{x^{m/2+k-1}}{(1+m \cdot x/n)^{m/2+n/2}}dx$$

$$= (n/m)^k \frac{\Gamma(m/2+n/2)}{\Gamma(m/2)\Gamma(n/2)} \int_0^\infty \frac{x^{(m+2k)/2-1}}{(1+x)^{(m+2k)/2+(n-2k)/2}}dx$$

$$= (n/m)^k \frac{\Gamma(m/2+k)\Gamma(n/2-k)}{\Gamma(m/2)\Gamma(n/2)}$$

$$= (n/m)^k \frac{\prod_{j=0}^{k-1}(m/2+j)}{\prod_{j=1}^{k}(n/2-j)},$$

where the last equality follows from the fact that, by (4.36), $\Gamma(\alpha+k) = \Gamma(\alpha)$ $\prod_{j=0}^{k-1}(\alpha+j)$ for $\alpha > 0$. Thus,

$$\mu_{m,n} = \int_0^\infty x h_{m,n}(x)dx = \frac{n}{n-2} \quad \text{if } n \geq 3, \mu_{m,n} = \infty \quad \text{if } n \leq 2,$$

$$(4.46)$$

$$\int_0^\infty x^2 h_{m,n}(x)dx = \frac{n^2(m+2)}{m(n-2)(n-4)} \quad \text{if } n \geq 5,$$

$$= \infty \quad \text{if } n \leq 4. \quad (4.47)$$

The results in (4.42) follow now from (4.46) and (4.47).

4.B. Proof of Theorem 4.4

For notational convenience I will prove Theorem 4.4 for the case $k = 2$ only. First note that the distribution of Y is absolutely continuous because, for arbitrary Borel sets B in $\mathbb{R}^2$,

$$P[Y \in B] = P[G(X) \in B] = P[X \in G^{-1}(B)] = \int_{G^{-1}(B)} f(x)dx.$$

If B has Lebesgue measure zero, then, because G is a one-to-one mapping, the Borel set $A = G^{-1}(B)$ has Lebesgue measure zero. Therefore, Y has density

$h(y)$, for instance, and thus for arbitrary Borel sets B in $\mathbb{R}^2$,

$$P[Y \in B] = \int_B h(y)dy.$$

Choose a fixed $y_0 = (y_{0,1}, y_{0,2})^T$ in the support $G(\mathbb{R}^2)$ of Y such that $x_0 = G^{-1}(y_0)$ is a continuity point of the density f of X and y_0 is a continuity point of the density h of Y. Let $Y(\delta_1, \delta_2) = [y_{0,1}, y_{0,1} + \delta_1] \times [y_{0,2}, y_{0,2} + \delta_2]$ for some positive numbers δ_1 and δ_2. Then, with λ the Lebesgue measure

$$P[Y \in Y(\delta_1, \delta_2)]$$

$$= \int_{G^{-1}(Y(\delta_1,\delta_2))} f(x)dx \leq \left(\sup_{x \in G^{-1}(Y(\delta_1,\delta_2))} f(x) \right) \lambda(G^{-1}(Y(\delta_1, \delta_2)))$$

$$= \left(\sup_{y \in Y(\delta_1,\delta_2)} f(G^{-1}(y)) \right) \lambda(G^{-1}(Y(\delta_1, \delta_2))), \tag{4.48}$$

and similarly,

$$P[Y \in Y(\delta_1, \delta_2)] \geq \left(\inf_{y \in Y(\delta_1,\delta_2)} f(G^{-1}(y)) \right) \lambda(G^{-1}(Y(\delta_1, \delta_2))). \tag{4.49}$$

It follows now from (4.48) and (4.49) that

$$h(y_0) = \lim_{\delta_1 \downarrow 0} \lim_{\delta_2 \downarrow 0} \frac{P[Y \in Y(\delta_1, \delta_2)]}{\delta_1 \delta_2}$$

$$= f(G^{-1}(y_0)) \lim_{\delta_1 \downarrow 0} \lim_{\delta_2 \downarrow 0} \frac{\lambda(G^{-1}(Y(\delta_1, \delta_2)))}{\delta_1 \delta_2}. \tag{4.50}$$

It remains to show that the latter limit is equal to $|\det[J(y_0)]|$.

If we let $G^{-1}(y) = (g_1^*(y), g_2^*(y))^T$, it follows from the mean value theorem that for each element $g_j^*(y)$ there exists a $\lambda_j \in [0, 1]$ depending on y and y_0 such that $g_j^*(y) = g_j^*(y_0) + J_j(y_0 + \lambda_j(y - y_0))(y - y_0)$, where $J_j(y)$ is the jth row of $J(y)$. Thus, writing

$$D_0(y) = \begin{pmatrix} J_1(y_0 + \lambda_1(y - y_0)) - J_1(y_0) \\ J_2(y_0 + \lambda_2(y - y_0)) - J_2(y_0) \end{pmatrix}$$

$$= \tilde{J}_0(y) - J(y_0), \tag{4.51}$$

for instance, we have $G^{-1}(y) = G^{-1}(y_0) + J(y_0)(y - y_0) + D_0(y)(y - y_0)$. Now, put $A = J(y_0)^{-1}$ and $b = y_0 - J(y_0)^{-1}G^{-1}(y_0)$. Then,

$$G^{-1}(y) = A^{-1}(y - b) + D_0(y)(y - y_0); \tag{4.52}$$

hence,

$$G^{-1}(Y(\delta_1, \delta_2)) = \{x \in \mathbb{R}^2 : x$$
$$= A^{-1}(y - b) + D_0(y)(y - y_0), y \in Y(\delta_1, \delta_2)\}.$$
(4.53)

The matrix A maps the set (4.53) onto

$$A[G^{-1}(Y(\delta_1, \delta_2))]$$
$$= \{x \in \mathbb{R}^2 : x = y - b + A \cdot D_0(y)(y - y_0), y \in Y(\delta_1, \delta_2)\},$$
(4.54)

where for arbitrary Borel sets B conformable with a matrix A, $A[B] \stackrel{\text{def.}}{=} \{x : x = Ay, y \in B\}$. Because the Lebesgue measure is invariant for location shifts (i.e., the vector b in (4.54)), it follows that

$$\lambda\left(A[G^{-1}(Y(\delta_1, \delta_2))]\right)$$
$$= \lambda\left(\{x \in \mathbb{R}^2 : x = y + A \cdot D_0(y)(y - y_0), y \in Y(\delta_1, \delta_2)\}\right).$$
(4.55)

Observe from (4.51) that

$$A \cdot D_0(y) = J(y_0)^{-1} D_0(y) = J(y_0)^{-1} \tilde{J}_0(y) - I_2$$
(4.56)

and

$$\lim_{y \to y_0} J(y_0)^{-1} \tilde{J}_0(y) = I_2.$$
(4.57)

Then

$$\lambda\left(A[G^{-1}(Y(\delta_1, \delta_2))]\right)$$
$$= \lambda\left(\{x \in \mathbb{R}^2 : x = y_0 + J(y_0)^{-1} \tilde{J}_0(y)(y - y_0), y \in Y(\delta_1, \delta_2)\}\right).$$
(4.58)

It can be shown, using (4.57), that

$$\lim_{\delta_1 \downarrow 0} \lim_{\delta_2 \downarrow 0} \frac{\lambda\left(A[G^{-1}(Y(\delta_1, \delta_2))]\right)}{\lambda\left(Y(\delta_1, \delta_2)\right)} = 1.$$
(4.59)

Recall from Appendix I that the matrix A can be written as $A = QDU$, where Q is an orthogonal matrix, D is a diagonal matrix, and U is an upper-triangular matrix with diagonal elements all equal to 1. Let $B = (0, 1) \times (0, 1)$. Then it is not hard to verify in the 2×2 case that U maps B onto a parallelogram $U[B]$ with the same area as B; hence, $\lambda(U[B]) = \lambda(B) = 1$. Consequently, the Lebesgue measure of the rectangle $D[B]$ is the same as the Lebesgue measure of the set $D[U[B]]$. Moreover, an orthogonal matrix rotates a set of points around the origin, leaving all the angles and distances the same. Therefore, the set $A[B]$

has the same Lebesgue measure as the rectangle $D[B]$: $\lambda(A[B]) = \lambda(D[B]) = |\det[D]| = |\det[A]|$. Along the same lines, the following more general result can be shown:

Lemma 4.B.1: *For a $k \times k$ matrix A and a Borel set B in $\mathbb{R}^k$, $\lambda(A[B]) = |\det[A]|\lambda(B)$, where λ is the Lebesgue measure on the Borel sets in $\mathbb{R}^k$.*

Thus, (4.59) now becomes

$$\lim_{\delta_1 \downarrow 0} \lim_{\delta_2 \downarrow 0} \frac{\lambda\left(A\left[G^{-1}(\mathrm{Y}(\delta_1, \delta_2))\right]\right)}{\lambda\left(\mathrm{Y}(\delta_1, \delta_2)\right)}$$

$$= |\det[A]| \lim_{\delta_1 \downarrow 0} \lim_{\delta_2 \downarrow 0} \frac{\lambda\left(G^{-1}(\mathrm{Y}(\delta_1, \delta_2))\right)}{\delta_1 \delta_2} = 1;$$

hence,

$$\lim_{\delta_1 \downarrow 0} \lim_{\delta_2 \downarrow 0} \frac{\lambda\left(G^{-1}(\mathrm{Y}(\delta_1, \delta_2))\right)}{\delta_1 \, \delta_2} = \frac{1}{|\det[A]|}$$

$$= |\det[A^{-1}]| = |\det[J(y_0)]|. \qquad (4.60)$$

Theorem 4.4 follows now from (4.50) and (4.60).

5   The Multivariate Normal Distribution and Its Application to Statistical Inference

5.1. Expectation and Variance of Random Vectors

Multivariate distributions employ the concepts of the expectation vector and variance matrix. The expected "value" or, more precisely, the expectation vector (sometimes also called the "mean vector") of a random vector $X = (x_1, \ldots, x_n)^{\mathrm{T}}$ is defined as the vector of expected values:

$$E(X) \stackrel{\text{def.}}{=} (E(x_1), \ldots, E(x_n))^{\mathrm{T}}.$$

Adopting the convention that the expectation of a random matrix is the matrix of the expectations of its elements, we can define the variance matrix of X as[1]

$$
\begin{aligned}
\mathrm{Var}(X) &\stackrel{\text{def.}}{=} E\left[(X - E(X))(X - E(X))^{\mathrm{T}}\right] \\
&= \begin{pmatrix}
\mathrm{cov}(x_1, x_1) & \mathrm{cov}(x_1, x_2) & \cdots & \mathrm{cov}(x_1, x_n) \\
\mathrm{cov}(x_2, x_1) & \mathrm{cov}(x_2, x_2) & \cdots & \mathrm{cov}(x_2, x_n) \\
\vdots & \vdots & \ddots & \vdots \\
\mathrm{cov}(x_n, x_1) & \mathrm{cov}(x_n, x_2) & \cdots & \mathrm{cov}(x_n, x_n)
\end{pmatrix}.
\end{aligned}
\tag{5.1}
$$

Recall that the diagonal elements of the matrix (5.1) are variances: $\mathrm{cov}(x_j, x_j) = \mathrm{var}(x_j)$. Obviously, a variance matrix is symmetric and positive (semi)definite. Moreover, note that (5.1) can be written as

$$\mathrm{Var}(X) = E[XX^{\mathrm{T}}] - (E[X])(E[X])^{\mathrm{T}}. \tag{5.2}$$

Similarly, the covariance matrix of a pair of random vectors X and Y is the matrix of covariances of their components:[2]

---

[1]   To distinguish the variance of a random variable from the variance matrix of a random vector, the latter will be denoted by Var with capital V.

[2]   The capital C in Cov indicates that this is a covariance matrix rather than a covariance of two random variables.

$$\text{Cov}(X, Y) \overset{\text{def.}}{=} E\left[(X - E(X))(Y - E(Y))^{\mathsf{T}}\right]. \tag{5.3}$$

Note that $\text{Cov}(Y, X) = \text{Cov}(X, Y)^{\mathsf{T}}$. Thus, for each pair X, Y there are two covariance matrices, one being the transpose of the other.

5.2. The Multivariate Normal Distribution

Now let the components of $X = (x_1, \ldots, x_n)^{\mathsf{T}}$ be independent, standard normally distributed random variables. Then, $E(X) = 0 \,(\in \mathbb{R}^n)$ and $\text{Var}(X) = I_n$. Moreover, the joint density $f(x) = f(x_1, \ldots, x_n)$ of X in this case is the product of the standard normal marginal densities:

$$
\begin{aligned}
f(x) = f(x_1, \ldots, x_n) &= \prod_{j=1}^{n} \frac{\exp\left(-x_j^2/2\right)}{\sqrt{2\pi}} \\
&= \frac{\exp\left(-\tfrac{1}{2}\sum_{j=1}^{n} x_j^2\right)}{(\sqrt{2\pi})^n} = \frac{\exp\left(-\tfrac{1}{2}x^{\mathsf{T}}x\right)}{(\sqrt{2\pi})^n}.
\end{aligned}
$$

The shape of this density for the case $n = 2$ is displayed in Figure 5.1.

Next, consider the following linear transformations of $X : Y = \mu + AX$, where $\mu = (\mu_1, \ldots, \mu_n)^{\mathsf{T}}$ is a vector of constants and A is a nonsingular $n \times n$ matrix with nonrandom elements. Because A is nonsingular and therefore invertible, this transformation is a one-to-one mapping with inverse $X = A^{-1}(Y - \mu)$. Then the density function $g(y)$ of Y is equal to

$$
\begin{aligned}
g(y) &= f(x)|\det(\partial x / \partial y)| \\
&= f(A^{-1}y - A^{-1}\mu)|\det(\partial(A^{-1}y - A^{-1}\mu)/\partial y)| \\
&= f(A^{-1}y - A^{-1}\mu)|\det(A^{-1})| = \frac{f(A^{-1}y - A^{-1}\mu)}{|\det(A)|} \\
&= \frac{\exp\left[-\tfrac{1}{2}(y - \mu)^{\mathsf{T}}(A^{-1})^{\mathsf{T}}A^{-1}(y - \mu)\right]}{(\sqrt{2\pi})^n |\det(A)|} \\
&= \frac{\exp\left[-\tfrac{1}{2}(y - \mu)^{\mathsf{T}}(AA^{\mathsf{T}})^{-1}(y - \mu)\right]}{(\sqrt{2\pi})^n \sqrt{|\det(AA^{\mathsf{T}})|}}.
\end{aligned}
$$

Observe that μ is the expectation vector of $Y : E(Y) = \mu + A\,(E(X)) = \mu$. But what is AA^{T}? We know from (5.2) that $\text{Var}(Y) = E[YY^{\mathsf{T}}] - \mu\mu^{\mathsf{T}}$. Therefore, substituting $Y = \mu + AX$ yields

$$
\begin{aligned}
\text{Var}(Y) &= E\left[(\mu + AX)(\mu^{\mathsf{T}} + X^{\mathsf{T}}A^{\mathsf{T}}) - \mu\mu^{\mathsf{T}}\right] \\
&= \mu(E(X^{\mathsf{T}}))A^{\mathsf{T}} + A(E(X))\mu^{\mathsf{T}} + A(E(XX^{\mathsf{T}}))A^{\mathsf{T}} = AA^{\mathsf{T}}
\end{aligned}
$$

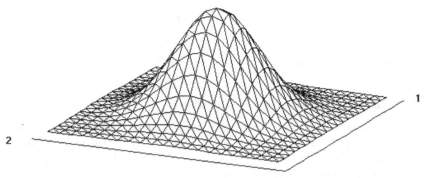

Figure 5.1. The bivariate standard normal density on $[-3, 3] \times [-3, 3]$.

because $E(X) = 0$ and $E[XX^\mathrm{T}] = I_n$. Thus, AA^T is the variance matrix of Y. This argument gives rise to the following definition of the n-variate normal distribution:

Definition 5.1: *Let Y be an $n \times 1$ random vector satisfying $E(Y) = \mu$ and $Var(Y) = \Sigma$, where Σ is nonsingular. Then Y is distributed $N_n(\mu, \Sigma)$ if the density $g(y)$ of Y is of the form*

$$g(y) = \frac{\exp\left[-\frac{1}{2}(y - \mu)^\mathrm{T}\Sigma^{-1}(y - \mu)\right]}{(\sqrt{2\pi})^n \sqrt{\det(\Sigma)}}. \tag{5.4}$$

In the same way as before we can show that a nonsingular (hence one-to-one) linear transformation of a normal distribution is normal itself:

Theorem 5.1: *Let $Z = a + BY$, where Y is distributed $N_n(\mu, \Sigma)$ and B is a nonsingular matrix of constants. Then Z is distributed $N_n(a + B\mu, B\Sigma B^\mathrm{T})$.*

Proof: First, observe that $Z = a + BY$ implies $Y = B^{-1}(Z - a)$. Let $h(z)$ be the density of Z and $g(y)$ the density of Y. Then

$$\begin{aligned}
h(z) &= g(y)|\det(\partial y/\partial z)| \\
&= g(B^{-1}z - B^{-1}a)|\det(\partial(B^{-1}z - B^{-1}a)/\partial z)| \\
&= \frac{g(B^{-1}z - B^{-1}a)}{|\det(B)|} = \frac{g(B^{-1}(z - a))}{\sqrt{\det(BB^\mathrm{T})}} \\
&= \frac{\exp\left[-\frac{1}{2}(B^{-1}(z - a) - \mu)^\mathrm{T}\Sigma^{-1}(B^{-1}(z - a) - \mu)\right]}{(\sqrt{2\pi})^n \sqrt{\det(\Sigma)}\sqrt{\det(BB^\mathrm{T})}} \\
&= \frac{\exp\left[-\frac{1}{2}(z - a - B\mu)^\mathrm{T}(B\Sigma B^\mathrm{T})^{-1}(z - a - B\mu)\right]}{(\sqrt{2\pi})^n \sqrt{\det(B\Sigma B^\mathrm{T})}}.
\end{aligned}$$

Q.E.D.

I will now relax the assumption in Theorem 5.1 that the matrix B is a nonsingular $n \times n$ matrix. This more general version of Theorem 5.1 can be proved using the moment-generating function or the characteristic function of the multivariate normal distribution.

Theorem 5.2: *Let Y be distributed $N_n(\mu, \Sigma)$. Then the moment-generating function of Y is $m(t) = exp(t^T\mu + t^T\Sigma t/2)$, and the characteristic of Y is $\varphi(t) = exp(i \cdot t^T\mu - t^T\Sigma t/2)$.*

Proof: We have

$m(t)$

$$= \int exp[t^Ty] \frac{exp\left[-\frac{1}{2}(y-\mu)^T\Sigma^{-1}(y-\mu)\right]}{(\sqrt{2\pi})^n\sqrt{\det(\Sigma)}} dy$$

$$= \int \frac{exp\left(-\frac{1}{2}[y^T\Sigma^{-1}y - 2\mu^T\Sigma^{-1}y + \mu^T\Sigma^{-1}\mu - 2t^Ty]\right)}{(\sqrt{2\pi})^n\sqrt{\det(\Sigma)}} dy$$

$$= \int \frac{exp\left(-\frac{1}{2}\left[y^T\Sigma^{-1}y - 2(\mu+\Sigma t)^T\Sigma^{-1}y + (\mu+\Sigma t)^T\Sigma^{-1}(\mu+\Sigma t)\right]\right)}{(\sqrt{2\pi})^n\sqrt{\det(\Sigma)}} dy$$

$$\times exp\left(\frac{1}{2}\left[(\mu+\Sigma t)^T\Sigma^{-1}(\mu+\Sigma t) - \mu^T\Sigma^{-1}\mu\right]\right)$$

$$= \int \frac{exp\left(-\frac{1}{2}(y-\mu-\Sigma t)^T\Sigma^{-1}(y-\mu-\Sigma t)\right)}{(\sqrt{2\pi})^n\sqrt{\det(\Sigma)}} dy \times exp\left(t^T\mu + \frac{1}{2}t^T\Sigma t\right).$$

Because the last integral is equal to 1, the result for the moment-generating function follows. The result for the characteristic function follows from $\varphi(t) = m(i \cdot t)$. Q.E.D.

Theorem 5.3: *Theorem 5.1 holds for any linear transformation $Z = a + BY$.*

Proof: Let $Z = a + BY$, where B is $m \times n$. It is easy to verify that the characteristic function of Z is $\varphi_Z(t) = E[exp(i \cdot t^TZ)] = E[exp(i \cdot t^T(a + BY))] = exp(i \cdot t^Ta)E[exp(i \cdot t^TBY)] = exp(i \cdot (a + B\mu)^Tt - \frac{1}{2}t^TB\Sigma B^Tt)$. Theorem 5.3 follows now from Theorem 5.2. Q.E.D.

Note that this result holds regardless of whether the matrix $B\Sigma B^T$ is nonsingular or not. In the latter case the normal distribution involved is called "singular":

Definition 5.2: *An $n \times 1$ random vector Y has a singular $N_n(\mu, \Sigma)$ distribution if its characteristic function is of the form $\varphi_Y(t) = exp(i \cdot t^T\mu - \frac{1}{2}t^T\Sigma t)$ with Σ a singular, positive semidefinite matrix.*

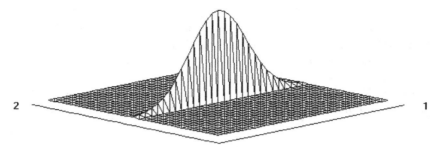

Figure 5.2. Density of a near-singular normal distribution on $[-3, 3] \times [-3, 3]$.

Because of the latter condition the distribution of the random vector Y involved is no longer absolutely continuous, but the form of the characteristic function is the same as in the nonsingular case – and that is all that matters.

For example, let $n = 2$ and

$$\mu = \begin{pmatrix} 0 \\ 0 \end{pmatrix}, \qquad \Sigma = \begin{pmatrix} 1 & 0 \\ 0 & \sigma^2 \end{pmatrix},$$

where $\sigma^2 > 0$ but small. The density of the corresponding $N_2(\mu, \Sigma)$ distribution of $Y = (Y_1, Y_2)^{\mathrm{T}}$ is

$$f(y_1, y_2|\sigma) = \frac{\exp\left(-y_1^2/2\right)}{\sqrt{2\pi}} \times \frac{\exp\left(-y_2^2/(2\sigma^2)\right)}{\sigma\sqrt{2\pi}}. \tag{5.5}$$

Then $\lim_{\sigma\downarrow 0} f(y_1, y_2|\sigma) = 0$ if $y_2 \neq 0$, and $\lim_{\sigma\downarrow 0} f(y_1, y_2|\sigma) = \infty$ if $y_2 = 0$. Thus, a singular multivariate normal distribution does not have a density.

In Figure 5.2 the density (5.5) for the near-singular case $\sigma^2 = 0.00001$ is displayed. The height of the picture is actually rescaled to fit in the box $[-3, 3] \times [-3, 3] \times [-3, 3]$. If we let σ approach zero, the height of the ridge corresponding to the marginal density of Y_1 will increase to infinity.

The next theorem shows that uncorrelated multivariate normally distributed random variables are independent. Thus, although for most distributions uncorrelatedness does not imply independence, for the multivariate normal distribution it does.

Theorem 5.4: *Let X be n-variate normally distributed, and let X_1 and X_2 be subvectors of components of X. If X_1 and X_2 are uncorrelated, that is, $Cov(X_1, X_2) = O$, then X_1 and X_2 are independent.*

Proof: Because X_1 and X_2 cannot have common components, we may without loss of generality assume that $X = (X_1^{\mathrm{T}}, X_2^{\mathrm{T}})^{\mathrm{T}}$, $X_1 \in \mathbb{R}^k$, $X_2 \in \mathbb{R}^m$. Partition the expectation vector and variance matrix of X conformably as

$$E(X) = \begin{pmatrix} \mu_1 \\ \mu_2 \end{pmatrix}, \qquad \mathrm{Var}(X) = \begin{pmatrix} \Sigma_{11} & \Sigma_{12} \\ \Sigma_{21} & \Sigma_{22} \end{pmatrix}.$$

Then $\Sigma_{12} = O$ and $\Sigma_{21} = O$ because they are covariance matrices, and X_1 and X_2 are uncorrelated; hence, the density of X is

$$f(x) = f(x_1, x_2)$$

$$= \frac{\exp\left(-\frac{1}{2}\left[\begin{pmatrix} x_1 \\ x_2 \end{pmatrix} - \begin{pmatrix} \mu_1 \\ \mu_2 \end{pmatrix}\right]^{\mathsf{T}} \begin{bmatrix} \Sigma_{11} & 0 \\ 0 & \Sigma_{22} \end{bmatrix}^{-1} \left[\begin{pmatrix} x_1 \\ x_2 \end{pmatrix} - \begin{pmatrix} \mu_1 \\ \mu_2 \end{pmatrix}\right]\right)}{(\sqrt{2\pi})^n \sqrt{\det\begin{pmatrix} \Sigma_{11} & 0 \\ 0 & \Sigma_{22} \end{pmatrix}}}$$

$$= \frac{\exp\left(-\frac{1}{2}(x_1 - \mu_1)^{\mathsf{T}} \Sigma_{11}^{-1} (x_1 - \mu_1)\right)}{(\sqrt{2\pi})^k \sqrt{\det(\Sigma_{11})}}$$

$$\times \frac{\exp\left(-\frac{1}{2}(x_2 - \mu_2)^{\mathsf{T}} \Sigma_{22}^{-1} (x_2 - \mu_2)\right)}{(\sqrt{2\pi})^m \sqrt{\det(\Sigma_{22})}}.$$

This implies independence of X_1 and X_2.   Q.E.D.

5.3. Conditional Distributions of Multivariate Normal Random Variables

Let Y be a scalar random variable and X be a k-dimensional random vector. Assume that

$$\begin{pmatrix} Y \\ X \end{pmatrix} \sim N_{k+1}\left[\begin{pmatrix} \mu_Y \\ \mu_X \end{pmatrix}, \begin{pmatrix} \Sigma_{YY} & \Sigma_{YX} \\ \Sigma_{XY} & \Sigma_{XX} \end{pmatrix}\right],$$

where $\mu_Y = E(Y)$, $\mu_X = E(X)$, and

$$\Sigma_{YY} = \text{Var}(Y), \ \Sigma_{YX} = \text{Cov}(Y, X)$$
$$= E\big[(Y - E(Y))(X - E(X))^{\mathsf{T}}\big],$$
$$\Sigma_{XY} = \text{Cov}(X, Y) = E(X - E(X))(Y - E(Y))$$
$$= \Sigma_{YX}^{\mathsf{T}}, \ \Sigma_{XX} = \text{Var}(X).$$

To derive the conditional distribution of Y, given X, let $U = Y - \alpha - \beta^{\mathsf{T}} X$, where α is a scalar constant and β is a $k \times 1$ vector of constants such that $E(U) = 0$ and U and X are independent. It follows from Theorem 5.1 that

$$\begin{pmatrix} U \\ X \end{pmatrix} = \begin{pmatrix} -\alpha \\ 0 \end{pmatrix} + \begin{pmatrix} 1 & -B^{\mathsf{T}} \\ 0 & I_k \end{pmatrix} \begin{pmatrix} Y \\ X \end{pmatrix}$$

$$\sim N_{k+1}\left[\begin{pmatrix} -\alpha + \mu_Y - \beta^{\mathsf{T}}\mu_X \\ \mu_X \end{pmatrix},\right.$$

$$\left. \begin{pmatrix} 1 & -\beta^{\mathsf{T}} \\ 0 & I_k \end{pmatrix} \begin{pmatrix} \Sigma_{YY} & \Sigma_{YX} \\ \Sigma_{XY} & \Sigma_{XX} \end{pmatrix} \begin{pmatrix} 1 & 0^{\mathsf{T}} \\ -\beta & I_k \end{pmatrix}\right].$$

The variance matrix involved can be rewritten as

$$\operatorname{Var}\begin{pmatrix} U \\ X \end{pmatrix} = \begin{pmatrix} \Sigma_{YY} - \Sigma_{YX}\beta - \beta^{\mathrm{T}}\Sigma_{XY} + \beta^{\mathrm{T}}\Sigma_{XX}\beta & \Sigma_{YX} - \beta^{\mathrm{T}}\Sigma_{XX} \\ \Sigma_{XY} - \Sigma_{XX}\beta & \Sigma_{XX} \end{pmatrix}.$$

$$(5.6)$$

Next, choose β such that U and X are uncorrelated and hence independent. In view of (5.6), a necessary and sufficient condition for that is $\Sigma_{XY} - \Sigma_{XX}\beta = 0$; hence, $\beta = \Sigma_{XX}^{-1}\Sigma_{XY}$. Moreover, $E(U) = 0$ if $\alpha = \mu_Y - \beta^{\mathrm{T}}\mu_X$. Then

$$\Sigma_{YY} - \Sigma_{YX}\beta - \beta^{\mathrm{T}}\Sigma_{XY} + \beta^{\mathrm{T}}\Sigma_{XX}\beta = \Sigma_{YY} - \Sigma_{YX}\Sigma_{XX}^{-1}\Sigma_{XY},$$
$$\Sigma_{YX} - \beta^{\mathrm{T}}\Sigma_{XX} = 0^{\mathrm{T}}, \ \Sigma_{XY} - \Sigma_{XX}\beta = 0,$$

and consequently

$$\begin{pmatrix} U \\ X \end{pmatrix} \sim N_{k+1}\left[\begin{pmatrix} 0 \\ \mu_X \end{pmatrix}, \begin{pmatrix} \Sigma_{YY} - \Sigma_{YX}\Sigma_{XX}^{-1}\Sigma_{XY} & 0^{\mathrm{T}} \\ 0 & \Sigma_{XX} \end{pmatrix}\right]. \qquad (5.7)$$

Thus, U and X are independent normally distributed, and consequently $E(U|X) = E(U) = 0$. Because $Y = \alpha + \beta^{\mathrm{T}}X + U$, we now have $E(Y|X) = \alpha + \beta^{\mathrm{T}}(E(X|X)) + E(U|X) = \alpha + \beta^{\mathrm{T}}X$. Moreover, it is easy to verify from (5.7) that the conditional density of Y, given $X = x$, is

$$f(y|x) = \frac{\exp\left[-\frac{1}{2}(y - \alpha - \beta^{\mathrm{T}}x)^2/\sigma_u^2\right]}{\sigma_u\sqrt{2\pi}},$$
$$\text{where} \quad \sigma_u^2 = \Sigma_{YY} - \Sigma_{YX}\Sigma_{XX}^{-1}\Sigma_{XY}.$$

Furthermore, note that σ_u^2 is just the conditional variance of Y, given X:

$$\sigma_u^2 = \operatorname{var}(Y|X) \stackrel{\text{def.}}{=} E\left[(Y - E(Y|X))^2|X\right].$$

These results are summarized in the following theorem.

Theorem 5.5: *Let*

$$\begin{pmatrix} Y \\ X \end{pmatrix} \sim N_{k+1}\left[\begin{pmatrix} \mu_Y \\ \mu_X \end{pmatrix}, \begin{pmatrix} \Sigma_{YY} & \Sigma_{YX} \\ \Sigma_{XY} & \Sigma_{XX} \end{pmatrix}\right],$$

where $Y \in \mathbb{R}$, $X \in \mathbb{R}^k$, and Σ_{XX} is nonsingular. Then, conditionally on X, Y is normally distributed with conditional expectation $E(Y|X) = \alpha + \beta^{\mathrm{T}}X$, where $\beta = \Sigma_{XX}^{-1}\Sigma_{XY}$ and $\alpha = \mu_Y - \beta^{\mathrm{T}}\mu_X$, and conditional variance $\operatorname{var}(Y|X) = \Sigma_{YY} - \Sigma_{YX}\Sigma_{XX}^{-1}\Sigma_{XY}.$

The result in Theorem 5.5 is the basis for linear regression analysis. Suppose that Y measures an economic activity that is partly caused or influenced by other economic variables measured by the components of the random vector X. In applied economics the relation between Y, called the dependent variable, and the components of X, called the independent variables or the regressors, is often modeled linearly as $Y = \alpha + \beta^{\mathrm{T}} X + U$, where α is the intercept, β is the vector of slope parameters (also called regression coefficients), and U is an error term that is usually assumed to be independent of X and normally $N(0, \sigma^2)$ distributed. Theorem 5.5 shows that if Y and X are jointly normally distributed, then such a linear relation between Y and X exists.

5.4. Independence of Linear and Quadratic Transformations of Multivariate Normal Random Variables

Let X be distributed $N_n(0, I_n)$ – that is, X is n-variate, standard, normally distributed. Consider the linear transformations $Y = BX$, where B is a $k \times n$ matrix of constants, and $Z = CX$, where C is an $m \times n$ matrix of constants. It follows from Theorem 5.4 that

$$\begin{pmatrix} Y \\ Z \end{pmatrix} \sim N_{k+m}\left[\begin{pmatrix} 0 \\ 0 \end{pmatrix}, \begin{pmatrix} BB^{\mathrm{T}} & BC^{\mathrm{T}} \\ CB^{\mathrm{T}} & CC^{\mathrm{T}} \end{pmatrix} \right].$$

Then Y and Z are uncorrelated and therefore independent if and only if $CB^{\mathrm{T}} = O$. More generally we have

Theorem 5.6: *Let X be distributed $N_n(0, I_n)$, and consider the linear transformations $Y = b + BX$, where b is a $k \times 1$ vector and B a $k \times n$ matrix of constants, and $Z = c + CX$, where c is an $m \times 1$ vector and C an $m \times n$ matrix of constants. Then Y and Z are independent if and only if $BC^{\mathrm{T}} = O$.*

This result can be used to set forth conditions for independence of linear and quadratic transformations of standard normal random vectors:

Theorem 5.7: *Let X and Y be defined as in Theorem 5.6, and let $Z = X^{\mathrm{T}} CX$, where C is a symmetric $n \times n$ matrix of constants. Then Y and Z are independent if $BC = O$.*

Proof: First, note that the latter condition only makes sense if C is singular, for otherwise $B = O$. Thus, let rank $(C) = m < n$. We can write $C = Q\Lambda Q^{\mathrm{T}}$, where Λ is a diagonal matrix with the eigenvalues of C on the diagonal, and Q is the orthogonal matrix of corresponding eigenvectors. Let $V = Q^{\mathrm{T}} X$, which is $N_n(0, I_n)$ distributed because $QQ^{\mathrm{T}} = I_n$. Because $n - m$ eigenvalues of C are zero, we can partition Q, Λ, and V such that

$$Q = (Q_1, Q_2), \qquad \Lambda = \begin{pmatrix} \Lambda_1 & O \\ O & O \end{pmatrix},$$

$$V = \begin{pmatrix} V_1 \\ V_2 \end{pmatrix} = \begin{pmatrix} Q_1^{\mathrm{T}} X \\ Q_2^{\mathrm{T}} X \end{pmatrix}, \qquad Z = V_1^{\mathrm{T}} \Lambda_1 V_1,$$

where Λ_1 is the diagonal matrix with the m nonzero eigenvalues of C on the diagonal. Then

$$BC = B(Q_1, Q_2)\begin{pmatrix} \Lambda_1 & O \\ O & O \end{pmatrix}\begin{pmatrix} Q_1^{\mathsf{T}} \\ Q_2^{\mathsf{T}} \end{pmatrix} = BQ_1\Lambda_1 Q_1^{\mathsf{T}} = O$$

implies $BQ_1\Lambda_1 = BQ_1\Lambda_1 Q_1^{\mathsf{T}}Q_1 = O$ (because $Q^{\mathsf{T}}Q = I_n$ implies $Q_1^{\mathsf{T}}Q_1 = I_m$), which in turn implies that $BQ_1 = O$. The latter is a sufficient condition for the independence of V_1 and Y and hence of the independence of Z and Y. Q.E.D.

Finally, consider the conditions for independence of two quadratic forms of standard normal random vectors:

Theorem 5.8: *Let $X \sim N_n(0, I_n)$, $Z_1 = X^{\mathsf{T}}AX$, and $Z_2 = X^{\mathsf{T}}BX$, where A and B are symmetric $n \times n$ matrices of constants. Then Z_1 and Z_2 are independent if and only if $AB = O$.*

The proof of Theorem 5.8 is not difficult but is quite lengthy; it is therefore given in Appendix 5.A.

5.5. Distributions of Quadratic Forms of Multivariate Normal Random Variables

As we will see in Section 5.6, quadratic forms of multivariate normal random variables play a key role in statistical testing theory. The two most important results are stated in Theorems 5.9 and 5.10:

Theorem 5.9: *Let X be distributed $N_n(0, \Sigma)$, where Σ is nonsingular. Then $X^{\mathsf{T}}\Sigma^{-1}X$ is distributed as χ_n^2.*

Proof: Denote $Y = (Y_1, \ldots, Y_n)^{\mathsf{T}} = \Sigma^{-\frac{1}{2}}X$. Then Y is n-variate, standard normally distributed; hence, $Y_1, \ldots, Y_n$ are independent identically distributed (i.i.d.) $N(0, 1)$, and thus, $X^{\mathsf{T}}\Sigma^{-1}X = Y^{\mathsf{T}}Y = \Sigma_{j=1}^{n}Y_j^2 \sim \chi_n^2$. Q.E.D.

The next theorem employs the concept of an *idempotent* matrix. Recall from Appendix I that a square matrix M is idempotent if $M^2 = M$. If M is also symmetric, we can write $M = Q\Lambda Q^{\mathsf{T}}$, where Λ is the diagonal matrix of eigenvalues of M and Q is the corresponding orthogonal matrix of eigenvectors. Then $M^2 = M$ implies $\Lambda^2 = \Lambda$; hence, the eigenvalues of M are either 1 or 0. If all eigenvalues are 1, then $\Lambda = I$; hence, $M = I$. Thus, the only nonsingular symmetric idempotent matrix is the unit matrix. Consequently, the concept of a symmetric idempotent matrix is only meaningful if the matrix involved is singular.

The rank of a symmetric idempotent matrix M equals the number of nonzero eigenvalues; hence, trace$(M) = $ trace$(Q \Lambda Q^{\mathrm{T}}) = $ trace$(\Lambda Q^{\mathrm{T}} Q) = $ trace$(\Lambda) = $ rank$(\Lambda) = $ rank(M), where trace(M) is defined as the sum of the diagonal elements of M. Note that we have used the property trace$(AB) = $ trace(BA) for conformable matrices A and B.

Theorem 5.10: *Let X be distributed $N_n(0, I)$, and let M be a symmetric idempotent $n \times n$ matrix of constants with rank k. Then $X^{\mathrm{T}} M X$ is distributed χ_k^2.*

Proof: We can write

$$ M = Q \begin{pmatrix} I_k & O \\ O & O \end{pmatrix} Q^{\mathrm{T}}, $$

where Q is the orthogonal matrix of eigenvectors. Because $Y = (Y_1, \dots, Y_n)^{\mathrm{T}} = Q^{\mathrm{T}} X \sim N_n(0, I)$, we now have

$$ X^{\mathrm{T}} M X = Y^{\mathrm{T}} \begin{pmatrix} I_k & O \\ O & O \end{pmatrix} Y = \sum_{j=1}^{k} Y_j^2 \sim \chi_k^2. $$

Q.E.D.

5.6. Applications to Statistical Inference under Normality

5.6.1. Estimation

Statistical inference is concerned with parameter estimation and parameter inference. The latter will be discussed next in this section.

In a broad sense, an estimator of a parameter is a function of the data that serves as an approximation of the parameter involved. For example, if $X_1, X_2, \dots, X_n$ is a random sample from the $N(\mu, \sigma^2)$-distribution, then the sample mean $\bar{X} = (1/n) \sum_{j=1}^{n} X_j$ may serve as an estimator of the unknown parameter μ (the population mean). More formally, given a data set $\{X_1, X_2, \dots, X_n\}$ for which the joint distribution function depends on an unknown parameter (vector) θ, an estimator of θ is a Borel-measurable function $\hat{\theta} = g_n(X_1, \dots, X_n)$ of the data that serves as an approximation of θ. Of course, the function g_n should not itself depend on unknown parameters.

In principle, we can construct many functions of the data that may serve as an approximation of an unknown parameter. For example, one may consider using X_1 only as an estimator of μ. How does one decide which function of the data should be used. To be able to select among the many candidates for an estimator, we need to formulate some desirable properties of estimators. The first one is "unbiasedness":

Definition 5.3: *An estimator $\hat{\theta}$ of a parameter (vector) θ is unbiased if $E[\hat{\theta}] = \theta$.*

The unbiasedness property is not specific to a particular value of the parameter involved but should hold for all possible values of this parameter in the sense that if we draw a new data set from the same type of distribution but with a different parameter value, the estimator should stay unbiased. In other words, if the joint distribution function of the data is $F_n(x_1, \ldots, x_n|\theta)$, where $\theta \in \Theta$ is an unknown parameter (vector) in a parameter space Θ (i.e., the space of all possible values of θ), and $\hat{\theta} = g_n(X_1, \ldots, X_n)$ is an unbiased estimator of θ, then $\int g_n(x_1, \ldots, x_n)dF_n(x_1, \ldots, x_n|\theta) = \theta$ for all $\theta \in \Theta$.

Note that in the preceding example both $\bar{X}$ and X_1 are unbiased estimators of μ. Thus, we need a further criterion in order to select an estimator. This criterion is efficiency:

Definition 5.4: *An unbiased estimator $\hat{\theta}$ of an unknown scalar parameter θ is efficient if, for all other unbiased estimators $\tilde{\theta}$, $var(\hat{\theta}) \leq var(\tilde{\theta})$. In the case in which θ is a parameter vector, the latter reads: $Var(\tilde{\theta}) - Var(\hat{\theta})$ is a positive semidefinite matrix.*

In our example, X_1 is not an efficient estimator of μ because $var(X_1) = \sigma^2$ and $var(\bar{X}) = \sigma^2/n$. But is $\bar{X}$ efficient? To answer this question, we need to derive the minimum variance of an unbiased estimator as follows. For notational convenience, stack the data in a vector X. Thus, in the univariate case $X = (X_1, X_2, \ldots, X_n)^{\mathrm{T}}$, and in the multivariate case $X = (X_1^{\mathrm{T}}, \ldots, X_n^{\mathrm{T}})^{\mathrm{T}}$. Assume that the joint distribution of X is absolutely continuous with density $f_n(x|\theta)$, which for each x is twice continuously differentiable in θ. Moreover, let $\hat{\theta} = g_n(X)$ be an unbiased estimator of θ. Then

$$\int g_n(x) f_n(x|\theta)dx = \theta. \tag{5.8}$$

Furthermore, assume for the time being that θ is a scalar, and let

$$\frac{d}{d\theta} \int g_n(x) f_n(x|\theta)dx = \int g_n(x)\frac{d}{d\theta} f_n(x|\theta)dx. \tag{5.9}$$

Conditions for (5.9) can be derived from the mean-value theorem and the dominated convergence theorem. In particular, (5.9) is true for all θ in an open set Θ if

$$\int |g_n(x)|\sup_{\theta \in \Theta}|d^2 f_n(x|\theta)/(d\theta)^2|dx < \infty.$$

Then it follows from (5.8) and (5.9) that

$$\int g_n(x) \left[\frac{d}{d\theta} \ln(f_n(x|\theta)) \right] f_n(x|\theta)dx = \int g_n(x) \frac{d}{d\theta} f_n(x|\theta)dx = 1.$$

$$(5.10)$$

Similarly, if

$$\frac{d}{d\theta} \int f_n(x|\theta)dx = \int \frac{d}{d\theta} f_n(x|\theta)dx, \qquad (5.11)$$

which is true for all θ in an open set Θ for which $\int \sup_{\theta \in \Theta} |d^2 f_n(x|\theta)/(d\theta)^2| dx < \infty$, then, because $\int f_n(x|\theta)dx = 1$, we have

$$\int \left[\frac{d}{d\theta} \ln(f_n(x|\theta)) \right] f_n(x|\theta)dx = \int \frac{d}{d\theta} f_n(x|\theta)dx = 0. \qquad (5.12)$$

If we let $\hat{\beta} = d \ln(f_n(X|\theta))/d\theta$, it follows now from (5.10) that $E[\hat{\theta} \cdot \hat{\beta}] = 1$ and from (5.12) that $E[\hat{\beta}] = 0$. Therefore, $\text{cov}(\hat{\theta}, \hat{\beta}) = E[\hat{\theta} \cdot \hat{\beta}] - E[\hat{\theta}]E[\hat{\beta}] = 1$. Because by the Cauchy–Schwartz inequality, $|\text{cov}(\hat{\theta}, \hat{\beta})| \leq \sqrt{\text{var}(\hat{\theta})}\sqrt{\text{var}(\hat{\beta})}$, we now have that $\text{var}(\hat{\theta}) \geq 1/\text{var}(\hat{\beta})$:

$$\text{var}(\hat{\theta}) \geq \frac{1}{E\left([d \ln(f_n(X|\theta))/d\theta]^2\right)}. \qquad (5.13)$$

This result is known as the Cramer–Rao inequality, and the right-hand side of (5.13) is called the Cramer–Rao lower bound. More generally, we have the following:

Theorem 5.11: *(Cramer–Rao) Let $f_n(x|\theta)$ be the joint density of the data stacked in a vector X, where θ is a parameter vector. Let $\hat{\theta}$ be an unbiased estimator of θ. Then $Var(\hat{\theta}) = (E[(\partial \ln(f_n(X|\theta)/\partial\theta^{\mathsf{T}})(\partial \ln(f_n(X|\theta)/\partial\theta)])^{-1} + D$, where D is a positive semidefinite matrix.*

Now let us return to our problem of whether the sample mean $\bar{X}$ of a random sample from the $N(\mu, \sigma^2)$ distribution is an efficient estimator of μ. In this case the joint density of the sample is $f_n(x|\mu, \sigma^2) = \prod_{j=1}^n \exp(-\frac{1}{2}(x_j - \mu)^2/\sigma^2)/\sqrt{\sigma^2 2\pi}$; hence, $\partial \ln(f_n(X|\mu, \sigma^2))/\partial\mu = \sum_{j=1}^n (X_j - \mu)/\sigma^2$, and thus the Cramer–Rao lower bound is

$$\frac{1}{E\left[(\partial \ln(f_n(X|\mu, \sigma^2))/\partial\mu)^2\right]} = \sigma^2/n. \qquad (5.14)$$

This is just the variance of the sample mean $\bar{X}$; hence, $\bar{X}$ is an efficient estimator of μ. This result holds for the multivariate case as well:

Theorem 5.12: *Let $X_1, X_2, \ldots, X_n$ be a random sample from the $N_k[\mu, \Sigma]$ distribution. Then the sample mean $\bar{X} = (1/n) \sum_{j=1}^{n} X_j$ is an unbiased and efficient estimator of μ.*

The sample variance of a random sample $X_1, X_2, \ldots, X_n$ from a univariate distribution with expectation μ and variance σ^2 is defined by

$$S^2 = (1/(n-1)) \sum_{j=1}^{n} (X_j - \bar{X})^2, \tag{5.15}$$

which serves as an estimator of σ^2. An alternative form of the sample variance is

$$\hat{\sigma}^2 = (1/n) \sum_{j=1}^{n} (X_j - \bar{X})^2 = \frac{n-1}{n} S^2, \tag{5.16}$$

but as I will show for the case of a random sample from the $N(\mu, \sigma^2)$ distribution, (5.15) is an unbiased estimator and (5.16) is not:

Theorem 5.13: *Let S^2 be the sample variance of a random sample $X_1, \ldots, X_n$ from the $N(\mu, \sigma^2)$ distribution. Then $(n-1)S^2/\sigma^2$ is distributed χ^2_{n-1}.*

The proof of Theorem 5.13 is left as an exercise. Because the expectation of the χ^2_{n-1} distribution is $n - 1$, this result implies that $E(S^2) = \sigma^2$, whereas by (5.16), $E(\hat{\sigma}^2) = \sigma^2(n-1)/n$. Moreover, given that the variance of the χ^2_{n-1} distribution is $2(n-1)$, it follows from Theorem 5.13 that

$$\text{var}(S^2) = 2\sigma^4/(n-1). \tag{5.17}$$

The Cramer–Rao lower bound for an unbiased estimator of σ^2 is $2\sigma^4/n$; thus, S^2 is not efficient, but it is close if n is large.

For a random sample $X_1, X_2, \ldots, X_n$ from a multivariate distribution with expectation vector μ and variance matrix Σ the sample variance matrix takes the form

$$\hat{\Sigma} = (1/(n-1)) \sum_{j=1}^{n} (X_j - \bar{X})(X_j - \bar{X})^{\mathsf{T}}. \tag{5.18}$$

This is also an unbiased estimator of $\Sigma = \text{Var}(X_j)$ even if the distribution involved is not normal.

5.6.2. Confidence Intervals

Because estimators are approximations of unknown parameters, the question of how close they are arises. I will answer this question for the sample mean and the sample variance in the case of a random sample $X_1, X_2, \ldots, X_n$ from the $N(\mu, \sigma^2)$ distribution.

It is almost trivial that $\bar{X} \sim N(\mu, \sigma^2/n)$; hence,

$$\sqrt{n}(\bar{X} - \mu)/\sigma \sim N(0, 1). \tag{5.19}$$

Therefore, for given $\alpha \in (0, 1)$ there exists a $\beta > 0$ such that

$$P[|\bar{X} - \mu| \le \beta\sigma/\sqrt{n}] = P[|\sqrt{n}(\bar{X} - \mu)/\sigma| \le \beta]$$

$$= \int_{-\beta}^{\beta} \frac{\exp(-u^2/2)}{\sqrt{2\pi}} du = 1 - \alpha. \tag{5.20}$$

For example, if we choose $\alpha = 0.05$, then $\beta = 1.96$ (see Appendix IV, Table IV.3), and thus in this case

$$P[\bar{X} - 1.96\sigma/\sqrt{n} \le \mu \le \bar{X} + 1.96\sigma/\sqrt{n}] = 0.95.$$

The interval $[\bar{X} - 1.96\sigma/\sqrt{n}, \bar{X} + 1.96\sigma/\sqrt{n}]$ is called the 95% confidence interval of μ. If σ is known, then this interval can be computed and will tell us how close $\bar{X}$ and μ are with a margin of error of 5%. But in general σ is not known, so how do we proceed then?

To solve this problem, we need the following corollary of Theorem 5.7:

Theorem 5.14: *Let $X_1, X_2, \ldots, X_n$ be a random sample from the $N(\mu, \sigma^2)$ distribution. Then the sample mean $\bar{X}$ and the sample variance S^2 are independent.*

Proof: Observe, for instance, that $X_* = ((X_1 - \mu)/\sigma, (X_2 - \mu)/\sigma, \ldots, (X_n - \mu)/\sigma)^{\mathrm{T}} \sim N_n(0, I_n)$, $\bar{X} = \mu + (\sigma/n, \ldots, \sigma/n)X_* = b + BX_*$, and

$$\begin{pmatrix} (X_1 - \bar{X})/\sigma \\ \vdots \\ (X_n - \bar{X})/\sigma \end{pmatrix} = \left(I - \frac{1}{n} \begin{pmatrix} 1 \\ 1 \\ \vdots \\ 1 \end{pmatrix} (1, 1, \ldots, 1) \right) X_* = CX_*.$$

The latter expression implies that $(n - 1)S^2/\sigma^2 = X_*^{\mathrm{T}}C^{\mathrm{T}}CX_* = X_*^{\mathrm{T}}C^2 X_* = X_*^{\mathrm{T}}CX_*$ because C is symmetric and idempotent with $\operatorname{rank}(C) = \operatorname{trace}(C) = n - 1$. Therefore, by Theorem 5.7, the sample mean and the sample variance are independent if $BC = 0$, which in the present case is equivalent to the condition $CB^{\mathrm{T}} = 0$. The latter is easily verified as follows:

$$CB^{\mathrm{T}} = \frac{\sigma}{n} \left(I - \frac{1}{n} \begin{pmatrix} 1 \\ 1 \\ \vdots \\ 1 \end{pmatrix} (1, \ldots, 1) \right) \begin{pmatrix} 1 \\ 1 \\ \vdots \\ 1 \end{pmatrix} = \frac{\sigma}{n} \left(\begin{pmatrix} 1 \\ 1 \\ \vdots \\ 1 \end{pmatrix} - \frac{1}{n} \begin{pmatrix} 1 \\ 1 \\ \vdots \\ 1 \end{pmatrix} n \right) = 0$$

Q.E.D.

It follows now from (5.19), Theorems 5.13 and 5.14, and the definition of the Student's t distribution that

Theorem 5.15: *Under the conditions of Theorem 5.14, $\sqrt{n}(\bar{X} - \mu)/S \sim t_{n-1}$.*

Recall from Chapter 4 that the t_{n-1} distribution has density

$$h_{n-1}(x) = \frac{\Gamma(n/2)}{\sqrt{(n-1)\pi} \, \Gamma((n-1)/2)(1 + x^2/(n-1))^{n/2}}, \tag{5.21}$$

where $\Gamma(y) = \int_0^\infty x^{y-1} \exp(-x)dx$, $y > 0$. Thus, as in (5.20), for each $\alpha \in (0, 1)$ and sample size n there exists a $\beta_n > 0$ such that

$$P[|\bar{X} - \mu| \le \beta_n S/\sqrt{n}] = \int_{-\beta_n}^{\beta_n} h_{n-1}(u)du = 1 - \alpha; \tag{5.22}$$

hence, $[\bar{X} - \beta_n S/\sqrt{n}, \bar{X} + \beta_n S/\sqrt{n}]$ is now the $(1 - \alpha) \times 100\%$ confidence interval of μ.

Similarly, on the basis of Theorem 5.13 we can construct confidence intervals of σ^2. Recall from Chapter 4 that the χ^2_{n-1} distribution has density

$$g_{n-1}(x) = \frac{x^{(n-1)/2-1} \exp(-x/2)}{\Gamma((n-1)/2)2^{(n-1)/2}}.$$

For a given $\alpha \in (0, 1)$ and sample size n we can choose $\beta_{1,n} < \beta_{2,n}$ such that

$$P\left[(n-1)S^2/\beta_{2,n} \le \sigma^2 \le (n-1)S^2/\beta_{1,n}\right]$$
$$= P\left[\beta_{1,n} \le (n-1)S^2/\sigma^2 \le \beta_{2,n}\right]$$
$$= \int_{\beta_{1,n}}^{\beta_{2,n}} g_{n-1}(u)du = 1 - \alpha. \tag{5.23}$$

There are different ways to choose $\beta_{1,n}$ and $\beta_{2,n}$ such that the last equality in (5.23) holds. Clearly, the optimal choice is such that $\beta_{1,n}^{-1} - \beta_{2,n}^{-1}$ is minimal because it will yield the smallest confidence interval, but that is computationally complicated. Therefore, in practice $\beta_{1,n}$ and $\beta_{2,n}$ are often chosen such that

$$\int_0^{\beta_{1,n}} g_{n-1}(u)du = \alpha/2, \quad \int_{\beta_{2,n}}^\infty g_{n-1}(u)du = \alpha/2. \tag{5.24}$$

Appendix IV contains tables from which you can look up the values of the β's in (5.20) and (5.22) for $\alpha \times 100\% = 5\%$ and $\alpha \times 100\% = 10\%$. These percentages are called significance levels (see the next section).

5.6.3. Testing Parameter Hypotheses

Suppose you consider starting a business to sell a new product in the United States such as a European car that is not yet being imported there. To determine whether there is a market for this car in the United States, you have randomly selected n persons from the population of potential buyers of this car. Each person j in the sample is asked how much he or she would be willing to pay for this car. Let the answer be Y_j. Moreover, suppose that the cost of importing this car is a fixed amount Z per car. Denote $X_j = \ln(Y_j/Z)$, and assume that X_j is $N(\mu, \sigma^2)$ distributed. If $\mu > 0$, then your planned car import business will be profitable; otherwise, you should forget about this idea.

To decide whether $\mu > 0$ or $\mu \le 0$, you need a decision rule based on the random sample $X = (X_1, X_2, \ldots, X_n)^{\mathrm{T}}$. Any decision rule takes the following form. Given a subset C of $\mathbb{R}^n$, to be determined below in this section, decide that $\mu > 0$ if $X \in C$, and decide that $\mu \le 0$ if $X \notin C$. Thus, you decide that the hypothesis $\mu \le 0$ is true if $I(X \in C) = 0$, and you decide that the hypothesis $\mu > 0$ is true if $I(X \in C) = 1$. In this case the hypothesis $\mu \le 0$ is called the *null hypothesis*, which is usually denoted by $H_0 : \mu \le 0$, and the hypothesis $\mu > 0$ is called the *alternative hypothesis* and is denoted by $H_1 : \mu > 0$. The procedure itself is called a *statistical test*.

This decision rule yields two types of errors. In the first one, called the *Type I error*, you decide that H_1 is true whereas in reality H_0 is true. In the other error, called the *Type II error*, H_0 is considered to be true whereas in reality H_1 is true. Both errors come with costs. If the Type I error occurs, you will incorrectly assume your car import business to be profitable, and thus you will lose your investment if you start up your business. If the Type II error occurs, you will forgo a profitable business opportunity. Clearly, the Type I error is the more serious of the two.

Now choose C such that $X \in C$ if and only if $\sqrt{n}(\bar{X}/S) > \beta$ for some fixed $\beta > 0$. Then

$$
\begin{aligned}
P[X \in C] &= P[\sqrt{n}(\bar{X}/S) > \beta] = P[\sqrt{n}(\bar{X} - \mu)/S + \sqrt{n}\mu/S > \beta] \\
&= P[\sqrt{n}(\bar{X} - \mu)/\sigma + \sqrt{n}\mu/\sigma > \beta \cdot S/\sigma] \\
&= \int_{-\infty}^{\infty} P[S/\sigma < (u + \sqrt{n}\mu/\sigma)/\beta] \exp[-u^2/2]/\sqrt{2\pi}\, du,
\end{aligned}
$$

$$(5.25)$$

where the last equality follows from Theorem 5.14 and (5.19). If $\mu \le 0$, this probability is that of a Type I error. Clearly, the probability (5.25) is an increasing function of μ; hence, the maximum probability of a Type I error is obtained for $\mu = 0$. But if $\mu = 0$, then it follows from Theorem 5.15 that $\sqrt{n}(\bar{X}/S) \sim t_{n-1}$; hence,

$$\max_{\mu \leq 0} P[X \in C] = \int_{\beta}^{\infty} h_{n-1}(u)du = \alpha, \tag{5.26}$$

for instance, where h_{n-1} is the density of the t_{n-1} distribution (see (5.21)). The probability (5.26) is called the *size* of the test of the null hypothesis involved, which is the maximum risk of a Type I error, and $\alpha \times 100\%$ is called the *significance level* of the test. Depending on how risk averse you are, you have to choose a size $\alpha \in (0, 1)$, and therefore $\beta = \beta_n$ must be chosen such that $\int_{\beta_n}^{\infty} h_{n-1}(u)du = \alpha$. This value β_n is called the *critical value* of the test involved, and because it is based on the distribution of $\sqrt{n}(\bar{X}/S)$, the latter is considered the test statistic involved. Moreover, $\alpha \times 100\%$ is called the *significance level* of the test.

If we replace β in (5.25) by β_n, 1 minus the probability of a Type II error is a function of $\mu/\sigma > 0$:

$$\rho_n(\mu/\sigma) = \int_{-\sqrt{n}\mu/\sigma}^{\infty} P[S/\sigma < (u + \sqrt{n}\mu/\sigma)/\beta_n] \frac{\exp(-u^2/2)}{\sqrt{2\pi}} du,$$

$$\mu > 0. \tag{5.27}$$

This function is called the *power function*, which is the probability of correctly rejecting the null hypothesis H_0 in favor of the alternative hypothesis H_1. Consequently, $1 - \rho_n(\mu/\sigma)$, $\mu > 0$, is the probability of a Type II error.

The test in this example is called a *t-test* because the critical value β_n is derived from the *t*-distribution.

A test is said to be *consistent* if the power function converges to 1 as $n \to \infty$ for all values of the parameter(s) under the alternative hypothesis. Using the results in the next chapter, one can show that the preceding test is consistent:

$$\lim_{n \to \infty} \rho_n(\mu/\sigma) = 1 \quad \text{if } \mu > 0. \tag{5.28}$$

Now let us consider the test of the null hypothesis $H_0 : \mu = 0$ against the alternative hypothesis $H_1: \mu \neq 0$. Under the null hypothesis, $\sqrt{n}(\bar{X}/S) \sim t_{n-1}$ exactly. Given the size $\alpha \in (0, 1)$, choose the critical value $\beta_n > 0$ as in (5.22). Then H_0 is accepted if $|\sqrt{n}(\bar{X}/S)| \leq \beta_n$ and rejected in favor of H_1 if $|\sqrt{n}(\bar{X}/S)| > \beta_n$. The power function of this test is

$$\rho_n(\mu/\sigma) = \int_{-\infty}^{\infty} P[S/\sigma < |u + \sqrt{n}\mu/\sigma|/\beta_n] \exp[-u^2/2]/\sqrt{2\pi} du,$$

$$\mu \neq 0. \tag{5.29}$$

This test is known as is the two-sided t-test with significance level $\alpha \times 100\%$. The critical values β_n for the 5% and 10% significance levels can be found in Table IV.1 in Appendix IV. Also, this test is consistent:

$$\lim_{n \to \infty} \rho_n(\mu/\sigma) = 1 \quad \text{if } \mu \neq 0. \tag{5.30}$$

5.7. Applications to Regression Analysis

5.7.1. The Linear Regression Model

Consider a random sample $Z_j = (Y_j, X_j^{\mathrm{T}})^{\mathrm{T}}, j = 1, 2, \ldots, n$ from a k-variate, nonsingular normal distribution, where $Y_j \in \mathbb{R}$, $X_j \in \mathbb{R}^{k-1}$. We have seen in Section 5.3 that one can write

$$Y_j = \alpha + X_j^{\mathrm{T}}\beta + U_j, U_j \sim N(0, \sigma^2), \quad j = 1, \ldots, n, \tag{5.31}$$

where $U_j = Y_j - E[Y_j|X_j]$ is independent of X_j. This is the classical linear regression model, where Y_j is the dependent variable, X_j is the vector of independent variables, also called the regressors, and U_j is the error term. This model is widely used in empirical econometrics – even in the case in which X_j is not known to be normally distributed.

If we let

$$Y = \begin{pmatrix} Y_1 \\ \vdots \\ Y_n \end{pmatrix}, \qquad X = \begin{pmatrix} 1 & X_1^{\mathrm{T}} \\ \vdots & \vdots \\ 1 & X_n^{\mathrm{T}} \end{pmatrix}, \qquad \theta_0 = \begin{pmatrix} \alpha \\ \beta \end{pmatrix}, \qquad U = \begin{pmatrix} U_1 \\ \vdots \\ U_n \end{pmatrix},$$

model (5.31) can be written in vector–matrix form as

$$Y = X\theta_0 + U, U|X \sim N_n[0, \sigma^2 I_n], \tag{5.32}$$

where $U|X$ is a shorthand notation for "U conditional on X."

In the remaining sections I will address the problems of how to estimate the parameter vector θ_0 and how to test various hypotheses about θ_0 and its components.

5.7.2. Least-Squares Estimation

Observe that

$$\begin{aligned} E[(Y - X\theta)^{\mathrm{T}}(Y - X\theta)] &= E\big[(U + X(\theta_0 - \theta))^{\mathrm{T}}(U + X(\theta_0 - \theta))\big] \\ &= E[U^{\mathrm{T}}U] + 2(\theta_0 - \theta)^{\mathrm{T}}E(X^{\mathrm{T}}E[U|X]) \\ &\quad + (\theta_0 - \theta)^{\mathrm{T}}(E[X^{\mathrm{T}}X])(\theta_0 - \theta) \\ &= n \cdot \sigma^2 + (\theta_0 - \theta)^{\mathrm{T}}(E[X^{\mathrm{T}}X])(\theta_0 - \theta). \end{aligned} \tag{5.33}$$

Hence, it follows from (5.33) that[3]

$$\theta_0 = \underset{\theta \in \mathbb{R}^k}{\operatorname{argmin}} E\big[(Y - X\theta)^{\mathrm{T}}(Y - X\theta)\big] = (E[X^{\mathrm{T}}X])^{-1} E[X^{\mathrm{T}}Y]$$

$$(5.34)$$

provided that the matrix $E[X^{\mathrm{T}}X]$ is nonsingular. However, the nonsingularity of the distribution of $Z_j = (Y_j, X_j^{\mathrm{T}})^{\mathrm{T}}$ guarantees that $E[X^{\mathrm{T}}X]$ is nonsingular because it follows from Theorem 5.5 that the solution (5.34) is unique if $\Sigma_{XX} = \mathrm{Var}(X_j)$ is nonsingular.

The expression (5.34) suggests estimating θ_0 by the ordinary[4] least-squares (OLS) estimator

$$\hat{\theta} = \underset{\theta \in \mathbb{R}^k}{\operatorname{argmin}}(Y - X\theta)^{\mathrm{T}}(Y - X\theta) = (X^{\mathrm{T}}X)^{-1}X^{\mathrm{T}}Y. \qquad (5.35)$$

It follows easily from (5.32) and (5.35) that

$$\hat{\theta} - \theta_0 = (X^{\mathrm{T}}X)^{-1}X^{\mathrm{T}}U; \qquad (5.36)$$

hence, $\hat{\theta}$ is conditionally unbiased: $E[\hat{\theta}|X] = \theta_0$ and therefore also unconditionally unbiased: $E[\hat{\theta}] = \theta_0$. More generally,

$$\hat{\theta}|X \sim N_k\big[\theta_0, \sigma^2(X^{\mathrm{T}}X)^{-1}\big]. \qquad (5.37)$$

Of course, the unconditional distribution of $\hat{\theta}$ is not normal.

Note that the OLS estimator is not efficient because $\sigma^2(E[X^{\mathrm{T}}X])^{-1}$ is the Cramer–Rao lower bound of an unbiased estimator of (5.37) and $\mathrm{Var}(\hat{\theta}) = \sigma^2 E[(X^{\mathrm{T}}X)^{-1}] \neq \sigma^2(E[X^{\mathrm{T}}X])^{-1}$. However, the OLS estimator is the most efficient of all conditionally unbiased estimators $\tilde{\theta}$ of (5.37) that are linear functions of Y. In other words, the OLS estimator is the best linear unbiased estimator (BLUE). This result is known as the Gauss–Markov theorem:

Theorem 5.16: *(Gauss–Markov theorem) Let $C(X)$ be a $k \times n$ matrix whose elements are Borel-measurable functions of the random elements of X, and let $\tilde{\theta} = C(X)Y$. If $E[\tilde{\theta}|X] = \theta_0$, then for some positive semidefinite $k \times k$ matrix D, $\mathrm{Var}[\tilde{\theta}|X] = \sigma^2 C(X)C(X)^{\mathrm{T}} = \sigma^2(X^{\mathrm{T}}X)^{-1} + D$.*

Proof: The conditional unbiasedness condition implies that $C(X)X = I_k$; hence, $\tilde{\theta} = \theta_0 + C(X)U$, and thus $\mathrm{Var}(\tilde{\theta}|X) = \sigma^2 C(X)C(X)^{\mathrm{T}}$. Now

$$\begin{aligned}
D &= \sigma^2\big[C(X)C(X)^{\mathrm{T}} - (X^{\mathrm{T}}X)^{-1}\big] \\
&= \sigma^2\big[C(X)C(X)^{\mathrm{T}} - C(X)X(X^{\mathrm{T}}X)^{-1}X^{\mathrm{T}}C(X)^{\mathrm{T}}\big] \\
&= \sigma^2 C(X)\big[I_n - X(X^{\mathrm{T}}X)^{-1}X^{\mathrm{T}}\big]C(X)^{\mathrm{T}} = \sigma^2 C(X)M C(X)^{\mathrm{T}},
\end{aligned}$$

---

[3] Recall that "argmin" stands for the argument for which the function involved takes a minimum.

[4] The OLS estimator is called "ordinary" to distinguish it from the nonlinear least-squares estimator. See Chapter 6 for the latter.

for instance, where the second equality follows from the unbiasedness condition $CX = I_k$. The matrix

$$M = I_n - X(X^\mathsf{T}X)^{-1}X^\mathsf{T} \tag{5.38}$$

is idempotent; hence, its eigenvalues are either 1 or 0. Because all the eigenvalues are nonnegative, M is positive semidefinite and so is $C(X)MC(X)^\mathsf{T}$. Q.E.D.

Next, we need an estimator of the error variance σ^2. If we observed the errors U_j, then we could use the sample variance $S^2 = (1/(n-1))\sum_{j=1}^{n}(U_j - \bar{U})^2$ of the U_j's as an unbiased estimator. This suggests using OLS *residuals*,

$$\hat{U}_j = Y_j - \tilde{X}_j^\mathsf{T}\hat{\theta}, \quad \text{where} \quad \tilde{X}_j = \begin{pmatrix} 1 \\ X_j \end{pmatrix}, \tag{5.39}$$

instead of the actual errors U_j in this sample variance. Taking into account that

$$\sum_{j=1}^{n} \hat{U}_j \equiv 0, \tag{5.40}$$

we find that the feasible variance estimator involved takes the form $\hat{S}^2 = (1/(n-1))\sum_{j=1}^{n} \hat{U}_j^2$. However, this estimator is not unbiased, but a minor correction will yield an unbiased estimator of σ^2, namely,

$$S^2 = (1/(n-k)) \sum_{j=1}^{n} \hat{U}_j^2, \tag{5.41}$$

which is called the OLS estimator of σ^2. The unbiasedness of this estimator is a by-product of the following more general result, which is related to the result of Theorem 5.13.

Theorem 5.17: *Conditional on X and well as unconditionally, $(n-k)S^2/\sigma^2 \sim \chi^2_{n-k}$; hence, $E[S^2] = \sigma^2$.*

Proof: Observe that

$$\sum_{j=1}^{n} \hat{U}_j^2 = \sum_{j=1}^{n} (Y_j - \tilde{X}_j^\mathsf{T}\hat{\theta})^2 = \sum_{j=1}^{n} (U_j - \tilde{X}_j^\mathsf{T}(\hat{\theta} - \theta_0))^2$$

$$= \sum_{j=1}^{n} U_j^2 - 2\left(\sum_{j=1}^{n} U_j\tilde{X}_j^\mathsf{T}\right)(\hat{\theta} - \theta_0)$$

$$+ (\hat{\theta} - \theta_0)^\mathsf{T}\left(\sum_{j=1}^{n} \tilde{X}_j^\mathsf{T}\tilde{X}_j\right)(\hat{\theta} - \theta_0)$$

$$= U^\mathsf{T}U - 2U^\mathsf{T}X(\hat{\theta} - \theta_0) + (\hat{\theta} - \theta_0)X^\mathsf{T}X(\hat{\theta} - \theta_0)$$

$$= U^\mathsf{T}U - U^\mathsf{T}X(X^\mathsf{T}X)^{-1}X^\mathsf{T}U = U^\mathsf{T}MU, \tag{5.42}$$

where the last two equalities follow from (5.36) and (5.38), respectively. Because the matrix M is idempotent with rank

$$\text{rank}(M) = \text{trace}(M) = \text{trace}(I_n) - \text{trace}\left(X(X^T X)^{-1} X^T\right)$$
$$= \text{trace}(I_n) - \text{trace}\left((X^T X)^{-1} X^T X\right) = n - k,$$

it follows from Theorem 5.10 that, conditional on X, (5.42) divided by σ^2 has a χ^2_{n-k} distribution

$$\sum_{j=1}^{n} \hat{U}_j^2 / \sigma^2 | X \sim \chi^2_{n-k}. \tag{5.43}$$

It is left as an exercise to prove that (5.43) also implies that the unconditional distribution of (5.42) divided by σ^2 is χ^2_{n-k}:

$$\sum_{j=1}^{n} \hat{U}_j^2 / \sigma^2 \sim \chi^2_{n-k}. \tag{5.44}$$

Because the expectation of the χ^2_{n-k} distribution is $n - k$, it follows from (5.44) that the OLS estimator (5.41) of σ^2 is unbiased.   Q.E.D.

Next, observe from (5.38) that $X^T M = O$, and thus by Theorem 5.7 $(X^T X)^{-1} X^T U$ and $U^T M U$ are independent conditionally on X, that is,

$$P[X^T U \le x \text{ and } U^T M U \le z | X]$$
$$= P[X^T U \le x | X] \cdot P[U^T M U \le z | X], \forall\, x \in \mathbb{R}^k, z \ge 0.$$

Consequently,

Theorem 5.18: *Conditional on X, $\hat{\theta}$ and S^2 are independent,*

but unconditionally they can be dependent.

Theorems 5.17 and 5.18 yield two important corollaries, which I will state in the next theorem. These results play a key role in statistical testing.

Theorem 5.19:

(a) *Let $c \in \mathbb{R}^k$ be a given nonrandom vector. Then*

$$\frac{c^T(\hat{\theta} - \theta_0)}{S\sqrt{c^T(X^T X)^{-1} c}} \sim t_{n-k}. \tag{5.45}$$

(b) *Let R be a given nonrandom $m \times k$ matrix with rank $m \le k$. Then*

$$\frac{(\hat{\theta} - \theta_0)^T R^T \left(R(X^T X)^{-1} R^T\right)^{-1} R(\hat{\theta} - \theta_0)}{m \cdot S^2} \sim F_{m,n-k}. \tag{5.46}$$

Proof of (5.45): It follows from (5.37) that $c^T(\hat{\theta} - \theta_0)|X \sim N[0, \sigma^2 c^T(X^T X)^{-1}c]$; hence,

$$\left.\frac{c^T(\hat{\theta} - \theta_0)}{\sigma\sqrt{c^T(X^T X)^{-1}c}}\right| X \sim N[0, 1]. \tag{5.47}$$

It follows now from Theorem 5.18 that, conditional on X, the random variable in (5.47) and S^2 are independent; hence, it follows from Theorem 5.17 and the definition of the t-distribution that (5.44) is true, conditional on X and therefore also unconditionally.

Proof of (5.46): It follows from (5.37) that $R(\hat{\theta} - \theta_0)|X \sim N_m[0, \sigma^2 R(X^T X)^{-1} R^T]$; hence, it follows from Theorem 5.9 that

$$\left.\frac{(\hat{\theta} - \theta_0)^T R^T \left(R(X^T X)^{-1} R^T\right)^{-1} R(\hat{\theta} - \theta_0)}{\sigma^2}\right| X \sim \chi_m^2. \tag{5.48}$$

Again it follows from Theorem 5.18 that, conditional on X, the random variable in (5.48) and S^2 are independent; hence, it follows from Theorem 5.17 and the definition of the F-distribution that (5.46) is true, conditional on X and therefore also unconditionally.   Q.E.D.

Note that the results in Theorem 5.19 do not hinge on the assumption that the vector X_j in model (5.31) has a multivariate normal distribution. The only conditions that matter for the validity of Theorem 5.19 are that in (5.32), $U|X \sim N_n(0, \sigma^2 I_n)$ and $P[0 < \det(X^T X) < \infty] = 1$.

5.7.3. Hypotheses Testing

Theorem 5.19 is the basis for hypotheses testing in linear regression analysis. First, consider the problem of whether a particular component of the vector X_j of explanatory variables in model (5.31) have an effect on Y_j or not. If not, the corresponding component of β is zero. Each component of β corresponds to a component $\theta_{i,0}$, $i > 0$, of θ_0. Thus, the null hypothesis involved is

$$H_0 : \theta_{i,0} = 0. \tag{5.49}$$

Let $\hat{\theta}_i$ be component i of $\hat{\theta}$, and let the vector e_i be column i of the unit matrix I_k. Then it follows from Theorem 5.19(a) that, under the null hypothesis (5.49),

$$\hat{t}_i = \frac{\hat{\theta}_i}{S\sqrt{e_i^T(X^T X)^{-1} e_i}} \sim t_{n-k}. \tag{5.50}$$

The statistic $\hat{t}_i$ in (5.50) is called the *t-statistic* or *t-value* of the coefficient $\theta_{i,0}$. If $\theta_{i,0}$ can take negative or positive values, the appropriate alternative hypothesis is

$$H_1: \theta_{i,0} \neq 0. \tag{5.51}$$

Given the size $\alpha \in (0, 1)$ of the test, the critical value γ corresponds to $P[|T| > \gamma] = \alpha$, where $T \sim t_{n-k}$. Thus, the null hypothesis (5.49) is accepted if $|\hat{t}_i| \leq \gamma$ and is rejected in favor of the alternative hypothesis (5.51) if $|\hat{t}_i| > \gamma$. In the latter case, we say that $\theta_{i,0}$ is significant at the $\alpha \times 100\%$ significance level. This test is called the two-sided t-test. The critical value γ can be found in Table IV.1 in Appendix IV for the 5% and 10% significance levels and degrees of freedom $n - k$ ranging from 1 to 30. As follows from the results in the next chapter, for larger values of $n - k$ one may use the critical values of the standard normal test in Table IV.3 of Appendix IV.

If the possibility that $\theta_{i,0}$ is negative can be excluded, the appropriate alternative hypothesis is

$$H_1^+: \theta_{i,0} > 0. \tag{5.52}$$

Given the size α, the critical value γ_+ involved now corresponds to $P[T > \gamma_+] = \alpha$, where again $T \sim t_{n-k}$. Thus, the null hypothesis (5.49) is accepted if $\hat{t}_i \leq \gamma_+$ and is rejected in favor of the alternative hypothesis (5.52) if $\hat{t}_i > \gamma_+$. This is the right-sided t-test. The critical value γ_+ can be found in Table IV.2 of Appendix IV for the 5% and 10% significance levels and degrees of freedom $n - k$ ranging from 1 to 30. Again, for larger values of $n - k$ one may use the critical values of the standard normal test in Table IV.3 of Appendix IV.

Similarly, if the possibility that $\theta_{i,0}$ is positive can be excluded, the appropriate alternative hypothesis is

$$H_1^-: \theta_{i,0} < 0. \tag{5.53}$$

Then the null hypothesis (5.49) is accepted if $\hat{t}_i \geq -\gamma_+$ and is rejected in favor of the alternative hypothesis (5.53) if $\hat{t}_i < -\gamma_+$. This is the left-sided t-test.

If the null hypothesis (5.49) is not true, then one can show, using the results in the next chapter, that for $n \to \infty$ and arbitrary $M > 0$, $P[\hat{t}_i > M] \to 1$ if $\theta_{i,0} > 0$ and $P[\hat{t}_i < -M] \to 1$ if $\theta_{i,0} < 0$. Therefore, the t-tests involved are consistent.

Finally, consider a null hypothesis of the form

$$H_0 : R\theta_0 = q, \tag{5.54}$$

where R is a given $m \times k$ matrix with rank $m \leq k$, and q is a given $m \times 1$ vector.

For example, the null hypothesis that the parameter vector β in model (5.31) is a zero vector corresponds to $R = (0, I_{k-1}), q = 0 \in \mathbb{R}^{k-1}, m = k - 1$. This hypothesis implies that none of the components of X_j have any effect on Y_j. In that case $Y_j = \alpha + U_j$, and because U_j and X_j are independent, so are Y_j and X_j.

It follows from Theorem 5.19(b) that, under the null hypothesis (5.54),

$$\hat{F} = \frac{(R\hat{\theta} - q)^{\mathsf{T}}\left(R(X^{\mathsf{T}}X)^{-1}R^{\mathsf{T}}\right)^{-1}(R\hat{\theta} - q)}{m \cdot S^2} \sim F_{m,n-k}. \qquad (5.55)$$

Given the size α, the critical value γ is chosen such that $P[F > \gamma] = \alpha$, where $F \sim F_{m,n-k}$. Thus, the null hypothesis (5.54) is accepted if $\hat{F} \leq \gamma$ and is rejected in favor of the alternative hypothesis $R\theta_0 \neq q$ if $\hat{F} > \gamma$. For obvious reasons, this test is called the F test. The critical value γ can be found in Appendix IV for the 5% and 10% significance levels. Moreover, one can show, using the results in the next chapter, that if the null hypothesis (5.54) is false, then for any $M > 0$, $\lim_{n \to \infty} P[\hat{F} > M] = 1$. Thus, the F test is a consistent test.

5.8. Exercises

1. Let

$$\binom{Y}{X} \sim N_2\left[\binom{1}{0}, \binom{4 \ \ 1}{1 \ \ 1}\right].$$

   (a) Determine $E(Y|X)$.
   (b) Determine $\text{var}(U)$, where $U = Y - E(Y|X)$.
   (c) Why are U and X independent?

2. Let X be n-variate standard normally distributed, and let A be a nonstochastic $n \times k$ matrix with rank $k < n$. The projection of X on the column space of A is a vector p such that the following two conditions hold:
   (1) p is a linear combination of the columns of A;
   (2) the distance between X and p, $\|X - p\| = \sqrt{(X - p)^{\mathsf{T}}(X - p)}$, is minimal.
   (a) Show that $p = A(A^{\mathsf{T}}A)^{-1}A^{\mathsf{T}}X$.
   (b) Is it possible to write down the density of p? If yes, do it. If no, why not?
   (c) Show that $\|p\|^2 = p^{\mathsf{T}}p$ has a χ^2 distribution. Determine the degrees of freedom involved.
   (d) Show that $\|X - p\|^2$ has a χ^2 distribution. Determine the degrees of freedom involved.
   (e) Show that $\|p\|$ and $\|X - p\|$ are independent.

3. Prove Theorem 5.13.

4. Show that (5.11) is true for θ in an open set Θ if $d^2 f_n(x|\theta)/(d\theta)^2$ is, for each x, continuous on Θ and $\int \sup_{\theta \in \Theta} |d^2 f_n(x|\theta)/(d\theta)^2| dx < \infty$. *Hint:* Use the mean-value theorem and the dominated convergence theorem.

5. Show that for a random sample $X_1, X_2, \ldots, X_n$ from a distribution with expectation μ and variance σ^2 the sample variance (5.15) is an unbiased estimator of σ^2 even if the distribution involved is not normal.

6. Prove (5.17).

7. Show that for a random sample $X_1, X_2, \ldots, X_n$ from a multivariate distribution with expectation vector μ and variance matrix Σ the sample variance matrix (5.18) is an unbiased estimator of Σ.

8. Given a random sample of size n from the $N(\mu, \sigma^2)$ distribution, prove that the Cramer–Rao lower bound for an unbiased estimator of σ^2 is $2\sigma^4/n$.

9. Prove Theorem 5.15.

10. Prove the second equalities in (5.34) and (5.35).

11. Show that the Cramer–Rao lower bound of an unbiased estimator of (5.37) is equal to $\sigma^2(E[X^T X])^{-1}$.

12. Show that the matrix (5.38) is idempotent.

13. Why is (5.40) true?

14. Why does (5.43) imply (5.44)?

15. Suppose your econometric software package reports that the OLS estimate of a regression parameter is 1.5, with corresponding t-value 2.4. However, you are only interested in whether the true parameter value is 1 or not. How would you test these hypotheses? Compute the test statistic involved. Moreover, given that the sample size is $n = 30$ and that your model has five other parameters, conduct the test at the 5% significance level.

APPENDIX

5.A. Proof of Theorem 5.8

Note again that the condition $AB = O$ only makes sense if both A and B are singular; if otherwise, either A, B or both are O. Write $A = Q_A \Lambda_A Q_A^T$, $B = Q_B \Lambda_B Q_B^T$, where Q_A and Q_B are orthogonal matrices of eigenvectors and Λ_A and Λ_B are diagonal matrices of corresponding eigenvalues. Then $Z_1 = X^T Q_A \Lambda_A Q_A^T X$, $Z_2 = X^T Q_B \Lambda_B Q_B^T X$. Because A and B are both singular, it follows that Λ_A and Λ_B are singular. Thus, let

$$\Lambda_A = \begin{pmatrix} \Lambda_1 & O & O \\ O & -\Lambda_2 & O \\ O & O & O \end{pmatrix},$$

where Λ_1 is the $k \times k$ diagonal matrix of positive eigenvalues and $-\Lambda_2$ the $m \times m$ diagonal matrix of negative eigenvalues of A with $k + m < n$. Then

$$
Z_1 = X^T Q_A \begin{pmatrix} \Lambda_1 & O & O \\ O & -\Lambda_2 & O \\ O & O & O \end{pmatrix} Q_A^T X
$$

$$
= X^T Q_A \begin{pmatrix} \Lambda_1^{\frac{1}{2}} & O & O \\ O & \Lambda_2^{\frac{1}{2}} & O \\ O & O & O \end{pmatrix} \begin{pmatrix} I_k & O & O \\ O & -I_m & O \\ O & O & I_{n-k-m} \end{pmatrix} \begin{pmatrix} \Lambda_1^{\frac{1}{2}} & O & O \\ O & \Lambda_2^{\frac{1}{2}} & O \\ O & O & O \end{pmatrix} Q_A^T X.
$$

Similarly, let

$$
\Lambda_B = \begin{pmatrix} \Lambda_1^* & O & O \\ O & -\Lambda_2^* & O \\ O & O & O \end{pmatrix},
$$

where Λ_1^* is the $p \times p$ diagonal matrix of positive eigenvalues and $-\Lambda_2^*$ is the $q \times q$ diagonal matrix of negative eigenvalues of B with $p + q < n$. Then

$$
Z_2 = X^T Q_B \begin{pmatrix} (\Lambda_1^*)^{\frac{1}{2}} & O & O \\ O & (\Lambda_2^*)^{\frac{1}{2}} & O \\ O & O & O \end{pmatrix} \begin{pmatrix} I_p & O & O \\ O & -I_q & O \\ O & O & I_{n-p-q} \end{pmatrix}
$$

$$
\times \begin{pmatrix} (\Lambda_1^*)^{\frac{1}{2}} & O & O \\ O & (\Lambda_2^*)^{\frac{1}{2}} & O \\ O & O & O \end{pmatrix} Q_B^T X.
$$

Next, for instance, let

$$
Y_1 = \begin{pmatrix} \Lambda_1^{\frac{1}{2}} & O & O \\ O & \Lambda_2^{\frac{1}{2}} & O \\ O & O & O \end{pmatrix} Q_A^T X = M_1 X,
$$

$$
Y_2 = \begin{pmatrix} (\Lambda_1^*)^{\frac{1}{2}} & O & O \\ O & (\Lambda_2^*)^{\frac{1}{2}} & O \\ O & O & O \end{pmatrix} Q_B^T X = M_2 X.
$$

Then, for instance,

$$
Z_1 = Y_1^T \begin{pmatrix} I_k & O & O \\ O & -I_m & O \\ O & O & I_{n-k-m} \end{pmatrix} Y_1 = Y_1^T D_1 Y_1,
$$

and

$$Z_2 = Y_2^T \begin{pmatrix} I_p & O & O \\ O & -I_q & O \\ O & O & I_{n-p-q} \end{pmatrix} Y_2 = Y_2^T D_2 Y_2,$$

where the diagonal matrices D_1 and D_2 are nonsingular but possibly different. Clearly, Z_1 and Z_2 are independent if Y_1 and Y_2 are independent. Now observe that

$$AB = Q_A \begin{pmatrix} \Lambda_1^{\frac{1}{2}} & O & O \\ O & \Lambda_2^{\frac{1}{2}} & O \\ O & O & I_{n-k-m} \end{pmatrix} \begin{pmatrix} I_k & O & O \\ O & -I_m & O \\ O & O & I_{n-k-m} \end{pmatrix}$$

$$\times \begin{pmatrix} \Lambda_1^{\frac{1}{2}} & O & O \\ O & \Lambda_2^{\frac{1}{2}} & O \\ O & O & O \end{pmatrix} Q_A^T Q_B \begin{pmatrix} (\Lambda_1^*)^{\frac{1}{2}} & O & O \\ O & (\Lambda_2^*)^{\frac{1}{2}} & O \\ O & O & O \end{pmatrix}$$

$$\times \begin{pmatrix} I_p & O & O \\ O & -I_q & O \\ O & O & I_{n-p-q} \end{pmatrix} \begin{pmatrix} (\Lambda_1^*)^{\frac{1}{6}} & O & O \\ O & (\Lambda_2^*)^{\frac{1}{2}} & O \\ O & O & I_{n-p-q} \end{pmatrix} Q_B^T.$$

The first three matrices are nonsingular and so are the last three. Therefore, $AB = O$ if and only if

$$M_1 M_2^T = \begin{pmatrix} \Lambda_1^{\frac{1}{2}} & O & O \\ O & \Lambda_2^{\frac{1}{2}} & O \\ O & O & O \end{pmatrix} Q_A^T Q_B \begin{pmatrix} (\Lambda_1^*)^{\frac{1}{2}} & O & O \\ O & (\Lambda_2^*)^{\frac{1}{2}} & O \\ O & O & O \end{pmatrix} = O.$$

It follows now from Theorem 5.7 that the latter implies that Y_1 and Y_2 are independent; hence, the condition $AB = O$ implies that Y_1 and Y_2 are independent. Q.E.D.

6 Modes of Convergence

6.1. Introduction

Toss a fair coin n times, and let $Y_j = 1$ if the outcome of the jth tossing is heads and $Y_j = -1$ if the outcome involved is tails. Denote $X_n = (1/n)\sum_{j=1}^{n} Y_j$. For the case $n = 10$, the left panel of Figure 6.1 displays the distribution function $F_n(x)$[1] of X_n on the interval $[-1.5, 1.5]$, and the right panel displays a typical plot of X_k for $k = 1, 2, \ldots, 10$ based on simulated Y_j's.[2]

Now let us see what happens if we increase n: First, consider the case $n = 100$ in Figure 6.2. The distribution function $F_n(x)$ becomes steeper for x close to zero, and X_n seems to tend towards zero.

These phenomena are even more apparent for the case $n = 1000$ in Figure 6.3.

What you see in Figures 6.1–6.3 is the law of large numbers: $X_n = (1/n)\sum_{j=1}^{n} Y_j \to E[Y_1] = 0$ in some sense to be discussed in Sections 6.2–6.3 and the related phenomenon that $F_n(x)$ converges pointwise in $x \neq 0$ to the distribution function $F(x) = I(x \geq 0)$ of a "random" variable X satisfying $P[X = 0] = 1$.

Next, let us have a closer look at the distribution function of $\sqrt{n}X_n$: $G_n(x) = F_n(x/\sqrt{n})$ with corresponding probabilities $P[\sqrt{n}X_n = (2k - n)/\sqrt{n}]$, $k = 0, 1, \ldots, n$ and see what happens if $n \to \infty$. These probabilities can be displayed

---

[1] Recall that $n(X_n + 1)/2 = \sum_{j=1}^{n}(Y_j + 1)/2$ has a binomial $(n, 1/2)$ distribution, and thus the distribution function $F_n(x)$ of X_n is

$$F_n(x) = P[X_n \leq x] = P[n(X_n + 1)/2 \leq n(x + 1)/2]$$
$$= \sum_{k=0}^{\min(n, [n(x+1)/2])} \binom{n}{k} (1/2)^n,$$

where $[z]$ denotes the largest integer $\leq z$, and the sum $\sum_{k=0}^{m}$ is zero if $m < 0$.

[2] The Y_j's have been generated as $Y_j = 2 \cdot I(U_j > 0.5) - 1$, where the U_j's are random drawings from the uniform $[0, 1]$ distribution and $I(\cdot)$ is the indicator function.

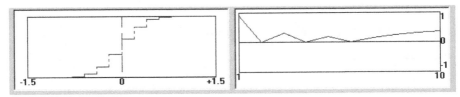

Figure 6.1. $n = 10$. Left: Distribution function of X_n. Right: Plot of X_k for $k = 1, 2, \ldots, n$.

in the form of a histogram:

$$H_n(x) = \frac{P\left[2(k-1)/\sqrt{n} - \sqrt{n} < \sqrt{n}X_n \leq 2k/\sqrt{n} - \sqrt{n}\right]}{2/\sqrt{n}}$$

$$if \ x \in \left(2(k-1)/\sqrt{n} - \sqrt{n}, 2k/\sqrt{n} - \sqrt{n}\right], k = 0, 1, \ldots, n,$$

$$H_n(x) = 0 \text{ elsewhere.}$$

Figures 6.4–6.6 compare $G_n(x)$ with the distribution function of the standard normal distribution and $H_n(x)$ with the standard normal density for $n = 10, 100$ and 1000.

What you see in the left-hand panels in Figures 6.4–6.6 is the central limit theorem:

$$\lim_{n \to \infty} G_n(x) = \int_{-\infty}^{x} \frac{\exp[-u^2/2]}{\sqrt{2\pi}} du,$$

pointwise in x, and what you see in the right-hand panels is the corresponding fact that

$$\lim_{\delta \downarrow 0} \lim_{n \to \infty} \frac{G_n(x + \delta) - G_n(x)}{\delta} = \frac{\exp[-x^2/2]}{\sqrt{2\pi}}.$$

The law of large numbers and the central limit theorem play a key role in statistics and econometrics. In this chapter I will review and explain these laws.

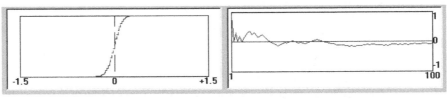

Figure 6.2. $n = 100$. Left: Distribution function of X_n. Right: Plot of X_k for $k = 1, 2, \ldots, n$.

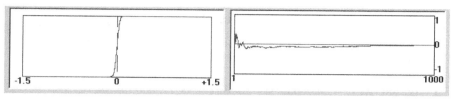

Figure 6.3. $n = 1000$. Left: Distribution function of X_n. Right: Plot of X_k for $k = 1, 2, \ldots, n$.

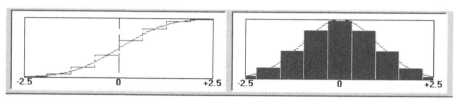

Figure 6.4. $n = 10$. Left: $G_n(x)$. Right: $H_n(x)$ compared with the standard normal distribution.

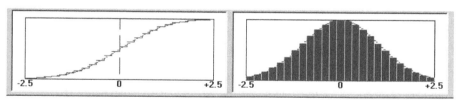

Figure 6.5. $n = 100$. Left: $G_n(x)$. Right: $H_n(x)$ compared with the standard normal distribution.

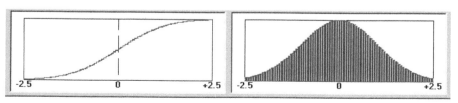

Figure 6.6. $n = 1000$. Left: $G_n(x)$. Right: $H_n(x)$ compared with the standard normal distribution.

6.2. Convergence in Probability and the Weak Law of Large Numbers

Let X_n be a sequence of random variables (or vectors) and let X be a random or constant variable (or conformable vector).

Definition 6.1: *We say that X_n converges in probability to X, also denoted as $plim_{n\to\infty}X_n = X$ or $X_n \to_p X$, if for an arbitrary $\varepsilon > 0$ we have $lim_{n\to\infty}P(|X_n - X| > \varepsilon) = 0$, or equivalently, $lim_{n\to\infty}P(|X_n - X| \leq \varepsilon) = 1$.*

In this definition, X may be a random variable or a constant. The latter case, where $P(X = c) = 1$ for some constant c, is the most common case in econometric applications. Also, this definition carries over to random vectors provided that the absolute value function $|x|$ is replaced by the Euclidean norm $\|x\| = \sqrt{x^T x}$.

The right panels of Figures 6.1–6.3 demonstrate the law of large numbers. One of the versions of this law is the weak law of large numbers (WLLN), which also applies to uncorrelated random variables.

Theorem 6.1: *(WLLN for uncorrelated random variables). Let $X_1, \ldots, X_n$ be a sequence of uncorrelated random variables with $E(X_j) = \mu$ and $var(X_j) = \sigma^2 < \infty$ and let $\bar{X} = (1/n)\sum_{j=1}^n X_j$. Then $plim_{n\to\infty}\bar{X} = \mu$.*

Proof: Because $E(\bar{X}) = \mu$ and $var(\bar{X}) = \sigma^2/n$, it follows from Chebishev inequality that $P(|\bar{X} - \mu| > \varepsilon) \leq \sigma^2/(n\varepsilon^2) \to 0$ if $n \to \infty$.   Q.E.D.

The condition of a finite variance can be traded in for the i.i.d. condition:

Theorem 6.2: *(The WLLN for i.i.d. random variables). Let $X_1, \ldots, X_n$ be a sequence of independent, identically distributed random variables with $E[|X_j|] < \infty$ and $E(X_j) = \mu$, and let $\bar{X} = (1/n)\sum_{j=1}^n X_j$. Then $plim_{n\to\infty}\bar{X} = \mu$.*

Proof: Let $Y_j = X_j \cdot I(|X_j| \leq j)$ and $Z_j = X_j \cdot I(|X_j| > j)$, and thus $X_j = Y_j + Z_j$. Then

$$E\left|(1/n)\sum_{j=1}^n (Z_j - E(Z_j))\right| \leq 2(1/n)\sum_{j=1}^n E[|Z_j|]$$

$$= 2(1/n)\sum_{j=1}^n E[|X_1|I(|X_1| > j)] \to 0, \tag{6.1}$$

and

$$E\left[\left|(1/n)\sum_{j=1}^n (Y_j - E(Y_j))\right|^2\right] \leq (1/n^2)\sum_{j=1}^n E[Y_j^2]$$

$$= (1/n^2)\sum_{j=1}^n E\left[X_1^2 I(|X_1| \leq j)\right]$$

$$= (1/n^2) \sum_{j=1}^{n} \sum_{k=1}^{j} E\left[X_1^2 \, I(k-1 < |X_1| \le k)\right]$$

$$\le (1/n^2) \sum_{j=1}^{n} \sum_{k=1}^{j} k \cdot E[|X_1| \cdot I(k-1 < |X_1| \le k)]$$

$$= (1/n^2) \sum_{j=1}^{n} \sum_{k=1}^{j-1} \sum_{i=k}^{j} E[|X_1| \cdot I(i-1 < |X_1| \le i)]$$

$$\le (1/n^2) \sum_{j=1}^{n} \sum_{k=1}^{j-1} E[|X_1| \cdot I(|X_1| > k-1)]$$

$$\le (1/n) \sum_{k=1}^{n} E[|X_1| \cdot I(|X_1| > k-1)] \to 0 \qquad (6.2)$$

as $n \to \infty$, where the last equality in (6.2) follows from the easy equality $\sum_{k=1}^{j} k \cdot \alpha_k = \sum_{k=1}^{j-1} \sum_{i=k}^{j} \alpha_i$, and the convergence results in (6.1) and (6.2) follow from the fact that $E[|X_1| I(|X_1| > j)] \to 0$ for $j \to \infty$ because $E[|X_1|] < \infty$. Using Chebishev's inequality, we find that it follows now from (6.1) and (6.2) that, for arbitrary $\varepsilon > 0$,

$$P\left[\left|(1/n) \sum_{j=1}^{n} (X_j - E(X_j))\right| > \varepsilon\right]$$

$$\le P\left[\left|(1/n) \sum_{j=1}^{n} (Y_j - E(Y_j))\right| + \left|(1/n) \sum_{j=1}^{n} (Z_j - E(Z_j))\right| > \varepsilon\right]$$

$$\le P\left[\left|(1/n) \sum_{j=1}^{n} (Y_j - E(Y_j))\right| > \varepsilon/2\right]$$

$$+ P\left[\left|(1/n) \sum_{j=1}^{n} (Z_j - E(Z_j))\right| > \varepsilon/2\right]$$

$$\le 4E\left[\left|(1/n) \sum_{j=1}^{n} (Y_j - E(Y_j))\right|^2\right] \Big/ \varepsilon^2$$

$$+ 2E\left[\left|(1/n) \sum_{j=1}^{n} (Z_j - E(Z_j))\right|\right] \Big/ \varepsilon \to 0 \qquad (6.3)$$

as $n \to \infty$. Note that the second inequality in (6.3) follows from the fact that, for nonnegative random variables X and Y, $P[X + Y > \varepsilon] \le P[X > \varepsilon/2] + P[Y > \varepsilon/2]$. The theorem under review follows now from (6.3), Definition 6.1, and the fact that ε is arbitrary. Q.E.D.

Note that Theorems 6.1 and 6.2 carry over to finite-dimensional random vectors X_j by replacing the absolute values $|\cdot|$ by Euclidean norms: $\|x\| =$

$\sqrt{x^\mathsf{T} x}$ and the variance by the variance matrix. The reformulation of Theorems 6.1 and 6.2 for random vectors is left as an easy exercise.

Convergence in probability carries over after taking continuous transformations. This result is often referred to as Slutsky's theorem:

Theorem 6.3: *(Slutsky's theorem). Let X_n a sequence of random vectors in $\mathbb{R}^k$ satisfying $X_n \to_p c$, where c is nonrandom. Let $\Psi(x)$ be an $\mathbb{R}^m$-valued function on $\mathbb{R}^k$ that is continuous in c. Then $\Psi(X_n) \to_p \Psi(c)$.*

Proof: Consider the case $m = k = 1$. It follows from the continuity of Ψ that for an arbitrary $\varepsilon > 0$ there exists a $\delta > 0$ such that $|x - c| \leq \delta$ implies $|\Psi(x) - \Psi(c)| \leq \varepsilon$; hence,

$$P(|X_n - c| \leq \delta) \leq P(|\Psi(X_n) - \Psi(c)| \leq \varepsilon).$$

Because $\lim_{n \to \infty} P(|X_n - c| \leq \delta) = 1$, the theorem follows for the case under review. The more general case with $m > 1$, $k > 1$, or both can be proved along the same lines.   Q.E.D.

The condition that c be constant is not essential. Theorem 6.3 carries over to the case in which c is a random variable or vector, as we will see in Theorem 6.7 below.

Convergence in probability does *not* automatically imply convergence of expectations. A counterexample is $X_n = X + 1/n$, where X has a Cauchy distribution (see Chapter 4). Then $E[X_n]$ and $E(X)$ are not defined, but $X_n \to_p X$. However,

Theorem 6.4: *(Bounded convergence theorem) If X_n is bounded, that is, $P(|X_n| \leq M) = 1$ for some $M < \infty$ and all n, then $X_n \to_p X$ implies $\lim_{n \to \infty} E(X_n) = E(X)$.*

Proof: First, X has to be bounded too, with the same bound M; otherwise, $X_n \to_p X$ is not possible. Without loss of generality we may now assume that $P(X = 0) = 1$ and that X_n is a nonnegative random variable by replacing X_n with $|X_n - X|$ because $E[|X_n - X|] \to 0$ implies $\lim_{n \to \infty} E(X_n) = E(X)$. Next, let $F_n(x)$ be the distribution function of X_n and let $\varepsilon > 0$ be arbitrary. Then

$$0 \leq E(X_n) = \int_0^M x \, dF_n(x)$$

$$= \int_0^\varepsilon x \, dF_n(x) + \int_\varepsilon^M x \, dF_n(x) \leq \varepsilon + M \cdot P(X_n \geq \varepsilon).$$

$$\tag{6.4}$$

Because the latter probability converges to zero (by the definition of convergence in probability and the assumption that X_n is nonnegative with zero probability limit), we have $0 \leq \limsup_{n\to\infty} E(X_n) \leq \varepsilon$ for all $\varepsilon > 0$; hence, $\lim_{n\to\infty} E(X_n) = 0$. Q.E.D.

The condition that X_n in Theorem 6.4 is bounded can be relaxed using the concept of uniform integrability:

Definition 6.2: *A sequence X_n of random variables is said to be uniformly integrable if $\lim_{M\to\infty} \sup_{n\geq1} E[|X_n| \cdot I(|X_n| > M)] = 0$.*

Note that Definition 6.2 carries over to random vectors by replacing the absolute value $|\cdot|$ with the Euclidean norm $\|\cdot\|$. Moreover, it is easy to verify that if $|X_n| \leq Y$ with probability 1 for all $n \geq 1$, where $E(Y) < \infty$, then X_n is uniformly integrable.

Theorem 6.5: *(Dominated convergence theorem) Let X_n be uniformly integrable. Then $X_n \to_p X$ implies $\lim_{n\to\infty} E(X_n) = E(X)$.*

Proof: Again, without loss of generality we may assume that $P(X = 0) = 1$ and that X_n is a nonnegative random variable. Let $0 < \varepsilon < M$ be arbitrary. Then, as in (6.4),

$$0 \leq E(X_n) = \int_0^\infty x\, dF_n(x) = \int_0^\varepsilon x\, dF_n(x) + \int_\varepsilon^M x\, dF_n(x) + \int_M^\infty x\, dF_n(x)$$

$$\leq \varepsilon + M \cdot P(X_n \geq \varepsilon) + \sup_{n\geq1} \int_M^\infty x\, dF_n(x). \qquad (6.5)$$

For fixed M the second term on the right-hand side of (6.5) converges to zero. Moreover, by uniform integrability we can choose M so large that the third term is smaller than ε. Hence, $0 \leq \limsup_{n\to\infty} E(X_n) \leq 2\varepsilon$ for all $\varepsilon > 0$, and thus $\lim_{n\to\infty} E(X_n) = 0$. Q.E.D.

Also Theorems 6.4 and 6.5 carry over to random vectors by replacing the absolute value function $|x|$ by the Euclidean norm $\|x\| = \sqrt{x^T x}$.

6.3. Almost-Sure Convergence and the Strong Law of Large Numbers

In most (but not all!) cases in which convergence in probability and the weak law of large numbers apply, we actually have a much stronger result:

Definition 6.3: *We say that X_n converges almost surely (or with probability 1) to X, also denoted by $X_n \to X$ a.s. (or w.p.1), if*

$$for\ all\ \varepsilon > 0,\ \lim_{n \to \infty} P(\sup_{m \geq n} |X_m - X| \leq \varepsilon) = 1, \tag{6.6}$$

or equivalently,

$$P(\lim_{n \to \infty} X_n = X) = 1. \tag{6.7}$$

The equivalence of conditions (6.6) and (6.7) will be proved in Appendix 6.B (Theorem 6.B.1).

It follows straightforwardly from (6.6) that almost-sure convergence implies convergence in probability. The converse, however, is not true. It is possible that a sequence X_n converges in probability but not almost surely. For example, let $X_n = U_n/n$, where the U_n's are i.i.d. nonnegative random variables with distribution function $G(u) = \exp(-1/u)$ for $u > 0$, $G(u) = 0$ for $u \leq 0$. Then, for arbitrary $\varepsilon > 0$,

$$P(|X_n| \leq \varepsilon) = P(U_n \leq n\varepsilon) = G(n\varepsilon)$$
$$= \exp(-1/(n\varepsilon)) \to 1 \text{ as } n \to \infty;$$

hence, $X_n \to_p 0$. On the other hand,

$$P(|X_m| \leq \varepsilon \text{ for all } m \geq n) = P(U_m \leq m\varepsilon \text{ for all } m \geq n)$$
$$= \prod_{m=n}^{\infty} G(m\varepsilon) = \exp\left(-\varepsilon^{-1} \sum_{m=n}^{\infty} m^{-1}\right)$$
$$= 0,$$

where the second equality follows from the independence of the U_n's and the last equality follows from the fact that $\sum_{m=1}^{\infty} m^{-1} = \infty$. Consequently, X_n does not converge to 0 almost surely.

Theorems 6.2–6.5 carry over to the almost-sure convergence case without additional conditions:

Theorem 6.6: *(Kolmogorov's strong law of large numbers). Under the conditions of Theorem 6.2, $\bar{X} \to \mu$ a.s.*

Proof: See Appendix 6.B.

The result of Theorem 6.6 is actually what you see happening in the right-hand panels of Figures 6.1–6.3.

Theorem 6.7: *(Slutsky's theorem). Let X_n a sequence of random vectors in $\mathbb{R}^k$ converging a.s. to a (random or constant) vector X. Let $\Psi(x)$ be an $\mathbb{R}^m$-valued function on $\mathbb{R}^k$ that is continuous on an open subset[3] B of $\mathbb{R}^k$ for which $P(X \in B) = 1$). Then $\Psi(X_n) \to \psi(X)$ a.s.*

---

[3] Recall that open subsets of a Euclidean space are Borel sets.

Proof: See Appendix 6.B.

Because a.s. convergence implies convergence in probability, it is trivial that

Theorem 6.8: *If $X_n \to X$ a.s., then the result of Theorem 6.4 carries over.*

Theorem 6.9: *If $X_n \to X$ a.s., then the result of Theorem 6.5 carries over.*

6.4. The Uniform Law of Large Numbers and Its Applications

6.4.1. The Uniform Weak Law of Large Numbers

In econometrics we often have to deal with means of random functions. A random function is a function that is a random variable for each fixed value of its argument. More precisely,

Definition 6.4: *Let $\{\Omega, \mathscr{F}, P\}$ be the probability space. A random function $f(\theta)$ on a subset Θ of a Euclidean space is a mapping $f(\omega, \theta): \Omega \times \Theta \to \mathbb{R}$ such that for each Borel set B in $\mathbb{R}$ and each $\theta \in \Theta$, $\{\omega \in \Omega : f(\omega, \theta) \in B\} \in \mathscr{F}$.*

Usually random functions take the form of a function $g(X, \theta)$ of a random vector X and a nonrandom vector θ. For such functions we can extend the weak law of large numbers for i.i.d. random variables to a uniform weak law of large numbers (UWLLN):

Theorem 6.10: *(UWLLN). Let $X_j, j = 1, \ldots, n$ be a random sample from a k-variate distribution, and let $\theta \in \Theta$ be nonrandom vectors in a closed and bounded (hence compact[4]) subset $\Theta \subset \mathbb{R}^m$. Moreover, let $g(x, \theta)$ be a Borel-measurable function on $\mathbb{R}^k \times \Theta$ such that for each x, $g(x, \theta)$ is a continuous function on Θ. Finally, assume that $E[\sup_{\theta \in \Theta} |g(X_j, \theta)|] < \infty$. Then $plim_{n \to \infty} \sup_{\theta \in \Theta} |(1/n) \sum_{j=1}^{n} g(X_j, \theta) - E[g(X_1, \theta)]| = 0$.*

Proof: See Appendix 6.A.

6.4.2. Applications of the Uniform Weak Law of Large Numbers

6.4.2.1. Consistency of M-Estimators

Chapter 5 introduced the concept of a parameter estimator and listed two desirable properties of estimators: unbiasedness and efficiency. Another obviously

---

[4] See Appendix II.

desirable property is that the estimator gets closer to the parameter to be estimated if we use more data information. This is the consistency property:

Definition 6.5: *An estimator $\hat{\theta}$ of a parameter θ, based on a sample of size n, is called consistent if $plim_{n\to\infty}\hat{\theta} = \theta$.*

Theorem 6.10 is an important tool in proving consistency of parameter estimators. A large class of estimators is obtained by maximizing or minimizing an objective function of the form $(1/n) \sum_{j=1}^{n} g(X_j, \theta)$, where g, X_j, and θ are the same as in Theorem 6.10. These estimators are called M-estimators (where the M indicates that the estimator is obtained by <u>M</u>aximizing or <u>M</u>inimizing a <u>M</u>ean of random functions). Suppose that the parameter of interest is $\theta_0 = argmax_{\theta\in\Theta}$ $E[g(X_1, \theta)]$, where Θ is a given closed and bounded set. Note that "argmax" is a shorthand notation for the argument for which the function involved is maximal. Then it seems a natural choice to use $\hat{\theta} = argmax_{\theta\in\Theta}(1/n) \sum_{j=1}^{n} g(X_j, \theta)$ as an estimator of θ_0. Indeed, under some mild conditions the estimator involved is consistent:

Theorem 6.11: *(Consistency of M-estimators) Let $\hat{\theta} = argmax_{\theta\in\Theta} \hat{Q}(\theta)$, $\theta_0 = argmax_{\theta\in\Theta} \bar{Q}(\theta)$, where $\hat{Q}(\theta) = (1/n)\sum_{j=1}^{n} g(X_j, \theta)$, and $\bar{Q}(\theta) = E[\hat{Q}(\theta)] = E[g(X_1, \theta)]$, with g, X_j, and θ the same as in Theorem 6.10. If θ_0 is unique, in the sense that for arbitrary $\varepsilon > 0$ there exists a $\delta > 0$ such that $\bar{Q}(\theta_0) - sup_{\|\theta-\theta_0\|>\varepsilon} \bar{Q}(\theta) > \delta$,[5] then $plim_{n\to\infty}\hat{\theta} = \theta_0$.*

Proof: First, note that $\hat{\theta} \in \Theta$ and $\theta_0 \in \Theta$ because $g(x, \theta)$ is continuous in θ. See Appendix II. By the definition of θ_0,

$$0 \leq \bar{Q}(\theta_0) - \bar{Q}(\hat{\theta}) = \bar{Q}(\theta_0) - \hat{Q}(\theta_0) + \hat{Q}(\theta_0) - \bar{Q}(\hat{\theta})$$
$$\leq \bar{Q}(\theta_0) - \hat{Q}(\theta_0) + \hat{Q}(\hat{\theta}) - \bar{Q}(\hat{\theta}) \leq 2 \sup_{\theta\in\Theta} |\hat{Q}(\theta) - \bar{Q}(\theta)|, \quad (6.8)$$

and it follows from Theorem 6.3 that the right-hand side of (6.8) converges in probability to zero. Thus,

$$\plim_{n\to\infty} \bar{Q}(\hat{\theta}) = \bar{Q}(\theta_0). \quad (6.9)$$

Moreover, the uniqueness condition implies that for arbitrary $\varepsilon > 0$ there exists a $\delta > 0$ such that $\bar{Q}(\theta_0) - \bar{Q}(\hat{\theta}) \geq \delta$ if $\|\hat{\theta} - \theta_0\| > \varepsilon$; hence,

$$P(\|\hat{\theta} - \theta_0\| > \varepsilon) \leq P(\bar{Q}(\theta_0) - \bar{Q}(\hat{\theta}) \geq \delta). \quad (6.10)$$

---

[5] It follows from Theorem II.6 in Appendix II that this condition is satisfied if Θ is compact and $\bar{Q}$ is continuous on Θ.

Combining (6.9) and (6.10), we find that the theorem under review follows from Definition 6.1. Q.E.D.

It is easy to verify that Theorem 6.11 carries over to the "argmin" case simply by replacing g by $-g$.

As an example, let $X_1, \ldots, X_n$ be a random sample from the noncentral Cauchy distribution with density $h(x|\theta_0) = 1/[\pi(1 + (x - \theta_0)^2]$ and suppose that we know that θ_0 is contained in a given closed and bounded interval Θ. Let $g(x, \theta) = f(x - \theta)$, where $f(x) = \exp(-x^2/2)/\sqrt{2\pi}$ is the density of the standard normal distribution. Then,

$$E[g(X_1, \theta)] = \int_{-\infty}^{\infty} \frac{\exp(-(x + \theta_0 - \theta)^2)/\sqrt{2\pi}}{\pi(1 + x^2)} dx$$

$$= \int_{-\infty}^{\infty} f(x - \theta + \theta_0)h(x|\theta)dx = \gamma(\theta - \theta_0), \tag{6.11}$$

for instance, where $\gamma(y)$ is a density itself, namely the density of $Y = U + Z$, with U and Z independent random drawings from the standard normal and standard Cauchy distribution, respectively. This is called the *convolution* of the two densities involved. The characteristic function of Y is $\exp(-|t| - t^2/2)$, and thus by the inversion formula for characteristic functions

$$\gamma(y) = \frac{1}{2\pi} \int_{-\infty}^{\infty} \cos(t \cdot y) \exp(-|t| - t^2/2) dt. \tag{6.12}$$

This function is maximal in $y = 0$, and this maximum is unique because, for fixed $y \neq 0$, the set $\{t \in \mathbb{R} : \cos(t \cdot y) = 1\}$ is countable and therefore has Lebesgue measure zero. In particular, it follows from (6.12) that, for arbitrary $\varepsilon > 0$,

$$\sup_{|y|\geq\varepsilon} \gamma(y) \leq \frac{1}{2\pi} \int_{-\infty}^{\infty} \sup_{|y|\geq\varepsilon} |\cos(t \cdot y)| \exp(-|t| - t^2/2) dt < \gamma(0).$$

$$\tag{6.13}$$

Combining (6.11) and (6.13) yields $\sup_{|\theta - \theta_0|\geq\varepsilon} E[g(X_1, \theta)] < E[g(X_1, \theta_0)]$. Thus, all the conditions of Theorem 6.11 are satisfied; hence, $\text{plim}_{n\to\infty}\hat{\theta} = \theta_0$.

Another example is the nonlinear least-squares estimator. Consider a random sample $Z_j = (Y_j, X_j^T)^T$, $j = 1, 2, \ldots, n$ with $Y_j \in \mathbb{R}$, $X_j \in \mathbb{R}^k$ and assume that

Assumption 6.1: *For a given function $f(x, \theta)$ on $\mathbb{R}^k \times \Theta$, with Θ a given compact subset of $\mathbb{R}^m$, there exists a $\theta_0 \in \Theta$ such that $P[E[Y_j|X_j] = f(X_j, \theta_0)] =$*

1. *Moreover, for each $x \in \mathbb{R}^k$, $f(x, \theta)$ is a continuous function on Θ, and for each $\theta \in \Theta$, $f(x, \theta)$ is a Borel-measurable function on $\mathbb{R}^k$. Furthermore, let $E[Y_1^2] < \infty$, $E[sup_{\theta \in \Theta} f(X_1, \theta)^2] < \infty$, and*

$$\inf_{\|\theta - \theta_0\| \geq \delta} E\left[(f(X_1, \theta) - f(X_1, \theta_0))^2\right] > 0 \quad for \quad \delta > 0.$$

Letting $U_j = Y_j - E[Y_j | X_j]$, we can write

$$Y_j = f(X_j, \theta_0) + U_j, \quad where \quad P(E[U_j | X_j] = 0) = 1. \tag{6.14}$$

This is the general form of a nonlinear regression model. I will show now that, under Assumption 6.1, the nonlinear least-squares estimator

$$\hat{\theta} = \underset{\theta \in \Theta}{\operatorname{argmin}}(1/n) \sum_{j=1}^{n} (Y_j - f(X_j, \theta))^2 \tag{6.15}$$

is a consistent estimator of θ_0.

Let $g(Z_j, \theta) = (Y_j - f(X_j, \theta))^2$. Then it follows from Assumption 6.1 and Theorem 6.10 that

$$\underset{n \to \infty}{\operatorname{plim}} \sup_{\theta \in \Theta} \left| (1/n) \sum_{j=1}^{n} [g(Z_j, \theta) - E[g(Z_1, \theta)]] \right| = 0.$$

Moreover,

$$\begin{aligned}
E[g(Z_1, \theta)] &= E\left[(U_j + f(X_j, \theta_0) - f(X_j, \theta))^2\right] \\
&= E\left[U_j^2\right] + 2E[E(U_j | X_j)(f(X_j, \theta_0) - f(X_j, \theta))] \\
&\quad + E\left[(f(X_j, \theta_0) - f(X_j, \theta))^2\right] \\
&= E\left[U_j^2\right] + E\left[(f(X_j, \theta_0) - f(X_j, \theta))^2\right];
\end{aligned}$$

hence, it follows from Assumption 6.1 that $\inf_{\|\theta - \theta_0\| \geq \delta} E[|g(Z_1, \theta)|] > 0$ for $\delta > 0$. Therefore, the conditions of Theorem 6.11 for the argmin case are satisfied, and, consequently, the nonlinear least-squares estimator (6.15) is consistent.

6.4.2.2. Generalized Slutsky's Theorem

Another easy but useful corollary of Theorem 6.10 is the following generalization of Theorem 6.3:

Theorem 6.12: *(Generalized Slutsky's theorem) Let X_n a sequence of random vectors in $\mathbb{R}^k$ converging in probability to a nonrandom vector c. Let $\Phi_n(x)$ be a sequence of random functions on $\mathbb{R}^k$ satisfying $\operatorname{plim}_{n \to \infty} \sup_{x \in B} |\Phi_n(x) -$*

$\Phi(x)| = 0$, where B is a closed and bounded subset of $\mathbb{R}^k$ containing c and Φ is a continuous nonrandom function on B. Then $\Phi_n(X_n) \to_p \Phi(c)$.

Proof: Exercise.

This theorem can be further generalized to the case in which $c = X$ is a random vector simply by adding the condition that $P[X \in B] = 1$, but the current result suffices for the applications of Theorem 6.12.

This theorem plays a key role in deriving the asymptotic distribution of an M-estimator together with the central limit theorem discussed in Section 6.7.

6.4.3. The Uniform Strong Law of Large Numbers and Its Applications

The results of Theorems 6.10–6.12 also hold almost surely. See Appendix 6.B for the proofs.

Theorem 6.13: *Under the conditions of Theorem 6.10, $\sup_{\theta \in \Theta} |(1/n) \sum_{j=1}^{n} g(X_j, \theta) - E[g(X_1, \theta)]| \to 0$ a.s.*

Theorem 6.14: *Under the conditions of Theorems 6.11 and 6.13, $\hat{\theta} \to \theta_0$ a.s.*

Theorem 6.15: *Under the conditions of Theorem 6.12 and the additional condition that $X_n \to c$ a.s., $\Phi_n(X_n) \to \Phi(c)$ a.s.*

6.5. Convergence in Distribution

Let X_n be a sequence of random variables (or vectors) with distribution functions $F_n(x)$, and let X be a random variable (or conformable random vector) with distribution function $F(x)$.

Definition 6.6: *We say that X_n converges to X in distribution (denoted by $X_n \to_d X$) if $\lim_{n \to \infty} F_n(x) = F(x)$ pointwise in x – possibly except in the discontinuity points of $F(x)$.*

Alternative notation: If X has a particular distribution, for example $N(0, 1)$, then $X_n \to_d X$ is also denoted by $X_n \to_d N(0, 1)$.

The reason for excluding discontinuity points of $F(x)$ in the definition of convergence in distribution is that $\lim_{n \to \infty} F_n(x)$ may not be right-continuous in these discontinuity points. For example, let $X_n = X + 1/n$. Then $F_n(x) = F(x - 1/n)$. Now if $F(x)$ is discontinuous in x_0, then $\lim_{n \to \infty} F(x_0 - 1/n) < F(x_0)$; hence $\lim_{n \to \infty} F_n(x_0) < F(x_0)$. Thus, without the exclusion of discontinuity points, $X + 1/n$ would not converge in distribution to the distribution of X, which would be counterintuitive.

If each of the components of a sequence of random vectors converges in distribution, then the random vectors themselves may *not* converge in distribution. As a counterexample, let

$$X_n = \begin{pmatrix} X_{1n} \\ X_{2n} \end{pmatrix} \sim N_2 \left(\begin{pmatrix} 0 \\ 0 \end{pmatrix}, \begin{pmatrix} 1 & (-1)^n/2 \\ (-1)^n/2 & 1 \end{pmatrix} \right). \qquad (6.16)$$

Then $X_{1n} \to_d N(0, 1)$ and $X_{2n} \to_d N(0, 1)$, but X_n does not converge in distribution.

Moreover, in general $X_n \to_d X$ does *not* imply that $X_n \to_p$. For example, if we replace X by an independent random drawing Z from the distribution of X, then $X_n \to_d X$ and $X_n \to_d Z$ are equivalent statements because they only say that the distribution function of X_n converges to the distribution function of X (or Z) pointwise in the continuity points of the latter distribution function. If $X_n \to_d X$ implied $X_n \to_p X$, then $X_n \to_p Z$ would imply that $X = Z$, which is not possible because X and Z are independent. The only exception is the case in which the distribution of X is degenerated: $P(X = c) = 1$ for some constant c:

Theorem 6.16: *If X_n converges in distribution to X, and $P(X = c) = 1$, where c is a constant, then X_n converges in probability to c.*

Proof: Exercise.

Note that this result is demonstrated in the left-hand panels of Figures 6.1–6.3. On the other hand,

Theorem 6.17: $X_n \to_p X$ *implies* $X_n \to_d X$.

Proof: Theorem 6.17 follows straightforwardly from Theorem 6.3, Theorem 6.4, and Theorem 6.18 below.   Q.E.D.

There is a one-to-one correspondence between convergence in distribution and convergence of expectations of bounded continuous functions of random variables:

Theorem 6.18: *Let X_n and X be random vectors in $\mathbb{R}^k$. Then $X_n \to_d X$ if and only if for all bounded continuous functions φ on $\mathbb{R}^k$ $\lim_{n\to\infty} E[\varphi(X_n)] = E[\varphi(X)]$.*

Proof: I will only prove this theorem for the case in which X_n and X are random variables. Throughout the proof the distribution function of X_n is denoted by $F_n(x)$ and the distribution function of X by $F(x)$.

Proof of the "only if" case: Let $X_n \to_d X$. Without loss of generality we may assume that $\varphi(x) \in [0, 1]$ for all x. For any $\varepsilon > 0$ we can choose continuity points a and b of $F(x)$ such that $F(b) - F(a) > 1 - \varepsilon$. Moreover, we can choose continuity points $a = c_1 < c_2 < \cdots < c_m = b$ of $F(x)$ such that, for $j = 1, \ldots, m-1$,

$$\sup_{x \in (c_j, c_{j+1}]} \varphi(x) - \inf_{x \in (c_j, c_{j+1}]} \varphi(x) \le \varepsilon. \tag{6.17}$$

Now define

$$\psi(x) = \inf_{x \in (c_j, c_{j+1}]} \varphi(x) \quad \text{for} \quad x \in (c_j, c_{j+1}],$$

$$j = 1, \ldots, m-1, \psi(x) = 0 \text{ elsewhere.} \tag{6.18}$$

Then $0 \le \varphi(x) - \psi(x) \le \varepsilon$ for $x \in (a, b]$, $0 \le \varphi(x) - \psi(x) \le 1$ for $x \notin (a, b]$; hence,

$$\limsup_{n \to \infty} |E[\psi(X_n)] - E[\varphi(X_n)]|$$

$$\le \limsup_{n \to \infty} \left(\int_{x \in (a,b]} |\psi(x) - \varphi(x)| dF_n(x) + \int_{x \notin (a,b]} |\psi(x) - \varphi(x)| dF_n(x) \right)$$

$$\le \varepsilon + 1 - \lim_{n \to \infty} (F_n(b) - F_n(a)) = \varepsilon + 1 - (F(b) - F(a)) \le 2\varepsilon. \tag{6.19}$$

Moreover, we have

$$|E[\psi(X)] - E[\varphi(X)]| \le 2\varepsilon, \tag{6.20}$$

and

$$\lim_{n \to \infty} E[\psi(X_n)] = E[\psi(X)]. \tag{6.21}$$

If we combine (6.19)–(6.21), the "only if" part easily follows.

Proof of the "if" case: Let $a < b$ be arbitrary continuity points of $F(x)$, and let

$$\varphi(x) = \begin{cases} = 0 & \text{if } x \ge b, \\ = 1 & \text{if } x < a, \\ = \frac{b-x}{b-a} & \text{if } a \le x < b. \end{cases} \tag{6.22}$$

Then clearly (6.22) is a bounded continuous function. Next, observe that

$$E[\varphi(X_n)] = \int \varphi(x) dF_n(x)$$

$$= F_n(a) + \int_a^b \frac{b-x}{b-a} dF_n(x) \ge F_n(a); \tag{6.23}$$

hence,

$$E[\varphi(X)] = \lim_{n \to \infty} E[\varphi(X_n)] \ge \limsup_{n \to \infty} F_n(a). \tag{6.24}$$

Moreover,

$$E[\varphi(X)] = \int \varphi(x)dF(x) = F(a) + \int_a^b \frac{b-x}{b-a}dF(x) \leq F(b). \quad (6.25)$$

Combining (6.24) and (6.25) yields $F(b) \geq \limsup_{n\to\infty} F_n(a)$; hence, because $b(> a)$ was arbitrary, letting $b \downarrow a$ it follows that

$$F(a) \geq \limsup_{n\to\infty} F_n(a). \quad (6.26)$$

Similarly, for $c < a$ we have $F(c) \leq \liminf_{n\to\infty} F_n(a)$; hence, if we let $c \uparrow a$, it follows that

$$F(a) \leq \liminf_{n\to\infty} F_n(a). \quad (6.27)$$

If we combine (6.26) and (6.27), the "if" part follows, that is, $F(a) = \lim_{n\to\infty} F_n(a)$. Q.E.D.

Note that the "only if" part of Theorem 6.18 implies another version of the bounded convergence theorem:

Theorem 6.19: *(Bounded convergence theorem) If X_n is bounded: $P(|X_n| \leq M) = 1$ for some $M < \infty$ and all n, then $X_n \to_d X$ implies $\lim_{n\to\infty} E(X_n) = E(X)$.*

Proof: Easy exercise.

On the basis of Theorem 6.18, it is not hard to verify that the following result holds.

Theorem 6.20: *(Continuous mapping theorem) Let X_n and X be random vectors in $\mathbb{R}^k$ such that $X_n \to_d X$, and let $\Phi(x)$ be a continuous mapping from $\mathbb{R}^k$ into $\mathbb{R}^m$. Then $\Phi(X_n) \to_d \Phi(X)$.*

Proof: Exercise.

The following are examples of Theorem 6.20 applications:

(1) Let $X_n \to_d X$, where X is $N(0, 1)$ distributed. Then $X_n^2 \to_d \chi_1^2$.
(2) Let $X_n \to_d X$, where X is $N_k(0, I)$ distributed. Then $X_n^{\mathrm{T}} X_n \to_d \chi_k^2$.

If $X_n \to_d X$, $Y_n \to_d Y$, and $\Phi(x, y)$ is a continuous function, then in general it does *not* follow that $\Phi(X_n, Y_n) \to_d \Phi(X, Y)$ except if either X or Y has a degenerated distribution:

Theorem 6.21: *Let X and X_n be random vectors in $\mathbb{R}^k$ such that $X_n \to_d X$, and let Y_n be a random vector in $\mathbb{R}^m$ such that $\mathrm{plim}_{n\to\infty} Y_n = c$, where $c \in \mathbb{R}^m$ is* *a nonrandom vector. Moreover, let* $\Phi(x, y)$ *be a continuous function on the set* $\mathbb{R}^k \times \{y \in \mathbb{R}^m : \|y - c\| < \delta\}$ *for some* $\delta > 0.$[6] *Then* $\Phi(X_n, Y_n) \to_d \Phi(X, c).$

Proof: Again, we prove the theorem for the case $k = m = 1$ only. Let $F_n(x)$ and $F(x)$ be the distribution functions of X_n and X, respectively, and let $\Phi(x, y)$ be a bounded continuous function on $\mathbb{R} \times (c - \delta, c + \delta)$ for some $\delta > 0$. Without loss of generality we may assume that $|\Phi(x, y)| \leq 1$. Next, let $\varepsilon > 0$ be arbitrary, and choose continuity points $a < b$ of $F(x)$ such that $F(b) - F(a) > 1 - \varepsilon$. Then for any $\gamma > 0$,

$$
\begin{aligned}
|E[\Phi(X_n, Y_n)] &- E[\Phi(X_n, c)]| \\
&\leq E[|\Phi(X_n, Y_n) - \Phi(X_n, c)|I(|Y_n - c| \leq \gamma)] \\
&\quad + E[|\Phi(X_n, Y_n) - \Phi(X_n, c)|I(|Y_n - c| > \gamma)] \\
&\leq E[|\Phi(X_n, Y_n) - \Phi(X_n, c)|I(|Y_n - c| \leq \gamma)I(X_n \in [a, b])] \\
&\quad + 2P(X_n \notin [a, b]) + 2P(|Y_n - c| > \gamma) \\
&\leq \sup_{x \in [a, b],\, |y - c| \leq \gamma} |\Phi(x, y) - \Phi(x, c)| + 2(1 - F_n(b) + F_n(a)) \\
&\quad + 2P(|Y_n - c| > \gamma).
\end{aligned}
\tag{6.28}
$$

Because a continuous function on a closed and bounded subset of Euclidean space is uniformly continuous on that subset (see Appendix II), we can choose γ so small that

$$
\sup_{x \in [a, b],\, |y - c| \leq \gamma} |\Phi(x, y) - \Phi(x, c)| < \varepsilon.
\tag{6.29}
$$

Moreover, $1 - F_n(b) + F_n(a) \to 1 - F(b) + F(a) < \varepsilon$, and $P(|Y_n - c| > \gamma) \to 0$. Therefore, it follows from (6.28) that

$$
\limsup_{n \to \infty} |E[\Phi(X_n, Y_n)] - E[\Phi(X_n, c)]| \leq 3\varepsilon.
\tag{6.30}
$$

The rest of the proof is left as an exercise. Q.E.D.

Corollary 6.1: *Let* Z_n *be t-distributed with n degrees of freedom. Then* $Z_n \to_d$ $N(0, 1)$.

Proof: By the definition of the *t*-distribution with n degrees of freedom we can write

$$
Z_n = \frac{U_0}{\sqrt{\frac{1}{n} \sum_{j=1}^{n} U_j^2}},
\tag{6.31}
$$

where $U_0, U_1, \ldots, U_n$ are i.i.d. $N(0, 1)$. Let $X_n = U_0$ and $X = U_0$ so that trivially $X_n \to_d X$. Let $Y_n = (1/n) \sum_{j=1}^{n} U_j^2$. Then by the weak law

---

[6] Thus, Φ is continuous in y on a little neighborhood of c.

of large numbers (Theorem 6.2) we have $\text{plim}_{n\to\infty} Y_n = E(U_1^2) = 1$. Let $\Phi(x, y) = x/\sqrt{y}$. Note that $\Phi(x, y)$ is continuous on $R \times (1 - \varepsilon, 1 + \varepsilon)$ for $0 < \varepsilon < 1$. Thus, by Theorem 6.21, $Z_n = \Phi(X_n, Y_n) \to \Phi(X, 1) = U_0 \sim N(0, 1)$ in distribution.   Q.E.D.

Corollary 6.2: *Let $U_1 \ldots U_n$ be a random sample from $N_k(\mu, \Sigma)$, where Σ is nonsingular. Denote $\bar{U} = (1/n) \sum_{j=1}^{n} U_j$, $\hat{\Sigma} = (1/(n-1)) \sum_{j=1}^{n} (U_j - \bar{U})(U_j - \bar{U})^{\text{T}}$, and let $Z_n = n(\bar{U} - \mu)^{\text{T}} \hat{\Sigma}^{-1} (\bar{U} - \mu)$. Then $Z_n \to_d \chi_k^2$.*

Proof: For a $k \times k$ matrix $A = (a_1, \ldots, a_k)$, let $\text{vec}(A)$ be the $k^2 \times 1$ vector of stacked columns a_j, $j = 1, \ldots, k$ of A : $\text{vec}(A) = (a_1^{\text{T}}, \ldots, a_k^{\text{T}})^{\text{T}} = b$, for instance, with inverse $\text{vec}^{-1}(b) = A$. Let $c = \text{vec}(\Sigma)$, $Y_n = \text{vec}(\hat{\Sigma})$, $X_n = \sqrt{n}(\bar{U} - \mu)$, $X \sim N_k(0, \Sigma)$, and $\Psi(x, y) = x^{\text{T}}(\text{vec}^{-1}(y))^{-1}x$. Because Σ is nonsingular, there exists a neighborhood $C(\delta) = \{y \in \mathbb{R}^{k \times k} : \|y - c\| < \delta\}$ of c such that for all y in $C(\delta)$, $\text{vec}^{-1}(y)$ is nonsingular (*Exercise*: Why?), and consequently, $\Psi(x, y)$ is continuous on $\mathbb{R}^k \times C(\delta)$ (*Exercise*: Why?). The corollary follows now from Theorem 6.21 (*Exercise*: Why?).   Q.E.D.

6.6. Convergence of Characteristic Functions

Recall that the characteristic function of a random vector X in $\mathbb{R}^k$ is defined as

$$\varphi(t) = E[\exp(it^{\text{T}}X)] = E[\cos(t^{\text{T}}X)] + i \cdot E[\sin(t^{\text{T}}X)]$$

for $t \in \mathbb{R}^k$, where $i = \sqrt{-1}$. The last equality obtains because $\exp(i \cdot x) = \cos(x) + i \cdot \sin(x)$.

Also recall that distributions are the same if and only if their characteristic functions are the same. This property can be extended to sequences of random variables and vectors:

Theorem 6.22: *Let X_n and X be random vectors in $\mathbb{R}^k$ with characteristic functions $\varphi_n(t)$ and $\varphi(t)$, respectively. Then $X_n \to_d X$ if and only if $\varphi(t) = \lim_{n\to\infty} \varphi_n(t)$ for all $t \in \mathbb{R}^k$.*

Proof: See Appendix 6.C for the case $k = 1$.

Note that the "only if" part of Theorem 6.22 follows from Theorem 6.18: $X_n \to_d X$ implies that, for any $t \in \mathbb{R}^k$,

$$\lim_{n\to\infty} E[\cos(t^{\text{T}}X_n)] = E[\cos(t^{\text{T}}X)];$$

$$\lim_{n\to\infty} E[\sin(t^{\text{T}}X_n)] = E[\sin(t^{\text{T}}X)];$$

hence,

$$\lim_{n\to\infty} \varphi_n(t) = \lim_{n\to\infty} E[\cos(t^{\text{T}}X_n)] + i \cdot \lim_{n\to\infty} E[\sin(t^{\text{T}}X_n)]$$
$$= E[\cos(t^{\text{T}}X)] + i \cdot E[\sin(t^{\text{T}}X)] = \varphi(t).$$

Theorem 6.22 plays a key role in the derivation of the central limit theorem in the next section.

6.7. The Central Limit Theorem

The prime example of the concept of convergence in distribution is the central limit theorem, which we have seen in action in Figures 6.4–6.6:

Theorem 6.23: *Let $X_1, \ldots, X_n$ be i.i.d. random variables satisfying $E(X_j) = \mu$, $var(X_j) = \sigma^2 < \infty$ and let $\bar{X} = (1/n) \sum_{j=1}^{n} X_j$. Then $\sqrt{n}(\bar{X} - \mu) \to_d N(0, \sigma^2)$.*

Proof: Without loss of generality we may assume that $\mu = 0$ and $\sigma = 1$. Let $\varphi(t)$ be the characteristic function of X_j. The assumptions $\mu = 0$ and $\sigma = 1$ imply that the first and second derivatives of $\varphi(t)$ at $t = 0$ are equal to $\varphi'(0) = 0$, $\varphi''(0) = -1$, respectively; hence by Taylor's theorem applied to $\text{Re}[\phi(t)]$ and $\text{Im}[\phi(t)]$ separately there exists numbers $\lambda_{1,t}, \lambda_{2,t} \in [0, 1]$ such that

$$\varphi(t) = \varphi(0) + t\varphi'(0) + \frac{1}{2}t^2 \left(\text{Re}[\varphi''(\lambda_{1,t} \cdot t)] + i \cdot \text{Im}[\varphi''(\lambda_{2,t} \cdot t)] \right)$$

$$= 1 - \frac{1}{2}t^2 + z(t)t^2,$$

for instance, where $z(t) = (1 + \text{Re}[\varphi''(\lambda_{1,t} \cdot t)] + i \cdot \text{Im}[\varphi''(\lambda_{2,t} \cdot t)])/2$. Note that $z(t)$ is bounded and satisfies $\lim_{t \to 0} z(t) = 0$.

Next, let $\varphi_n(t)$ be the characteristic function of $\sqrt{n}\bar{X}$. Then

$$\varphi_n(t) = \left(\varphi(t/\sqrt{n}) \right)^n$$

$$= \left(1 - \frac{1}{2}t^2/n + z(t/\sqrt{n})\, t^2/n \right)^n$$

$$= \left(1 - \frac{1}{2}t^2/n \right)^n$$

$$+ \sum_{m=1}^{n} \binom{n}{m} \left(1 - \frac{1}{2}t^2/n \right)^{n-m} \left(z(t/\sqrt{n})t^2/n \right)^m. \qquad (6.32)$$

For n so large that $t^2 < 2n$ we have

$$\left| \sum_{m=1}^{n} \binom{n}{m} \left(1 - \frac{1}{2}t^2/n \right)^{n-m} \left(z(t/\sqrt{n})t^2/n \right)^m \right|$$

$$\leq \sum_{m=1}^{n} \binom{n}{m} \left(|z(t/\sqrt{n})|t^2/n \right)^m = \left(1 + |z(t/\sqrt{n})| \, t^2/n \right)^n - 1.$$

$$(6.33)$$

Now observe that, for any real-valued sequence a_n that converges to a,

$$\lim_{n\to\infty} \ln\left((1 + a_n/n)^n\right) = \lim_{n\to\infty} n\ln(1 + a_n/n)$$

$$= \lim_{n\to\infty} a_n \times \lim_{n\to\infty} \frac{\ln(1 + a_n/n) - \ln(1)}{a_n/n}$$

$$= a \times \lim_{\delta\to 0} \frac{\ln(1 + \delta) - \ln(1)}{\delta} = a;$$

hence,

$$\lim_{n\to\infty} a_n = a \Rightarrow \lim_{n\to\infty} (1 + a_n/n)^n = e^a. \tag{6.34}$$

If we let $a_n = |z(t/\sqrt{n})|t^2$, which has limit $a = 0$, it follows from (6.34) that the right-hand expression in (6.33) converges to zero, and if we let $a_n = a = -t^2/2$ it follows then from (6.32) that

$$\lim_{n\to\infty} \varphi_n(t) = e^{-t^2/2}. \tag{6.35}$$

The right-hand side of (6.35) is the characteristic function of the standard normal distribution. The theorem follows now from Theorem 6.22.   Q.E.D.

There is also a multivariate version of the central limit theorem:

Theorem 6.24: *Let* $X_1, \ldots, X_n$ *be i.i.d. random vectors in* $\mathbb{R}^k$ *satisfying* $E(X_j) = \mu$, *Var*$(X_j) = \Sigma$, *where* Σ *is finite, and let* $\bar{X} = (1/n)\sum_{j=1}^n X_j$. *Then* $\sqrt{n}(\bar{X} - \mu) \to_d N_k(0, \Sigma)$.

Proof: Let $\xi \in \mathbb{R}^k$ be arbitrary but not a zero vector. Then it follows from Theorem 6.23 that $\sqrt{n}\xi^T(\bar{X} - \mu) \to_d N(0, \xi^T\Sigma\xi)$; hence, it follows from Theorem 6.22 that for all $t \in \mathbb{R}$, $\lim_{n\to\infty} E(\exp[i \cdot t\sqrt{n}\,\xi^T(\bar{X} - \mu)]) = \exp(-t^2\xi^T\Sigma\xi/2)$. Choosing $t = 1$, we thus have that, for arbitrary $\xi \in \mathbb{R}^k$, $\lim_{n\to\infty} E(\exp[i \cdot \xi^T\sqrt{n}(\bar{X} - \mu)]) = \exp(-\xi^T\Sigma\xi/2)$. Because the latter is the characteristic function of the $N_k(0, \Sigma)$ distribution, Theorem 6.24 follows now from Theorem 6.22.   Q.E.D.

Next, let Φ be a continuously differentiable mapping from $\mathbb{R}^k$ to $\mathbb{R}^m$, and let the conditions of Theorem 6.24 hold. The question is, What is the limiting distribution of $\sqrt{n}(\Phi(\bar{X}) - \Phi(\mu))$, if any? To answer this question, assume for the time being that $k = m = 1$ and let var$(X_j) = \sigma^2$; thus, $\sqrt{n}(\bar{X} - \mu) \to_d N(0, \sigma^2)$. It follows from the mean value theorem (see Appendix II) that there exists a random variable $\lambda \in [0, 1]$ such that

$$\sqrt{n}(\Phi(\bar{X}) - \Phi(\mu)) = \sqrt{n}(\bar{X} - \mu)\Phi'(\mu + \lambda(\bar{X} - \mu)).$$

Because $\sqrt{n}(\bar{X} - \mu) \to_d N(0, \sigma^2)$ implies $(\bar{X} - \mu) \to_d 0$, which by Theorem 6.16 implies that $\bar{X} \to_p \mu$, it follows that $\mu + \lambda(\bar{X} - \mu) \to_p \mu$. Moreover, because the derivative Φ' is continuous in μ it follows now from Theorem 6.3

that $\Phi'(\mu + \lambda(\bar{X} - \mu)) \to_p \Phi'(\mu)$. Therefore, it follows from Theorem 6.21 that $\sqrt{n}(\Phi(\bar{X}) - \Phi(\mu)) \to_d N[0, \sigma^2(\Phi'(\mu))^2]$. Along similar lines, if we apply the mean value theorem to each of the components of Φ separately, the following more general result can be proved. This approach is known as the *δ-method*.

Theorem 6.25: *Let X_n be a random vector in $\mathbb{R}^k$ satisfying $\sqrt{n}(X_n - \mu) \to_d N_k[0, \Sigma]$, where $\mu \in \mathbb{R}^k$ is nonrandom. Moreover, let $\Phi(x) = (\Phi_1(x), \dots, \Phi_m(x))^\mathsf{T}$ with $x = (x_1, \dots, x_k)^\mathsf{T}$ be a mapping from $\mathbb{R}^k$ to $\mathbb{R}^m$ such that the $m \times k$ matrix of partial derivatives*

$$\Delta(x) = \begin{pmatrix} \partial\Phi_1(x)/\partial x_1 & \dots & \partial\Phi_1(x)/\partial x_k \\ \vdots & \ddots & \vdots \\ \partial\Phi_m(x)/\partial x_1 & \dots & \partial\Phi_m(x)/\partial x_k \end{pmatrix} \tag{6.36}$$

exists in an arbitrary, small, open neighborhood of μ and its elements are continuous in μ. Then $\sqrt{n}(\varphi(X_n) - \Phi(\mu)) \to_d N_m[0, \Delta(\mu)\Sigma\Delta(\mu)^\mathsf{T}]$.

6.8. Stochastic Boundedness, Tightness, and the O_p and o_p Notations

The stochastic boundedness and related tightness concepts are important for various reasons, but one of the most important is that they are necessary conditions for convergence in distribution.

Definition 6.7: *A sequence of random variables or vectors X_n is said to be stochastically bounded if, for every $\varepsilon \in (0, 1)$, there exists a finite $M > 0$ such that $\inf_{n \geq 1} P[\|X_n\| \leq M] > 1 - \varepsilon$.*

Of course, if X_n is bounded itself (i.e., $P[\|X_n\| \leq M] = 1$ for all n), it is stochastically bounded as well, but the converse may not be true. For example, if the X_n's are equally distributed (but not necessarily independent) random variables with common distribution function F, then for every $\varepsilon \in (0, 1)$ we can choose continuity points $-M$ and M of F such that $P[|X_n| \leq M] = F(M) - F(-M) = 1 - \varepsilon$. Thus, the stochastic boundedness condition limits the *heterogeneity* of the X_n's.

Stochastic boundedness is usually denoted by $O_p(1)$: $X_n = O_p(1)$ means that the sequence X_n is stochastically bounded. More generally,

Definition 6.8: *Let a_n be a sequence of positive nonrandom variables. Then $X_n = O_p(a_n)$ means that X_n/a_n is stochastically bounded and $O_p(a_n)$ by itself represents a generic random variable or vector X_n such that $X_n = O_p(a_n)$.*

The necessity of stochastic boundedness for convergence in distribution follows from the fact that

Theorem 6.26: *Convergence in distribution implies stochastic boundedness.*

Proof: Let X_n and X be random variables with corresponding distribution functions F_n and F, respectively, and assume that $X_n \to_d X$. Given an $\varepsilon \in (0, 1)$ we can choose continuity points $-M_1$ and M_1 of F such that $F(M_1) > 1 - \varepsilon/4$, $F(-M_1) < \varepsilon/4$. Because $\lim_{n\to\infty} F_n(M_1) = F(M_1)$ there exists an index n_1 such that $|F_n(M_1) - F(M_1)| < \varepsilon/4$ if $n \geq n_1$; hence, $F_n(M_1) > 1 - \varepsilon/2$ if $n \geq n_1$. Similarly, there exists an index n_2 such that $F_n(-M_1) < \varepsilon/2$ if $n \geq n_2$. Let $m = \max(n_1, n_2)$. Then $\inf_{n\geq m} P[|X_n| \leq M_1] > 1 - \varepsilon$. Finally, we can always choose an M_2 so large that $\min_{1\leq n\leq m-1} P[|X_n| \leq M_2] > 1 - \varepsilon$. If we take $M = \max(M_1, M_2)$, the theorem follows. The proof of the multivariate case is almost the same.   Q.E.D.

Note that, because convergence in probability implies convergence in distribution, it follows trivially from Theorem 6.26 that convergence in probability implies stochastic boundedness.

For example, let $S_n = \sum_{j=1}^{n} X_j$, where the X_j's are i.i.d. random variables with expectation μ and variance $\sigma^2 < \infty$. If $\mu = 0$, then $S_n = O_p(\sqrt{n})$ because, by the central limit theorem, $S_n/\sqrt{n}$ converges in distribution to $N(0, \sigma^2)$. However, if $\mu \neq 0$, then only $S_n = O_p(n)$ because then $S_n/\sqrt{n} - \mu\sqrt{n} \to_d N(0, \sigma^2)$; hence, $S_n/\sqrt{n} = O_p(1) + O_p(\sqrt{n})$ and thus $S_n = O_p(\sqrt{n}) + O_p(n) = O_p(n)$.

In Definition 6.2 I have introduced the concept of uniform integrability. It is left as an exercise to prove that

Theorem 6.27: *Uniform integrability implies stochastic boundedness.*

Tightness is the version of stochastic boundedness for probability measures:

Definition 6.9: *A sequence of probability measures μ_n on the Borel sets in $\mathbb{R}^k$ is called tight if, for an arbitrary $\varepsilon \in (0, 1)$ there exists a compact subset K of $\mathbb{R}^k$ such that $\inf_{n\geq 1} \mu_n(K) > 1 - \varepsilon$.*

Clearly, if $X_n = O_p(1)$, then the sequence of corresponding induced probability measures μ_n is tight because the sets of the type $K = \{x \in \mathbb{R}^k : \|x\| \leq M\}$ are closed and bounded for $M < \infty$ and therefore compact.

For sequences of random variables and vectors the tightness concept does not add much over the stochastic boundedness concept, but the tightness concept is fundamental in proving so-called functional central limit theorems.

If $X_n = O_p(1)$, then obviously for any $\delta > 0$, $X_n = O_p(n^\delta)$. But X_n/n^δ is now more than stochastically bounded because then we also have that $X_n/n^\delta \to_p 0$. The latter is denoted by $X_n = o_p(n^\delta)$:

Definition 6.10: *Let a_n be a sequence of positive nonrandom variables. Then $X_n = o_p(a_n)$ means that X_n/a_n converges in probability to zero (or a zero vector*

if X_n is a vector), and $o_p(a_n)$ by itself represents a generic random variable or vector X_n such that $X_n = o_p(a_n)$. Moreover, the sequence $1/a_n$ represents the rate of convergence of X_n.

Thus, $X_n \to_p X$ can also be denoted by $X_n = X + o_p(1)$. This notation is handy if the difference of X_n and X is a complicated expression. For example, the result of Theorem 6.25 is obtained because, by the mean value theorem, $\sqrt{n}(\varphi(X_n) - \Phi(\mu)) = \tilde{\Delta}_n(\mu)\sqrt{n}(X_n - \mu) = \Delta(\mu)\sqrt{n}(X_n - \mu) + o_p(1)$, where

$$\tilde{\Delta}_n(\mu)$$

$$= \begin{pmatrix} \partial\Phi_1(x)/\partial x|_{x=\mu+\lambda_{1,n}(X_n-\mu)} \\ \vdots \\ \partial\Phi_m(x)/\partial x|_{x=\mu+\lambda_{k,n}(X_n-\mu)} \end{pmatrix}, \quad \text{with} \quad \lambda_{j,n} \in [0, 1], j = 1, \ldots, k.$$

The remainder term $(\tilde{\Delta}_n(\mu) - \Delta(\mu))\sqrt{n}(X_n - \mu)$ can now be represented by $o_p(1)$, because $\tilde{\Delta}_n(\mu) \to_p \Delta(\mu)$ and $\sqrt{n}(X_n - \mu) \to_d N_k[0, \Sigma]$; hence, by Theorem 6.21 this remainder term converges in distribution to the zero vector and thus also in probability to the zero vector.

6.9. Asymptotic Normality of M-Estimators

This section sets forth conditions for the asymptotic normality of M-estimators in addition to the conditions for consistency. An estimator $\hat{\theta}$ of a parameter $\theta_0 \in \mathbb{R}^m$ is asymptotically normally distributed if an increasing sequence of positive numbers a_n and a positive semidefinite $m \times m$ matrix Σ exist such that $a_n(\hat{\theta} - \theta_0) \to_d N_m[0, \Sigma]$. Usually, $a_n = \sqrt{n}$, but there are exceptions to this rule.

Asymptotic normality is fundamental for econometrics. Most of the econometric tests rely on it. Moreover, the proof of the asymptotic normality theorem in this section also nicely illustrates the usefulness of the main results in this chapter.

Given that the data are a random sample, we only need a few additional conditions over those of Theorems 6.10 and 6.11:

Theorem 6.1: *Let, in addition to the conditions of Theorems 6.10 and 6.11, the following conditions be satisfied:*

(a) *Θ is convex.*
(b) *θ_0 is an interior point of Θ.*
(c) *For each $x \in \mathbb{R}^k$, $g(x, \theta)$ is twice continuously differentiable on Θ.*
(d) *For each pair $\theta_{i_1}, \theta_{i_2}$ of components of θ, $E[\sup_{\theta\in\Theta}|\partial^2 g(X_1, \theta)/(\partial\theta_{i_1}\partial\theta_{i_2})|] < \infty$.*

(e)   The $m \times m$ matrix $A = E\left[\frac{\partial^2 g(X_1, \theta_0)}{\partial \theta_0 \partial \theta_0^{\mathsf{T}}}\right]$ is nonsingular.

(f)   The $m \times m$ matrix $B = E\left[\left(\frac{\partial g(X_1, \theta_0)}{\partial \theta_0^{\mathsf{T}}}\right)\left(\frac{\partial g(X_1, \theta_0)}{\partial \theta_0}\right)\right]$ is finite.

Then $\sqrt{n}(\hat{\theta} - \theta_0) \to_d N_m[0,\, A^{-1}BA^{-1}]$.

Proof: I will prove the theorem for the case $m = 1$ only, leaving the general case as an exercise.

I have already established in Theorem 6.11 that $\hat{\theta} \to_p \theta_0$. Because θ_0 is an interior point of Θ, the probability that $\hat{\theta}$ is an interior point converges to 1, and consequently the probability that the first-order condition for a maximum of $\hat{Q}(\theta) = (1/n)\sum_{j=1}^{n} g(X_j, \theta)$ in $\theta = \hat{\theta}$ holds converges to 1. Thus,

$$\lim_{n \to \infty} P[\hat{Q}'(\hat{\theta}) = 0] = 1, \tag{6.37}$$

where, as usual, $\hat{Q}'(\theta) = d\hat{Q}(\theta)/d\theta$. Next, observe from the mean value theorem that there exists a $\hat{\lambda} \in [0, 1]$ such that

$$\sqrt{n}\,\hat{Q}'(\hat{\theta}) = \sqrt{n}\,\hat{Q}'(\theta_0) + \hat{Q}''(\theta_0 + \hat{\lambda}(\hat{\theta} - \theta_0))\sqrt{n}(\hat{\theta} - \theta_0), \tag{6.38}$$

where $\hat{Q}''(\theta) = d^2\hat{Q}(\theta)/(d\theta)^2$. Note that, by the convexity of Θ,

$$P[\theta_0 + \hat{\lambda}(\hat{\theta} - \theta_0) \in \Theta] = 1, \tag{6.39}$$

and by the consistency of $\hat{\theta}$,

$$\plim_{n \to \infty}[\theta_0 + \hat{\lambda}(\hat{\theta} - \theta_0)] = \theta_0. \tag{6.40}$$

Moreover, it follows from Theorem 6.10 and conditions (c) and (d), with the latter adapted to the univariate case, that

$$\plim_{n \to \infty} \sup_{\theta \in \Theta} |\hat{Q}''(\theta) - \bar{Q}''(\theta)| = 0, \tag{6.41}$$

where $\bar{Q}''(\theta)$ is the second derivative of $\bar{Q}(\theta) = E[g(X_1, \theta)]$. Then it follows from (6.39)–(6.41) and Theorem 6.12 that

$$\plim_{n \to \infty} \hat{Q}''(\theta_0 + \hat{\lambda}(\hat{\theta} - \theta_0)) = \bar{Q}''(\theta_0) \neq 0. \tag{6.42}$$

Note that $\bar{Q}''(\theta_0)$ corresponds to the matrix A in condition (e), and thus $\bar{Q}''(\theta_0)$ is positive in the "argmin" case and negative in the "argmax" case. Therefore, it follows from (6.42) and Slutsky's theorem (Theorem 6.3) that

$$\plim_{n \to \infty} \hat{Q}''(\theta_0 + \hat{\lambda}(\hat{\theta} - \theta_0))^{-1} = \bar{Q}''(\theta_0)^{-1} = A^{-1}. \tag{6.43}$$

Now (6.38) can be rewritten as

$$\sqrt{n}(\hat{\theta} - \theta_0) = -\hat{Q}''(\theta_0 + \hat{\lambda}(\hat{\theta} - \theta_0))^{-1}\sqrt{n}\hat{Q}'(\theta_0)$$
$$+ \hat{Q}''(\theta_0 + \hat{\lambda}(\hat{\theta} - \theta_0))^{-1}\sqrt{n}\hat{Q}'(\hat{\theta})$$
$$= -\hat{Q}''(\theta_0 + \hat{\lambda}(\hat{\theta} - \theta_0))^{-1}\sqrt{n}\hat{Q}'(\theta_0) + o_p(1), \qquad (6.44)$$

where the $o_p(1)$ term follows from (6.37), (6.43), and Slutsky's theorem.

Because of condition (b), the first-order condition for θ_0 applies, that is,

$$\bar{Q}'(\theta_0) = E[dg(X_1, \theta_0)/d\theta_0] = 0. \qquad (6.45)$$

Moreover, condition (f), adapted to the univariate case, now reads as follows:

$$\text{var}[dg(X_1, \theta_0)/d\theta_0] = B \in (0, \infty). \qquad (6.46)$$

Therefore, it follows from (6.45), (6.46), and the central limit theorem (Theorem 6.23) that

$$\sqrt{n}\hat{Q}'(\theta_0) = (1/\sqrt{n})\sum_{j=1}^{n} dg(X_j, \theta_0)/d\theta_0 \to_d N[0, B]. \qquad (6.47)$$

Now it follows from (6.43), (6.47), and Theorem 6.21 that

$$-\hat{Q}''(\theta_0 + \hat{\lambda}(\hat{\theta} - \theta_0))^{-1}\sqrt{n}\hat{Q}'(\theta_0) \to_d N[0, A^{-1}BA^{-1}]; \qquad (6.48)$$

hence, the result of the theorem under review for the case $m = 1$ follows from (6.44), (6.48), and Theorem 6.21.   Q.E.D.

The result of Theorem 6.28 is only useful if we are able to estimate the asymptotic variance matrix $A^{-1}BA^{-1}$ consistently because then we will be able to design tests of various hypotheses about the parameter vector θ_0.

Theorem 6.29: *Let*

$$\hat{A} = \frac{1}{n}\sum_{j=1}^{n} \frac{\partial^2 g(X_j, \hat{\theta})}{\partial\hat{\theta}\partial\hat{\theta}^{\mathrm{T}}}, \qquad (6.49)$$

and

$$\hat{B} = \frac{1}{n}\sum_{j=1}^{n} \left(\frac{\partial g(X_j, \hat{\theta})}{\partial\hat{\theta}^{\mathrm{T}}}\right)\left(\frac{\partial g(X_j, \hat{\theta})}{\partial\hat{\theta}}\right). \qquad (6.50)$$

Under the conditions of Theorem 6.28, $plim_{n\to\infty}\hat{A} = A$, and under the additional condition that $E[sup_{\theta\in\Theta}\|\partial g(X_1, \theta)/\partial\theta^{\mathrm{T}}\|^2] < \infty$, $plim_{n\to\infty}\hat{B} = B$. Consequently, $plim_{n\to\infty}\hat{A}^{-1}\hat{B}\hat{A}^{-1} = A^{-1}BA^{-1}$.

Proof: The theorem follows straightforwardly from the uniform weak law of large numbers and various Slutsky's theorems – in particular Theorem 6.21.

6.10. Hypotheses Testing

As an application of Theorems 6.28 and 6.29, consider the problem of testing a null hypothesis against an alternative hypothesis of the form

$$H_0 : R\theta_0 = q, \; H_1 : R\theta_0 \neq q, \tag{6.51}$$

respectively, where R is a given $r \times m$ matrix of rank $r \leq m$ and q is a given $r \times 1$ vector. Under the null hypothesis in (6.51) and the conditions of Theorem 6.2, $\sqrt{n}(R\hat{\theta} - q) \to_d N_r[0, RA^{-1}BA^{-1}R^{\mathrm{T}}]$, and if the matrix B is nonsingular then the asymptotic variance matrix involved is nonsingular. Then it follows from Theorem 6.21 that

Theorem 6.30: *Under the conditions of Theorems 6.28 and 6.29, the additional condition that B is nonsingular, and the null hypothesis in (6.51) with R of full rank r,*

$$W_n = n(R\hat{\theta} - q)^{\mathrm{T}}\left(R\hat{A}^{-1}\hat{B}\hat{A}^{-1}R^{\mathrm{T}}\right)^{-1}(R\hat{\theta} - q) \to_d \chi_r^2. \tag{6.52}$$

On the other hand, under the alternative hypothesis in (6.51),

$$W_n/n \to_p (R\theta_0 - q)^{\mathrm{T}}\left(RA^{-1}BA^{-1}R^{\mathrm{T}}\right)^{-1}(R\theta_0 - q) > 0. \tag{6.53}$$

The statistic W_n is now the test statistic of the Wald test of the null hypothesis in (6.51). Given the size $\alpha \in (0, 1)$, choose a critical value β such that, for a χ_r^2-distributed random variable Z, $P[Z > \beta] = \alpha$ and thus under the null hypothesis in (6.51), $P[W_n > \beta] \to \alpha$. Then the null hypothesis is accepted if $W_n \leq \beta$ and rejected in favor of the alternative hypothesis if $W_n > \beta$. Owing to (6.53), this test is consistent. Note that the critical value β can be found in Table IV.4 in Appendix IV for the 5% and 10% significance levels and degrees of freedom r ranging from 1 to 30.

If $r = 1$, so that R is a row vector, we can modify (6.52) to

$$t_n = \sqrt{n}\left(R\hat{A}^{-1}\hat{B}\hat{A}^{-1}R^{\mathrm{T}}\right)^{-1/2}(R\hat{\theta} - q) \to_d N(0, 1), \tag{6.54}$$

whereas under the alternative hypothesis (6.53) becomes

$$t_n/\sqrt{n} \to_p \left(RA^{-1}BA^{-1}R^{\mathrm{T}}\right)^{-1/2}(R\theta_0 - q) \neq 0. \tag{6.55}$$

These results can be used to construct a two or one-sided test in a way similar to the t-test we have seen before in the previous chapter. In particular,

Theorem 6.31: *Assume that the conditions of Theorem 6.30 hold. Let $\theta_{i,0}$ be component i of θ_0, and let $\hat{\theta}_i$ be component i of $\hat{\theta}$. Consider the hypotheses $H_0 : \theta_{i,0} = \theta_{i,0}^*, \; H_1 : \theta_{i,0} \neq \theta_{i,0}^*$, where $\theta_{i,0}^*$ is given (often the value $\theta_{i,0}^* = 0$ is of special interest). Let the vector e_i be column i of the unit matrix I_m. Then, under H_0,*

$$\hat{t}_i = \frac{\sqrt{n}(\hat{\theta}_i - \theta_{i,0}^*)}{\sqrt{e_i^T \hat{A}^{-1} \hat{B} \hat{A}^{-1} e_i)}} \to_d N(0, 1), \tag{6.56}$$

whereas under H_1,

$$\hat{t}_i / \sqrt{n} \to_p \frac{\hat{\theta}_{i,0} - \theta_{i,0}^*}{\sqrt{e_i^T A^{-1} B A^{-1} e_i)}} \neq 0. \tag{6.57}$$

Given the size $\alpha \in (0, 1)$, choose a critical value β such that, for a standard, normally distributed random variable U, $P[|U| > \beta] = \alpha$, and thus by (6.56), $P[|\hat{t}_i| > \beta] \to \alpha$ if the null hypothesis is true. Then the null hypothesis is accepted if $|\hat{t}_i| \leq \beta$ and rejected in favor of the alternative hypothesis if $|\hat{t}_i| > \beta$. It is obvious from (6.57) that this test is consistent.

The statistic $\hat{t}_i$ in (6.56) is usually referred to as a t-test statistic because of the similarity of this test to the t-test in the normal random sample case. However, its finite sample distribution under the null hypothesis may not be of the t-distribution type at all. Moreover, in the case $\theta_{i,0}^* = 0$ the statistic $\hat{t}_i$ is called the t-value (or pseudo t-value) of the estimator $\hat{\theta}_i$, and if the test rejects the null hypothesis this estimator is said to be significant at the $\alpha \times 100\%$ significance level. Note that the critical value β involved can be found in Table IV.3 in Appendix IV, for the 5% and 10% significance levels.

6.11. Exercises

1. Let $X_n = (X_{1,n}, \ldots, X_{k,n})^T$ and $c = (c_1, \ldots, c_k)^T$. Prove that $\text{plim}_{n\to\infty} X_n = c$ if and only if $\text{plim}_{n\to\infty} X_{i,n} = c_i$ for $i = 1, \ldots, k$.

2. Prove that if $P(|X_n| \leq M) = 1$ and $X_n \to_p X$ then $P(|X| \leq M) = 1$.

3. Prove Theorem 6.12.

4. Explain why the random vector X_n in (6.16) does not converge in distribution.

5. Prove Theorem 6.16.

6. Prove Theorem 6.17.

7. Prove (6.21).

8. Prove Theorem 6.19.

9. Prove Theorem 6.20, using Theorem 6.18.

10. Finish the proof of Theorem 6.21.

11. Answer the questions Why? in the proof of Corollary 6.2.

12. Prove that the limit (6.35) is just the characteristic function of the standard normal distribution.

13. Prove the first and the last equality in (6.32).

14. Prove Theorem 6.25.

15. Prove Theorem 6.27. *Hint:* Use Chebishev's inequality for first absolute moments.

16. Adapt the proof of Theorem 6.28 for $m = 1$ to the multivariate case $m > 1$.

17. Prove Theorem 6.29.

18. Formulate the conditions (additional to Assumption 6.1) for the asymptotic normality of the nonlinear least-squares estimator (6.15) for the special case that $P[E(U_1^2|X_1) = \sigma^2] = 1$.

APPENDIXES

6.A. Proof of the Uniform Weak Law of Large Numbers

First, recall that "sup" denotes the smallest upper bound of the function involved, and similarly, "inf" is the largest lower bound. Now for arbitrary $\delta > 0$ and $\theta_* \in \Theta$, let $\Theta_\delta(\theta_*) = \{\theta \in \Theta : \|\theta - \theta_*\| < \delta\}$. Using the fact that $\sup_x |f(x)| \leq \max\{|\sup_x f(x)|, |\inf_x f(x)|\} \leq |\sup_x f(x)| + |\inf_x f(x)|$, we find that

$$
\sup_{\theta \in \Theta_\delta(\theta_*)} \left| (1/n) \sum_{j=1}^n g(X_j, \theta) - E[g(X_1, \theta)] \right|
$$

$$
\leq \left| \sup_{\theta \in \Theta_\delta(\theta_*)} \left\{ (1/n) \sum_{j=1}^n g(X_j, \theta) - E[g(X_1, \theta)] \right\} \right|
$$

$$
+ \left| \inf_{\theta \in \Theta_\delta(\theta_*)} \left\{ (1/n) \sum_{j=1}^n g(X_j, \theta) - E[g(X_1, \theta)] \right\} \right| \tag{6.58}
$$

Moreover,

$$
\sup_{\theta \in \Theta_\delta(\theta_*)} \left\{ (1/n) \sum_{j=1}^n g(X_j, \theta) - E[g(X_1, \theta)] \right\}
$$

$$
\leq (1/n) \sum_{j=1}^n \sup_{\theta \in \Theta_\delta(\theta_*)} g(X_j, \theta) - \inf_{\theta \in \Theta_\delta(\theta_*)} E[g(X_1, \theta)]
$$

$$
\leq \left| (1/n) \sum_{j=1}^n \sup_{\theta \in \Theta_\delta(\theta_*)} g(X_j, \theta) - E\left[\sup_{\theta \in \Theta_\delta(\theta_*)} g(X_1, \theta) \right] \right|
$$

$$
+ E\left[\sup_{\theta \in \Theta_\delta(\theta_*)} g(X_1, \theta) \right] - E\left[\inf_{\theta \in \Theta_\delta(\theta_*)} g(X_1, \theta) \right], \tag{6.59}
$$

and similarly

$$
\inf_{\theta \in \Theta_\delta(\theta_*)} \left\{ (1/n) \sum_{j=1}^n g(X_j, \theta) - E[g(X_1, \theta)] \right\}
$$

$$
\geq (1/n) \sum_{j=1}^n \inf_{\theta \in \Theta_\delta(\theta_*)} g(X_j, \theta) - \sup_{\theta \in \Theta_\delta(\theta_*)} E[g(X_1, \theta)]
$$

$$
\geq - \left| (1/n) \sum_{j=1}^n \inf_{\theta \in \Theta_\delta(\theta_*)} g(X_j, \theta) - E\left[\inf_{\theta \in \Theta_\delta(\theta_*)} g(X_1, \theta) \right] \right|
$$

$$
+ E\left[\inf_{\theta \in \Theta_\delta(\theta_*)} g(X_1, \theta) \right] - E\left[\sup_{\theta \in \Theta_\delta(\theta_*)} g(X_1, \theta) \right]. \tag{6.60}
$$

Hence,

$$
\left| \sup_{\theta \in \Theta_\delta(\theta_*)} \left\{ (1/n) \sum_{j=1}^n g(X_j, \theta) - E[g(X_1, \theta)] \right\} \right|
$$

$$
\leq \left| (1/n) \sum_{j=1}^n \sup_{\theta \in \Theta_\delta(\theta_*)} g(X_j, \theta) - E\left[\sup_{\theta \in \Theta_\delta(\theta_*)} g(X_1, \theta) \right] \right|
$$

$$
+ \left| (1/n) \sum_{j=1}^n \inf_{\theta \in \Theta_\delta(\theta_*)} g(X_j, \theta) - E\left[\inf_{\theta \in \Theta_\delta(\theta_*)} g(X_1, \theta) \right] \right|
$$

$$
+ E\left[\sup_{\theta \in \Theta_\delta(\theta_*)} g(X_1, \theta) \right] - E\left[\inf_{\theta \in \Theta_\delta(\theta_*)} g(X_1, \theta) \right], \tag{6.61}
$$

and similarly

$$
\left| \inf_{\theta \in \Theta_\delta(\theta_*)} \left\{ (1/n) \sum_{j=1}^n g(X_j, \theta) - E[g(X_1, \theta)] \right\} \right|
$$

$$
\leq \left| (1/n) \sum_{j=1}^n \sup_{\theta \in \Theta_\delta(\theta_*)} g(X_j, \theta) - E\left[\sup_{\theta \in \Theta_\delta(\theta_*)} g(X_1, \theta) \right] \right|
$$

$$
+ \left| (1/n) \sum_{j=1}^n \inf_{\theta \in \Theta_\delta(\theta_*)} g(X_j, \theta) - E\left[\inf_{\theta \in \Theta_\delta(\theta_*)} g(X_1, \theta) \right] \right|
$$

$$
+ E\left[\sup_{\theta \in \Theta_\delta(\theta_*)} g(X_1, \theta) \right] - E\left[\inf_{\theta \in \Theta_\delta(\theta_*)} g(X_1, \theta) \right]. \tag{6.62}
$$

If we combine (6.58), (6.61), and (6.62), it follows that

$$
\sup_{\theta \in \Theta_\delta(\theta_*)} \left| (1/n) \sum_{j=1}^{n} g(X_j, \theta) - E[g(X_1, \theta)] \right|
$$

$$
\leq 2 \left| (1/n) \sum_{j=1}^{n} \sup_{\theta \in \Theta_\delta(\theta_*)} g(X_j, \theta) - E \left[\sup_{\theta \in \Theta_\delta(\theta_*)} g(X_1, \theta) \right] \right|
$$

$$
+ 2 \left| (1/n) \sum_{j=1}^{n} \inf_{\theta \in \Theta_\delta(\theta_*)} g(X_j, \theta) - E \left[\inf_{\theta \in \Theta_\delta(\theta_*)} g(X_1, \theta) \right] \right|
$$

$$
+ 2 \left(E \left[\sup_{\theta \in \Theta_\delta(\theta_*)} g(X_1, \theta) \right] - E \left[\inf_{\theta \in \Theta_\delta(\theta_*)} g(X_1, \theta) \right] \right). \quad (6.63)
$$

It follows from the continuity of $g(x, \theta)$ in θ and the dominated convergence theorem [Theorem 6.5] that

$$
\limsup_{\delta \downarrow 0} \sup_{\theta_* \in \Theta} E \left[\sup_{\theta \in \Theta_\delta(\theta_*)} g(X_1, \theta) - \inf_{\theta \in \Theta_\delta(\theta_*)} g(X_1, \theta) \right]
$$

$$
\leq \lim_{\delta \downarrow 0} E \sup_{\theta_* \in \Theta} \left[\sup_{\theta \in \Theta_\delta(\theta_*)} g(X_1, \theta) - \inf_{\theta \in \Theta_\delta(\theta_*)} g(X_1, \theta) \right] = 0;
$$

hence, we can choose δ so small that

$$
\sup_{\theta_* \in \Theta} E \left[\sup_{\theta \in \Theta_\delta(\theta_*)} g(X_1, \theta) - \inf_{\theta \in \Theta_\delta(\theta_*)} g(X_1, \theta) \right] < \varepsilon/4. \quad (6.64)
$$

Furthermore, by the compactness of Θ it follows that there exist a finite number of θ_*'s, for instance $\theta_1, \ldots, \theta_{N(\delta)}$ such that

$$
\Theta \subset \bigcup_{i=1}^{N(\delta)} \Theta_\delta(\theta_i). \quad (6.65)
$$

Therefore, it follows from Theorem 6.2 and (6.63)–(6.65) that

$$
P \left(\sup_{\theta \in \Theta} \left| (1/n) \sum_{j=1}^{n} g(X_j, \theta) - E[g(X_1, \theta)] \right| > \varepsilon \right)
$$

$$
\leq P \left(\max_{1 \leq i \leq N(\delta)} \sup_{\theta \in \Theta_\delta(\theta_i)} \left| (1/n) \sum_{j=1}^{n} g(X_j, \theta) - E[g(X_1, \theta)] \right| > \varepsilon \right)
$$

$$
\leq \sum_{i=1}^{N(\delta)} P \left(\sup_{\theta \in \Theta_\delta(\theta_i)} \left| (1/n) \sum_{j=1}^{n} g(X_j, \theta) - E[g(X_1, \theta)] \right| > \varepsilon \right)
$$

$$\leq \sum_{i=1}^{N(\delta)} P\left(\left|(1/n)\sum_{j=1}^{n}\sup_{\theta\in\Theta_\delta(\theta_*)} g(X_j,\theta) - E\left[\sup_{\theta\in\Theta_\delta(\theta_*)} g(X_1,\theta)\right]\right.\right.$$

$$\left.\left. + \left|(1/n)\sum_{j=1}^{n}\inf_{\theta\in\Theta_\delta(\theta_*)} g(X_j,\theta) - E\left[\inf_{\theta\in\Theta_\delta(\theta_*)} g(X_1,\theta)\right]\right| > \varepsilon/4\right)\right.$$

$$\leq \sum_{i=1}^{N(\delta)} P\left(\left|(1/n)\sum_{j=1}^{n}\sup_{\theta\in\Theta_\delta(\theta_*)} g(X_j,\theta) - E\left[\sup_{\theta\in\Theta_\delta(\theta_*)} g(X_1,\theta)\right]\right| > \varepsilon/8\right)$$

$$+ \sum_{i=1}^{N(\delta)} P\left(\left|(1/n)\sum_{j=1}^{n}\inf_{\theta\in\Theta_\delta(\theta_*)} g(X_j,\theta) - E\left[\inf_{\theta\in\Theta_\delta(\theta_*)} g(X_1,\theta)\right]\right| > \varepsilon/8\right)$$

$$\to 0 \text{ as } n \to \infty. \tag{6.66}$$

6.B. Almost-Sure Convergence and Strong Laws of Large Numbers

6.B.1. Preliminary Results

First, I will show the equivalence of (6.6) and (6.7) in Definition 6.3:

Theorem 6.B.1: *Let X_n and X be random variables defined on a common probability space $\{\Omega, \mathscr{F}, P\}$. Then $\lim_{n\to\infty} P(|X_m - X| \leq \varepsilon \text{ for all } m \geq n) = 1$ for arbitrary $\varepsilon > 0$ if and only if $P(\lim_{n\to\infty} X_n = X) = 1$. This result carries over to random vectors by replacing $|\cdot|$ with the Euclidean norm $\|\cdot\|$.*

Proof: Note that the statement $P(\lim_{n\to\infty} X_n = X) = 1$ reads as follows: There exists a set $N \in \mathscr{F}$ with $P(N) = 0$ such that $\lim_{n\to\infty} X_n(\omega) = X(\omega)$ pointwise in $\omega \in \Omega\backslash N$. Such a set N is called a *null set*.

Let

$$A_n(\varepsilon) = \bigcap_{m=n}^{\infty} \{\omega \in \Omega : |X_m(\omega) - X(\omega)| \leq \varepsilon\}. \tag{6.67}$$

First, assume that for arbitrary $\varepsilon > 0$, $\lim_{n\to\infty} P(A_n(\varepsilon)) = 1$. Because $A_n(\varepsilon) \subset A_{n+1}(\varepsilon)$ it follows that $P[\cup_{n=1}^{\infty} A_n(\varepsilon)] = \lim_{n\to\infty} P(A_n(\varepsilon)) = 1$; hence, $N(\varepsilon) = \Omega\backslash\cup_{n=1}^{\infty} A_n(\varepsilon)$ is a null set and so is the countable union $N = \cup_{k=1}^{\infty} N(1/k)$. Now let $\omega \in \Omega\backslash N$. Then $\omega \in \Omega\backslash\cup_{k=1}^{\infty} N(1/k) = \cap_{k=1}^{\infty} \tilde{N}(1/k) = \cap_{k=1}^{\infty} \cup_{n=1}^{\infty} A_n(1/k)$; hence, for each positive integer k, $\omega \in \cup_{n=1}^{\infty} A_n(1/k)$. Because $A_n(1/k) \subset A_{n+1}(1/k)$ it follows now that for each positive integer k there exists a positive integer $n_k(\omega)$ such that $\omega \in A_n(1/k)$ for all $n \geq n_k(\omega)$. Let $k(\varepsilon)$ be the smallest integer $\geq 1/\varepsilon$, and let $n_0(\omega, \varepsilon) = n_{k(\varepsilon)}(\omega)$. Then for arbitrary $\varepsilon > 0$, $|X_n(\omega) - X(\omega)| \leq \varepsilon$ if $n \geq n_0(\omega, \varepsilon)$. Therefore, $\lim_{n\to\infty} X_n(\omega) = X(\omega)$ pointwise in $\omega \in \Omega\backslash N$ and hence $P(\lim_{n\to\infty} X_n = X) = 1$.

Next, assume that the latter holds, that is, there exists a null set N such that $\lim_{n\to\infty} X_n(\omega) = X(\omega)$ pointwise in $\omega \in \Omega\backslash N$. Then for arbitrary $\varepsilon > 0$ and $\omega \in \Omega\backslash N$ there exists a positive integer $n_0(\omega, \varepsilon)$ such that $\omega \in A_{n_0(\omega,\varepsilon)}(\varepsilon)$ and therefore also $\omega \in \cup_{n=1}^{\infty} A_n(\varepsilon)$. Thus, $\Omega\backslash N \subset \cup_{n=1}^{\infty} A_n(\varepsilon)$, and consequently $1 = P(\Omega\backslash N) \le P[\cup_{n=1}^{\infty} A_n(\varepsilon)]$. Because $A_n(\varepsilon) \subset A_{n+1}(\varepsilon)$, it follows now that $\lim_{n\to\infty} P(A_n(\varepsilon)) = P[\cup_{n=1}^{\infty} A_n(\varepsilon)] = 1$.   Q.E.D.

The following theorem, known as the Borel–Cantelli lemma, provides a convenient condition for almost-sure convergence.

Theorem 6.B.2: *(Borel–Cantelli). If for arbitrary $\varepsilon > 0$, $\sum_{n=1}^{\infty} P(|X_n - X| > \varepsilon) < \infty$, then $X_n \to X$ a.s.*

Proof: Let $\tilde{A}_n(\varepsilon)$ be the complement of the set $A_n(\varepsilon)$ in (6.67). Then

$$P(\tilde{A}_n(\varepsilon)) = P\left[\bigcup_{m=n}^{\infty} \{\omega \in \Omega : |X_m(\omega) - X(\omega)| > \varepsilon\} \right]$$

$$\le \sum_{m=n}^{\infty} P[|X_n - X| > \varepsilon] \to 0,$$

where the latter conclusion follows from the condition that $\sum_{n=1}^{\infty} P(|X_n - X| > \varepsilon) < \infty$.[7] Thus, $\lim_{n\to\infty} P(\tilde{A}_n(\varepsilon)) = 0$; hence, $\lim_{n\to\infty} P(A_n(\varepsilon)) = 1$.   Q.E.D.

The following theorem establishes the relationship between convergence in probability and almost-sure convergence:

Theorem 6.B.3: $X_n \to_p X$ *if and only if every subsequence n_m of $n = 1, 2, 3, \ldots$ contains a further subsequence $n_m(k)$ such that for $k \to \infty$, $X_{n_m(k)} \to X$ a.s.*

Proof: Suppose that $X_n \to_p X$ is not true but that every subsequence n_m of $n = 1, 2, 3, \ldots$ contains a further subsequence $n_m(k)$ such that for $k \to \infty$, $X_{n_m(k)} \to X$ a.s. Then there exist numbers $\varepsilon > 0, \delta \in (0, 1)$ and a subsequence n_m such that $\sup_{m\ge 1} P[|X_{n_m} - X| \le \varepsilon] \le 1 - \delta$. Clearly, the same holds for every further subsequence $n_m(k)$, which contradicts the assumption that there exists a further subsequence $n_m(k)$ such that for $k \to \infty$, $X_{n_m(k)} \to X$ a.s. This proves the "only if" part.

Next, suppose that $X_n \to_p X$. Then for every subsequence n_m, $X_{n_m} \to_p X$. Consequently, for each positive integer k, $\lim_{m\to\infty} P[|X_{n_m} - X| > k^{-2}] = 0$; hence, for each k we can find a positive integer $n_m(k)$ such that $P[|X_{n_m(k)} -$

---

[7] Let $a_m, m \ge 1$, be a sequence of nonnegative numbers such that $\sum_{m=1}^{\infty} a_m = K < \infty$. Then $\sum_{m=1}^{n-1} a_m$ is monotonic nondecreasing in $n \ge 2$ with limit $\lim_{n\to\infty} \sum_{m=1}^{n-1} a_m = \sum_{m=1}^{\infty} a_m = K$; hence, $K = \sum_{m=1}^{\infty} a_m = \lim_{n\to\infty} \sum_{m=1}^{n-1} a_m + \lim_{n\to\infty} \sum_{m=n}^{\infty} a_m = K + \lim_{n\to\infty} \sum_{m=n}^{\infty} a_m$. Thus, $\lim_{n\to\infty} \sum_{m=n}^{\infty} a_m = 0$.

$X| > k^{-2}] \leq k^{-2}$. Thus, $\sum_{k=1}^{\infty} P[|X_{n_m(k)} - X| > k^{-2}] \leq \sum_{k=1}^{\infty} k^{-2} < \infty$. The latter implies that $\sum_{k=1}^{\infty} P[|X_{n_m(k)} - X| > \varepsilon] < \infty$ for each $\varepsilon > 0$; hence, by Theorem 6.B.2, $X_{n_m(k)} \to X$ a.s. Q.E.D.

6.B.2. Slutsky's Theorem

Theorem 6.B.1 can be used to prove Theorem 6.7. Theorem 6.3 was only proved for the special case that the probability limit X is constant. However, the general result of Theorem 6.3 follows straightforwardly from Theorems 6.7 and 6.B.3.

Let us restate Theorems 6.3 and 6.7 together:

Theorem 6.B.4: *(Slutsky's theorem). Let X_n a sequence of random vectors in $\mathbb{R}^k$ converging a.s. (in probability) to a (random or constant) vector X. Let $\Psi(x)$ be an $\mathbb{R}^m$-valued function on $\mathbb{R}^k$ that is continuous on an open (Borel) set B in $\mathbb{R}^k$ for which $P(X \in B) = 1$. Then $\Psi(X_n)$ converges a.s. (in probability) to $\Psi(X)$.*

Proof: Let $X_n \to X$ a.s. and let $\{\Omega, \mathscr{F}, P\}$ be the probability space involved. According to Theorem 6.B.1 there exists a null set N_1 such that $\lim_{n\to\infty} X_n(\omega) = X(\omega)$ pointwise in $\omega \in \Omega \backslash N_1$. Moreover, let $N_2 = \{\omega \in \Omega : X(\omega) \notin B\}$. Then N_2 is also a null set and so is $N = N_1 \cup N_2$. Pick an arbitrary $\omega \in \Omega \backslash N$. Because Ψ is continuous in $X(\omega)$ it follows from standard calculus that $\lim_{n\to\infty} \Psi(X_n(\omega)) = \Psi(X(\omega))$. By Theorem 6.B.1 this result implies that $\Psi(X_n) \to \Psi(X)$ a.s. Because the latter convergence result holds along any subsequence, it follows from Theorem 6.B.3 that $X_n \to_p X$ implies $\Psi(X_n) \to_p \Psi(X)$. Q.E.D.

6.B.3. Kolmogorov's Strong Law of Large Numbers

I will now provide the proof of Kolmogorov's strong law of large numbers based on the elegant and relatively simple approach of Etemadi (1981). This proof (and other versions of the proof as well) employs the notion of equivalent sequences.

Definition 6.B.1: *Two sequences of random variables, X_n and Y_n, $n \geq 1$, are said to be equivalent if $\sum_{n=1}^{\infty} P[X_n \neq Y_n] < \infty$.*

The importance of this concept lies in the fact that if one of the equivalent sequences obeys a strong law of large numbers, then so does the other one:

Lemma 6.B.1: *If X_n and Y_n are equivalent and $(1/n)\sum_{j=1}^{n} Y_j \to \mu$ a.s., then $(1/n)\sum_{j=1}^{n} X_j \to \mu$ a.s.*

Proof: Without loss of generality we may assume that $\mu = 0$. Let $\{\Omega, \mathscr{F}, P\}$ be the probability space involved and let

$$A_n = \bigcup_{m=n}^{\infty} \{\omega \in \Omega : X_m(\omega) \neq Y_m(\omega)\}.$$

Then $P(A_n) \leq \sum_{m=n}^{\infty} P(X_m \neq Y_m) \to 0$; hence, $\lim_{n\to\infty} P(A_n) = 0$ and thus $P(\cap_{n=1}^{\infty} A_n) = 0$. The latter implies that for each $\omega \in \Omega \backslash \{\cap_{n=1}^{\infty} A_n\}$ there exists a natural number $n_*(\omega)$ such that $X_n(\omega) = Y_n(\omega)$ for all $n \geq n_*(\omega)$ because, if not, there exists a countable infinite subsequence $n_m(\omega), m = 1, 2, 3, \ldots$ such that $X_{n_k(\omega)}(\omega) \neq Y_{n_k(\omega)}(\omega)$; hence, $\omega \in A_n$ for all $n \geq 1$ and thus $\omega \in \cap_{n=1}^{\infty} A_n$. Now let N_1 be the null set on which $(1/n) \sum_{j=1}^{n} Y_j \to 0$ a.s. fails to hold, and let $N = N_1 \cup \{\cap_{n=1}^{\infty} A_n\}$. Because for each $\omega \in \Omega \backslash N$, $X_j(\omega)$ and $Y_j(\omega)$ differ for at most a finite number of j's and $\lim_{n\to\infty}(1/n) \sum_{j=1}^{n} Y_j(\omega) = 0$, it follows also that $\lim_{n\to\infty}(1/n) \sum_{j=1}^{n} X_j(\omega) = 0$.   Q.E.D.

The following construction of equivalent sequences plays a key role in the proof of the strong law of large numbers.

Lemma 6.B.2: *Let $X_n, n \geq 1$, be i.i.d., with $E[|X_n|] < \infty$, and let $Y_n = X_n \cdot I(|X_n| \leq n)$. Then X_n and Y_n are equivalent.*

Proof: The lemma follows from

$$\sum_{n=1}^{\infty} P[X_n \neq Y_n] = \sum_{n=1}^{\infty} P[|X_n| > n]$$

$$= \sum_{n=1}^{\infty} P[|X_1| > n] \leq \int_0^{\infty} P[|X_1| > t]dt$$

$$= \int_0^{\infty} E[I(|X_1| > t)]dt \leq E\left[\int_0^{\infty} I(|X_1| > t)]dt\right]$$

$$= E\left[\int_0^{|X_1|} dt\right] = E[|X_1|] < \infty.$$

Q.E.D.

Now let $X_n, n \geq 1$ be the sequence in Lemma 6.B.2, and suppose that $(1/n) \sum_{j=1}^{n} \max(0, X_j) \to E[\max(0, X_1)]$ a.s. and $(1/n) \sum_{j=1}^{n} \max(0, -X_j) \to E[\max(0, -X_1)]$ a.s. Then it is easy to verify from Theorem 6.B.1, by taking the union of the null sets involved, that

$$\frac{1}{n} \sum_{j=1}^{n} \left(\begin{array}{c} \max(0, X_j) \\ \max(0, -X_j) \end{array} \right) \to \left(\begin{array}{c} E[\max(0, X_1)] \\ E[\max(0, -X_1)] \end{array} \right) \text{ a.s.}$$

Applying Slutsky's theorem (Theorem 6.B.4) with $\Phi(x, y) = x - y$, we find that $(1/n) \sum_{j=1}^{n} X_j \to E[X_1]$ a.s. Therefore, the proof of Kolmogorov's strong law of large numbers is completed by Lemma 6.B.3 below.

Lemma 6.B.3: *Let the conditions of Lemma 6.B.2 hold, and assume in addition that $P[X_n \geq 0] = 1$. Then $(1/n) \sum_{j=1}^{n} X_j \to E[X_1]$ a.s.*

Proof: Let $Z(n) = (1/n) \sum_{j=1}^{n} Y_j$ and observe that

$$\mathrm{var}(Z(n)) \leq (1/n^2) \sum_{j=1}^{n} E[Y_j^2] = (1/n^2) \sum_{j=1}^{n} E[X_j^2 I(X_j \leq j)]$$

$$\leq n^{-1} E[X_1^2 I(X_1 \leq n)]. \tag{6.68}$$

Next let $\alpha > 1$ and $\varepsilon > 0$ be arbitrary. It follows from (6.68) and Chebishev's inequality that

$$\sum_{n=1}^{\infty} P[|Z([\alpha^n]) - E[Z([\alpha^n])]| > \varepsilon]$$

$$\leq \sum_{n=1}^{\infty} \mathrm{var}(Z([\alpha^n]))/\varepsilon^2 \leq \sum_{n=1}^{\infty} \frac{E[X_1^2 I(X_1 \leq [\alpha^n])]}{\varepsilon^2 [\alpha^n]}$$

$$\leq \varepsilon^{-2} E\left[X_1^2 \sum_{n=1}^{\infty} I(X_1 \leq [\alpha^n])/[\alpha^n]\right], \tag{6.69}$$

where $[\alpha^n]$ is the integer part of α^n. Let k be the smallest natural number such that $X_1 \leq [\alpha^k]$, and note that $[\alpha^n] > \alpha^n/2$. Then the last sum in (6.69) satisfies

$$\sum_{n=1}^{\infty} I(X_1 \leq [\alpha^n])/[\alpha^n] \leq 2 \sum_{n=k}^{\infty} \alpha^{-n}$$

$$= 2 \cdot \left(\sum_{n=0}^{\infty} \alpha^{-n}\right) \alpha^{-k} \leq \frac{2\alpha}{(\alpha - 1)X_1};$$

hence,

$$E\left[X_1^2 \sum_{n=1}^{\infty} I(X_1 \leq [\alpha^n])/[\alpha^n]\right] \leq \frac{2\alpha}{\alpha - 1} E[X_1] < \infty.$$

Consequently, it follows from the Borel–Cantelli lemma that $Z([\alpha^n]) - E[Z([\alpha^n])] \to 0$ a.s. Moreover, it is easy to verify that $E[Z([\alpha^n])] \to E[X_1]$. Hence, $Z([\alpha^n]) \to E[X_1]$ a.s.

For each natural number $k > \alpha$ there exists a natural number n_k such that $[\alpha^{n_k}] \leq k \leq [\alpha^{n_k+1}]$, and since the X_j's are nonnegative we have

$$\frac{[\alpha^{n_k}]}{[\alpha^{n_k+1}]} Z([\alpha^{n_k}]) \leq Z(k) \leq \frac{[\alpha^{n_k+1}]}{[\alpha^{n_k}]} Z([\alpha^{n_k+1}]). \qquad (6.70)$$

The left-hand expression in (6.70) converges a.s. to $E[X_1]/\alpha$ as $k \to \infty$, and the right-hand side converges a.s. to $\alpha E[X_1]$; hence, we have, with probability 1,

$$\frac{1}{\alpha} E[X_1] \leq \liminf_{k \to \infty} Z(k) \leq \limsup_{k \to \infty} Z(k) \leq \alpha E[X_1].$$

In other words, if we let $\underline{Z} = \liminf_{k \to \infty} Z(k)$, $\bar{Z} = \limsup_{k \to \infty} Z(k)$, there exists a null set N_α (depending on α) such that for all $\omega \in \Omega \backslash N_\alpha$, $E[X_1]/\alpha \leq \underline{Z}(\omega) \leq \bar{Z}(\omega) \leq \alpha E[X_1]$. Taking the union N of N_α over all *rational* $\alpha > 1$, so that N is also a null set,[8] we find that the same holds for all $\omega \in \Omega \backslash N$ and all rational $\alpha > 1$. Letting $\alpha \downarrow 1$ along the rational values then yields $\lim_{k \to \infty} Z(k) = \underline{Z}(\omega) = \bar{Z}(\omega) = E[X_1]$ for all $\omega \in \Omega \backslash N$. Therefore, by Theorem 6.B.1, $(1/n)\sum_{j=1}^{n} Y_j \to E[X_1]$ a.s., which by Lemmas 6.B.2 and 6.B.3 implies that $(1/n)\sum_{j=1}^{n} X_j \to E[X_1]$. *a.s.*   Q.E.D.

This completes the proof of Theorem 6.6.

6.B.5. The Uniform Strong Law of Large Numbers and Its Applications

Proof of Theorem 6.13: It follows from (6.63), (6.64), and Theorem 6.6 that

$$\limsup_{n \to \infty} \sup_{\theta \in \Theta_\delta(\theta_*)} \left| (1/n) \sum_{j=1}^{n} g(X_j, \theta) - E[g(X_1, \theta)] \right|$$

$$\leq 2 \left(E \left[\sup_{\theta \in \Theta_\delta(\theta_*)} g(X_1, \theta) \right] - E \left[\inf_{\theta \in \Theta_\delta(\theta_*)} g(X_1, \theta) \right] \right) < \varepsilon/2 \text{ a.s.;}$$

hence, (6.65) can now be replaced by

$$\limsup_{n \to \infty} \sup_{\theta \in \Theta} \left| (1/n) \sum_{j=1}^{n} g(X_j, \theta) - E[g(X_1, \theta)] \right|$$

$$\leq \limsup_{n \to \infty} \max_{1 \leq i \leq N(\delta)} \sup_{\theta \in \Theta_\delta(\theta_i)} \left| (1/n) \sum_{j=1}^{n} g(X_j, \theta) - E[g(X_1, \theta)] \right|$$

$$\leq \varepsilon/2 \text{ a.s.} \qquad (6.71)$$

With $\varepsilon/2$ replaced by $1/m, m \geq 1$, the last inequality in (6.71) reads as follows:

---

[8] Note that $\cup_{\alpha \in (1, \infty)} N_\alpha$ is an uncountable union and may therefore not be a null set. Consequently, we need to confine the union to all rational $\alpha > 1$, which is countable.

Let $\{\Omega, \mathscr{F}, P\}$ be the probability space involved. For $m = 1, 2, 3, \ldots$ there exist null sets N_m such that for all $\omega \in \Omega \backslash N_m$,

$$\limsup_{n \to \infty} \sup_{\theta \in \Theta} \left| (1/n) \sum_{j=1}^{n} g(X_j(\omega), \theta) - E[g(X_1, \theta)] \right| \le 1/m, \qquad (6.72)$$

and the same holds for all $\omega \in \Omega \backslash \cup_{k=1}^{\infty} N_k$ uniformly in m. If we get $m \to \infty$ in (6.72), Theorem 6.13 follows.

Note that this proof is based on a seminal paper by Jennrich (1969).

An issue that has not yet been addressed is whether $\sup_{\theta \in \Theta} |(1/n) \sum_{j=1}^{n} g(X_j, \theta) - E[g(X_1, \theta)]|$ is a well-defined random variable. If so, we must have that for arbitrary $y > 0$,

$$\left\{ \omega \in \Omega : \sup_{\theta \in \Theta} \left| (1/n) \sum_{j=1}^{n} g(X_j(\omega), \theta) - E[g(X_1, \theta)] \right| \le y \right\}$$

$$= \bigcap_{\theta \in \Theta} \left\{ \omega \in \Omega : \left| (1/n) \sum_{j=1}^{n} g(X_j(\omega), \theta) - E[g(X_1, \theta)] \right| \le y \right\} \in \mathscr{F}.$$

However, this set is an uncountable intersection of sets in $\mathscr{F}$ and therefore not necessarily a set in $\mathscr{F}$ itself. The following lemma, which is due to Jennrich (1969), shows that in the case under review there is no problem.

Lemma 6.B.4: *Let $f(x, \theta)$ be a real function on $B \times \Theta$, $B \subset \mathbb{R}^k$, $\Theta \subset \mathbb{R}^m$, where B is a Borel set and Θ is compact (hence Θ is a Borel set) such that for each x in B, $f(x, \theta)$ is continuous in $\theta \in \Theta$, and for each $\theta \in \Theta$, $f(x, \theta)$ is Borel measurable. Then there exists a Borel-measurable mapping $\theta(x) : B \to \Theta$ such that $f(x, \theta(x)) = \inf_{\theta \in \Theta} f(x, \theta)$; hence, the latter is Borel measurable itself. The same result holds for the "sup" case.*

Proof: I will only prove this result for the special case $k = m = 1$, $B = \mathbb{R}$, $\Theta = [0, 1]$. Denote $\Theta_n = \cup_{j=1}^{n} \{0, 1/j, 2/j, \ldots, (j-1)/j, 1\}$, and observe that $\Theta_n \subset \Theta_{n+1}$ and that $\Theta_* = \cup_{n=1}^{\infty} \Theta_n$ is the set of all rational numbers in $[0, 1]$. Because Θ_n is finite, for each positive integer n there exists a Borel-measurable function $\theta_n(x) : \mathbb{R} \to \Theta_n$ such that $f(x, \theta_n(x)) = \inf_{\theta \in \Theta_n} f(x, \theta)$. Let $\theta(x) = \liminf_{n \to \infty} \theta_n(x)$. Note that $\theta(x)$ is Borel measurable. For each x there exists a subsequence n_j (which may depend on x) such that $\theta(x) = \lim_{j \to \infty} \theta_{n_j}(x)$. Hence, by continuity, $f(x, \theta(x)) = \lim_{j \to \infty} f(x, \theta_{n_j}(x)) = \lim_{j \to \infty} \inf_{\theta \in \Theta_{n_j}} f(x, \theta)$. Now suppose that for some $\varepsilon > 0$ the latter is greater or equal to $\varepsilon + \inf_{\theta \in \Theta_*} f(x, \theta)$. Then, because for $m \le n_j$, $\inf_{\theta \in \Theta_*} f(x, \theta) \le \inf_{\theta \in \Theta_m} f(x, \theta)$, and the latter is monotonic nonincreasing in m, it follows that, for all $n \ge 1$, $\inf_{\theta \in \Theta_n} f(x, \theta) \ge \varepsilon + \inf_{\theta \in \Theta_*} f(x, \theta)$. It is not too hard to show, using the continuity of $f(x, \theta)$ in θ, that this is not possible.

Therefore, $f(x, \theta(x)) = \inf_{\theta \in \Theta_*} f(x, \theta)$; hence, by continuity, $f(x, \theta(x)) = \inf_{\theta \in \Theta} f(x, \theta)$. Q.E.D.

Proof of Theorem 6.14: Let $\{\Omega, \mathscr{F}, P\}$ be the probability space involved, and denote $\theta_n = \hat{\theta}$. Now (6.9) becomes $\bar{Q}(\theta_n) \to \bar{Q}(\theta_0)$ a.s., that is, there exists a null set N such that for all $\omega \in \Omega \backslash N$,

$$\lim_{n \to \infty} \bar{Q}(\theta_n(\omega)) = \bar{Q}(\theta_0). \tag{6.73}$$

Suppose that for some $\omega \in \Omega \backslash N$ there exists a subsequence $n_m(\omega)$ and an $\varepsilon > 0$ such that $\inf_{m \geq 1} \|\theta_{n_m(\omega)}(\omega) - \theta_0\| > \varepsilon$. Then by the uniqueness condition there exists a $\delta(\omega) > 0$ such that $\bar{Q}(\theta_0) - \bar{Q}(\theta_{n_m(\omega)}(\omega)) \geq \delta(\omega)$ for all $m \geq 1$, which contradicts (6.73). Hence, for every subsequence $n_m(\omega)$ we have $\lim_{m \to \infty} \theta_{n_m(\omega)}(\omega) = \theta_0$, which implies that $\lim_{n \to \infty} \theta_n(\omega) = \theta_0$.

Proof of Theorem 6.15: The condition $X_n \to c$ a.s. translates as follows: There exists a null set N_1 such that for all $\omega \in \Omega \backslash N_1$, $\lim_{n \to \infty} X_n(\omega) = c$. By the continuity of Φ on B the latter implies that $\lim_{n \to \infty} |\Phi(X_n(\omega)) - \Phi(c)| = 0$ and that for at most a finite number of indices n, $X_n(\omega) \notin B$. Similarly, the uniform a.s. convergence condition involved translates as follows: There exists a null set N_2 such that for all $\omega \in \Omega \backslash N_2$, $\lim_{n \to \infty} \sup_{x \in B} |\Phi_n(x, \omega) - \Phi(x)| \to 0$. Take $N = N_1 \cup N_2$. Then for all $\omega \in \Omega \backslash N$,

$$\limsup_{n \to \infty} |\Phi_n(X_n(\omega), \omega) - \Phi(c)|$$
$$\leq \limsup_{n \to \infty} |\Phi_n(X_n(\omega), \omega) - \Phi(X_n(\omega))|$$
$$+ \limsup_{n \to \infty} |\Phi(X_n(\omega)) - \Phi(c)| \leq \limsup_{n \to \infty} \sup_{x \in B} |\Phi_n(x, \omega) - \Phi(x)|$$
$$+ \limsup_{n \to \infty} |\Phi(X_n(\omega)) - \Phi(c)| = 0.$$

6.C. Convergence of Characteristic Functions and Distributions

In this appendix I will provide the proof of the univariate version of Theorem 6.22. Let F_n be a sequence of distribution functions on $\mathbb{R}$ with corresponding characteristic functions $\varphi_n(t)$, and let F be a distribution function on $\mathbb{R}$ with characteristic function $\varphi(t) = \lim_{n \to \infty} \varphi_n(t)$. Let

$$\underline{F}(x) = \lim_{\delta \downarrow 0} \liminf_{n \to \infty} F_n(x + \delta), \overline{F}(x) = \lim_{\delta \downarrow 0} \limsup_{n \to \infty} F_n(x + \delta).$$

The function $\underline{F}(x)$ is right continuous and monotonic nondecreasing in x but not necessarily a distribution function itself because $\lim_{x \uparrow \infty} \underline{F}(x)$ may be less than 1 or even 0. On the other hand, it is easy to verify that $\lim_{x \downarrow -\infty} \underline{F}(x) = 0$. Therefore, if $\lim_{x \to \infty} \underline{F}(x) = 1$, then $\underline{F}$ is a distribution function. The same applies to $\overline{F}(x)$: If $\lim_{x \to \infty} \overline{F}(x) = 1$, then $\overline{F}$ is a distribution function.

I will first show that $\lim_{x \to \infty} \underline{F}(x) = \lim_{x \to \infty} \bar{F}(x) = 1$ and then that $\underline{F}(x) = \bar{F}(x)$.

Lemma 6.C.1: *Let F_n be a sequence of distribution functions on $\mathbb{R}$ with corresponding characteristic functions $\varphi_n(t)$ and suppose that $\varphi(t) = \lim_{n \to \infty} \varphi_n(t)$ pointwise for each t in $\mathbb{R}$, where φ is continuous in $t = 0$. Then $\underline{F}(x) = \lim_{\delta \downarrow 0} \liminf_{n \to \infty} F_n(x + \delta)$ is a distribution function and so is $\bar{F}(x) = \lim_{\delta \downarrow 0} \limsup_{n \to \infty} F_n(x + \delta)$.*

Proof: For $T > 0$ and $A > 0$ we have

$$
\frac{1}{2T} \int_{-T}^{T} \varphi_n(t)dt = \frac{1}{2T} \int_{-T}^{T} \int_{-\infty}^{\infty} \exp(i \cdot t \cdot x)dF_n(x)dt
$$

$$
= \frac{1}{2T} \int_{-\infty}^{\infty} \int_{-T}^{T} \exp(i \cdot t \cdot x)dt dF_n(x)
$$

$$
= \frac{1}{2T} \int_{-\infty}^{\infty} \int_{-T}^{T} \cos(t \cdot x)dt dF_n(x)
$$

$$
= \int_{-\infty}^{\infty} \frac{\sin(Tx)}{Tx}dF_n(x)
$$

$$
= \int_{-2A}^{2A} \frac{\sin(Tx)}{Tx}dF_n(x) + \int_{-\infty}^{-2A} \frac{\sin(Tx)}{Tx}dF_n(x)
$$

$$
+ \int_{2A}^{\infty} \frac{\sin(Tx)}{Tx}dF_n(x). \tag{6.74}
$$

Because $|\sin(x)/x| \leq 1$ and $|Tx|^{-1} \leq (2TA)^{-1}$ for $|x| > 2A$ it follows from (6.74) that

$$
\left| \frac{1}{T} \int_{-T}^{T} \varphi_n(t)dt \right| \leq 2 \int_{-2A}^{2A} dF_n(x) + \frac{1}{AT} \int_{-\infty}^{-2A} dF_n(x) + \frac{1}{AT} \int_{2A}^{\infty} dF_n(x)
$$

$$
= 2\left(1 - \frac{1}{2AT}\right) \int_{-2A}^{2A} dF_n(x) + \frac{1}{AT}
$$

$$
= 2\left(1 - \frac{1}{2AT}\right) \mu_n([-2A, 2A]) + \frac{1}{AT}, \tag{6.75}
$$

where μ_n is the probability measure on the Borel sets in $\mathbb{R}$ corresponding to F_n. Hence, if we put $T = A^{-1}$ it follows from (6.75) that

$$\mu_n([-2A, 2A]) \geq \left| A \int_{-1/A}^{1/A} \varphi_n(t)dt \right| - 1, \tag{6.76}$$

which can be rewritten as

$$F_n(2A) \geq \left| A \int_{-1/A}^{1/A} \varphi_n(t)dt \right| - 1 + F_n(-2A) - \mu_n(\{-2A\}). \tag{6.77}$$

Now let $2A$ and $-2A$ be continuity points of $\underline{F}$. Then it follows from (6.77), the condition that $\varphi(t) = \lim_{n \to \infty} \varphi_n(t)$ pointwise for each t in $\mathbb{R}$, and the bounded[9] convergence theorem that

$$\underline{F}(2A) \geq \left| A \int_{-1/A}^{1/A} \varphi(t)dt \right| - 1 + \underline{F}(-2A). \tag{6.78}$$

Because $\varphi(0) = 1$ and φ is continuous in 0 the integral in (6.78) converges to 2 for $A \to \infty$.

Moreover, $\underline{F}(-2A) \downarrow 0$ if $A \to \infty$. Consequently, it follows from (6.78) that $\lim_{A \to \infty} \underline{F}(2A) = 1$. By the same argument it follows that $\lim_{A \to \infty} \bar{F}(2A) = 1$. Thus, $\underline{F}$ and $\bar{F}$ are distribution functions.   Q.E.D.

Lemma 6.C.2: *Let F_n be a sequence of distribution functions on $\mathbb{R}$ such that $\underline{F}(x) = \lim_{\delta \downarrow 0} \liminf_{n \to \infty} F_n(x + \delta)$ and $\bar{F}(x) = \lim_{\delta \downarrow 0} \limsup_{n \to \infty} F_n(x + \delta)$ are distribution functions. Then for every bounded continuous function φ on $\mathbb{R}$ and every $\varepsilon > 0$ there exist subsequences $\underline{n}_k(\varepsilon)$ and $\bar{n}_k(\varepsilon)$ such that*

$$\limsup_{k \to \infty} \left| \int \varphi(x)dF_{\underline{n}_k(\varepsilon)}(x) - \int \varphi(x)d\underline{F}(x) \right| < \varepsilon,$$

$$\limsup_{k \to \infty} \left| \int \varphi(x)dF_{\bar{n}_k(\varepsilon)}(x) - \int \varphi(x)d\bar{F}(x) \right| < \varepsilon.$$

Proof: Without loss of generality we may assume that $\varphi(x) \in [0, 1]$ for all x. For any $\varepsilon > 0$ we can choose continuity points $a < b$ of $\underline{F}(x)$ such that $\underline{F}(b) - \bar{F}(a) > 1 - \varepsilon$. Moreover, we can choose continuity points $a = c_1 <$

---

[9] Note that $|\varphi(t)| \leq 1$.

$c_2 < \cdots < c_m = b$ of $\underline{F}(x)$ such that, for $j = 1, \ldots, m - 1$,

$$\sup_{x \in (c_j, c_{j+1}]} \varphi(x) - \inf_{x \in (c_j, c_{j+1}]} \varphi(x) \le \varepsilon. \tag{6.79}$$

Furthermore, there exists a subsequence n_k (possibly depending on ε) such that

$$\lim_{k \to \infty} F_{n_k}(c_j) = \underline{F}(c_j) \quad \text{for} \quad j = 1, 2, \ldots, m. \tag{6.80}$$

Now define

$$\psi(x) = \inf_{x \in (c_j, c_{j+1}]} \varphi(x) \quad \text{for} \quad x \in (c_j, c_{j+1}], j = 1, \ldots, m - 1,$$

$$\psi(x) = 0 \text{ elsewhere.} \tag{6.81}$$

Then by (6.79), $0 \le \varphi(x) - \psi(x) \le \varepsilon$ for $x \in (a, b]$ and $0 \le \varphi(x) - \psi(x) \le 1$ for $x \notin (a, b]$; hence,

$$\limsup_{n \to \infty} \left| \int \psi(x) dF_n(x) - \int \varphi(x) dF_n(x) \right|$$

$$\le \limsup_{n \to \infty} \left(\int_{x \in (a,b]} |\psi(x) - \varphi(x)| dF_n(x) + \int_{x \notin (a,b]} |\psi(x) - \varphi(x)| dF_n(x) \right)$$

$$\le \varepsilon + 1 - \limsup_{n \to \infty} (F_n(b) - F_n(a)) \le \varepsilon + 1 - (\bar{F}(b) - \bar{F}(a)) \le 2\varepsilon. \tag{6.82}$$

Moreover, if follows from (6.79) and (6.81) that

$$\left| \int \psi(x) d\underline{F}(x) - \int \varphi(x) d\underline{F}(x) \right| \le 2\varepsilon \tag{6.83}$$

and from (6.80) that

$$\lim_{k \to \infty} \int \psi(x) dF_{n_k}(x) = \int \psi(x) d\underline{F}(x). \tag{6.84}$$

Combining (6.82)–(6.84) we find that

$$\limsup_{k \to \infty} \left| \int \varphi(x) dF_{n_k}(x) - \int \varphi(x) d\underline{F}(x) \right|$$

$$\le \limsup_{k \to \infty} \left| \int \varphi(x) dF_{n_k}(x) - \int \psi(x) dF_{n_k}(x) \right|$$

$$+ \limsup_{k \to \infty} \left| \int \psi(x) dF_{n_k}(x) - \int \psi(x) d\underline{F}(x) \right|$$

$$+ \limsup_{k \to \infty} \left| \int \psi(x) d\underline{F}(x) - \int \varphi(x) d\underline{F}(x) \right| < 4\varepsilon. \tag{6.85}$$

A similar result holds for the case $\bar{F}$. Q.E.D.

Let $\varphi_*(t)$ be the characteristic function of $\underline{F}$. Because $\varphi(t) = \lim_{n \to \infty} \varphi_n(t)$, it follows from Lemma 6.C.2 that for each t and arbitrary $\varepsilon > 0$, $|\varphi(t) - \varphi_*(t)| < \varepsilon$; hence, $\varphi(t) = \varphi_*(t)$. The same result holds for the characteristic function $\varphi^*(t)$ of $\bar{F} : \varphi(t) = \varphi^*(t)$. Consequently, $\varphi(t) = \lim_{n \to \infty} \varphi_n(t)$ is the characteristic function of both $\underline{F}$ and $\bar{F}$, which by Lemma 6.C.1 are distribution functions. By the uniqueness of characteristic functions (see Appendix 2.C in Chapter 2) it follows that both distributions are equal: $\underline{F}(x) = \bar{F}(x) = F(x)$, for instance. Thus, for each continuity point x of F, $F(x) = \lim_{n \to \infty} F_n(x)$.

Note that we have not assumed from the outset that $\varphi(t) = \lim_{n \to \infty} \varphi_n(t)$ is a characteristic function but only that this pointwise limit exists and is continuous in zero. Consequently, the univariate version of the "if" part of Theorem 6.22 can be restated more generally as follows:

Lemma 6.C.1: *Let X_n be a sequence of random variables with corresponding characteristic functions $\varphi_n(t)$. If $\varphi(t) = \lim\limits_{n \to \infty} \varphi_n(t)$ exists for all $t \in \mathbb{R}$ and $\varphi(t)$ is continuous in $t = 0$ (i.e., $\lim_{t \to 0} \varphi(t) = 1$), then*

(a) *$\varphi(t)$ is a characteristic function itself;*
(b) *$X_n \to_d X$, where X is a random variable with characteristic function $\varphi(t)$.*

This result carries over to the multivariate case, but the proof is rather complicated and is therefore omitted. See Section 29 in Billingsley (1986).

7 Dependent Laws of Large Numbers and Central Limit Theorems

Chapter 6 I focused on the convergence of sums of i.i.d. random variables – in particular the law of large numbers and the central limit theorem. However, macroeconomic and financial data are time series data for which the independence assumption does not apply. Therefore, in this chapter I will generalize the weak law of large numbers and the central limit theorem to certain classes of time series.

7.1. Stationarity and the Wold Decomposition

Chapter 3 introduced the concept of strict stationarity, which for convenience will be restated here:

Definition 7.1: *A time series process X_t is said to be strictly stationary if, for arbitrary integers $m_1 < m_2 < \cdots < m_n$, the joint distribution of $X_{t-m_1}, \ldots, X_{t-m_n}$ does not depend on the time index t.*

A weaker version of stationarity is covariance stationarity, which requires that the first and second moments of any set $X_{t-m_1}, \ldots, X_{t-m_n}$ of time series variables do not depend on the time index t.

Definition 7.2: *A time series process $X_t \in \mathbb{R}^k$ is covariance stationary (or weakly stationary) if $E[\|X_t\|^2] < \infty$ and, for all integers t and m, $E[X_t] = \mu$ and $E[(X_t - \mu)(X_{t-m} - \mu)^{\mathrm{T}}] = \Gamma(m)$ do not depend on the time index t.*

Clearly, a strictly stationary time series process X_t is covariance stationary if $E[\|X_t\|^2] < \infty$.

For zero-mean covariance stationary processes the famous Wold (1938) decomposition theorem holds. This theorem is the basis for linear time series analysis and forecasting – in particular the Box–Jenkins (1979) methodology – and vector autoregression innovation response analysis. See Sims (1980, 1982, 1986) and Bernanke (1986) for the latter.

Theorem 7.1: *(Wold decomposition) Let $X_t \in \mathbb{R}$ be a zero-mean covariance stationary process. Then we can write $X_t = \sum_{j=0}^{\infty} \alpha_j U_{t-j} + W_t$, where $\alpha_0 = 1$, $\sum_{j=0}^{\infty} \alpha_j^2 < \infty$, the U_t's are zero-mean covariance stationary and uncorrelated random variables, and W_t is a deterministic process, that is, there exist coefficients β_j such that $P[W_t = \sum_{j=1}^{\infty} \beta_j W_{t-j}] = 1$. Moreover, $U_t = X_t - \sum_{j=1}^{\infty} \beta_j X_{t-j}$ and $E[U_{t+m} W_t] = 0$ for all integers m and t.*

Intuitive proof: The exact proof employs Hilbert space theory and will therefore be given in the appendix to this chapter. However, the intuition behind the Wold decomposition is not too difficult.

It is possible to find a sequence β_j, $j = 1, 2, 3, \ldots$ of real numbers such that $E[(X_t - \sum_{j=1}^{\infty} \beta_j X_{t-j})^2]$ is minimal. The random variable

$$\hat{X}_t = \sum_{j=1}^{\infty} \beta_j X_{t-j} \tag{7.1}$$

is then called the *linear projection* of X_t on X_{t-j}, $j \geq 1$. If we let

$$U_t = X_t - \sum_{j=1}^{\infty} \beta_j X_{t-j}, \tag{7.2}$$

it follows from the first-order condition $\partial E[(X_t - \sum_{j=1}^{\infty} \beta_j X_{t-j})^2]/\partial \beta_j = 0$ that

$$E[U_t X_{t-m}] = 0 \quad \text{for} \quad m = 1, 2, 3, \ldots. \tag{7.3}$$

Note that (7.2) and (7.3) imply

$$E[U_t] = 0, \qquad E[U_t U_{t-m}] = 0 \quad \text{for} \quad m = 1, 2, 3, \ldots. \tag{7.4}$$

Moreover, note that by (7.2) and (7.3),

$$E\left[X_t^2\right] = E\left[\left(U_t + \sum_{j=1}^{\infty} \beta_j X_{t-j}\right)^2\right]$$

$$= E\left[U_t^2\right] + E\left[\left(\sum_{j=1}^{\infty} \beta_j X_{t-j}\right)^2\right],$$

and thus by the covariance stationarity of X_t,

$$E\left[U_t^2\right] = \sigma_u^2 \leq E\left[X_t^2\right] \tag{7.5}$$

and

$$E[\hat{X}_t^2] = E\left[\left(\sum_{j=1}^{\infty} \beta_j X_{t-j}\right)^2\right] = \sigma_{\hat{X}}^2 \leq E\left[X_t^2\right] \tag{7.6}$$

for all t. Hence it follows from (7.4) and (7.5) that U_t is a zero-mean covariance stationary time series process itself.

Next, substitute $X_{t-1} = U_{t-1} + \sum_{j=1}^{\infty} \beta_j X_{t-1-j}$ in (7.1). Then (7.1) becomes

$$
\hat{X}_t = \beta_1 \left(U_{t-1} + \sum_{j=1}^{\infty} \beta_j X_{t-1-j} \right) + \sum_{j=2}^{\infty} \beta_j X_{t-j}
$$

$$
= \beta_1 U_{t-1} + \sum_{j=2}^{\infty} (\beta_j + \beta_1 \beta_{j-1}) X_{t-j}
$$

$$
= \beta_1 U_{t-1} + \left(\beta_2 + \beta_1^2 \right) X_{t-2} + \sum_{j=3}^{\infty} (\beta_j + \beta_1 \beta_{j-1}) X_{t-j}. \tag{7.7}
$$

Now replace X_{t-2} in (7.7) by $U_{t-2} + \sum_{j=1}^{\infty} \beta_j X_{t-2-j}$. Then (7.7) becomes

$$
\hat{X}_t = \beta_1 U_{t-1} + \left(\beta_2 + \beta_1^2 \right) \left(U_{t-2} + \sum_{j=1}^{\infty} \beta_j X_{t-2-j} \right) + \sum_{j=3}^{\infty} (\beta_j + \beta_1 \beta_{j-1}) X_{t-j}
$$

$$
= \beta_1 U_{t-1} + \left(\beta_2 + \beta_1^2 \right) U_{t-2} + \sum_{j=3}^{\infty} \left[\left(\beta_2 + \beta_1^2 \right) \beta_{j-2} + (\beta_j + \beta_1 \beta_{j-1}) \right] X_{t-j}
$$

$$
= \beta_1 U_{t-1} + \left(\beta_2 + \beta_1^2 \right) U_{t-2} + \left[\left(\beta_2 + \beta_1^2 \right) \beta_1 + (\beta_3 + \beta_1 \beta_2) \right] X_{t-3}
$$

$$
+ \sum_{j=4}^{\infty} \left[\left(\beta_2 + \beta_1^2 \right) \beta_{j-2} + (\beta_j + \beta_1 \beta_{j-1}) \right] X_{t-j}.
$$

Repeating this substitution m times yields an expression of the type

$$
\hat{X}_t = \sum_{j=1}^{m} \alpha_j U_{t-j} + \sum_{j=m+1}^{\infty} \theta_{m,j} X_{t-j}, \tag{7.8}
$$

for instance. It follows now from (7.3), (7.4), (7.5), and (7.8) that

$$
E[\hat{X}_t^2] = \sigma_u^2 \sum_{j=1}^{m} \alpha_j^2 + E \left[\left(\sum_{j=m+1}^{\infty} \theta_{m,j} X_{t-j} \right)^2 \right].
$$

Hence, letting $m \to \infty$, we have

$$
E[\hat{X}_t^2] = \sigma_u^2 \sum_{j=1}^{\infty} \alpha_j^2 + \lim_{m \to \infty} E \left[\left(\sum_{j=m+1}^{\infty} \theta_{m,j} X_{t-j} \right)^2 \right] = \sigma_{\hat{X}}^2 < \infty.
$$

Therefore, we can write X_t as

$$
X_t = \sum_{j=0}^{\infty} \alpha_j U_{t-j} + W_t, \tag{7.9}
$$

where $\alpha_0 = 1$ and $\sum_{j=0}^{\infty} \alpha_j^2 < \infty$ with $W_t = \text{plim}_{m \to \infty} \sum_{j=m+1}^{\infty} \theta_{m,j} X_{t-j}$ a remainder term that satisfies

$$E[U_{t+m} W_t] = 0 \quad \text{for all integers } m \text{ and } t. \tag{7.10}$$

Finally, observe from (7.2) and (7.9) that

$$
\begin{aligned}
U_t - \left(W_t - \sum_{j=1}^{\infty} \beta_j W_{t-j} \right) &= (X_t - W_t) - \sum_{j=1}^{\infty} \beta_j (X_{t-j} - W_{t-j}) \\
&= \sum_{j=0}^{\infty} \alpha_j \left(U_{t-j} - \sum_{m=1}^{\infty} \beta_m U_{t-j-m} \right) \\
&= U_t + \sum_{j=1}^{\infty} \delta_j U_{t-j}, \text{ for instance.}
\end{aligned}
$$

It follows now straightforwardly from (7.4), (7.5), and (7.10) that $\delta_j = 0$ for all $j \geq 1$; hence, $W_t = \sum_{j=1}^{\infty} \beta_j W_{t-j}$ with probability 1.   Q.E.D.

Theorem 7.1 carries over to vector-valued covariance stationary processes:

Theorem 7.2: *(Multivariate Wold decomposition) Let $X_t \in \mathbb{R}^k$ be a zero-mean covariance stationary process. Then we can write $X_t = \sum_{j=0}^{\infty} A_j U_{t-j} + W_t$, where $A_0 = I_k$, $\sum_{j=0}^{\infty} A_j A_j^{\mathsf{T}}$ is finite, the U_t's are zero-mean covariance stationary and uncorrelated random vectors (i.e., $E[U_t U_{t-m}^{\mathsf{T}}] = O$ for $m \geq 1$), and W_t is a deterministic process (i.e., there exist matrices B_j such that $P[W_t = \sum_{j=1}^{\infty} B_j W_{t-j}] = 1$). Moreover, $U_t = X_t - \sum_{j=1}^{\infty} B_j X_{t-j}$, and $E[U_{t+m} W_t^{\mathsf{T}}] = O$ for all integers m and t.*

Although the process W_t is deterministic in the sense that it is perfectly predictable from its past values, it still may be random. If so, let $\mathscr{F}_W^t = \sigma(W_t, W_{t-1}, W_{t-2}, \ldots)$ be the σ-algebra generated by W_{t-m} for $m \geq 0$. Then all W_t's are measurable $\mathscr{F}_W^{t-m}$ for arbitrary natural numbers m; hence, all W_t's are measurable $\mathscr{F}_W^{-\infty} = \cap_{t=0}^{\infty} \mathscr{F}_W^{-t}$. However, it follows from (7.2) and (7.9) that each W_t can be constructed from X_{t-j} for $j \geq 0$; hence, $\mathscr{F}_X^t = \sigma(X_t, X_{t-1}, X_{t-2}, \ldots) \supset \mathscr{F}_W^t$, and consequently, all W_t's are measurable $\mathscr{F}_X^{-\infty} = \cap_{t=0}^{\infty} \mathscr{F}_X^{-t}$. This implies that $W_t = E[W_t | \mathscr{F}_X^{-\infty}]$. See Chapter 3.

The σ-algebra $\mathscr{F}_X^{-\infty}$ represents the information contained in the remote past of X_t. Therefore, $\mathscr{F}_X^{-\infty}$ is called the remote σ-algebra, and the events therein are called the remote events. If $\mathscr{F}_X^{-\infty}$ is the trivial σ-algebra $\{\Omega, \emptyset\}$, and thus the remote past of X_t is uninformative, then $E[W_t | \mathscr{F}_X^{-\infty}] = E[W_t]$; hence, $W_t = 0$. However, the same result holds if all the remote events have either probability 0 or 1, as is easy to verify from the definition of conditional expectations with respect to a σ-algebra. This condition follows automatically from Kolmogorov's zero-one law if the X_t's are independent (see Theorem 7.5 below), but for dependent processes this is not guaranteed. Nevertheless, for economic time series this is not too farfetched an assumption, for in reality they always start from scratch somewhere in the far past (e.g., 500 years ago for U.S. time series).

Definition 7.3: *A time series process X_t has a vanishing memory if the events in the remote σ-algebra $\mathscr{F}_X^{-\infty} = \cap_{t=0}^{\infty} \sigma(X_{-t}, X_{-t-1}, X_{-t-2}, \ldots)$ have either probability 0 or 1.*

Thus, under the conditions of Theorems 7.1 and 7.2 and the additional assumption that the covariance stationary time series process involved has a vanishing memory, the deterministic term W_t in the Wold decomposition is 0 or is a zero vector, respectively.

7.2. Weak Laws of Large Numbers for Stationary Processes

I will show now that covariance stationary time series processes with a vanishing memory obey a weak law of large numbers and then specialize this result to strictly stationary processes.

Let $X_t \in \mathbb{R}$ be a covariance stationary process, that is, for all t, $E[X_t] = \mu$, $\text{var}[X_t] = \sigma^2$ and $\text{cov}(X_t, X_{t-m}) = \gamma(m)$. If X_t has a vanishing memory, then by Theorem 7.1 there exist uncorrelated random variables $U_t \in \mathbb{R}$ with zero expectations and common finite variance σ_u^2 such that $X_t - \mu = \sum_{m=0}^{\infty} \alpha_m U_{t-m}$, where $\sum_{m=0}^{\infty} \alpha_m^2 < \infty$. Then

$$\gamma(k) = E\left[\left(\sum_{m=0}^{\infty} \alpha_{m+k} U_{t-m}\right)\left(\sum_{m=0}^{\infty} \alpha_m U_{t-m}\right)\right]. \tag{7.11}$$

Because $\sum_{m=0}^{\infty} \alpha_m^2 < \infty$, it follows that $\lim_{k\to\infty} \sum_{m=k}^{\infty} \alpha_m^2 = 0$. Hence, it follows from (7.11) and the Schwarz inequality that

$$|\gamma(k)| \le \sigma_u^2 \sqrt{\sum_{m=k}^{\infty} \alpha_m^2} \sqrt{\sum_{m=0}^{\infty} \alpha_m^2} \to 0 \text{ as } k \to \infty.$$

Consequently,

$$\begin{aligned}
\text{var}\left((1/n)\sum_{t=1}^{n} X_t\right) &= \sigma^2/n + 2(1/n^2)\sum_{t=1}^{n-1}\sum_{m=1}^{n-t} \gamma(m) \\
&= \sigma^2/n + 2(1/n^2)\sum_{m=1}^{n-1}(n-m)\gamma(m) \\
&\le \sigma^2/n + 2(1/n)\sum_{m=1}^{\infty} |\gamma(m)| \to 0 \text{ as } n \to \infty.
\end{aligned} \tag{7.12}$$

From Chebishev's inequality, it follows now from (7.12) that

Theorem 7.3: *If X_t is a covariance stationary time series process with vanishing memory, then $\text{plim}_{n\to\infty}(1/n)\sum_{t=1}^{n} X_t = E[X_1]$.*

This result requires that the second moment of X_t be finite. However, this condition can be relaxed by assuming strict stationarity:

Theorem 7.4: *If X_t is a strictly stationary time series process with vanishing memory, and $E[|X_1|] < \infty$, then $plim_{n \to \infty}(1/n) \sum_{t=1}^n X_t = E[X_1]$.*

Proof: Assume first that $P[X_t \geq 0] = 1$. For any positive real number M, $X_t I(X_t \leq M)$ is a covariance stationary process with vanishing memory; hence, by Theorem 7.3,

$$\operatorname*{plim}_{n \to \infty}(1/n) \sum_{t=1}^n (X_t I(X_t \leq M) - E[X_1 I(X_1 \leq M)]) = 0. \qquad (7.13)$$

Next, observe that

$$\left| (1/n) \sum_{t=1}^n (X_t - E[X_1]) \right|$$

$$\leq \left| (1/n) \sum_{t=1}^n (X_t I(X_t \leq M) - E[X_1 I(X_1 \leq M)]) \right|$$

$$+ \left| (1/n) \sum_{t=1}^n (X_t I(X_t > M) - E[X_1 I(X_1 > M)]) \right| \qquad (7.14)$$

Because, for nonnegative random variables Y and Z, $P[Y + Z > \varepsilon] \leq P[Y > \varepsilon/2] + P[Z > \varepsilon/2]$, it follows from (7.14) that for arbitrary $\varepsilon > 0$,

$$P\left[\left| (1/n) \sum_{t=1}^n (X_t - E[X_1]) \right| > \varepsilon \right]$$

$$\leq P\left[\left| (1/n) \sum_{t=1}^n (X_t I(X_t \leq M) - E[X_1 I(X_1 \leq M)]) \right| > \varepsilon/2 \right]$$

$$+ P\left[\left| (1/n) \sum_{t=1}^n (X_t I(X_t > M) - E[X_1 I(X_1 > M)]) \right| > \varepsilon/2 \right].$$

$$(7.15)$$

For an arbitrary $\delta \in (0, 1)$, we can choose M so large that $E[X_1 I(X_1 > M)] < \varepsilon \delta/8$. Hence, if we use Chebishev's inequality for first moments, the last probability in (7.15) can be bounded by $\delta/2$:

$$P\left[\left| (1/n) \sum_{t=1}^n (X_t I(X_t > M) - E[X_1 I(X_1 > M)]) \right| > \varepsilon/2 \right]$$

$$\leq 4E[X_1 I(X_1 > M)]/\varepsilon < \delta/2. \qquad (7.16)$$

Moreover, it follows from (7.13) that there exists a natural number $n_0(\varepsilon, \delta)$ such that

$$P\left[\left|(1/n)\sum_{t=1}^{n}(X_t I(X_t \leq M) - E[X_1 I(X_1 \leq M)])\right| > \varepsilon/2\right]$$
$$< \delta/2 \quad \text{if } n \geq n_0(\varepsilon, \delta). \tag{7.17}$$

If we combine (7.15)–(7.17), the theorem follows for the case $P[X_t \geq 0] = 1$. The general case follows easily from $X_t = \max(0, X_t) - \max(0, -X_t)$ and Slutsky's theorem.   Q.E.D.

Most stochastic dynamic macroeconomic models assume that the model variables are driven by independent random shocks, and thus the model variables involved are functions of these independent random shocks and their past. These random shock are said to form a base for the model variables involved:

Definition 7.4: *A time series process U_t is a base for a time series process X_t if, for each t, X_t is measurable $\mathscr{F}_{-\infty}^{t} = \sigma(U_t, U_{t-1}, U_{t-2}, \ldots)$.*

If X_t has an independent base, then it has a vanishing memory owing to Kolmogorov's zero-one law:

Theorem 7.5: *(Kolmogorov's zero-one law) Let X_t be a sequence of independent random variables or vectors, and let $\mathscr{F}_{-\infty}^{t} = \sigma(X_t, X_{t-1}, X_{t-2}, \ldots)$. Then the sets in the remote σ-algebra $\mathscr{F}_{-\infty} = \cap_{t=1}^{\infty}\mathscr{F}_{-\infty}^{t}$ have either probability $\emptyset$ or 1.*

Proof: Denote by $\mathscr{F}_{t}^{t+k}$ the σ-algebra generated by $X_t, \ldots, X_{t+k}$. Moreover, denote by $\mathscr{F}_{t-m}^{t-1}$ the σ-algebra generated by $X_{t-1}, \ldots, X_{t-m}$. Each set A_1 in $\mathscr{F}_{t}^{t+k}$ takes the form

$$A_1 = \{\omega \in \Omega : (X_t(\omega), \ldots, X_{t+k}(\omega))^{\mathsf{T}} \in B_1\}$$

for some Borel set $B_1 \in \mathbb{R}^{k+1}$. Similarly, each set A_2 in $\cup_{m=1}^{\infty}\mathscr{F}_{t-m}^{t-1}$ takes the form

$$A_2 = \{\omega \in \Omega : (X_{t-1}(\omega), \ldots, X_{t-m}(\omega))^{\mathsf{T}} \in B_2\}$$

for some $m \geq 1$ and some Borel set $B_2 \in \mathbb{R}^{m}$. Clearly, A_1 and A_2 are independent.

I will now show that the same holds for sets A_2 in $\mathscr{F}_{-\infty}^{t-1} = \sigma(\cup_{m=1}^{\infty}\mathscr{F}_{t-m}^{t-1})$, the smallest σ-algebra containing $\cup_{m=1}^{\infty}\mathscr{F}_{t-m}^{t-1}$. Note that $\cup_{m=1}^{\infty}\mathscr{F}_{t-m}^{t-1}$ may not be a σ-algebra itself, but it is easy to verify that it is an algebra because $\mathscr{F}_{t-m}^{t-1} \subset \mathscr{F}_{t-m-1}^{t-1}$. For a given set C in $\mathscr{F}_{t}^{t+k}$ with positive probability and for all sets A in $\cup_{m=1}^{\infty}\mathscr{F}_{t-m}^{t-1}$, we have $P(A|C) = P(A)$. Thus, $P(\cdot|C)$ is a probability measure on the algebra $\cup_{m=1}^{\infty}\mathscr{F}_{t-m}^{t-1}$, which has a unique extension to the smallest σ-algebra containing $\cup_{m=1}^{\infty}\mathscr{F}_{t-m}^{t-1}$ (see Chapter 1). Consequently, $P(A|C) = P(A)$

is true for all sets A in $\mathscr{F}_{-\infty}^{t-1}$. Moreover, if C has probability zero, then $P(A \cap C) \leq P(C) = 0 = P(A)P(C)$. Thus, for all sets C in $\mathscr{F}_t^{t+k}$ and all sets A in $\mathscr{F}_{-\infty}^{t-1}$, $P(A \cap C) = P(A)P(C)$.

Next, let $A \in \cap_t \mathscr{F}_{-\infty}^{t}$, where the intersection is taken over all integers t, and let $C \in \cup_{k=1}^{\infty} \mathscr{F}_{t-k}^{t}$. Then for some k, C is a set in $\mathscr{F}_{t-k}^{t}$ and A is a set in $\mathscr{F}_{-\infty}^{m}$ for all m; therefore, $A \in \mathscr{F}_{-\infty}^{t-k-1}$ and hence $P(A \cap C) = P(A)P(C)$. By a similar argument it can be shown that $P(A \cap C) = P(A)P(C)$ for all sets $A \in \cap_t \mathscr{F}_{-\infty}^{t-1}$ and $C \in \sigma(\cup_{k=1}^{\infty} \mathscr{F}_{t-k}^{t})$. But $\mathscr{F}_{-\infty} = \cap_t \mathscr{F}_{-\infty}^{t-1} \subset \sigma(\cup_{k=1}^{\infty} \mathscr{F}_{t-k}^{t})$, and thus we may choose $C = A$. Consequently, for all sets $A \in \cap_t \mathscr{F}_{-\infty}^{t-1}$, $P(A) = P(A)^2$, which implies that $P(A)$ is either zero or one.   Q.E.D.

7.3. Mixing Conditions

Inspection of the proof of Theorem 7.5 reveals that the independence assumption can be relaxed. We only need independence of an arbitrary set A in $\mathscr{F}_{-\infty}$ and an arbitrary set C in $\mathscr{F}_{t-k}^{t} = \sigma(X_t, X_{t-1}, X_{t-2}, \ldots, X_{t-k})$ for $k \geq 1$. A sufficient condition for this is that the process X_t is α-mixing or φ-mixing:

Definition 7.5: *Let* $\mathscr{F}_{-\infty}^{t} = \sigma(X_t, X_{t-1}, X_{t-2}, \ldots)$, $\mathscr{F}_t^{\infty} = \sigma(X_t, X_{t+1}, X_{t+2}, \ldots)$ *and*

$$\alpha(m) = \sup_t \sup_{A \in \mathscr{F}_t^{\infty}, \, B \in \mathscr{F}_{-\infty}^{t-m}} |P(A \cap B) - P(A) \cdot P(B)|,$$

$$\varphi(m) = \sup_t \sup_{A \in \mathscr{F}_t^{\infty}, \, B \in \mathscr{F}_{-\infty}^{t-m}} |P(A|B) - P(A)|.$$

If $\lim_{m \to \infty} \alpha(m) = 0$, *then the time series process* X_t *involved is said to be* α-mixing; *if* $\lim_{m \to \infty} \varphi(m) = 0$, X_t *is said to be* φ-mixing.

Note in the α-mixing case that

$$\sup_{A \in \mathscr{F}_{t-k}^{t}, \, B \in \mathscr{F}_{-\infty}} |P(A \cap B) - P(A) \cdot P(B)|$$

$$\leq \limsup_{m \to \infty} \sup_t \sup_{A \in \mathscr{F}_{t-k}^{\infty}, \, B \in \mathscr{F}_{-\infty}^{t-k-m}} |P(A \cap B) - P(A) \cdot P(B)|$$

$$= \limsup_{m \to \infty} \alpha(m) = 0;$$

hence, the sets $A \in \mathscr{F}_{t-k}^{t}$, $B \in \mathscr{F}_{-\infty}$ are independent. Moreover, note that $\alpha(m) \leq \varphi(m)$, and thus φ-mixing implies α-mixing. Consequently, the latter is the weaker condition, which is sufficient for a zero-one law:

Theorem 7.6: *Theorem 7.5 carries over for* α-*mixing processes.*

Therefore, the following theorem is another version of the weak law of large numbers:

Theorem 7.7: *If X_t is a strictly stationary time series process with an α-mixing base and $E[|X_1|] < \infty$, then $plim_{n\to\infty}(1/n)\sum_{t=1}^{n} X_t = E[X_1]$.*

7.4. Uniform Weak Laws of Large Numbers

7.4.1. Random Functions Depending on Finite-Dimensional Random Vectors

On the basis of Theorem 7.7, all the convergence in probability results in Chapter 6 for i.i.d. random variables or vectors carry over to strictly stationary time series processes with an α-mixing base. In particular, the uniform weak law of large numbers can now be restated as follows:

Theorem 7.8(a): *(UWLLN) Let X_t be a strictly stationary k-variate time series process with an α-mixing base, and let $\theta \in \Theta$ be nonrandom vectors in a compact subset $\Theta \subset \mathbb{R}^m$. Moreover, let $g(x, \theta)$ be a Borel-measurable function on $\mathbb{R}^k \times \Theta$ such that for each x, $g(x, \theta)$ is a continuous function on Θ. Finally, assume that $E[\sup_{\theta\in\Theta}|g(X_j, \theta)|] < \infty$. Then*

$$plim_{n\to\infty} \sup_{\theta\in\Theta} \left| (1/n) \sum_{j=1}^{n} g(X_j, \theta) - E[g(X_1, \theta)] \right| = 0.$$

Theorem 7.8(a) can be proved along the same lines as the proof of the uniform weak law of large numbers for the i.i.d. case in Appendix 6.A of Chapter 6 simply by replacing the reference to the weak law of large numbers for i.i.d. random variables by a reference to Theorem 7.7.

7.4.2. Random Functions Depending on Infinite-Dimensional Random Vectors

In time series econometrics we quite often have to deal with random functions that depend on a countable infinite sequence of random variables or vectors. As an example, consider the time series process

$$Y_t = \beta_0 Y_{t-1} + X_t, \quad \text{with} \quad X_t = V_t - \gamma_0 V_{t-1}, \tag{7.18}$$

where the V_t's are i.i.d. with zero expectation and finite variance σ^2 and the parameters involved satisfy $|\beta_0| < 1$ and $|\gamma_0| < 1$. The part

$$Y_t = \beta_0 Y_{t-1} + X_t \tag{7.19}$$

is an autoregression of order 1, denoted by AR(1), and the part

$$X_t = V_t - \gamma_0 V_{t-1} \tag{7.20}$$

is a moving average process or order 1, denoted by MA(1). Therefore, model (7.18) is called an ARMA(1, 1) model (see Box and Jenkins 1976). The condition $|\beta_0| < 1$ is necessary for the strict stationarity of Y_t because then, by backwards substitution of (7.18), we can write model (7.18) as

$$
\begin{aligned}
Y_t &= \sum_{j=0}^{\infty} \beta_0^j (V_{t-j} - \gamma_0 V_{t-1-j}) \\
&= V_t + (\beta_0 - \gamma_0) \sum_{j=1}^{\infty} \beta_0^{j-1} V_{t-j}.
\end{aligned}
\tag{7.21}
$$

This is the Wold decomposition of Y_t. The MA(1) model (7.20) can be written as an AR(1) model in V_t:

$$
V_t = \gamma_0 V_{t-1} + U_t.
\tag{7.22}
$$

If $|\gamma_0| < 1$, then by backwards substitution of (7.22) we can write (7.20) as

$$
X_t = -\sum_{j=1}^{\infty} \gamma_0^j X_{t-j} + V_t.
\tag{7.23}
$$

If we substitute $X_t = Y_t - \beta_0 Y_{t-1}$ in (7.23), the ARMA(1, 1) model (7.18) can now be written as an infinite-order AR model:

$$
\begin{aligned}
Y_t &= \beta_0 Y_{t-1} - \sum_{j=1}^{\infty} \gamma_0^j (Y_{t-j} - \beta_0 Y_{t-1-j}) + V_t \\
&= (\beta_0 - \gamma_0) \sum_{j=1}^{\infty} \gamma_0^{j-1} Y_{t-j} + V_t.
\end{aligned}
\tag{7.24}
$$

Note that if $\beta_0 = \gamma_0$, then (7.24) and (7.21) reduce to $Y_t = V_t$; thus, there is no way to identify the parameters. Consequently, we need to assume that $\beta_0 \neq \gamma_0$. Moreover, observe from (7.21) that Y_t is strictly stationary with an independent (hence α-mixing) base.

There are different ways to estimate the parameters β_0, γ_0 in model (7.18) on the basis of observations on Y_t for $t = 0, 1, \ldots, n$ only. If we assume that the V_t's are normally distributed, we can use maximum likelihood (see Chapter 8). But it is also possible to estimate the model by nonlinear least squares (NLLS).

If we would observe all the Y_t's for $t < n$, then the nonlinear least-squares estimator of $\theta_0 = (\beta_0, \gamma_0)^{\mathrm{T}}$ is

$$
\hat{\theta} = \underset{\theta \in \Theta}{\operatorname{argmin}} (1/n) \sum_{t=1}^{n} (Y_t - f_t(\theta))^2,
\tag{7.25}
$$

where

$$
f_t(\theta) = (\beta - \gamma) \sum_{j=1}^{\infty} \gamma^{j-1} Y_{t-j}, \quad \text{with} \quad \theta = (\beta, \gamma)^{\mathrm{T}},
\tag{7.26}
$$

and

$$
\Theta = [-1 + \varepsilon, 1 - \varepsilon] \times [-1 + \varepsilon, 1 - \varepsilon], \quad \varepsilon \in (0, 1),
\tag{7.27}
$$

for instance, where ε is a small number. If we only observe the Y_t's for $t = 0, 1, \ldots, n$, which is the usual case, then we can still use NLLS by setting the Y_t's for $t < 0$ to zero. This yields the feasible NLLS estimator

$$\tilde{\theta} = \underset{\theta \in \Theta}{\text{argmin}}(1/n) \sum_{t=1}^{n} (Y_t - \tilde{f}_t(\theta))^2, \tag{7.28}$$

where

$$\tilde{f}_t(\theta) = (\beta - \gamma) \sum_{j=1}^{t} \gamma^{j-1} Y_{t-j}. \tag{7.29}$$

For proving the consistency of (7.28) we need to show first that

$$\underset{n \to \infty}{\text{plim}} \sup_{\theta \in \Theta} \left| (1/n) \sum_{t=1}^{n} \left((Y_t - \tilde{f}_t(\theta))^2 - (Y_t - f_t(\theta))^2 \right) \right| = 0 \tag{7.30}$$

(*Exercise*), and

$$\underset{n \to \infty}{\text{plim}} \sup_{\theta \in \Theta} \left| (1/n) \sum_{t=1}^{n} \left((Y_t - f_t(\theta))^2 - E[(Y_1 - f_1(\theta))^2] \right) \right| = 0. \tag{7.31}$$

(*Exercise*) However, the random functions $g_t(\theta) = (Y_t - f_t(\theta))^2$ depend on infinite-dimensional random vectors $(Y_t, Y_{t-1}, Y_{t-2}, Y_{t-2}, \ldots)^{\mathsf{T}}$, and thus Theorem 7.8(a) is not applicable to (7.31). Therefore, we need to generalize Theorem 7.8(a) to prove (7.31):

Theorem 7.8(b): (*UWLLN*) *Let* $\mathscr{F}_t = \sigma(V_t, V_{t-1}, V_{t-2}, \ldots)$, *where* V_t *is a time series process with an* α-*mixing base. Let* $g_t(\theta)$ *be a sequence of random functions on a compact subset* Θ *of a Euclidean space. Write* $N_\delta(\theta_*) = \{\theta \in \Theta : \|\theta - \theta_*\| \le \delta\}$ *for* $\theta_* \in \Theta$ *and* $\delta \ge 0$. *If for each* $\theta_* \in \Theta$ *and each* $\delta \ge 0$,

(a) $\sup_{\theta \in N_\delta(\theta_*)} g_t(\theta)$ *and* $\inf_{\theta \in N_\delta(\theta_*)} g_t(\theta)$ *are measurable* $\mathscr{F}_t$ *and strictly stationary*,

(b) $E[\sup_{\theta \in N_\delta(\theta_*)} g_t(\theta)] < \infty$ *and* $E[\inf_{\theta \in N_\delta(\theta_*)} g_t(\theta)] > -\infty$,

(c) $\lim_{\delta \downarrow 0} E[\sup_{\theta \in N_\delta(\theta_*)} g_t(\theta)] = \lim_{\delta \downarrow 0} E[\inf_{\theta \in N_\delta(\theta_*)} g_t(\theta)] = E[g_t(\theta_*)]$;

then, $\text{plim}_{n \to \infty} \sup_{\theta \in \Theta} |(1/n) \sum_{t=1}^{n} g_t(\theta) - E[g_1(\theta)]| = 0$.

Theorem 7.8(b) can also be proved easily along the lines of the proof of the uniform weak law of large numbers in Appendix 6.A of Chapter 6.

Note that it is possible to strengthen the (uniform) weak laws of large numbers to corresponding strong laws or large numbers by imposing conditions on the speed of convergence to zero of $\alpha(m)$ (see McLeish 1975).

It is not too hard (but rather tedious) to verify that the conditions of Theorem 7.8(b) apply to the random functions $g_t(\theta) = (Y_t - f_t(\theta))^2$ with Y_t defined by (7.18) and $f_t(\theta)$ by (7.26).

7.4.3. Consistency of M-Estimators

Further conditions for the consistency of M-estimators are stated in the next theorem, which is a straightforward generalization of a corresponding result in Chapter 6 for the i.i.d. case:

Theorem 7.9: *Let the conditions of Theorem 7.8(b) hold, and let* $\theta_0 = argmax_{\theta \in \Theta} E[g_1(\theta)]$, $\hat{\theta} = argmax_{\theta \in \Theta}(1/n) \sum_{t=1}^{n} g_t(\theta)$. *If for* $\delta > 0$, $sup_{\theta \in \Theta \setminus N_\delta(\theta_0)} E[g_1(\theta)] < E[g_1(\theta_0)]$, *then* $plim_{n \to \infty} \hat{\theta} = \theta_0$. *Similarly, if* $\theta_0 = argmin_{\theta \in \Theta} E[g_1(\theta)]$, $\hat{\theta} = argmin_{\theta \in \Theta}(1/n) \sum_{t=1}^{n} g_t(\theta)$, *and for* $\delta > 0$, $inf_{\theta \in \Theta \setminus N_\delta(\theta_0)} E[g_1(\theta)] > E[g_1(\theta_0)]$, *then* $plim_{n \to \infty} \hat{\theta} = \theta_0$.

Again, it is not too hard (but rather tedious) to verify that the conditions of Theorem 7.9 apply to (7.25) with Y_t defined by (7.18) and $f_t(\theta)$ by (7.26). Thus the feasible NLLS estimator (7.28) is consistent.

7.5. Dependent Central Limit Theorems

7.5.1. Introduction

As is true of the conditions for asymptotic normality of M-estimators in the i.i.d. case (see Chapter 6), the crucial condition for asymptotic normality of the NLLS estimator (7.25) is that

$$\frac{1}{\sqrt{n}} \sum_{t=1}^{n} V_t \left(\partial f_t(\theta_0)/\partial \theta_0^\mathsf{T} \right) \to_d N_2[0, B], \tag{7.32}$$

where

$$B = E \left[V_1^2 \left(\partial f_1(\theta_0)/\partial \theta_0^\mathsf{T} \right) \left(\partial f_1(\theta_0)/\partial \theta_0 \right) \right]. \tag{7.33}$$

It follows from (7.21) and (7.26) that

$$f_t(\theta_0) = (\beta_0 - \gamma_0) \sum_{j=1}^{\infty} \beta_0^{j-1} V_{t-j}, \tag{7.34}$$

which is measurable $\mathscr{F}_{t-1} = \sigma(V_{t-1}, V_{t-2}, V_{t-3}, \ldots)$, and thus

$$\partial f_t(\theta_0)/\partial \theta_0^\mathsf{T}$$
$$= \left(\sum_{j=1}^{\infty} (\beta_0 + (\beta_0 - \gamma_0)(j-1)) \beta_0^{j-2} V_{t-j} - \sum_{j=1}^{\infty} \beta_0^{j-1} V_{t-j} \right).$$

Therefore, it follows from the law of iterated expectations (see Chapter 3) that

$$B = \sigma^2 E\left[(\partial f_1(\theta_0)/\partial\theta_0^{\mathsf{T}})(\partial f_1(\theta_0)/\partial\theta_0)\right]$$

$$= \sigma^4 \begin{pmatrix} \sum_{j=1}^{\infty}(\beta_0 + (\beta_0 - \gamma_0)(j-1))^2\beta_0^{2(j-2)} & -\sum_{j=1}^{\infty}(\beta_0 + (\beta_0 - \gamma_0)(j-1))\beta_0^{2(j-2)} \\ -\sum_{j=1}^{\infty}(\beta_0 + (\beta_0 - \gamma_0)(j-1))\beta_0^{2(j-2)} & \sum_{j=1}^{\infty}\beta_0^{2(j-1)} \end{pmatrix}$$

$$\tag{7.35}$$

and

$$P\left(E[V_t(\partial f_t(\theta_0)/\partial\theta_0^{\mathsf{T}})|\mathscr{F}_{t-1}] = 0\right) = 1. \tag{7.36}$$

The result (7.36) makes $V_t(\partial f_t(\theta_0)/\partial\theta_0^{\mathsf{T}})$ a bivariate martingale difference process, and for an arbitrary nonrandom $\xi \in \mathbb{R}^2, \xi \neq 0$, the process $U_t = V_t\xi^{\mathsf{T}}(\partial f_t(\theta_0)/\partial\theta_0^{\mathsf{T}})$ is then a univariate martingale difference process:

Definition 7.4: *Let U_t be a time series process defined on a common probability space $\{\Omega, \mathscr{F}, P\}$, and let $\mathscr{F}_t$ be a sequence of sub-σ-algebras of $\mathscr{F}$. If for each t,*

  (a) U_t is measurable $\mathscr{F}_t$,
  (b) $\mathscr{F}_{t-1} \subset \mathscr{F}_t$,
  (c) $E[|U_t|] < \infty$, and
  (d) $P(E[U_t|\mathscr{F}_{t-1}] = 0) = 1$,

then $\{U_t, \mathscr{F}_t\}$ is called a martingale difference process.

If condition (d) is replaced by $P(E[U_t|\mathscr{F}_{t-1}] = U_{t-1}) = 1$, then $\{U_t, \mathscr{F}_t\}$ is called a martingale. In that case $\Delta U_t = U_t - U_{t-1} = U_t - E[U_t|\mathscr{F}_{t-1}]$ satisfies $P(E[\Delta U_t|\mathscr{F}_{t-1}] = 0) = 1$. This is the reason for calling the process in Definition 7.4 a martingale difference process.

Thus, what we need for proving (7.32) is a martingale difference central limit theorem.

7.5.2. A Generic Central Limit Theorem

In this section I will explain McLeish's (1974) central limit theorems for dependent random variables with an emphasis on stationary martingale difference processes.

The following approximation of $\exp(i \cdot x)$ plays a key role in proving central limit theorems for dependent random variables.

Lemma 7.1: *For $x \in \mathbb{R}$ with $|x| < 1$, $\exp(i \cdot x) = (1 + i \cdot x)\exp(-x^2/2 + r(x))$, where $|r(x)| \leq |x|^3$.*

Proof: It follows from the definition of the complex logarithm and the series expansion of $\log(1 + i \cdot x)$ for $|x| < 1$ (see Appendix III) that

$$\log(1 + i \cdot x) = i \cdot x + x^2/2 + \sum_{k=3}^{\infty} (-1)^{k-1} i^k x^k / k + i \cdot m \cdot \pi$$

$$= i \cdot x + x^2/2 - r(x) + i \cdot m \cdot \pi,$$

where $r(x) = -\sum_{k=3}^{\infty} (-1)^{k-1} i^k x^k / k$. Taking the exp of both sides of the equation for $\log(1 + i \cdot x)$ yields $\exp(i \cdot x) = (1 + i \cdot x) \exp(-x^2/2 + r(x))$. To prove the inequality $|r(x)| \leq |x|^3$, observe that

$$r(x) = -\sum_{k=3}^{\infty} (-1)^{k-1} i^k x^k / k = x^3 \sum_{k=0}^{\infty} (-1)^k i^{k+1} x^k / (k + 3)$$

$$= x^3 \sum_{k=0}^{\infty} (-1)^{2k} i^{2k+1} x^{2k} / (2k + 3)$$

$$+ x^3 \sum_{k=0}^{\infty} (-1)^{2k+1} i^{2k+2} x^{2k+1} / (2k + 4)$$

$$= x^3 \sum_{k=0}^{\infty} (-1)^k x^{2k+1} / (2k + 4) + i \cdot x^3 \sum_{k=0}^{\infty} (-1)^k x^{2k} / (2k + 3)$$

$$= \sum_{k=0}^{\infty} (-1)^k x^{2k+4} / (2k + 4) + i \cdot \sum_{k=0}^{\infty} (-1)^k x^{2k+3} / (2k + 3)$$

$$= \int_0^x \frac{y^3}{1 + y^2} dy + i \cdot \int_0^x \frac{y^2}{1 + y^2} dy, \qquad (7.37)$$

where the last equality in (7.37) follows from

$$\frac{d}{dx} \sum_{k=0}^{\infty} (-1)^k x^{2k+4} / (2k + 4) = \sum_{k=0}^{\infty} (-1)^k x^{2k+3}$$

$$= x^3 \sum_{k=0}^{\infty} (-x^2)^k = \frac{x^3}{1 + x^2}$$

for $|x| < 1$, and similarly

$$\frac{d}{dx} \sum_{k=0}^{\infty} (-1)^k x^{2k+3} / (2k + 3) = \frac{x^2}{1 + x^2}.$$

The theorem now follows from (7.37) and the easy inequalities

$$\left| \int_0^x \frac{y^3}{1 + y^2} dy \right| \leq \int_0^{|x|} y^3 dy = \frac{1}{4} |x|^4 \leq |x|^3 / \sqrt{2}$$

and

$$\left| \int_0^x \frac{y^2}{1+y^2} dy \right| \leq \int_0^{|x|} y^2 dy = \frac{1}{3}|x|^3 \leq |x|^3/\sqrt{2},$$

which hold for $|x| < 1$.   Q.E.D.

The result of Lemma 7.1 plays a key role in the proof of the following generic central limit theorem:

Lemma 7.2: *Let $X_t, t = 1, 2, \ldots, n, \ldots$ be a sequence of random variables satisfying the following four conditions:*

$$plim_{n\to\infty} \max_{1\leq t\leq n} |X_t|/\sqrt{n} = 0, \tag{7.38}$$

$$plim_{n\to\infty}(1/n) \sum_{t=1}^n X_t^2 = \sigma^2 \in (0, \infty), \tag{7.39}$$

$$\lim_{n\to\infty} E\left[\prod_{t=1}^n (1 + i \cdot \xi \cdot X_t/\sqrt{n})\right] = 1, \quad \forall \xi \in \mathbb{R}, \tag{7.40}$$

and

$$\sup_{n\geq 1} E\left[\prod_{t=1}^n \left(1 + \xi^2 X_t^2/n\right)\right] < \infty, \quad \forall \xi \in \mathbb{R}. \tag{7.41}$$

Then

$$\frac{1}{\sqrt{n}} \sum_{t=1}^n X_t \to_d N(0, \sigma^2). \tag{7.42}$$

Proof: Without loss of generality we may assume that $\sigma^2 = 1$ because, if not, we may replace X_t by X_t/σ. It follows from the first part of Lemma 7.1 that

$$\exp\left(i\xi(1/\sqrt{n}) \sum_{t=1}^n X_t\right) = \left[\prod_{t=1}^n (1 + i\xi X_t/\sqrt{n})\right]$$

$$\times \exp\left(-(\xi^2/2)(1/n) \sum_{t=1}^n X_t^2\right) \exp\left(\sum_{t=1}^n r(\xi X_t/\sqrt{n})\right). \tag{7.43}$$

Condition (7.39) implies that

$$plim_{n\to\infty} \exp\left(-(\xi^2/2)(1/n) \sum_{t=1}^n X_t^2\right) = \exp(-\xi^2/2). \tag{7.44}$$

Moreover, it follows from (7.38), (7.39), and the inequality $|r(x)| \leq |x|^3$ for $|x| < 1$ that

$$\left| \sum_{t=1}^{n} r(\xi X_t/\sqrt{n}) I(|\xi X_t/\sqrt{n}| < 1) \right|$$

$$\leq \frac{|\xi|^3}{n\sqrt{n}} \sum_{t=1}^{n} |X_j|^3 I\left(|\xi X_t/\sqrt{n}| < 1\right)$$

$$\leq |\xi|^3 \frac{\max_{1 \leq t \leq n} |X_t|}{\sqrt{n}} \left((1/n) \sum_{t=1}^{n} X_t^2 \right) \to_p 0.$$

Next, observe that

$$\left| \sum_{t=1}^{n} r(\xi X_t/\sqrt{n}) I(|\xi X_t/\sqrt{n}| \geq 1) \right|$$

$$\leq \sum_{t=1}^{n} \left| r(\xi X_t/\sqrt{n}) \right| I(|\xi X_t/\sqrt{n}| \geq 1)$$

$$\leq I\left(|\xi| \cdot \max_{1 \leq t \leq n} |X_t|/\sqrt{n} \geq 1 \right) \sum_{t=1}^{n} \left| r(\xi X_t/\sqrt{n}) \right|. \qquad (7.45)$$

The result (7.45) and condition (7.38) imply that

$$P\left[\sum_{t=1}^{n} r(\xi X_t/\sqrt{n}) I(|\xi X_t/\sqrt{n}| \geq 1) = 0 \right]$$

$$\geq P\left(|\xi| \cdot \max_{1 \leq t \leq n} |X_t|/\sqrt{n} < 1 \right) \to 1. \qquad (7.46)$$

Therefore, it follows from (7.38), (7.39), and (7.46) that

$$\operatorname*{plim}_{n \to \infty} \exp\left(\sum_{t=1}^{n} r(\xi X_t/\sqrt{n}) \right) = 1. \qquad (7.47)$$

Thus, we can write

$$\exp\left(i\xi(1/\sqrt{n}) \sum_{t=1}^{n} X_t \right) = \left[\prod_{t=1}^{n} (1 + i\xi X_t/\sqrt{n}) \right] \exp(-\xi^2/2)$$

$$+ \left[\prod_{t=1}^{n} (1 + i\xi X_t/\sqrt{n}) \right] Z_n(\xi), \qquad (7.48)$$

where

$$Z_n(\xi) = \exp(-\xi^2/2) - \exp\left(-(\xi^2/2)(1/n)\sum_{t=1}^{n} X_t^2\right)$$

$$\times \exp\left(\sum_{t=1}^{n} r(\xi X_t/\sqrt{n})\right) \to_p 0.$$
(7.49)

Because $|Z_n(\xi)| \leq 2$ with probability 1 given that

$$| \exp(-x^2/2 + r(x))| \leq 1,$$
(7.50)

it follows from (7.49) and the dominated-convergence theorem that

$$\lim_{n\to\infty} E\left[|Z_n(\xi)|^2\right] = 0.$$
(7.51)

Moreover, condition (7.41) implies (using $\overline{zw} = \bar{z} \cdot \bar{w}$ and $|z| = \sqrt{z\bar{z}}$) that

$$\sup_{n\geq 1} E\left[\left|\prod_{t=1}^{n}(1 + i\xi X_t/\sqrt{n})\right|^2\right]$$

$$= \sup_{n\geq 1} E\left[\prod_{t=1}^{n}(1 + i\xi X_t/\sqrt{n})(1 - i\xi X_t/\sqrt{n})\right]$$

$$= \sup_{n\geq 1} E\left[\prod_{t=1}^{n}(1 + \xi^2 X_t^2/n)\right] < \infty.$$
(7.52)

Therefore, it follows from the Cauchy–Schwarz inequality and (7.51) and (7.52) that

$$\left|\lim_{n\to\infty} E\left[Z_n(\xi)\prod_{t=1}^{n}(1 + i\xi X_t/\sqrt{n})\right]\right|$$

$$\leq \sqrt{\lim_{n\to\infty} E[|Z_n(\xi)|^2]} \sqrt{\sup_{n\geq 1} E\left[\prod_{t=1}^{n}(1 + \xi^2 X_t^2/n)\right]} = 0$$
(7.53)

Finally, it follows now from (7.40), (7.48), and (7.53) that

$$\lim_{n\to\infty} E\left[\exp\left(i\xi(1/\sqrt{n})\sum_{t=1}^{n} X_t\right)\right] = \exp(-\xi^2/2).$$
(7.54)

Because the right-hand side of (7.54) is the characteristic function of the $N(0, 1)$ distribution, the theorem follows for the case $\sigma^2 = 1$ Q.E.D.

Lemma 7.2 is the basis for various central limit theorems for dependent processes. See, for example, Davidson's (1994) textbook. In the next section, I will specialize Lemma 7.2 to martingale difference processes.

7.5.3. Martingale Difference Central Limit Theorems

Note that Lemma 7.2 carries over if we replace the X_t's by a double array $X_{n,t}, t = 1, 2, \ldots, n, n = 1, 2, 3, \ldots$. In particular, let

$$Y_{n,1} = X_1,$$

$$Y_{n,t} = X_t I\left((1/n)\sum_{k=1}^{t-1} X_k^2 \le \sigma^2 + 1\right) \quad \text{for} \quad t \ge 2. \tag{7.55}$$

Then, by condition (7.39),

$$P[Y_{n,t} \ne X_t \text{ for some } t \le n] \le P[(1/n)\sum_{t=1}^{n} X_t^2 > \sigma^2 + 1] \to 0; \tag{7.56}$$

hence, (7.42) holds if

$$\frac{1}{\sqrt{n}}\sum_{t=1}^{n} Y_{n,t} \to_d N(0, \sigma^2). \tag{7.57}$$

Therefore, it suffices to verify the conditions of Lemma 7.2 for (7.55).

First, it follows straightforwardly from (7.56) that condition (7.39) implies

$$\plim_{n\to\infty}(1/n)\sum_{t=1}^{n} Y_{n,t}^2 = \sigma^2. \tag{7.58}$$

Moreover, if X_t is strictly stationary with an σ-mixing base and $E[X_1^2] = \sigma^2 \in (0, \infty)$, then it follows from Theorem 7.7 that (7.39) holds and so does (7.58).

Next, let us have a closer look at condition (7.38). It is not hard to verify that, for arbitrary $\varepsilon > 0$,

$$P\left[\max_{1\le t\le n} |X_t|/\sqrt{n} > \varepsilon\right] = P\left[(1/n)\sum_{t=1}^{n} X_t^2 I(|X_t|/\sqrt{n} > \varepsilon) > \varepsilon^2\right]. \tag{7.59}$$

Hence, (7.38) is equivalent to the condition that, for arbitrary $\varepsilon > 0$,

$$(1/n)\sum_{t=1}^{n} X_t^2 I(|X_t| > \varepsilon\sqrt{n}) \to_p 0. \tag{7.60}$$

Note that (7.60) is true if X_t is strictly stationary because then

$$E\left[(1/n)\sum_{t=1}^{n} X_t^2 I(|X_t| > \varepsilon\sqrt{n})\right] = E\left[X_1^2 I(|X_1| > \varepsilon\sqrt{n})\right] \to 0.$$

Now consider condition (7.41) for the $Y_{n,t}$'s. Observe that

$$\prod_{t=1}^{n}(1 + \xi^2 Y_{n,t}^2/n)$$

$$= \prod_{t=1}^{n}\left[1 + \xi^2 X_t^2 I\left((1/n)\sum_{k=1}^{t-1} X_k^2 \le \sigma^2 + 1\right)\Big/n\right]$$

$$= \prod_{t=1}^{J_n}\left[1 + \xi^2 X_t^2/n\right],$$

where

$$J_n = 1 + \sum_{t=2}^{n} I\left((1/n)\sum_{k=1}^{t-1} X_k^2 \le \sigma^2 + 1\right). \tag{7.61}$$

Hence,

$$\ln\left[\prod_{t=1}^{n}(1 + \xi^2 Y_{n,t}^2/n)\right] = \sum_{t=1}^{J_n-1}\ln\left[1 + \xi^2 X_t^2/n\right] + \ln\left[1 + \xi^2 X_{J_n}^2/n\right]$$

$$\le \xi^2\frac{1}{n}\sum_{t=1}^{J_n-1} X_t^2 + \ln\left[1 + \xi^2 X_{J_n}^2/n\right]$$

$$\le (\sigma^2 + 1)\xi^2 + \ln\left[1 + \xi^2 X_{J_n}^2/n\right], \tag{7.62}$$

where the last inequality in (7.62) follows (7.61). Therefore,

$$\sup_{n\ge 1} E\left[\prod_{t=1}^{n}(1 + \xi^2 Y_{n,t}^2/n)\right]$$

$$\le \exp((\sigma^2 + 1)\xi^2)\left[1 + \xi^2\sup_{n\ge 1} E\left[X_{J_n}^2\right]/n\right]$$

$$\le \exp((\sigma^2 + 1)\xi^2)\left[1 + \xi^2\sup_{n\ge 1}\left((1/n)\sum_{t=1}^{n} E\left[X_t^2\right]\right)\right]. \tag{7.63}$$

Thus, (7.63) is finite if $\sup_{n\ge 1}(1/n)\sum_{t=1}^{n} E[X_t^2] < \infty$, which in its turn is true if X_t is covariance stationary.

Finally, it follows from the law of iterated expectations that, for a martingale difference process X_t, $E[\prod_{t=1}^{n}(1 + i\xi X_t/\sqrt{n})] = E[\prod_{t=1}^{n}(1 +$

$i\xi E[X_t|\mathscr{F}_{t-1}]/\sqrt{n})] = 1, \forall \xi \in \mathbb{R},$ and therefore also $E[\prod_{t=1}^n (1 + i\xi Y_{n,t}/\sqrt{n})] = E[\prod_{t=1}^n (1 + i\xi E[Y_{n,t}|\mathscr{F}_{t-1}]/\sqrt{n})] = 1, \forall \xi \in \mathbb{R}.$

We can now specialize Lemma 7.2 to martingale difference processes:

Theorem 7.10: *Let $X_t \in \mathbb{R}$ be a martingale difference process satisfying the following three conditions:*

(a) $(1/n) \sum_{t=1}^n X_t^2 \to_p \sigma^2 \in (0, \infty);$
(b) *For arbitrary* $\varepsilon > 0, (1/n) \sum_{t=1}^n X_t^2 I(|X_t| > \varepsilon \sqrt{n}) \to_p 0;$
(c) $\sup_{n \geq 1}(1/n) \sum_{t=1}^n E[X_t^2] < \infty.$

Then, $(1/\sqrt{n}) \sum_{t=1}^n X_t \to_d N(0, \sigma^2).$

Moreover, it is not hard to verify that the conditions of Theorem 7.10 hold if the martingale difference process X_t is strictly stationary with an α-mixing base and $E[X_1^2] = \sigma^2 \in (0, \infty)$:

Theorem 7.11: *Let $X_t \in \mathbb{R}$ be a strictly stationary martingale difference process with an α-mixing base satisfying $E[X_1^2] = \sigma^2 \in (0, \infty)$. Then $(1/\sqrt{n}) \sum_{t=1}^n X_t \to_d N(0, \sigma^2).$*

7.6. Exercises

1. Let U and V be independent standard normal random variables, and let $X_t = U \cdot \cos(\lambda t) + V \cdot \sin(\lambda t)$ for all integers t and some nonrandom number $\lambda \in (0, \pi)$. Prove that X_t is covariance stationary and deterministic.

2. Show that the process X_t in problem 1 does not have a vanishing memory but that nevertheless $\text{plim}_{n \to \infty}(1/n) \sum_{t=1}^n X_t = 0.$

3. Let X_t be a time series process satisfying $E[|X_t|] < \infty$, and suppose that the events in the remote σ-algebra $\mathscr{F}_{-\infty} = \cap_{t=0}^\infty \sigma(X_{-t}, X_{-t-1}, X_{-t-2}, \ldots)$ have either probability 0 or 1. Show that $P(E[X_t|\mathscr{F}_{-\infty}] = E[X_t]) = 1.$

4. Prove (7.30).

5. Prove (7.31) by verifying the conditions on Theorem 7.8(b) for $g_t(\theta) = (Y_t - f_t(\theta))^2$ with Y_t defined by (7.18) and $f_t(\theta)$ by (7.26).

6. Verify the conditions of Theorem 7.9 for $g_t(\theta) = (Y_t - f_t(\theta))^2$ with Y_t defined by (7.18) and $f_t(\theta)$ by (7.26).

7. Prove (7.50).

8. Prove (7.59).

APPENDIX

7.A. Hilbert Spaces

7.A.1. Introduction

In general terms, a Hilbert space is a space of elements for which properties similar to those of Euclidean spaces hold. We have seen in Appendix I that the Euclidean space $\mathbb{R}^n$ is a special case of a vector space, that is, a space of elements endowed with two arithmetic operations: addition, denoted by "+," and scalar multiplication, denoted by a dot. In particular, a space V is a vector space if for all x, y, and z in V and all scalars c, c_1, and c_2,

(a) $x + y = y + x$;
(b) $x + (y + z) = (x + y) + z$;
(c) There is a unique zero vector 0 in V such that $x + 0 = x$;
(d) For each x there exists a unique vector $-x$ in V such that $x + (-x) = 0$;
(e) $1 \cdot x = x$;
(f) $(c_1 c_2) \cdot x = c_1 \cdot (c_2 \cdot x)$;
(g) $c \cdot (x + y) = c \cdot x + c \cdot y$;
(h) $(c_1 + c_2) \cdot x = c_1 \cdot x + c_2 \cdot x$.

Scalars are real or complex numbers. If the scalar multiplication rules are confined to real numbers, the vector space V is a real vector space. In the sequel I will only consider real vector spaces.

The inner product of two vectors x and y in $\mathbb{R}^n$ is defined by $x^{\mathsf{T}} y$. If we denote $\langle x, y \rangle = x^{\mathsf{T}} y$, it is trivial that this inner product obeys the rules in the more general definition of the term:

Definition 7.A.1: *An inner product on a real vector space V is a real function $\langle x, y \rangle$ on $V \times V$ such that for all x, y, z in V and all c in $\mathbb{R}$,*

(1) $\langle x, y \rangle = \langle y, x \rangle$;
(2) $\langle cx, y \rangle = c \langle x, y \rangle$;
(3) $\langle x + y, z \rangle = \langle x, z \rangle + \langle y, z \rangle$;
(4) $\langle x, x \rangle > 0$ when $x \neq 0$.

A vector space endowed with an inner product is called an inner-product space. Thus, $\mathbb{R}^n$ is an inner-product space. In $\mathbb{R}^n$ the norm of a vector x is defined by $\|x\| = \sqrt{x^{\mathsf{T}} x}$. Therefore, the norm on a real inner-product space is defined similarly as $\|x\| = \sqrt{\langle x, x \rangle}$. Moreover, in $\mathbb{R}^n$ the distance between two vectors x and y is defined by $\|x - y\| = \sqrt{(x - y)^{\mathsf{T}} (x - y)}$. Therefore, the distance between two vectors x and y in a real inner-product space is defined similarly as $\|x - y\| = \sqrt{\langle x - y, x - y \rangle}$. The latter is called a metric.

An inner-product space with associated norm and metric is called a pre-Hilbert space. The reason for the "pre" is that still one crucial property of $\mathbb{R}^n$ is missing, namely, that every Cauchy sequence in $\mathbb{R}^n$ has a limit in $\mathbb{R}^n$.

Definition 7.A.2: *A sequence of elements X_n of an inner-product space with associated norm and metric is called a Cauchy sequence if, for every $\varepsilon > 0$, there exists an n_0 such that for all $k, m \geq n_0$, $\|x_k - x_m\| < \varepsilon$.*

Theorem 7.A.1: *Every Cauchy sequence in $\mathbb{R}^\ell$, $\ell < \infty$ has a limit in the space involved.*

Proof: Consider first the case $\mathbb{R}$. Let $\bar{x} = \text{limsup}_{n \to \infty} x_n$, where x_n is a Cauchy sequence. I will show first that $\bar{x} < \infty$.

There exists a subsequence n_k such that $\bar{x} = \lim_{k \to \infty} x_{n_k}$. Note that x_{n_k} is also a Cauchy sequence. For arbitrary $\varepsilon > 0$ there exists an index k_0 such that $|x_{n_k} - x_{n_m}| < \varepsilon$ if $k, m \geq k_0$. If we keep k fixed and let $m \to \infty$, it follows that $|x_{n_k} - \bar{x}| < \varepsilon$; hence, $\bar{x} < \infty$, Similarly, $\underline{x} = \text{liminf}_{n \to \infty} x_n > -\infty$. Now we can find an index k_0 and subsequences n_k and n_m such that for $k, m \geq k_0$, $|x_{n_k} - \bar{x}| < \varepsilon$, $|x_{n_m} - \underline{x}| < \varepsilon$, and $|x_{n_k} - x_{n_m}| < \varepsilon$; hence, $|\underline{x} - \bar{x}| < 3\varepsilon$. Because ε is arbitrary, we must have $\underline{x} = \bar{x} = \lim_{n \to \infty} x_n$. If we apply this argument to each component of a vector-valued Cauchy sequence, the result for the case $\mathbb{R}^\ell$ follows.   Q.E.D.

For an inner-product space to be a Hilbert space, we have to require that the result in Theorem 7.A1 carry over to the inner-product space involved:

Definition 7.A.3: *A Hilbert space H is a vector space endowed with an inner product and associated norm and metric such that every Cauchy sequence in H has a limit in H.*

7.A.2. A Hilbert Space of Random Variables

Let $\mathfrak{R}_0$ be the vector space of zero-mean random variables with finite second moments defined on a common probability space $\{\Omega, \mathscr{F}, P\}$ endowed with the inner product $\langle X, Y \rangle = E[X \cdot Y]$, norm $\|X\| = \sqrt{E[X^2]}$, and metric $\|X - Y\|$.

Theorem 7.A.2: *The space $\mathfrak{R}_0$ defined above is a Hilbert space.*

Proof: To demonstrate that $\mathfrak{R}_0$ is a Hilbert space, we need to show that every Cauchy sequence X_n, $n \geq 1$, has a limit in $\mathfrak{R}_0$. Because, by Chebishev's inequality,

$$P[|X_n - X_m| > \varepsilon] \leq E[(X_n - X_m)^2]/\varepsilon^2$$
$$= \|X_n - X_m\|^2/\varepsilon^2 \to 0 \quad \text{as} \quad n, m \to \infty$$

for every $\varepsilon > 0$, it follows that $|X_n - X_m| \to_p 0$ as $n, m \to \infty$. In Appendix 6.B of Chapter 6, we have seen that convergence in probability implies convergence a.s. along a subsequence. Therefore, there exists a subsequence n_k such that $|X_{n_k} - X_{n_m}| \to 0$ a.s. as $n, m \to \infty$. The latter implies that there exists a null set N such that for every $\omega \in \Omega \backslash N$, $X_{n_k}(\omega)$ is a Cauchy sequence in $\mathbb{R}$; hence, $\lim_{k \to \infty} X_{n_k}(\omega) = X(\omega)$ exists for every $\omega \in \Omega \backslash N$. Now for every fixed m,

$$(X_{n_k} - X_m)^2 \to (X - X_m)^2 \text{ a.s. as } k \to \infty.$$

By Fatou's lemma (see Lemma 7.A.1) and the Cauchy property, the latter implies that

$$\|X - X_m\|^2 = E\left[(X - X_m)^2\right]$$
$$\leq \liminf_{k \to \infty} E\left[(X_{n_k} - X_m)^2\right] \to 0 \text{ as } m \to \infty.$$

Moreover, it is easy to verify that $E[X] = 0$ and $E[X^2] < \infty$. Thus, every Cauchy sequence in $\mathfrak{R}_0$ has a limit in $\mathfrak{R}_0$; hence, $\mathfrak{R}_0$ is a Hilbert space.   Q.E.D.

Lemma 7.A.1: *(Fatou's lemma). Let X_n, $n \geq 1$, be a sequence of nonnegative random variables. Then $E[\liminf_{n \to \infty} X_n] \leq \liminf_{n \to \infty} E[X_n]$.*

Proof: Put $X = \liminf_{n \to \infty} X_n$ and let φ be a simple function satisfying $0 \leq \varphi(x) \leq x$. Moreover, put $Y_n = \min(\varphi(X), X_n)$. Then $Y_n \to_p \varphi(X)$ because, for arbitrary $\varepsilon > 0$,

$$P[|Y_n - \varphi(X)| > \varepsilon] = P[X_n < \varphi(X) - \varepsilon] \leq P[X_n < X - \varepsilon] \to 0.$$

Given that $E[\varphi(X)] < \infty$ because φ is a simple function, and $Y_n \leq \varphi(X)$, it follows from $Y_n \to_p \varphi(X)$ and the dominated convergence theorem that

$$E[\varphi(X)] = \lim_{n \to \infty} E[Y_n] = \liminf_{n \to \infty} E[Y_n] \leq \liminf_{n \to \infty} E[X_n]. \tag{7.64}$$

If we take the supremum over all simple functions φ satisfying $0 \leq \varphi(x) \leq x$, it follows now from (7.64) and the definition of $E[X]$ that $E[X] \leq \liminf_{n \to \infty} E[X_n]$.   Q.E.D.

7.A.3. Projections

As for the Hilbert space $\mathbb{R}^n$, two elements x and y in a Hilbert space H are said to be orthogonal if $\langle x, y \rangle = 0$, and orthonormal if, in addition, $\|x\| = 1$ and $\|y\| = 1$. Thus, in the Hilbert space $\mathfrak{R}_0$, two random variables are orthogonal if they are uncorrelated.

Definition 7.A.4: *A linear manifold of a real Hilbert space H is a nonempty subset M of H such that for each pair x, y in M and all real numbers α and β,*

$\alpha \cdot x + \beta \cdot y \in M$. *The closure $\bar{M}$ of M is called a subspace of H. The subspace spanned by a subset C of H is the closure of the intersection of all linear manifolds containing C.*

In particular, if S is the subspace spanned by a countable infinite sequence $x_1, x_2, x_3, \ldots$ of vectors in H, then each vector x in S takes the form $x = \sum_n^\infty c_n \cdot x_n$, where the coefficients c_n are such that $\|x\| < \infty$.

It is not hard to verify that a subspace of a Hilbert space is a Hilbert space itself.

Definition 7.A.5: *The projection of an element y in a Hilbert space H on a subspace S of H is an element x of S such that $\|y - x\| = \min_{z \in S}\|y - z\|$.*

For example, if S is a subspace spanned by vectors $x_1, \ldots, x_k$ in H and $y \in H \backslash S$, then the projection of y on S is a vector $x = c_1 \cdot x_1 + \cdots + c_k \cdot x_k \in S$, where the coefficients c_j are chosen such that $\|y - c_1 \cdot x_1 - \cdots - c_k \cdot x_k\|$ is minimal. Of course, if $y \in S$, then the projection of y on S is y itself.

Projections always exist and are unique:

Theorem 7.A.3: *(Projection theorem) If S is a subspace of a Hilbert space H and y is a vector in H, then there exists a unique vector x in S such that $\|y - x\| = \min_{z \in S}\|y - z\|$. Moreover, the residual vector $u = y - x$ is orthogonal to any z in S.*

Proof: Let $y \in H \backslash S$ and $\inf_{z \in S}\|y - z\| = \delta$. By the definition of infimum it is possible to select vectors x_n in S such that $\|y - x_n\| \leq \delta + 1/n$. The existence of the projection x of y on S then follows by showing that x_n is a Cauchy sequence as follows. Observe that

$$\|x_n - x_m\|^2 = \|(x_n - y) - (x_m - y)\|^2$$
$$= \|x_n - y\|^2 + \|x_m - y\|^2 - 2\langle x_n - y, x_m - y \rangle$$

and

$$4\|(x_n + x_m)/2 - y\|^2 = \|(x_n - y) + (x_m - y)\|^2$$
$$= \|x_n - y\|^2 + \|x_m - y\|^2 + 2\langle x_n - y, x_m - y \rangle.$$

Adding these two equations up yields

$$\|x_n - x_m\|^2 = 2\|x_n - y\|^2 + 2\|x_m - y\|^2 - 4\|(x_n + x_m)/2 - y\|^2.$$
$$(7.65)$$

Because $(x_n + x_m)/2 \in S$, it follows that $\|(x_n + x_m)/2 - y\|^2 \geq \delta^2$; hence, it follows from (7.65) that

$$\|x_n - x_m\|^2 \leq 2\|x_n - y\|^2 + 2\|x_m - y\|^2 - 4\delta^2$$
$$\leq 4\delta/n + 1/n^2 + 4\delta/m + 1/m^2.$$

Thus, x_n is a Cauchy sequence in S, and because S is a Hilbert space itself, x_n has a limit x in S.

As to the orthogonality of $u = y - x$ with any vector z in S, note that for every real number c and every z in S, $x + c \cdot z$ is a vector in S, and thus

$$\delta^2 \le \|y - x - c \cdot z\|^2 = \|u - c \cdot z\|^2$$
$$= \|y - x\|^2 + \|c \cdot z\|^2 - 2\langle u, c \cdot z \rangle$$
$$= \delta^2 + c^2 \|z\|^2 - 2c\langle u, z \rangle. \tag{7.66}$$

Minimizing the right-hand side of (7.66) to c yields the solution $c_0 = \langle u, z \rangle / \|z\|^2$, and substituting this solution in (7.66) yields the inequality $(\langle u, z \rangle)^2 / \|z\|^2 \le 0$. Thus, $\langle u, z \rangle = 0$.

Finally, suppose that there exists another vector p in S such that $\|y - p\| = \delta$. Then $y - p$ is orthogonal to any vector z in $S : \langle y - p, z \rangle = 0$. But $x - p$ is a vector in S, and thus $\langle y - p, x - p \rangle = 0$ and $\langle y - x, x - p \rangle = 0$; hence, $0 = \langle y - p, x - p \rangle - \langle y - x, x - p \rangle = \langle x - p, x - p \rangle = \|x - p\|^2$. Therefore, $p = x$.   Q.E.D.

7.A.5. Proof of the Wold Decomposition

Let X_t be a zero-mean covariance stationary process and $E[X_t^2] = \sigma^2$. Then the X_t's are members of the Hilbert space $\Re_0$ defined in Section 7.A.2. Let $S_{-\infty}^{t-1}$ be the subspace spanned by $X_{t-j}, j \ge 1$, and let $\hat{X}_t$ be the projection of X_t on $S_{-\infty}^{t-1}$. Then $U_t = X_t - \hat{X}_t$ is orthogonal to all $X_{t-j}, j \ge 1$, that is, $E[U_t X_{t-j}] = 0$ for $j \ge 1$. Because $U_{t-j} \in S_{-\infty}^{t-1}$ for $j \ge 1$, the U_t's are also orthogonal to each other: $E[U_t U_{t-j}] = 0$ for $j \ge 1$.

Note that, in general, $\hat{X}_t$ takes the form $\hat{X}_t = \sum_{j=1}^{\infty} \beta_{t,j} X_{t-j}$, where the coefficients $\beta_{t,j}$ are such that $\|Y_t\|^2 = E[Y_t^2] < \infty$. However, because X_t is covariance stationary the coefficients $\beta_{t,j}$ do not depend on the time index t, for they are the solutions of the normal equations

$$\gamma(m) = E[X_t X_{t-m}] = \sum_{j=1}^{\infty} \beta_j E[X_{t-j} X_{t-m}]$$

$$= \sum_{j=1}^{\infty} \beta_j \gamma(|j - m|), \quad m = 1, 2, 3, \ldots.$$

Thus, the projections $\hat{X}_t = \sum_{j=1}^{\infty} \beta_j X_{t-j}$ are covariance stationary and so are the U_t's because

$$\sigma^2 = \|X_t\|^2 = \|U_t + \hat{X}_t\|^2 = \|U_t\|^2 + \|\hat{X}_t\|^2 + 2\langle U_t, \hat{X}_t \rangle$$
$$= \|U_t\|^2 + \|\hat{X}_t\|^2 = E[U_t^2] + E[\hat{X}_t^2];$$

thus, $E[U_t^2] = \sigma_u^2 \le \sigma^2$.

Next, let $Z_{t,m} = \sum_{j=1}^{m} \alpha_j U_{t-j}$, where $\alpha_j = \langle X_t, U_{t-j} \rangle = E[X_t U_{t-j}]$. Then

$$
\|X_t - Z_{t,m}\|^2 = \left\| X_t - \sum_{j=1}^{m} \alpha_j U_{t-j} \right\|^2
$$

$$
= E\left[X_t^2\right] - 2\sum_{j=1}^{m} \alpha_j E[X_t U_{t-j}]
$$

$$
+ \sum_{i=1}^{m} \sum_{j=1}^{m} \alpha_i \alpha_j E[U_i U_j] = E\left[X_t^2\right] - \sum_{j=1}^{m} \alpha_j^2 \geq 0
$$

for all $m \geq 1$; hence, $\sum_{j=1}^{\infty} \alpha_j^2 < \infty$. The latter implies that $\sum_{j=m}^{\infty} \alpha_j^2 \rightarrow 0$ for $m \rightarrow \infty$, and thus for fixed t, $Z_{t,m}$ is a Cauchy sequence in $S_{-\infty}^{t-1}$, and $X_t - Z_{t,m}$ is a Cauchy sequence in $S_{-\infty}^{t}$. Consequently, $Z_t = \sum_{j=1}^{\infty} \alpha_j U_{t-j} \in S_{-\infty}^{t-1}$ and $W_t = X_t - \sum_{j=1}^{\infty} \alpha_j U_{t-j} \in S_{-\infty}^{t}$ exist.

As to the latter, it follows easily from (7.8) that $W_t \in S_{-\infty}^{t-m}$ for every m; hence,

$$
W_t \in \bigcap_{-\infty < t < \infty} S_{-\infty}^{t}. \tag{7.67}
$$

Consequently, $E[U_{t+m} W_t] = 0$ for all integers t and m. Moreover, it follows from (7.67) that the projection of W_t on any $S_{-\infty}^{t-m}$ is W_t itself; hence, W_t is perfectly predictable from any set $\{X_{t-j}, j \geq 1\}$ of past values of X_t as well as from any set $\{W_{t-j}, j \geq 1\}$ of past values of W_t.

8 Maximum Likelihood Theory

8.1. Introduction

Consider a random sample $Z_1, \ldots, Z_n$ from a k-variate distribution with density $f(z|\theta_0)$, where $\theta_0 \in \Theta \subset \mathbb{R}^m$ is an unknown parameter vector with Θ a given parameter space. As is well known, owing to the independence of the Z_j's, the joint density function of the random vector $Z = (Z_1^{\mathrm{T}}, \ldots, Z_n^{\mathrm{T}})^{\mathrm{T}}$ is the product of the marginal densities, $\prod_{j=1}^n f(z_j \mid \theta_0)$. The likelihood function in this case is defined as this joint density with the nonrandom arguments z_j replaced by the corresponding random vectors Z_j, and θ_0 by θ:

$$\hat{L}_n(\theta) = \prod_{j=1}^n f(Z_j|\theta). \tag{8.1}$$

The maximum likelihood (ML) estimator of θ_0 is now $\hat{\theta} = \mathrm{argmax}_{\theta \in \Theta} \hat{L}_n(\theta)$, or equivalently,

$$\hat{\theta} = \underset{\theta \in \Theta}{\mathrm{argmax}} \ln(\hat{L}_n(\theta)), \tag{8.2}$$

where "argmax" stands for the argument for which the function involved takes its maximum value.

The ML estimation method is motivated by the fact that, in this case,

$$E[\ln(\hat{L}_n(\theta))] \le E[\ln(\hat{L}_n(\theta_0))]. \tag{8.3}$$

To see this, note that $\ln(u) = u - 1$ for $u = 1$ and $\ln(u) < u - 1$ for $0 < u < 1$ and $u > 1$. Therefore, if we take $u = f(Z_j|\theta)/f(Z_j|\theta_0)$ it follows that, for all θ, $\ln(f(Z_j|\theta)/f(Z_j|\theta_0)) \le f(Z_j|\theta)/f(Z_j|\theta_0) - 1$, and if we take expectations it follows now that

$$E[\ln(f(Z_j|\theta)/f(Z_j|\theta_0))] \leq E[f(Z_j|\theta)/f(Z_j|\theta_0)] - 1$$

$$= \int_{\mathbb{R}^k} \frac{f(z|\theta)}{f(z|\theta_0)} f(z|\theta_0)dz - 1$$

$$= \int_{\{z\in\mathbb{R}^k:f(z|\theta_0)>0\}} f(z|\theta)dz - 1 \leq 0.$$

Summing up for $j = 1, 2, \ldots, n$, (8.3) follows.

This argument reveals that neither the independence assumption of the data $Z = (Z_1^T, \ldots, Z_n^T)^T$ nor the absolute continuity assumption is necessary for (8.3). The only condition that matters is that

$$E[\hat{L}_n(\theta)/\hat{L}_n(\theta_0)] \leq 1 \tag{8.4}$$

for all $\theta \in \Theta$ and $n \geq 1$. Moreover, if the support of Z_j is not affected by the parameters in θ_0 – that is, if in the preceding case the set $\{z \in \mathbb{R}^m : f(z|\theta) > 0\}$ is the same for all $\theta \in \Theta$ – then the inequality in (8.4) becomes an equality:

$$E[\hat{L}_n(\theta)/\hat{L}_n(\theta_0)] = 1 \tag{8.5}$$

for all $\theta \in \Theta$ and $n \geq 1$. Equality (8.5) is the most common case in econometrics.

To show that absolute continuity is not essential for (8.3), suppose that the Z_j's are independent and identically *discrete* distributed with support Ξ, that is, for all $z \in \Xi$, $P[Z_j = z] > 0$ and $\sum_{z\in\Xi} P[Z_j = z] = 1$. Moreover, now let $f(z|\theta_0) = P[Z_j = z]$, where $f(z|\theta)$ is the probability model involved. Of course, $f(z|\theta)$ should be specified such that $\sum_{z\in\Xi} f(z|\theta) = 1$ for all $\theta \in \Theta$. For example, suppose that the Z_j's are independent Poisson (θ_0) distributed, and thus $f(z|\theta) = e^{-\theta}\theta^z/z!$ and $\Xi = \{0, 1, 2, \ldots\}$. Then the likelihood function involved also takes the form (8.1), and

$$E[f(Z_j|\theta)/f(Z_j|\theta_0)] = \sum_{z\in\Xi} \frac{f(z|\theta)}{f(z|\theta_0)} f(z|\theta_0) = \sum_{z\in\Xi} f(z|\theta) = 1;$$

hence, (8.5) holds in this case as well and therefore so does (8.3).

In this and the previous case the likelihood function takes the form of a product. However, in the dependent case we can also write the likelihood function as a product. For example, let $Z = (Z_1^T, \ldots, Z_n^T)^T$ be absolutely continuously distributed with joint density $f_n(z_n, \ldots, z_1|\theta_0)$, where the Z_j's are no longer independent. It is always possible to decompose a joint density as a product of conditional densities and an initial marginal density. In particular, letting, for $t \geq 2$,

$$f_t(z_t|z_{t-1}, \ldots, z_1, \theta) = f_t(z_t, \ldots, z_1|\theta)/f_{t-1}(z_{t-1}, \ldots, z_1|\theta),$$

we can write

$$f_n(z_n, \ldots, z_1|\theta) = f_1(z_1|\theta) \prod_{t=2}^{n} f_t(z_t|z_{t-1}, \ldots, z_1, \theta).$$

Therefore, the likelihood function in this case can be written as

$$\hat{L}_n(\theta) = f_n(Z_n, \ldots, Z_1|\theta) = f_1(Z_1|\theta) \prod_{t=2}^{n} f_t(Z_t|Z_{t-1}, \ldots, Z_1, \theta).$$

$$(8.6)$$

It is easy to verify that in this case (8.5) also holds, and therefore so does (8.3). Moreover, it follows straightforwardly from (8.6) and the preceding argument that

$$P\left(E\left[\left.\frac{\hat{L}_t(\theta)/\hat{L}_{t-1}(\theta)}{\hat{L}_t(\theta_0)/\hat{L}_{t-1}(\theta_0)}\right| Z_{t-1}, \ldots, Z_1\right] \leq 1\right) = 1$$

$$\text{for} \quad t = 2, 3, \ldots, n; \qquad (8.7)$$

hence,

$$P(E[\ln(\hat{L}_t(\theta)/\hat{L}_{t-1}(\theta)) - \ln(\hat{L}_t(\theta_0)/\hat{L}_{t-1}(\theta_0))|Z_{t-1}, \ldots, Z_1] \leq 0)$$

$$= 1 \quad \text{for} \quad t = 2, 3, \ldots, n. \qquad (8.8)$$

Of course, these results hold in the independent case as well.

8.2. Likelihood Functions

There are many cases in econometrics in which the distribution of the data is neither absolutely continuous nor discrete. The Tobit model discussed in Section 8.3 is such a case. In these cases we cannot construct a likelihood function in the way I have done here, but still we can define a likelihood function indirectly, using the properties (8.4) and (8.7):

Definition 8.1: *A sequence $\hat{L}_n(\theta)$, $n \geq 1$, of nonnegative random functions on a parameter space Θ is a sequence of likelihood functions if the following conditions hold:*

(a) *There exists an increasing sequence $\mathscr{F}_n$, $n \geq 0$, of σ-algebras such that for each $\theta \in \Theta$ and $n \geq 1$, $\hat{L}_n(\theta)$ is measurable $\mathscr{F}_n$.*
(b) *There exists a $\theta_0 \in \Theta$ such that for all $\theta \in \Theta$, $P(E[L_1(\theta)/L_1(\theta_0)|\mathscr{F}_0] \leq 1) = 1$, and, for $n \geq 2$,*

$$P\left(E\left[\left.\frac{\hat{L}_n(\theta)/\hat{L}_{n-1}(\theta)}{\hat{L}_n(\theta_0)/\hat{L}_{n-1}(\theta_0)}\right| \mathscr{F}_{n-1}\right] \leq 1\right) = 1.$$

(c) For all $\theta_1 \neq \theta_2$ in Θ, $P[\hat{L}_1(\theta_1) = \hat{L}_1(\theta_2)|\mathscr{F}_0] < 1$, and for $n \geq 2$,

$$P[\hat{L}_n(\theta_1)/\hat{L}_{n-1}(\theta_1) = \hat{L}_n(\theta_2)/\hat{L}_{n-1}(\theta_2)|\mathscr{F}_{n-1}] < 1.^{[1]}$$

The conditions in (c) exclude the case that $\hat{L}_n(\theta)$ is constant on Θ. Moreover, these conditions also guarantee that $\theta_0 \in \Theta$ is unique:

Theorem 8.1: *For all $\theta \in \Theta \backslash \{\theta_0\}$ and $n \geq 1$, $E[\ln(\hat{L}_n(\theta)/\hat{L}_n(\theta_0))] < 0$.*

Proof: First, let $n = 1$. I have already established that $\ln(\hat{L}_1(\theta)/\hat{L}_1(\theta_0)) <$ $\hat{L}_1(\theta)/\hat{L}_1(\theta_0) - 1$ if $\hat{L}_n(\theta)/\hat{L}_n(\theta_0) \neq 1$. Thus, letting $Y(\theta) = \hat{L}_n(\theta)/\hat{L}_n(\theta_0) -$ $\ln(\hat{L}_n(\theta)/\hat{L}_n(\theta_0)) - 1$ and $X(\theta) = \hat{L}_n(\theta)/\hat{L}_n(\theta_0)$, we have $Y(\theta) \geq 0$, and $Y(\theta) > 0$ if and only if $X(\theta) \neq 1$. Now suppose that $P(E[Y(\theta)|\mathscr{F}_0] = 0) = 1$. Then $P[Y(\theta) = 0|\mathscr{F}_0] = 1$ a.s. because $Y(\theta) \geq 0$; hence, $P[X(\theta) = 1|\mathscr{F}_0] =$ 1 a.s. Condition (c) in Definition 8.1 now excludes the possibility that $\theta \neq \theta_0$; hence, $P(E[\ln(\hat{L}_1(\theta)/\hat{L}_1(\theta_0))|\mathscr{F}_0] < 0) = 1$ if and only if $\theta \neq \theta_0$. In its turn this result implies that

$$E[\ln(\hat{L}_1(\theta)/\hat{L}_1(\theta_0))] < 0 \quad \text{if } \theta \neq \theta_0. \tag{8.9}$$

By a similar argument it follows that, for $n \geq 2$,

$$E[\ln(\hat{L}_n(\theta)/\hat{L}_{n-1}(\theta)) - \ln(\hat{L}_n(\theta_0)/\hat{L}_{n-1}(\theta_0))] < 0 \quad \text{if } \theta \neq \theta_0. \tag{8.10}$$

The theorem now follows from (8.9) and (8.10).   Q.E.D.

As we have seen for the case (8.1), if the support $\{z : f(z|\theta) > 0\}$ of $f(z|\theta)$ does not depend on θ, then the inequalities in condition (b) become equalities, with $\mathscr{F}_n = \sigma(Z_n, \ldots, Z_1)$ for $n \geq 1$, and $\mathscr{F}_0$ the trivial σ-algebra. Therefore,

Definition 8.2: *The sequence $\hat{L}_n(\theta)$, $n \geq 1$, of likelihood functions has invariant support if, for all $\theta \in \Theta$, $P(E[\hat{L}_1(\theta)/\hat{L}_1(\theta_0)|\mathscr{F}_0] = 1) = 1$, and, for $n \geq 2$,*

$$P\left(E\left[\left.\frac{\hat{L}_n(\theta)/\hat{L}_{n-1}(\theta)}{\hat{L}_n(\theta_0)/\hat{L}_{n-1}(\theta_0)}\right|\mathscr{F}_{n-1}\right] = 1\right) = 1.$$

As noted before, this is the most common case in econometrics.

---

[1] See Chapter 3 for the definition of these conditional probabilities.

8.3. Examples

8.3.1. The Uniform Distribution

Let Z_j, $j = 1, \ldots, n$ be independent random drawings from the uniform $[0, \theta_0]$ distribution, where $\theta_0 > 0$. The density function of Z_j is $f(z|\theta_0) = \theta_0^{-1} I(0 \leq z \leq \theta_0)$, and thus the likelihood function involved is

$$\hat{L}_n(\theta) = \theta^{-n} \prod_{j=1}^{n} I(0 \leq Z_j \leq \theta). \tag{8.11}$$

In this case $\mathscr{F}_n = \sigma(Z_n, \ldots, Z_1)$ for $n \geq 1$, and we may choose for $\mathscr{F}_0$ the trivial σ-algebra $\{\Omega, \emptyset\}$. The conditions (b) in Definition 8.1 now read

$$E[\hat{L}_1(\theta)/\hat{L}_1(\theta_0)|\mathscr{F}_0] = E[\hat{L}_1(\theta)/\hat{L}_1(\theta_0)|] = \min(\theta, \theta_0)/\theta \leq 1,$$

$$E\left[\left.\frac{\hat{L}_n(\theta)/\hat{L}_{n-1}(\theta)}{\hat{L}_n(\theta_0)/\hat{L}_{n-1}(\theta_0)}\right| \mathscr{F}_{n-1}\right] = E[\hat{L}_1(\theta)/\hat{L}_1(\theta_0)|]$$

$$= \min(\theta, \theta_0)/\theta \leq 1 \quad \text{for} \quad n \geq 2.$$

Moreover, the conditions (c) in Definition 8.1 read

$$P\left[\theta_1^{-1} I(0 \leq Z_1 \leq \theta_1) = \theta_2^{-1} I(0 \leq Z_1 \leq \theta_2)\right]$$

$$= P(Z_1 > \max(\theta_1, \theta_2)) < 1 \quad \text{if} \quad \theta_1 \neq \theta_2.$$

Hence, Theorem 8.1 applies. Indeed,

$$E[\ln(\hat{L}_n(\theta)/\hat{L}_n(\theta_0))] = n \ln(\theta_0/\theta) + n E[\ln(I(0 \leq Z_1 \leq \theta))]$$

$$- E[\ln(I(0 \leq Z_1 \leq \theta_0))]$$

$$= n \ln(\theta_0/\theta) + n E[\ln(I(0 \leq Z_1 \leq \theta))]$$

$$= \begin{cases} -\infty & \text{if } \theta < \theta_0, \\ n \ln(\theta_0/\theta) < 0 & \text{if } \theta > \theta_0, \\ 0 & \text{if } \theta = \theta_0. \end{cases}$$

8.3.2. Linear Regression with Normal Errors

Let $Z_j = (Y_j, X_j^T)^T$, $j = 1, \ldots, n$ be independent random vectors such that

$$Y_j = \alpha_0 + \beta_0^T X_j + U_j, \ U_j|X_j \sim N(0, \sigma_0^2),$$

where the latter means that the conditional distribution of U_j, given X_j, is a normal $N(0, \sigma_0^2)$ distribution. The conditional density of Y_j, given

X_j, is

$$f(y|\theta_0, X_j) = \frac{\exp\left[-\frac{1}{2}\left(y - \alpha_0 - \beta_0^T X_j\right)^2 / \sigma_0^2\right]}{\sigma_0 \sqrt{2\pi}},$$

where $\theta_0 = \left(\alpha_0, \beta_0^T, \sigma_0^2\right)^T$.

Next, suppose that the X_j's are absolutely continuously distributed with density $g(x)$. Then the likelihood function is

$$\hat{L}_n(\theta) = \left(\prod_{j=1}^n f(Y_j|\theta, X_j)\right)\left(\prod_{j=1}^n g(X_j)\right)$$

$$= \frac{\exp\left[-\frac{1}{2}\sum_{j=1}^n \left(Y_j - \alpha - \beta^T X_j\right)^2/\sigma^2\right]}{\sigma^n(\sqrt{2\pi})^n}\prod_{j=1}^n g(X_j), \quad (8.12)$$

where $\theta = (\alpha, \beta^T, \sigma^2)^T$. However, note that in this case the marginal distribution of X_j does not matter for the ML estimator $\hat{\theta}$ because this distribution does not depend on the parameter vector θ_0. More precisely, the functional form of the ML estimator $\hat{\theta}$ as a function of the data is invariant to the marginal distributions of the X_j's, although the asymptotic properties of the ML estimator (implicitly) depend on the distributions of the X_j's. Therefore, without loss of generality, we may ignore the distribution of the X_j's in (8.12) and work with the conditional likelihood function:

$$\hat{L}_n^c(\theta) = \prod_{j=1}^n f(Y_j|\theta, X_j) = \frac{\exp\left[-\frac{1}{2}\sum_{j=1}^n \left(Y_j - \alpha - \beta^T X_j\right)^2/\sigma^2\right]}{\sigma^n(\sqrt{2\pi})^n},$$

where $\theta = (\alpha, \beta^T, \sigma^2)^T$. $\quad (8.13)$

As to the σ-algebras involved, we may choose $\mathscr{F}_0 = \sigma(\{X_j\}_{j=1}^\infty)$ and, for $n \geq 1$, $\mathscr{F}_n = \sigma(\{Y_j\}_{j=1}^n) \vee \mathscr{F}_0$, where $\vee$ denotes the operation "take the smallest σ-algebra containing the two σ-algebras involved."[2] The conditions (b) in Definition 8.1 then read

$$E\left[\hat{L}_1^c(\theta)/\hat{L}_1^c(\theta_0)|\mathscr{F}_0\right] = E[f(Y_1|\theta, X_1)/f(Y_1|\theta_0, X_1)|X_1] = 1,$$

$$E\left[\left.\frac{\hat{L}_n^c(\theta)/\hat{L}_{n-1}^c(\theta)}{\hat{L}_n^c(\theta_0)/\hat{L}_{n-1}^c(\theta_0)}\right|\mathscr{F}_{n-1}\right] = E[f(Y_n|\theta, X_n)/f(Y_n|\theta_0, X_n)|X_n]$$

$$= 1 \quad \text{for} \quad n \geq 2.$$

Thus, Definition 8.2 applies. Moreover, it is easy to verify that the conditions (c) of Definition 8.1 now read as $P[f(Y_n|\theta_1, X_n) = f(Y_n|\theta_2, X_n)|X_n] < 1$ if $\theta_1 \neq \theta_2$. This is true but is tedious to verify.

---

[2] Recall from Chapter 1 that the union of σ-algebras is not necessarily a σ-algebra.

8.3.3. Probit and Logit Models

Again, let $Z_j = (Y_j, X_j^T)^T$, $j = 1, \ldots, n$ be independent random vectors, but now Y_j takes only two values, 0 and 1, with conditional Bernoulli probabilities

$$P(Y_j = 1|\theta_0, X_j) = F(\alpha_0 + \beta_0^T X_j),$$
$$P(Y_j = 0|\theta_0, X_j) = 1 - F(\alpha_0 + \beta_0^T X_j), \tag{8.14}$$

where F is a given distribution function and $\theta_0 = (\alpha_0, \beta_0^T)^T$. For example, let the sample be a survey of households, where Y_j indicates home ownership and X_j is a vector of household characteristics such as marital status, number of children living at home, and income.

If F is the logistic distribution function, $F(x) = 1/[1 + \exp(-x)]$, then model (8.14) is called the Logit model; if F is the distribution function of the standard normal distribution, then model (8.14) is called the Probit model.

In this case the conditional likelihood function is

$$\hat{L}_n^c(\theta) = \prod_{j=1}^{n} [Y_j F(\alpha + \beta^T X_j) + (1 - Y_j)(1 - F(\alpha + \beta^T X_j))],$$
$$\text{where} \quad \theta = (\alpha, \beta^T)^T. \tag{8.15}$$

Also in this case, the marginal distribution of X_j does not affect the functional form of the ML estimator as a function of the data.

The σ-algebras involved are the same as in the regression case, namely, $\mathscr{F}_0 = \sigma(\{X_j\}_{j=1}^{\infty})$ and, for $n \geq 1$, $\mathscr{F}_n = \sigma(\{Y_j\}_{j=1}^{n}) \vee \mathscr{F}_0$. Moreover, note that

$$E[\hat{L}_1^c(\theta)/\hat{L}_1^c(\theta_0)|\mathscr{F}_0] = \sum_{y=0}^{1} [y F(\alpha + \beta^T X_1)$$
$$+ (1 - y)(1 - F(\alpha + \beta^T X_1))] = 1,$$

and similarly

$$E\left[\frac{\hat{L}_n^c(\theta)/\hat{L}_{n-1}^c(\theta)}{\hat{L}_n^c(\theta_0)/\hat{L}_{n-1}^c(\theta_0)}\middle|\mathscr{F}_{n-1}\right] = \sum_{y=0}^{1} [y F(\alpha + \beta^T X_n)$$
$$+ (1 - y)(1 - F(\alpha + \beta^T X_n))] = 1;$$

hence, the conditions (b) of Definition 8.1 and the conditions of Definition 8.2 apply. Also the conditions (c) in Definition 8.1 apply, but again it is rather tedious to verify this.

8.3.4. The Tobit Model

Let $Z_j = (Y_j, X_j^\mathrm{T})^\mathrm{T}$, $j = 1, \ldots, n$ be independent random vectors such that

$$Y_j = \max(Y_j^*, 0), \quad \text{where} \quad Y_j^* = \alpha_0 + \beta_0^\mathrm{T} X_j + U_j$$
$$\text{with} \quad U_j | X_j \sim N(0, \sigma_0^2). \tag{8.16}$$

The random variables Y_j^* are only observed if they are positive. Note that

$$\begin{aligned} P[Y_j = 0 | X_j] &= P[\alpha_0 + \beta_0^\mathrm{T} X_j + U_j \leq 0 | X_j] \\ &= P[U_j > \alpha_0 + \beta_0^\mathrm{T} X_j | X_j] = 1 - \Phi\left((\alpha_0 + \beta_0^\mathrm{T} X_j)/\sigma_0\right), \end{aligned}$$

$$\text{where} \quad \Phi(x) = \int_{-\infty}^{x} \exp(-u^2/2)/\sqrt{2\pi}\, du.$$

This is a Probit model. Because model (8.16) was proposed by Tobin (1958) and involves a Probit model for the case $Y_j = 0$, it is called the *Tobit* model. For example, let the sample be a survey of households, where Y_j is the amount of money household j spends on tobacco products and X_j is a vector of household characteristics. But there are households in which nobody smokes, and thus for these households $Y_j = 0$.

In this case the setup of the conditional likelihood function is not as straight-forward as in the previous examples because the conditional distribution of Y_j given X_j is neither absolutely continuous nor discrete. Therefore, in this case it is easier to derive the likelihood function indirectly from Definition 8.1 as follows.

First note that the conditional distribution function of Y_j, given X_j and $Y_j > 0$, is

$$\begin{aligned} P[Y_j \leq y | X_j, Y_j > 0] &= \frac{P[0 < Y_j \leq y | X_j]}{P[Y_j > 0 | X_j]} \\ &= \frac{P[-\alpha_0 - \beta_0^\mathrm{T} X_j < U_j \leq y - \alpha_0 - \beta_0^\mathrm{T} X_j | X_j]}{P[Y_j > 0 | X_j]} \\ &= \frac{\Phi\left((y - \alpha_0 - \beta_0^\mathrm{T} X_j)/\sigma_0\right) - \Phi\left((-\alpha_0 - \beta_0^\mathrm{T} X_j)/\sigma_0\right)}{\Phi\left((\alpha_0 + \beta_0^\mathrm{T} X_j)/\sigma_0\right)} I(y > 0); \end{aligned}$$

hence, the conditional density function of Y_j, given X_j and $Y_j > 0$, is

$$h(y|\theta_0, X_j, Y_j > 0) = \frac{\varphi\left((y - \alpha_0 - \beta_0^\mathrm{T} X_j)/\sigma_0\right)}{\sigma_0 \Phi\left((\alpha_0 + \beta_0^\mathrm{T} X_j)/\sigma_0\right)} I(y > 0),$$

$$\text{where} \quad \varphi(x) = \frac{\exp(-x^2/2)}{\sqrt{2\pi}}.$$

Next, observe that, for any Borel-measurable function g of (Y_j, X_j) such that $E[|g(Y_j, X_j)|] < \infty$, we have

$$E[g(Y_j, X_j)|X_j]$$
$$= g(0, X_j)P[Y_j = 0|X_j] + E[g(Y_j, X_j)I(Y_j > 0)|X_j]$$
$$= g(0, X_j)P[Y_j = 0|X_j]$$
$$\quad + E\left(E[g(Y_j, X_j)|X_j, Y_j > 0]|X_j]I(Y_j > 0)|X_j\right)$$
$$= g(0, X_j)\left(1 - \Phi\left((\alpha_0 + \beta_0^{\mathrm{T}}X_j)/\sigma_0\right)\right)$$
$$\quad + E\left(\int_0^\infty g(y, X_j)h(y|\theta_0, X_j, Y_j > 0)dy \cdot I(Y_j > 0)|X_j\right)$$
$$= g(0, X_j)\left(1 - \Phi\left((\alpha_0 + \beta_0^{\mathrm{T}}X_j)/\sigma_0\right)\right)$$
$$\quad + \int_0^\infty g(y, X_j)h(y|\theta_0, X_j, Y_j > 0)dy \cdot \Phi\left((\alpha_0 + \beta_0^{\mathrm{T}}X_j)/\sigma_0\right)$$
$$= g(0, X_j)\left(1 - \Phi\left((\alpha_0 + \beta_0^{\mathrm{T}}X_j)/\sigma_0\right)\right)$$
$$\quad + \frac{1}{\sigma_0}\int_0^\infty g(y, X_j)\varphi\left((y - \alpha_0 - \beta_0^{\mathrm{T}}X_j)/\sigma_0\right)dy. \qquad (8.17)$$

Hence, if we choose

$$g(Y_j, X_j)$$
$$= \frac{(1 - \Phi((\alpha + \beta^{\mathrm{T}}X_j)/\sigma))I(Y_j = 0) + \sigma^{-1}\varphi((Y_j - \alpha - \beta^{\mathrm{T}}X_j)/\sigma)I(Y_j > 0)}{(1 - \Phi((\alpha_0 + \beta_0^{\mathrm{T}}X_j)/\sigma_0))I(Y_j = 0) + \sigma_0^{-1}\varphi(Y_j - \alpha_0 - \beta_0^{\mathrm{T}}X_j)/\sigma_0)I(Y_j > 0)},$$
$$\qquad (8.18)$$

it follows from (8.17) that

$$E[g(Y_j, X_j)|X_j] = 1 - \Phi\left((\alpha + \beta^{\mathrm{T}}X_j)/\sigma\right)$$
$$\quad + \frac{1}{\sigma}\int_0^\infty \varphi\left((y - \alpha - \beta^{\mathrm{T}}X_j)/\sigma\right)dy$$
$$= 1 - \Phi\left((\alpha + \beta^{\mathrm{T}}X_j)/\sigma\right)$$
$$\quad + 1 - \Phi\left((-\alpha - \beta^{\mathrm{T}}X_j)/\sigma\right) = 1. \qquad (8.19)$$

In view of Definition 8.1, (8.18) and (8.19) suggest defining the conditional likelihood function of the Tobit model as

$$\hat{L}_n^c(\theta) = \prod_{j=1}^n \left[\left(1 - \Phi\left((\alpha + \beta^{\mathrm{T}}X_j)/\sigma\right)\right)I(Y_j = 0)\right.$$
$$\left. + \sigma^{-1}\varphi\left((Y_j - \alpha - \beta^{\mathrm{T}}X_j)/\sigma\right)I(Y_j > 0)\right].$$

The conditions (b) in Definition 8.1 now follow from (8.19) with the σ-algebras involved defined as in the regression case. Moreover, the conditions (c) also apply.

Finally, note that

$$E[Y_j|X_j, Y_j > 0] = \alpha_0 + \beta_0^T X_j + \frac{\sigma_0 \varphi\left((\alpha_0 + \beta_0^T X_j)/\sigma_0\right)}{\Phi\left((\alpha_0 + \beta_0^T X_j)/\sigma_0\right)}. \quad (8.20)$$

Therefore, if one estimated a linear regression model using only the observations with $Y_j > 0$, the OLS estimates would be inconsistent, owing to the last term in (8.20).

8.4. Asymptotic Properties of ML Estimators

8.4.1. Introduction

Without the conditions (c) in Definition 8.1, the solution $\theta_0 = \text{argmax}_{\theta \in \Theta} E[\ln(\hat{L}_n(\theta))]$ may not be unique. For example, if $Z_j = \cos(X_j + \theta_0)$ with the X_j's independent absolutely continuously distributed random variables with common density, then the density function $f(z|\theta_0)$ of Z_j satisfies $f(z|\theta_0) = f(z|\theta_0 + 2s\pi)$ for all integers s. Therefore, the parameter space Θ has to be chosen small enough to make θ_0 unique.

Also, the first- and second-order conditions for a maximum of $E[\ln(\hat{L}_n(\theta))]$ at $\theta = \theta_0$ may not be satisfied. The latter is, for example, the case for the likelihood function (8.11): if $\theta < \theta_0$, then $E[\ln(\hat{L}_n(\theta))] = -\infty$; if $\theta \geq \theta_0$, then $E[\ln(\hat{L}_n(\theta))] = -n \cdot \ln(\theta)$, and thus the left derivative of $E[\ln(\hat{L}_n(\theta))]$ in $\theta = \theta_0$ is $\lim_{\delta\downarrow0}(E[\ln(\hat{L}_n(\theta_0))] - E[\ln(\hat{L}_n(\theta_0 - \delta))])/\delta = \infty$, and the right-derivative is $\lim_{\delta\downarrow0}(E[\ln(\hat{L}_n(\theta_0 + \delta))] - E[\ln(\hat{L}_n(\theta_0))])/\delta = -n/\theta_0$. Because the first- and second-order conditions play a crucial role in deriving the asymptotic normality and efficiency of the ML estimator (see the remainder of this section), the rest of this chapter does not apply to the case (8.11).

8.4.2. First- and Second-Order Conditions

The following conditions guarantee that the first- and second-order conditions for a maximum hold.

Assumption 8.1: *The parameter space Θ is convex and θ_0 is an interior point of Θ. The likelihood function $\hat{L}_n(\theta)$ is, with probability 1, twice continuously differentiable in an open neighborhood Θ_0 of θ_0, and, for $i_1, i_2 = 1, 2, 3, \ldots, m$,*

$$E\left[\sup_{\theta \in \Theta_0}\left|\frac{\partial^2 \hat{L}_n(\theta)}{\partial \theta_{i_1} \partial \theta_{i_2}}\right|\right] < \infty \quad (8.21)$$

and

$$E\left[\sup_{\theta \in \Theta_0}\left|\frac{\partial^2 ln(\hat{L}_n(\theta))}{\partial \theta_{i_1} \partial \theta_{i_2}}\right|\right] < \infty. \tag{8.22}$$

Theorem 8.2: *Under Assumption 8.1,*

$$E\left(\frac{\partial ln(\hat{L}_n(\theta))}{\partial \theta^{\mathrm{T}}}\bigg|_{\theta=\theta_0}\right) = 0 \quad and \quad E\left(\frac{\partial^2 ln(\hat{L}_n(\theta))}{\partial \theta \partial \theta^{\mathrm{T}}}\bigg|_{\theta=\theta_0}\right)$$

$$= -Var\left(\frac{\partial ln(\hat{L}_n(\theta))}{\partial \theta^{\mathrm{T}}}\bigg|_{\theta=\theta_0}\right).$$

Proof: For notational convenience I will prove this theorem for the univariate parameter case $m = 1$ only. Moreover, I will focus on the case that $Z = (Z_1^{\mathrm{T}}, \ldots, Z_n^{\mathrm{T}})^{\mathrm{T}}$ is a random sample from an absolutely continuous distribution with density $f(z|\theta_0)$.

Observe that

$$E[ln(\hat{L}_n(\theta))/n] = \frac{1}{n}\sum_{j=1}^{n} E[ln(f(Z_j|\theta))] = \int ln(f(z|\theta))f(z|\theta_0)dz, \tag{8.23}$$

It follows from Taylor's theorem that, for $\theta \in \Theta_0$ and every $\delta \neq 0$ for which $\theta + \delta \in \Theta_0$, there exists a $\lambda(z, \delta) \in [0, 1]$ such that

$$ln(f(z|\theta + \delta)) - ln(f(z|\theta))$$
$$= \delta\frac{d\, ln(f(z|\theta))}{d\theta} + \frac{1}{2}\delta^2\frac{d^2\, ln(f(z|\theta + \lambda(z, \delta)\delta))}{(d(\theta + \lambda(z, \delta)\delta))^2}. \tag{8.24}$$

Note that, by the convexity of Θ, $\theta_0 + \lambda(z, \delta)\delta \in \Theta$. Therefore, it follows from condition (8.22), the definition of a derivative, and the dominated convergence theorem that

$$\frac{d}{d\theta}\int ln(f(z|\theta))f(z|\theta_0)dz = \int \frac{d\, ln(f(z|\theta))}{d\theta}f(z|\theta_0)dz. \tag{8.25}$$

Similarly, it follows from condition (8.21), Taylor's theorem, and the dominated convergence theorem that

$$\int \frac{df(z|\theta)}{d\theta}dz = \frac{d}{d\theta}\int f(z|\theta)dz = \frac{d}{d\theta}1 = 0. \tag{8.26}$$

Moreover,

$$\int \frac{d\ln(f(z|\theta))}{d\theta} f(z|\theta_0)dz|_{\theta=\theta_0} = \int \frac{df(z|\theta)/d\theta}{f(z|\theta)} f(z|\theta_0)dz|_{\theta=\theta_0}$$

$$= \int \frac{df(z|\theta)}{d\theta} dz|_{\theta=\theta_0} \qquad (8.27)$$

The first part of Theorem 8.2 now follows from (8.23) through (8.27).

As is the case for (8.25) and (8.26), it follows from the mean value theorem and conditions (8.21) and (8.22) that

$$\frac{d^2}{(d\theta)^2} \int \ln(f(z|\theta)) f(z|\theta_0)dz = \int \frac{d^2 \ln(f(z|\theta))}{(d\theta)^2} f(z|\theta_0)dz \qquad (8.28)$$

and

$$\int \frac{d^2 f(z|\theta)}{(d\theta)^2} dz = \frac{d}{(d\theta)^2} \int f(z|\theta)dz = 0. \qquad (8.29)$$

The second part of the theorem follows now from (8.28), (8.29), and

$$\int \frac{d^2 \ln(f(z|\theta))}{(d\theta)^2} f(z|\theta_0)dz|_{\theta=\theta_0} = \int \frac{d^2 f(z|\theta)}{(d\theta)^2} \frac{f(z|\theta_0)}{f(z|\theta)} dz|_{\theta=\theta_0}$$

$$- \int \left(\frac{df(z|\theta)/d\theta}{f(z|\theta)}\right)^2 f(z|\theta_0)dz|_{\theta=\theta_0} = \int \frac{d^2 f(z|\theta)}{(d\theta)^2} dz|_{\theta=\theta_0}$$

$$- \int (d\ln(f(z|\theta))/d\theta)^2 f(z|\theta_0)dz|_{\theta=\theta_0}.$$

The adaptation of the proof to the general case is reasonably straightforward and is therefore left as an exercise.   Q.E.D.

The matrix

$$H_n = \text{Var}(\partial \ln(\hat{L}_n(\theta))/\partial\theta^{\mathsf{T}}|_{\theta=\theta_0}) \qquad (8.30)$$

is called the *Fisher information matrix*. As we have seen in Chapter 5, the inverse of the Fisher information matrix is just the Cramer–Rao lower bound of the variance matrix of an unbiased estimator of θ_0.

8.4.3. Generic Conditions for Consistency and Asymptotic Normality

The ML estimator is a special case of an M-estimator. In Chapter 6, the generic conditions for consistency and asymptotic normality of M-estimators, which in most cases apply to ML estimators as well, were derived. The case (8.11) is one of the exceptions, though. In particular, if

Assumption 8.2: $plim_{n\to\infty} sup_{\theta\in\Theta}|ln(\hat{L}_n(\theta)/\hat{L}_n(\theta_0)) - E[ln(\hat{L}_n(\theta)/\hat{L}_n(\theta_0))]$
$| = 0$ and $lim_{n\to\infty} sup_{\theta\in\Theta}|E[ln(\hat{L}_n(\theta)/\hat{L}_n(\theta_0))] - \ell(\theta|\theta_0)| = 0$, where $\ell(\theta|\theta_0)$
is a continuous function in θ_0 such that, for arbitrarily small $\delta > 0$,
$sup_{\theta\in\Theta:||\theta-\theta_0||\geq\delta}\ell(\theta|\theta_0) < 0$,

then the ML estimator is consistent.

Theorem 8.3: *Under Assumption 8.2, $plim_{n\to\infty}\hat{\theta} = \theta_0$.*

The conditions in Assumption 8.2 need to be verified on a case-by-case basis. In particular, the uniform convergence in probability condition has to be verified from the conditions of the uniform weak law of large numbers. Note that it follows from Theorem II.6 in Appendix II that the last condition in Assumption 8.2, that is, $sup_{\theta\in\Theta:||\theta-\theta_0||\geq\delta} \ell(\theta|\theta_0) < 0$, holds if the parameter space Θ is compact, $\ell(\theta|\theta_0)$ is continuous on Θ, and θ_0 is unique. The latter follows from Theorem 8.1.

Some of the conditions for asymptotic normality of the ML estimator are already listed in Assumption 8.1 – in particular the convexity of the parameter space Θ and the condition that θ_0 be an interior point of Θ. The other (high-level) conditions are

Assumption 8.3: *For $i_1, i_2 = 1, 2, 3, \ldots, m$,*

$$plim_{\substack{n\to\infty\ \theta\in\Theta}} sup \left| \frac{\partial^2 \ln(\hat{L}_n(\theta))/n}{\partial\theta_{i_1}\partial\theta_{i_2}} - E\left[\frac{\partial^2 \ln(\hat{L}_n(\theta))/n}{\partial\theta_{i_1}\partial\theta_{i_2}}\right]\right| = 0 \qquad (8.31)$$

and

$$lim_{\substack{n\to\infty\ \theta\in\Theta}} sup \left| E\left[\frac{\partial^2 \ln(\hat{L}_n(\theta))/n}{\partial\theta_{i_1}\partial\theta_{i_2}}\right] + h_{i_1,i_2}(\theta)\right| = 0, \qquad (8.32)$$

where $h_{i_1,i_2}(\theta)$ is continuous in θ_0. Moreover, the $m \times m$ matrix $\bar{H}$ with elements $h_{i_1,i_2}(\theta_0)$ is nonsingular. Furthermore,

$$\frac{\partial ln(\hat{L}_n(\theta_0))/\sqrt{n}}{\partial\theta_0^T} \to_d N_m[0, \bar{H}]. \qquad (8.33)$$

Note that the matrix $\bar{H}$ is just the limit of H_n/n, where H_n is the Fisher information matrix (8.30). Condition (8.31) can be verified from the uniform weak law of large numbers. Condition (8.32) is a regularity condition that accommodates data heterogeneity. In quite a few cases we may take $h_{i_1,i_2}(\theta) = -n^{-1}E[\partial^2 \ln(\hat{L}_n(\theta))/(\partial\theta_{i_1}\partial\theta_{i_2})]$. Finally, condition (8.33) can be verified from the central limit theorem.

Theorem 8.4: *Under Assumptions 8.1–8.3, $\sqrt{n}(\hat{\theta} - \theta_0) \to_d N_m[0, \bar{H}^{-1}]$.*

Proof: It follows from the mean value theorem (see Appendix II) that for each $i \in \{1, \ldots, m\}$ there exists a $\hat{\lambda}_i \in [0, 1]$ such that

$$\left. \frac{\partial \ln(\hat{L}_n(\theta))/\sqrt{n}}{\partial \theta_i} \right|_{\theta=\hat{\theta}}$$

$$= \left. \frac{\partial \ln(\hat{L}_n(\theta))/\sqrt{n}}{\partial \theta_i} \right|_{\theta=\theta_0} + \left(\left. \frac{\partial^2 \ln(\hat{L}(\theta))/n}{\partial \theta \partial \theta_i} \right|_{\theta=\theta_0+\hat{\lambda}_i(\hat{\theta}-\theta_0)} \right) \sqrt{n}(\hat{\theta} - \theta_0),$$

$$(8.34)$$

The first-order condition for (8.2) and the condition that θ_0 be an interior point of Θ imply

$$\operatorname*{plim}_{n \to \infty} n^{-1/2} \partial \ln(\hat{L}_n(\theta))/\partial \theta_i |_{\theta=\hat{\theta}} = 0. \qquad (8.35)$$

Moreover, the convexity of Θ guarantees that the mean value $\theta_0 + \hat{\lambda}_i(\hat{\theta} - \theta_0)$ is contained in Θ. It follows now from the consistency of $\hat{\theta}$ and the conditions (8.31) and (8.32) that

$$\tilde{H} = \begin{pmatrix} \left. \frac{\partial^2 \ln(\hat{L}_n(\theta))/n}{\partial \theta \partial \theta_1} \right|_{\theta=\theta_0+\hat{\lambda}_1(\hat{\theta}-\theta_0)} \\ \vdots \\ \left. \frac{\partial^2 \ln(\hat{L}_n(\theta))/n}{\partial \theta \partial \theta_m} \right|_{\theta=\theta_0+\hat{\lambda}_m(\hat{\theta}-\theta_0)} \end{pmatrix} \to_p \bar{H}. \qquad (8.36)$$

The condition that $\bar{H}$ is nonsingular allows us to conclude from (8.36) and Slutsky's theorem that

$$\operatorname*{plim}_{n \to \infty} \tilde{H}^{-1} = \bar{H}^{-1}; \qquad (8.37)$$

hence, it follows from (8.34) and (8.35) that

$$\sqrt{n}(\hat{\theta} - \theta_0) = -\tilde{H}^{-1} \left(\partial \ln(\hat{L}_n(\theta_0))/\partial \theta_0^{\mathsf{T}} \right)/\sqrt{n} + o_p(1). \qquad (8.38)$$

Theorem 8.4 follows now from condition (8.33) and the results (8.37) and (8.38).   Q.E.D.

In the case of a random sample $Z_1, \ldots, Z_n$, the asymptotic normality condition (8.33) can easily be derived from the central limit theorem for i.i.d. random variables. For example, again let the Z_j's be k-variate distributed with density $f(z|\theta_0)$. Then it follows from Theorem 8.2 that, under Assumption 8.1,

$$E\left[\partial \ln(f(Z_j|\theta_0))/\partial \theta_0^{\mathsf{T}} \right] = n^{-1} E\left[\partial \ln(\hat{L}_n(\theta_0))/\partial \theta_0^{\mathsf{T}} \right] = 0$$

and

$$\text{Var}\big[\partial \ln(f(Z_j|\theta_0))/\partial\theta_0^\text{T}\big] = n^{-1}\text{Var}\big[\partial \ln(\hat{L}_n(\theta_0))/\partial\theta_0^\text{T}\big] = \bar{H},$$

and thus (8.33) straightforwardly follows from the central limit theorem for i.i.d. random vectors.

8.4.4. Asymptotic Normality in the Time Series Case

In the time series case (8.6) we have

$$\frac{\partial \ln(\hat{L}_n(\theta_0))/\partial\theta_0^\text{T}}{\sqrt{n}} = \frac{1}{\sqrt{n}}\sum_{t=1}^{n} U_t, \tag{8.39}$$

where

$$U_1 = \partial \ln(f_1(Z_1|\theta_0))/\partial\theta_0^\text{T},$$
$$U_t = \partial \ln(f_t(Z_t|Z_{t-1},\dots,Z_1,\theta_0))/\partial\theta_0^\text{T} \quad \text{for} \quad t \geq 2. \tag{8.40}$$

The process U_t is a martingale difference process (see Chapter 7): Letting $\mathscr{F}_t = \sigma(Z_1,\dots,Z_t)$ for $t \geq 1$ and designating $\mathscr{F}_0$ as the trivial σ-algebra $\{\Omega, \emptyset\}$, it is easy to verify that, for $t \geq 1$, $E[U_t|\mathscr{F}_{t-1}] = 0$ a.s. Therefore, condition (8.33) can in principle be derived from the conditions of the martingale difference central limit theorems (Theorems 7.10 and 7.11) in Chapter 7.

Note that, even if Z_t is a strictly stationary process, the U_t's may not be strictly stationary. In that case condition (8.33) can be proved by specializing Theorem 7.10 in Chapter 7.

An example of condition (8.33) following from Theorem 7.11 in Chapter 7 is the autoregressive (AR) model of order 1:

$$Z_t = \alpha + \beta Z_{t-1} + \varepsilon_t,$$
$$\text{where} \quad \varepsilon_t \text{ is i.i.d. } N(0, \sigma^2) \quad \text{and} \quad |\beta| < 1. \tag{8.41}$$

The condition $|\beta| < 1$ is necessary for strict stationarity of Z_t. Then, for $t \geq 2$, the conditional distribution of Z_t, given $\mathscr{F}_{t-1} = \sigma(Z_1,\dots,Z_{t-1})$, is $N(\alpha + \beta Z_{t-1}, \sigma^2)$, and thus, with $\theta_0 = (\alpha, \beta, \sigma^2)^\text{T}$, (8.40) becomes

$$U_t = \frac{\partial(-\frac{1}{2}(Z_t - \alpha - \beta Z_{t-1})^2/\sigma^2 - \frac{1}{2}\ln(\sigma^2) - \ln(\sqrt{2\pi}))}{\partial(\alpha, \beta, \sigma^2)}$$
$$= \frac{1}{\sigma^2}\begin{pmatrix} \varepsilon_t \\ \varepsilon_t Z_{t-1} \\ \frac{1}{2}(\varepsilon_t^2/\sigma^2 - 1) \end{pmatrix}. \tag{8.42}$$

Because the ε_t's are i.i.d. $N(0, \sigma^2)$ and ε_t and Z_{t-1} are mutually independent, it follows that (8.42) is a martingale difference process not only with respect to $\mathscr{F}_t = \sigma(Z_1, \ldots, Z_t)$ but also with respect to $\mathscr{F}_{-\infty}^t = \sigma(\{Z_{t-j}\}_{j=0}^{\infty})$, that is, $E[U_t|\mathscr{F}_{-\infty}^{t-1}] = 0$ a.s.

By backwards substitution of (8.41) it follows that $Z_t = \sum_{j=0}^{\infty} \beta^j(\alpha + \varepsilon_{t-j})$; hence, the marginal distribution of Z_1 is $N[\alpha/(1-\beta), \sigma^2/(1-\beta^2)]$. However, there is no need to derive U_1 in this case because this term is irrelevant for the asymptotic normality of (8.39). Therefore, the asymptotic normality of (8.39) in this case follows straightforwardly from the stationary martingale difference central limit theorem with asymptotic variance matrix

$$\bar{H} = \text{Var}(U_t) = \frac{1}{\sigma^2} \begin{pmatrix} 1 & \frac{\alpha}{1-\beta} & 0 \\ \frac{\alpha}{1-\beta} & \frac{\alpha^2}{(1-\beta)^2} + \frac{\sigma^2}{1-\beta^2} & 0 \\ 0 & 0 & \frac{1}{2\sigma^2} \end{pmatrix}.$$

8.4.5. Asymptotic Efficiency of the ML Estimator

The ML estimation approach is a special case of the M-estimation approach discussed in Chapter 6. However, the position of the ML estimator among the M-estimators is a special one, namely, the ML estimator is, under some regularity conditions, asymptotically efficient.

To explain and prove asymptotic efficiency, let

$$\tilde{\theta} = \underset{\theta \in \Theta}{\text{argmax}}(1/n) \sum_{j=1}^{n} g(Z_j, \theta) \tag{8.43}$$

be an M-estimator of

$$\theta_0 = \underset{\theta \in \Theta}{\text{argmax}} \, E[g(Z_1, \theta)], \tag{8.44}$$

where again $Z_1, \ldots, Z_n$ is a random sample from a k-variate, absolutely continuous distribution with density $f(z|\theta_0)$, and $\Theta \subset \mathbb{R}^m$ is the parameter space. In Chapter 6, I have set forth conditions such that

$$\sqrt{n}(\tilde{\theta} - \theta_0) \to_d N_m[0, A^{-1}BA^{-1}], \tag{8.45}$$

where

$$A = E\left[\frac{\partial^2 g(Z_1, \theta_0)}{\partial \theta_0 \partial \theta_0^{\text{T}}}\right] = \int_{\mathbb{R}^k} \frac{\partial^2 g(z, \theta_0)}{\partial \theta_0 \partial \theta_0^{\text{T}}} f(z|\theta_0) dz \tag{8.46}$$

and

$$B = E\left[(\partial g(Z_1, \theta_0)/\partial \theta_0^{\text{T}})(\partial g(Z_1, \theta_0)/\partial \theta_0)\right]$$
$$= \int_{\mathbb{R}^k} (\partial g(z, \theta_0)/\partial \theta_0^{\text{T}})(\partial g(z, \theta_0)/\partial \theta_0) f(z|\theta_0) dz. \tag{8.47}$$

As will be shown below in this section, the matrix $A^{-1}BA^{-1} - \bar{H}^{-1}$ is positive semidefinite; hence, the asymptotic variance matrix of $\tilde{\theta}$ is "larger" (or at least not smaller) than the asymptotic variance matrix $\bar{H}^{-1}$ of the ML estimator $\tilde{\theta}$. In other words, the ML estimator is an *asymptotically efficient* M-estimator.

This proposition can be motivated as follows. Under some regularity conditions, as in Assumption 8.1, it follows from the first-order condition for (8.44) that

$$\int_{\mathbb{R}^k} \left(\partial g(z, \theta_0)/\partial \theta_0^{\mathsf{T}} \right) f(z|\theta_0)dz = 0. \tag{8.48}$$

Because equality (8.48) does not depend on the value of θ_0 it follows that, for all θ,

$$\int_{\mathbb{R}^k} (\partial g(z, \theta)/\partial \theta^{\mathsf{T}}) f(z|\theta)dz = 0. \tag{8.49}$$

Taking derivatives inside and outside the integral (8.49) again yields

$$\int_{\mathbb{R}^k} \frac{\partial^2 g(z, \theta)}{\partial \theta \partial \theta^{\mathsf{T}}} f(z|\theta)dz + \int_{\mathbb{R}^k} (\partial g(z, \theta)/\partial \theta^{\mathsf{T}})(\partial f(z|\theta)/\partial \theta)dz$$

$$= \int_{\mathbb{R}^k} \frac{\partial^2 g(z, \theta)}{\partial \theta \partial \theta^{\mathsf{T}}} f(z|\theta)dz + \int_{\mathbb{R}^k} (\partial g(z, \theta)/\partial \theta^{\mathsf{T}})$$

$$\times (\partial \ln(f(z|\theta))/\partial \theta)f(z|\theta)dz = O. \tag{8.50}$$

If we replace θ by θ_0, it follows from (8.46) and (8.50) that

$$E\left[\left(\frac{\partial g(Z_1, \theta_0)}{\partial \theta_0^{\mathsf{T}}} \right) \left(\frac{\partial \ln(f(Z_1|\theta_0))}{\partial \theta_0} \right) \right] = -A. \tag{8.51}$$

Because the two vectors in (8.51) have zero expectations, (8.51) also reads

$$\text{Cov}\left(\frac{\partial g(Z_1, \theta_0)}{\partial \theta_0^{\mathsf{T}}}, \frac{\partial \ln(f(Z_1|\theta_0))}{\partial \theta_0^{\mathsf{T}}} \right) = -A. \tag{8.52}$$

It follows now from (8.47), (8.52), and Assumption 8.3 that

$$\text{Var}\left(\begin{matrix} \partial g(Z_1, \theta_0)/\partial \theta_0^{\mathsf{T}} \\ \partial \ln(f(Z_1|\theta_0))/\partial \theta_0^{\mathsf{T}} \end{matrix} \right) = \left(\begin{matrix} B & -A \\ -A & \bar{H} \end{matrix} \right),$$

which of course is positive semidefinite, and therefore so is

$$\left(A^{-1}, \bar{H}^{-1}\right) \begin{pmatrix} B & -A \\ -A & \bar{H} \end{pmatrix} \begin{pmatrix} A^{-1} \\ \bar{H}^{-1} \end{pmatrix} = A^{-1} B A^{-1} - \bar{H}^{-1}.$$

Note that this argument does not hinge on the independence and absolute continuity assumptions made here. We only need that (8.45) holds for some positive definite matrices A and B and that

$$\frac{1}{\sqrt{n}} \begin{pmatrix} \sum_{j=1}^{n} \partial g(Z_j, \theta_0) / \partial \theta_0^{\mathrm{T}} \\ \partial \ln(\hat{L}_n(\theta_0)) / \partial \theta_0^{\mathrm{T}} \end{pmatrix} \to_d N_{2m} \left[\begin{pmatrix} 0 \\ 0 \end{pmatrix}, \begin{pmatrix} B & -A \\ -A & \bar{H} \end{pmatrix} \right].$$

8.5. Testing Parameter Restrictions

8.5.1. The Pseudo t-Test and the Wald Test

In view of Theorem 8.2 and Assumption 8.3, the matrix $\bar{H}$ can be estimated consistently by the matrix $\hat{H}$ in (8.53):

$$\hat{H} = -\left. \frac{\partial^2 \ln(\hat{L}_n(\theta)) / n}{\partial \theta \partial \theta^{\mathrm{T}}} \right|_{\theta = \hat{\theta}} \to_p \bar{H}. \tag{8.53}$$

If we denote the ith column of the unit matrix I_m by e_i it follows now from (8.53), Theorem 8.4, and the results in Chapter 6 that

Theorem 8.5: *(Pseudo t-test) under Assumptions 8.1–8.3, $\hat{t}_i = \sqrt{n} e_i^{\mathrm{T}} \hat{\theta} / \sqrt{e_i^{\mathrm{T}} \hat{H}^{-1} e_i} \to_d N(0, 1)$ if $e_i^{\mathrm{T}} \theta_0 = 0$.*

Thus, the null hypothesis $H_0 : e_i^{\mathrm{T}} \theta_0 = 0$, which amounts to the hypothesis that the ith component of θ_0 is zero, can now be tested by the pseudo t-value $\hat{t}_i$ in the same way as for M-estimators.

Next, consider the partition

$$\theta_0 = \begin{pmatrix} \theta_{1,0} \\ \theta_{2,0} \end{pmatrix}, \quad \theta_{1,0} \in \mathbb{R}^{m-r}, \quad \theta_{2,0} \in \mathbb{R}^r \tag{8.54}$$

and suppose that we want to test the null hypothesis $\theta_{2,0} = 0$. This hypothesis corresponds to the linear restriction $R\theta_0 = 0$, where $R = (O, I_r)$. It follows from Theorem 8.4 that under this null hypothesis

$$\sqrt{n} R\hat{\theta} \to_d N_r(0, R\bar{H}^{-1} R^{\mathrm{T}}). \tag{8.55}$$

Partitioning $\hat{\theta}$, $\hat{H}^{-1}$ and $\bar{H}^{-1}$ conformably to (8.54) as

$$\hat{\theta} = \begin{pmatrix} \hat{\theta}_1 \\ \hat{\theta}_2 \end{pmatrix}, \quad \hat{H}^{-1} = \begin{pmatrix} \hat{H}^{(1,1)} & \hat{H}^{(1,2)} \\ \hat{H}^{(2,1)} & \hat{H}^{(2,2)} \end{pmatrix},$$

$$\bar{H}^{-1} = \begin{pmatrix} \bar{H}^{(1,1)} & \bar{H}^{(1,2)} \\ \bar{H}^{(2,1)} & \bar{H}^{(2,2)} \end{pmatrix}, \tag{8.56}$$

we find that $\hat{\theta}_2 = R\hat{\theta}$, $\hat{H}^{(2,2)} = R\hat{H}^{-1}R^{\mathrm{T}}$, and $\bar{H}^{(2,2)} = R\bar{H}^{-1}R^{\mathrm{T}}$; hence, it follows from (8.55) that $(\hat{H}^{(2,2)})^{-1/2} \sqrt{n}\hat{\theta}_2 \to_d N_r(0, I_r)$.

Theorem 8.6: *(Wald test) Under Assumptions 8.1–8.3, $n\hat{\theta}_2^{\mathrm{T}}(\hat{H}^{(2,2)})^{-1}\hat{\theta}_2 \to_d \chi_r^2$ if $\theta_{2,0} = 0$.*

8.5.2. The Likelihood Ratio Test

An alternative to the Wald test is the likelihood ratio (LR) test, which is based on the ratio

$$\hat{\lambda} = \frac{\max_{\theta \in \Theta : \theta_2 = 0} \hat{L}_n(\theta)}{\max_{\theta \in \Theta} \hat{L}_n(\theta)} = \frac{\hat{L}_n(\tilde{\theta})}{\hat{L}_n(\hat{\theta})},$$

where θ is partitioned conformably to (8.54) as

$$\theta = \begin{pmatrix} \theta_1 \\ \theta_2 \end{pmatrix}$$

and

$$\tilde{\theta} = \begin{pmatrix} \tilde{\theta}_1 \\ \tilde{\theta}_2 \end{pmatrix} = \begin{pmatrix} \tilde{\theta}_1 \\ 0 \end{pmatrix} = \underset{\theta \in \Theta : \theta_2 = 0}{\mathrm{argmax}} \; \hat{L}_n(\theta) \tag{8.57}$$

is the restricted ML estimator. Note that $\hat{\lambda}$ is always between 0 and 1. The intuition behind the LR test is that, if $\theta_{2,0} = 0$, then $\hat{\lambda}$ will approach 1 (in probability) as $n \to \infty$ because then both the unrestricted ML estimator $\hat{\theta}$ and the restricted ML estimator $\tilde{\theta}$ are consistent. On the other hand, if the null hypothesis is false, then $\hat{\lambda}$ will converge in probability to a value less than 1.

Theorem 8.7: *(LR test) Under Assumptions 8.1–8.3, $-2\ln(\hat{\lambda}) \to_d \chi_r^2$ if $\theta_{2,0} = 0$.*

Proof: As in (8.38) we have

$$\sqrt{n}(\tilde{\theta}_1 - \theta_{1,0}) = -\bar{H}_{1,1}^{-1} \left(\frac{\partial \ln(\hat{L}_n(\theta))/\sqrt{n}}{\partial \theta_1^{\mathrm{T}}} \bigg|_{\theta = \theta_0} \right) + o_p(1),$$

where $\bar{H}_{1,1}$ is the upper-left $(m - r) \times (m - r)$ block of $\bar{H}$

$$\bar{H} = \begin{pmatrix} \bar{H}_{1,1} & \bar{H}_{1,2} \\ \bar{H}_{2,1} & \bar{H}_{2,2} \end{pmatrix},$$

and consequently

$$\sqrt{n}(\tilde{\theta} - \theta_0) = -\begin{pmatrix} \bar{H}_{1,1}^{-1} & O \\ O & O \end{pmatrix} \left(\frac{\partial \ln(\hat{L}_n(\theta_0))/\sqrt{n}}{\partial \theta_0^{\mathrm{T}}} \right) + o_p(1). \quad (8.58)$$

Subtracting (8.58) from (8.34) and using condition (8.33) yield

$$\sqrt{n}(\hat{\theta} - \tilde{\theta}_0) = -\left(\bar{H}^{-1} - \begin{pmatrix} \bar{H}_{1,1}^{-1} & O \\ O & O \end{pmatrix} \right) \left(\frac{\partial \ln(\hat{L}_n(\theta_0))/\sqrt{n}}{\partial \theta_0^{\mathrm{T}}} \right)$$
$$+ o_p(1) \to_d N_m(0, \Delta), \quad (8.59)$$

where

$$\Delta = \left(\bar{H}^{-1} - \begin{pmatrix} \bar{H}_{1,1}^{-1} & O \\ O & O \end{pmatrix} \right) \bar{H} \left(\bar{H}^{-1} - \begin{pmatrix} \bar{H}_{1,1}^{-1} & O \\ O & O \end{pmatrix} \right)$$
$$= \bar{H}^{-1} - \begin{pmatrix} \bar{H}_{1,1}^{-1} & O \\ O & O \end{pmatrix}. \quad (8.60)$$

The last equality in (8.60) follows straightforwardly from the partition (8.56).

Next, it follows from the second-order Taylor expansion around the unrestricted ML estimator $\hat{\theta}$ that, for some $\hat{\eta} \in [0, 1]$,

$$\ln(\hat{\lambda}) = \ln(\hat{L}_n(\tilde{\theta})) - \ln(\hat{L}_n(\hat{\theta})) = (\tilde{\theta} - \hat{\theta})^{\mathrm{T}} \left(\left. \frac{\partial \ln(\hat{L}_n(\theta))}{\partial \theta^{\mathrm{T}}} \right|_{\theta = \hat{\theta}} \right)$$
$$+ \frac{1}{2} \sqrt{n}(\tilde{\theta} - \hat{\theta})^{\mathrm{T}} \left(\left. \frac{\partial^2 \ln(\hat{L}_n(\theta))/n}{\partial \theta \partial \theta^{\mathrm{T}}} \right|_{\theta = \hat{\theta} + \hat{\eta}(\tilde{\theta} - \hat{\theta})} \right) \sqrt{n}(\tilde{\theta} - \hat{\theta})$$
$$= -\frac{1}{2} \sqrt{n}(\tilde{\theta} - \hat{\theta})^{\mathrm{T}} \bar{H} \sqrt{n}(\tilde{\theta} - \hat{\theta}) + o_p(1), \quad (8.61)$$

where the last equality in (8.61) follows because, as in (8.36),

$$\left. \frac{\partial^2 \ln(\hat{L}(\theta))/n}{\partial \theta \partial \theta^{\mathrm{T}}} \right|_{\theta = \hat{\theta} + \hat{\eta}(\tilde{\theta} - \hat{\theta})} \to_p -\bar{H}. \quad (8.62)$$

Thus, we have

$$-2 \ln(\hat{\lambda}) = \left(\Delta^{-1/2} \sqrt{n}(\hat{\theta} - \tilde{\theta}) \right)^{\mathrm{T}} \left(\Delta^{1/2} \bar{H} \Delta^{1/2} \right) \left(\Delta^{-1/2} \sqrt{n}(\hat{\theta} - \tilde{\theta}) \right)$$
$$+ o_p(1). \quad (8.63)$$

Because, by (8.59), $\Delta^{-1/2} \sqrt{n}(\hat{\theta} - \tilde{\theta}) \to_d N_m(0, I_m)$, and by (8.60) the matrix $\Delta^{1/2} \bar{H} \Delta^{1/2}$ is idempotent with rank $(\Delta^{1/2} \bar{H} \Delta^{1/2}) =$ trace $(\Delta^{1/2} \bar{H} \Delta^{1/2}) = r$, the theorem follows from the results in Chapters 5 and 6. Q.E.D.

8.5.3. The Lagrange Multiplier Test

The restricted ML estimator $\tilde{\theta}$ can also be obtained from the first-order conditions of the Lagrange function $\mathscr{L}(\theta, \mu) = \ln(\hat{L}_n(\theta)) - \theta_2^T \mu$, where $\mu \in \mathbb{R}^r$ is a vector of Lagrange multipliers. These first-order conditions are

$$\partial \mathscr{L}(\theta, \mu)/\partial \theta_1^T|_{\theta=\tilde{\theta}, \mu=\tilde{\mu}} = \partial \ln(\hat{L}(\theta))/\partial \theta_1^T|_{\theta=\tilde{\theta}} = 0,$$

$$\partial \mathscr{L}(\theta, \mu)/\partial \theta_2^T|_{\theta=\tilde{\theta}, \mu=\tilde{\mu}} = \partial \ln(\hat{L}(\theta))/\partial \theta_2^T|_{\theta=\tilde{\theta}} - \tilde{\mu} = 0,$$

$$\partial \mathscr{L}(\theta, \mu)/\partial \mu^T|_{\theta=\tilde{\theta}, \mu=\tilde{\mu}} = \tilde{\theta}_2 = 0.$$

Hence,

$$\frac{1}{\sqrt{n}} \begin{pmatrix} 0 \\ \tilde{\mu} \end{pmatrix} = \frac{\partial \ln(\hat{L}(\theta))/\sqrt{n}}{\partial \theta^T}\bigg|_{\theta=\tilde{\theta}}.$$

Again, using the mean value theorem, we can expand this expression around the unrestricted ML estimator $\hat{\theta}$, which then yields

$$\frac{1}{\sqrt{n}} \begin{pmatrix} 0 \\ \tilde{\mu} \end{pmatrix} = -\bar{H} \sqrt{n}(\tilde{\theta} - \hat{\theta}) + o_p(1) \to_d N(0, \bar{H} \Delta \bar{H}), \tag{8.64}$$

where the last conclusion in (8.64) follows from (8.59). Hence,

$$\frac{\tilde{\mu}^T \bar{H}^{(2,2)} \tilde{\mu}}{n} = \frac{1}{n}(0^T, \tilde{\mu}^T) \bar{H}^{-1} \begin{pmatrix} 0 \\ \tilde{\mu} \end{pmatrix}$$

$$= \sqrt{n}(\tilde{\theta} - \hat{\theta})^T \bar{H} \sqrt{n}(\tilde{\theta} - \hat{\theta}) + o_p(1) \to_d \chi_r^2, \tag{8.65}$$

where the last conclusion in (8.65) follows from (8.61). Replacing $\bar{H}$ in expression (8.65) by a consistent estimator on the basis of the restricted ML estimator $\tilde{\theta}$, for instance,

$$\tilde{H} = -\frac{\partial^2 \ln(\hat{L}_n(\theta))/n}{\partial \theta \partial \theta^T}\bigg|_{\theta=\tilde{\theta}}. \tag{8.66}$$

and partitioning $\tilde{H}^{-1}$ conformably to (8.56) as

$$\tilde{H}^{-1} = \begin{pmatrix} \tilde{H}^{(1,1)} & \tilde{H}^{(1,2)} \\ \tilde{H}^{(2,1)} & \tilde{H}^{(2,2)} \end{pmatrix},$$

we have

Theorem 8.8: *(LM test) Under Assumptions 8.1–8.3,* $\tilde{\mu}^T \tilde{H}^{(2,2)} \tilde{\mu}/n \to_d \chi_r^2$ *if* $\theta_{2,0} = 0$.

8.5.4. Selecting a Test

The Wald, LR, and LM tests basically test the same null hypothesis against the same alternative, so which one should we use? The Wald test employs only the unrestricted ML estimator $\hat{\theta}$, and thus this test is the most convenient if we have to conduct unrestricted ML estimation anyway. The LM test is entirely based on the restricted ML estimator $\tilde{\theta}$, and there are situations in which we start with restricted ML estimation or where restricted ML estimation is much easier to do than unrestricted ML estimation, or even where unrestricted ML estimation is not feasible because, without the restriction imposed, the model is incompletely specified. Then the LM test is the most convenient test. Both the Wald and the LM tests require the estimation of the matrix $\bar{H}$. That may be a problem for complicated models because of the partial derivatives involved. In that case I recommend using the LR test.

Although I have derived the Wald, LR, and LM tests for the special case of a null hypothesis of the type $\theta_{2,0} = 0$, the results involved can be modified to general linear hypotheses of the form $R\theta_0 = q$, where R is a $r \times m$ matrix of rank r, by reparametrizing the likelihood function as follows. Specify a $(m - r) \times m$ matrix R_* such that the matrix

$$Q = \begin{pmatrix} R_* \\ R \end{pmatrix}$$

is nonsingular. Then define new parameters by

$$\beta = \begin{pmatrix} \beta_1 \\ \beta_2 \end{pmatrix} = \begin{pmatrix} R_* \theta \\ R\theta \end{pmatrix} - \begin{pmatrix} 0 \\ q \end{pmatrix} = Q\theta - \begin{pmatrix} 0 \\ q \end{pmatrix}.$$

If we substitute

$$\theta = Q^{-1}\beta + Q^{-1}\begin{pmatrix} 0 \\ q \end{pmatrix}$$

in the likelihood function, the null hypothesis involved is equivalent to $\beta_2 = 0$.

8.6. Exercises

1. Derive $\hat{\theta} = \text{argmax}_\theta \hat{L}_n(\theta)$ for the case (8.11) and show that, if $Z_1, \ldots, Z_n$ is a random sample, then the ML estimator involved is consistent.

2. Derive $\hat{\theta} = \text{argmax}_\theta \hat{L}_n(\theta)$ for the case (8.13).

3. Show that the log-likelihood function of the Logit model is unimodal, that is, the matrix $\partial^2 \ln[\hat{L}_n(\theta)]/(\partial\theta\partial\theta^\top)$ is negative-definite for all θ.

4. Prove (8.20).

5. Extend the proof of Theorem 8.2 to the multivariate parameter case.

6. Let $(Y_1, X_1), \ldots, (Y_n, X_n)$ be a random sample from a bivariate continuous distribution with conditional density

    $$f(y|x, \theta_0) = (x/\theta_0)\exp(-y \cdot x/\theta_0) \quad \text{if } x > 0 \quad \text{and} \quad y > 0;$$
    $$f(y|x, \theta_0) = 0 \text{ elsewhere},$$

    where $\theta_0 > 0$ is an unknown parameter. The marginal density $h(x)$ of X_j is unknown, but we do know that h does not depend on θ_0 and $h(x) = 0$ for $x \leq 0$.
    (a) Specify the conditional likelihood function $\hat{L}_n^c(\theta)$.
    (b) Derive the maximum likelihood estimator $\hat{\theta}$ of θ_0.
    (c) Show that $\hat{\theta}$ is unbiased.
    (d) Show that the variance of $\hat{\theta}$ is equal to θ_0^2/n.
    (e) Verify that this variance is equal to the Cramer–Rao lower bound.
    (f) Derive the test statistic of the LR test of the null hypothesis $\theta_0 = 1$ in the form for which it has an asymptotic χ_1^2 null distribution.
    (g) Derive the test statistic of the Wald test of the null hypothesis $\theta_0 = 1$.
    (h) Derive the test statistic of the LM test of the null hypothesis $\theta_0 = 1$.
    (i) Show that under the null hypothesis $\theta_0 = 1$ the LR test in part (f) has a limiting χ_1^2 distribution.

7. Let $Z_1, \ldots, Z_n$ be a random sample from the (nonsingular) $N_k[\mu, \Sigma]$ distribution. Determine the maximum likelihood estimators of μ and Σ.

8. In the case in which the dependent variable Y is a duration (e.g., an unemployment duration spell), the conditional distribution of Y given a vector X of explanatory variables is often modeled by the proportional hazard model

    $$P[Y \leq y|X = x] = 1 - \exp\left(-\varphi(x)\int_0^y \lambda(t)dt\right), \quad y > 0, \tag{8.68}$$

    where $\lambda(t)$ is a positive function on $(0, \infty)$ such that $\int_0^\infty \lambda(t)dt = \infty$ and φ is a positive function.

    The reason for calling this model a proportional hazard model is the following. Let $f(y|x)$ be the conditional density of Y given $X = x$, and let $G(y|x) = \exp\left(-\varphi(x)\int_0^y \lambda(t)dt\right), y > 0$. The latter function is called the conditional survival function. Then $f(y|x)/G(y|x) = \varphi(x)\lambda(y)$ is called the hazard function because, for a small $\delta > 0$, $\delta f(y|x)/G(y|x)$ is approximately the conditional probability (hazard) that $Y \in (y, y + \delta]$ given that $Y > y$ and $X = x$.

    Convenient specifications of $\lambda(t)$ and $\varphi(x)$ are

    $$\lambda(t) = \gamma t^{\gamma-1}, \gamma > 0 \text{ (Weibull specification)}$$
    $$\varphi(x) = \exp(\alpha + \beta^{\mathsf{T}} x). \tag{8.69}$$

    Now consider a random sample of size n of unemployed workers. Each unemployed worker j is interviewed twice. The first time, worker j tells the interviewer how long he or she has been unemployed and reveals his or her vector X_j of characteristics. Call this time $Y_{1,j}$. A fixed period of length T later the interviewer asks worker j whether he or she is still (uninterruptedly) unemployed and, if not, how long it took during this period to find employment for the first time. Call this duration $Y_{2,j}$. In the latter case the observed unemployment duration is $Y_j = Y_{1,j} + Y_{2,j}$, but if the worker is still unemployed we only know that $Y_j > Y_{1,j} + T$. The latter is called censoring. On the assumption that the X_j's do not change over time, set up the conditional likelihood function for this case, using the specifications (8.68) and (8.69).

Appendix I – Review of Linear Algebra

I.1. Vectors in a Euclidean Space

A vector is a set of coordinates that locates a point in a Euclidean space. For example, in the two-dimensional Euclidean space $\mathbb{R}^2$ the vector

$$a = \begin{pmatrix} a_1 \\ a_2 \end{pmatrix} = \begin{pmatrix} 6 \\ 4 \end{pmatrix} \tag{I.1}$$

is the point whose location in a plane is determined by moving $a_1 = 6$ units away from the origin along the horizontal axis (axis 1) and then moving $a_2 = 4$ units away parallel to the vertical axis (axis 2), as displayed in Figure I.1. The distances a_1 and a_2 are called the *components* of the vector a involved.

An alternative interpretation of the vector a is a force pulling from the origin (the intersection of the two axes). This force is characterized by its direction (the angle of the line in Figure I.1) and its strength (the length of the line piece between point a and the origin). As to the latter, it follows from the Pythagorean theorem that this length is the square root of the sum of the squared distances of point a from the vertical and horizontal axes, $\sqrt{a_1^2 + a_2^2} = \sqrt{6^2 + 4^2} = 3\sqrt{6}$, and is denoted by $\|a\|$. More generally, the length of a vector

$$x = \begin{pmatrix} x_1 \\ x_2 \\ \vdots \\ x_n \end{pmatrix} \tag{I.2}$$

in $\mathbb{R}^n$ is defined by

$$\|x\| \stackrel{\text{def.}}{=} \sqrt{\sum_{j=1}^{n} x_j^2}. \tag{I.3}$$

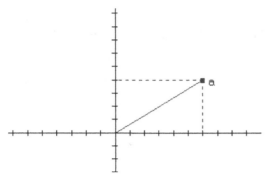

Figure I.1. A vector in $\mathbb{R}^2$.

Two basic operations apply to vectors in $\mathbb{R}^n$. The first basic operation is scalar multiplication:

$$c \cdot x \overset{\text{def.}}{=} \begin{pmatrix} c \cdot x_1 \\ c \cdot x_2 \\ \vdots \\ c \cdot x_n \end{pmatrix}, \tag{I.4}$$

where $c \in \mathbb{R}$ is a scalar. Thus, vectors in $\mathbb{R}^n$ are multiplied by a scalar by multiplying each of the components by this scalar. The effect of scalar multiplication is that the point x is moved a factor c along the line through the origin and the original point x. For example, if we multiply the vector a in Figure I.1 by $c = 1.5$, the effect is the following:

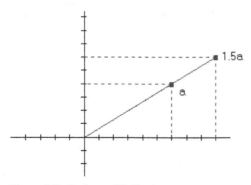

Figure I.2. Scalar multiplication.

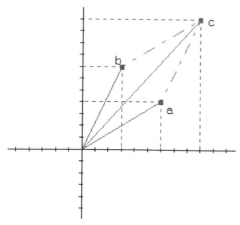

Figure I.3. $c = a + b$.

The second operation is addition. Let x be the vector (I.2), and let

$$y = \begin{pmatrix} y_1 \\ y_2 \\ \vdots \\ y_n \end{pmatrix}. \tag{I.5}$$

Then

$$x + y \stackrel{\text{def.}}{=} \begin{pmatrix} x_1 + y_1 \\ x_2 + y_2 \\ \vdots \\ x_n + y_n \end{pmatrix}. \tag{I.6}$$

Thus, vectors are added by adding up the corresponding components. Of course, this operation is only defined for *conformable* vectors, that is, vectors with the same number of components.

As an example of the addition operation, let a be the vector (I.1), and let

$$b = \begin{pmatrix} b_1 \\ b_2 \end{pmatrix} = \begin{pmatrix} 3 \\ 7 \end{pmatrix}. \tag{I.7}$$

Then

$$a + b = \begin{pmatrix} 6 \\ 4 \end{pmatrix} + \begin{pmatrix} 3 \\ 7 \end{pmatrix} = \begin{pmatrix} 9 \\ 11 \end{pmatrix} = c, \tag{I.8}$$

for instance. This result is displayed in Figure I.3. We see from Figure I.3 that the origin together with the points a, b, and $c = a + b$ form a parallelogram (which is easy to prove). In terms of forces, the combined forces represented by the vectors a and b result in the force represented by the vector $c = a + b$.

The distance between the vectors a and b in Figure I.3 is $\|a - b\|$. To see this, observe that the length of the horizontal line piece between the vertical line through b and point a is $a_1 - b_1$, and similarly the vertical line piece between b and the horizontal line through a has length $b_2 - a_2$. These two line pieces, together with the line piece connecting the points a and b, form a triangle for which the Pythagorean theorem applies: The squared distance between a and b is equal to $(a_1 - b_1)^2 + (a_2 - b_2)^2 = \|a - b\|^2$. More generally,

The distance between the vector x in (I.2) *and the vector y in* (I.5) *is*

$$\|x - y\| = \sqrt{\sum_{j=1}^{n}(x_j - y_j)^2}. \tag{I.9}$$

Moreover, it follows from (I.9) and the law of cosines[1] that

The angle φ between the vector x in (I.2) *and the vector y in* (I.5) *satisfies*

$$\cos(\varphi) = \frac{\|x\|^2 + \|y\|^2 - \|x - y\|^2}{2\|x\| \cdot \|y\|} = \frac{\sum_{j=1}^{n} x_j y_j}{\|x\| \cdot \|y\|}. \tag{I.10}$$

I.2. Vector Spaces

The two basic operations, addition and scalar multiplication, make a Euclidean space $\mathbb{R}^n$ a special case of a vector space:

Definition I.1: *Let V be a set endowed with two operations: the operation "addition," denoted by "$+$," which maps each pair (x, y) in $V \times V$ into V, and the operation "scalar multiplication" denoted by a dot $(\cdot)$ that maps each pair (c, x) in $\mathbb{R} \times V$ into V. The set V is called a vector space if the addition and multiplication operations involved satisfy the following rules for all x, y, and z in V and all scalars c, c_1, and c_2 in $\mathbb{R}$:*

(a) $x + y = y + x$;
(b) $x + (y + z) = (x + y) + z$;
(c) *There is a unique zero vector 0 in V such that $x + 0 = x$;*
(d) *For each x there exists a unique vector $-x$ in V such that $x + (-x) = 0$;*
(e) $1 \cdot x = x$;
(f) $(c_1 c_2) \cdot x = c_1 \cdot (c_2 \cdot x)$;
(g) $c \cdot (x + y) = c \cdot x + c \cdot y$;
(h) $(c_1 + c_2) \cdot x = c_1 \cdot x + c_2 \cdot x$.

---

[1] *Law of cosines:* Consider a triangle ABC, let φ be the angle between the legs $C \to A$ and $C \to B$, and denote the lengths of the legs opposite to the points A, B, and C by α, β, and γ, respectively. Then $\gamma^2 = \alpha^2 + \beta^2 - 2\alpha\beta \cos(\varphi)$.

It is trivial to verify that, with addition "$+$" defined by (I.6) and scalar multiplication $c \cdot x$ defined by (I.4), the Euclidean space $\mathbb{R}^n$ is a vector space. However, the notion of a vector space is much more general. For example, let V be the space of all continuous functions on $\mathbb{R}$ with pointwise addition and scalar multiplication defined the same way as for real numbers. Then it is easy to verify that this space is a vector space.

Another (but weird) example of a vector space is the space V of positive real numbers endowed with the "addition" operation $x + y = x \cdot y$ and the "scalar multiplication" $c \cdot x = x^c$. In this case the null vector 0 is the number 1, and $-x = 1/x$.

Definition I.2: *A subspace V_0 of a vector space V is a nonempty subset of V that satisfies the following two requirements:*

(a) For any pair x, y in V_0, $x + y$ is in V_0;
(b) For any x in V_0 and any scalar c, $c \cdot x$ is in V_0.

It is not hard to verify that a subspace of a vector space is a vector space itself because the rules (a) through (h) in Definition I.1 are inherited from the "host" vector space V. In particular, any subspace contains the null vector 0, as follows from part (b) of Definition I.2 with $c = 0$. For example, the line through the origin and point a in Figure I.1 extended indefinitely in both directions is a subspace of $\mathbb{R}^2$. This subspace is said to be *spanned* by the vector a. More generally,

Definition I.3: *Let $x_1, x_2, \ldots, x_n$ be vectors in a vector space V. The space V_0 spanned by $x_1, x_2, \ldots, x_n$ is the space of all linear combinations of $x_1, x_2, \ldots, x_n$, that is, each y in V_0 can be written as $y = \sum_{j=1}^{n} c_j x_j$ for some coefficients c_j in $\mathbb{R}$.*

Clearly, this space V_0 is a subspace of V.

For example, the two vectors a and b in Figure I.3 span the whole Euclidean space $\mathbb{R}^2$ because any vector x in $\mathbb{R}^2$ can be written as

$$ x = \begin{pmatrix} x_1 \\ x_2 \end{pmatrix} = c_1 \begin{pmatrix} 6 \\ 4 \end{pmatrix} + c_2 \begin{pmatrix} 3 \\ 7 \end{pmatrix} = \begin{pmatrix} 6c_1 + 3c_2 \\ 4c_1 + 7c_2 \end{pmatrix}, $$

where

$$ c_1 = \frac{7}{30}x_1 - \frac{1}{10}x_2, \qquad c_2 = -\frac{2}{15}x_1 + \frac{1}{5}x_2. $$

The same applies to the vectors a, b, and c in Figure I.3: They also span the whole Euclidean space $\mathbb{R}^2$. However, in this case any pair of a, b, and c does the same, and thus one of these three vectors is redundant because each of the vectors a, b, and c can already be written as a linear combination of the other two. Such vectors are called *linear dependent*:

Definition I.4: *A set of vectors $x_1, x_2, \ldots, x_n$ in a vector space V is linear dependent if one or more of these vectors can be written as a linear combination of the other vectors, and the set is called linear independent if none of them can be written as a linear combination of the other vectors. In particular, $x_1, x_2, \ldots, x_n$ are linear independent if and only if $\sum_{j=1}^{n} c_j x_j = 0$ implies that $c_1 = c_2 = \cdots = c_n = 0$.*

For example, the vectors a and b in Figure I.3 are linear independent because, if not, then would exist a scalar c such that $b = c \cdot a$; hence, $6 = 3c$ and $4 = 7c$, which is impossible. A set of such linear-independent vectors is called a *basis* for the vector space they span:

Definition I.5: *A basis for a vector space is a set of vectors having the following two properties:*

(a) They are linear independent;
(b) They span the vector space involved.

We have seen that each of the subsets $\{a, b\}$, $\{a, c\}$, and $\{b, c\}$ of the set $\{a, b, c\}$ of vectors in Figure I.3 is linear independent and spans the vector space $\mathbb{R}^2$. Thus, there are in general many bases for the same vector space, but what they have in common is their number. This number is called the dimension of V.

Definition I.6: *The number of vectors that form a basis of a vector space is called the dimension of this vector space.*

To show that this definition is unambiguous, let $\{x_1, x_2, \ldots, x_n\}$ and $\{y_1, y_2, \ldots, y_m\}$ be two different bases for the same vector space, and let $m = n + 1$. Each of the y_i's can be written as a linear combination of $x_1, x_2, \ldots, x_n : y_i = \sum_{j=1}^{n} c_{i,j} x_j$. If $\{y_1, y_2, \ldots, y_{n+1}\}$ is linear independent, then $\sum_{i=1}^{n+1} z_i y_i = \sum_{j=1}^{n} \sum_{i=1}^{n+1} z_i c_{i,j} x_j = 0$ if and only if $z_1 = \cdots = z_{n+1} = 0$. But because $\{x_1, x_2, \ldots, x_n\}$ is linear independent we must also have that $\sum_{i=1}^{n+1} z_i c_{i,j} = 0$ for $j = 1, \ldots, n$. The latter is a system of n linear equations in $n + 1$ unknown variables z_i and therefore has a nontrivial solution in the sense that there exists a solution $z_1, \ldots, z_{n+1}$ such that at least one of the z's is nonzero. Consequently, $\{y_1, y_2, \ldots, y_{n+1}\}$ cannot be linear independent.

Note that in principle the dimension of a vector space can be infinite. For example, consider the space $\mathbb{R}^{\infty}$ of all countable infinite sequences

$x = (x_1, x_2, x_3, \ldots)$ of real numbers endowed with the addition operation

$$x + y = (x_1, x_2, x_3, \ldots) + (y_1, y_2, y_3, \ldots)$$
$$= (x_1 + y_1, x_2 + y_2, x_3 + y_3, \ldots)$$

and the scalar multiplication operation

$$c \cdot x = (c \cdot x_1, c \cdot x_2, c \cdot x_3, \ldots).$$

Let y_i be a countable infinite sequence of zeros except for the ith element in this sequence, which is equal to 1. Thus, $y_1 = (1, 0, 0, \ldots)$, $y_2 = (0, 1, 0, \ldots)$, and so on. Then $\{y_1, y_2, y_3, \ldots\}$ is a basis for $\mathbb{R}^\infty$ with dimension ∞. Also in this case there are many different bases; for example, another basis for $\mathbb{R}^\infty$ is $y_1 = (1, 0, 0, 0, \ldots)$, $y_2 = (1, 1, 0, 0, \ldots)$, $y_3 = (1, 1, 1, 0, \ldots)$, and so on.

I.3. Matrices

In Figure I.3 the location of point c can be determined by moving nine units away from the origin along the horizontal axis 1 and then moving eleven units away from axis 1 parallel to the vertical axis 2. However, given the vectors a and b, an alternative way of determining the location of point c is to move $\|a\|$ units away from the origin along the line through the origin and point a (the subspace spanned by a) and then move $\|b\|$ units away parallel to the line through the origin and point b (the subspace spanned by b). Moreover, if we take $\|a\|$ as the new distance unit along the subspace spanned by a, and $\|b\|$ as the new distance unit along the subspace spanned by b, then point c can be located by moving one (new) unit away from the origin along the new axis 1 formed by the subspace spanned by a and then moving one (new) unit away from this new axis 1 parallel to the subspace spanned by b (which is now the new axis 2). We may interpret this as moving the point $\binom{1}{1}$ to a new location: point c. This is precisely what a matrix does: moving points to a new location by changing the coordinate system. In particular, the matrix

$$A = (a, b) = \begin{pmatrix} 6 & 3 \\ 4 & 7 \end{pmatrix} \tag{I.11}$$

moves any point

$$x = \begin{pmatrix} x_1 \\ x_2 \end{pmatrix} \tag{I.12}$$

to a new location by changing the original perpendicular coordinate system to a new coordinate system in which the new axis 1 is the subspace spanned by the first column, a, of the matrix A with new unit distance the length of a, and the new axis 2 is the subspace spanned by the second column, b, of A with new unit distance the length of b. Thus, this matrix A moves point x to point

$$
\begin{aligned}
y = Ax &= x_1 \cdot a + x_2 \cdot b \\
&= x_1 \cdot \begin{pmatrix} 6 \\ 4 \end{pmatrix} + x_2 \cdot \begin{pmatrix} 3 \\ 7 \end{pmatrix} = \begin{pmatrix} 6x_1 + 3x_2 \\ 4x_1 + 7x_2 \end{pmatrix}.
\end{aligned}
\tag{I.13}
$$

In general, an $m \times n$ matrix

$$
A = \begin{pmatrix} a_{1,1} & \cdots & a_{1,n} \\ \vdots & \ddots & \vdots \\ a_{m,1} & \cdots & a_{m,n} \end{pmatrix}
\tag{I.14}
$$

moves the point in $\mathbb{R}^n$ corresponding to the vector x in (I.2) to a point in the subspace of $\mathbb{R}^m$ spanned by the columns of A, namely, to point

$$
y = Ax = \sum_{j=1}^{n} x_j \begin{pmatrix} a_{1,j} \\ \vdots \\ a_{m,j} \end{pmatrix} = \begin{pmatrix} \sum_{j=1}^{n} a_{1,j} x_j \\ \vdots \\ \sum_{j=1}^{n} a_{m,j} x_j \end{pmatrix} = \begin{pmatrix} y_1 \\ \vdots \\ y_m \end{pmatrix}.
\tag{I.15}
$$

Next, consider the $k \times m$ matrix

$$
B = \begin{pmatrix} b_{1,1} & \cdots & b_{1,m} \\ \vdots & \ddots & \vdots \\ b_{k,1} & \cdots & b_{k,m} \end{pmatrix},
\tag{I.16}
$$

and let y be given by (I.15). Then

$$
\begin{aligned}
By = B(Ax) &= \begin{pmatrix} b_{1,1} & \cdots & b_{1,m} \\ \vdots & \ddots & \vdots \\ b_{k,1} & \cdots & b_{k,m} \end{pmatrix} \begin{pmatrix} \sum_{j=1}^{n} a_{1,j} x_j \\ \vdots \\ \sum_{j=1}^{n} a_{m,j} x_j \end{pmatrix} \\
&= \begin{pmatrix} \sum_{j=1}^{n} \left(\sum_{s=1}^{m} b_{1,s} a_{s,j} \right) x_j \\ \vdots \\ \sum_{j=1}^{n} \left(\sum_{s=1}^{m} b_{k,s} a_{s,j} \right) x_j \end{pmatrix} = Cx,
\end{aligned}
\tag{I.17}
$$

where

$$
C = \begin{pmatrix} c_{1,1} & \cdots & c_{1,n} \\ \vdots & \ddots & \vdots \\ c_{k,1} & \cdots & c_{k,n} \end{pmatrix} \quad \text{with} \quad c_{i,j} = \sum_{s=1}^{m} b_{i,s} a_{s,j}.
$$

This matrix C is called the product of the matrices B and A and is denoted by BA. Thus, with A given by (I.14) and B given by (I.16),

$$
BA = \begin{pmatrix} b_{1,1} & \cdots & b_{1,m} \\ \vdots & \ddots & \vdots \\ b_{k,1} & \cdots & b_{k,m} \end{pmatrix} \begin{pmatrix} a_{1,1} & \cdots & a_{1,n} \\ \vdots & \ddots & \vdots \\ a_{m,1} & \cdots & a_{m,n} \end{pmatrix}
$$
$$
= \begin{pmatrix} \sum_{s=1}^{m} b_{1,s} a_{s,1} & \cdots & \sum_{s=1}^{m} b_{1,s} a_{s,n} \\ \vdots & \ddots & \vdots \\ \sum_{s=1}^{m} b_{k,s} a_{s,1} & \cdots & \sum_{s=1}^{m} b_{k,s} a_{s,n} \end{pmatrix},
$$

which is a $k \times n$ matrix. Note that the matrix BA only exists if the number of columns of B is equal to the number of rows of A. Such matrices are described as being *conformable*. Moreover, note that if A and B are also conformable, so that AB is defined,[2] then the commutative law does not hold, that is, in general $AB \neq BA$. However, the associative law $(AB)C = A(BC)$ does hold, as is easy to verify.

Let A be the $m \times n$ matrix (I.14), and now let B be another $m \times n$ matrix:

$$
B = \begin{pmatrix} b_{1,1} & \cdots & b_{1,n} \\ \vdots & \ddots & \vdots \\ b_{m,1} & \cdots & b_{m,n} \end{pmatrix}.
$$

As argued before, A maps a point $x \in \mathbb{R}^n$ to a point $y = Ax \in \mathbb{R}^m$, and B maps x to a point $z = Bx \in \mathbb{R}^m$. It is easy to verify that $y + z = Ax + Bx = (A + B)x = Cx$, for example, where $C = A + B$ is the $m \times n$ matrix formed by adding up the corresponding elements of A and B:

$$
A + B = \begin{pmatrix} a_{1,1} & \cdots & a_{1,n} \\ \vdots & \ddots & \vdots \\ a_{m,1} & \cdots & a_{m,n} \end{pmatrix} + \begin{pmatrix} b_{1,1} & \cdots & b_{1,n} \\ \vdots & \ddots & \vdots \\ b_{m,1} & \cdots & b_{m,n} \end{pmatrix}
$$
$$
= \begin{pmatrix} a_{1,1} + b_{1,1} & \cdots & a_{1,n} + b_{1,n} \\ \vdots & \ddots & \vdots \\ a_{m,1} + b_{m,1} & \cdots & a_{m,n} + b_{m,n} \end{pmatrix}.
$$

Thus, conformable matrices are added up by adding up the corresponding elements.

---

[2]   In writing a matrix product it is from now on implicitly assumed that the matrices involved are conformable.

Moreover, for any scalar c we have $A(c \cdot x) = c \cdot (Ax) = (c \cdot A)x$, where $c \cdot A$ is the matrix formed by multiplying each element of A by the scalar c:

$$c \cdot A = c \cdot \begin{pmatrix} a_{1,1} & \cdots & a_{1,n} \\ \vdots & \ddots & \vdots \\ a_{m,1} & \cdots & a_{m,n} \end{pmatrix} = \begin{pmatrix} c \cdot a_{1,1} & \cdots & c \cdot a_{1,n} \\ \vdots & \ddots & \vdots \\ c \cdot a_{m,1} & \cdots & c \cdot a_{m,n} \end{pmatrix}.$$

Now with addition and scalar multiplication defined in this way, it is easy to verify that all the conditions in Definition I.1 hold for matrices as well (i.e., the set of all $m \times n$ matrices is a vector space). In particular, the "zero" element involved is the $m \times n$ matrix with all elements equal to zero:

$$O_{m,n} = \begin{pmatrix} 0 & \cdots & 0 \\ \vdots & \ddots & \vdots \\ 0 & \cdots & 0 \end{pmatrix}.$$

Zero matrices are usually denoted by O only without subscripts indicating the size.

I.4. The Inverse and Transpose of a Matrix

I will now address the question of whether, for a given $m \times n$ matrix A, there exists an $n \times m$ matrix B such that, with $y = Ax$, $By = x$. If so, the action of A is undone by B, that is, B moves y back to the original position x.

If $m < n$, there is no way to undo the mapping $y = Ax$. In other words, there does not exist an $n \times m$ matrix B such that $By = x$. To see this, consider the 1×2 matrix $A = (2, 1)$. Then, with x as in (I.12), $Ax = 2x_1 + x_2 = y$, but if we know y and A we only know that x is located on the line $x_2 = y - 2x_1$; however, there is no way to determine where on this line.

If $m = n$ in (I.14), thus making the matrix A involved a *square* matrix, we can undo the mapping A if the columns[3] of the matrix A are linear independent. Take for example the matrix A in (I.11) and the vector y in (I.13), and let

$$B = \begin{pmatrix} \frac{7}{30} & -\frac{1}{10} \\ -\frac{2}{15} & \frac{1}{5} \end{pmatrix}.$$

Then

$$By = \begin{pmatrix} \frac{7}{30} & -\frac{1}{10} \\ -\frac{2}{15} & \frac{1}{5} \end{pmatrix} \begin{pmatrix} 6x_1 + 3x_2 \\ 4x_1 + 7x_2 \end{pmatrix} = \begin{pmatrix} x_1 \\ x_2 \end{pmatrix} = x,$$

---

[3] Here and in the sequel the columns of a matrix are interpreted as vectors.

and thus this matrix B moves the point $y = Ax$ back to x. Such a matrix is called the *inverse* of A and is denoted by A^{-1}. Note that, for an invertible $n \times n$ matrix A, $A^{-1}A = I_n$, where I_n is the $n \times n$ *unit matrix*:

$$I_n = \begin{pmatrix} 1 & 0 & 0 & \ldots & 0 \\ 0 & 1 & 0 & \ldots & 0 \\ 0 & 0 & 1 & \ldots & 0 \\ \vdots & \vdots & \vdots & \ddots & \vdots \\ 0 & 0 & 0 & \ldots & 1 \end{pmatrix}. \tag{I.18}$$

Note that a unit matrix is a special case of a *diagonal matrix*, that is, a square matrix with all off-diagonal elements equal to zero.

We have seen that the inverse of A is a matrix A^{-1} such that $A^{-1}A = I$.[4] But what about AA^{-1}? Does the order of multiplication matter? The answer is no:

Theorem I.1: *If A is invertible, then $AA^{-1} = I$, that is, A is the inverse of A^{-1},*

because it is trivial that

Theorem I.2: *If A and B are invertible matrices, then $(AB)^{-1} = B^{-1}A^{-1}$.*

Now let us give a formal proof of our conjecture that

Theorem I.3: *A square matrix is invertible if and only if its columns are linear independent.*

Proof: Let A be $n \times n$ the matrix involved. I will show first that

(a) *The columns $a_1, \ldots, a_n$ of A are linear independent if and only if for every $b \in \mathbb{R}^n$ the system of n linear equations $Ax = b$ has a unique solution.*

To see this, suppose that there exists another solution $y : Ay = b$. Then $A (x - y) = 0$ and $x - y \neq 0$, which imply that the columns $a_1, \ldots, a_n$ of A are linear dependent. Similarly, if for every $b \in \mathbb{R}^n$ the system $Ax = b$ has a unique solution, then the columns $a_1, \ldots, a_n$ of A must be linear independent because, if not, then there exists a vector $c \neq 0$ in $\mathbb{R}^n$ such that $Ac = 0$; hence, if x is a solution of $Ax = b$, then so is $x + c$.

Next, I will show that

(b) *A is invertible if and only if for every $b \in \mathbb{R}^n$ the system of n linear equations $Ax = b$ has a unique solution.*

---

[4] Here and in the sequel I denotes a generic unit matrix.

First, if A is invertible then the solution of $Ax = b$ is $x = A^{-1}b$, which for each $b \in \mathbb{R}^n$ is unique. Second, let $b = e_i$ be the ith column of the unit matrix I_n, and let x_i be the unique solution of $Ax_i = e_i$. Then the matrix X with columns $x_1, \ldots, x_n$ satisfies

$$AX = A(x_1, \ldots, x_n) = (Ax_1, \ldots, Ax_n) = (e_1, \ldots, e_n) = I_n;$$

hence, A is the inverse of $X : A = X^{-1}$. It follows now from Theorem I.1 that X is the inverse of $A : X = A^{-1}$.   Q.E.D.

If the columns of a square matrix A are linear dependent, then Ax maps point x into a lower-dimensional space, namely, the subspace spanned by the columns of A. Such a mapping is called a *singular* mapping, and the corresponding matrix A is therefore called *singular*. Consequently, a square matrix with linear independent columns is described as *nonsingular*. It follows from Theorem I.3 that nonsingularity is equivalent to invertibility and singularity is equivalent to the absence of invertibility.

If $m > n$ in (I.14), and thus the matrix A involved has more rows than columns, we can also undo the action of A if the columns of the matrix A are linear independent as follows. First, consider the *transpose*[5] A^{T} of the matrix A in (I.14):

$$A^{\mathrm{T}} = \begin{pmatrix} a_{1,1} & \cdots & a_{m,1} \\ \vdots & \ddots & \vdots \\ a_{1,n} & \cdots & a_{m,n} \end{pmatrix},$$

that is, A^{T} is formed by filling its columns with the elements of the corresponding rows of A. Note that

Theorem I.4: $(AB)^{\mathrm{T}} = B^{\mathrm{T}}A^{\mathrm{T}}$. *Moreover, if A and B are square and invertible, then* $(A^{\mathrm{T}})^{-1} = (A^{-1})^{\mathrm{T}}$, $((AB)^{-1})^{\mathrm{T}} = (B^{-1}A^{-1})^{\mathrm{T}} = (A^{-1})^{\mathrm{T}}(B^{-1})^{\mathrm{T}} = (A^{\mathrm{T}})^{-1}(B^{\mathrm{T}})^{-1}$, *and similarly,* $((AB)^{\mathrm{T}})^{-1} = (B^{\mathrm{T}}A^{\mathrm{T}})^{-1} = (A^{\mathrm{T}})^{-1}(B^{\mathrm{T}})^{-1} = (A^{-1})^{\mathrm{T}}(B^{-1})^{\mathrm{T}}$.

Proof: Exercise.

Because a vector can be interpreted as a matrix with only one column, the transpose operation also applies to vectors. In particular, the transpose of the vector x in (I.2) is

$$x^{\mathrm{T}} = (x_1, x_2, \ldots, x_n),$$

which may be interpreted as a $1 \times n$ matrix.

---

[5]   The transpose of a matrix A is also denoted in the literature by A'.

Now if $y = Ax$, then $A^T y = A^T A x$, where $A^T A$ is an $n \times n$ matrix. If $A^T A$ is invertible, then $(A^T A)^{-1} A^T y = x$ and thus the action of the matrix A is undone by the $n \times m$ matrix $(A^T A)^{-1} A^T$. Consequently, it remains to be shown that

Theorem I.5: $A^T A$ *is invertible if and only if the columns of the matrix A are linear independent.*

Proof: Let $a_1, \ldots, a_n$ be the columns of A. Then $A^T a_1, \ldots, A^T a_n$ are the columns of $A^T A$. Thus, the columns of $A^T A$ are linear combinations of the columns of A. Suppose that the columns of $A^T A$ are linear dependent. Then there exist coefficients c_j not all equal to zero such that $c_1 A^T a_1 + \cdots + c_n A^T a_n = 0$. This equation can be rewritten as $A^T(c_1 a_1 + \cdots + c_n a_n) = 0$. Because $a_1, \ldots, a_n$ are linear independent, we have $c_1 a_1 + \cdots + c_n a_n \neq 0$; hence, the columns of A^T are linear dependent. However, this is impossible because of the next theorem. Therefore, if the columns of A are linear independent, then so are the columns of $A^T A$. Thus, the theorem under review follows from Theorem I.3 and Theorem I.6 below.

Theorem I.6: *The dimension of the subspace spanned by the columns of a matrix A is equal to the dimension of the subspace spanned by the columns of its transpose A^T.*

The proof of Theorem I.6 has to be postponed because we need for it the results in the next sections. In particular, Theorem I.6 follows from Theorems I.11, I.12, and I.13.

Definition I.7: *The dimension of the subspace spanned by the columns of a matrix A is called the rank of A.*

Thus, a square matrix is invertible if and only if its rank equals its size, and if a matrix is invertible then so is its transpose.

I.5. Elementary Matrices and Permutation Matrices

Let A be the $m \times n$ matrix in (I.14). An elementary $m \times m$ matrix E is a matrix such that the effect of EA is the addition of a multiple of one row of A to another row of A. For example, let $E_{i,j}(c)$ be an elementary matrix such that the effect of $E_{i,j}(c)A$ is that c times row j is added to row $i < j$:

$$E_{i,j}(c)A = \begin{pmatrix} a_{1,1} & \cdots & a_{1,n} \\ \vdots & \ddots & \vdots \\ a_{i-1,1} & \cdots & a_{i-1,n} \\ a_{i,1} + ca_{j,1} & \cdots & a_{i,n} + ca_{j,n} \\ a_{i+1,1} & \cdots & a_{i+1,n} \\ \vdots & \ddots & \vdots \\ a_{j,1} & \cdots & a_{j,n} \\ \vdots & \ddots & \vdots \\ a_{m,1} & \cdots & a_{m,n} \end{pmatrix}. \tag{I.19}$$

Then $E_{i,j}(c)^6$ is equal to the unit matrix I_m (compare (I.18)) except that the zero in the (i, j)'s position is replaced by a nonzero constant c. In particular, if $i = 1$ and $j = 2$ in (I.19), and thus $E_{1,2}(c)A$ adds c times row 2 of A to row 1 of A, then

$$E_{1,2}(c) = \begin{pmatrix} 1 & c & 0 & \cdots & 0 \\ 0 & 1 & 0 & \cdots & 0 \\ 0 & 0 & 1 & \cdots & 0 \\ \vdots & \vdots & \vdots & \ddots & \vdots \\ 0 & 0 & 0 & \cdots & 1 \end{pmatrix}.$$

This matrix is a special case of an *upper-triangular* matrix, that is, a square matrix with all the elements below the diagonal equal to zero. Moreover, $E_{2,1}(c)A$ adds c times row 1 of A to row 2 of A:

$$E_{2,1}(c) = \begin{pmatrix} 1 & 0 & 0 & \cdots & 0 \\ c & 1 & 0 & \cdots & 0 \\ 0 & 0 & 1 & \cdots & 0 \\ \vdots & \vdots & \vdots & \ddots & \vdots \\ 0 & 0 & 0 & \cdots & 1 \end{pmatrix}, \tag{I.20}$$

which is a special case of a *lower-triangular* matrix, that is, a square matrix with all the elements above the diagonal equal to zero.

Similarly, if E is an elementary $n \times n$ matrix, then the effect of AE is that one of the columns of A times a nonzero constant is added to another column of A. Thus,

---

[6] The notation $E_{i,j}(c)$ will be used for a specific elementary matrix, and a generic elementary matrix will be denoted by "E."

Definition I.8: *An elementary matrix is a unit matrix with one off-diagonal zero element replaced by a nonzero constant.*

Note that the columns of an elementary matrix are linear independent; hence, an elementary matrix is invertible. The inverse of an elementary matrix is easy to determine: If the effect of EA is that c times row j of A is added to row i of A, then E^{-1} is an elementary matrix such that the effect of $E^{-1}EA$ is that $-c$ times row j of EA is added to row i of A; thus, $E^{-1}EA$ restores A. For example, the inverse of the elementary matrix (I.20) is

$$
E_{2,1}(c)^{-1} = \begin{pmatrix} 1 & 0 & 0 & \dots & 0 \\ c & 1 & 0 & \dots & 0 \\ 0 & 0 & 1 & \dots & 0 \\ \vdots & \vdots & \vdots & \ddots & \vdots \\ 0 & 0 & 0 & \dots & 1 \end{pmatrix}^{-1} = \begin{pmatrix} 1 & 0 & 0 & \dots & 0 \\ -c & 1 & 0 & \dots & 0 \\ 0 & 0 & 1 & \dots & 0 \\ \vdots & \vdots & \vdots & \ddots & \vdots \\ 0 & 0 & 0 & \dots & 1 \end{pmatrix}
$$

$$
= E_{2,1}(-c).
$$

We now turn to permutation matrices.

Definition I.9: *An elementary permutation matrix is a unit matrix with two columns or rows swapped. A permutation matrix is a matrix whose columns or rows are permutations of the columns or rows of a unit matrix.*

In particular, the elementary permutation matrix that is formed by swapping the columns i and j of a unit matrix will be denoted by $P_{i,j}$.

The effect of an (elementary) permutation matrix on A is that PA swaps two rows, or permutates the rows, of A. Similarly, AP swaps or permutates the columns of A. Whether you swap or permutate columns or rows of a unit matrix does not matter because the resulting (elementary) permutation matrix is the same. An example of an elementary permutation matrix is

$$
P_{1,2} = \begin{pmatrix} 0 & 1 & 0 & \dots & 0 \\ 1 & 0 & 0 & \dots & 0 \\ 0 & 0 & 1 & \dots & 0 \\ \vdots & \vdots & \vdots & \ddots & \vdots \\ 0 & 0 & 0 & \dots & 1 \end{pmatrix}.
$$

Note that a permutation matrix P can be formed as a product of elementary permutation matrices, for example, $P = P_{i_1, j_1} \dots P_{i_k, j_k}$. Moreover, note that if an elementary permutation matrix $P_{i,j}$ is applied to itself (i.e., $P_{i,j} P_{i,j}$), then the swap is undone and the result is the unit matrix: Thus, *the inverse of an elementary permutation matrix* $P_{i,j}$ *is* $P_{i,j}$ *itself.* This result holds only for elementary permutation matrices, though. In the case of the permutation matrix $P = P_{i_1, j_1} \dots P_{i_k, j_k}$ we have $P^{-1} = P_{i_k, j_k} \dots P_{i_1, j_1}$. Because elementary permutation matrices are symmetric (i.e., $P_{i,j} = P_{i,j}^{\mathrm{T}}$), it follows that $P^{-1} = P_{i_k,j_k}^{\mathrm{T}} \cdots P_{i_1,j_1}^{\mathrm{T}} = P^{\mathrm{T}}$. Moreover, if E is an elementary matrix and $P_{i,j}$ an elementary permutation matrix, then $P_{i,j} E = EP_{i,j}$. Combining these results, we obtain the following theorem:

Theorem I.7: *If E is an elementary matrix and P is a permutation matrix, then $PE = EP^{\mathrm{T}}$. Moreover, $P^{-1} = P^{\mathrm{T}}$.*

I.6. Gaussian Elimination of a Square Matrix and the Gauss–Jordan Iteration for Inverting a Matrix

I.6.1. Gaussian Elimination of a Square Matrix

The results in the previous section are the tools we need to derive the following result:

Theorem I.8: *Let A be a square matrix.*

(a) *There exists a permutation matrix P, possibly equal to the unit matrix I, a lower-triangular matrix L with diagonal elements all equal to 1, a diagonal matrix D, and an upper-triangular matrix U with diagonal elements all equal to 1 such that $PA = LDU$.*

(b) *If A is nonsingular and $P = I$, this decomposition is unique; that is, if $A = LDU = L_* D_* U_*$, then $L_* = L$, $D_* = D$, and $U_* = U$.*

The proof of part (b) is as follows: $LDU = L_* D_* U_*$ implies

$$L^{-1} L_* D_* = DUU_*^{-1}. \tag{I.21}$$

It is easy to verify that the inverse of a lower-triangular matrix is lower triangular and that the product of lower-triangular matrices is lower triangular. Thus the left-hand side of (I.21) is lower triangular. Similarly, the right-hand side of (I.21) is upper triangular. Consequently, the off-diagonal elements in both sides are zero: Both matrices in (I.21) are diagonal. Because D_* is diagonal and nonsingular, it follows from (I.21) that $L^{-1} L_* = DUU_*^{-1} D_*^{-1}$ is diagonal. Moreover, because the diagonal elements of L^{-1} and L_* are all equal to 1, the same applies to $L^{-1} L_*$, that is, $L^{-1} L_* = I$; hence, $L = L_*$. Similarly, we have $U = U_*$. Then $D = L^{-1} AU^{-1}$ and $D_* = L^{-1} AU^{-1}$.

Rather than giving a formal proof of part (a) of Theorem I.8, I will demonstrate the result involved by two examples, one for the case that A is nonsingular and the other for the case that A is singular.

Example 1: A is nonsingular.

Let

$$A = \begin{pmatrix} 2 & 4 & 2 \\ 1 & 2 & 3 \\ -1 & 1 & -1 \end{pmatrix}. \tag{I.22}$$

We are going to multiply A by elementary matrices and elementary permutation matrices such that the final result will be an upper-triangular matrix. This is called *Gaussian elimination*.

First, add $-1/2$ times row 1 to row 2 in (I.22). This is equivalent to multiplying A by the elementary matrix $E_{2,1}(-1/2)$. (Compare (I.20) with $c = -1/2$.) Then

$$E_{2,1}(-1/2)A = \begin{pmatrix} 1 & 0 & 0 \\ -0.5 & 1 & 0 \\ 0 & 0 & 1 \end{pmatrix} \begin{pmatrix} 2 & 4 & 2 \\ 1 & 2 & 3 \\ -1 & 1 & -1 \end{pmatrix} = \begin{pmatrix} 2 & 4 & 2 \\ 0 & 0 & 2 \\ -1 & 1 & -1 \end{pmatrix}.$$

(I.23)

Next, add $1/2$ times row 1 to row 3, which is equivalent to multiplying (I.23) by the elementary matrix $E_{3,1}(1/2)$:

$$E_{3,1}(1/2)E_{2,1}(-1/2)A = \begin{pmatrix} 1 & 0 & 0 \\ 0 & 1 & 0 \\ 0.5 & 0 & 1 \end{pmatrix} \begin{pmatrix} 2 & 4 & 2 \\ 0 & 0 & 2 \\ -1 & 1 & -1 \end{pmatrix}$$

$$= \begin{pmatrix} 2 & 4 & 2 \\ 0 & 0 & 2 \\ 0 & 3 & 0 \end{pmatrix}.$$

(I.24)

Now swap rows 2 and 3 of the right-hand matrix in (I.24). This is equivalent to multiplying (I.24) by the elementary permutation matrix $P_{2,3}$ formed by swapping the columns 2 and 3 of the unit matrix I_3. Then

$$P_{2,3}E_{3,1}(1/2)E_{2,1}(-1/2)A$$

$$= \begin{pmatrix} 1 & 0 & 0 \\ 0 & 0 & 1 \\ 0 & 1 & 0 \end{pmatrix} \begin{pmatrix} 2 & 4 & 2 \\ 0 & 0 & 2 \\ 0 & 3 & 0 \end{pmatrix} = \begin{pmatrix} 2 & 4 & 2 \\ 0 & 3 & 0 \\ 0 & 0 & 2 \end{pmatrix}$$

$$= \begin{pmatrix} 2 & 0 & 0 \\ 0 & 3 & 0 \\ 0 & 0 & 2 \end{pmatrix} \begin{pmatrix} 1 & 2 & 1 \\ 0 & 1 & 0 \\ 0 & 0 & 1 \end{pmatrix} = DU,$$

(I.25)

for instance. Moreover, because $P_{2,3}$ is an elementary permutation matrix we have that $P_{2,3}^{-1} = P_{2,3}$; hence, it follows from Theorem I.7 and (I.25) that

$$P_{2,3}E_{3,1}(1/2)E_{2,1}(-1/2)A = E_{3,1}(1/2)P_{2,3}E_{2,1}(-1/2)A$$
$$= E_{3,1}(1/2)E_{2,1}(-1/2)P_{2,3}A$$
$$= DU.$$

(I.26)

Furthermore, observe that

$$E_{3,1}(1/2)E_{2,1}(-1/2)$$

$$= \begin{pmatrix} 1 & 0 & 0 \\ -0.5 & 1 & 0 \\ 0 & 0 & 1 \end{pmatrix} \begin{pmatrix} 1 & 0 & 0 \\ 0 & 1 & 0 \\ 0.5 & 0 & 1 \end{pmatrix} = \begin{pmatrix} 1 & 0 & 0 \\ -0.5 & 1 & 0 \\ 0.5 & 0 & 1 \end{pmatrix};$$

hence,

$$(E_{3,1}(1/2)E_{2,1}(-1/2))^{-1} = \begin{pmatrix} 1 & 0 & 0 \\ -0.5 & 1 & 0 \\ 0.5 & 0 & 1 \end{pmatrix}^{-1}$$

$$= \begin{pmatrix} 1 & 0 & 0 \\ 0.5 & 1 & 0 \\ -0.5 & 0 & 1 \end{pmatrix} = L, \qquad (I.27)$$

for instance. Combining (I.26) and (I.27), we find now that $P_{2,3}A = LDU$.

Example 2: A is singular.

Theorem I.8 also holds for singular matrices. The only difference with the nonsingular case is that, if A is singular, then the diagonal matrix D will have zeros on the diagonal. To demonstrate this, let

$$A = \begin{pmatrix} 2 & 4 & 2 \\ 1 & 2 & 1 \\ -1 & 1 & -1 \end{pmatrix}. \qquad (I.28)$$

Because the first and last column of the matrix (I.28) are equal, the columns are linear dependent; hence, (I.28) is singular. Now (I.23) becomes

$$E_{2,1}(-1/2)A = \begin{pmatrix} 1 & 0 & 0 \\ -0.5 & 1 & 0 \\ 0 & 0 & 1 \end{pmatrix} \begin{pmatrix} 2 & 4 & 2 \\ 1 & 2 & 1 \\ -1 & 1 & -1 \end{pmatrix} = \begin{pmatrix} 2 & 4 & 2 \\ 0 & 0 & 0 \\ -1 & 1 & -1 \end{pmatrix},$$

(I.24) becomes

$$E_{3,1}(1/2)E_{2,1}(-1/2)A = \begin{pmatrix} 1 & 0 & 0 \\ 0 & 1 & 0 \\ 0.5 & 0 & 1 \end{pmatrix} \begin{pmatrix} 2 & 4 & 2 \\ 0 & 0 & 0 \\ -1 & 1 & -1 \end{pmatrix}$$

$$= \begin{pmatrix} 2 & 4 & 2 \\ 0 & 0 & 0 \\ 0 & 3 & 0 \end{pmatrix},$$

and (I.25) becomes

$$P_{2,3}E_{3,1}(1/2)E_{2,1}(-1/2)A = \begin{pmatrix} 1 & 0 & 0 \\ 0 & 0 & 1 \\ 0 & 1 & 0 \end{pmatrix} \begin{pmatrix} 2 & 4 & 2 \\ 0 & 0 & 0 \\ 0 & 3 & 0 \end{pmatrix} = \begin{pmatrix} 2 & 4 & 2 \\ 0 & 3 & 0 \\ 0 & 0 & 0 \end{pmatrix}$$

$$= \begin{pmatrix} 2 & 0 & 0 \\ 0 & 3 & 0 \\ 0 & 0 & 0 \end{pmatrix} \begin{pmatrix} 1 & 2 & 1 \\ 0 & 1 & 0 \\ 0 & 0 & 1 \end{pmatrix} = DU. \quad (I.29)$$

The formal proof of part (a) of Theorem I.8 is similar to the argument in these two examples and is therefore omitted.

Note that the result (I.29) demonstrates that

Theorem I.9: *The dimension of the subspace spanned by the columns of a square matrix A is equal to the number of nonzero diagonal elements of the matrix D in Theorem I.8.*

Example 3: A is symmetric and nonsingular

Next, consider the case that A is symmetric, that is, $A^T = A$. For example, let

$$A = \begin{pmatrix} 2 & 4 & 2 \\ 4 & 0 & 1 \\ 2 & 1 & -1 \end{pmatrix}.$$

Then

$$E_{3,2}(-3/8)E_{2,1}(-1)E_{2,1}(-2)AE_{1,2}(-2)E_{1,3}(-1)E_{2,3}(-3/8)$$
$$= \begin{pmatrix} 2 & 0 & 0 \\ 0 & -8 & 0 \\ 0 & 0 & -15/8 \end{pmatrix} = D;$$

hence,

$$A = (E_{3,2}(-3/8)E_{3,1}(-1)E_{2,1}(-2))^{-1}$$
$$\times D(E_{1,2}(-2)E_{1,3}(-1)E_{2,3}(-3/8))^{-1} = LDL^T.$$

Thus, in the symmetric case we can eliminate each pair of nonzero elements opposite the diagonal jointly by multiplying A from the left by an appropriate elementary matrix and multiplying A from the right by the transpose of the same elementary matrix.

Example 4: A is symmetric and singular

Although I have demonstrated this result for a nonsingular symmetric matrix, it holds for the singular case as well. For example, let

$$A = \begin{pmatrix} 2 & 4 & 2 \\ 4 & 0 & 4 \\ 2 & 4 & 2 \end{pmatrix}.$$

Then

$$E_{3,1}(-1)E_{2,1}(-2)AE_{1,2}(-2)E_{1,3}(-1) = \begin{pmatrix} 2 & 0 & 0 \\ 0 & -8 & 0 \\ 0 & 0 & 0 \end{pmatrix} = D.$$

Example 5: A is symmetric and has a zero in a pivot position

If there is a zero in a pivot position,[7] then we need a row exchange. In that case the result $A = LDL^T$ will no longer be valid. For example, let

$$A = \begin{pmatrix} 0 & 4 & 2 \\ 4 & 0 & 4 \\ 2 & 4 & 2 \end{pmatrix}.$$

Then

$$E_{3,2}(-1)E_{3,1}(-1/2)P_{1,2}A = \begin{pmatrix} 4 & 0 & 4 \\ 0 & 4 & 2 \\ 0 & 0 & -2 \end{pmatrix}$$

$$= \begin{pmatrix} 4 & 0 & 0 \\ 0 & 4 & 0 \\ 0 & 0 & -2 \end{pmatrix} \begin{pmatrix} 1 & 0 & 1 \\ 0 & 1 & 1/2 \\ 0 & 0 & 1 \end{pmatrix} = DU,$$

but

$$L = (E_{3,2}(-1)E_{3,1}(-1/2))^{-1} = E_{3,1}(1/2)E_{3,2}(1)$$

$$= \begin{pmatrix} 1 & 0 & 0 \\ 0 & 1 & 0 \\ 1/2 & 1 & 1 \end{pmatrix} \neq U^T.$$

Thus, examples 3, 4, and 5 demonstrate that

Theorem I.10: *If A is symmetric and the Gaussian elimination can be conducted without the need for row exchanges, then there exists a lower-triangular matrix L with diagonal elements all equal to 1 and a diagonal matrix D such that $A = LDL^T$.*

I.6.2. The Gauss–Jordan Iteration for Inverting a Matrix

The Gaussian elimination of the matrix A in the first example in the previous section suggests that this method can also be used to compute the inverse of A as follows. Augment the matrix A in (I.22) to a 3×6 matrix by augmenting the columns of A with the columns of the unit matrix I_3:

$$B = (A, I_3) = \begin{pmatrix} 2 & 4 & 2 & 1 & 0 & 0 \\ 1 & 2 & 3 & 0 & 1 & 0 \\ -1 & 1 & -1 & 0 & 0 & 1 \end{pmatrix}.$$

Now follow the same procedure as in Example 1, up to (I.25), with A replaced

---

[7] A pivot is an element on the diagonal to be used to wipe out the elements below that diagonal element.

by B. Then (I.25) becomes

$$P_{2,3}E_{3,1}(1/2)E_{2,1}(-1/2)B$$

$$= (P_{2,3}E_{3,1}(1/2)E_{2,1}(-1/2)A, \; P_{2,3}E_{3,1}(1/2)E_{2,1}(-1/2))$$

$$= \begin{pmatrix} 2 & 4 & 2 & & 1 & 0 & 0 \\ 0 & 3 & 0 & & 0.5 & 0 & 1 \\ 0 & 0 & 2 & & -0.5 & 1 & 0 \end{pmatrix} = (U_*, C), \tag{I.30}$$

for instance, where U_* in (I.30) follows from (I.25) and

$$C = P_{2,3}E_{3,1}(1/2)E_{2,1}(-1/2) = \begin{pmatrix} 1 & 0 & 0 \\ 0.5 & 0 & 1 \\ -0.5 & 1 & 0 \end{pmatrix}. \tag{I.31}$$

Now multiply (I.30) by elementary matrix $E_{13}(-1)$, that is, subtract row 3 from row 1:

$$(E_{1,3}(-1)P_{2,3}E_{3,1}(1/2)E_{2,1}(-1/2)A,$$

$$E_{1,3}(-1)P_{2,3}E_{3,1}(1/2)E_{2,1}(-1/2))$$

$$= \begin{pmatrix} 2 & 4 & 0 & & 1.5 & -1 & 0 \\ 0 & 3 & 0 & & 0.5 & 0 & 1 \\ 0 & 0 & 2 & & -0.5 & 1 & 0 \end{pmatrix}; \tag{I.32}$$

multiply (I.32) by elementary matrix $E_{12}(-4/3)$, that is, subtract $4/3$ times row 3 from row 1:

$$(E_{1,2}(-4/3)E_{1,3}(-1)P_{2,3}E_{3,1}(1/2)E_{2,1}(-1/2)A,$$

$$E_{1,2}(-4/3)E_{1,3}(-1)P_{2,3}E_{3,1}(1/2)E_{2,1}(-1/2))$$

$$= \begin{pmatrix} 2 & 0 & 0 & & 5/6 & -1 & -4/3 \\ 0 & 3 & 0 & & 0.5 & 0 & 1 \\ 0 & 0 & 2 & & -0.5 & 1 & 0 \end{pmatrix}; \tag{I.33}$$

and finally, divide row 1 by pivot 2, row 2 by pivot 3, and row 3 by pivot 2, or equivalently, multiply (I.33) by a diagonal matrix D_* with diagonal elements $1/2$, $1/3$ and $1/2$:

$$(D_*E_{1,2}(-4/3)E_{1,3}(-1)P_{2,3}E_{3,1}(1/2)E_{2,1}(-1/2)A,$$

$$D_*E_{1,2}(-4/3)E_{1,3}(-1)P_{2,3}E_{3,1}(1/2)E_{2,1}(-1/2))$$

$$= (I_3, \; D_*E_{1,2}(-4/3)E_{1,3}(-1)P_{2,3}E_{3,1}(1/2)E_{2,1}(-1/2))$$

$$= \begin{pmatrix} 1 & 0 & 0 & & 5/12 & -1/2 & -2/3 \\ 0 & 1 & 0 & & 1/6 & 0 & 1/3 \\ 0 & 0 & 1 & & -1/4 & 1/2 & 0 \end{pmatrix}. \tag{I.34}$$

Observe from (I.34) that the matrix (A, I_3) has been transformed into a matrix of the type $(I_3, A^*) = (A^*A, A^*)$, where $A^* = D_*E_{1,2}(-4/3) \times$

$E_{1,3}(-1)P_{2,3}E_{3,1}(1/2)E_{2,1}(-1/2)$ is the matrix consisting of the last three columns of (I.34). Consequently, $A^* = A^{-1}$.

This way of computing the inverse of a matrix is called the *Gauss–Jordan iteration*. In practice, the Gauss–Jordan iteration is done in a slightly different but equivalent way using a sequence of tableaux. Take again the matrix A in (I.22). The Gauss–Jordan iteration then starts from the initial tableau:

Tableau 1

A			I		
2	4	2	1	0	0
1	2	3	0	1	0
−1	1	−1	0	0	1

If there is a zero in a pivot position, you have to swap rows, as we will see later in this section. In the case of Tableau 1 there is not yet a problem because the first element of row 1 is nonzero.

The first step is to make all the nonzero elements in the first column equal to one by dividing all the rows by their first element provided that they are nonzero. Then we obtain

Tableau 2

1	2	1	1/2	0	0
1	2	3	0	1	0
1	−1	1	0	0	−1

Next, wipe out the first elements of rows 2 and 3 by subtracting row 1 from them:

Tableau 3

1	2	1	1/2	0	0
0	0	2	−1/2	1	0
0	−3	0	−1/2	0	−1

Now we have a zero in a pivot position, namely, the second zero of row 2. Therefore, swap rows 2 and 3:

Tableau 4

1	2	1	1/2	0	0
0	−3	0	−1/2	0	−1
0	0	2	−1/2	1	0

Divide row 2 by −3 and row 3 by 2:

Tableau 5

1	2	1	1/2	0	0
0	1	0	1/6	0	1/3
0	0	1	−1/4	1/2	0

The left 3×3 block is now upper triangular.

Next, we have to wipe out, one by one, the elements in this block above the diagonal. Thus, subtract row 3 from row 1:

Tableau 6

1	2	0	3/4	−1/2	0
0	1	0	1/6	0	1/3 .
0	0	1	−1/4	1/2	0

Finally, subtract two times row 2 from row 1:

Tableau 7

	I			A^{-1}	
1	0	0	5/12	−1/2	−2/3
0	1	0	1/6	0	1/3 .
0	0	1	−1/4	1/2	0

This is the final tableau. The last three columns now form A^{-1}.

Once you have calculated A^{-1}, you can solve the linear system $Ax = b$ by computing $x = A^{-1}b$. However, you can also incorporate the latter in the Gauss–Jordan iteration, as follows. Again let A be the matrix in (I.22), and let, for example,

$$b = \begin{pmatrix} 1 \\ 1 \\ 1 \end{pmatrix}.$$

Insert this vector in Tableau 1:

Tableau 1*

	A		*b*		*I*	
2	4	2	1	1	0	0
1	2	3	1	0	1	0 .
−1	1	−1	1	0	0	1

and perform the same row operations as before. Then Tableau 7 becomes

Tableau 7*

	I		$A^{-1}b$		A^{-1}	
1	0	0	−5/12	5/12	−1/2	−2/3
0	1	0	1/2	1/6	0	1/3 .
0	0	1	−1/4	−1/4	1/2	0

This is how matrices were inverted and systems of linear equations were solved fifty and more years ago using only mechanical calculators. Nowadays of course you would use a computer, but the Gauss–Jordan method is still handy and not too time consuming for small matrices like the one in this example.

I.7. Gaussian Elimination of a Nonsquare Matrix

The Gaussian elimination of a nonsquare matrix is similar to the square case except that in the final result the upper-triangular matrix now becomes an echelon matrix:

Definition I.10: *An $m \times n$ matrix U is an echelon matrix if, for $i = 2, \ldots, m$, the first nonzero element of row i is farther to the right than the first nonzero element of the previous row $i - 1$.*

For example, the matrix

$$U = \begin{pmatrix} 2 & 0 & 1 & 0 \\ 0 & 0 & 3 & 1 \\ 0 & 0 & 0 & 4 \end{pmatrix}$$

is an echelon matrix, and so is

$$U = \begin{pmatrix} 2 & 0 & 1 & 0 \\ 0 & 0 & 0 & 1 \\ 0 & 0 & 0 & 0 \end{pmatrix}.$$

Theorem I.8 can now be generalized to

Theorem I.11: *For each matrix A there exists a permutation matrix P, possibly equal to the unit matrix I, a lower-triangular matrix L with diagonal elements all equal to 1, and an echelon matrix U such that $PA = LU$. If A is a square matrix, then U is an upper-triangular matrix. Moreover, in that case $PA = LDU$, where now U is an upper-triangular matrix with diagonal elements all equal to 1 and D is a diagonal matrix.*[8]

Again, I will only prove the general part of this theorem by examples. The parts for square matrices follow trivially from the general case.

First, let

$$A = \begin{pmatrix} 2 & 4 & 2 & 1 \\ 1 & 2 & 3 & 1 \\ -1 & 1 & -1 & 0 \end{pmatrix}, \tag{I.35}$$

---

[8] Note that the diagonal elements of D are the diagonal elements of the former upper-triangular matrix U.

which is the matrix (I.22) augmented with an additional column. Then it follows from (I.31) that

$$P_{2,3}E_{3,1}(1/2)E_{2,1}(-1/2)A = \begin{pmatrix} 1 & 0 & 0 \\ 0.5 & 0 & 1 \\ -0.5 & 1 & 0 \end{pmatrix}\begin{pmatrix} 2 & 4 & 2 & 1 \\ 1 & 2 & 3 & 1 \\ -1 & 1 & -1 & 0 \end{pmatrix}$$

$$= \begin{pmatrix} 2 & 4 & 2 & 1 \\ 0 & 3 & 0 & 1/2 \\ 0 & 0 & 2 & 1/2 \end{pmatrix} = U,$$

where U is now an echelon matrix.

As another example, take the transpose of the matrix A in (I.35):

$$A^{\mathrm{T}} = \begin{pmatrix} 2 & 1 & -1 \\ 4 & 2 & 1 \\ 2 & 3 & -1 \\ 1 & 1 & 0 \end{pmatrix}.$$

Then

$$P_{2,3}E_{4,2}(-1/6)E_{4,3}(1/4)E_{2,1}(-2)E_{3,1}(-1)E_{4,1}(-1/2)A^{\mathrm{T}}$$

$$= \begin{pmatrix} 2 & 1 & -1 \\ 0 & 2 & 0 \\ 0 & 0 & 3 \\ 0 & 0 & 0 \end{pmatrix} = U,$$

where again U is an echelon matrix.

I.8. Subspaces Spanned by the Columns and Rows of a Matrix

The result in Theorem I.9 also reads as follows: $A = BU$, where $B = P^{-1}L$ is a nonsingular matrix. Moreover, note that the size of U is the same as the size of A, that is, if A is an $m \times n$ matrix, then so is U. If we denote the columns of U by $u_1, \ldots, u_n$, it follows therefore that the columns $a_1, \ldots, a_n$ of A are equal to $Bu_1, \ldots, Bu_n$, respectively. This suggests that the subspace spanned by the columns of A has the same dimension as the subspace spanned by the columns of U. To prove this conjecture, let V_A be the subspace spanned by the columns of A and let V_U be the subspace spanned by the columns of U. Without loss or generality we may reorder the columns of A such that the first k columns $a_1, \ldots, a_k$ of A form a basis for V_A. Now suppose that $u_1, \ldots, u_k$ are linear dependent, that is, there exist constants $c_1, \ldots, c_k$ not all equal to zero such that $\sum_{j=1}^{k} c_j u_j = 0$. But then also $\sum_{j=1}^{k} c_j Bu_j = \sum_{j=1}^{k} c_j a_j = 0$, which by the linear independence of $a_1, \ldots, a_k$ implies that all the c_j's are equal to zero.

Hence, $u_1, \ldots, u_k$ are linear independent, and therefore the dimension of V_U is greater or equal to the dimension of V_A. But because $U = B^{-1}A$, the same argument applies the other way around: the dimension of V_A is greater or equal to the dimension of V_U. Thus, we have

Theorem I.12: *The subspace spanned by the columns of A has the same dimension as the subspace spanned by the columns of the corresponding echelon matrix U in Theorem I.9.*

Next, I will show that

Theorem I.13: *The subspace spanned by the columns of A^{T} is the same as the subspace spanned by the columns of the transpose U^{T} of the corresponding echelon matrix U in Theorem I.9.*

Proof: Let A be an $m \times n$ matrix. The equality $A = BU$ implies that $A^{\mathsf{T}} = U^{\mathsf{T}} B^{\mathsf{T}}$. The subspace spanned by the columns of A^{T} consists of all vectors $x \in \mathbb{R}^m$ for which there exists a vector $c_1 \in \mathbb{R}^n$ such that $x = A^{\mathsf{T}} c_1$, and similarly the subspace spanned by the columns of U^{T} consists of all vectors $x \in \mathbb{R}^m$ for which there exists a vector $c_2 \in \mathbb{R}^n$ such that $x = U^{\mathsf{T}} c_2$. If we let $c_2 = B^{\mathsf{T}} c_1$, the theorem follows.   Q.E.D.

Now let us have a closer look at a typical echelon matrix:

$$
U = \begin{pmatrix}
0 & \ldots & 0 & ☺ & \ldots & * & * & \ldots & * & * & \ldots & * & * & \ldots & * \\
0 & \ldots & 0 & 0 & \ldots & 0 & ☺ & \ldots & * & * & \ldots & * & * & \ldots & * \\
0 & \ldots & 0 & 0 & \ldots & 0 & 0 & \ldots & 0 & ☺ & \ldots & * & * & \ldots & * \\
0 & \ldots & 0 & 0 & \ldots & 0 & 0 & \ldots & 0 & 0 & \ldots & 0 & ☺ & \ldots & * \\
\vdots & \ddots & \vdots & \vdots & \ddots & \vdots & \vdots & \ddots & \vdots & \vdots & \ddots & \vdots & \vdots & \ldots & \vdots \\
0 & \ldots & 0 & 0 & \ldots & 0 & 0 & \ldots & 0 & 0 & \ldots & 0 & 0 & \ldots & 0
\end{pmatrix},
$$

(I.36)

where each symbol ☺ indicates the first nonzero elements of the row involved called the *pivot*. The elements indicated by * may be zero or nonzero. Because the elements below a pivot ☺ are zero, the columns involved are linear independent. In particular, it is impossible to write a column with a pivot as a linear combination of the previous ones. Moreover, it is easy to see that all the columns without a pivot can be formed as linear combinations of the columns with a pivot. Consequently, the columns of U with a pivot form a basis for the subspace spanned by the columns of U. But the transpose U^{T} of U is also an echelon matrix, and the number of rows of U with a pivot is the same as the number of columns with a pivot; hence,

Theorem I.14: *The dimension of the subspace spanned by the columns of an echelon matrix U is the same as the dimension of the subspace spanned by the columns of its transpose U^T.*

If we combine Theorems I.11, I.12 and I.13, it now follows that Theorem I.6 holds.

The subspace spanned by the columns of a matrix A is called the **column space** of A and is denoted by $\mathcal{R}(A)$. The *row space* of A is the space spanned by the columns of A^T, that is, the row space of A is $\mathcal{R}(A^T)$. Theorem I.14 implies that the dimension of $\mathcal{R}(A)$ is equal to the dimension of $\mathcal{R}(A^T)$.

There is also another space associated with a matrix A, namely, the *null space* of A denoted by $\mathcal{N}(A)$. This is the space of all vectors x for which $Ax = 0$, which is also a subspace of a vector space. If A is square and nonsingular, then $\mathcal{N}(A) = \{0\}$; if not it follows from Theorem I.12 that $\mathcal{N}(A) = \mathcal{N}(U)$, where U is the echelon matrix in Theorem I.12.

To determine the dimension of $\mathcal{N}(U)$, suppose that A is an $m \times n$ matrix with rank r, and thus U is an $m \times n$ matrix with rank r. Let R be an $n \times n$ permutation matrix such that the first r columns of UR are the r columns of U with a pivot. Clearly, the dimension of $\mathcal{N}(U)$ is the same as the dimension of $\mathcal{N}(UR)$. We can partition UR as (U_r, U_{n-r}), where U_r is the $m \times r$ matrix consisting of the columns of U with a pivot, and U_{n-r} is the $m \times (n-r)$ matrix consisting of the other columns of U. Partitioning a vector x in $\mathcal{N}(UR)$ accordingly – that is, $x = (x_r^T, x_{n-r}^T)^T$ – we have

$$URx = U_r x_r + U_{n-r} x_{n-r} = 0. \tag{I.37}$$

It follows from Theorem I.5 that $U_r^T U_r$ is invertible; hence, it follows from (I.37) and the partition $x = (x_r^T, x_{n-r}^T)^T$ that

$$x = \begin{pmatrix} -\left(U_r^T U_r\right)^{-1} U_r^T U_{n-r} \\ I_{n-r} \end{pmatrix} x_{n-r}. \tag{I.38}$$

Therefore, $\mathcal{N}(UR)$ is spanned by the columns of the matrix in (I.38), which has rank $n - r$, and thus the dimension of $\mathcal{N}(A)$ is $n - r$. By the same argument it follows that the dimension of $\mathcal{N}(A^T)$ is $m - r$.

The subspace $\mathcal{N}(A^T)$ is called the *left null space* of A because it consists of all vectors y for which $y^T A = 0^T$.

In summary, it has been shown that the following results hold.

Theorem I.15: *Let A be an $m \times n$ matrix with rank r. Then $\mathcal{R}(A)$ and $\mathcal{R}(A^T)$ have dimension r, $\mathcal{N}(A)$ has dimension $n - r$, and $\mathcal{N}(A^T)$ has dimension $m - r$.*

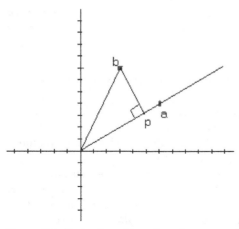

Figure I.4. Projection of b on the subspace spanned by a.

Note that in general the rank of a product AB is not determined by the ranks r and s of A and B, respectively. At first sight one might guess that the rank of AB is $\min(r, s)$, but that in general is not true. For example, let $A = (1, 0)$ and $B^\mathsf{T} = (0, 1)$. Then A and B have rank 1, but $AB = 0$, which has rank zero. The only thing we know for sure is that the rank of AB cannot exceed $\min(r, s)$. Of course, if A and B are conformable, invertible matrices, then AB is invertible; hence, the rank of AB is equal to the rank of A and the rank of B, but that is a special case. The same applies to the case in Theorem I.5.

I.9. Projections, Projection Matrices, and Idempotent Matrices

Consider the following problem: Which point on the line through the origin and point a in Figure I.3 is the closest to point b? The answer is point p in Figure I.4. The line through b and p is perpendicular to the subspace spanned by a, and therefore the distance between b and any other point in this subspace is larger than the distance between b and p. Point p is called the *projection* of b on the subspace spanned by a. To find p, let $p = c \cdot a$, where c is a scalar. The distance between b and p is now $\|b - c \cdot a\|$; consequently, the problem is to find the scalar c that minimizes this distance. Because $\|b - c \cdot a\|$ is minimal if and only if

$$\|b - c \cdot a\|^2 = (b - c \cdot a)^\mathsf{T}(b - c \cdot a) = b^\mathsf{T}b - 2c \cdot a^\mathsf{T}b + c^2 a^\mathsf{T}a$$

is minimal, the answer is $c = a^\mathsf{T}b/a^\mathsf{T}a$; hence, $p = (a^\mathsf{T}b/a^\mathsf{T}a) \cdot a$.

Similarly, we can project a vector y in $\mathbb{R}^n$ on the subspace of $\mathbb{R}^n$ spanned by a basis $\{x_1, \ldots, x_k\}$ as follows. Let X be the $n \times k$ matrix with columns

$x_1, \ldots, x_k$. Any point p in the column space $\mathscr{R}(X)$ of X can be written as $p = Xb$, where $b \in \mathbb{R}^k$. Then the squared distance between y and $p = Xb$ is

$$
\begin{aligned}
\|y - Xb\|^2 &= (y - Xb)^\mathsf{T}(y - Xb) \\
&= y^\mathsf{T}y - b^\mathsf{T}X^\mathsf{T}y - y^\mathsf{T}Xb + b^\mathsf{T}X^\mathsf{T}Xb \\
&= y^\mathsf{T}y - 2b^\mathsf{T}X^\mathsf{T}y + b^\mathsf{T}X^\mathsf{T}Xb,
\end{aligned}
\tag{I.39}
$$

where the last equality follows because $y^\mathsf{T}Xb$ is a scalar (or, equivalently, a 1×1 matrix); hence, $y^\mathsf{T}Xb = (y^\mathsf{T}Xb)^\mathsf{T} = b^\mathsf{T}X^\mathsf{T}y$. Given X and y, (I.39) is a quadratic function of b. The first-order condition for a minimum of (I.39) is given by

$$
\frac{\partial \|y - Xb\|^2}{\partial b^\mathsf{T}} = -2X^\mathsf{T}y + 2X^\mathsf{T}Xb = 0,
$$

which has the solution

$$
b = (X^\mathsf{T}X)^{-1}X^\mathsf{T}y.
$$

Thus, the vector p in $\mathscr{R}(X)$ closest to y is

$$
p = X(X^\mathsf{T}X)^{-1}X^\mathsf{T}y,
\tag{I.40}
$$

which is the projection of y on $\mathscr{R}(X)$.

Matrices of the type in (I.40) are called projection matrices:

Definition I.11: *Let A be an $n \times k$ matrix with rank k. Then the $n \times n$ matrix $P = A(A^\mathsf{T}A)^{-1}A^\mathsf{T}$ is called a projection matrix: For each vector x in $\mathbb{R}^n$, Px is the projection of x on the column space of A.*

Note that this matrix P is such that $PP = A(A^\mathsf{T}A)^{-1}A^\mathsf{T}A(A^\mathsf{T}A)^{-1}A^\mathsf{T}) = A(A^\mathsf{T}A)^{-1}A^\mathsf{T} = P$. This is not surprising, though, because $p = Px$ is already in $\mathscr{R}(A)$; hence, the point in $\mathscr{R}(A)$ closest to p is p itself.

Definition I.12: *An $n \times n$ matrix M is called idempotent if $MM = M$.*

Thus, projection matrices are idempotent.

I.10. Inner Product, Orthogonal Bases, and Orthogonal Matrices

It follows from (I.10) that the cosine of the angle φ between the vectors x in (I.2) and y in (I.5) is

$$
\cos(\varphi) = \frac{\sum_{j=1}^{n} x_j y_j}{\|x\| \cdot \|y\|} = \frac{x^\mathsf{T}y}{\|x\| \cdot \|y\|}.
\tag{I.41}
$$

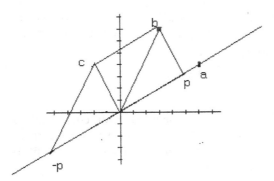

Figure I.5. Orthogonalization.

Definition I.13: *The quantity $x^T y$ is called the inner product of the vectors x and y.*

If $x^T y = 0$, then $\cos(\varphi) = 0$; hence, $\varphi = \pi/2$ or $\varphi = 3\pi/4$. This corresponds to angles of 90 and 270°, respectively; hence, x and y are perpendicular. Such vectors are said to be orthogonal.

Definition I.14: *Conformable vectors x and y are orthogonal if their inner product $x^T y$ is zero. Moreover, they are orthonormal if, in addition, their lengths are $1 : \|x\| = \|y\| = 1$.*

In Figure I.4, if we flip point p over to the other side of the origin along the line through the origin and point a and add b to $-p$, then the resulting vector $c = b - p$ is perpendicular to the line through the origin and point a. This is illustrated in Figure I.5. More formally,

$$a^T c = a^T (b - p) = a^T (b - (a^T b/\|a\|^2))a$$
$$= a^T b - (a^T b/\|a\|^2)\|a\|^2 = 0.$$

This procedure can be generalized to convert any basis of a vector space into an orthonormal basis as follows. Let $a_1, \ldots, a_k, k \leq n$ be a basis for a subspace of $\mathbb{R}^n$, and let $q_1 = \|a_1\|^{-1} \cdot a_1$. The projection of a_2 on q_1 is now $p = (q_1^T a_2) \cdot q_1$; hence, $a_2^* = a_2 - (q_1^T a_2) \cdot q_1$ is orthogonal to q_1. Thus, let $q_2 = \|a_2^*\|^{-1} a_2^*$. The next step is to erect a_3 perpendicular to q_1 *and* q_2, which can be done by subtracting from a_3 its projections on q_1 and q_2, that is, $a_3^* = a_3 - (a_3^T q_1)q_1 - (a_3^T q_2)q_2$. Using the facts that, by construction,

$$q_1^T q_1 = 1, \qquad q_2^T q_2 = 1, \qquad q_1^T q_2 = 0, \qquad q_2^T q_1 = 0,$$

we have indeed that $q_1^T a_3^* = q_1^T a_3 - (a_3^T q_1)q_1^T q_1 - (a_3^T q_2)q_1^T q_2 = q_1^T a_3 - a_3^T q_1 = 0$ and similarly, $q_2^T a_3^* = 0$. Thus, now let $q_3 = \|a_3^*\|^{-1} a_3^*$. Repeating this procedure yields

Theorem I.16: *Let* $a_1, \ldots, a_k$ *be a basis for a subspace of* $\mathbb{R}^n$, *and construct* $q_1, \ldots, q_k$ *recursively by*

$$q_1 = \|a_1\|^{-1} \cdot a_1 \quad and \quad a_j^* = a_j - \sum_{i=1}^{j-1} \left(a_j^\mathrm{T} q_i\right) q_i,$$

$$q_j = \|a_j^*\|^{-1} a_j^* \quad for \quad j = 2, 3, \ldots, k. \tag{I.42}$$

Then $q_1, \ldots, q_k$ *is an orthonormal basis for the subspace spanned by* $a_1, \ldots, a_k$.

The construction (I.42) is known as the *Gram–Smidt* process. The orthonormality of $q_1, \ldots, q_k$ has already been shown, but it still has to be shown that $q_1, \ldots, q_k$ spans the same subspace as $a_1, \ldots, a_k$. To show this, observe from (I.42) that $a_1, \ldots, a_k$ is related to $q_1, \ldots, q_k$ by

$$a_j = \sum_{i=1}^{j} u_{i,j} q_i, \quad j = 1, 2, \ldots, k, \tag{I.43}$$

where

$$u_{j,j} = \|a_j^*\|, u_{i,j} = q_i^\mathrm{T} a_j \quad for \quad i < j,$$
$$u_{i,j} = 0 \quad for \quad i > j, i, j = 1, \ldots, k \tag{I.44}$$

with $a_1^* = a_1$. It follows now from (I.43) that $a_1, \ldots, a_k$ are linear combinations of $q_1, \ldots, q_k$, and it follows from (I.42) that $q_1, \ldots, q_k$ are linear combinations of $a_1, \ldots, a_k$; hence, the two bases span the same subspace.

Observe from (I.44) that the $k \times k$ matrix U with elements $u_{i,j}$ is an upper-triangular matrix with positive diagonal elements. Moreover, if we denote by A the $n \times k$ matrix with columns $a_1, \ldots, a_k$ and by Q the $n \times k$ matrix with columns $q_1, \ldots, q_k$, it follows from (I.43) that $A = QU$. Thus, Theorem I.17 follows from Theorem I.16, (I.43), and (I.44):

Theorem I.17: *Let* A *be an* $n \times k$ *matrix with rank* k. *There exists an* $n \times k$ *matrix* Q *with orthonormal columns and an upper-triangular* $k \times k$ *matrix* U *with positive diagonal elements such that* $A = QU$.

In the case $k = n$, the matrix Q in Theorem I.17 is called an orthogonal matrix:

Definition I.15: *An orthogonal matrix* Q *is a square matrix with orthonormal columns:* $Q^\mathrm{T} Q = I$.

In particular, if Q is an orthogonal $n \times n$ matrix with columns $q_1, \ldots, q_n$, then the elements of the matrix $Q^\mathrm{T} Q$ are $q_i^\mathrm{T} q_j = I(i = j)$, where $I(\cdot)$ is the indicator function[9]; hence, $Q^TQ = I_n$. Thus, $Q^T = Q^{-1}$. It follows now from Theorem I.1 also that $QQ^T = I_n$, that is, the rows of an orthogonal matrix are also orthonormal.

Orthogonal transformations of vectors leave the angles between the vectors, and their lengths, the same. In particular, let x and y be vectors in $\mathbb{R}^n$ and let Q be an orthogonal $n \times n$ matrix. Then $(Qx)^T(Qy) = x^TQ^TQy = x^Ty$, $\|Qx\| = \sqrt{(Qx)^T(Qx)} = \sqrt{x^Tx} = \|x\|$; hence, it follows from (I.41) that the angle between Qx and Qy is the same as the angle between x and y.

In the case $n = 2$, the effect of an orthogonal transformation is a rotation. A typical orthogonal 2×2 matrix takes the form

$$Q = \begin{pmatrix} \cos(\theta) & \sin(\theta) \\ \sin(\theta) & -\cos(\theta) \end{pmatrix}. \tag{I.45}$$

This matrix transforms the unit vector $e_1 = (1,0)^T$ into the vector $q_\theta = (\cos(\theta), \sin(\theta))^T$, and it follows from (I.41) that θ is the angle between the two. By moving θ from 0 to 2π, the vector q_θ rotates counterclockwise from the initial position e_1 back to e_1.

I.11. Determinants: Geometric Interpretation and Basic Properties

The area enclosed by the parallelogram in Figure I.3 has a special meaning, namely, the *determinant* of the matrix

$$A = (a, b) = \begin{pmatrix} a_1 & b_1 \\ a_2 & b_2 \end{pmatrix} = \begin{pmatrix} 6 & 3 \\ 4 & 7 \end{pmatrix}. \tag{I.46}$$

The determinant is denoted by $\det(A)$. This area is two times the area enclosed by the triangle formed by the origin and the points a and b in Figure I.3 and in its turn is the sum of the areas enclosed by the triangle formed by the origin, point b, and the projection

$$p = (a^Tb/a^Ta) \cdot a = (a^Tb/\|a\|^2) \cdot a$$

of b on a and the triangle formed by the points p, a, and b in Figure I.4. The first triangle has area $1/2\|b - p\|$ times the distance of p to the origin, and the second triangle has area equal to $1/2\|b - p\|$ times the distance between p and a; hence, the determinant of A is

$$\begin{aligned} \det(A) &= \|b - p\| \cdot \|a\| = \|b - (a^Tb/\|a\|^2)\| \cdot \|a\| \\ &= \sqrt{\|a\|^2\|b\|^2 - (a^Tb)^2} \\ &= \sqrt{(a_1^2 + a_2^2)(b_1^2 + b_2^2) - (a_1b_1 + a_2b_2)^2} \\ &= \sqrt{(a_1b_2 - b_1a_2)^2} = \pm|a_1b_2 - b_1a_2| = a_1b_2 - b_1a_2. \end{aligned} \tag{I.47}$$

---

[9] $I(true) = 1$, $I(false) = 0$.

The last equality in (I.47) is a matter of normalization inasmuch as $-(a_1 b_2 - b_1 a_2)$ would also fit (I.47), but the chosen normalization is appropriate for (I.46) because, then,

$$\det(A) = a_1 b_2 - b_1 a_2 = 6 \times 7 - 3 \times 4 = 30. \tag{I.48}$$

However, as I will show for the matrix (I.50) below, a determinant can be negative or zero.

Equation (I.47) reads in words:

Definition I.16: *The determinant of a 2×2 matrix is the product of the diagonal elements minus the product of the off-diagonal elements.*

We can also express (I.47) in terms of the angles φ_a and φ_b of the vectors a and b, respectively, with the right-hand side of the horizontal axis:

$$a_1 = \|a\| \cos(\varphi_a), \qquad a_2 = \|a\| \sin(\varphi_a),$$
$$b_1 = \|b\| \cos(\varphi_b), \qquad b_2 = \|b\| \sin(\varphi_b);$$

hence,

$$\begin{aligned}
\det(A) &= a_1 b_2 - b_1 a_2 \\
&= \|a\| \cdot \|b\| \cdot (\cos(\varphi_a) \sin(\varphi_b) - \sin(\varphi_a) \cos(\varphi_b)) \\
&= \|a\| \cdot \|b\| \cdot \sin(\varphi_b - \varphi_a).
\end{aligned} \tag{I.49}$$

Because, in Figure I.3, $0 < \varphi_b - \varphi_a < \pi$, we have that $\sin(\varphi_b - \varphi_a) > 0$.

As an example of a negative determinant, let us swap the columns of A and call the result matrix B:

$$B = A P_{1,2} = (b, a) = \begin{pmatrix} b_1 & a_1 \\ b_2 & a_2 \end{pmatrix} = \begin{pmatrix} 3 & 6 \\ 7 & 4 \end{pmatrix}, \tag{I.50}$$

where

$$P_{1,2} = \begin{pmatrix} 0 & 1 \\ 1 & 0 \end{pmatrix}$$

is the elementary permutation matrix involved. Then

$$\det(B) = b_1 a_2 - a_1 b_2 = -30.$$

At first sight this seems odd because the area enclosed by the parallelogram in Figure I.3 has not been changed. However, it has! Recall the interpretation of a matrix as a mapping: A matrix moves a point to a new location by replacing the original perpendicular coordinate system by a new system formed by the

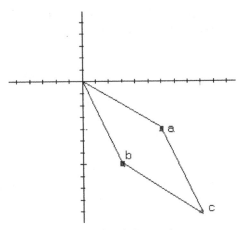

Figure I.6. Backside of Figure I.3.

columns space of the matrix involved with new units of measurement the lengths of the columns. In the case of the matrix B in (I.50) we have

$$
\begin{array}{ccc}
 & \textit{Unit vectors} & \\
\textit{Axis} & \textit{Original} & \textit{New} \\
1: & e_1 = \begin{pmatrix} 1 \\ 0 \end{pmatrix} & \rightarrow \quad b = \begin{pmatrix} 3 \\ 7 \end{pmatrix} \\
2: & e_2 = \begin{pmatrix} 0 \\ 1 \end{pmatrix} & \rightarrow \quad a = \begin{pmatrix} 6 \\ 4 \end{pmatrix}
\end{array}
$$

Thus, b is now the first unit vector, and a is the second. If we adopt the convention that the natural position of unit vector 2 is above the line spanned by the first unit vector, as is the case for e_1 and e_2, then we are actually looking at the parallelogram in Figure I.3 from the *backside*, as in Figure I.6.

Thus, the effect of swapping the columns of the matrix A in (I.46) is that Figure I.3 is *flipped over vertically* $180°$. Because we are now looking at Figure I.3 from the back, which is the negative side, the area enclosed by the parallelogram is negative too! Note that this corresponds to (I.49): If we swap the columns of A, then we swap the angles φ_a and φ_b in (I.49); consequently, the determinant flips sign.

As another example, let a be as before, but now position b in the southwest quadrant, as in Figures I.7 and I.8. The fundamental difference between these two cases is that in Figure I.7 point b is *above* the line through a and the origin, and thus $\varphi_b - \varphi_a < \pi$, whereas in Figure I.8 point b is *below* that line: $\varphi_b - \varphi_a > \pi$. Therefore, the area enclosed by the parallelogram in Figure I.7 is positive, whereas the area enclosed by the parallelogram in Figure I.8 is

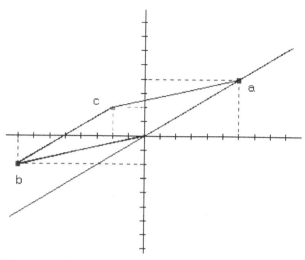

Figure I.7. $\det(a, b) > 0$.

negative. Hence, in the case of Figure I.7, $\det(a, b) > 0$, and in the case of Figure I.8, $\det(a, b) < 0$. Again, in Figure I.8 we are looking at the backside of the picture; you have to flip it vertically to see the front side.

What I have demonstrated here for 2×2 matrices is that, if the columns are interchanged, then the determinant changes sign. It is easy to see that the same

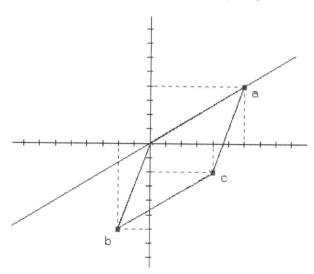

Figure I.8. $\det(a, b) < 0$.

applies to the rows. This property holds for general $n \times n$ matrices as well in the following way.

Theorem I.18: *If two adjacent columns or rows of a square matrix are swapped,*[10] *then the determinant changes sign only.*

Next, let us consider determinants of special 2×2 matrices. The first special case is the orthogonal matrix. Recall that the columns of an orthogonal matrix are perpendicular and have unit length. Moreover, recall that an orthogonal 2×2 matrix *rotates* a set of points around the origin, leaving angles and distances the same. In particular, consider the set of points in the unit square formed by the vectors $(0, 0)^T$, $(0, 1)^T$, $(1, 0)^T$, and $(1, 1)^T$. Clearly, the area of this unit square equals 1, and because the unit square corresponds to the 2×2 unit matrix I_2, the determinant of I_2 equals 1. Now multiply I_2 by an orthogonal matrix Q. The effect is that the unit square is rotated without affecting its shape or size. Therefore,

Theorem I.19: *The determinant of an orthogonal matrix is either* 1 *or* -1, *and the determinant of a unit matrix is* 1.

The "either–or" part follows from Theorem I.18: swapping adjacent columns of an orthogonal matrix preserves orthonormality of the columns of the new matrix but switches the sign of the determinant. For example, consider the orthogonal matrix Q in (I.45). Then it follows from Definition I.16 that

$$\det(Q) = -\cos^2(\theta) - \sin^2(\theta) = -1.$$

Now swap the columns of the matrix (I.45):

$$Q = \begin{pmatrix} \sin(\theta) & -\cos(\theta) \\ \cos(\theta) & \sin(\theta) \end{pmatrix}.$$

Then it follows from Definition I.16 that

$$\det(Q) = \sin^2(\theta) + \cos^2(\theta) = 1.$$

Note that Theorem I.19 is not confined to the 2×2 case; it is true for orthogonal and unit matrices of any size.

Next, consider the lower-triangular matrix

$$L = \begin{pmatrix} a & 0 \\ b & c \end{pmatrix}.$$

---

[10] The operation of swapping a pair of adjacent columns or rows is also called a column or row exchange, respectively.

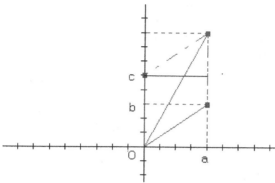

Figure I.9. det(L).

According to Definition I.16, $\det(L) = a \cdot c - 0 \cdot c = a \cdot c$, and thus in the 2×2 case the determinant of a lower-triangular matrix is the product of the diagonal elements. This is illustrated in Figure I.9. The determinant of L is the area in the parallelogram, which is the same as the area in the rectangle formed by the vectors $(a, 0)^T$ and $(0, c)^T$. This area is $a \cdot c$. Thus, you can move b freely along the vertical axis without affecting the determinant of L. If you were to flip the picture over vertically, which corresponds to replacing a by $-a$, the parallelogram would be viewed from the backside; hence, the determinant flips sign.

The same result applies of course to upper-triangular and diagonal 2×2 matrices. Thus, we have

Theorem I.20: *The determinant of a lower-triangular matrix is the product of the diagonal elements. The same applies to an upper-triangular matrix and a diagonal matrix.*

Again, this result is not confined to the 2×2 case but holds in general.

Now consider the determinant of a transpose matrix. In the 2×2 case the transpose A^T of A can be formed by first swapping the columns and then swapping the rows. Then it follows from Theorem I.18 that in each of the two steps only the sign flips; hence,

Theorem I.21: $det(A) = det(A^T)$.

The same applies to the general case: the transpose of A can be formed by a sequence of column exchanges and a corresponding sequence of row exchanges, and the total number of column and row exchanges is an even number.

It follows from Theorem I.11 that, in the case of a square matrix A, there exist a permutation matrix P possibly equal to the unit matrix I, a lower-triangular matrix L with diagonal elements all equal to 1, a diagonal matrix D, and an upper-triangular matrix U with diagonal elements all equal to 1 such that $PA = LDU$. Moreover, recall that a permutation matrix is orthogonal because it consists of permutations of the columns of the unit matrix. Thus, we can write $A = P^{\mathrm{T}}LDU$.

Now consider the parallelogram formed by the columns of U. Because the diagonal elements of U are 1, the area of this parallelogram is the same as the area of the unit square: $\det(U) = \det(I)$. Therefore, the effect of the transformation $P^{\mathrm{T}}LD$ on the area of the parallelogram formed by the columns of U is the same as the effect of $P^{\mathrm{T}}LD$ on the area of the unit square, and consequently $\det(P^{\mathrm{T}}LDU) = \det(P^{\mathrm{T}}LD)$. The effect of multiplying D by L is that the rectangle formed by the columns of D is tilted and squeezed without affecting the area itself. Therefore, $\det(LD) = \det(D)$, and consequently $\det(P^{\mathrm{T}}LDU) = \det(P^{\mathrm{T}}D)$. Next, P^{T} permutates the rows of D, and so the effect on $\det(D)$ is a sequence of sign switches only. The number of sign switches involved is the same as the number of column exchanges of P^{T} necessary to convert P^{T} into the unit matrix. If this number of swaps is even, then $\det(P) = \det(P^{\mathrm{T}}) = 1$; otherwise, $\det(P) = \det(P^{\mathrm{T}}) = -1$. Thus, in the 2×2 case (as well as in the general case) we have

Theorem I.22: $det(A) = det(P) \cdot det(D)$, where P and D are the permutation matrix and the diagonal matrix, respectively, in the decomposition $PA = LDU$ in Theorem I.11 for the case of a square matrix A.

This result yields two important corollaries. First,

Theorem I.23: *The determinant of a singular matrix is zero.*

To see this, observe from the decomposition $PA = LDU$ that A is singular if and only if D is singular. If D is singular, then at least one of the diagonal elements of D is zero; hence, $\det(D) = 0$.

Second, for conformable square matrices A and B we have

Theorem I.24: $det(AB) = det(A) \cdot det(B)$.

This result can be shown in the same way as Theorem I.22, that is, by showing that $\det(A) = \det(P^{\mathrm{T}}LDUB) = \det(P) \cdot \det(DB)$ and $\det(DB) = \det(D) \cdot \det(B)$.

Moreover, Theorems I.20 and I.24 imply that

Theorem I.25: *Adding or subtracting a constant times a row or column to another row or column, respectively, does not change the determinant.*

The reason is that this operation is equivalent to multiplying a matrix by an elementary matrix and that an elementary matrix is triangular with diagonal elements equal to 1.

Furthermore, we have

Theorem I.26: *Let A be an $n \times n$ matrix and let c be a scalar. If one of the columns or rows is multiplied by c, then the determinant of the resulting matrix is $c \cdot det(A)$. Consequently, $det(c \cdot A) = c^n \cdot det(A)$.*

This theorem follows straightforwardly from Theorems I.20 and I.24. For example, let B be a diagonal matrix with diagonal elements 1, except for one element, such as diagonal element i, which equals c. Then BA is the matrix A with the ith column multiplied by c. Because, by Theorem I.20, $det(B) = c$, the first part of Theorem I.26 for the "column" case follows from Theorem I.24, and the "row" case follows from $det(AB) = det(A) \cdot det(B) = c \cdot det(A)$. The second part follows by choosing $B = c \cdot I_n$.

The results in this section merely serve as a motivation for what a determinant is as well as its geometric interpretation and basic properties. All the results so far can be derived from three fundamental properties, namely, the results in Theorems I.18, I.20, and I.21. If we were to *assume* that the results in Theorems I.18, I.20, and I.21 hold and treat these properties as axioms, all the other results would follow from these properties and the decomposition $PA = LDU$. Moreover, the function involved is unique.

As to the latter, suppose that $\delta(A)$ is a function satisfying

(a) If two adjacent rows or columns are swapped, then δ switches sign only.
(b) If A is triangular, then $\delta(A)$ is the product of the diagonal elements of A.
(c) $\delta(AB) = \delta(A) \cdot \delta(B)$.

Then it follows from the decomposition $A = P^T LDU$ and axiom (c) that

$$\delta(A) = \delta(P^T)\delta(L)\delta(D)\delta(U).$$

Moreover, it follows from axiom (b) that $\delta(L) = \delta(U) = 1$ and $\delta(D) = det(D)$. Finally, it follows from axiom (b) that the functions $\delta(\cdot)$ and $det(\cdot)$ coincide for unit matrices and therefore by axiom (a), $\delta(P^T) = \delta(P) = det(P)$. Thus, $\delta(A) = det(A)$; hence, the determinant is uniquely defined by the axioms (a), (b), and (c). Consequently,

Definition I.17: *The determinant of a square matrix is uniquely defined by three fundamental properties*:

(a) *If two adjacent rows or columns are swapped, then the determinant switches sign only.*

(b) *The determinant of a triangular matrix is the product of the diagonal elements.*

(c) *The determinant of AB is the product of the determinants of A and B.*

These three axioms can be used to derive a general expression for the determinant together with the results in the next section regarding determinants of block-triangular matrices.

I.12. Determinants of Block-Triangular Matrices

Consider a square matrix A partitioned as

$$A = \begin{pmatrix} A_{1,1} & A_{1,2} \\ A_{2,1} & A_{2,2} \end{pmatrix},$$

where $A_{1,1}$ and $A_{2,2}$ are submatrices of size $k \times k$ and $m \times m$, respectively, $A_{1,2}$ is a $k \times m$ matrix, and $A_{2,1}$ is an $m \times k$ matrix. This matrix A is block-triangular if either $A_{1,2}$ or $A_{2,1}$ is a zero matrix, and it is block-diagonal if both $A_{1,2}$ and $A_{2,1}$ are zero matrices. In the latter case

$$A = \begin{pmatrix} A_{1,1} & O \\ O & A_{2,2} \end{pmatrix},$$

where the two O blocks represent zero elements. For each block $A_{1,1}$ and $A_{2,2}$ we can apply Theorem I.11, that is, $A_{1,1} = P_1^{\mathrm{T}} L_1 D_1 U_1$, $A_{2,2} = P_2^{\mathrm{T}} L_2 D_2 U_2$; hence,

$$\begin{aligned}
A &= \begin{pmatrix} P_1^{\mathrm{T}} L_1 D_1 U_1 & O \\ O & P_2^{\mathrm{T}} L_2 D_2 U_2 \end{pmatrix} \\
&= \begin{pmatrix} P_1 & O \\ O & P_2 \end{pmatrix}^{\mathrm{T}} \cdot \begin{pmatrix} L_1 & O \\ O & L_2 \end{pmatrix} \cdot \begin{pmatrix} D_1 & O \\ O & D_2 \end{pmatrix} \begin{pmatrix} U_1 & O \\ O & U_2 \end{pmatrix} = P^{\mathrm{T}} L D U,
\end{aligned}$$

for instance. Then $\det(A) = \det(P) \cdot \det(D) = \det(P_1) \cdot \det(P_2) \cdot \det(D_1) \cdot \det(D_2) = \det(A_{1,1}) \cdot \det(A_{2,2})$. More generally, we have that

Theorem I.27: *The determinant of a block-diagonal matrix is the product of the determinants of the diagonal blocks.*

Next, consider the lower block-diagonal matrix

$$A = \begin{pmatrix} A_{1,1} & O \\ A_{2,1} & A_{2,2} \end{pmatrix},$$

where again $A_{1,1}$ and $A_{2,2}$ are $k \times k$ and $m \times m$ matrices, respectively, and $A_{2,1}$ is an $m \times k$ matrix. Then it follows from Theorem I.25 that for any $k \times m$

matrix C,

$$\det(A) = \det\left[\begin{pmatrix} A_{1,1} & O \\ A_{2,1} - CA_{1,1} & A_{2,2} \end{pmatrix}\right].$$

If $A_{1,1}$ is nonsingular, then we can choose $C = A_{1,1}^{-1}A_{2,1}$ so that $A_{2,1} - CA_{1,1} = O$. In that case it follows from Theorem I.27 that $\det(A) = \det(A_{1,1}) \cdot \det(A_{2,2})$. If $A_{1,1}$ is singular, then the rows of $A_{1,1}$ are linear dependent, and so are the first k rows of A. Hence, if $A_{1,1}$ is singular, then A is singular; thus, by Theorem I.23, $\det(A) = \det(A_{1,1}) \cdot \det(A_{2,2}) = 0$. Consequently,

Theorem I.28: *The determinant of a block-triangular matrix is the product of the determinants of the diagonal blocks.*

I.13. Determinants and Cofactors

Consider the $n \times n$ matrix

$$A = \begin{pmatrix} a_{1,1} & \cdots & a_{1,n} \\ \vdots & \ddots & \vdots \\ a_{n,1} & \cdots & a_{n,n} \end{pmatrix} \tag{I.51}$$

and define the following matrix-valued function of A:

Definition I.18: *The transformation $\rho(A|i_1, i_2, \ldots, i_n)$ is a matrix formed by replacing all but the i_k's element a_{k,i_k} by zeros in rows $k = 1, \ldots, n$ of matrix (I.51). Similarly, the transformation $\kappa(A|i_1, i_2, \ldots, i_n)$ is a matrix formed by replacing all but the i_k's element $a_{i_k,k}$ by zeros in columns $k = 1, \ldots, n$ of matrix (I.51).*

For example, in the 3×3 case,

$$\rho(A|2, 3, 1) = \begin{pmatrix} 0 & a_{1,2} & 0 \\ 0 & 0 & a_{2,3} \\ a_{3,1} & 0 & 0 \end{pmatrix},$$

$$\kappa(A|2, 3, 1) = \begin{pmatrix} 0 & 0 & a_{1,3} \\ a_{2,1} & 0 & 0 \\ 0 & a_{3,2} & 0 \end{pmatrix}.$$

Recall that a permutation of the numbers $1, 2, \ldots, n$ is an ordered set of these n numbers and that there are $n!$ of these permutations, including the trivial permutation $1, 2, \ldots, n$. Moreover, it is easy to verify that, for each permutation $i_1, i_2, \ldots, i_n$ of $1, 2, \ldots, n$, there exists a unique permutation $j_1, j_2, \ldots, j_n$

such that $\rho(A|i_1, i_2, \ldots, i_n) = \kappa(A|j_1, j_2, \ldots, j_n)$ and vice versa. Now define the function

$$
\begin{aligned}
\delta(A) &= \sum \det[\rho(A|i_1, i_2, \ldots, i_n)] \\
&= \sum \det[\kappa(A|i_1, i_2, \ldots, i_n)],
\end{aligned} \tag{I.52}
$$

where the summation is over all permutations $i_1, i_2, \ldots, i_n$ of $1, 2, \ldots, n$.

Note that $\det[\rho(A|i_1, i_2, \ldots, i_n)] = \pm a_{1,i_1} a_{2,i_2} \cdots a_{n,i_n}$, where the sign depends on how many row or column exchanges are needed to convert $\rho(A|i_1, i_2, \ldots, i_n)$ into a diagonal matrix. If the number of exchanges is even, the sign is $+$; the sign is $-$ if this number is odd. Clearly, this sign is the same as the sign of the determinant of the permutation matrix $\rho(E_n|i_1, i_2, \ldots, i_n)$, where E_n is the $n \times n$ matrix with all elements equal to 1.

I will show now that $\delta(A)$ in (I.52) satisfies the axioms in Definition I.17, and thus:

Theorem I.29: *The function $\delta(A)$ in (I.52) is the determinant of $A : \delta(A) = det(A)$.*

Proof: First, exchange rows of A such as rows 1 and 2, for example. The new matrix is $P_{12}A$, where P_{12} is the elementary permutation matrix involved, that is, the unit matrix with the first two columns exchanged. Then $\rho(P_{12}A|i_1, i_2, \ldots, i_n) = P_{12}\rho(A|i_1, i_2, \ldots, i_n)$; hence, $\delta(P_{12}A) = \det(P_{1,2})\delta(A) = -\delta(A)$. Thus, $\delta(A)$ satisfies axiom (a) in Definition I.17.

Second, let A be lower triangular. Then $\rho(A|i_1, i_2, \ldots, i_n)$ is lower triangular but has at least one zero diagonal element for all permutations $i_1, i_2, \ldots, i_n$ except for the trivial permutation $1, 2, \ldots, n$. Thus, in this case $\delta(A) = \det[\rho(A|1, 2, \ldots, n) = \det(A)$. The same applies, of course, to upper-triangular and diagonal matrices. Consequently $\delta(A)$ satisfies axiom (b) in Definition I.17.

Finally, observe that $\rho(AB|i_1, i_2, \ldots, i_n)$ is a matrix with elements $\sum_{k=1}^{n} a_{m,k} b_{k,i_m}$ in position (m, i_m), $m = 1, \ldots, n$ and zeros elsewhere. Hence,

$$\rho(AB|i_1, i_2, \ldots, i_n) = A \cdot \rho(B|i_1, i_2, \ldots, i_n),$$

which implies that

$$\delta(AB) = \det(A) \cdot \delta(B). \tag{I.53}$$

Now write B as $B = P^{\mathsf{T}}LDU$, and observe from (I.53) and axiom (b) that $\delta(B) = \delta((P^{\mathsf{T}}LD)U) = \det(P^{\mathsf{T}}LD)\delta(U) = \det(P^{\mathsf{T}}LD)\det(U) = \det(B)$. The same applies to A. Thus,

$$\delta(AB) = \det(A) \cdot \det(B) = \delta(A) \cdot \delta(B). \tag{I.54}$$

Q.E.D.

Next, consider the following transformation.

Definition I.19: *The transformation $\tau(A|k, m)$ is a matrix formed by replacing all elements in row k and column m by zeros except element $a_{k,m}$ itself.*

For example, in the 3×3 case,

$$\tau(A|2, 3) = \begin{pmatrix} a_{1,1} & a_{1,2} & 0 \\ 0 & 0 & a_{2,3} \\ a_{3,1} & a_{3,2} & 0 \end{pmatrix}. \tag{I.55}$$

Then it follows from (I.52) and Theorem I.29 that

$$\det[\tau(A|k, m)] = \sum_{i_k=m} \det[\rho(A|i_1, i_2, \ldots, i_n)]$$

$$= \sum_{i_k=k} \det[\kappa(A|i_1, i_2, \ldots, i_n)]; \tag{I.56}$$

hence,

Theorem I.30: *For $n \times n$ matrices A, $\det(A) = \sum_{m=1}^{n} \det[\tau(A|k, m)]$ for $k = 1, 2, \ldots, n$ and $\det(A) = \sum_{k=1}^{n} \det[\tau(A|k, m)]$ for $m = 1, 2, \ldots, n$.*

Now let us evaluate the determinant of the matrix (I.55). Swap rows 1 and 2, and then recursively swap columns 2 and 3 and columns 1 and 2. The total number of row and column exchanges is 3; hence,

$$\det[\tau(A|2, 3)] = (-1)^3 \det \left[\begin{pmatrix} a_{2,3} & 0 & 0 \\ 0 & a_{1,1} & a_{1,2} \\ 0 & a_{3,1} & a_{3,2} \end{pmatrix} \right]$$

$$= a_{2,3}(-1)^{2+3} \det \left[\begin{pmatrix} a_{1,1} & a_{1,2} \\ a_{3,1} & a_{3,2} \end{pmatrix} \right] = a_{2,3} \text{cof}_{2,3}(A),$$

for instance, where $\text{cof}_{2,3}(A)$ is the *cofactor* of element $a_{2,3}$ of A. Note that the second equality follows from Theorem I.27. Similarly, we need $k - 1$ row exchanges and $m - 1$ column exchanges to convert $\tau(A|k, m)$ into a block-diagonal matrix. More generally,

Definition I.20: *The cofactor $\text{cof}_{k,m}(A)$ of an $n \times n$ matrix A is the determinant of the $(n - 1) \times (n - 1)$ matrix formed by deleting row k and column m times $(-1)^{k+m}$.*

Thus, Theorem I.30 now reads as follows:

Theorem I.31: *For $n \times n$ matrices A, $\det(A) = \sum_{m=1}^{n} a_{k,m} cof_{k,m}(A)$ for $k = 1, 2, \ldots, n$, and also $\det(A) = \sum_{k=1}^{n} a_{k,m} cof_{k,m}(A)$ for $m = 1, 2, \ldots, n$.*

I.14. Inverse of a Matrix in Terms of Cofactors

Theorem I.31 now enables us to write the inverse of a matrix A in terms of cofactors and the determinant as follows. Define

Definition I.20: *The matrix*

$$A_{adjoint} = \begin{pmatrix} cof_{1,1}(A) & \cdots & cof_{n,1}(A) \\ \vdots & \ddots & \vdots \\ cof_{1,n}(A) & \cdots & cof_{n,n}(A) \end{pmatrix} \tag{I.57}$$

is called the adjoint matrix of A.

Note that the adjoint matrix is the transpose of the matrix of cofactors with typical (i, j)'s element $cof_{i,j}(A)$. Next, observe from Theorem I.31 that $\det(A) = \sum_{k=1}^{n} a_{i,k} cof_{i,k}(A)$ is just the diagonal element i of $A \cdot A_{adjoint}$. Moreover, suppose that row j of A is replaced by row i, and call this matrix B. This has no effect on $cof_{j,k}(A)$, but $\sum_{k=1}^{n} a_{i,k} cof_{j,k}(A) = \sum_{k=1}^{n} a_{i,k} cof_{i,k}(B)$ is now the determinant of B. Because the rows of B are linear dependent, $\det(B) = 0$. Thus, we have

$$\begin{aligned} \sum_{k=1}^{n} a_{i,k} cof_{j,k}(A) &= \det(A) \quad \text{if } i = j, \\ &= 0 \quad \text{if } i \neq j; \end{aligned}$$

hence,

Theorem I.32: *If $\det(A) \neq 0$, then $A^{-1} = \frac{1}{\det(A)} A_{adjoint}$.*

Note that the cofactors $cof_{j,k}(A)$ do not depend on $a_{i,j}$. It follows therefore from Theorem I.31 that

$$\frac{\partial \det(A)}{\partial a_{i,j}} = cof_{i,j}(A). \tag{I.58}$$

Using the well-known fact that $d \ln(x)/dx = 1/x$, we find now from Theorem I.32 and (I.58) that

Theorem I.33: *If $\det(A) > 0$ then*

$$\frac{\partial \ln[\det(A)]}{\partial A} \overset{def.}{=} \begin{pmatrix} \frac{\partial \ln[\det(A)]}{\partial a_{1,1}} & \cdots & \frac{\partial \ln[\det(A)]}{\partial a_{n,1}} \\ \vdots & \ddots & \vdots \\ \frac{\partial \ln[\det(A)]}{\partial a_{1,n}} & \cdots & \frac{\partial \ln[\det(A)]}{\partial a_{n,n}} \end{pmatrix} = A^{-1}. \tag{I.59}$$

Note that (I.59) generalizes the formula $d \ln(x)/dx = 1/x$ to matrices. This result will be useful in deriving the maximum likelihood estimator of the variance matrix of the multivariate normal distribution.

I.15. Eigenvalues and Eigenvectors

I.15.1. Eigenvalues

Eigenvalues and eigenvectors play a key role in modern econometrics – in particular in cointegration analysis. These econometric applications are confined to eigenvalues and eigenvectors of symmetric matrices, that is, square matrices A for which $A = A^\mathrm{T}$. Therefore, I will mainly focus on the symmetric case.

Definition I.21: *The eigenvalues*[11] *of an $n \times n$ matrix A are the solutions for λ of the equation $\det(A - \lambda I_n) = 0$.*

It follows from Theorem I.29 that $\det(A) = \sum \pm a_{1,i_1} a_{2,i_2} \dots a_{n,i_n}$, where the summation is over all permutations $i_1, i_2, \dots, i_n$ of $1, 2, \dots, n$. Therefore, if we replace A by $A - \lambda I_n$ it is not hard to verify that $\det(A - \lambda I_n)$ is a polynomial of order n in λ, $\det(A - \lambda I_n) = \sum_{k=0}^{n} c_k \lambda^k$, where the coefficients c_k are functions of the elements of A.

For example, in the 2×2 case

$$A = \begin{pmatrix} a_{1,1} & a_{1,2} \\ a_{2,1} & a_{2,2} \end{pmatrix}$$

we have

$$\det(A - \lambda I_2) = \det \left[\begin{pmatrix} a_{1,1} - \lambda & a_{1,2} \\ a_{2,1} & a_{2,2} - \lambda \end{pmatrix} \right]$$
$$= (a_{1,1} - \lambda)(a_{2,2} - \lambda) - a_{1,2} a_{2,1}$$
$$= \lambda^2 - (a_{1,1} + a_{2,2})\lambda + a_{1,1} a_{2,2} - a_{1,2} a_{2,1},$$

which has two roots, that is, the solutions of $\lambda^2 - (a_{1,1} + a_{2,2})\lambda + a_{1,1} a_{2,2} - a_{1,2} a_{2,1} = 0$:

$$\lambda_1 = \frac{a_{1,1} + a_{2,2} + \sqrt{(a_{1,1} - a_{2,2})^2 + 4 a_{1,2} a_{2,1}}}{2},$$

$$\lambda_2 = \frac{a_{1,1} + a_{2,2} - \sqrt{(a_{1,1} - a_{2,2})^2 + 4 a_{1,2} a_{2,1}}}{2}.$$

There are three cases to be distinguished. If $(a_{1,1} - a_{2,2})^2 + 4 a_{1,2} a_{2,1} > 0$, then

---

[11] Eigenvalues are also called characteristic roots. The name "eigen" comes from the German adjective *eigen*, which means "inherent," or "characteristic."

λ_1 and λ_2 are different and real valued. If $(a_{1,1} - a_{2,2})^2 + 4a_{1,2}a_{2,1} = 0$, then $\lambda_1 = \lambda_2$ and they are real valued. However, if $(a_{1,1} - a_{2,2})^2 + 4a_{1,2}a_{2,1} < 0$, then λ_1 and λ_2 are different but complex valued:

$$\lambda_1 = \frac{a_{1,1} + a_{2,2} + i \cdot \sqrt{-(a_{1,1} - a_{2,2})^2 - 4a_{1,2}a_{2,1}}}{2},$$

$$\lambda_2 = \frac{a_{1,1} + a_{2,2} - i \cdot \sqrt{-(a_{1,1} - a_{2,2})^2 - 4a_{1,2}a_{2,1}}}{2},$$

where $i = \sqrt{-1}$. In this case λ_1 and λ_2 are complex conjugate: $\lambda_2 = \bar{\lambda}_1$.[12] Thus, eigenvalues can be complex valued!

Note that if the matrix A involved is symmetric (i.e., $a_{1,2} = a_{2,1}$), then

$$\lambda_1 = \frac{a_{1,1} + a_{2,2} + \sqrt{(a_{1,1} - a_{2,2})^2 + 4a_{1,2}^2}}{2},$$

$$\lambda_2 = \frac{a_{1,1} + a_{2,2} - \sqrt{(a_{1,1} - a_{2,2})^2 + 4a_{1,2}^2}}{2},$$

and thus in the symmetric 2×2 case the eigenvalues are always real valued. It will be shown in Section I.15.3 that this is true for all symmetric $n \times n$ matrices.

I.15.2. Eigenvectors

By Definition I.21 it follows that if λ is an eigenvalue of an $n \times n$ matrix A, then $A - \lambda I_n$ is a singular matrix (possibly complex valued!). Suppose first that λ is real valued. Because the rows of $A - \lambda I_n$ are linear dependent there exists a vector $x \in \mathbb{R}^n$ such that $(A - \lambda I_n)x = 0$ $(\in R^n)$; hence, $Ax = \lambda x$. Such a vector x is called an eigenvector of A corresponding to the eigenvalue λ. Thus, in the real eigenvalue case:

Definition I.22: *An eigenvector*[13] *of an $n \times n$ matrix A corresponding to an eigenvalue λ is a vector x such that $Ax = \lambda x$.*

However, this definition also applies to the complex eigenvalue case, but then the eigenvector x has complex-valued components: $x \in \mathbb{C}^n$. To show the latter, consider the case that λ is complex valued: $\lambda = \alpha + i \cdot \beta$, $\alpha, \beta \in \mathbb{R}$, $\beta \neq 0$. Then

$$A - \lambda I_n = A - \alpha I_n - i \cdot \beta I_n$$

---

[12] Recall that the complex conjugate of $x = a + i \cdot b$, $a, b \in \mathbb{R}$, is $\bar{x} = a - i \cdot b$. See Appendix III.

[13] Eigenvectors are also called characteristic vectors.

is complex valued with linear-dependent rows in the following sense. There exists a vector $x = a + i \cdot b$ with $a, b \in \mathbb{R}^n$ and length[14] $\|x\| = \sqrt{a^{\mathsf{T}} a + b^{\mathsf{T}} b} > 0$ such that

$$(A - \alpha I_n - i \cdot \beta I_n)(a + i \cdot b)$$
$$= [(A - \alpha I_n)a + \beta b] + i \cdot [(A - \alpha I_n)b - \beta a] = 0 (\in \mathbb{R}^n).$$

Consequently, $(A - \alpha I_n)a + \beta b = 0$ and $(A - \alpha I_n)b - \beta a = 0$; thus,

$$\begin{pmatrix} A - \alpha I_n & \beta I_n \\ -\beta I_n & A - \alpha I_n \end{pmatrix} \begin{pmatrix} a \\ b \end{pmatrix} = \begin{pmatrix} 0 \\ 0 \end{pmatrix} \in \mathbb{R}^{2n}. \tag{I.60}$$

Therefore, in order for the length of x to be positive, the matrix in (I.60) has to be singular; then $\binom{a}{b}$ can be chosen from the null space of this matrix.

I.15.3. Eigenvalues and Eigenvectors of Symmetric Matrices

On the basis of (I.60) it is easy to show that, in the case of a symmetric matrix A, $\beta = 0$ and $b = 0$:

Theorem I.34: *The eigenvalues of a symmetric $n \times n$ matrix A are all real valued, and the corresponding eigenvectors are contained in $\mathbb{R}^n$.*

Proof: First, note that (I.60) implies that, for arbitrary $\xi \in \mathbb{R}$,

$$0 = \begin{pmatrix} b \\ \xi a \end{pmatrix}^{\mathsf{T}} \begin{pmatrix} A - \alpha I_n & \beta I_n \\ -\beta I_n & A - \alpha I_n \end{pmatrix} \begin{pmatrix} a \\ b \end{pmatrix}$$
$$= \xi a^{\mathsf{T}} A b + b^{\mathsf{T}} A a - \alpha b^{\mathsf{T}} a - \xi \alpha a^{\mathsf{T}} b + \beta b^{\mathsf{T}} b - \xi \beta a^{\mathsf{T}} a.$$

Next observe that $b^{\mathsf{T}} a = a^{\mathsf{T}} b$ and by symmetry, $b^{\mathsf{T}} A a = (b^{\mathsf{T}} A a)^{\mathsf{T}} = a^{\mathsf{T}} A^{\mathsf{T}} b = a^{\mathsf{T}} A b$, where the first equality follows because $b^{\mathsf{T}} A a$ is a scalar (or 1×1 matrix). Then we have for arbitrary $\xi \in \mathbb{R}$,

$$(\xi + 1)a^{\mathsf{T}} A b - \alpha (\xi + 1)a^{\mathsf{T}} b + \beta (b^{\mathsf{T}} b - \xi a^{\mathsf{T}} a) = 0. \tag{I.61}$$

If we choose $\xi = -1$ in (I.61), then $\beta(b^{\mathsf{T}} b + a^{\mathsf{T}} a) = \beta \cdot \|x\|^2 = 0$; consequently, $\beta = 0$ and thus $\lambda = \alpha \in \mathbb{R}$. It is now easy to see that b no longer matters, and we may therefore choose $b = 0$. Q.E.D.

There is more to say about the eigenvectors of symmetric matrices, namely,

---

[14] Recall (see Appendix III) that the length (or norm) of a complex number $x = a + i \cdot b$, $a, b \in \mathbb{R}$, is defined as $|x| = \sqrt{(a + i \cdot b) \cdot (a - i \cdot b)} = \sqrt{a^2 + b^2}$. Similarly, in the vector case $x = a + i \cdot b$, $a, b \in \mathbb{R}^n$, the length of x is defined as $\|x\| = \sqrt{(a + i \cdot b)^{\mathsf{T}}(a - i \cdot b)} = \sqrt{a^{\mathsf{T}} a + b^{\mathsf{T}} b}$.

Theorem I.35: *The eigenvectors of a symmetric $n \times n$ matrix A can be chosen orthonormal.*

Proof: First assume that all the eigenvalues $\lambda_1, \lambda_2, \ldots, \lambda_n$ of A are different. Let $x_1, x_2, \ldots, x_n$ be the corresponding eigenvectors. Then for $i \neq j$, $x_i^T A x_j = \lambda_j x_i^T x_j$ and $x_j^T A x_i = \lambda_i x_j^T x_i$; hence, $(\lambda_i - \lambda_j) x_i^T x_j = 0$ because, by symmetry,

$$x_i^T A x_j = \left(x_i^T A x_j \right)^T = x_j^T A^T x_i = x_j^T A x_i.$$

Because $\lambda_i \neq \lambda_j$, it follows now that $x_i^T x_j = 0$. Upon normalizing the eigenvectors as $q_j = \|x_j\|^{-1} x_j$, we obtain the result.

The case in which two or more eigenvalues are equal requires a completely different proof. First, normalize the eigenvectors as $q_j = \|x_j\|^{-1} x_j$. Using the approach in Section I.10, we can always construct vectors $y_2, \ldots, y_n \in \mathbb{R}^n$ such that $q_1, y_2, \ldots, y_n$ is an orthonormal basis of $\mathbb{R}^n$. Then $Q_1 = (q_1, y_2, \ldots, y_n)$ is an orthogonal matrix. The first column of $Q_1^T A Q_1$ is $Q_1^T A q_1 = \lambda Q_1^T q_1$. But by the orthogonality of Q_1, $q_1^T Q_1 = q_1^T (q_1, y_2, \ldots, y_n) = (q_1^T q_1, q_1^T y_2, \ldots, q_1^T y_n) = (1, 0, 0, \ldots, 0)$; hence, the first column of $Q_1^T A Q_1$ is $(\lambda_1, 0, 0, \ldots, 0)^T$ and, by symmetry of $Q_1^T A Q_1$, the first row is $(\lambda_1, 0, 0, \ldots, 0)$. Thus, $Q_1^T A Q_1$ takes the form

$$Q_1^T A Q_1 = \begin{pmatrix} \lambda_1 & 0^T \\ 0 & A_{n-1} \end{pmatrix}.$$

Next, observe that

$$
\begin{aligned}
\det \left(Q_1^T A Q_1 - \lambda I_n \right) &= \det \left(Q_1^T A Q_1 - \lambda Q_1^T Q_1 \right) \\
&= \det \left[Q_1^T (A - \lambda I_n) Q_1 \right] \\
&= \det \left(Q_1^T \right) \det(A - \lambda I_n) \det(Q_1) \\
&= \det(A - \lambda I_n),
\end{aligned}
$$

and thus the eigenvalues of $Q_1^T A Q_1$ are the same as the eigenvalues of A; consequently, the eigenvalues of A_{n-1} are $\lambda_2, \ldots, \lambda_n$. Applying the preceding argument to A_{n-1}, we obtain an orthogonal $(n-1) \times (n-1)$ matrix Q_2^* such that

$$Q_2^{*T} A_{n-1} Q_2^* = \begin{pmatrix} \lambda_2 & 0^T \\ 0 & A_{n-2} \end{pmatrix}.$$

Hence, letting

$$Q_2 = \begin{pmatrix} 1 & 0^T \\ 0 & Q_2^* \end{pmatrix},$$

which is an orthogonal $n \times n$ matrix, we can write

$$Q_2^T Q_1^T A Q_1 Q_2 = \begin{pmatrix} \Lambda_2 & O \\ O & A_{n-2} \end{pmatrix},$$

where Λ_2 is a diagonal matrix with diagonal elements λ_1 and λ_2. Repeating this procedure $n-3$ more times yields

$$Q_n^{\mathrm{T}} \cdots Q_2^{\mathrm{T}} Q_1^{\mathrm{T}} A Q_1 Q_2 \dots Q_n = \Lambda,$$

where Λ_2 is the diagonal matrix with diagonal elements $\lambda_1, \lambda_2, \dots, \lambda_n$.

Note that $Q = Q_1 Q_2 \dots Q_n$, is an orthogonal matrix itself, and it is now easy to verify that the columns of Q are the eigenvectors of A.   Q.E.D.

In view of this proof, we can now restate Theorem I.35 as follows:

Theorem I.36: *A symmetric matrix A can be written as $A = Q\Lambda Q^{\mathrm{T}}$, where Λ is a diagonal matrix with the eigenvalues of A on the diagonal and Q is the orthogonal matrix with the corresponding eigenvectors as columns.*

This theorem yields several useful corollaries. The first one is trivial:

Theorem I.37: *The determinant of a symmetric matrix is the product of its eigenvalues.*

The next corollary concerns idempotent matrices (see Definition I.12):

Theorem I.38: *The eigenvalues of a symmetric idempotent matrix are either 0 or 1. Consequently, the only nonsingular symmetric idempotent matrix is the unit matrix I.*

Proof: Let the matrix A in Theorem I.36 be idempotent: $A \cdot A = A$. Then, $A = Q\Lambda Q^{\mathrm{T}} = A \cdot A = Q\Lambda Q^{\mathrm{T}} Q\Lambda Q^{\mathrm{T}} = Q\Lambda^2 Q^{\mathrm{T}}$; hence, $\Lambda = \Lambda^2$. Because Λ is diagonal, each diagonal element λ_j satisfies $\lambda_j = \lambda_j^2$; hence, $\lambda_j(1 - \lambda_j) = 0$. Moreover, if A is nonsingular and idempotent, then none of the eigenvalues can be zero; hence, they are all equal to $1 : \Lambda = I$. Then $A = QIQ^{\mathrm{T}} = A = QQ^{\mathrm{T}} = I$.   Q.E.D.

I.16. Positive Definite and Semidefinite Matrices

Another set of corollaries of Theorem I.36 concern positive (semi)definite matrices. Most of the symmetric matrices we will encounter in econometrics are positive (semi)definite or negative (semi)definite. Therefore, the following results are of the utmost importance to econometrics.

Definition I.23: *An $n \times n$ matrix A is called positive definite if, for arbitrary vectors $x \in \mathbb{R}^n$ unequal to the zero vector, $x^{\mathrm{T}} A x > 0$, and it is called positive semidefinite if for such vectors x, $x^{\mathrm{T}} A x \geq 0$. Moreover, A is called negative (semi)definite if $-A$ is positive (semi)definite.*

Note that symmetry is not required for positive (semi)definiteness. However, $x^T A x$ can always be written as

$$x^T A x = x^T \left(\frac{1}{2} A + \frac{1}{2} A^T \right) x = x^T A_s x, \tag{I.62}$$

for example, where A_s is symmetric; thus, A is positive or negative (semi)definite if and only if A_s is positive or negative (semi)definite.

Theorem I.39: *A symmetric matrix is positive (semi)definite if and only if all its eigenvalues are positive (nonnegative).*

Proof: This result follows easily from $x^T A x = x^T Q \Lambda Q^T x = y^T \Lambda y = \sum_j \lambda_j y_j^2$, where $y = Q^T x$ with components y_j. Q.E.D.

On the basis of Theorem I.39, we can now define arbitrary powers of positive definite matrices:

Definition I.24: *If A is a symmetric positive (semi)definite $n \times n$ matrix, then for $\alpha \in \mathbb{R}$ [$\alpha > 0$] the matrix A to the power α is defined by $A^\alpha = Q \Lambda^\alpha Q^T$, where Λ^α is a diagonal matrix with diagonal elements the eigenvalues of A to the power α: $\Lambda^\alpha = diag(\lambda_1^\alpha, \dots, \lambda_n^\alpha)$ and Q is the orthogonal matrix of corresponding eigenvectors.*

The following theorem is related to Theorem I.8.

Theorem I.40: *If A is symmetric and positive semidefinite, then the Gaussian elimination can be conducted without need for row exchanges. Consequently, there exists a lower-triangular matrix L with diagonal elements all equal to 1 and a diagonal matrix D such that $A = LDL^T$.*

Proof: First note that by Definition I.24 with $\alpha = 1/2$, $A^{1/2}$ is symmetric and $(A^{1/2})^T A^{1/2} = A^{1/2} A^{1/2} = A$. Second, recall that, according to Theorem I.17 there exists an orthogonal matrix Q and an upper-triangular matrix U such that $A^{1/2} = QU$; hence, $A = (A^{1/2})^T A^{1/2} = U^T Q^T Q U = U^T U$. The matrix U^T is lower triangular and can be written as $U^T = LD_*$, where D_* is a diagonal matrix and L is a lower-triangular matrix with diagonal elements all equal to 1. Thus, $A = LD_* D_* L^T = LDL^T$, where $D = D_* D_*$. Q.E.D.

I.17. Generalized Eigenvalues and Eigenvectors

The concepts of generalized eigenvalues and eigenvectors play a key role in cointegration analysis. Cointegration analysis is an advanced econometric time series topic and will therefore not likely be covered in an introductory Ph.D.-level econometrics course for which this review of linear algebra is intended.

Nevertheless, to conclude this review I will briefly discuss what generalized eigenvalues and eigenvectors are and how they relate to the standard case.

Given two $n \times n$ matrices A and B, the generalized eigenvalue problem is to find the values of λ for which

$$\det(A - \lambda B) = 0. \tag{I.63}$$

Given a solution λ, which is called the *generalized eigenvalue* of A relative to B, the corresponding *generalized eigenvector* (relative to B) is a vector x in $\mathbb{R}^n$ such that $Ax = \lambda Bx$.

However, if B is singular, then the generalized eigenvalue problem may not have n solutions as in the standard case and may even have no solution at all. To demonstrate this, consider the 2×2 case:

$$A = \begin{pmatrix} a_{1,1} & a_{1,2} \\ a_{2,1} & a_{2,2} \end{pmatrix}, \qquad B = \begin{pmatrix} b_{1,1} & b_{1,2} \\ b_{2,1} & b_{2,2} \end{pmatrix}.$$

Then,

$$
\begin{aligned}
\det(A - \lambda B) &= \det\left[\begin{pmatrix} a_{1,1} - \lambda b_{1,1} & a_{1,2} - \lambda b_{1,2} \\ a_{2,1} - \lambda b_{2,1} & a_{2,2} - \lambda b_{2,2} \end{pmatrix} \right] \\
&= (a_{1,1} - \lambda b_{1,1})(a_{2,2} - \lambda b_{2,2}) \\
&\quad - (a_{1,2} - \lambda b_{1,2})(a_{2,1} - \lambda b_{2,1}) \\
&= a_{1,1}a_{2,2} - a_{1,2}a_{2,1} \\
&\quad + (a_{2,1}b_{1,2} - a_{2,2}b_{1,1} - a_{1,1}b_{2,2} + b_{2,1}a_{1,2})\lambda \\
&\quad + (b_{1,1}b_{2,2} - b_{2,1}b_{1,2})\lambda^2.
\end{aligned}
$$

If B is singular, then $b_{1,1}b_{2,2} - b_{2,1}b_{1,2} = 0$, and thus the quadratic term vanishes. But the situation can even be worse! It is also possible that the coefficient of λ vanishes, whereas the constant term $a_{1,1}a_{2,2} - a_{1,2}a_{2,1}$ remains nonzero. In that case the generalized eigenvalues do not exist at all. This is, for example, the case if

$$A = \begin{pmatrix} 1 & 0 \\ 0 & -1 \end{pmatrix}, \qquad B = \begin{pmatrix} 1 & 1 \\ 1 & 1 \end{pmatrix}.$$

Then

$$
\begin{aligned}
\det(A - \lambda B) &= \det\left[\begin{pmatrix} 1 - \lambda & -\lambda \\ -\lambda & -1 - \lambda \end{pmatrix} \right] \\
&= -(1 - \lambda)(1 + \lambda) - \lambda^2 = -1,
\end{aligned}
$$

and thus the generalized eigenvalue problem involved has no solution.

Therefore, in general we need to require that the matrix B be nonsingular. In that case the solutions of (I.63) are the same as the solutions of the standard eigenvalue problems $\det(AB^{-1} - \lambda I) = 0$ and $\det(B^{-1}A - \lambda I) = 0$.

The generalized eigenvalue problems we will encounter in advanced econometrics always involve a pair of symmetric matrices A and B with B positive definite. Then the solutions of (I.63) are the same as the solutions of the symmetric, standard eigenvalue problem

$$\det(B^{-1/2}AB^{-1/2} - \lambda I) = 0. \tag{I.64}$$

The generalized eigenvectors relative to B corresponding to the solutions of (I.63) can be derived from the eigenvectors corresponding to the solutions of (I.64):

$$B^{-1/2}AB^{-1/2}x = \lambda x = \lambda B^{1/2}B^{-1/2}x \Rightarrow A(B^{-1/2}x)$$
$$= \lambda B(B^{-1/2}x). \tag{I.65}$$

Thus, if x is an eigenvector corresponding to a solution λ of (I.64), then $y = B^{-1/2}x$ is the generalized eigenvector relative to B corresponding to the generalized eigenvalue λ.

Finally, note that generalized eigenvectors are in general not orthogonal even if the two matrices involved are symmetric. However, in the latter case the generalized eigenvectors are "orthogonal with respect to the matrix B" in the sense that, for different generalized eigenvectors y_1 and y_2, $y_1^T B y_2 = 0$. This follows straightforwardly from the link $y = B^{-1/2}x$ between generalized eigenvectors y and standard eigenvectors x.

I.18. Exercises

1. Consider the matrix

$$A = \begin{pmatrix} 2 & 1 & 1 \\ 4 & -6 & 0 \\ -2 & 7 & 2 \end{pmatrix}.$$

   (a) Conduct the Gaussian elimination by finding a sequence E_j of elementary matrices such that $(E_k E_{k-1} \dots E_2 \cdot E_1) A = U = $ upper triangular.
   (b) Then show that, by undoing the elementary operations E_j involved, one gets the LU decomposition $A = LU$ with L a lower-triangular matrix with all diagonal elements equal to 1.
   (c) Finally, find the LDU factorization.

2. Find the 3×3 permutation matrix that swaps rows 1 and 3 of a 3×3 matrix.

3. Let

$$A = \begin{pmatrix} 1 & v_1 & 0 & 0 \\ 0 & v_2 & 0 & 0 \\ 0 & v_3 & 1 & 0 \\ 0 & v_4 & 0 & 1 \end{pmatrix},$$

   where $v_2 \neq 0$.

(a) Factorize A into LU.

(b) Find A^{-1}, which has the same form as A.

4. Compute the inverse of the matrix

$$A = \begin{pmatrix} 1 & 2 & 0 \\ 2 & 6 & 4 \\ 0 & 4 & 11 \end{pmatrix}$$

by any method.

5. Consider the matrix

$$A = \begin{pmatrix} 1 & 2 & 0 & 2 & 1 \\ -1 & -2 & 1 & 1 & 0 \\ 1 & 2 & -3 & -7 & -2 \end{pmatrix},$$

(a) Find the echelon matrix U in the factorization $PA = LU$.

(b) What is the rank of A?

(c) Find a basis for the null space of A.

(d) Find a basis for the column space of A.

6. Find a basis for the following subspaces of $\mathbb{R}^4$:

(a) The vectors $(x_1, x_2, x_3, x_4)^T$ for which $x_1 = 2x_4$.

(b) The vectors $(x_1, x_2, x_3, x_4)^T$ for which $x_1 + x_2 + x_3 = 0$ and $x_3 + x_4 = 0$.

(c) The subspace spanned by $(1, 1, 1, 1)^T$, $(1, 2, 3, 4)^T$, and $(2, 3, 4, 5)^T$.

7. Let

$$A = \begin{pmatrix} 1 & 2 & 0 & 3 \\ 0 & 0 & 0 & 0 \\ 2 & 4 & 0 & 1 \end{pmatrix} \quad \text{and} \quad b = \begin{pmatrix} b_1 \\ b_2 \\ b_3 \end{pmatrix}.$$

(a) Under what conditions on b does $Ax = b$ have a solution?

(b) Find a basis for the nullspace of A.

(c) Find the general solution of $Ax = b$ when a solution exists.

(d) Find a basis for the column space of A.

(e) What is the rank of A^T?

8. Apply the Gram–Smidt process to the vectors

$$a = \begin{pmatrix} 0 \\ 0 \\ 1 \end{pmatrix}, \qquad b = \begin{pmatrix} 0 \\ 1 \\ 1 \end{pmatrix}, \qquad c = \begin{pmatrix} 1 \\ 1 \\ 1 \end{pmatrix}$$

and write the result in the form $A = QU$, where Q is an orthogonal matrix and U is upper triangular.

9. With a, b, and c as in problem 8, find the projection of c on the space spanned by a and b.

10. Find the determinant of the matrix A in problem 1.

11. Consider the matrix

$$A = \begin{pmatrix} 1 & a \\ -1 & 1 \end{pmatrix}.$$

For which values of a has this matrix
(a) two different real-valued eigenvalues?
(b) two complex-valued eigenvalues?
(c) two equal real-valued eigenvalues?
(d) at least one zero eigenvalue?

12. For the case $a = -4$, find the eigenvectors of the matrix A in problem 11 and standardize them to unit length.

13. Let A be a matrix with eigenvalues 0 and 1 and corresponding eigenvectors $(1, 2)^{\mathrm{T}}$ and $(2, -1)^{\mathrm{T}}$.
(a) How can you tell in advance that A is symmetric?
(b) What is the determinant of A?
(c) What is A?

14. The trace of a square matrix is the sum of the diagonal elements. Let A be a positive definite $k \times k$ matrix. Prove that the maximum eigenvalue of A can be found as the limit of the ratio $\mathrm{trace}(A^n)/\mathrm{trace}(A^{n-1})$ for $n \to \infty$.

Appendix II – Miscellaneous Mathematics

This appendix reviews various mathematical concepts, topics, and related results that are used throughout the main text.

II.1. Sets and Set Operations

II.1.1. General Set Operations

The union $A \cup B$ of two sets A and B is the set of elements that belong to either A or B or to both. Thus, if we denote "belongs to" or "is an element of" by the symbol $\in$, $x \in A \cup B$ implies that $x \in A$ or $x \in B$, or in both, and vice versa. A finite union $\cup_{j=1}^{n} A_j$ of sets $A_1, \ldots, A_n$ is the set having the property that for each $x \in \cup_{j=1}^{n} A_j$ there exists an index i, $1 \leq i \leq n$, for which $x \in A_i$, and vice versa: If $x \in A_i$ for some index i, $1 \leq i \leq n$, then $x \in \cup_{j=1}^{n} A_j$. Similarly, the countable union $\cup_{j=1}^{\infty} A_j$ of an infinite sequence of sets A_j, $j = 1, 2, 3, \ldots$ is a set with the property that for each $x \in \cup_{j=1}^{\infty} A_j$ there exists a finite index $i \geq 1$ for which $x \in A_i$, and vice versa: If $x \in A_i$ for some finite index $i \geq 1$, then $x \in \cup_{j=1}^{\infty} A_j$.

The intersection $A \cap B$ of two sets A and B is the set of elements that belong to both A and B. Thus, $x \in A \cap B$ implies that $x \in A$ and $x \in B$, and vice versa. The finite intersection $\cap_{j=1}^{n} A_j$ of sets $A_1, \ldots, A_n$ is the set with the property that, if $x \in \cap_{j=1}^{n} A_j$, then for all $i = 1, \ldots, n$, $x \in A_i$ and vice versa: If $x \in A_i$ for all $i = 1, \ldots, n$, then $x \in \cap_{j=1}^{n} A_j$. Similarly, the countable intersection $\cap_{j=1}^{\infty} A_j$ of an infinite sequence of sets A_j, $j = 1, 2, \ldots$ is a set with the property that, if $x \in \cap_{j=1}^{\infty} A_j$, then for all indices $i \geq 1$, $x \in A_i$, and vice versa: If $x \in A_i$ for all indices $i \geq 1$, then $x \in \cap_{j=1}^{\infty} A_j$.

A set A is a subset of a set B, denoted by $A \subset B$, if all the elements of A are contained in B. If $A \subset B$ and $B \subset A$, then $A = B$.

The difference $A \backslash B$ (also denoted by $A - B$) of sets A and B is the set of elements of A that are not contained in B. The symmetric difference of two sets A and B is denoted and defined by $A \triangle B = (A/B) \cup (B/A)$.

If $A \subset B$, then the set $\tilde{A} = B/A$ (also denoted by $\sim A$) is called the complement of A with respect to B. If A_j for $j = 1, 2, 3, \ldots$ are subsets of B, then $\sim \cup_j A_j = \cap_j \tilde{A}_j$ and $\sim \cap_j A_j = \cup_j \tilde{A}_j$ for finite as well as countable infinite unions and intersections.

Sets A and B are disjoint if they do not have elements in common: $A \cap B = \emptyset$, where $\emptyset$ denotes the empty set, that is, a set without elements. Note that $A \cup \emptyset = A$ and $A \cap \emptyset = \emptyset$. Thus, the empty set $\emptyset$ is a subset of any set, including $\emptyset$ itself. Consequently, the empty set is disjoint with any other set, including $\emptyset$ itself. In general, a finite or countable infinite sequence of sets is disjoint if their finite or countable intersection is the empty set $\emptyset$.

For every sequence of sets $A_j, j = 1, 2, 3, \ldots$, there exists a sequence $B_j, j = 1, 2, 3, \ldots$ of disjoint sets such that for each j, $B_j \subset A_j$, and $\cup_j A_j = \cup_j B_j$. In particular, let $B_1 = A_1$ and $B_n = A_n \setminus \cup_{j=1}^{n-1} A_j$ for $n = 2, 3, 4, \ldots$.

The order in which unions are taken does not matter, and the same applies to intersections. However, if you take unions and intersections sequentially, it matters what is done first. For example, $(A \cup B) \cap C = (A \cap C) \cup (B \cap C)$, which is in general different from $A \cup (B \cap C)$ except if $A \subset C$. Similarly, $(A \cap B) \cup C = (A \cup C) \cap (B \cup C)$, which is in general different from $A \cap (B \cup C)$ except if $A \subset B$.

II.1.2. Sets in Euclidean Spaces

An open ε-neighborhood of a point x in a Euclidean space $\mathbb{R}^k$ is a set of the form

$$N_\varepsilon(x) = \{y \in \mathbb{R}^k : \|y - x\| < \varepsilon\}, \varepsilon > 0,$$

and a closed ε-neighborhood is a set of the form

$$\bar{N}_\varepsilon(x) = \{y \in \mathbb{R}^k : \|y - x\| \leq \varepsilon\}, \varepsilon > 0.$$

A set A is considered *open* if for *every* $x \in A$ there exists a small open ε-neighborhood $N_\varepsilon(x)$ contained in A. In shorthand notation: $\forall x \in A \; \exists \varepsilon > 0: N_\varepsilon(x) \subset A$, where $\forall$ stands for "for all" and $\exists$ stands for "there exists." Note that the ε's may be different for different x.

A point x is called a *point of closure* of a subset A of $\mathbb{R}^k$ if every open ε-neighborhood $N_\varepsilon(x)$ contains a point in A as well as a point in the complement $\tilde{A}$ of A. Note that points of closure may not exist, and if one exists it may not be contained in A. For example, the Euclidean space $\mathbb{R}^k$ itself has no points of closure because its complement is empty. Moreover, the interval $(0,1)$ has two points of closure, 0 and 1, both not included in $(0,1)$. The *boundary* of a set A, denoted by ∂A, is the set of points of closure of A. Again, ∂A may be empty. A set A is closed if it contains all its points of closure provided they exist. In other words, A is closed if and only if $\partial A \neq \emptyset$ and $\partial A \subset A$. Similarly, a set A is open if either $\partial A = \emptyset$ or $\partial A \subset \tilde{A}$. The *closure* of a set A, denoted by $\bar{A}$, is the union of A and its boundary ∂A: $\bar{A} = A \cup \partial A$. The set $A \backslash \partial A$ is the interior of A.

Finally, if for each pair x, y of points in a set A and an arbitrary $\lambda \in [0, 1]$ the convex combination $z = \lambda x + (1 - \lambda)y$ is also a point in A, then the set A is called *convex*.

II.2. Supremum and Infimum

The supremum of a sequence of real numbers, or a real function, is akin to the notion of a maximum value. In the latter case the maximum value is taken at some element of the sequence, or in the function case some value of the argument. Take for example the sequence $a_n = (-1)^n/n$ for $n = 1, 2, \ldots$, that is, $a_1 = -1, a_2 = 1/2, a_3 = -1/3, a_4 = 1/4, \ldots$. Then clearly the maximum value is $1/2$, which is taken by a_2. The latter is what distinguishes a maximum from a supremum. For example, the sequence $a_n = 1 - 1/n$ for $n = 1, 2, \ldots$ is bounded by 1: $a_n < 1$ for all indices $n \geq 1$, and the upper bound 1 is the lowest possible upper bound; however, a finite index n for which $a_n = 1$ does not exist. More formally, the (finite) supremum of a sequence $a_n(n = 1, 2, 3, \ldots)$ is a number b denoted by $\sup_{n \geq 1} a_n$ such that $a_n \leq b$ for all indices $n \geq 1$, and for every arbitrary small positive number ε there exists a finite index n such that $a_n > b - \varepsilon$. Clearly, this definition fits a maximum as well: a maximum is a supremum, but a supremum is not always a maximum.

If the sequence a_n is unbounded from above in the sense that for every arbitrary, large real number M there exists an index $n \geq 1$ for which $a_n > M$, then we say that the supremum is infinite: $\sup_{n \geq 1} a_n = \infty$.

The notion of a supremum also applies to functions. For example, the function $f(x) = \exp(-x^2)$ takes its maximum 1 at $x = 0$, but the function $f(x) = 1 - \exp(-x^2)$ does not have a maximum; it has supremum 1 because $f(x) \leq 1$ for all x, but there does not exist a finite x for which $f(x) = 1$. As another example, let $f(x) = x$ on the interval $[a, b]$. Then b is the maximum of $f(x)$ on $[a, b]$, but b is only the supremum $f(x)$ on $[a, b)$ because b is not contained in $[a, b)$. More generally, the finite supremum of a real function $f(x)$ on a set A, denoted by $\sup_{x \in A} f(x)$, is a real number b such that $f(x) \leq b$ for all x in A, and for every arbitrary, small positive number ε there exists an x in A such that $f(x) > b - \varepsilon$. If $f(x) = b$ for some x in A, then the supremum coincides with the maximum. Moreover, the supremum involved is infinite, $\sup_{x \in A} f(x) = \infty$, if for every arbitrary large real number M there exists an x in A for which $f(x) > M$.

The minimum versus infimum cases are similar:

$$\inf_{n \geq 1} a_n = -\sup_{n \geq 1}(-a_n) \quad \text{and} \quad \inf_{x \in A} f(x) = -\sup_{x \in A}(-f(x)).$$

The concepts of supremum and infimum apply to any collection $\{c_\alpha, \alpha \in A\}$ of real numbers, where the index set A may be uncountable, for we may interpret c_α as a real function on the index set A – for instance, $c_\alpha = f(\alpha)$.

II.3. Limsup and Liminf

Let $a_n(n = 1, 2, \ldots)$ be a sequence of real numbers, and define the sequence b_n as

$$b_n = \sup_{m \geq n} a_m. \tag{II.1}$$

Then b_n is a nonincreasing sequence: $b_n \geq b_{n+1}$ because, if a_n is greater than the smallest upper bound of $a_{n+1}, a_{n+2}, a_{n+3}, \ldots$, then a_n is the maximum of $a_n, a_{n+1}, a_{n+2}, a_{n+3}, \ldots$; hence, $b_n = a_n > b_{n+1}$ and, if not, then $b_n = b_{n+1}$. Nonincreasing sequences always have a limit, although the limit may be $-\infty$. The limit of b_n in (II.1) is called the limsup of a_n:

$$\limsup_{n \to \infty} a_n \overset{\text{def.}}{=} \lim_{n \to \infty} \left(\sup_{m \geq n} a_m \right). \tag{II.2}$$

Note that because b_n is nonincreasing, the limit of b_n is equal to the infimum of b_n. Therefore, the limsup of a_n may also be defined as

$$\limsup_{n \to \infty} a_n \overset{\text{def.}}{=} \inf_{n \geq 1} \left(\sup_{m \geq n} a_m \right). \tag{II.3}$$

Note that the limsup may be $+\infty$ or $-\infty$, for example, in the cases $a_n = n$ and $a_n = -n$, respectively.

Similarly, the liminf of a_n is defined by

$$\liminf_{n \to \infty} a_n \overset{\text{def.}}{=} \lim_{n \to \infty} \left(\inf_{m \geq n} a_m \right) \tag{II.4}$$

or equivalently by

$$\liminf_{n \to \infty} a_n \overset{\text{def.}}{=} \sup_{n \geq 1} \left(\inf_{m \geq n} a_m \right). \tag{II.5}$$

Again, it is possible that the liminf is $+\infty$ or $-\infty$.

Note that $\liminf_{n \to \infty} a_n \leq \limsup_{n \to \infty} a_n$ because $\inf_{m \geq n} a_m \leq \sup_{m \geq n} a_m$ for all indices $n \geq 1$, and therefore the inequality must hold for the limits as well.

Theorem II.1:

(a) If $\liminf_{n\to\infty} a_n = \limsup_{n\to\infty} a_n$, then $\lim_{n\to\infty} a_n = \limsup_{n\to\infty} a_n$, and if $\liminf_{n\to\infty} a_n < \limsup_{n\to\infty} a_n$, then the limit of a_n does not exist.

(b) Every sequence a_n contains a subsequence a_{n_k} such that $\lim_{k\to\infty} a_{n_k} = \limsup_{n\to\infty} a_n$, and a_n also contains a subsequence a_{n_m} such that $\lim_{m\to\infty} a_{n_m} = \liminf_{n\to\infty} a_n$.

Proof: The proof of (a) follows straightforwardly from (II.2), (II.4), and the definition of a limit. The construction of the subsequence a_{n_k} in part (b) can be done recursively as follows. Let $b = \limsup_{n\to\infty} a_n < \infty$. Choose $n_1 = 1$, and suppose that we have already constructed a_{n_j} for $j = 1, \ldots, k \geq 1$. Then there exists an index $n_{k+1} > n_k$ such that $a_{n_{k+1}} > b - 1/(k+1)$ because, otherwise, $a_m \leq b - 1/(k+1)$ for all $m \geq n_k$, which would imply that $\limsup_{n\to\infty} a_n \leq b - 1/(k+1)$. Repeating this construction yields a subsequence a_{n_k} such that, from large enough k onwards, $b - 1/k < a_{n_k} \leq b$. If we let $k \to \infty$, the limsup case of part (b) follows. If $\limsup_{n\to\infty} a_n = \infty$, then, for each index n_k we can find an index $n_{k+1} > n_k$ such that $a_{n_{k+1}} > k + 1$; hence, $\lim_{k\to\infty} a_{n_k} = \infty$. The subsequence in the case $\limsup_{n\to\infty} a_n = -\infty$ and in the liminf case can be constructed similarly. Q.E.D.

The concept of a supremum can be generalized to sets. In particular, the countable union $\cup_{j=1}^{\infty} A_j$ may be interpreted as the supremum of the sequence of sets A_j, that is, the smallest set containing all the sets A_j. Similarly, we may interpret the countable intersection $\cap_{j=1}^{\infty} A_j$ as the infimum of the sets A_j, that is, the largest set contained in each of the sets A_j. Now let $B_n = \cup_{j=n}^{\infty} A_j$ for $n = 1, 2, 3, \ldots$. This is a nonincreasing sequence of sets: $B_{n+1} \subset B_n$; hence, $\cap_{j=1}^{n} B_n = B_n$. The limit of this sequence of sets is the limsup of A_n for $n \to \infty$, that is, as in (II.3) we have

$$\limsup_{n\to\infty} A_n \overset{\text{def.}}{=} \bigcap_{n=1}^{\infty} \left(\bigcup_{j=n}^{\infty} A_j \right).$$

Next, let $C_n = \cap_{j=n}^{\infty} A_j$ for $n = 1, 2, 3, \ldots$. This is a nondecreasing sequence of sets: $C_n \subset C_{n+1}$; hence, $\cup_{j=1}^{n} C_n = C_n$. The limit of this sequence of sets is the liminf of A_n for $n \to \infty$, that is, as in (II.5) we have

$$\liminf_{n\to\infty} A_n \overset{\text{def.}}{=} \bigcup_{n=1}^{\infty} \left(\bigcap_{j=n}^{\infty} A_j \right).$$

II.4. Continuity of Concave and Convex Functions

A real function φ on a subset of a Euclidean space is convex if, for each pair of points a, b and every $\lambda \in [0, 1]$, $\varphi(\lambda a + (1 - \lambda)b) \geq \lambda \varphi(a) + (1 - \lambda)\varphi(b)$. For example, $\varphi(x) = x^2$ is a convex function on the real line, and so is $\varphi(x) =$

$\exp(x)$. Similarly, φ is concave if, for each pair of points a, b and every $\lambda \in [0, 1]$, $\varphi(\lambda a + (1 - \lambda)b) \leq \lambda\varphi(a) + (1 - \lambda)\varphi(b)$.

I will prove the continuity of convex and concave functions by contradiction. Suppose that φ is convex but not continuous in a point a. Then

$$\varphi(a+) = \lim_{b \downarrow a} \varphi(b) \neq \varphi(a) \qquad (\text{II}.6)$$

or

$$\varphi(a-) = \lim_{b \uparrow a} \varphi(b) \neq \varphi(a), \qquad (\text{II}.7)$$

or both. In the case of (II.6) we have

$$\varphi(a+) = \lim_{b \downarrow a} \varphi(a + 0.5(b - a)) = \lim_{b \downarrow a} \varphi(0.5a + 0.5b)$$
$$\leq 0.5\varphi(a) + 0.5 \lim_{b \downarrow a} \varphi(b) = 0.5\varphi(a) + 0.5\varphi(a+);$$

hence, $\varphi(a+) \leq \varphi(a)$, and therefore by (II.6), $\varphi(a+) < \varphi(a)$. Similarly, if (II.7) is true, then $\varphi(a-) < \varphi(a)$. Now let $\delta > 0$. By the convexity of φ, it follows that

$$\varphi(a) = \varphi(0.5(a - \delta) + 0.5(a + \delta)) \leq 0.5\varphi(a - \delta) + 0.5\varphi(a + \delta),$$

and consequently, letting $\delta \downarrow 0$ and using the fact that $\varphi(a+) < \varphi(a)$, or $\varphi(a-) < \varphi(a)$, or both, we have $\varphi(a) \leq 0.5\varphi(a-) + 0.5\varphi(a+) < \varphi(a)$. Because this result is impossible, it follows that (II.6) and (II.7) are impossible; hence, φ is continuous.

If φ is concave, then $-\varphi$ is convex and thus continuous; hence, concave functions are continuous.

II.5. Compactness

An (open) covering of a subset Θ of a Euclidean space $\mathbb{R}^k$ is a collection of (open) subsets $U(\alpha), \alpha \in A$, of $\mathbb{R}^k$, where A is a possibly uncountable index set such that $\Theta \subset \cup_{\alpha \in A} U(\alpha)$. A set is described as *compact* if every open covering has a finite subcovering; that is, if $U(\alpha), \alpha \in A$ is an open covering of Θ and Θ is compact, then there exists a finite subset B of A such that $\Theta \subset \cup_{\alpha \in B} U(\alpha)$.

The notion of compactness extends to more general spaces than only Euclidean spaces. However,

Theorem II.2: *Closed and bounded subsets of Euclidean spaces are compact.*

Proof: I will prove the result for sets Θ in $\mathbb{R}$ only. First note that boundedness is a necessary condition for compactness because a compact set can always be covered by a finite number of bounded open sets.

Next let Θ be a closed and bounded subset of the real line. By boundedness, there exist points a and b such that Θ is contained in $[a, b]$. Because every open covering of Θ can be extended to an open covering of $[a, b]$, we may without loss of generality assume that $\Theta = [a, b]$. For notational convenience, let $\Theta = [0, 1]$. There always exists an open covering of $[0, 1]$ because, for arbitrary $\varepsilon > 0$, $[0, 1] \subset \cup_{0 \le x \le 1}(x - \varepsilon, x + \varepsilon)$. Let $U(\alpha)$, $\alpha \in A$, be an open covering of $[0, 1]$. Without loss of generality we may assume that each of the open sets $U(\alpha)$ takes the form $(a(\alpha), b(\alpha))$. Moreover, if for two different indices α and β, $a(\alpha) = a(\beta)$, then either $(a(\alpha), b(\alpha)) \subset (a(\beta), b(\beta))$, so that $(a(\alpha), b(\alpha))$ is superfluous, or $(a(\alpha), b(\alpha)) \supset (a(\beta), b(\beta))$, so that $(a(\beta), b(\beta))$ is superfluous. Thus, without loss of generality we may assume that the $a(\alpha)$'s are all distinct and can be arranged in increasing order. Consequently, we may assume that the index set A is the set of the $a(\alpha)$'s themselves, that is, $U(a) = (a, b(a))$, $a \in A$, where A is a subset of $\mathbb{R}$ such that $[0, 1] \subset \cup_{a \in A}(a, b(a))$. Furthermore, if $a_1 < a_2$, then $b(a_1) < b(a_2)$, for otherwise $(a_2, b(a_2))$ is superfluous. Now let $0 \in (a_1, b(a_1))$, and define for $n = 2, 3, 4, \ldots$, $a_n = (a_{n-1} + b(a_{n-1}))/2$. Then $[0, 1] \subset \cup_{n=1}^{\infty}(a_n, b(a_n))$. This implies that $1 \in \cup_{n=1}^{\infty}(a_n, b(a_n))$; hence, there exists an n such that $1 \in (a_n, b(a_n))$. Consequently, $[0, 1] \subset \cup_{j=1}^{n}(a_j, b(a_j))$. Thus, $[0, 1]$ is compact. This argument extends to arbitrary closed and bounded subsets of a Euclidean space.   Q.E.D.

A *limit point* of a sequence x_n of real numbers is a point x_* such that for every $\varepsilon > 0$ there exists an index n for which $|x_n - x_*| < \varepsilon$. Consequently, a limit point is a limit along a subsequence. Sequences x_n confined to an interval $[a, b]$ always have at least one limit point, and these limit points are contained in $[a, b]$ because $\limsup_{n \to \infty} x_n$ and $\liminf_{n \to \infty} x_n$ are limit points contained in $[a, b]$ and any other limit point must lie between $\liminf_{n \to \infty} x_n$ and $\limsup_{n \to \infty} x_n$. This property carries over to general compact sets:

Theorem II.3: *Every infinite sequence θ_n of points in a compact set Θ has at least one limit point, and all the limit points are contained in Θ.*

Proof: Let Θ be a compact subset of a Euclidean space and let Θ_k, $k = 1, 2, \ldots$ be a decreasing sequence of compact subsets of Θ each containing infinitely many θ_n's to be constructed as follows. Let $\Theta_0 = \Theta$ and $k \ge 0$. There exist a finite number of points $\theta_{k,j}^*$, $j = 1, \ldots, m_k$ such that, with $U_k(\theta^*) = \{\theta : \|\theta - \theta^*\| < 2^{-k}\}$, Θ_k is contained in $\cup_{j=1}^{m_k} U_k(\theta_{k,j}^*)$. Then at least one of these open sets contains infinitely many points θ_n, say $U_k(\theta_{k,1}^*)$. Next, let

$$\Theta_{k+1} = \{\theta : \|\theta - \theta_{k,1}^*\| \le 2^{-k}\} \cap \Theta_k,$$

which is compact and contains infinitely many points θ_n. Repeating this construction, we can easily verify that $\cap_{k=0}^{\infty} \Theta_k$ is a singleton and that this singleton is a limit point contained in Θ. Finally, if a limit point θ^* is located outside Θ, then, for some large k, $U_k(\theta^*) \cap \Theta = \emptyset$, which contradicts the requirement that $U_k(\theta^*)$ contain infinitely many θ_n's.   Q.E.D.

Theorem II.4: *Let θ_n be a sequence of points in a compact set Θ. If all the limit points of θ_n are the same, then $\lim_{n\to\infty}\theta_n$ exists and is a point in Θ.*

Proof: Let $\theta_* \in \Theta$ be the common limit point. If the limit does not exist, then there exists a $\delta > 0$ and an infinite subsequence θ_{n_k} such that $|\theta_{n_k} - \theta_*| \geq \delta$ for all k. But θ_{n_k} also has limit point θ_*, and thus there exists a further subsequence $\theta_{n_k(m)}$ that converges to θ_*. Therefore, the theorem follows by contradiction. Q.E.D.

Theorem II.5: *For a continuous function g on a compact set Θ, $\sup_{\theta\in\Theta} g(\theta) = \max_{\theta\in\Theta} g(\theta)$ and $\inf_{\theta\in\Theta} g(\theta) = \min_{\theta\in\Theta} g(\theta)$. Consequently, $\mathrm{argmax}_{\theta\in\Theta} g(\theta) \in \Theta$ and $\mathrm{argmin}_{\theta\in\Theta} g(\theta) \in \Theta$.*

Proof: It follows from the definition of $\sup_{\theta\in\Theta} g(\theta)$ that for each $k \geq 1$ there exists a point $\theta_k \in \Theta$ such that $g(\theta_k) > \sup_{\theta\in\Theta} g(\theta) - 2^{-k}$; hence, $\lim_{k\to\infty} g(\theta_k) = \sup_{\theta\in\Theta} g(\theta)$. Because Θ is compact, the sequence θ_k has a limit point $\theta_* \in \Theta$ (see Theorem II.3); hence, by the continuity of g, $g(\theta_*) = \sup_{\theta\in\Theta} g(\theta)$. Consequently, $\sup_{\theta\in\Theta} g(\theta) = \max_{\theta\in\Theta} g(\theta) = g(\theta_*)$.   Q.E.D.

Theorem II.6: *Let g be a continuous function on a compact set Θ, and let $\theta_0 = \mathrm{argmin}_{\theta\in\Theta} g(\theta)$ be unique. Then there exists a $\bar{\delta} > 0$ such that for all $\delta \in (0, \bar{\delta})$, $\inf_{\theta\in\Theta:\|\theta-\theta_0\|\geq\delta} g(\theta) > g(\theta_0)$. Similarly, if $\theta_0 = \mathrm{argmax}_{\theta\in\Theta} g(\theta)$ is unique, then there exists a $\bar{\delta} > 0$ such that for all $\delta \in (0, \bar{\delta})$, $\sup_{\theta\in\Theta:\|\theta-\theta_0\|\geq\delta} g(\theta) < g(\theta_0)$.*

Proof: It follows from Theorem II.5 that $\theta_0 = \mathrm{argmin}_{\theta\in\Theta} g(\theta) \in \Theta$. Let $\Theta_\delta = \{\theta \in \Theta : \|\theta - \theta_0\| \geq \delta\}$ for $\delta > 0$. If Θ_δ is nonempty, then it is compact. To see this, let $\{\Theta_\alpha, \alpha \in A\}$ be an open covering of Θ_δ : $\Theta_\delta \subset \cup_{\alpha\in A} \Theta_\alpha$, and let $\Theta_* = \{\theta : \|\theta - \theta_0\| < \delta\}$. Then $\Theta \subset \Theta_* \cup (\cup_{\alpha\in A} \Theta_\alpha)$, and thus by the compactness of Θ there exists a finite subcovering $\Theta \subset \cup_{j=1}^n \Theta_j$. Without loss of generality we may assume that $\Theta_* = \Theta_0$ and thus that $\Theta_\delta \subset \cup_{j=0}^n \Theta_j$; hence, Θ_δ is compact. Then by Theorem II.5, $\theta_\delta = \mathrm{argmin}_{\theta\in\Theta_\delta} g(\theta) \in \Theta_\delta \subset \Theta$. Because θ_0 is unique we have $g(\theta_0) < g(\theta_\delta)$. The argmax case follows by a similar argument.   Q.E.D.

II.6. Uniform Continuity

A function g on $\mathbb{R}^k$ is called uniformly continuous if for every $\varepsilon > 0$ there exists a $\delta > 0$ such that $|g(x) - g(y)| < \varepsilon$ if $\|x - y\| < \delta$. In particular,

Theorem II.7: *If a function g is continuous on a compact subset Θ of $\mathbb{R}^k$, then it is uniformly continuous on Θ.*

Proof: Let $\varepsilon > 0$ be arbitrary, and observe from the continuity of g that, for each x in Θ, there exists a $\delta(x) > 0$ such that $|g(x) - g(y)| < \varepsilon/2$ if $\|x - y\| < 2\delta(x)$. Now let $U(x) = \{y \in \mathbb{R}^k : \|y - x\| < \delta(x)\}$. Then the collection $\{U(x), x \in \Theta\}$ is an open covering of Θ; hence, by compactness of Θ there exists a finite number of points $\theta_1, \ldots, \theta_n$ in Θ such that $\Theta \subset \cup_{j=1}^{n} U(\theta_j)$. Next, let $\delta = \min_{1 \leq j \leq n} \delta(\theta_j)$. Each point $x \in \Theta$ belongs to at least one of the open sets $U(\theta_j) : x \in U(\theta_j)$ for some j. Then $\|x - \theta_j\| < \delta(\theta_j) < 2\delta(\theta_j)$ and hence $|g(x) - g(\theta_j)| < \varepsilon/2$. Moreover, if $\|x - y\| < \delta$, then

$$\|y - \theta_j\| = \|y - x + x - \theta_j\| \leq \|x - y\|$$
$$+ \|x - \theta_j\| < \delta + \delta(\theta_j) \leq 2\delta(\theta_j);$$

hence, $|g(y) - g(\theta_j)| < \varepsilon/2$. Consequently, $|g(x) - g(y)| \leq |g(x) - g(\theta_j)| + |g(y) - g(\theta_j)| < \varepsilon$ if $\|x - y\| < \delta$. Q.E.D.

II.7. Derivatives of Vector and Matrix Functions

Consider a real function $f(x) = f(x_1, \ldots, x_n)$ on $\mathbb{R}^n$, where $x = (x_1, \ldots, x_n)^{\mathsf{T}}$. Recall that the partial derivative of f to a component x_i of x is denoted and defined by

$$\frac{\partial f(x)}{\partial x_i} = \frac{\partial f(x_1, \ldots, x_n)}{\partial x_i}$$

$$\overset{\text{def.}}{=} \lim_{\delta \to 0} \frac{f(x_1, \ldots, x_{i-1}, x_i + \delta, x_{i+1}, \ldots, x_n) - f(x_1, \ldots, x_{i-1}, x_i, x_{i+1}, \ldots, x_n)}{\delta}.$$

For example, let $f(x) = \beta^{\mathsf{T}} x = x^{\mathsf{T}} \beta = \beta_1 x_1 + \cdots \beta_n x_n$. Then

$$\begin{pmatrix} \partial f(x)/\partial x_1 \\ \vdots \\ \partial f(x)/\partial x_n \end{pmatrix} = \begin{pmatrix} \beta_1 \\ \vdots \\ \beta_n \end{pmatrix} = \beta.$$

This result could also have been obtained by treating x^{T} as a scalar and taking the derivative of $f(x) = x^{\mathsf{T}} \beta$ to $x^{\mathsf{T}} : \partial(x^{\mathsf{T}} \beta)/\partial x^{\mathsf{T}} = \beta$. This motivates the convention to denote the *column* vector of a partial derivative of $f(x)$ by $\partial f(x)/\partial x^{\mathsf{T}}$. Similarly, if we treat x as a scalar and take the derivative of $f(x) = \beta^{\mathsf{T}} x$ to x, then the result is a *row* vector: $\partial(\beta^{\mathsf{T}} x)/\partial x = \beta^{\mathsf{T}}$. Thus, in general,

$$\frac{\partial f(x)}{\partial x^{\mathsf{T}}} \overset{\text{def.}}{=} \begin{pmatrix} \partial f(x)/\partial x_1 \\ \vdots \\ \partial f(x)/\partial x_n \end{pmatrix}, \quad \frac{\partial f(x)}{\partial x} \overset{\text{def.}}{=} (\partial f(x)/\partial x_1, \ldots, \partial f(x)/\partial x_n).$$

If the function H is vector valued, for instance $H(x) = (h_1(x), \ldots,$ $h_m(x))^T$, $x \in \mathbb{R}^n$, then applying the operation $\partial/\partial x$ to each of the components yields an $m \times n$ matrix:

$$\frac{\partial H(x)}{\partial x} \overset{\text{def.}}{=} \begin{pmatrix} \partial h_1(x)/\partial x \\ \vdots \\ \partial h_m(x)/\partial x \end{pmatrix} = \begin{pmatrix} \partial h_1(x)/\partial x_1 & \cdots & \partial h_1(x)/\partial x_n \\ \vdots & & \vdots \\ \partial h_m(x)/\partial x_1 & \cdots & \partial h_m(x)/\partial x_n \end{pmatrix}.$$

Moreover, applying the latter to a column vector of partial derivatives of a real function f yields

$$\frac{\partial(\partial f(x)/\partial x^T)}{\partial x} = \begin{pmatrix} \dfrac{\partial^2 f(x)}{\partial x_1 \partial x_1} & \cdots & \dfrac{\partial^2 f(x)}{\partial x_1 \partial x_n} \\ \vdots & \ddots & \vdots \\ \dfrac{\partial^2 f(x)}{\partial x_n \partial x_1} & \cdots & \dfrac{\partial^2 f(x)}{\partial x_n \partial x_n} \end{pmatrix} = \frac{\partial^2 f(x)}{\partial x \partial x^T},$$

for instance.

In the case of an $m \times n$ matrix X with columns $x_1, \ldots, x_n \in \mathbb{R}^k$, $x_j = (x_{1,j}, \ldots, x_{m,j})^T$ and a differentiable function $f(X)$ on the vector space of $k \times n$ matrices, we may interpret $X = (x_1, \ldots, x_n)$ as a "row" of column vectors, and thus

$$\frac{\partial f(X)}{\partial X} = \frac{\partial f(X)}{\partial(x_1, \ldots, x_n)} \overset{\text{def.}}{=} \begin{pmatrix} \partial f(X)/\partial x_1 \\ \vdots \\ \partial f(X)/\partial x_n \end{pmatrix}$$

$$\overset{\text{def.}}{=} \begin{pmatrix} \partial f(X)/\partial x_{1,1} & \cdots & \partial f(X)/\partial x_{m,1} \\ \vdots & \ddots & \vdots \\ \partial f(X)/\partial x_{1,n} & \cdots & \partial f(X)/\partial x_{m,n} \end{pmatrix}$$

is an $n \times m$ matrix. For the same reason, $\partial f(X)/\partial X^T \overset{\text{def.}}{=} (\partial f(X)/\partial X)^T$. An example of such a derivative to a matrix is given by Theorem I.33 in Appendix I, which states that if X is a square nonsingular matrix, then $\partial \ln[\det(X)]/\partial X = X^{-1}$.

Next, consider the quadratic function $f(x) = a + x^T b + x^T C x$, where

$$x = \begin{pmatrix} x_1 \\ \vdots \\ x_n \end{pmatrix}, \quad b = \begin{pmatrix} b_1 \\ \vdots \\ b_n \end{pmatrix}, \quad C = \begin{pmatrix} c_{1,1} & \cdots & c_{1,n} \\ \vdots & \cdots & \vdots \\ c_{n,1} & \cdots & c_{n,n} \end{pmatrix} \text{ with } c_{i,j} = c_{j,i}.$$

Thus, C is a symmetric matrix. Then

$$\partial f(x)/\partial x_k = \frac{\partial \left(a + \sum_{i=1}^n b_i x_i + \sum_{i=1}^n \sum_{j=1}^n x_i c_{i,j} x_j \right)}{\partial x_k}$$

$$= \sum_{i=1}^n b_i \frac{\partial x_i}{\partial x_k} + \sum_{i=1}^n \sum_{j=1}^n \frac{\partial x_i c_{i,j} x_j}{\partial x_k}$$

$$= b_k + 2 c_{k,k} x_k + \sum_{\substack{i=1 \\ i \neq k}}^n x_i c_{i,k} + \sum_{\substack{j=1 \\ j \neq k}}^n c_{k,j} x_j$$

$$= b_k + 2 \sum_{j=1}^n c_{k,j} x_j, \quad k = 1, \ldots, n;$$

hence, stacking these partial derivatives in a column vector yields

$$\partial f(x)/\partial x^\mathrm{T} = b + 2Cx. \tag{II.8}$$

If C is not symmetric, we may without loss of generality replace C in the function $f(x)$ by the symmetric matrix $C/2 + C^\mathrm{T}/2$ because $x^\mathrm{T}Cx = (x^\mathrm{T}Cx)^\mathrm{T} = x^\mathrm{T}C^\mathrm{T}x$, and thus

$$\partial f(x)/\partial x^\mathrm{T} = b + Cx + C^\mathrm{T}x.$$

The result (II.8) for the case $b = 0$ can be used to give an interesting alternative interpretation of eigenvalues and eigenvectors of symmetric matrices, namely, as the solutions of a quadratic optimization problem under quadratic restrictions. Consider the optimization problem

$$\text{max or min} \, x^\mathrm{T} Ax \, \text{s} \cdot \text{t} \cdot x^\mathrm{T}x = 1, \tag{II.9}$$

where A is a symmetric matrix and "max" and "min" include local maxima and minima and saddle-point solutions. The Lagrange function for solving this problem is

$$\mathcal{L}(x, \lambda) = x^\mathrm{T}Ax + \lambda(1 - x^\mathrm{T}x)$$

with first-order conditions

$$\partial \mathcal{L}(x, \lambda)/\partial x^\mathrm{T} = 2Ax - 2\lambda x = 0 \Rightarrow Ax = \lambda x, \tag{II.10}$$

$$\partial \mathcal{L}(x, \lambda)/\partial \lambda = 1 - x^\mathrm{T}x = 0 \Rightarrow \|x\| = 1. \tag{II.11}$$

Condition (II.10) defines the Lagrange multiplier λ as the eigenvalue and the solution for x as the corresponding eigenvector of A, and (II.11) is the normalization of the eigenvector to unit length. If we combine (II.10) and (II.11), it follows that $\lambda = x^\mathrm{T}Ax$.

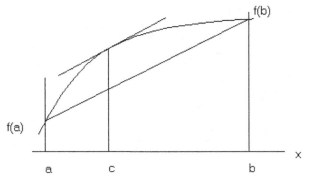

Figure II.1. The mean value theorem.

II.8. The Mean Value Theorem

Consider a differentiable real function $f(x)$ displayed as the curved line in Figure II.1. We can always find a point c in the interval $[a, b]$ such that the slope of $f(x)$ at $x = c$, which is equal to the derivative $f'(c)$, is the same as the slope of the straight line connecting the points $(a, f(a))$ and $(b, f(b))$ simply by shifting the latter line parallel to the point where it becomes tangent to $f(x)$. The slope of this straight line through the points $(a, f(a))$ and $(b, f(b))$ is $(f(b) - f(a))/(b - a)$. Thus, at $x = c$ we have $f'(c) = (f(b) - f(a))/(b - a)$, or equivalently, $f(b) = f(a) + (b - a)f'(c)$. This easy result is called the mean value theorem. Because this point c can also be expressed as $c = a + \lambda(b - a)$, with $0 \leq \lambda = (c - a)/(b - a) \leq 1$, we can now state the mean value theorem as follows:

Theorem II.8(a): *Let $f(x)$ be a differentiable real function on an interval $[a, b]$ with derivative $f'(x)$. For any pair of points $x, x_0 \in [a, b]$ there exists a $\lambda \in [0, 1]$ such that $f(x) = f(x_0) + (x - x_0)f'(x_0 + \lambda(x - x_0))$.*

This result carries over to real functions of more than one variable:

Theorem II.8(b): *Let $f(x)$ be a differentiable real function on a convex subset C of $\mathbb{R}^k$. For any pair of points $x, x_0 \in C$ there exists a $\lambda \in [0, 1]$ such that*

$$f(x) = f(x_0) + (x - x_0)^T (\partial/\partial y^T) f(y)|_{y=x_0+\lambda(x-x_0)}.$$

II.9. Taylor's Theorem

The mean value theorem implies that if, for two points $a < b$, $f(a) = f(b)$, then there exists a point $c \in [a, b]$ such that $f'(c) = 0$. This fact is the core of the proof of Taylor's theorem:

Theorem II.9(a): *Let $f(x)$ be an n-times, continuously differentiable real function on an interval $[a, b]$ with the nth derivative denoted by $f^{(n)}(x)$. For any pair of points $x, x_0 \in [a, b]$ there exists a $\lambda \in [0, 1]$ such that*

$$f(x) = f(x_0) + \sum_{k=1}^{n-1} \frac{(x - x_0)^k}{k!} f^{(k)}(x_0)$$

$$+ \frac{(x - x_n)^n}{n!} f^{(n)}(x_0 + \lambda(x - x_0)).$$

Proof: Let $a \le x_0 < x \le b$. We can always write

$$f(x) = f(x_0) + \sum_{k=1}^{n-1} \frac{(x - x_0)^k}{k!} f^{(k)}(x_0) + R_n, \tag{II.12}$$

where R_n is the remainder term. Now let $a \le x_0 < x \le b$ be fixed, and consider the function

$$g(u) = f(x) - f(u) - \sum_{k=1}^{n-1} \frac{(x - u)^k}{k!} f^{(k)}(u) - \frac{R_n(x - u)^n}{(x - x_0)^n}$$

with derivative

$$g'(u) = -f'(u) + \sum_{k=1}^{n-1} \frac{(x - u)^{k-1}}{(k - 1)!} f^{(k)}(u) - \sum_{k=1}^{n-1} \frac{(x - u)^k}{k!} f^{(k+1)}(u)$$

$$+ \frac{nR_n(x - u)^{n-1}}{(x - x_0)^n} = -f'(u) + \sum_{k=0}^{n-2} \frac{(x - u)^k}{k!} f^{(k+1)}(u)$$

$$- \sum_{k=1}^{n-1} \frac{(x - u)^k}{k!} f^{(k+1)}(u) + \frac{nR_n(x - u)^{n-1}}{(x - x_0)^n}$$

$$= - \frac{(x - u)^{n-1}}{(n - 1)!} f^{(n)}(u) + \frac{nR_n(x - u)^{n-1}}{(x - x_0)^n}.$$

Then $g(x) = g(x_0) = 0$; hence, there exists a point $c \in [x_0, x]$ such that $g'(c) = 0$:

$$0 = - \frac{(x - c)^{n-1}}{(n - 1)!} f^{(n)}(c) + \frac{nR_n(x - c)^{n-1}}{(x - x_0)^n}.$$

Therefore,

$$R_n = \frac{(x - x_n)^n}{n!} f^{(n)}(c) = \frac{(x - x_n)^n}{n!} f^{(n)}(x_0 + \lambda(x - x_0)), \tag{II.13}$$

where $c = x_0 + \lambda (x - x_0)$. If we combine (II.12) and (II.13), the theorem follows.   Q.E.D.

Also, Taylor's theorem carries over to real functions of more than one variable, but the result involved is awkward to display for $n > 2$. Therefore, we only state the second-order Taylor expansion theorem involved:

Theorem II.9(b): *Let $f(x)$ be a twice continuously differentiable real function on a convex subset Ξ of $\mathbb{R}^n$. For any pair of points $x, x_0 \in \Xi$ there exists a $\lambda \in [0, 1]$ such that*

$$f(x) = f(x_0) + (x - x_0)^{\mathrm{T}} \left(\left. \frac{\partial f(y)}{\partial y^{\mathrm{T}}} \right|_{y=x_0} \right)$$

$$+ \frac{1}{2}(x - x_0)^{\mathrm{T}} \left(\left. \frac{\partial^2 f(y)}{\partial y \partial y^{\mathrm{T}}} \right|_{y=x_0+\lambda(x-x_0)} \right)(x - x_0). \tag{II.14}$$

II.10. Optimization

Theorem II.9(b) shows that the function $f(x)$ involved is locally quadratic. Therefore, the conditions for a maximum or a minimum of $f(x)$ in a point $x_0 \in \Xi$ can be derived from (II.14) and the following theorem.

Theorem II.10: *Let C be a symmetric $n \times n$ matrix, and let $f(x) = a + x^{\mathrm{T}}b + x^{\mathrm{T}}Cx, \in \mathbb{R}^n$, where a is a given scalar and b is a given vector in $\mathbb{R}^n$. If C is positive (negative) definite, then $f(x)$ takes a unique minimum (maximum) at $x = -1/2\, C^{-1}b$.*

Proof: The first-order condition for a maximum or minimum is $\partial f(x)/\partial x^{\mathrm{T}} = 0 (\in \mathbb{R}^n)$; hence, $x = -1/2 C^{-1}b$. As to the uniqueness issue and the question of whether the optimum is a minimum or a maximum, recall that $C = Q \Lambda Q^{\mathrm{T}}$, where Λ is the diagonal matrix of the eigenvalues of C and Q is the corresponding matrix of eigenvectors. Thus, we can write $f(x)$ as $f(x) = a + x^{\mathrm{T}} QQ^{\mathrm{T}}b + x^{\mathrm{T}}Q \Lambda Q^{\mathrm{T}}x$. Let $y = Q^{\mathrm{T}}x = (y_1, \ldots, y_n)^{\mathrm{T}}$ and $\beta = Q^{\mathrm{T}}b = (\beta_1, \ldots, \beta_n)^{\mathrm{T}}$. Then $f(Qy) = a + y^{\mathrm{T}}\beta + y^{\mathrm{T}}\Lambda\, y = a + \sum_{j=1}^{n}(\beta_j y_j + \lambda_j y_j^2)$. The latter is a sum of quadratic functions in one variable that each have a unique minimum if $\lambda_j > 0$ and a unique maximum if $\lambda_j < 0$.   Q.E.D.

It follows now from (II.14) and Theorem II.10 that

Theorem II.11: *The function $f(x)$ in Theorem II.9(b) takes a local maximum (minimum) in a point $x_0 \in \Xi$, that is, x_0 is contained in an open subset Ξ_0 of Ξ such that, for all $x \in \Xi_0 \backslash \{x_0\}, f(x) < f(x_0)(f(x) > f(x_0))$ if and only if $\partial f(x_0)/\partial x_0^{\mathrm{T}} = 0 (\in \mathbb{R}^n)$, and the matrix $\partial^2 f(x_0)/(\partial x_0 \partial x_0^{\mathrm{T}})$ is negative (positive) definite.*

A practical application of Theorems II.8(a), II.9, and II.10 is the Newton iteration for finding a minimum or a maximum of a function. Suppose that the function $f(x)$ in Theorem II.9(b) takes a unique global maximum at $x_* \in \Xi$. Starting from an initial guess x_0 of x_*, for $k \geq 0$ let,

$$x_{k+1} = x_k - \left(\frac{\partial^2 f(x_k)}{\partial x_k \partial x_k^{\mathrm{T}}}\right)^{-1} \left(\frac{\partial f(x_k)}{\partial x_k^{\mathrm{T}}}\right).$$

Thus, the Newton iteration maximizes or minimizes the local quadratic approximation of f in x_k. The iteration is stopped if for some small threshold $\varepsilon > 0$, $\| x_{k+1} - x_k \| < \varepsilon$.

Appendix III – A Brief Review
of Complex Analysis

III.1. The Complex Number System

Complex numbers have many applications. The complex number system allows computations to be conducted that would be impossible to perform in the real world. In probability and statistics we mainly use complex numbers in dealing with characteristic functions, but in time series analysis complex analysis plays a key role. See for example Fuller (1996).

Complex numbers are actually two-dimensional vectors endowed with arithmetic operations that make them act as numbers. Therefore, complex numbers are introduced here in their "real" form as vectors in $\mathbb{R}^2$.

In addition to the usual addition and scalar multiplication operators on the elements of $\mathbb{R}^2$ (see Appendix I), we define the vector multiplication operator "$\times$" by

$$\begin{pmatrix} a \\ b \end{pmatrix} \times \begin{pmatrix} c \\ d \end{pmatrix} \stackrel{\text{def.}}{=} \begin{pmatrix} a \cdot c - b \cdot d \\ b \cdot c + a \cdot d \end{pmatrix}. \tag{III.1}$$

Observe that

$$\begin{pmatrix} a \\ b \end{pmatrix} \times \begin{pmatrix} c \\ d \end{pmatrix} = \begin{pmatrix} c \\ d \end{pmatrix} \times \begin{pmatrix} a \\ b \end{pmatrix}.$$

Moreover, define the inverse operator "-1" by

$$\begin{pmatrix} a \\ b \end{pmatrix}^{-1} \stackrel{\text{def.}}{=} \frac{1}{a^2 + b^2} \begin{pmatrix} a \\ -b \end{pmatrix} \text{ provided that } a^2 + b^2 > 0, \tag{III.2}$$

and thus

$$\begin{pmatrix} a \\ b \end{pmatrix}^{-1} \times \begin{pmatrix} a \\ b \end{pmatrix} = \begin{pmatrix} a \\ b \end{pmatrix} \times \begin{pmatrix} a \\ b \end{pmatrix}^{-1}$$

$$= \frac{1}{a^2 + b^2} \begin{pmatrix} a \\ -b \end{pmatrix} \times \begin{pmatrix} a \\ b \end{pmatrix} = \begin{pmatrix} 1 \\ 0 \end{pmatrix}.$$

The latter vector plays the same role as the number 1 in the real number system. Furthermore, we can now define the division operator "/" by

$$\begin{pmatrix} a \\ b \end{pmatrix} \Big/ \begin{pmatrix} c \\ d \end{pmatrix} \overset{\text{def.}}{=} \begin{pmatrix} a \\ b \end{pmatrix} \times \begin{pmatrix} c \\ d \end{pmatrix}^{-1} = \frac{1}{c^2+d^2} \begin{pmatrix} a \\ b \end{pmatrix} \times \begin{pmatrix} c \\ -d \end{pmatrix}$$

$$= \frac{1}{c^2+d^2} \begin{pmatrix} a \cdot c + b \cdot d \\ b \cdot c - a \cdot d \end{pmatrix}$$

$$\tag{III.3}$$

provided that $c^2 + d^2 > 0$. Note that

$$\begin{pmatrix} 1 \\ 0 \end{pmatrix} \Big/ \begin{pmatrix} c \\ d \end{pmatrix} = \frac{1}{c^2+d^2} \begin{pmatrix} c \\ -d \end{pmatrix} = \begin{pmatrix} c \\ d \end{pmatrix}^{-1}.$$

In the subspace $\mathbb{R}_1^2 = \{(x, 0)^{\mathrm{T}}, x \in \mathbb{R}\}$ these operators work the same as for real numbers:

$$\begin{pmatrix} a \\ 0 \end{pmatrix} \times \begin{pmatrix} c \\ 0 \end{pmatrix} = \begin{pmatrix} a \cdot c \\ 0 \end{pmatrix}, \qquad \begin{pmatrix} c \\ 0 \end{pmatrix}^{-1} = \begin{pmatrix} 1/c \\ 0 \end{pmatrix},$$

$$\begin{pmatrix} a \\ 0 \end{pmatrix} \Big/ \begin{pmatrix} c \\ 0 \end{pmatrix} = \begin{pmatrix} a/c \\ 0 \end{pmatrix}$$

provided that $c \neq 0$. Therefore, all the basic arithmetic operations (addition, subtraction, multiplication, division) of the real number system $\mathbb{R}$ apply to $\mathbb{R}_1^2$, and vice versa.

In the subspace $\mathbb{R}_2^2 = \{(0, x)^{\mathrm{T}}, x \in \mathbb{R}\}$ the multiplication operator "$\times$" yields

$$\begin{pmatrix} 0 \\ b \end{pmatrix} \times \begin{pmatrix} 0 \\ d \end{pmatrix} = \begin{pmatrix} -b \cdot d \\ 0 \end{pmatrix}.$$

In particular, note that

$$\begin{pmatrix} 0 \\ 1 \end{pmatrix} \times \begin{pmatrix} 0 \\ 1 \end{pmatrix} = \begin{pmatrix} -1 \\ 0 \end{pmatrix}. \tag{III.4}$$

Now let

$$a + i \cdot b \overset{\text{def.}}{=} \begin{pmatrix} 1 \\ 0 \end{pmatrix} a + \begin{pmatrix} 0 \\ 1 \end{pmatrix} b, \quad \text{where} \quad i = \begin{pmatrix} 0 \\ 1 \end{pmatrix} \tag{III.5}$$

and interpret $a + i.0$ as the mapping

$$a + i \cdot 0 : \begin{pmatrix} a \\ 0 \end{pmatrix} \rightarrow a. \tag{III.6}$$

Then it follows from (III.1) and (III.5) that

$$(a + i \cdot b) \times (c + i \cdot d) = \begin{pmatrix} a \\ b \end{pmatrix} \times \begin{pmatrix} c \\ d \end{pmatrix} = \begin{pmatrix} a \cdot c - b \cdot d \\ b \cdot c + a \cdot d \end{pmatrix}$$
$$= (a \cdot c - b \cdot d) + i \cdot (b \cdot c + a \cdot d). \quad \text{(III.7)}$$

However, the same result can be obtained by using standard arithmetic operations and treating the identifier i as $\sqrt{-1}$:

$$(a + i \cdot b) \times (c + i \cdot d) = a \cdot c + i^2 \cdot b \cdot d + i \cdot b \cdot c + i \cdot a \cdot d$$
$$= (a \cdot c - b \cdot d) + i \cdot (b \cdot c + a \cdot d). \quad \text{(III.8)}$$

In particular, it follows from (III.4)–(III.6) that

$$i \times i = \begin{pmatrix} 0 \\ 1 \end{pmatrix} \times \begin{pmatrix} 0 \\ 1 \end{pmatrix} = \begin{pmatrix} -1 \\ 0 \end{pmatrix} = -1 + i \cdot 0 \to -1,$$

which can also be obtained by standard arithmetic operations with treated i as $\sqrt{-1}$ and $i.0$ as 0.

Similarly, we have

$$(a + i \cdot b)/(c + i \cdot d) = \begin{pmatrix} a \\ b \end{pmatrix} \Big/ \begin{pmatrix} c \\ d \end{pmatrix} = \frac{1}{c^2 + d^2} \begin{pmatrix} a \cdot c + b \cdot d \\ b \cdot c - a \cdot d \end{pmatrix}$$
$$= \frac{a \cdot c + b \cdot d}{c^2 + d^2} + i \cdot \frac{b \cdot c - a \cdot d}{c^2 + d^2}$$

provided that $c^2 + d^2 > 0$. Again, this result can also be obtained by standard arithmetic operations with i treated as $\sqrt{-1}$:

$$(a + i \cdot b)/(c + i \cdot d) = \frac{a + i \cdot b}{c + i \cdot d} \times \frac{c - i \cdot d}{c - i \cdot d}$$
$$= \frac{(a + i \cdot b) \times (c - i \cdot d)}{(c + i \cdot d) \times (c - i \cdot d)}$$
$$= \frac{a \cdot c + b \cdot d}{c^2 + d^2} + i \cdot \frac{b \cdot c - a \cdot d}{c^2 + d^2}.$$

The Euclidean space $\mathbb{R}^2$ endowed with the arithmetic operations (III.1)–(III.3) resembles a number system except that the "numbers" involved cannot be ordered. However, it is possible to measure the distance between these "numbers" using the Euclidean norm:

$$|a + i \cdot b| \stackrel{\text{def.}}{=} \left\| \begin{pmatrix} a \\ b \end{pmatrix} \right\| = \sqrt{a^2 + b^2}$$
$$= \sqrt{(a + i \cdot b) \times (a - i \cdot b)}. \quad \text{(III.9)}$$

If the "numbers" in this system are denoted by (III.5) and standard arithmetic operations are applied with i treated as $\sqrt{-1}$ and $i.0$ as 0, the results are the same as for the arithmetic operations (III.1), (III.2), and (III.3) on the elements of $\mathbb{R}^2$. Therefore, we may interpret (III.5) as a number, bearing in mind that this number has two dimensions if $b \neq 0$.

From now on I will use the standard notation for multiplication, that is, $(a + i \cdot b)(c + i \cdot d)$ instead of (III.8).

The "a" of $a + i \cdot b$ is called the real part of the complex number involved, denoted by $\text{Re}(a + i \cdot b) = a$, and b is called the imaginary part, denoted by $\text{Im}(a + i \cdot b) = b$. Moreover, $a - i \cdot b$ is called the complex conjugate of $a + i \cdot b$ and vice versa. The complex conjugate of $z = a + i \cdot b$ is denoted by a bar: $\bar{z} = a - i \cdot b$. It follows from (III.7) that, for $z = a + i \cdot b$ and $w = c + i \cdot d$, $\overline{zw} = \bar{z} \cdot \bar{w}$. Moreover, $|z| = \sqrt{z \bar{z}}$. Finally, the complex number system itself is denoted by $\mathbb{C}$.

III.2. The Complex Exponential Function

Recall that, for real-valued x the exponential function e^x, also denoted by $\exp(x)$, has the series representation

$$e^x = \sum_{k=0}^{\infty} \frac{x^k}{k!}. \tag{III.10}$$

The property $e^{x+y} = e^x e^y$ corresponds to the equality

$$\sum_{k=0}^{\infty} \frac{(x+y)^k}{k!} = \sum_{k=0}^{\infty} \frac{1}{k!} \sum_{m=0}^{k} \binom{k}{m} x^{k-m} y^m$$

$$= \sum_{k=0}^{\infty} \sum_{m=0}^{k} \frac{x^{k-m}}{(k-m)!} \frac{y^m}{m!}$$

$$= \left(\sum_{k=0}^{\infty} \frac{x^k}{k!} \right) \left(\sum_{m=0}^{\infty} \frac{y^m}{m!} \right). \tag{III.11}$$

The first equality in (III.11) results from the binomial expansion, and the last equality follows easily by rearranging the summation. It is easy to see that (III.11) also holds for complex-valued x and y. Therefore, we can define the complex exponential function by the series expansion (III.10):

$$e^{a+i \cdot b} \stackrel{\text{def.}}{=} \sum_{k=0}^{\infty} \frac{(a + i \cdot b)^k}{k!}$$

$$= \sum_{k=0}^{\infty} \frac{a^k}{k!} \sum_{m=0}^{\infty} \frac{(i \cdot b)^m}{m!} = e^a \sum_{m=0}^{\infty} \frac{i^m \cdot b^m}{m!}$$

$$= e^a \left[\sum_{m=0}^{\infty} \frac{(-1)^m \cdot b^{2m}}{(2m)!} + i \cdot \sum_{m=0}^{\infty} \frac{(-1)^m \cdot b^{2m+1}}{(2m+1)!} \right]. \tag{III.12}$$

Moreover, it follows from Taylor's theorem that

$$\cos(b) = \sum_{m=0}^{\infty} \frac{(-1)^m \cdot b^{2m}}{(2m)!}, \quad \sin(b) = \sum_{m=0}^{\infty} \frac{(-1)^m \cdot b^{2m+1}}{(2m+1)!}, \quad \text{(III.13)}$$

and thus (III.12) becomes

$$e^{a+i \cdot b} = e^a[\cos(b) + i \cdot \sin(b)]. \quad \text{(III.14)}$$

Setting $a = 0$, we find that the latter equality yields the following expressions for the cosines and sine in terms of the complex exponential function:

$$\cos(b) = \frac{e^{i \cdot b} + e^{-i \cdot b}}{2}, \quad \sin(b) = \frac{e^{i \cdot b} - e^{-i \cdot b}}{2 \cdot i}.$$

These expressions are handy in recovering the sine-cosine formulas:

$$\sin(a)\sin(b) = [\cos(a - b) - \cos(a + b)]/2$$
$$\sin(a)\cos(b) = [\sin(a + b) + \sin(a - b)]/2$$
$$\cos(a)\sin(b) = [\sin(a + b) - \sin(a - b)]/2$$
$$\cos(a)\cos(b) = [\cos(a + b) + \cos(a - b)]/2$$
$$\sin(a + b) = \sin(a)\cos(b) + \cos(a)\sin(b)$$
$$\cos(a + b) = \cos(a)\cos(b) - \sin(a)\sin(b)$$
$$\sin(a - b) = \sin(a)\cos(b) - \cos(a)\sin(b)$$
$$\cos(a - b) = \cos(a)\cos(b) + \sin(a)\sin(b).$$

Moreover, it follows from (III.14) that, for natural numbers n,

$$e^{i \cdot n \cdot b} = [\cos(b) + i \cdot \sin(b)]^n = \cos(n \cdot b) + i \cdot \sin(n \cdot b). \quad \text{(III.15)}$$

This result is known as DeMoivre's formula. It also holds for real numbers n, as we will see in Section III.3.

Finally, note that any complex number $z = a + i \cdot b$ can be expressed as

$$z = a + i \cdot b = |z| \cdot \left[\frac{a}{\sqrt{a^2 + b^2}} + i \cdot \frac{b}{\sqrt{a^2 + b^2}} \right]$$
$$= |z| \cdot [\cos(2\pi\varphi) + i \cdot \sin(2\pi\varphi)] = |z| \cdot \exp(i \cdot 2\pi\varphi),$$

where $\varphi \in [0, 1]$ is such that $2\pi\varphi = \arccos(a/\sqrt{a^2 + b^2}) = \arcsin(b/\sqrt{a^2 + b^2})$.

III.3. The Complex Logarithm

Like the natural logarithm $\ln(\cdot)$, the complex logarithm $\log(z)$, $z \in \mathbb{C}$ is a complex number $a + i \cdot b = \log(z)$ such that $\exp(a + i \cdot b) = z$; hence, it follows from (III.15) that $z = \exp(a)[\cos(b) + i \cdot \sin(b)]$ and consequently, because

$$| \exp(-a) \cdot z| = | \cos(b) + i \cdot \sin(b)| = \sqrt{\cos^2(b) + \sin^2(b)} = 1,$$

we have that $\exp(a) = |z|$ and $\exp(i \cdot b) = z/|z|$. The first equation has a unique solution, $a = \ln(|z|)$, as long as $z \neq 0$. The second equation reads as

$$\cos(b) + i \cdot \sin(b) = (\text{Re}(z) + i \cdot \text{Im}(z))/|z|; \tag{III.16}$$

hence $\cos(b) = \text{Re}(z)/|z|$, $\sin(b) = \text{Im}(z)/|z|$, and thus $b = \arctan(\text{Im}(z)/\text{Re}(z))$. However, equation (III.16) also holds if we add or subtract multiples of π to or from b because $\tan(b) = \tan(b + m \cdot \pi)$ for arbitrary integers m; hence,

$$\log(z) = \ln(|z|) + i \cdot [\arctan(\text{Im}(z)/\text{Re}(z)) + m\pi],$$
$$m = 0, \pm 1, \pm 2, \pm 3, \dots . \tag{III.17}$$

Therefore, the complex logarithm is not uniquely defined.

The imaginary part of (III.17) is usually denoted by

$$\arg(z) = \arctan(\text{Im}(z)/\text{Re}(z)) + m\pi, \quad m = 0, \pm 1, \pm 2, \pm 3, \dots .$$

It is the angle in radians indicated in Figure III.1 eventually rotated multiples of $180°$ clockwise or counterclockwise: Note that $\text{Im}(z)/\text{Re}(z)$ is the tangents of the angle $\arg(z)$; hence, $\arctan(\text{Im}(z)/\text{Re}(z))$ is the angle itself.

With the complex exponential function and logarithm defined, we can now define the power z^w as the complex number $a + i \cdot b$ such that $a + i \cdot b = \exp(w \cdot \log(z))$, which exists if $|z| > 0$. Consequently, DeMoivre's formula carries over to all real-valued powers n:

$$[\cos(b) + i \cdot \sin(b)]^n = \left(e^{i \cdot b}\right)^n = e^{i \cdot n \cdot b} = \cos(n \cdot b) + i \cdot \sin(n \cdot b).$$

III.4. Series Expansion of the Complex Logarithm

For the case $x \in \mathbb{R}$, $|x| < 1$, it follows from Taylor's theorem that $\ln(1 + x)$ has the series representation

$$\ln(1 + x) = \sum_{k=1}^{\infty} (-1)^{k-1} x^k / k. \tag{III.18}$$

I will now address the issue of whether this series representation carries over if we replace x by $i \cdot x$ because this will yield a useful approximation of $\exp(i \cdot x)$,

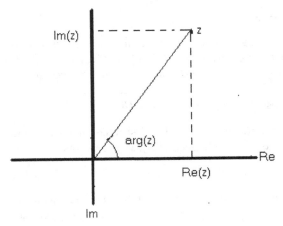

Figure III.1. arg(z).

which plays a key role in proving central limit theorems for dependent random variables.[1] See Chapter 7.

If (III.18) carries over we can write, for arbitrary integers m,

$$\log(1 + i \cdot x) = \sum_{k=1}^{\infty} (-1)^{k-1} i^k x^k / k + i \cdot m\pi$$

$$= \sum_{k=1}^{\infty} (-1)^{2k-1} i^{2k} x^{2k} / (2k)$$

$$+ \sum_{k=1}^{\infty} (-1)^{2k-1-1} i^{2k-1} x^{2k-1} / (2k-1) + i \cdot m\pi$$

$$= \sum_{k=1}^{\infty} (-1)^{k-1} x^{2k} / (2k)$$

$$+ i \cdot \sum_{k=1}^{\infty} (-1)^{k-1} x^{2k-1} / (2k-1) + i \cdot m\pi. \quad \text{(III.19)}$$

On the other hand, it follows from (III.17) that

$$\log(1 + i \cdot x) = \frac{1}{2} \ln(1 + x^2) + i \cdot [\arctan(x) + m\pi].$$

Therefore, we need to verify that, for $x \in \mathbb{R}$, $|x| < 1$,

$$\frac{1}{2} \ln(1 + x^2) = \sum_{k=1}^{\infty} (-1)^{k-1} x^{2k} / (2k) \quad \text{(III.20)}$$

---

[1] For $x \in \mathbb{R}$ with $|x| < 1$, $\exp(i \cdot x) = (1 + i \cdot x) \exp(-x^2/2 + r(x))$, where $|r(x)| \le |x|^3$.

and

$$\arctan(x) = \sum_{k=1}^{\infty}(-1)^{k-1}x^{2k-1}/(2k-1). \tag{III.21}$$

Equation (III.20) follows from (III.18) by replacing x with x^2. Equation (III.21) follows from

$$\frac{d}{dx}\sum_{k=1}^{\infty}(-1)^{k-1}x^{2k-1}/(2k-1) = \sum_{k=1}^{\infty}(-1)^{k-1}x^{2k-2}$$

$$= \sum_{k=0}^{\infty}(-x^2)^k = \frac{1}{1+x^2}$$

and the facts that arctan $(0) = 0$ and

$$\frac{d\arctan(x)}{dx} = \frac{1}{1+x^2}.$$

Therefore, the series representation (III.19) is true.

III.5. Complex Integration

In probability and statistics we encounter complex integrals mainly in the form of characteristic functions, which for absolutely continuous random variables are integrals over complex-valued functions with real-valued arguments. Such functions take the form

$$f(x) = \varphi(x) + i \cdot \psi(x), x \in \mathbb{R},$$

where φ and ψ are real-valued functions on $\mathbb{R}$. Therefore, we may define the (Lebesgue) integral of f over an interval $[a, b]$ simply as

$$\int_a^b f(x)dx = \int_a^b \varphi(x)dx + i \cdot \int_a^b \psi(x)dx$$

provided of course that the latter two integrals are defined. Similarly, if μ is a probability measure on the Borel sets in $\mathbb{R}^k$ and $\text{Re}(f(x))$ and $\text{Im}(f(x))$ are Borel-measurable-real functions on $\mathbb{R}^k$, then

$$\int f(x)d\mu(x) = \int \text{Re}(f(x))d\mu(x) + i \cdot \int \text{Im}(f(x))d\mu(x),$$

provided that the latter two integrals are defined.

Integrals of complex-valued functions of complex variables are much trickier, though. See, for example, Ahlfors (1966). However, these types of integrals have limited applicability in econometrics and are therefore not discussed here.

Appendix IV – Tables of Critical Values

Table IV.1: *Critical values of the two-sided t_k test at the 5% and 10% significance levels*

k	5%	10%	k	5%	10%	k	5%	10%
1	12.704	6.313	11	2.201	1.796	21	2.080	1.721
2	4.303	2.920	12	2.179	1.782	22	2.074	1.717
3	3.183	2.353	13	2.160	1.771	23	2.069	1.714
4	2.776	2.132	14	2.145	1.761	24	2.064	1.711
5	2.571	2.015	15	2.131	1.753	25	2.059	1.708
6	2.447	1.943	16	2.120	1.746	26	2.056	1.706
7	2.365	1.895	17	2.110	1.740	27	2.052	1.703
8	2.306	1.859	18	2.101	1.734	28	2.048	1.701
9	2.262	1.833	19	2.093	1.729	29	2.045	1.699
10	2.228	1.813	20	2.086	1.725	30	2.042	1.697

Table IV.2: *Critical values of the right-sided t_k test at the 5% and* 10%
significance levels

k	5%	10%	k	5%	10%	k	5%	10%
1	6.313	3.078	11	1.796	1.363	21	1.721	1.323
2	2.920	1.886	12	1.782	1.356	22	1.717	1.321
3	2.353	1.638	13	1.771	1.350	23	1.714	1.319
4	2.132	1.533	14	1.761	1.345	24	1.711	1.318
5	2.015	1.476	15	1.753	1.341	25	1.708	1.316
6	1.943	1.440	16	1.746	1.337	26	1.706	1.315
7	1.895	1.415	17	1.740	1.333	27	1.703	1.314
8	1.859	1.397	18	1.734	1.330	28	1.701	1.313
9	1.833	1.383	19	1.729	1.328	29	1.699	1.311
10	1.813	1.372	20	1.725	1.325	30	1.697	1.310

Note: For $k > 30$ the critical values of the t_k test are approximately equal to the critical values of
the standard normal test in Table IV.3.

Table IV.3: *Critical values of the $N(0, 1)$ test*

Significance levels:	5%	10%
Two-sided:	1.960	1.645
Right-sided:	1.645	1.282

Table IV.4: *Critical values of the χ^2_k test at the 5% and* 10% *significance levels*

k	5%	10%	k	5%	10%	k	5%	10%
1	3.841	2.705	11	19.675	17.275	21	32.671	29.615
2	5.991	4.605	12	21.026	18.549	22	33.925	30.814
3	7.815	6.251	13	22.362	19.812	23	35.172	32.007
4	9.488	7.780	14	23.684	21.064	24	36.414	33.196
5	11.071	9.237	15	24.995	22.307	25	37.653	34.381
6	12.591	10.645	16	26.296	23.541	26	38.885	35.563
7	14.067	12.017	17	27.588	24.769	27	40.114	36.741
8	15.507	13.361	18	28.869	25.990	28	41.336	37.916
9	16.919	14.683	19	30.144	27.204	29	42.557	39.088
10	18.307	15.987	20	31.410	28.412	30	43.772	40.256

Note: Because the χ^2_k test is used to test parameter restrictions with the degrees of freedom k equal
to the number of restrictions, it is unlikely that you will need the critical values of the χ^2_k test for
$k > 30$.

Table IV.5: *Critical values of the $F_{k,m}$ test at the 5% significance level*

m\k	1	2	3	4	5	6	7	8	9	10	11	12	13	14	15
1	161.	199.	216.	225.	230.	234.	237.	239.	241.	242.	243.	244.	245.	245.	246.
2	18.5	19.0	19.2	19.2	19.3	19.3	19.4	19.4	19.4	19.4	19.4	19.4	19.4	19.4	19.4
3	10.1	9.55	9.28	9.12	9.01	8.94	8.89	8.84	8.81	8.79	8.76	8.75	8.73	8.72	8.70
4	7.71	6.94	6.59	6.39	6.26	6.16	6.09	6.04	6.00	5.96	5.94	5.91	5.89	5.87	5.86
5	6.61	5.79	5.41	5.19	5.05	4.95	4.88	4.82	4.77	4.73	4.70	4.68	4.66	4.64	4.62
6	5.99	5.14	4.76	4.53	4.39	4.28	4.21	4.15	4.10	4.06	4.03	4.00	3.98	3.96	3.94
7	5.59	4.74	4.35	4.12	3.97	3.87	3.79	3.73	3.68	3.64	3.60	3.57	3.55	3.53	3.51
8	5.32	4.46	4.07	3.84	3.69	3.58	3.50	3.44	3.39	3.35	3.31	3.28	3.26	3.24	3.22
9	5.12	4.26	3.86	3.63	3.48	3.37	3.29	3.23	3.18	3.14	3.10	3.07	3.05	3.03	3.01
10	4.96	4.10	3.71	3.48	3.33	3.22	3.14	3.07	3.02	2.98	2.94	2.91	2.89	2.86	2.84
11	4.84	3.98	3.59	3.36	3.20	3.09	3.01	2.95	2.90	2.85	2.82	2.79	2.76	2.74	2.72
12	4.75	3.89	3.49	3.26	3.11	3.00	2.91	2.85	2.80	2.75	2.72	2.69	2.66	2.64	2.62
13	4.67	3.81	3.41	3.18	3.03	2.92	2.83	2.77	2.71	2.67	2.63	2.60	2.58	2.55	2.53
14	4.60	3.74	3.34	3.11	2.96	2.85	2.76	2.70	2.65	2.60	2.57	2.53	2.51	2.48	2.46
15	4.54	3.68	3.29	3.06	2.90	2.79	2.71	2.64	2.59	2.54	2.51	2.48	2.45	2.42	2.40
16	4.49	3.63	3.24	3.01	2.85	2.74	2.66	2.59	2.54	2.49	2.46	2.42	2.40	2.37	2.35
17	4.45	3.59	3.20	2.96	2.81	2.70	2.61	2.55	2.49	2.45	2.41	2.38	2.35	2.33	2.31
18	4.41	3.55	3.16	2.93	2.77	2.66	2.58	2.51	2.46	2.41	2.37	2.34	2.31	2.29	2.27
19	4.38	3.52	3.13	2.90	2.74	2.63	2.54	2.48	2.42	2.38	2.34	2.31	2.28	2.26	2.23
20	4.35	3.49	3.10	2.87	2.71	2.60	2.51	2.45	2.39	2.35	2.31	2.28	2.25	2.22	2.20
21	4.32	3.47	3.07	2.84	2.68	2.57	2.49	2.42	2.37	2.32	2.28	2.25	2.22	2.20	2.18
22	4.30	3.44	3.05	2.82	2.66	2.55	2.46	2.40	2.34	2.30	2.26	2.23	2.20	2.17	2.15
23	4.28	3.42	3.03	2.80	2.64	2.53	2.44	2.37	2.32	2.27	2.24	2.20	2.18	2.15	2.13
24	4.26	3.40	3.01	2.78	2.62	2.51	2.42	2.35	2.30	2.25	2.22	2.18	2.15	2.13	2.11
25	4.24	3.39	2.99	2.76	2.60	2.49	2.40	2.34	2.28	2.24	2.20	2.16	2.14	2.11	2.09

$m\backslash k$	16	17	18	19	20	21	22	23	24	25	26	27	28	29	30
1	247.	247.	247.	248.	248.	248.	249.	249.	249.	249.	250.	250.	250.	250.	250.
2	19.4	19.4	19.4	19.4	19.4	19.5	19.5	19.5	19.5	19.5	19.5	19.5	19.5	19.5	19.5
3	8.69	8.68	8.67	8.67	8.66	8.65	8.65	8.64	8.64	8.63	8.63	8.63	8.62	8.62	8.62
4	5.84	5.83	5.82	5.81	5.80	5.79	5.79	5.78	5.77	5.77	5.76	5.76	5.75	5.75	5.75
5	4.60	4.59	4.58	4.57	4.56	4.55	4.54	4.53	4.53	4.52	4.52	4.51	4.51	4.50	4.50
6	3.92	3.91	3.90	3.88	3.87	3.86	3.86	3.85	3.84	3.83	3.83	3.82	3.82	3.81	3.81
7	3.49	3.48	3.47	3.46	3.44	3.43	3.43	3.42	3.41	3.40	3.40	3.39	3.39	3.38	3.38
8	3.20	3.19	3.17	3.16	3.15	3.14	3.13	3.12	3.12	3.11	3.10	3.10	3.09	3.08	3.08
9	2.99	2.97	2.96	2.95	2.94	2.93	2.92	2.91	2.90	2.89	2.89	2.88	2.87	2.87	2.86
10	2.83	2.81	2.80	2.79	2.77	2.76	2.75	2.75	2.74	2.73	2.72	2.72	2.71	2.70	2.70
11	2.70	2.69	2.67	2.66	2.65	2.64	2.63	2.62	2.61	2.60	2.59	2.59	2.58	2.58	2.57
12	2.60	2.58	2.57	2.56	2.54	2.53	2.52	2.51	2.51	2.50	2.49	2.48	2.48	2.47	2.47
13	2.52	2.50	2.48	2.47	2.46	2.45	2.44	2.43	2.42	2.41	2.40	2.40	2.39	2.39	2.38
26	4.22	3.37	2.98	2.74	2.59	2.47	2.39	2.32	2.27	2.22	2.18	2.15	2.12	2.09	2.07
27	4.21	3.35	2.96	2.73	2.57	2.46	2.37	2.31	2.25	2.20	2.17	2.13	2.10	2.08	2.06
28	4.20	3.34	2.95	2.71	2.56	2.45	2.36	2.29	2.24	2.19	2.15	2.12	2.09	2.06	2.04
29	4.18	3.33	2.93	2.70	2.55	2.43	2.35	2.28	2.22	2.18	2.14	2.10	2.08	2.05	2.03
30	4.17	3.32	2.92	2.69	2.53	2.42	2.33	2.27	2.21	2.16	2.13	2.09	2.06	2.04	2.01
40	4.08	3.23	2.84	2.61	2.45	2.34	2.25	2.18	2.12	2.08	2.04	2.00	1.97	1.95	1.92
50	4.03	3.18	2.79	2.56	2.40	2.29	2.20	2.13	2.07	2.03	1.99	1.95	1.92	1.89	1.87
60	4.00	3.15	2.76	2.53	2.37	2.25	2.17	2.10	2.04	1.99	1.95	1.92	1.89	1.86	1.84
70	3.98	3.13	2.74	2.50	2.35	2.23	2.14	2.07	2.02	1.97	1.93	1.89	1.86	1.84	1.81
80	3.96	3.11	2.72	2.49	2.33	2.21	2.13	2.06	2.00	1.95	1.91	1.88	1.84	1.82	1.79
90	3.95	3.10	2.71	2.47	2.32	2.20	2.11	2.04	1.99	1.94	1.90	1.86	1.83	1.80	1.78
100	3.94	3.09	2.70	2.46	2.31	2.19	2.10	2.03	1.97	1.93	1.89	1.85	1.82	1.79	1.77

(*continued*)

Table IV.5 (continued)

m\k	16	17	18	19	20	21	22	23	24	25	26	27	28	29	30
14	2.44	2.43	2.41	2.40	2.39	2.38	2.37	2.36	2.35	2.34	2.33	2.33	2.32	2.31	2.31
15	2.38	2.37	2.35	2.34	2.33	2.32	2.31	2.30	2.29	2.28	2.27	2.27	2.26	2.25	2.25
16	2.33	2.32	2.30	2.29	2.28	2.26	2.25	2.24	2.24	2.23	2.22	2.21	2.21	2.20	2.19
17	2.29	2.27	2.26	2.24	2.23	2.22	2.21	2.20	2.19	2.18	2.17	2.17	2.16	2.15	2.15
18	2.25	2.23	2.22	2.20	2.19	2.18	2.17	2.16	2.15	2.14	2.13	2.13	2.12	2.11	2.11
19	2.21	2.20	2.18	2.17	2.16	2.14	2.13	2.12	2.11	2.11	2.10	2.09	2.08	2.08	2.07
20	2.18	2.17	2.15	2.14	2.12	2.11	2.10	2.09	2.08	2.07	2.07	2.06	2.05	2.05	2.04
21	2.16	2.14	2.12	2.11	2.10	2.08	2.07	2.06	2.05	2.05	2.04	2.03	2.02	2.02	2.01
22	2.13	2.11	2.10	2.08	2.07	2.06	2.05	2.04	2.03	2.02	2.01	2.00	2.00	1.99	1.98
23	2.11	2.09	2.08	2.06	2.05	2.04	2.02	2.01	2.01	2.00	1.99	1.98	1.97	1.97	1.96
24	2.09	2.07	2.05	2.04	2.03	2.01	2.00	1.99	1.98	1.97	1.97	1.96	1.95	1.95	1.94
25	2.07	2.05	2.04	2.02	2.01	2.00	1.98	1.97	1.96	1.96	1.95	1.94	1.93	1.93	1.92
26	2.05	2.03	2.02	2.00	1.99	1.98	1.97	1.96	1.95	1.94	1.93	1.92	1.91	1.91	1.90
27	2.04	2.02	2.00	1.99	1.97	1.96	1.95	1.94	1.93	1.92	1.91	1.90	1.90	1.89	1.88
28	2.02	2.00	1.99	1.97	1.96	1.95	1.93	1.92	1.91	1.91	1.90	1.89	1.88	1.88	1.87
29	2.01	1.99	1.97	1.96	1.94	1.93	1.92	1.91	1.90	1.89	1.88	1.88	1.87	1.86	1.85
30	1.99	1.98	1.96	1.95	1.93	1.92	1.91	1.90	1.89	1.88	1.87	1.86	1.85	1.85	1.84
40	1.90	1.89	1.87	1.85	1.84	1.83	1.81	1.80	1.79	1.78	1.77	1.77	1.76	1.75	1.74
50	1.85	1.83	1.81	1.80	1.78	1.77	1.76	1.75	1.74	1.73	1.72	1.71	1.70	1.69	1.69
60	1.82	1.80	1.78	1.76	1.75	1.73	1.72	1.71	1.70	1.69	1.68	1.67	1.66	1.66	1.65
70	1.79	1.77	1.75	1.74	1.72	1.71	1.70	1.68	1.67	1.66	1.65	1.65	1.64	1.63	1.62
80	1.77	1.75	1.73	1.72	1.70	1.69	1.68	1.67	1.65	1.64	1.63	1.63	1.62	1.61	1.60
90	1.76	1.74	1.72	1.70	1.69	1.67	1.66	1.65	1.64	1.63	1.62	1.61	1.60	1.59	1.59
100	1.75	1.73	1.71	1.69	1.68	1.66	1.65	1.64	1.63	1.62	1.61	1.60	1.59	1.58	1.57

Table IV.6: *Critical values of the $F_{k,m}$ test at the 10% significance level*

m\k	1	2	3	4	5	6	7	8	9	10	11	12	13	14	15
1	39.9	49.5	53.6	55.8	57.2	58.2	58.9	59.4	59.8	60.2	60.5	60.7	60.9	61.1	61.2
2	8.53	9.00	9.16	9.24	9.29	9.33	9.35	9.37	9.38	9.39	9.40	9.41	9.41	9.42	9.42
3	5.54	5.46	5.39	5.34	5.31	5.28	5.27	5.25	5.24	5.23	5.22	5.22	5.21	5.20	5.20
4	4.54	4.32	4.19	4.11	4.05	4.01	3.98	3.95	3.94	3.92	3.91	3.90	3.89	3.88	3.87
5	4.06	3.78	3.62	3.52	3.45	3.40	3.37	3.34	3.32	3.30	3.28	3.27	3.26	3.25	3.24
6	3.78	3.46	3.29	3.18	3.11	3.05	3.01	2.98	2.96	2.94	2.92	2.90	2.89	2.88	2.87
7	3.59	3.26	3.07	2.96	2.88	2.83	2.78	2.75	2.72	2.70	2.68	2.67	2.65	2.64	2.63
8	3.46	3.11	2.92	2.81	2.73	2.67	2.62	2.59	2.56	2.54	2.52	2.50	2.49	2.48	2.46
9	3.36	3.01	2.81	2.69	2.61	2.55	2.51	2.47	2.44	2.42	2.40	2.38	2.36	2.35	2.34
10	3.29	2.92	2.73	2.61	2.52	2.46	2.41	2.38	2.35	2.32	2.30	2.28	2.27	2.26	2.24
11	3.23	2.86	2.66	2.54	2.45	2.39	2.34	2.30	2.27	2.25	2.23	2.21	2.19	2.18	2.17
12	3.18	2.81	2.61	2.48	2.39	2.33	2.28	2.24	2.21	2.19	2.17	2.15	2.13	2.12	2.10
13	3.14	2.76	2.56	2.43	2.35	2.28	2.23	2.20	2.16	2.14	2.12	2.10	2.08	2.07	2.05
14	3.10	2.73	2.52	2.39	2.31	2.24	2.19	2.15	2.12	2.10	2.07	2.05	2.04	2.02	2.01
15	3.07	2.70	2.49	2.36	2.27	2.21	2.16	2.12	2.09	2.06	2.04	2.02	2.00	1.99	1.97
16	3.05	2.67	2.46	2.33	2.24	2.18	2.13	2.09	2.06	2.03	2.01	1.99	1.97	1.95	1.94
17	3.03	2.64	2.44	2.31	2.22	2.15	2.10	2.06	2.03	2.00	1.98	1.96	1.94	1.93	1.91
18	3.01	2.62	2.42	2.29	2.20	2.13	2.08	2.04	2.00	1.98	1.95	1.93	1.92	1.90	1.89
19	2.99	2.61	2.40	2.27	2.18	2.11	2.06	2.02	1.98	1.96	1.93	1.91	1.89	1.88	1.86
20	2.97	2.59	2.38	2.25	2.16	2.09	2.04	2.00	1.96	1.94	1.91	1.89	1.87	1.86	1.84
21	2.96	2.57	2.36	2.23	2.14	2.08	2.02	1.98	1.95	1.92	1.90	1.88	1.86	1.84	1.83
22	2.95	2.56	2.35	2.22	2.13	2.06	2.01	1.97	1.93	1.90	1.88	1.86	1.84	1.83	1.81
23	2.94	2.55	2.34	2.21	2.11	2.05	1.99	1.95	1.92	1.89	1.87	1.84	1.83	1.81	1.80
24	2.93	2.54	2.33	2.19	2.10	2.04	1.98	1.94	1.91	1.88	1.85	1.83	1.81	1.80	1.78
25	2.92	2.53	2.32	2.18	2.09	2.02	1.97	1.93	1.89	1.87	1.84	1.82	1.80	1.79	1.77

(continued)

Table IV.6 (continued)

m\k	1	2	3	4	5	6	7	8	9	10	11	12	13	14	15
26	2.91	2.52	2.31	2.17	2.08	2.01	1.96	1.92	1.88	1.85	1.83	1.81	1.79	1.77	1.76
27	2.90	2.51	2.30	2.17	2.07	2.00	1.95	1.91	1.87	1.85	1.82	1.80	1.78	1.76	1.75
28	2.89	2.50	2.29	2.16	2.06	2.00	1.94	1.90	1.87	1.84	1.81	1.79	1.77	1.75	1.74
29	2.89	2.50	2.28	2.15	2.06	1.99	1.93	1.89	1.86	1.83	1.80	1.78	1.76	1.75	1.73
30	2.88	2.49	2.28	2.14	2.05	1.98	1.93	1.88	1.85	1.82	1.79	1.77	1.75	1.74	1.72
40	2.84	2.44	2.23	2.09	2.00	1.93	1.87	1.83	1.79	1.76	1.74	1.71	1.70	1.68	1.66
50	2.81	2.41	2.20	2.06	1.97	1.90	1.84	1.80	1.76	1.73	1.70	1.68	1.66	1.64	1.63
60	2.79	2.39	2.18	2.04	1.95	1.87	1.82	1.77	1.74	1.71	1.68	1.66	1.64	1.62	1.60
70	2.78	2.38	2.16	2.03	1.93	1.86	1.80	1.76	1.72	1.69	1.66	1.64	1.62	1.60	1.59
80	2.77	2.37	2.15	2.02	1.92	1.85	1.79	1.75	1.71	1.68	1.65	1.63	1.61	1.59	1.57
90	2.76	2.36	2.15	2.01	1.91	1.84	1.78	1.74	1.70	1.67	1.64	1.62	1.60	1.58	1.56
100	2.76	2.36	2.14	2.00	1.91	1.83	1.78	1.73	1.69	1.66	1.64	1.61	1.59	1.57	1.56

m\k	16	17	18	19	20	21	22	23	24	25	26	27	28	29	30
1	61.4	61.5	61.6	61.7	61.7	61.8	61.9	61.9	62.0	62.1	62.1	62.2	62.2	62.2	62.3
2	9.43	9.43	9.44	9.44	9.44	9.44	9.45	9.45	9.45	9.45	9.45	9.45	9.46	9.46	9.46
3	5.20	5.19	5.19	5.19	5.18	5.18	5.18	5.18	5.18	5.18	5.17	5.17	5.17	5.17	5.17
4	3.86	3.86	3.85	3.85	3.84	3.84	3.84	3.83	3.83	3.83	3.83	3.82	3.82	3.82	3.82
5	3.23	3.22	3.22	3.21	3.21	3.20	3.20	3.19	3.19	3.19	3.18	3.18	3.18	3.18	3.17
6	2.86	2.85	2.85	2.84	2.84	2.83	2.83	2.82	2.82	2.81	2.81	2.81	2.81	2.80	2.80
7	2.62	2.61	2.61	2.60	2.59	2.59	2.58	2.58	2.58	2.57	2.57	2.56	2.56	2.56	2.56
8	2.45	2.45	2.44	2.43	2.42	2.42	2.41	2.41	2.40	2.40	2.40	2.39	2.39	2.39	2.38
9	2.33	2.32	2.31	2.30	2.30	2.29	2.29	2.28	2.28	2.27	2.27	2.26	2.26	2.26	2.25
10	2.23	2.22	2.22	2.21	2.20	2.19	2.19	2.18	2.18	2.17	2.17	2.17	2.16	2.16	2.16
11	2.16	2.15	2.14	2.13	2.12	2.12	2.11	2.11	2.10	2.10	2.09	2.09	2.08	2.08	2.08

12	2.01	2.01	2.02	2.02	2.03	2.03	2.04	2.04	2.05	2.05	2.06	2.07	2.08	2.08	2.09
13	1.96	1.96	1.96	1.97	1.97	1.98	1.98	1.99	1.99	2.00	2.01	2.01	2.02	2.03	2.04
14	1.91	1.92	1.92	1.92	1.93	1.93	1.94	1.94	1.95	1.96	1.96	1.97	1.98	1.99	2.00
15	1.87	1.88	1.88	1.88	1.89	1.89	1.90	1.90	1.91	1.92	1.92	1.93	1.94	1.95	1.96
16	1.84	1.84	1.85	1.85	1.86	1.86	1.87	1.87	1.88	1.88	1.89	1.90	1.91	1.92	1.93
17	1.81	1.81	1.82	1.82	1.83	1.83	1.84	1.84	1.85	1.85	1.86	1.87	1.88	1.89	1.90
18	1.78	1.79	1.79	1.80	1.80	1.80	1.81	1.82	1.82	1.83	1.84	1.84	1.85	1.86	1.87
19	1.76	1.76	1.77	1.77	1.78	1.78	1.79	1.79	1.80	1.81	1.81	1.82	1.83	1.84	1.85
20	1.74	1.74	1.75	1.75	1.76	1.76	1.77	1.77	1.78	1.79	1.79	1.80	1.81	1.82	1.83
21	1.72	1.72	1.73	1.73	1.74	1.74	1.75	1.75	1.76	1.77	1.78	1.78	1.79	1.80	1.81
22	1.70	1.71	1.71	1.72	1.72	1.73	1.73	1.74	1.74	1.75	1.76	1.77	1.78	1.79	1.80
23	1.69	1.69	1.70	1.70	1.70	1.71	1.72	1.72	1.73	1.74	1.74	1.75	1.76	1.77	1.78
24	1.67	1.68	1.68	1.69	1.69	1.70	1.70	1.71	1.71	1.72	1.73	1.74	1.75	1.76	1.77
25	1.66	1.66	1.67	1.67	1.68	1.68	1.69	1.70	1.70	1.71	1.72	1.73	1.74	1.75	1.76
26	1.65	1.65	1.66	1.66	1.67	1.67	1.68	1.68	1.69	1.70	1.71	1.71	1.72	1.73	1.75
27	1.64	1.64	1.64	1.65	1.65	1.66	1.67	1.67	1.68	1.69	1.70	1.70	1.71	1.72	1.74
28	1.63	1.63	1.63	1.64	1.64	1.65	1.66	1.66	1.67	1.68	1.69	1.69	1.70	1.71	1.73
29	1.62	1.62	1.62	1.63	1.63	1.64	1.65	1.65	1.66	1.67	1.68	1.68	1.69	1.71	1.72
30	1.61	1.61	1.62	1.62	1.63	1.63	1.64	1.64	1.65	1.66	1.67	1.68	1.69	1.70	1.71
40	1.54	1.55	1.55	1.56	1.56	1.57	1.57	1.58	1.59	1.60	1.61	1.61	1.62	1.64	1.65
50	1.50	1.51	1.51	1.52	1.52	1.53	1.54	1.54	1.55	1.56	1.57	1.58	1.59	1.60	1.61
60	1.48	1.48	1.49	1.49	1.50	1.50	1.51	1.52	1.53	1.53	1.54	1.55	1.56	1.58	1.59
70	1.46	1.46	1.47	1.47	1.48	1.49	1.49	1.50	1.51	1.52	1.53	1.54	1.55	1.56	1.57
80	1.44	1.45	1.45	1.46	1.47	1.47	1.48	1.48	1.49	1.50	1.51	1.52	1.53	1.55	1.56
90	1.43	1.44	1.44	1.45	1.45	1.46	1.47	1.48	1.48	1.49	1.50	1.51	1.52	1.54	1.55
100	1.42	1.43	1.43	1.44	1.45	1.45	1.46	1.47	1.48	1.48	1.49	1.50	1.52	1.53	1.54

Notes: For $m > 100$ the critical values of the $F_{k,m}$ test are approximately equal to the critical values of the χ_k^2 test divided by k. Because the $F_{k,m}$ test is used to test parameter restrictions with the degrees of freedom k equal to the number of restrictions, it is unlikely that you will need the critical values of the $F_{k,m}$ test for $k > 30$.

References

Ahlfors, L. V. (1966): *Complex Analysis*. New York: McGraw-Hill.

Bernanke, B. S. (1986): "Alternative Explanations of the Money–Income Correlation," *Carnegie–Rochester Conference Series on Public Policy* 25, 49–100.

Bierens, H. J. (1994): *Topics in Advanced Econometrics: Estimation, Testing, and Specification of Cross-Section and Time Series Models*. Cambridge, UK: Cambridge University Press.

Billingsley, P. (1986): *Probability and Measure*. New York: John Wiley.

Box, G. E. P., and G. M. Jenkins (1976): *Time Series Analysis: Forecasting and Control*. San Francisco: Holden-Day.

Chung, K. L. (1974): *A Course in Probability Theory* (Second edition). New York: Academic Press.

Davidson, J. (1994): *Stochastic Limit Theory*. Oxford, UK: Oxford University Press.

Etemadi, N. (1981): "An Elementary Proof of the Strong Law of Large Numbers," *Zeitschrift für Wahrscheinlichkeitstheorie und Verwandte Gebiete* 55, 119–122.

Fuller, W. A. (1996): *Introduction to Statistical Time Series*. New York: John Wiley.

Gallant, A. R. (1997): *An Introduction to Econometric Theory*. Princeton, NJ.: Princeton University Press.

Jennrich, R. I. (1969): "Asymptotic Properties of Non-Linear Least Squares Estimators," *Annals of Mathematical Statistics* 40, 633–643.

McLeish, D. L. (1974): "Dependent Central Limit Theorems and Invariance Principles," *Annals of Probability* 2, 620–628.

McLeish, D. L. (1975): "A Maximal Inequality and Dependent Strong Laws," *Annals of Probability* 3, 329–339.

Press, W. H., B. P. Flannery, S. A Teukolsky, and W. T. Vetterling (1989): *Numerical Recipes (FORTRAN Version)*. Cambridge, UK: Cambridge University Press.

Royden, H. L. (1968): *Real Analysis*. London: Macmillan.

Sims, C. A. (1980): "Macroeconomics and Reality," *Econometrica* 48, 1–48.

Sims, C. A. (1982): "Policy Analysis with Econometric Models," *Brookings Papers on Economics Activity* 1, 107–152.

Sims, C. A. (1986): "Are Forecasting Models Usable for Policy Analysis?", *Federal Reserve Bank of Minneapolis Quarterly Review*, 1–16.

Stokey, N. L., R. E. Lucas, and E. Prescott (1989): *Recursive Methods in Economic Dynamics*. Cambridge, MA: Harvard University Press.

Tobin, J. (1958): "Estimation of Relationships for Limited Dependent Variables," *Econometrica* 26, 24–36.

Wold, H. (1938): *A Study in the Analysis of Stationary Time Series*. Upsala, Sweden: Almqvist and Wiksell.

Index

absolute value, 140, 141–142
adjoint matrix, 272
algebras
  defined, 4
  events and, 3
  infinite sets and, 11
  measure and, 16–17, 18
  properties of, 11
  of subsets, 11
  See also sets; σ-algebra
almost sure convergence, 143, 144, 167, 168
alternative hypothesis, 125, 131, 162
approximation, 119. *See* estimation
area, 19
argmax, 205
argmin, 128n.3, 147
asymptotic normality, 159, 190, 217, 219
asymptotic theory, xvi, xvii
asymptotic variance matrix, 161, 162, 221
autoregression, 179–180, 187, 219

basis, 234, 257
Bayesian statistics, 26, 27, 28, 31, 66, 79
Bernoulli probabilities, 211
best linear unbiased estimator (BLUE), 128
binomial distribution, 8–9, 24, 60, 87, 89
binomial expansion, 2
binomial numbers, 2
BLUE. *See* best linear unbiased estimator
Boolean functions, 32
Borel-Cantelli lemma, 168, 171
Borel fields, 14, 15
Borel measure, 37, 38, 41, 42, 48–49
  area and, 19
  continuity and, 41

definition of, 78
functions and, 40, 78
integration and, 37, 42, 43, 44, 48
length and, 19
limit and, 44
mathematical expectations, 49
measure theory, 37, 41, 42
probability measure and, 42
random variables and, 39
random vectors and, 77
randomness and, 20–21, 39, 77
Riemann integrals, 43
simple functions, 40
stationarity and, 82
Borel sets, 13, 17, 21, 39, 305
  Borel measure. *See* Borel measure
  defined, 13, 14
  integration and, 305
  interval in, 18
  Lebesgue measure and, 19, 20, 25, 26, 107
  partition of, 39–40
  probability and, 17, 18
  random variables, 20–21
  σ-algebra. *See* σ-algebra
  simple functions and, 39–40
bounded convergence theorem, 62, 142, 152
Box-Jenkins method, 179–180
Box-Muller algorithm, 102

car import example, 125
Cauchy distribution, 58, 60, 100, 103, 142, 147
Cauchy-Schwartz inequality, 52, 121, 195